Ethical Issues in Behavioral Research

Basic and Applied Perspectives

Second Edition

ALLAN J. KIMMEL

Blackwell Publishing

© 1996, 2007 by Allan J. Kimmel

BLACKWELL PUBLISHING
350 Main Street, Malden, MA 02148-5020, USA
9600 Garsington Road, Oxford OX4 2DQ, UK
550 Swanston Street, Carlton, Victoria 3053, Australia

The right of Allan J. Kimmel to be identified as the Author of this Work has been asserted in accordance with the UK Copyright, Designs, and Patents Act 1988.

First edition published 1996

Second edition published 2007 by Blackwell Publishing Ltd

1   2007

Library of Congress Cataloging-in-Publication Data

Kimmel, Allan J.
   Ethical issues in behavioral research: basic and applied perspectives / Allan J. Kimmel.— 2nd ed.
      p. cm.
   Includes bibliographical references and indexes.
      ISBN-13: 978-1-4051-3439-2 (pbk.)
    1. Psychology—Research—Moral and ethical aspects. 2. Human experimentation in psychology—Moral and ethical aspects. 3. Animal experimentation—Moral and ethical aspects. I. Title.

BF76.4.K55 2007
174′.915—dc22

                                                                              2006027508

A catalogue record for this title is available from the British Library.

Set in 10/12.5pt Meridien
by SPi Publisher Services, Pondicherry, India
Printed and bound in Singapore
by Markono Print Media Pte Ltd

The publisher's policy is to use permanent paper from mills that operate a sustainable forestry policy, and which has been manufactured from pulp processed using acid-free and elementary chlorine-free practices. Furthermore, the publisher ensures that the text paper and cover board used have met acceptable environmental accreditation standards.

For further information on
Blackwell Publishing, visit our website:
www.blackwellpublishing.com

ETHICAL ISSUES IN BEHAVIORAL RESEARCH

To Marie-Ange

And it is best to err, if err one must
As you have done, upon the side of trust.

                Tartuffe, by Molière (English translation by Richard Wilbur)

Contents

List of Boxes

List of Figures

List of Tables

Foreword

To someone like myself, who received his graduate training in psychology in 1947–51, the idea of a text on ethical issues in behavioral research is still wondrously strange. Prior to the 1960s, there was no conception of research ethics as a formal component of the training and practice of behavioral scientists. Not that researchers were oblivious to ethical concerns: clearly, they did not feel free to cause or risk physical harm to research participants, or to disclose confidential information. Beyond that, there were various proactive efforts in those years to raise the moral quality of research – such as the development of action research, which fostered the active participation of individuals and communities in studies that addressed their own needs and problems. But the idea that systematic attention to investigators' moral obligations to research participants and to the larger society is an integral component of the research process had not yet taken hold.

As a result, certain deceptive, invasive, manipulative, subtly coercive, and otherwise ethically questionable procedures – which are now matters of active concern in the field, as readers of this book will discover – were routinely used in those days, because of their methodological advantages, with little attention to their implications for the rights of research participants or the integrity of societal values. Here and there, questions were raised about these practices, but such questions tended to be viewed as intrusions on the scientific enterprise rather than legitimate parts of it.

This state of affairs began to change in the 1960s for various reasons, discussed by Allan Kimmel. First, several cases involving serious abuse of research participants came to light, which led to official inquiries, public debate, national commissions, and eventually government regulations. The most notorious cases were in the field of biomedical research, but there were also several controversial pieces of behavioral research (described in some detail in the present volume) that focused public and professional attention on the ethics of research. Second, the logic of the various human rights movements that sprang up in the 1960s was extended to the rights of human subjects – of the individuals, groups, communities, and societies that provided the data for research. (The issue of animal rights – as discussed in chapter 9 – did not enter into the debate until the next decade.) Framing the debate in human rights terms helped to direct particular attention to the exploitation of powerless, disadvantaged, and captive populations, whose informed consent to research procedures could more easily be bypassed. Third, the reexamination of established methodological assumptions, in which many social scientists engaged in the 1960s, provided a hospitable context for raising ethical issues. In social psychology, for example, the growing recognition that the experimental situation involves a real human relationship to which subjects bring their own expectations and purposes, provided an opening for questioning both the effectiveness and the ethical acceptability of deception in our experiments. The relationship between ethical and methodological issues is one of the important recurring themes in this book.

In the ensuing years, the role of ethical considerations in the work of behavioral scientists has become markedly different from what it was in my graduate student days. The change is reflected in the detailed guidelines for research ethics that have been developed by various professional associations around the world, as documented by Allan Kimmel; in the growing literature and curricular offerings on research ethics; and, above all, in the government regulations that mandate ethical review of research proposals and in the institutional review boards at universities and other research centers – at least in the United States – that enforce these regulations. The regulations and review boards require researchers to think about the ethical implications of their procedures and to develop appropriate mechanisms for obtaining informed consent, for assuring the welfare of research participants, for protecting the confidentiality of data, for providing adequate feedback to the individuals and communities who make the research possible.

Cynics might account for the observed changes by the fact that adherence to the regulations is a condition for obtaining government funding for research. There is no doubt some truth in this proposition: the fear of losing research funds has a way of concentrating the minds of researchers and research administrators. Institutionalization – the formal requirement to spell out how ethical concerns will be handled and to obtain committee approval – also contributes to maintaining at least minimal ethical standards. But I am convinced that, beyond the regulations and the routinized formalities, there has been a genuine change in consciousness about ethical issues within the behavioral research community.

The evidence presented in this book is not entirely reassuring about the depth of the changes that have occurred. For example, deception is still widely used in psychological research; subject pools at university departments do not always ensure free choice and commensurate benefits to research participants; in different areas of applied research participants' privacy continues to be compromised. Where the rules circumscribe a particular practice but do not absolutely prohibit it – as in the use of deception – there is often a tendency to push the limits. The minimal safeguards stipulated by the regulations have a way of becoming maximal when translated into practice. It is still too often the case that ethical considerations are treated as afterthoughts or as obstacles to be gotten out of the way so that the researcher's "real" work can proceed. In short, the ethical dimension has not been fully internalized by the research community.

Yet there have been enormous changes in the atmosphere, of which the present book is an outstanding manifestation. Ethical issues are now a legitimate part of the research enterprise. They are discussed within the profession, included in the curriculum, and empirically investigated. Government regulations, institutional mechanisms, and professional guidelines are all contributing to raising consciousness about these issues. The next frontier is conceptualizing ethical concerns as an integral component of the research process itself, on a par with theoretical and methodological concerns – based on the proposition that what we learn through our research is intimately linked to how we learn it. It is in this context that I value this book's thoughtful, balanced, and scholarly exposition, as a model not only for advanced students, but also for practicing behavioral scientists.

Herbert C. Kelman
Harvard University

Preface to the Second Edition

It is safe to say that since publication of the first edition of *Ethical Issues*, the scope and degree of interest in the ethics of research have grown dramatically, consistent with societal, scientific, and technological developments. This has made a revision of the original volume a somewhat daunting task, especially considering the degree to which the relevant literature base has grown during the past decade. A Google search (which did not exist when this book was first published) of the term "research ethics" today results in more than three million "hits."

This evolving subject area has expanded beyond the boundaries of traditional behavioral research practices. For example, during the past decade, the Internet has emerged as an important research tool; ethnographic research practices have begun to attract an increasing number of adherents (e.g. in the area of consumer research), consistent with the emergence of postmodern thinking and growing disillusionment among some researchers with the experimental laboratory approach; and applied studies in business contexts have come to occupy a central role in the marketing decisions of brand and product managers who find themselves operating in an increasingly competitive consumer marketplace. Developments in ethical codification at the professional, governmental, and corporate levels, and ongoing modifications to the research review process, also have significantly altered the face of the research environment, adding to apprehensions among researchers that increasing ethical regulation has begun to have a "chilling effect" on the pursuit of some scientific questions.

The ever-changing nature of the ethical climate in research areas coincides with greater sensitivity to institutional ethics in other domains, especially in light of scandals involving such global corporations as Enron, WorldCom, and Panatene, and ethical controversies that have swirled around the Olympic Games, the Church, and such bastions of journalism as *The New York Times* and *Le Monde*. Indeed, adherence to basic values of integrity represents a fundamental matter of concern as we progress into the 21st century.

These and other ongoing developments argued for an up-to-date and expanded edition of *Ethical Issues*. This new edition builds upon the original volume by offering a discussion of the recent empirical literature on a wide range of topics related to research ethics, along with a consideration of new and emerging ethical issues. Included in the new edition is a focus on the research community's response to current ethical demands that have arisen in professional and public contexts; the issues imposed by new research technologies that have emerged during the past decade; and the ethical challenges that arise in the application of research approaches in the helping professions and in business and management settings. Additionally, it devotes added attention to some of the ethical issues and conflicts encountered in the context of cross-cultural and international research, reflecting the growing tendency of both fundamental and applied researchers to carry out their studies in foreign settings.

During the past decade, an emerging trend has been discerned in the coverage of ethical issues in academic settings. Most major universities now offer courses and seminars on research ethics, and advanced training in ethics currently represents a mainstay of the business school curriculum. To illustrate, the following comments, which appeared in an edition of the University of Wisconsin newspaper *The Badger Herald* (October 23, 2003), reflect a growing awareness of the need for education in research ethics:

> At colleges and universities across the United States, graduate students are enrolling in courses specifically dealing with proper research ethics. After several high profile cases developed involving real or perceived scientific misconduct, the National Institutes of Health mandated in 1990 that all graduate students whose research is federally funded must study responsible research conduct. Even before the federal mandate took place, however, universities recognized that the best way to prepare researchers for potential ethical dilemmas would be through education. Such classes are a response to concerns that as graduate students become more and more directly involved with research work, they will face ethical questions while still in school, without having the maturity of a few years "on the job" to use as a frame of reference.

With such observations in mind, I took care to include in this new edition coverage of research issues that emerge in the conduct of student research, along with recommendations for approval procedures and review of student investigations. Moreover, although the focus in this edition again largely centers on psychology research, I recognized that researchers wrestle with many of the same issues and concerns in related disciplines. Thus, in writing this edition, I envisioned a readership that includes not only psychologists, but sociologists, nurses, counselors, managers, and anyone else who at some point in their professional lives might be expected to consume research results or directly participate in the gathering of data. The added emphasis in this edition on research in applied fields is highlighted by the book's new subtitle, "Basic and Applied Perspectives."

NEW TO THE EDITION

Among the expanded coverage and many new features included in this edition are the following:

- a bulleted list of the major topics at the beginning of each chapter, which is intended to serve as a "cognitive map" of the material covered;
- discussion of the revised (2002) ethical principles and code of conduct of the American Psychological Association, including a focus on key changes in comparison with the 1992 code;
- focus on ethical aspects of participant research on the Internet;
- practical recommendations for ethical decision making;
- expanded coverage of ethical issues in the helping professions, industrial-organizational psychology, and marketing and opinion research, exemplified by the addition of a second chapter on applied research issues;
- expanded coverage of ethical issues that arise in the conduct of ethnographic research;
- coverage of recent ethical developments outside the United States, including (a) an update of the survey of international codes of ethics that appeared in the first edition, and (b) recommendations for avoiding some of the ethical pitfalls that are encountered in cross-national research, as researchers gather data outside their home countries;
- expanded discussion of the delicate balance involving methodological and ethical research demands, including an updated assessment of the effectiveness of deception as an artifact coping mechanism;
- useful Internet links devoted to ethical issues in research and codes of conduct;
- expanded discussion of the ethical review process, including practical steps for researchers in the preparation of research proposals for committee review and coverage of student research review issues.

Preface to the First Edition

When I originally conceived the idea of writing this volume on research ethics, I envisioned a final product quite different from the one presently in the reader's hands. My original intent was to write a brief (less than a hundred pages), introductory level paperback for undergraduate psychology students to be used as a supplement in research methods courses. Fortunately, my original contacts at Blackwell had something else in mind, a more thorough, in-depth volume applicable to senior honors students and graduate students who themselves will be undertaking individual research projects, not only in psychology but in related behavioral and social science disciplines as well. I say "fortunately" because in retrospect I realize that it would not have been possible to complete the briefer overview that I originally had in mind and at the same time done justice to the many complex ethical and methodological issues involved in conducting worthwhile research. I now feel that a brief introduction to the issues would have misled readers into believing that the ethical issues are overly simplistic and the ethical dilemmas more readily resolvable than actually is the case.

Although I was successfully dissuaded from writing a short introductory volume on ethical issues for psychology undergraduates, I am confident that beginning level students in psychology, sociology, and related fields can benefit from this volume's extensive coverage of ethical issues and methodological approaches in the conduct of behavioral research. However, the primary audience that I envisioned while working on this book is one consisting of advanced undergraduates and graduate students in the behavioral sciences. This is a book that was written from the perspective of pragmatic and common-sense considerations, emphasizing actual (and hypothetical) research cases, in the hope that it may serve as a useful resource during all phases of the research process. With this in mind, the book should also be of benefit to many research professionals.

Let me briefly explain why I believe this volume represents an important contribution to the field. Currently, there does not appear to be an up-to-date text on research ethics. While there are several texts dealing with ethical issues in psychology and other helping professions, these volumes are either dated or they provide more generic surveys of issues that emerge in biomedical, therapeutic, consulting, and testing contexts (in addition to research issues). In the past fifteen years, ethical guidelines have been revised, new codes have appeared, additional ethical problems have been identified in applied and non-experimental areas, and unique approaches to resolving ethical dilemmas have been proposed. As an indication of the voluminous work that has been added to the literature, this book contains nearly 250 references that have appeared since 1982.

Despite the growing level of concern about ethical issues in the behavioral sciences during the past two decades, there does not appear to have been a corresponding increase in emphasis on research ethics at the college or university level. A 1984 survey conducted by the Committee for the Protection of Human Participants in Research (CPHPR) revealed that there were few courses offered by psychology departments on research ethics and there is little evidence suggesting that this situation has changed during the past decade.

The serious exploration of ethical issues for students of psychology tends to occur as a topical area within the research methods and experimental psychology courses. Thus, the primary sources of information about research ethics for psychology students are their textbooks in such courses and their course instructors. However, recent content analyses of psychology textbooks have revealed that the coverage of ethical issues in psychological research tends to be incomplete and highly selective. All too often, I am afraid, the "ethical issues" topic on course syllabi gets relegated to the "if time permits" category. Following an analysis of psychology textbooks published after 1979, one investigator concluded "that it is unlikely that students learn much about research ethics from these texts and will rarely be exposed to arguments opposing deceptive research" (Korn, 1984, p. 146). In this light, it is hoped that the present volume will provide a more complete and balanced coverage of research ethics than that which students have been receiving. The availability of this book, at least in part, might ameliorate the apparent lack in formal ethical training of behavioral scientists by stimulating university instructors to devote more time in their courses to research ethics and to begin to offer courses on the topic.

Towards satisfying these goals, this volume includes numerous case studies of controversial studies from a variety of disciplines, offers suggestions for resolving ethical conflicts and developing research alternatives, and compares professional ethical principles, governmental research guidelines, and self regulation. Informed consent, the weighing of costs and benefits, deception and debriefing, privacy and confidentiality, investigator/participant role relationships, the humane treatment of animals in laboratory research, and professional responsibilities in the accurate reporting of research findings are among the topics given central attention in this book.

When one considers the wide-ranging considerations involved in carrying out an investigation with human or animal subjects, it may appear that the research process is akin to a "high wire act," in which there are certain potential benefits and risks inherent in the activity that must be weighed. Like the inexperienced tightrope walker who freezes in the middle of a performance, unable to continue forward and too scared to turn back, researchers also may find themselves confronting unanticipated dilemmas and dealing with them in ineffective ways once an investigation is under way. Like other balancing acts, the research process typically is equipped with "safety nets" for the protection of researchers and their participants, in the form of ethical review committees, informed consent forms, and the like, in order to avoid serious undesirable consequences. In the spirit of the compromises that frequently must be reached in conducting an investigation, an attempt is made throughout this book to strike a balance between the rights and welfare of the participants of behavioral research and the rights of researchers to seek a fuller understanding of behavior.

Finally, I have selected the Molière quote as an epigraph for the book for several reasons, but mostly because of its emphasis on trust. Trust is a word that frequently appears in discussions of ethical issues in research, with good reason. Trust lies at the heart of virtually every decision that must be made by the researcher, and all human participants in the research process depend on the trust of others at all levels. Research subjects trust the researcher to treat them with dignity and respect, to protect their well-being, and to safeguard them from potential dangers or risks of harm. Researchers trust their subjects to maintain honesty in their responding, to respect the seriousness of the research enterprise, and to maintain their promises not to reveal certain aspects of a study to future participants. Society lends its trust to researchers to pursue worthwhile research questions which stand to benefit humanity, to protect participants from research abuses, and to maintain honesty and objectivity throughout the research process. In turn, researchers trust society to apply research findings cautiously and in an ethically responsible manner. The scientific community expects individual researchers to carry out their research in ways deemed appropriate by other members of the profession, to report their findings honestly and accurately, and to place the interests of others ahead of personal ambition in the conduct of research. Researchers trust their peers who serve on ethics committees and journal review boards to evaluate their research objectively and fairly. And so on. A breach of trust in any of these relationships will inevitably give rise to ethical problems.

This book is intended as a guide for researchers in anticipating ethical problems before they emerge, coping with them once they have become apparent, and perhaps avoiding them altogether. There are no guarantees that one will choose the most reasonable course of action that protects the greatest number of interests, or that ethical dilemmas will be resolved in the fairest and most reasonable ways. My main hope in having written this book is that it will contribute at least in some small way to shaping the values of individual researchers so that their judgments are made, in the words of Molière, "upon the side of trust."

Allan J. Kimmel
Paris, France

Acknowledgments

There are many people to whom I am deeply indebted for their assistance, inspiration, and support, and without whom this volume never would have come to fruition. I am sincerely grateful that Susan Milmoe, a past Executive Editor at Blackwell, recognized the need for a comprehensive text on research ethics and granted me the opportunity to write the first edition. I also owe a great deal of thanks to Christine Cardone, who encouraged and supported this revised edition, and to Sarah Coleman, who helped guide the book through to production. This volume also greatly benefited from the feedback provided by several anonymous reviewers who commented on my revised edition proposal.

Ralph Rosnow and Herbert Kelman are two persons who stand out as having had a substantial influence on the shaping of many of the ideas presented in this book and for having sparked my interest in research issues. Ralph has been an inspiring force throughout my career and his prodigious body of work on research methods and statistical analysis, ethics, and social psychology has provided unending intellectual stimulation. As for Herb Kelman, I am honored that the person who has significantly contributed to the ethical sensitivities in contemporary psychology agreed to be associated with this volume by accepting to have his foreword from the first edition reprinted here.

The author and publishers are grateful to the following for permission to use copyright material: American Counseling Association, *ACA Code of Ethics and Standards of Practice*, 2002; American Marketing Association, *Code of Ethics*, 1962, revised 1972; American Psychological Association, *Ethical Principles in the Conduct of Research with Human Participants*, 1973, revised 1982; American Psychological Association, "Ethical Principles of Psychologists and Code of Conduct," *American Psychologist*, 2002; American Scientific Affiliation Company; American Sociological Association, *Code of Ethics*, 1989; L.J. Bradley; The Boston Globe Newspaper Company; The British Psychological Society, *Code of Conduct, Ethical Principles and Guidelines*, 1995, Leicester, UK; The British Psychological Society, *Guidelines for the*

Use of Animals in Research, 1995, Leicester UK; The British Veterinary Association; The Canadian Psychological Association, *Canadian Code of Ethics for Psychologists*, revised edition, 1991; G. Chastain; Framingham State College, Massachusetts; C.B. Hendricks; The Institute of Business Ethics; The International Association of Marriage and Family Counselors; E. Landrum; D.C. Malloy; Pearson Education; R. Pitter; G. Raney, Department of Psychology, University of Illinois at Chicago; *Social Research Update*.

1

Introduction to Research Ethics

"The Environmental Protection Agency (EPA) ... is seeking input on a new proposed study in which infants in participating low income families will be monitored for health impacts as they undergo exposure to known toxic chemicals over the course of two years. The study entitled Children's Environmental Exposure Research Study (CHEERS) will look at how chemicals can be ingested, inhaled or absorbed by children ranging from babies to 3 years old. For taking part in these studies, each family will receive $970, a free video camera, a T-shirt, and a framed certificate of appreciation."

Organic Consumers Association, 2004

Chapter Topics

☞ Defining research ethics and related concepts
☞ Factors influencing ethical decision making
☞ Historical developments underlying the emergence of research ethics
☞ Illustrative research examples

On November 12, 2004, the EPA announced that it had suspended plans to pursue the ironically named CHEERS project in which families would be paid to allow researchers to study the effects that potentially dangerous pesticides have on their children. Soon after word began to spread about the planned US$9 million federal project, co-sponsored by the American Chemistry Council, it aroused considerable outrage from various consumer, medical, and political quarters. Democratic US Senators threatened to block the confirmation of Stephen Johnson, EPA's acting administrator, if the research was allowed to continue. Specifically, it was argued that the study unfairly targeted low-income, minority families through the allure of desirable incentives. Such families were unlikely to fully appreciate the health consequences for their children, such as the possibility of neurological damage, especially in light of claims on EPA's CHEERS website that the study would not entail any risks. Other critics, including some EPA scientists, asserted that the study's objective was precisely contrary to EPA's pesticide management policy, which is intended to protect children from the effects of pesticides and household cleaners, not to expose them to their potential dangers. Environmentalists joined the ranks of CHEERS critics by pointing to various public health and environmental concerns.

In defense of the EPA study, spokespersons for the study's sponsors argued that the potential benefits in terms of providing information about how small children are affected by harmful chemicals clearly justified the research. Further, it was pointed out that the study's design had been independently reviewed by scientists and public health officials, and was subject to broad mischaracterizations when described by critics. Despite these arguments, the study was suspended, forcing the EPA to reexamine the study's design and to resubmit it to an independent panel of experts at a later date.

The rapidity of the critical response and the ultimate judgment resulting in a halt to the pesticide study, at least for the foreseeable future, are indications of just how much ethical sensitivities have been raised in recent years. Not too long ago, such an investigation might have been carried out without a word of protest, bringing terrible consequences for an untold number of people. As recently as a half century ago, thousands of unwitting research participants were not as fortunate.

THE HUMAN RADIATION STUDIES

Albert Stevens. Elmer Allen. Eda Schultz Charlton. John Mousso. These are the names of but a few of the persons whose lives were tragically altered as a result of their participation in secret radiation experiments carried out by the United States Energy Department during the 1940s and 1950s. In contrast to earlier reports suggesting that the government-sponsored research involved fewer than 50 chronically ill patients, it now is estimated that thousands of relatively healthy human subjects were studied in several hundred experiments (Hilts, 1994b; Kong, 1994). Among the participants, who received no apparent medical benefits and in some cases suffered harmful consequences as a result of the experimental treatments, were pregnant women, infants, terminally ill patients, poor people, and other vulnerable groups (see Table 1.1).

Details regarding the number and breadth of the radiation experiments began to emerge in 1994 following a six-month inquiry by a government committee created to investigate Energy Department files and other relevant documents. Although there were earlier indications that ethically dubious radiation studies had been conducted, serious attention to the research was stimulated by a series of articles that appeared in a New Mexico newspaper, the *Albuquerque Tribune*, focusing on one experiment in which 18 patients were injected with plutonium in order to track its course in the human body. The exposé was compiled by Eileen Welsome, a distinguished journalist who had begun investigating the experiment in 1987 after discovering a footnote about it in a declassified government report on animal experimentation at a military base. Welsome eventually was able to trace the identities and backgrounds of some of the research participants, and her articles provided a human face to what many now view as a scientific tragedy. In her words, "I was shocked by the experiment. Once I got to know some of the

Table 1.1 Human radiation experiments

Studies	Example	Purpose
Fifteen studies involving about 130 black people	Tulane University and New Orleans' Charity Hospital researchers created and cut off blisters on subjects' forearms, then injected radioactive mercury	To study action of mercurial diuretic, used for patients with congestive heart failure, but study subjects did not have that health problem. Officials say patients volunteered
Eight studies involving about 140 infants and children	Washington University medical researchers injected children, most of them healthy newborns or premature infants with radioactive sodium	To study "sodium space," or electrolyte balance. One independent expert viewed the study as useful in understanding how to prevent infant death from diarrhea, but added it probably would not be approved today
Seven studies involving about 880 women, most of them pregnant	Columbia University researchers gave women tracer doses of radioactive sodium	To study sodium balance during pregnancy. A spokeswoman said the university has had a policy of getting consent from research participants since the 1950s
Eleven studies involving about 100 terminally ill patients	Beth Israel Hospital researchers injected tracer doses of radioactive sodium into terminally ill patients	To study a blood plasma substitute widely used during World War II. Level of consent obtained from patients and their families unknown
Three studies involving about 530 psychiatric patients	Researchers from University of California at Berkeley gave tracer doses of radioactive isotopes to Peruvian natives living at high altitude and to prisoners	To study blood metabolism in people living at high altitudes (in the case of the Peruvians) and to study body water (in the case of prisoner volunteers). Level of consent obtained from the Peruvians unknown

Breakdown of studies involving 1800 people from vulnerable populations who were given radioactive isotopes. The research offered no apparent medical benefit to the participants.

Source: Dolores Kong, "1800 tested in radiation experiments," *The Boston Globe*, February 20, 1994, pp. 1, 22. Reprinted courtesy of *The Boston Globe*.

stories behind the patients and actually met their relatives, I became even more shocked" (Welsome, 1993). The radiation experiments, which have now been extensively catalogued by the Office of Human Radiation Experiments, have been condemned as a blatant example of ethical abuse that has tarnished the reputation of American science worldwide (e.g. Advisory Committee, 1996; Cantwell, 2001; Welsome, 1999).

The radiation studies bear certain similarities to another government sponsored research project that to many observers represents one of the most notorious cases of ethical misuse and abuse of human subjects. This is the Tuskegee syphilis study, the longest non-therapeutic experiment on humans in medical history (Jones, 1993; Thomas and Quinn, 1991). The Tuskegee study was begun in

1932 by the US Public Health Service to investigate the long-term effects of untreated syphilis in 399 semi-literate black men in Macon County, Alabama. Although these men were diagnosed as having syphilis, treatment for the disease purposely was withheld so that the researchers could observe its "natural" course. Also included in the study were 201 black men without syphilis who served as control subjects.

As in many of the radiation experiments, the Tuskegee participants were not correctly informed about the nature of the non-therapeutic experiment and crucial information was withheld from them. Specifically, the syphilitic subjects were told that they were being treated for "bad blood," a term allegedly under-stood by the researchers to be a local euphemism for syphilis, but which the local blacks associated with unrelated ailments. In order to encourage continued participation in the study and monitor participants over time, the researchers promised the subjects "special free treatments" (which included painful, non-therapeutic spinal taps) on a periodic basis.

It was not long before it became clear that the infected subjects were suffering from more medical complications than the controls. By the mid-1940s, mortality rates were found to be twice as high for the untreated syphilitic subjects. The researchers estimated that between 28 and 100 deaths as of 1969 were due to syphilis-related conditions. Nevertheless, treatment was not provided until after the experiment was exposed in a 1972 *New York Times* article.

Because many details of the radiation and syphilis experiments were kept secret, it is perhaps understandable that the studies were allowed to continue for as long as they did without arousing public outrage about the lack of existing mechanisms for protecting the research participants. Contrary to the belief that there was little debate about the appropriateness of the radiation experimentation during the 1950s, government documents have revealed that serious ethical discussions had indeed taken place at high levels of the military and scientific establishment (Hilts, 1994b). However, despite some protests from officials within the Atomic Energy Commission, the experiments continued, some of the most dangerous involving the total-body irradiation of cancer patients. Additionally, a decision was reached to withhold all documentation referring to the experiments that could result in legal suits or adversely affect public opinion. As for the syphilis research, the investigators apparently believed that they were serving the best interest of humanity by carrying out important research on a deadly disease (Jones, 1993). Of course, it is difficult to imagine such research even being contemplated today without a recognition of the potential dangers it poses to unsuspecting research participants.

Within the behavioral sciences there are no known cases of research abuse in which comparable risks have seriously endangered the lives of human subjects. However, for anyone with at least a smattering of training in psychology, sociology, and related disciplines, the phrase "research ethics" conjures up some equally dramatic images. Many students of psychology know something about Stanley Milgram's studies of behavioral obedience, in which subjects were placed in the highly uncomfortable role of teacher, responsible for the delivery of severe "shocks" to a confederate learner. Others may have learned about the Stanford prison study, a study in which male college students participated in a simulated prison scenario playing the roles of prisoners or guards; the situation quickly developed into a psychological and emotional nightmare for several of the participants. Many of us have seen troubling pictures of research animals in textbooks and in the mass media depicting apparently painful surgical implants in monkeys, mice, and other animals, presumably sacrificed at the conclusion of the studies. In the realm of sociological research, many Americans are aware of some of the details of John Griffin's disguised participant observation, an informal investigation in which he himself served as the sole subject. Griffin, a white man, altered his appearance and lived for several months as a "black" in the southern United States. His experiences, as recounted in his famous book *Black Like Me*, offer a chilling insight into the treatment of American minorities during the 1950s (Griffin, 1961).

Whatever additional concerns these situations raise for us, it is clear that each case gives rise to several ethical questions: Were appropriate safeguards taken by the researchers to protect the well-being of their subjects? Should these studies have been conducted in the first place? What are the potential risks or harms involved in conducting such research, and what are the anticipated benefits or gains? Are such investigations justified by their benefits, regardless of the risks involved? Do researchers have a right to inflict pain on innocent research animals? Are there laws or guidelines that prohibit such research? These kinds of questions help us understand the issues involved in research ethics.

RESEARCH ETHICS DEFINED

At the start, these questions seem to have something to do with the acceptability of one's conduct or, more specifically, the appropriateness of one's approach in pursuing scientific truths. Indeed, "ethics" and the related term "morality" have similarly developed from terms that pertain to accepted (i.e. customary or usual) practice (Reese and Fremouw, 1984). The word "ethics" is derived from the Greek *ethos*, meaning a person's character or disposition, whereas the related term "morality" is derived from the Latin *moralis*, meaning custom, manners, or character. Philosophers typically describe moral judgments as involving matters of right or wrong, ought or ought not, a good action or a bad one. Whenever the question "Should I conduct this study?" is raised in the context of research, a moral issue is at stake.

Moral philosophers and others are apt to make subtle distinctions between the similar terms "moral" and "ethical," and to use these terms in different ways. In contrast to moral concerns, which question whether specific acts are consistent with accepted notions of right or wrong, the term "ethical" often is used to connote rules of behavior or conformity to a code or set of principles (Frankena, 1973; Reynolds, 1979). As an illustration, consider a case in which a psychologist deceived her research subjects but in so doing did not violate her profession's codified rules of proper behavior, as detailed in accepted ethical guidelines. In subsequent chapters we will see that some professional ethics codes do indeed condone the use of deceit under certain specified circumstances. Thus, although the psychologist may not have crossed the bounds of ethical propriety as defined by her profession's code of conduct, we may still feel that her behavior was not right in a moral sense by arguing that deceiving others can never be justified. This case does not necessarily imply a distinction between the terms, but rather a difference in the principles used to judge the psychologist's behavior (the profession's standards and those of a critic of deception). The psychologist's behavior was viewed as proper according to one set of principles (those by which professional psychologists are guided), but not according to another (a broader and more general set of moral principles). Thus, the terms "ethical" and "moral" may be used interchangeably to refer to rules of proper conduct, although we may prefer to distinguish between them in a context where codified principles are relevant.

Most people would agree that the terms ethical and moral are related to values, and may choose to describe the terms as referring to behaviors about which members of society hold certain values (Reese and Fremouw, 1984). When defining ethics from the perspective of values, a major emphasis is placed on ethical decisions. This approach to ethics suggests that the ethical or moral researcher makes judgments about research practices on the basis of his or her own values, and not by blindly following codified ethical guidelines. However, the ethical decision maker is one who is educated about ethical guidelines, and is able to carefully examine the various alternatives and take responsibility for choices. In essence, choices for conduct in each research situation are related to the decision maker's values, and these values must be weighed carefully when important decisions are to be made. To summarize, we can say that *research ethics* comprises principles and standards that, along with underlying values, guide appropriate conduct relevant to research decisions (see Figure 1.1). In essence, ethics provides researchers with the tools required to determine whether or not a certain action should be carried out and the extent to which a past action was justified (Malloy and Pitter, 2006).

When moral problems reflect an uncertainty about how to balance competing values we say that the situation poses an ethical (or moral) dilemma (Smith, 1985). An *ethical dilemma* is apparent in research situations in which two or more desirable values present themselves in a seemingly mutually exclusive way, with each value suggesting a different course of action that cannot be maximized simultaneously. It will become apparent throughout this book that many of the ethical issues that arise in behavioral research result from conflicting sets of values involving the goals, processes, or outcomes of an investigation. For example, one very common dilemma in psychological research emerges when investigators attempt to observe behavior as it naturally occurs in various social settings (a methodological approach known as "naturalistic observation"). In such situations, researchers must weigh the scientific requirements of validity (i.e. in obtaining an objective and valid measure of behavior) against the ethical importance of informing participants about their intentions prior to the observation in order to protect subjects' privacy rights. This ethical dilemma involves the important ethical procedure of "informed consent," which is discussed in detail in subsequent chapters.

Figure 1.1 The role of ethics and values in behavior.
Source: Adapted from Malloy and Pitter (2006). Reprinted with permission of the authors.

FACTORS INFLUENCING THE ETHICAL DECISION MAKING PROCESS

In the behavioral sciences, ethical decision making is often complicated by the fact that there are multiple interests that the researcher is obliged to serve, including members of the local community, employers, sponsors, granting agencies, professional affiliates, students, consumers, and other persons who ultimately may be affected by research findings. Generally speaking, the behavioral science investigator has recourse to three sources of guidance for ethical decision making and the resolution of ethical dilemmas: (1) personal, (2) professional, and (3) regulatory.

Personal ethical decision making

The investigator's decisions about what is appropriate or inappropriate conduct is to a great extent guided by his or her own personal value system, which is shaped by upbringing, education, and professional training. For example, a consumer researcher may decide that it is always wrong to conduct research on the effectiveness of persuasive tactics that will enable marketers to enhance the attractiveness of potentially harmful products (such as cigarettes and alcoholic beverages) for children, regardless of the incentives for doing so and even if the risks have been judged as minimal. This means-oriented approach to ethics reflects a reliance on general principles, rules, or policies to guide behavior (e.g. "do no harm"). In this sense, how one behaves is viewed as more relevant than the outcomes of one's actions (see Box 1.1). By contrast, an ends-oriented approach focuses on the consequences of an action, suggesting that the ends can justify questionable means. This perspective is consistent with a cost–benefit approach to ethical decision making. That is, an action is considered acceptable to the extent that it results in a favorable ratio of desirable (or good) outcomes to undesirable (or bad) ones. Consistent with this more utilitarian approach, a researcher may decide that it is ethically acceptable to conduct an investigation on the effects of racist imagery in television and advertising content that is likely to significantly advance understanding about how prejudicial attitudes are shaped, despite the possibility that some research participants members may be offended by the images to which they are exposed during the study (see Box 1.2).

Box 1.1   Ethical theories

Over its long history, moral philosophy has produced many ethical theories from which we might derive principles to guide research decisions. These theories are predominantly either consequentialist or non-consequentialist. Under consequentialist theories, the morally right research activity would be the one that produces at least as good a ratio of good to bad consequences (e.g. in terms of welfare or utility) as any other course of action, including not carrying out the action at all. Under non-consequentialist theories, the ethical evaluation of a research practice would generally reflect an assessment of its consistency with binding moral rules or duties, and consequences would not be of primary importance. One such duty might be to tell the truth.

The consequentialist analysis is akin to the familiar idea of cost–benefit assessment found in many professional ethics codes, whereas overriding obligations (e.g. one must always be completely honest with potential respondents) are more consistent with duty-based non-consequentialist reasoning. Although many provisions in formal ethics codes are in keeping with ethical theory, they are not in general directly informed by moral philosophy and their guidelines may reflect either a means-based (non-consequential) or ends-based (consequential) perspective.

Box 1.2   Three simple tests for a personal ethical decision

Test 1. Transparency
Do I mind others knowing what I have decided?

Test 2. Effect
Whom does my decision affect or hurt?

Test 3. Fairness
Would my decision be considered fair by those affected?

Source: Institute of Business Ethics (2005). (www.ibe.org.uk)

Professional ethical standards

As a member of a profession, the behavioral scientist is expected to adhere to the set of ethical standards that have been agreed upon by a majority of the profession's members. These standards are meant to apply to professional role behaviors and not to personal behavior, a distinction that may not always be clear-cut (Pipes, Holstein, and Aguirre, 2005). Although professional standards may be implicit, they often are explicitly presented in the form of ethics codes, which have been adopted by various professional organizations, such as the American Psychological Association (APA), the British Psychological Society (BPS), and the International Chamber of Commerce/European Society for Opinion and Marketing Research (ICC/ESOMAR), among many others (see appendix 2). In recent years, a growing number of social, political, and corporate organizations have developed codes of conduct that are useful for providing guidance to researchers working in applied contexts.

Ethics codes reflect the commitment of behavioral scientists to ethical professional conduct in all their dealings with persons with whom they interact in the research process. Despite a great degree of variance in the ways they are drafted, adherence to codified standards are completely voluntary, although disciplinary actions can be taken against researchers who violate them. Specific professional ethics guidelines are discussed in detail in chapter 2.

Regulatory mechanisms

In addition to voluntary ethical standards, researchers are required to adhere to a wide range of legally enforceable regulations for research practice. These legal strictures typically supersede ethical principles; in fact, many ethics codes explicitly stipulate that ethical decisions are to be carried out within the framework of legal mechanisms. For example, when conducting research with children, researchers must be cognizant of legal requirements pertaining to necessary consent procedures prior to the involvement of minors in the research process. In many countries, agreement must be obtained from legal guardians in addition to non-adult participants.

It should be noted that what is legal in one country setting may not be permissible in others. This is particularly evident with regard to the recruitment of participants, consent procedures, privacy, and confidentiality requirements. Researchers may be required to submit their research to special review in a foreign country to assure that the rights of participants receive necessary protections and that any special cultural factors are taken into consideration. Because a substantive amount of research is now carried out cross-culturally, with international research teams working in applied settings, these legal issues are more important than ever.

Thus, in addition to the recognition that personal ethical decision making in the behavioral sciences takes place within the context of legal strictures, it also must be acknowledged that ethical practices are governed by the larger system of society, with its corresponding set of ethical norms (such as freedom, due process, free trade, privacy, and fairness) and cultural values. Accordingly, we see that various forces influence the decision-making process for the ethical researcher and, as a result, many questions pertaining to acceptable or unacceptable practice fall within gray areas with no easy solutions, and often must be handled on a case by case basis.

HISTORICAL BACKGROUND: THE RISE OF ETHICAL CONCERNS IN THE BEHAVIORAL SCIENCES

As an expression of our values and a guide to achieving them, research ethics help to ensure that our scientific endeavors are compatible with our values and goals, through shared guidelines, principles, and unwritten laws. As recently as the 1960s, however, researchers in the behavioral sciences proceeded with few, if any, serious concerns about the ethical implications of their investigations. Discussions about ethical issues were rare, although studies involving deceptive manipulations, invasions of privacy, and threats to confidentiality were commonplace and altogether consistent with traditional ways of conducting scientific research. In fact, discussing ethical issues was likely to be seen as an indication that one had not outgrown a pre-scientific nature, bringing into the scientific domain issues that did not belong there. In other words, to have ethical concerns about methodological procedures that were so widely accepted and utilized was taken as a sign that one was not yet ready to participate fully in the scientific enterprise. Today, students in the behavioral sciences are trained in a very different kind of environment than previous generations. Ethical issues now are part and parcel of a broader framework of scientific issues that comprise the critical training of future researchers.

It was during the 1960s that behavioral scientists seriously began to attend to ethical issues pertinent to the conduct of their investigations. For example, in the discipline of social psychology, attention and debate focused on the issue of deception, largely because at that time most social psychological research on topics ranging from attitudes (e.g. Festinger and Carlsmith, 1959) to aggression (e.g. Berkowitz, 1969; Geen, 1968) and obedience (e.g. Milgram, 1963) involved laboratory experimentation based on the use of deception. Elsewhere, critics both within and outside the behavioral sciences began to grapple with issues arising in cross-cultural research, research in foreign areas, intelligence testing, and the like. These issues raised questions about the impact the research findings would have on the status of the groups from which data were derived. For the past quarter century, researchers have wrestled with these and other ethical issues that arise throughout the research process, from hypothesis generation to the reporting and application of the study's results (see Table 1.2).

There are several possible reasons for the increase of attention to ethical issues in psychology and related disciplines, and many of these reasons will be discussed in depth in the following chapters. One that bears mentioning at the outset has to do with the increasing number of cases involving human subject abuse that came to public attention during the 1960s. For example, in one of the first cases to receive widespread publicity, researchers at the Jewish Chronic Disease Hospital in Brooklyn, New York, injected live cancer cells into 26 chronically ill, elderly patients who were receiving care from hospital staff (Edsall, 1969; Schuler, 1982). The researchers hoped to demonstrate that the ill patients would react to the foreign cells by rejecting them rather quickly, as had been shown in experiments with healthy volunteer prisoners. This result indeed was

Table 1.2 Some ethical considerations before, during, and after a study

A. *Ethical considerations during the research planning stage*
- Does the researcher have the competence to conduct the research?
- Is the researcher aware of alternative approaches for meeting research objectives?
- Is the researcher knowledgeable about ethical guidelines, legal requirements, and local customs and norms?
- Has the research been evaluated by relevant ethics committees or review boards?
- Has the researcher recruited and selected participants fairly and in ways that are consistent with extant ethical guidelines?

B. *Ethical considerations during the conduct of the research*
- Are participants fully protected from physical and psychological harm?
- Are the participants' rights to informed consent, privacy, confidentiality, protection from deception, and debriefing protected?
- Are participants able to withdraw from the research at any time without fear of penalty?
- Does the researcher accurately record participant responses and other data?

C. *Ethical considerations once the research is completed*
- Does the researcher keep all promises made to participants and other relevant parties (e.g. employers, granting agencies, colleagues)?
- Are all incentives for participation delivered as promised?
- Are the study's results accurately represented in research reports?
- Is authorship credit justified?
- Does the researcher readily provide data for replication?

Source: Based in part on Aguinis and Henle (2004).

obtained, but when word got out about the researchers' invasive and potentially life-threatening procedure people reacted with shock and dismay. Many agreed that the apparent fact that none of the patients developed cancer could not justify the methods used by the researchers. Although some of the patients were told that something was going to be done to them of an experimental nature, none was informed about the cancer cell injections, nor were any of them asked to give written consent for the procedure. Thus, the participants were unaware of the nature of the risks imposed by the study.

Although the interventions utilized by behavioral researchers tend to be far less extreme than in the case described here, it is a common practice for researchers to withhold crucial information so as not to bias their subjects' reactions to experimental treatments. This sort of practice (often combined with research deceptions of an active sort) raises some complex ethical dilemmas in studies involving human subjects, and represents one of many conflicts between the methodological requirements of a study and societal standards considered throughout this book.

Before leaving the New York cancer cell study, the reader might be curious to learn about the fate of the researchers who were responsible for the investigation. The two researchers who had received federal funds for conducting the study subsequently were found guilty of fraud, deceit, and unprofessional conduct, and were censured and placed on a year's probation by the Board of Regents of the State University of New York (Faden and Beauchamp, 1986). A few years later, one of the researchers was elected president of the American Association for Cancer Research.

The cancer cell study was but one of many similar biomedical experiments that had been carried out without the informed consent of human participants (see Beecher, 1959, 1966). Several of these studies (in addition to the cancer cell research) are documented in psychiatrist Jay Katz's exhaustive anthology and casebook, *Experimentation with Human Beings*, which was published in 1972. Katz provides research examples from a number of fields, including sociology, psychology, medicine, and law, and traces the origins of political concern about the use of humans in research to the experiments conducted on prisoners in Nazi concentration camps during World War II.

The publication of Katz's book coincided with public disclosures of the Tuskegee syphilis study. People reacted in disbelief that the Tuskegee research could have been carried out over such an extended period, especially with governmental approval, and many critics openly questioned why a study of the long-term effects of syphilis was necessary in the first place. Medical annals are filled with case reports describing the effects of untreated syphilis. However, it must be considered that progress in science proceeds largely through systematic, controlled observations; researchers cannot rely solely on anecdotal reports and isolated cases. By carefully studying a large number of infected individuals, the Tuskegee researchers had an opportunity to obtain more objective and precise measurements for gaining insight into the nature of a serious disease. We also must keep in mind that the researchers who carried out investigations like those described here likely did not intend to cause harm or pose dangers to their research subjects, and no doubt viewed their methods as justified by the expected gains from conducting the studies. This "ends justify the means" variant of moral reasoning is one that continues to underlie the ethical decision making of many contemporary behavioral researchers. In some cases, however, as undoubtedly occurred in the cancer cell, syphilis, and radiation studies, researchers can be blinded to the potential risks posed by a research methodology while overemphasizing the anticipated merits of their investigations.

In the following chapters, we will consider the various ethical guidelines that have been developed by governments and professional associations in recent years; but it suffices to say at this juncture that behavioral and biomedical researchers now are required by most ethical codes to carefully weigh the expected benefits against the potential risks before deciding to proceed with a study. In studies where more than minimal risks are evident, research subjects must give their informed agreement beforehand that they understand the risks and agree to participate in the investigation.

The studies described above could not be legitimately carried out today because the ethical climate in the United States and other industrial nations has changed. For example, research involving even minimal levels of radiation would now be required to go through a rigorous review process in order to determine the adequacy of the study design and to make sure that proper mechanisms for protecting subjects' rights were in place (Kong, 1994). As suggested above, it was public awareness of earlier investigations like the New York cancer cell study and the Tuskegee syphilis study that in part led to stricter ethical standards for research. More specifically, such studies raised the awareness of public agency officials about the actual and potential risks to human participants in clinical investigations. They also highlighted the uncertain legal position of government agencies and functioned as a significant precedent in the eventual development of federal research guidelines (Faden and Beauchamp, 1986; Frankel, 1975). For example, the Tuskegee experiment indirectly led to the formation of a US governmental commission responsible for formulating some of the initial federal guidelines for behavioral and biomedical research (see chapter 2).

While these cases primarily occurred in the context of biomedical research, controversial cases also came to light in other disciplines. For example, in political science, a government-sponsored study known as Project Camelot gave rise to a wide-reaching ethical controversy. Project Camelot was a US$6 million project conducted under the auspices of the US Department of Defense by the Special Operations Research Office of the American University, Washington, DC.

Beginning in December 1964 (shortly after the United States had sent marines to the Dominican Republic), the project sponsors hoped to determine the conditions that gave rise to internal conflict in various Latin American countries, and the effects of actions taken by the indigenous governments to deal with those preconditions. In short, the goal of the research was to provide a systematic description of the events that preceded, occurred during, and followed either a peaceful or a violent change in government (Horowitz, 1967). The investigation was to involve various surveys and other field studies in Latin American countries, and a number of social scientists from various disciplines were recruited to serve as research consultants. However, the project was quickly condemned on ethical grounds by social scientists who viewed the project as a blatant attempt by the Department of Defense to intervene in the internal affairs of Latin American countries by sponsoring research designed to reduce the likelihood of revolution. The study was canceled in June 1965, prior to initiation of the actual fieldwork. One outcome of the controversy was a presidential communication instructing the US State Department to review all federally funded investigations involving research activities in other nations potentially affecting foreign policy.

Project Camelot is a particularly interesting case because it demonstrates the potential drawbacks of research conducted under the sponsorship of organizations such as the army, whose primary function is that of control. It also suggests how ethical issues can intensify as social scientists attempt to orient their research in the direction of broader human concerns while accepting support from specific social organizations (Kimmel, 1988a; Levin, 1981; Sjoberg, 1967).

Another landmark case is the 1954 Wichita Jury Study, which consisted of a series of investigations conducted on a Ford Foundation grant by a group of law professors from the University of Chicago. In an attempt to study the adequacy of the jury decision-making process, the researchers used hidden microphones to record the jury deliberations of six separate civil court cases. The study was carried out with the prior knowledge and approval of opposing counsel and the judges involved in the cases, but the jurors, defendants, and plaintiffs were not informed about any aspect of the research. It was agreed that the recordings would not be listened to until after the cases had been closed and all appeals exhausted, and that care would be taken to ensure the anonymity of all participants involved.

When the public became aware of the taped jury deliberations, a national uproar ensued (Faden and Beauchamp, 1986; Katz, 1972; Reynolds, 1979). The primary criticism centered on the methods used to collect the information for the study, given that secret jury deliberations are essential to the American judicial system and guaranteed by the Seventh Amendment to the US constitution. Serious questions also were raised about the confidentiality and privacy of those who were unaware of their participation in the research, and the possibility that general knowledge of the existence of the project might influence the decisions of other juries. The investigators defended their research by emphasizing the special care taken to minimize any effects on the jury members or the parties to the civil cases being considered. They also suggested that the project's successful completion could have resulted in recommendations for positive change in the judicial decision-making process or else could have boosted confidence in the current jury system. Interestingly, it was the controversy surrounding the Wichita study that ultimately resulted in legislation prohibiting intrusions upon the privacy of juries, including the tape recording of their deliberations (Faden and Beauchamp, 1986).

OVERVIEW AND ILLUSTRATIVE EXAMPLES

In each behavioral and social science discipline, it is possible to point to one or two controversial studies, like Project Camelot in the political realm and the Wichita Jury Study in the legal spectrum, that served to sensitize researchers within those fields and society in general about important ethical issues. In the remainder of this chapter, some additional studies are summarized in order to point out several of the ethical issues discussed in subsequent chapters.

Ethical issues can arise in laboratory or non-laboratory settings, in survey research, in the recruitment, selection, and study of human or animal subjects, and in the reporting of research findings. The ethical issues arising in each of these research contexts comprise a primary focus of chapters 3 through 10. (Chapter 2 and appendix 2 describe the professional and governmental guidelines that regulate research in the behavioral sciences.) This chapter concludes with a consideration of some basic reasons for studying research ethics.

Milgram's obedience experiments

Chapters 3 and 4 present an overview and analysis of the ethical issues that emerge in the conduct of laboratory research involving human participants. The Milgram obedience project, mentioned at the beginning of this chapter, is often cited as the behavioral research most responsible for contributing to sensitivities to ethical problems in the conduct of experimental laboratory research (e.g. Blass, 2004; Kimmel, 2003; Schuler, 1982; Slater, 2004). The central issue discussed in reference to Milgram's studies is that of the problem of deception of subjects. A brief summary of the research and an overview of the ethical debate that ensued appears below; we refer back to the obedience experiments periodically in other chapters.

In a series of laboratory experiments conducted between 1960 and 1964, Stanley Milgram, a social psychologist at Yale University, led his volunteer subjects to believe that they were giving dangerous electric shocks to innocent victims. These subjects were recruited to participate in an experiment allegedly on the effects of punishment on learning, and were assigned the task of teaching a list of words to a learner (actually an experimental "confederate") for a test of memory. The "teachers" (actual subjects) were required to "punish" the learner's mistakes by delivering increasingly stronger electric shocks (up to 450 volts).

As was typically the case in social psychology laboratory experiments at that time, Milgram's procedure was rigged; in this case, the learner did not actually receive shocks, but made a number of preplanned mistakes and feigned pain upon receiving the "shocks." For example, in one variation of the procedure, although the learner was in another room and could not be seen by subjects, his agonizing screams could be heard through the laboratory walls. As is now widely known, Milgram's actual intent was to observe the extent to which subjects obeyed the authority of the experimenter, who ordered subjects to proceed with the procedure despite their protests and the confederate's apparent agony. Milgram drew an explicit analogy between his experiments and Nazi atrocities committed in obedience to the commands of malevolent authorities during World War II.

Contrary to the expectations of several experts consulted by Milgram (1964) prior to conducting his research, a high degree of obedience was obtained in the experiments. In one typical study, twenty-six out of forty subjects (65 percent) continued to obey the orders of the experimenter to the end of the procedure, despite their apparent signs of discomfort and stress (Milgram, 1963). This outcome was unsettling in that it demonstrated the extent to which ordinary citizens might engage in brutal behavior at the direction of a person in a position of authority.

Milgram described his initial obedience experiments in 1961 in an unpublished research report. It was not until he published a series of articles about the project in 1963 that serious attention began to be paid to it, launching an unprecedented discussion in the profession of psychology. (The lay public first learned of the research in 1974 with publication of Milgram's book, *Obedience to Authority*.) Milgram received high praise for his ingenious experiments, and he was awarded the American Association for the Advancement of Science's (AAAS) prize for research in 1964. Although the target of scathing attacks for many years, Milgram's research received renewed attention by those who praised its insights into obedient behavior (Miller, Collins, and Brief, 1995). But it is in the context of discussions about ethical issues in laboratory research that his studies have attracted the most ink.

Psychologist Diana Baumrind (1964) was the first to criticize Milgram's research on ethical grounds, but several other colleagues soon followed. Milgram (e.g. 1964, 1974) steadfastly defended himself in print, attempting to answer all of the most important points of criticism. In brief, because we will return to these issues in chapter 3, the critics argued that there were not adequate measures taken to protect the participants from undue harm; that the entire program should have been terminated at the first indications of discomfort on the part of the participants; and that the participants would be alienated from future participation in psychological research because of the intensity of experience associated with laboratory procedures (Baumrind, 1964; Kelman, 1967).

Milgram (1964) countered these assertions by arguing that adequate measures were taken to protect the participants from harm; that subjects were allowed to withdraw from the study at any time; and that the deception was thoroughly explained to the participants at the end of the experiment. He further maintained that there was no reason to terminate the research because there were no indications of injurious effects apparent in the subjects. In fact, subjects indicated in follow-up questionnaires that the experiment was worthwhile and their responses suggested that they were not alienated from psychological research.

Milgram offered another compelling argument in defense of his obedience studies by suggesting that condemnation of his research procedure may have been fundamentally tied to the disturbing results he obtained. That is, if his results had turned out differently and subjects had refused to obey the experimenter-authority, then critics like Baumrind might not have perceived the deception as morally objectionable. In fact, there is some support for this contention, suggesting that perceptions of Milgram's research may be contingent more upon the subjects' responses than the experimental manipulations used (Bickman and Zarantonello, 1978). Whether or not one agrees with Milgram's points, it is clear that the use of deceptive and stressful methodologies in laboratory studies are obvious sources of ethical dilemmas. Such dilemmas force the ethical

researcher to consider alternative non-laboratory research approaches for pursuing the answers to scientific questions of interest.

The "tearoom trade" study

A basic alternative to laboratory research is for the behavioral scientist to observe
human behavior in more natural settings. Chapter 5 presents an overview of
various field research (i.e. non-laboratory) methodologies and the ethical issues
they entail. One of the advantages to conducting behavioral research in the field
is that observations can be carried out on unsuspecting participants, thus providing the researcher with a more natural reading of human reactions than might
be obtained in the laboratory. Of course, the drawback to this sort of approach
is that certain forms of disguised field research often threaten the research
participant's right to privacy.

A controversial investigation conducted by sociologist Laud Humphreys serves
as an illustration of the ethical problems that can emerge in disguised research in
public settings. For his doctoral research at Washington University, Humphreys
sought to describe the interactions among men who congregated in "tearooms,"
the name given to public restrooms where homosexuals illegally gathered to
engage in sexual activity. He also intended to learn about the lifestyles and
motives of the men whom he observed. To do so, Humphreys assumed the role
of "watchqueen" who was allowed to observe the sexual acts without
actually taking part in them, in exchange for serving as a lookout to warn
of approaching strangers. But Humphreys was on the lookout for more than
approaching strangers – he also noted the license plate numbers of the automobiles owned by the tearoom participants. By pretending to be a market
researcher, he next traced the registration numbers of the automobiles in order
to determine the tearoom participants' home addresses. One year later, Humphreys altered his appearance and, claiming to be a health service interviewer,
questioned the men at home. Once responses were obtained, Humphreys
destroyed the names of the participants so their identities could not be revealed.

The results revealed that a majority of the men Humphreys had observed
apparently led normal heterosexual lives as accepted members of their communities and did not view themselves as either homosexual or bisexual. Another
finding was that many of the participants' marriages were characterized by a high
degree of tension. Despite these interesting results, held by many as helpful in
dispelling some of the stereotypes and myths about the gay community, Humphreys's approach aroused strong criticism. Critics argued that although he had
taken precautions to protect his subjects, he nevertheless failed to protect their
right to privacy and used questionable strategies for obtaining information about
them. This negative reaction to Humphreys's research was so intense that it
prompted an (unsuccessful) attempt to have his doctoral degree rescinded.

Several specific ethical questions are raised by disguised field research like
the tearoom trade study (Sieber, 1982c). To what extent is deception justified by
the importance of an investigation? How might one go about studying illegal

behavior in scientifically valid and ethically justifiable ways? How can researchers protect their subjects' right to privacy in studies in which it is impossible to first obtain their voluntary consent? The primary ethical dilemma in the tearoom trade study involved a conflict between the interests of the scientist in obtaining knowledge and the interests of society in the protection of privacy and other rights.

Women and Love: the 1987 Hite Reports

Although ethical dilemmas may often seem more salient in research methodologies that involve the direct observation and measurement of behavior, problems also are encountered when indirect measurement tools, such as surveys, are used. In chapters 6 and 7 we consider the ethical issues that emerge in applied research, including studies in which behavioral scientists investigate human behavior through the use of interviews and written questionnaires. Concerns about privacy rights also emerge as relevant issues in this context, although in different ways than in field research. To what extent can survey researchers probe the private, personal lives of their subjects for research purposes, even when subjects' voluntary consent is obtained for doing so? Related and equally important issues in applied research in general involve protection of subject anonymity and response confidentiality.

In chapter 8, ethical issues in the recruitment and selection of research participants are described. These are issues that are relevant to all forms of human subject research, and bear a strong relationship to some subtle issues that arise in the context of survey research. One example of behavioral science research that serves to illustrate some of the issues covered in chapters 6–8 is found in the survey investigations conducted by Shere Hite (1976–1987). In order to illustrate Hite's research approach we shall focus here on her publication *Women and Love: A Cultural Revolution in Progress* (1987), the final volume of a trilogy of Hite Reports on the intimate lives of men and women. In this book, Hite argues that most American women are unhappy with their romantic, intimate relationships with men. Further, she contends that it is the men who largely are to blame for the dissatisfaction of their partners: men do not listen to their female partners, they refuse to discuss their feelings and to address tensions in their relationships, and they often unfairly criticize and ridicule their romantic partners. These assertions are based on the responses of more than 4,500 women who completed and returned her lengthy mail questionnaire.

It is not surprising that the contents of *Women and Love* quickly generated controversy, given the social climate of growing tensions between American men and women at the time of the book's publication. However, the loudest criticism of the Hite Report was voiced by leading survey research specialists and social scientists who decried Hite's research methodology. These research experts agreed that the report's methodology was seriously flawed because the findings were not based on a representative sample of American women.

The fact that Hite obtained such a large number of completed questionnaires may seem impressive at first, until one considers the large number of questionnaires that were *not* returned. To complete her research, Hite mailed 100,000 questionnaires to various feminist groups (such as the National Organization of Women, abortion rights groups, and university women's centers) and other women's groups (church groups, garden clubs, etc.). Thus, the 4,500 completed surveys represent a very low return rate of 4.5 percent, far below the standard return rate of between 40 and 70 percent for social science research surveys. (These figures reflect the fact that social scientists typically send follow-ups after the first mailing of questionnaires. Hite's return rate is closer to the average rate of 2.5–3.0 percent for commercial direct mail surveys.) Given the low rate of response to her survey, Hite's report merely reflects the relationship status and corresponding reactions of a small, non-representative sample of women who voluntarily chose to answer the 127 essay questions. Nevertheless, Hite claimed that the responses she obtained are "typical" and that her sample "quite closely mirrors" the US adult female population (Hochschild, 1987). Thus, she asks us to accept that 70 percent of women married for five years or more are having extramarital affairs, despite other reports by social scientists that the rate is closer to 30 percent. She also wants us to believe her finding that 92 percent of all women who divorce actually initiate the divorce proceedings.

Even Hite's staunchest critics appear to agree that she obtained some remarkable insights into the emotional toll of unsatisfying relationships experienced by the women who chose to reveal their life stories to her. Where most social scientists have problems, however, is in her claim that the stories are "typical." Instead, the critics suggest that these respondents represent a group of women who probably had suffered a very high level of emotional pain and were strongly motivated to answer the survey questions. But simply having a great many completed questionnaires does not make them typical if only those who have suffered feel strongly enough to respond. Hite defended her methodology by arguing that she purposely eschews random sampling in order to get more honest and personal responses. Her error is in then claiming that her responses are representative of a larger population.

On one level, the Hite Report gives rise to ethical concerns regarding privacy rights. Given the very personal and private nature of the written responses she obtained, an important consideration is whether Hite took precautionary steps to protect the anonymity of her subjects and to maintain the confidentiality of their responses. Additionally, did her respondents experience a recurrence of emotional and psychological pain as a result of completing the essays on the questionnaire? On another level, Hite's research demonstrates how ethical issues are an inevitable consequence of drawing unwarranted conclusions from one's research data. For example, Robert Groves, a sociologist who specializes in survey research, went so far as to criticize Hite's methodology as "the equivalent of medical malpractice in our field" and called the report "such a public display of incompetence that all others who are involved [in survey research] in a serious way are associated by default" (Mehren, 1987). Others similarly questioned the possible negative impact Hite's research would have on all other survey research, especially given the extensive publicity that the books received. These sorts of concerns also arose following publication of the first two Hite Reports, which dealt, respectively, with female and male sexuality. Clearly, procedures that produce misleading results are not beneficial, and thus are questionable on ethical grounds.

Taub's deafferented monkeys

The research examples described in this chapter thus far have all involved human subjects. In chapter 9, the ethical issues pertaining to behavioral research with animals are addressed. In recent years, the ethics of experimentation on non-human species has become a highly charged topic. Members and supporters of animal rights groups have created an atmosphere in which behavioral scientists now are pressured to justify research methods that may expose animal subjects to pain and suffering in the name of potential human benefit.

Various defenders of behavioral research on animals have cited a wide range of studies that have made significant contributions to the welfare of animals and humans (e.g. Cole, 1992; Miller, 1985; Orlans, 1993). Among this research is the controversial work of physiological psychologist Edward Taub and his associates (Taub et al., 1965). Taub's research represented a follow-up of some valuable early experiments conducted by Sherrington (1906). Using anesthetized dogs and cats, Sherrington's research demonstrated the importance of sensory information obtained from receptors in muscles, tendons, and joints in controlling reflexes necessary for balance, walking, and other motor activities. In one series of experiments, for example, Sherrington deprived his animal subjects of sensations from a limb by cutting the sensory nerves that served it (Mott and Sherrington, 1895). This procedure, known as deafferentation, resulted in a permanent loss of use of that limb after the animal had recovered from the surgery, despite the fact that the motor nerve pathways to the limb still were intact. Sherrington was awarded a Nobel Prize for his work, which provided useful information about reflexes necessary for the development of traditional techniques for the rehabilitation of persons suffering from neuro-muscular disorders.

Years after Sherrington's experiments, Taub and his colleagues challenged the untested assumption that animals could not be trained to regain use of a deafferented limb. Taub hypothesized that experimental animals were falling far short of their full potential for recovery after deafferentation. Using monkeys as his subjects, Taub demonstrated that much of the functioning of a forelimb that had been lost due to damage to sensory pathways indeed could be regained by restraining the use of the animal's good limb (Taub et al., 1965). Apparently, the restraints motivated the animal to attend more closely to any sensory information still available from the deafferented limb, and to relearn through trial and error to make maximum use of it.

These experiments clearly demonstrated that special training could enable deafferented animals to recover skills thought to be permanently lost. The findings, consistent with Taub's hypothesis of learned disuse, have contributed to successful efforts to treat patients who lost the use of their limbs as a result of stroke, brain injury, and other neurological damage. Patients now are better able to maximize their potential for recovery when conventional methods of physical therapy are supplemented with special training procedures. For example, as a direct result of Taub's work, doctors have successfully treated patients who were paralyzed on one side by restraining the movements of their undamaged arm (Miller, 1985). These patients, who appeared to have reached the limits of improvement through more conventional methods, were able to significantly improve their control over their damaged limbs following the restraining procedure.

While it is clear that the research reported here has led to important human benefits, the experiments nevertheless were vehemently criticized by those whose primary concern was the well-being of the animal subjects. Sherrington, for example, was accused of having performed painful surgery on animals without the use of anesthetics, in spite of the fact that his publications clearly stated that surgical anesthesia had accompanied the procedures (Keen, 1914). Faring much worse than his predecessor, however, was Taub, whose research became one of the first major targets of the growing anti-vivisection movement in the United States. Anti-vivisectionists are persons who oppose the practice of subjecting living animals to surgical procedures in order to advance scientific knowledge. When a group of animal rights activists, known as People for the Ethical Treatment of Animals (PETA), learned of Taub's research they filed a formal complaint charging Taub of animal abuse (Holden, 1986).

At issue were eight rhesus monkeys in Taub's laboratory at the Institute for Behavioral Research in Silver Spring, Maryland that had the sensory nerves removed from their forelimbs. Seven other monkeys in the laboratory served as controls in experiments on nerve regeneration. The charges were filed based on evidence of negligent conditions gathered by five scientists who toured Taub's laboratory in 1981. The evidence included slides taken in the laboratory that showed monkeys in undersized cages with mutilations believed to have been self-inflicted due to the loss of sensation in limbs caused by the experimental procedures. A court convicted Taub of animal cruelty, placed his monkeys in the custody of the National Institutes of Health (NIH), and revoked the unused portion of the more than US$200,000 in grant money he had received from the government to conduct his research. The conviction eventually was overturned by the Maryland Court of Appeals, which ruled that the state animal-cruelty law did not apply to federal research programs such as Taub's. His reputation still intact among his peers, Taub was awarded a Guggenheim Fellowship in 1983 to support additional research on the sensory mechanisms of monkeys, further angering animal rights activists who feared for the well-being of his research animals.

Since the controversy surrounding Taub's experiments, more stringent governmental policies regarding animal research have been instituted. There are lingering fears, however, that more limiting legislation supported by animal protectionists will curtail future human benefits derived from animal research.

The case of Sir Cyril Burt

The final chapter of this book focuses on some integral professional issues that pertain to the ethical review of behavioral research and the communication of research findings (chapter 10). Objective ethical review and the fair and accurate reporting of results are essential ingredients of ethical scientific conduct. An example of research that ultimately met these issues head on is found in the work of British psychologist Sir Cyril Burt on the inheritance of intelligence.

Burt, the founding father of British educational psychology, conducted a number of twin studies that figured prominently in the public debate about racial differences in intelligence. For more than twenty years, he generated copious data in support of his views about the relative importance of genetic factors as opposed to environmental ones in determining intelligence. For example, his studies of identical twins separated very early in life revealed high correlation values, despite the fact that the twins were reared in very different environments. Burt's data were not questioned at the time because he was a scientist of considerable influence in the sphere of mental measurement, and was widely respected for his research and statistical skills. Following his death in 1971, however, a different portrait of the man began to emerge, and it is now believed that Burt fabricated much of his data, perpetuating one of the most infamous frauds in the history of science (Hearnshaw, 1981; Mackintosh, 1995; Tucker, 1997).

Suspicions about Burt's research were first brought to the public's attention in a 1974 book by Princeton University psychologist Leon Kamin, *The Science and Politics of IQ*. Kamin pointed out numerous inaccuracies, inconsistencies, and methodological implausibilities that he had discovered in Burt's twins data. In one example, Burt had reported similar key correlation values (to three decimal places) for three different sample sizes (21 in 1955, over 30 in 1958, and 66 in 1966), a consistency that defies the laws of mathematical possibility. Kamin also discovered indications that Burt may have taken data from one study and pieced them into other studies so that the results would more conveniently fit his genetics hypotheses. Of course, Burt is not around to defend himself against these charges of scientific misconduct, so we may never know whether the statistical anomalies were a result of carelessness or a premeditated distortion of research evidence. In recent years, questions also have arisen about the accuracy and fairness of some of the arguments raised against Burt and his research integrity (see Joynson, 1989; Mackintosh, 1995).

About the same time Kamin's book appeared, Oliver Gillie, a London medical correspondent who had been commissioned to write a book on the heritability of intelligence, reported being unable to locate two of Burt's collaborators, despite an intensive search (Evans, 1976). Burt had published articles during the 1950s in which the names of two co-authors appeared. It is now widely believed that these collaborators may never have existed and that Burt invented them in order to increase the credibility of his research reports.

After these initial reports of possible cheating by Burt, other researchers described their own suspicions, suggesting that his data were often too good to be true – that is, they were too often a perfect fit for his theories (Evans, 1976; McAskie, 1978). Leslie Hearnshaw, whose authoritative biography of Burt appeared in 1979, added that Burt went beyond fabricating data and research assistants by authoring suspicious letters to prominent scientific journals (including the *British Journal of Statistical Psychology*, for which Burt served as editor) using pseudonyms to conceal his identity. These letters typically expressed praise for the work of Sir Cyril Burt and sometimes attacked his critics, thus providing Burt with a convenient device for calling attention to his own achievements and for further expressing his views. On occasion, Burt used these letters as an excuse to reply in print under his own name. According to Hearnshaw (1979), well over half of the 40 "contributors" of reviews, notes, and letters to the *British Journal of Statistical Psychology* during Burt's editorship are unidentifiable, but show enough consistency in style and content to suggest that Burt was their author.

Since the initial accusations of scientific fraud, Burt's research and reputation have been defended by scholars who have argued that the evidence against him is not as convincing as the many sensationalist reports surrounding the scandal have suggested. For example, Jensen (1974, 1978), a strong hereditarian, maintained that the statistical anomalies in Burt's published research were few and minor (see also Eysenck, 1981). More recently, persuasive cases have been made that many of the charges against Burt were unfounded, and that some of his initial detractors may have been bent on character assassination (Fletcher, 1991; Joynson, 1989). Despite the accumulated evidence on both sides of the debate, we probably will never know with complete certitude whether Burt deliberately falsified his data, although it appears that the charges against him have been excessive (Green, 1992).

Many observers maintain the view that Burt probably was so committed to his stance on the nature–nurture debate that he chose to use data in ways that would convince others of what he already believed to be true. Based on his thorough assessment of the man, Hearnshaw (1979) concluded that Burt's apparent deceit may have been a function of certain defects in character, which ultimately served to tarnish the reputation of an otherwise brilliant scientist. Although extreme cases of scientific fakery appear to be rare in the behavioral sciences, when they occur their effects can be serious and far reaching. For instance, the British school tier system was based largely on Burt's findings regarding the heritability of intelligence (Diener and Crandall, 1978).

CONCLUSION: WHY STUDY RESEARCH ETHICS?

In this chapter some well-known examples of ethically questionable research in the behavioral sciences and related fields have been described. These cases represent only a small portion of the many other examples examined in this book. This is not to suggest that such studies are indicative of the majority of research in the behavioral and social sciences. In fact, much research in these fields is free of ethical problems and poses no threat to the participants studied or to society at large. However, an examination of the research controversies can sensitize readers to some of the important considerations that are relevant to research ethics, including the difficulties that confront researchers in ethical decision making, and the consequences of their decisions.

A primary goal of this chapter has been to convey a better appreciation for the study of research ethics. Too often it seems that students (and, it is feared, seasoned investigators) approach the subject matter of research ethics as comprised of dry philosophical discourse, and view the many ethical issues and dilemmas as mere roadblocks to the exciting "stuff" of research – investigating interesting behavioral problems, designing complex studies, observing behavior, interviewing people, and the like. The examples considered in the previous pages, however, present a quite different picture of what this book is all about. Recognizing and attempting to resolve the ethical dilemmas that threaten scientific progress in a field of inquiry can be as challenging as developing a complex research strategy and design for testing a hypothesis of interest (see Blanck et al., 1992). Research that is shrouded by ethical questions ultimately can lead to the destruction of reputations and careers, can threaten funding for research projects, can give rise to radical movements (such as the anti-vivisection campaign), and can stimulate ongoing, passionate debate. As Diener and Crandall (1978, p. 2) argued, rather than being associated "with sermons about morality and with endless philosophical debate," research ethics more appropriately should be viewed as "a set of dynamic personal principles that appeal to vigorous and active scientists who face difficult real-world ethical decisions."

The study of research ethics helps to prevent research abuses and it assists us in understanding our responsibilities as ethical scientists. Ethically educated investigators can become better able to anticipate ethical problems in their studies before they occur, in order to avoid them entirely or else to become more skillful in coping with them. Too often, it seems that individuals do not fully appreciate the complexities of ethical dilemmas until they are caught up in them. By then, it may be too late to cope effectively with the problems in a reasoned and objective manner, and less than satisfactory compromises are likely to result.

The next chapter describes the ethical guidelines and standards that have evolved over the years to protect against the research abuses of the past. Such principles are intended to provide a workable framework within which researchers who seek guidance can analyze the issues relevant to the demands of their research, in order to make decisions that do not compromise either scientific truth or human rights.

2

Ethical Principles in Behavioral Research: Professional and Governmental Guidelines

"Ethical guidelines are necessary to clarify the conditions under which psychological research is acceptable."

British Psychological Society, 2005

"A code of ethics is always an expression of a profession's self-comprehension."

German Professional Code of Ethics, 1986

Chapter Topics

☞ Background to professional codes of ethics
☞ The American Psychological Association code of ethics
☞ Cost–benefit approach to ethics
☞ Ethical codes of sociology and anthropology
☞ Governmental and legal regulation of behavioral research

Psychologists have a professional responsibility to evaluate carefully and thoroughly the ethics of their investigations. Ethical decision making involves a set of balancing considerations as to how best to contribute to science and human welfare. Such decision making occurs not in a vacuum, but in the context of the shared principles of a profession, government regulations, and the characteristic values of the general public.

This chapter presents a summary of the various ethical principles and governmental regulations that guide behavioral scientists in the conduct of their research. In the following pages, we consider the scope of their coverage, provide some background as to their development, and clarify their various functions. A single set of ethical rules of conduct is not available to behavioral scientists, who may work in a variety of disciplines and settings, each having its own working set of standards for human and animal research. However, there are enough similarities among the principles for researchers to obtain a clear idea of the essential ethical concerns when conducting behavioral investigations. In this chapter the APA guidelines receive particular emphasis because they are widely viewed as representing the most extensive and elaborate statement of ethics among those adopted by behavioral scientists. Our overview of ethical regulation begins with a brief history of professional codes of ethics and concludes with a consideration of the role that government has played in the research process.

THE DEVELOPMENT OF PROFESSIONAL CODES OF ETHICS

Federal regulations and professional codes of ethics have replaced the so-called unwritten ethic that individuals would act in fair and compassionate ways with regard to the rights of others. The earliest ethical principles for regulating human research are those that were developed for medical research and therapy. These early principles can be considered as the forebears to those eventually developed for research in the behavioral sciences.

The current ethical principles for medicine were developed after World War II, as is similarly the case for the biomedical and behavioral research fields. It is possible to find much earlier versions of medical codes, including the Hippocratic oath, which dates back to Hellenic times. Thomas Percival's book *Medical Ethics*, published in 1803, was a significant contribution to ethics during the nineteenth century. The major emphasis in Percival's book was placed on the practitioner's obligation to provide appropriate medical treatment to others. Perhaps because scant systematic experimentation was being carried out at the time, Percival devoted little attention to the ethical issues pertinent to the doctor–patient relationship, such as the need to fully inform treated individuals of procedures and risks. His book later served as the basis for the American Medical Association's (AMA's) Code of Ethics in 1847, and subsequent revisions (Katz, 1970). The AMA's ethics code has been refined and elaborated over the years, with its most significant changes occurring in response to the moral outcry over atrocities committed during World War II by scientists in Nazi Germany.

The Nuremberg Code of Ethics

The contemporary origins of formal standards for guidance and control in the behavioral sciences can be traced to the Nazi abuses of human subjects during World War II. As is now widely known, horrific experiments were conducted on prisoners in Nazi concentration camps; after the war, these scientific cruelties were revealed and documented at the Nuremberg trials (*United States v. Karl Brandt et al.*). Among the studies carried out by Nazi physicians were experiments involving healthy prisoners' reactions to various diseases (such as malaria and typhoid fever), poisons, extreme temperatures, and simulated high altitudes. In one of these experiments, subjects were immersed in freezing water to determine how long it would take for them to die (Angell, 1990). Other studies were conducted to observe the course of infections and to test the effectiveness of treatments for different types of experimentally inflicted wounds (Katz, 1972). The Nuremberg trials ended in August 1947 with either death sentences or extensive prison terms imposed on the defendants, each of whom had been found guilty of committing war crimes and crimes against humanity.

In recent years much has been written about the abhorrent acts committed by the Nazi physicians in the name of research (e.g. Evans, 2004; Lifton, 2000), and even this apparently clear-cut illustration of ethical abuse has not escaped debate and controversy. For example, while some authors (e.g. Mitscherlich and Mielke, 1960; Proctor, 1999) have documented how some of the studies actually contributed to medical knowledge and other scientific achievements, others have questioned the use of knowledge obtained through such inhumane means. Attempts have been made to explain how the Nazi physicians were able to cope with their involvement in carrying out tasks that must have conflicted with their moral and professional values, citing complex medical-ethical rationalizations for their participation and prevailing German authoritarian political and social values (Lifton, 2000; Ravitch et al., 1987). Ravitch et al. have described how the researchers may have deluded themselves into believing they were undertaking noble medical and scientific work, a point that echoed earlier suggestions that the physicians felt a sense of duty to contribute to the German struggle for existence (Katz, 1972; Mitscherlich and Mielke, 1960).

An important outcome of the Nuremberg trials was the formulation of a code of ethics to prevent future atrocities like those perpetrated under the guise of "medical science" by the Nazi researchers (Annas and Grodin, 1995). The ten-point Nuremberg Code did not proscribe investigation as such, but instead attempted to outline permissible limits for experimentation (see Box 2.1). For example, the first principle of the code is particularly important for introducing the concept of "voluntary, informed consent," describing it as "absolutely essential" in research with humans. According to this principle, voluntary consent to participate in a study must be obtained from human subjects who are fully informed of the nature and risks of the experimental procedure. The other principles further delineate the criteria for an ethically acceptable investigation, including the necessity for the research to be carried out by competent, highly qualified researchers; that the subject has the freedom to discontinue participation in a study at any time; and that precautions are taken to avoid unnecessary physical and psychological risks.

It is difficult to imagine that the Nuremberg Code would have prevented Nazi atrocities had it been in place earlier, and, as we have seen in the case of the American radiation experiments and the Tuskegee syphilis study, additional examples of scientific cruelty have surfaced since the Nuremberg trials. The existence of ethical codes is no guarantee that research abuses will be prevented, but they do serve certain useful functions. By codifying a set of value judgments in a formal document, an ethical code defines the grounds by which a research procedure can be evaluated as morally right or wrong and thereby helps to

Box 2.1   The Nuremberg Code

The following ten principles of the 1946 Nuremberg Code were taken from Katz (1972, pp. 305–6) and appear in abridged form.

1   The voluntary consent of the human subject is absolutely essential.
2   The experiment should be such as to yield fruitful results for the good of society, unprocurable by other methods or means of study, and not random and unnecessary in nature.
3   The experiment should be so designed . . . that the anticipated results will justify the performance of the experiment.
4   The experiment should be so conducted as to avoid all unnecessary physical and mental suffering and injury.
5   No experiment should be conducted where there is an a priori reason to believe that death or disabling injury will occur; except, perhaps, in those experiments where the experimental physicians also serve as subjects.
6   The degree of risk to be taken should never exceed that determined by the humanitarian importance of the problem to be solved by the experiment.
7   Proper preparations should be made and adequate facilities provided to protect the experimental subject . . .
8   The experiment should be conducted only by scientifically qualified persons.
9   During the course of the experiment the human subject should be at liberty to bring the experiment to an end if he has reached the physical or mental state where continuation of the experiment seems to him to be impossible.
10 During the course of the experiment the scientist in charge must be prepared to terminate the experiment at any stage, if he has probable cause to believe that a continuation of the experiment is likely to result in injury, disability, or death to the experimental subject.

promote the fair treatment of participants in the research process. With its adoption, the Nuremberg Code offered at least some degree of protection to research participants and stimulated ethical codification in various research disciplines.

Ethical standards for psychology

Psychology's first complete set of ethical guidelines for human subject research were formulated by an APA ad hoc committee in 1973, although a more generic code detailing ethical considerations in research, teaching, and professional practice had been in place since 1953. Since its inception, the primary purpose of the

APA code of ethics has been to establish minimum standards for the conduct of psychologists, and its content reflects the association's concern for public welfare, protection of the profession of psychology, public relations, and education of members of the profession (Knapp and VandeCreek, 2003). The development of ethical standards for research in psychology is interesting historically because of the process by which the standards evolved and the changing political and social climates they reflected (Reese and Fremouw, 1984). Thus, the process of ethical codification in psychology provides an informative case study in the evolution of professional guidelines for research.

The beginnings of a code of ethics in psychology date back to 1938 when the APA Committee on Scientific and Professional Ethics was formed to consider the advisability of drafting an ethical code for the profession. Despite the decision to consider complaints of unethical conduct by psychologists, it was not until 1947 that formal work began on the development of a written set of guidelines. The decision to begin the drafting of an ethics code came about as a result of several converging forces, including raised sensitivities about ethical issues stemming from the Nuremberg trials, and the emergence of some problematic cases regarding the conduct of professional psychologists in both research and clinical contexts.

Ethical developments in psychology also came about as a result of psychologists' extensive involvement in and contributions to the war effort during World War II. Psychologists had been called on to initiate a variety of testing programs, including the intelligence testing of thousands of recruits for screening and placement purposes, and the situational stress testing of other military personnel for sensitive intelligence and espionage missions. When the war ended, there were accelerated demands for research applications in civilian contexts, such as personnel testing and training in business and industrial settings, which inevitably gave rise to questions about privacy, confidentiality, and the misuse of test results. The call for a code of ethics thus seems to have come about, at least in part, as a result of increased emphasis on the problems of professional psychology. The emergence of applied psychology essentially shattered the previously held assumption that research in the discipline was invariably ethical and value free, and ultimately would serve in the best interests of human welfare (Diener and Crandall, 1978).

APA's empirical approach

A unique approach was taken by the APA to accomplish the formidable undertaking of developing an ethics code. A committee of experts was formed, but the group eschewed any attempt to generate deductively a set of guidelines on its own, as had been done by elite groups in some other professions. Instead, the committee solicited the participation of all members of the professional association, who were asked to describe specific situations that actually had raised ethical problems for them. Thousands of responses were received by the committee, and an attempt was then made to determine inductively the primary areas of ethical issues encountered by psychologists in their work. Based on the critical incidents received, a set of provisional ethical standards was drafted and submitted to all APA members for review and comment. Proposals for the ethical standards were published in 1950 and 1951, and numerous reactions appeared in two important psychology journals, *American Psychologist* and *Psychological Bulletin*. The standards were revised and modified throughout this review process, and finally were approved in 1953.

The formal code, *Ethical Standards of Psychologists*, has since undergone numerous revisions over the past 50 years, most recently resulting in the 2002 version, *Ethical Principles and Code of Conduct* (APA, 2002). Each revision is undertaken by an APA ethics committee (now referred to as the Ethics Committee Task Force, or ECTF), which solicits comments from the entire APA membership prior to adoption.

The 1953 standards were generic in that they presented ethical principles in areas of consideration related to research, teaching, and professional practice. Very little in the initial code dealt directly with the ethical use of human subjects in research. A short section on the researcher's relationship to subjects presented four principles that focused on such issues as exposing research participants to harmful effects; deception and the withholding of information from subjects; confidentiality of data; and fulfillment of obligations to participants. The most prohibitive principles were those requiring that the identity of research participants could be revealed only with their "explicit permission" (thus emphasizing the importance of confidentiality), and that psychologists were "obliged" to fulfill all responsibilities to participants. The 1959 revision added the requirements of voluntary informed consent and removal of negative consequences in studies in which harmful after-effects were expected.

It is not surprising that the initial reaction to psychology's first formal ethical standards was for researchers to ignore them or else not to take them very seriously (Vinacke, 1954). Like other early professional codes of ethics, psychology's initial code was comprised of guidelines that were overly general and largely unenforceable, perhaps reflecting the uncertainty of the period as to the necessity for explicit research guidelines (Sieber, 1982c). However, by the late 1960s a changing scientific climate within psychology had begun to emerge and with it came a great deal of concern about the adequacy of the current standards as they pertained to human subject research. Laboratory experimentation with human subjects had increased dramatically, along with the regular use of deception and other ethically questionable research procedures. A number of methodological concerns were raised about the implications of these laboratory procedures, especially deception (see chapters 3 and 4). An interest in ethical issues seemed to go hand in hand with rising concerns over issues related to the methodology of experimentation, and it often is the case that developments toward ethical regulation tend to follow in the wake of disclosures of ethical misconduct or questionable practices (Kuschel, 1998). Thus, it was not until the debate over some highly controversial studies, like the Wichita Jury Study and Milgram's obedience research, that psychologists seriously began to wrestle with the issues of deception, privacy, and confidentiality in human subject research.

The rise in social conscience and the emphasis on the protection of individual rights ushered in during the late 1960s gave rise to additional ethical problems as psychologists began to focus their investigations on socially relevant problems, such as violence and crime, drug abuse, and minority issues. To a certain extent, the greater attention given to the rights of research subjects can be seen as part of the larger human rights movement in the United States during that time. In short, it was a combination of factors that led to a significant reevaluation in 1971 of the ethics of research in psychology.

The 1973 research principles

Repeating the method used to develop the original ethical standards, an ad hoc Committee on Ethical Standards for Research, chaired by Stuart W. Cook, developed a separate set of standards dealing solely with human subject research. Once again, the empirical process used to develop the principles was a time consuming and painstaking one, involving the participation of numerous psychologists who were asked to complete questionnaires, to provide examples of research situations that had raised ethical questions for them, and to respond to two draft versions of the principles. Much heated debate ensued, with some psychologists arguing that the principles threatened to limit scientific freedoms (e.g. Gergen, 1973a), and others maintaining that the principles were not strict enough to provide adequate protection for research participants (Baumrind, 1971, 1972). Eventually, a document consisting of ten research principles was adopted by the APA Council of Representatives in 1972 and was published in the January 1973 issue of *American Psychologist*. The research standards collectively appeared as principle 9 in the *Ethical Principles of Psychologists* and were detailed in an APA booklet with sample cases and extensive commentary (*Ethical Principles in the Conduct of Research with Human Participants*; APA, 1973, 1982).

The ten research principles (see Box 2.2) pertained to the following seven areas of concern: (1) making the decision to conduct an investigation (principles A–C); (2) obtaining subjects' informed consent to participate (principles D and E); (3) assuring freedom from coercion to participate (principle F); (4) maintaining fairness in the research relationship (principle F); (5) protecting subjects from physical and mental harm (principle G); (6) observing responsibilities to participants once the research is completed (principles H and I); and (7) guaranteeing anonymity of research participants and confidentiality of data (principle J).

A few noteworthy points about the profession's first substantive set of principles stand out. First, the principles deal only with the use of humans in psychological research; a separate set of guidelines for animal research constituted principle 10 of *Ethical Principles of Psychologists* (APA, 1990) and are described in detail in chapter 9. One unique aspect of the 1973 document (and subsequent revisions) is that it uses the term "participant" throughout, instead of the more common "subject," to refer to the individuals who are studied in psychological research. This choice of terminology was a conscious one on the part of the ad hoc

Box 2.2   Ethical principles for human subjects research (APA, 1973)

The following principles represent the initial set of APA standards specific to research. They are superseded by the 2002 version of the APA ethics code.

A   In planning a study, the investigator has the responsibility to make a careful evaluation of its ethical acceptability. To the extent that the weighing of scientific and human values suggests a compromise of any principle, the investigator incurs a correspondingly serious obligation to seek ethical advice and to observe stringent safeguards to protect the rights of human participants.

B   Considering whether a participant in a planned study will be a "subject at risk" or a "subject at minimal risk," according to recognized standards, is of primary ethical concern to the investigator.

C   The investigator always retains the responsibility for ensuring ethical practice in research. The investigator is also responsible for the ethical treatment of research participants by collaborators, assistants, students, and employees, all of whom, however, incur similar obligations.

D   Except in minimal-risk research, the investigator establishes a clear and fair agreement with research participants, prior to their participation, that clarifies the obligations and responsibilities of each. The investigator has the obligation to honor all promises and commitments included in that agreement. The investigator informs the participants of all aspects of the research that might reasonably be expected to influence willingness to participate and explains all other aspects of the research about which the participants inquire. Failure to make full disclosure prior to obtaining informed consent requires additional safeguards to protect the welfare and dignity of the research participants. Research with children or with participants who have impairments that would limit understanding and/or communication requires special safeguarding procedures.

E   Methodological requirements of a study may make the use of concealment or deception necessary. Before conducting such a study, the investigator has a special responsibility to (1) determine whether the use of such techniques is justified by the study's prospective scientific, educational, or applied value; (2) determine whether alternative procedures are available that do not use concealment or deception; and (3) ensure that the participants are provided with sufficient explanation as soon as possible.

F   The investigator respects the individual's freedom to decline to participate in or to withdraw from the research at any time. The obligation to protect this freedom requires careful thought and consideration when the investigator is in a position of authority or influence over the participant. Such positions of authority include, but are not limited to, situations in which research participation is required as part of employment or in which the participant is a student, client, or employee of the investigator.

Box 2.2   (Continued)

G The investigator protects the participant from physical and mental discomfort, harm, and danger that may arise from research procedures. If
risks of such consequences exist, the investigator informs the participant
of that fact. Research procedures likely to cause serious or lasting harm
to a participant are not used unless the failure to use these procedures
might expose the participant to risk of greater harm or unless the
research has great potential benefit and fully informed and voluntary
consent is obtained from each participant. The participant should be
informed of procedures for contacting the investigator within a reasonable time period following participation should stress, potential harm,
or related questions or concerns arise.

H After the data are collected, the investigator provides the participant
with information about the nature of the study and attempts to remove
any misconceptions that may have arisen. Where scientific or humane
values justify delaying or withholding this information, the investigator
incurs a special responsibility to monitor the research and to ensure that
there are no damaging consequences for the participant.

I Where research procedures result in undesirable consequences for the
individual participant, the investigator has the responsibility to detect
and remove or correct these consequences, including long-term effects.

J Information obtained about a research participant during the course of
an investigation is confidential unless otherwise agreed upon in
advance. When the possibility exists that others may obtain access to
such information, this possibility, together with the plans for protecting
confidentiality, is explained to the participant as part of the procedure
for obtaining informed consent.

Source: American Psychological Association (1973) *Ethical Principles in the
Conduct of Research with Human Participants*. Washington, DC. American
Psychological Association (1982) *Ethics in Research with Human Participants*
(2000). Washington, DC. Copyright © 1973 and 1982 American Psychological
Association. Reprinted with permission. APA cautions that the guidelines
and information provided in the 1973 and 1982 *Ethical Principles in the
Conduct of Research with Human Participants* are no longer current but
may be of educative value to psychologists, courts, and professional bodies.

committee, which recognized the various pejorative connotations associated with
the term "subject," including the subordinate role it seems to imply for investigators and the "objects" of their studies.

Historically, subjects were subservient to the divine rights of kings; in medical
practice, "subject" is sometimes used to refer to a cadaver for dissection and
demonstration. Given these associations, it has been argued that contemporary
usage of the term in the behavioral research context leads to a depersonalization

of members of the sample and implies a passive and subservient role in the research process (Oliver, 2003). One critic of the labeling of research participants as "subjects" argued that the term undermines "the individual and social qualities of the human being" (Riegel, 1979, p. 88). More recently, it has been suggested that a shift in terminology from "experimenter/subject" to "researcher/participant" can enhance the public character of science and thereby facilitate better research (see Box 2.3). The author agrees that the use of "subject" to refer to research participants can have negative associations in research contexts, and that the reader should be mindful of that possibility. What is more important, however, is that we remember to treat the individuals who assist us in

---

Box 2.3   From "subject" to "participant"

Traditionally, the use of the terms "experimenter" and "subject" in behavioral research reflected a rigid hierarchical distinction between the researcher as "expert" on human behavior and the research subject as "novice" (Young et al., 1995). This distinction is at the heart of the power differential that typically bestows greater authority upon the researcher in his or her interactions with subjects (Kelman, 1972). That is, generally it is the researcher who is fully informed about the nature of the research procedure, its purpose, and its theoretical underpinnings (the exception being when "blind" experimenters are employed to carry out the data collection but are left unaware of certain aspects of the study). Research subjects are presumed to be naive about these things and, as a result, are left relatively powerless in the situation, passively subject to the researcher's procedures.

In recent years, as sensitivities regarding the ethical treatment of others have increased, there have been calls for the establishment of a more egalitarian and respectful relationship between researchers and subjects. One indication of movement in this direction was apparent in recent revisions of the American Psychological Association's *Publication Manual*, an influential guide intended to aid authors in the preparation of manuscripts. The guide advocates a shift in terminology from "subject" to "participant" when referring to human beings. Such a shift towards eliminating the term "subject" in psychology publications also has been noted in psychology journals in recent years (Young et al., 1995).

According to Young et al. (1995), the move to replace the term "subject" with "participant" is a positive development that can serve to facilitate better research. In their view, "participant" more accurately reflects the ideal that persons involved in research are actively engaged in the scientific process, and wider adoption of the term represents a step in the direction of recognizing them as true collaborators. As a result, researchers may be more apt to establish a collaborative relationship with research participants (e.g. by obtaining their input during the formulation of questionnaires and interview protocols), ultimately serving to enhance the public image of psychological science.

the research process with respect and dignity, no matter how we choose to refer to them. Thus, the terms "subject" and "participant" are used interchangeably throughout this book. At other times, especially in references to surveys and research in other disciplines, the more general term "respondent" is used.

Another point regarding the ethical principles is that, like the 1953 standards, responsibility for ethical decision making was placed on the individual investigator. This emphasis subsequently has been a source of contention for those who feel that researchers are not always in the best position to objectively evaluate the ethicality of their own investigations. In chapter 9 we review some evidence that indeed supports this view. Although principle A recommends that the researcher should seek the advice of others when decisions suggest deviations from a principle, some scientists and laypersons believe that independent review committees should have the responsibility to oversee the ethics of human subject research. This, in fact, is an approach to ethical review that in recent years has taken on increasing importance in many research institutions, and is a government requirement for federally funded research in the United States.

Also a source of much controversy both before and after their approval is that few of the statements contained within the ethical principles consisted of absolute prohibitions. In some obvious cases, the principles are straightforward; for example, principle G states that procedures are not to be used if they pose the risk of serious harm to research participants. But for the most part, it is clear that the APA had not developed a set of "Ten Commandments" for research, prefaced by phrases like "thou shalt not," but instead took an approach emphasizing the *weighing* of considerations that maximize positive outcomes ("benefits" or "gains") relative to negative ones ("costs" or "risks"). This so-called "cost–benefit approach," of course, is consistent with a consequentialist approach that places responsibility for ethical decision making on the investigator, who is expected to evaluate prior to carrying out an investigation whether the anticipated benefits of the study outweigh the potential costs.

A cost–benefit approach to ethical decision making is consistent with a moral theory known as *utilitarianism*, which asserts that an action or rule of conduct is right if it produces the greatest well-being of everyone affected by it (Bentham, 1789). Based in part on the nineteenth-century British philosopher John Stuart Mill's (1957) "principle of utility," this perspective suggests that an individual ought to take the course of action that promotes the greatest good, happiness, or satisfaction for the most people. Utilitarians thus maintain that when a person is considering alternative moral choices, the net consequences of each of the available alternative actions must be considered.

In the context of behavioral research, utilitarians would argue that scientific ends sometimes justify the use of means that would necessarily sacrifice individual subjects' welfare, particularly when the research promises the "greatest good for the greatest number." For example, a research procedure that poses serious risk of harm to a group of human subjects would be justified from a utilitarian perspective if the study shows promise for developing a medical treatment that could save thousands of lives. This philosophical approach, essentially a variation of the moral suggestion that the ends justify the means, can be contrasted with *deontological* ethical theories, which hold that at least some basic actions are good in and of themselves without regard to whether they maximize positive consequences. "Deontologism" is a term that stems from a Greek word for duty or bindingness and thus is used to refer to duty-based moral theories (Atwell, 1981). Such theories suggest that general principles can be formulated that describe right or appropriate behavior, and that individuals must strive not to violate these general principles or allow for exceptions. Although deontologists often differ in their views about what is good or right, they generally minimize the role of consequences in ethical decision making. A deontological principle such as "do no harm" would suggest that the study described above should not be carried out, even though many individuals might benefit from its results.

Given the wide range of views espoused by psychologists during the two-year process of developing the profession's research principles, the Cook Committee, in the spirit of compromise, chose not to propose ethical statements in the form of absolute (or deontological) prohibitions. Instead, the research code that emerged was a utilitarian one, consisting of so-called "qualified" principles phrased in such a way as to guide rather than to direct individual decision making. Consider, for example, the important concept of voluntary informed consent. Principle D states that the investigator must inform participants of all aspects of the research that might influence their decision to participate. However, this principle is qualified by the next sentence, "Failure to make full disclosure ... requires additional safeguards." In short, while the code promoted the importance of informed consent, it allowed for exceptions. A researcher thus might choose *not* to obtain the informed consent of participants if it is believed that there are good reasons for withholding information or misleading subjects about certain aspects of the study. Other principles, such as those pertaining to the use of concealment or deception (principle E) and debriefing (principle H), are similarly qualified. Exceptions to these ethical principles often are warranted in psychological research on certain topics, such as conformity and attitude change, which could not meaningfully be studied in the laboratory with subjects' complete awareness. As discussed below, later revisions of the APA code offer clearer language regarding adherence to the basic principles and for clarifying the research situations in which exceptions might be justified.

The weighing of benefits and costs

In deciding whether or not an exception to an ethical principle is justified, the investigator must consider the benefits and costs of carrying out the study in the intended way. From a utilitarian perspective, the study would be deemed ethical if the benefits outweighed the costs (to participants, science, or society), assuming the potential costs were not too extreme. Among the possible benefits of conducting a study are monetary or other incentives for participants, the discovery of new information, the replication of results obtained from previous studies, etc. The costs of a research project could include physical or psychological discomfort for participants, invasion of privacy, expenditures of money or time, reduction of trust or respect for science, etc.

As an illustration of cost–benefit decision making, we can imagine the sort of decision making Stanley Milgram might have engaged in to evaluate the ethicality of his obedience experiments. (The reader should keep in mind that the 1973 principles were not in place at the time Milgram conducted his obedience research, and that the available ethical guidelines were vague at best. There is good reason to believe, based on some of his subsequent writings, that Milgram did ruminate at length about the benefits and costs of deceiving subjects prior to conducting the studies.)

Among the possible costs or disadvantages of a deceptive research procedure are that subjects might be offended by the deception, their self-esteem could be lowered, their relationships with others could be impaired, their subsequent actions might be modeled after the experimenter's deceptive behavior, and their perception of behavioral research might be so negatively affected as to give psychologists and other researchers a bad name. Additionally, with regard to the deception in Milgram's experiments, subjects' trust in authority figures could be diminished and subjects might be more prone to behave disobediently when later confronted by legitimate authorities.

Among the possible benefits or advantages of a deceptive procedure are the theoretical or social advances gained from the research findings, the avoidance of misleading findings that might have resulted from the study had subjects not been deceived, and the fact that subjects would have an opportunity to learn something about psychology, to perhaps gain some positive insight about their own behavior, and to feel good about their contribution to the research enterprise. Milgram's deceptive procedure provided the necessary "technical illusions" for studying the power of a malevolent authority to elicit obedience. He later suggested that his results provided tangible evidence of the psychological potential in human nature to perpetrate horrendous acts such as those committed by the Nazis during World War II.

Of course, once a listing of costs and benefits is developed, the decision must be made as to whether the particular study should be carried out. Unfortunately, the APA code does not provide any sort of simple equation or formula for arriving at such a decision. A cost–benefit assessment would require the researcher to consider the likelihood and degree of the risks involved in carrying out the study against the importance of anticipated gains. After weighing the considerations listed above, and after consulting several experts, Milgram might have decided that the potential theoretical and social advances far outweighed the potential risks involved; that without the use of deception, it would not have been possible to obtain new knowledge about the psychological mechanisms underlying obedience to authority; and that the probabilities of the costs were not great enough to justify abandoning the research as designed.

It is not difficult to imagine some of the criticisms that the APA research principles generated in psychology. Some individuals believed that the cost–benefit approach and the qualified nature of the principles would simply make it easier for researchers to justify ethically questionable methods in light of worthwhile research goals (e.g. Bok, 1978; Waterman, 1974). In this view, the personal rights of subjects are seen as violable at the researcher's discretion. Bok

interpreted the informed consent qualification as suggesting that when investigators can persuade themselves that a procedure lacking the fully informed
consent of subjects is for a good purpose and presents no harm, they can proceed
with secrecy and lies (Bok, 1992). Lying, which involves falsehoods that are
intended to deceive, is considered morally problematic by virtually all major
philosophical traditions and religions. It is a way of making people act against
their will and is the most common reason for distrust.

Baumrind (1975) also objected to cost–benefit calculations for resolving ethical
conflicts, asserting that such analyses inevitably lead to moral dilemmas. Since in
her view the function of a system of moral philosophy is precisely to avoid such
dilemmas, she attacked the code for failing to set forth clearly what is right or
wrong in order to provide the researcher with guidance in dealing with specific
ethical questions. Moreover, Baumrind argued that a code based on a system of
moral evaluation in which principles of informed consent, protection from psychological harm, and deception are qualified represents a move towards legitim-
izing improper conduct and desensitizes, rather than elevates, ethical sensibilities.
Similar complaints were voiced in response to the British Psychological Society's
1978 ethical principles for human subject research (Aitkenhead and Dordoy,
1983).

Others critics wrote extensively about the various practical problems that a
researcher could encounter in using the principles as a guide to ethical decision
making. Diener and Crandall (1978) summarized these practical problems by
pointing to five serious drawbacks to cost–benefit analyses. First, costs and benefits are impossible to accurately predict prior to conducting a study. A poorly
designed or otherwise methodologically flawed investigation likely will yield no
benefits, and most probably will have negative consequences for those individuals
involved. However, how does one predict the extent to which a study will have
positive consequences? As a further complication, some researchers (e.g. Haywood, 1976; Rosenthal and Rosnow, 1984) have argued that ethical decision
making should involve a consideration not only of the costs and benefits of *doing*
a study, but also of the costs and benefits of *not doing* the study (see Table 2.1).
How does one effectively predict the benefits of *not* doing something?

Second, potential research outcomes are impossible to measure or quantify
with any degree of precision. Without some sort of scale by which costs and
benefits can be numerically measured and weighted, the balancing of the two
against each other cannot be managed objectively. For example, a college student
who volunteers for an experiment in order to earn some desperately needed cash
(e.g. a US$15 incentive for participation) may be willing to risk a loss of self-
esteem in the process. On the other hand, a psychologist might view a student's
loss of self-esteem as the outcome having the greater consequence. In this case,
the two individuals obviously would be using different weights for quantifying
the possible consequences of the experiment. Even behavioral scientists tend to
disagree among themselves about the value of many studies that already have
been completed.

A third problem with cost–benefit decisions is that there often are different
recipients of the costs and benefits of a behavioral science investigation; for many

Table 2.1 Possible costs and benefits of behavioral research decisions

Recipient	Benefits	Costs
A. *Decision "to do" research*		
Subjects	Self-insight Extrinsic rewards (e.g. course credit or monetary payment) Increased understanding of science Feeling of having contributed to science	Mental anguish (e.g. stress or frustration) Physical discomfort Inflicted insight Loss of time Image of science lowered Mistrust of others Embarrassment Lessening of self-worth
Researcher	Satisfaction of desire for knowledge or scientific interest Professional success and career benefits Recognition Altruistic satisfaction	Investment of time and effort Forgoing other activities Legal sanctions (e.g. if confidentiality breached) Undermines integrity and commitment to truth (e.g. if deception used) Feelings of shame
Profession	Empirical tests of theories Attracts qualified researchers Provides for replications of earlier research	Exhausts pool of naive subjects Jeopardizes community support for the research enterprise
Society	Scientific advancement and progress Applications towards the betterment of humanity Increased understanding of behavior and interpersonal relations	Undermines trust in expert authorities and science Increased suspiciousness (e.g. self-consciousness in public places) Increased disregard for the rights of individuals Desensitizes people to needs of others

B. *Decision "not to do" research* (In general, the benefits and costs are the reverse of those for the decision to do research. The following list is thus simplified by providing only a few of the possible benefits and costs that could have been listed.)

Subjects	Avoidance of physical or mental harm More time for other activities	Loss of opportunity for self-insight, monetary incentives, understanding of science, etc.
Researcher	Increased opportunities for other activities Avoidance of ethical dilemmas involving the treatment of subjects	Fewer opportunities for professional advancement and status among peers
Profession	Use of available funds for other purposes Less likely to have image tarnished by controversial studies	Greater difficulties in determining the validity of theories, previous research, and assessment instruments
Society	Reduces opportunity for invading the privacy of others Maintains trust in expert authorities	Loss of opportunity to better society (e.g. by studying ways to reduce violence, prejudice, or mental illness)

Source: Bassett, Basinger, and Livermore (1982), Baumrind (1985), Forsyth (1987), Rosenthal and Rosnow (1991), Schuler (1982).

studies, individual subjects incur the costs while society in general stands to reap the benefits. This sort of outcome is contrary to the spirit of cost–benefit decision making, which had its roots in medical situations in which the individual patient faced both the risks and potential gains of a treatment. It is more difficult to justify exposing research participants to certain risks in studies that promise positive outcomes for others only (Kimble, 1976; Smith, 1976; Smith, Klein, and Kimmel, 2005).

A fourth drawback to cost–benefit analysis pertains to the fact that the assessment typically must be completed by the very person who has a vested interest in a favorable decision. Because of the researcher's conflict of interest in the decision-making process, objective cost–benefit analyses may be impossible to achieve. Many scientists are apt to overrate the importance of their work and to underestimate potential harms as they move closer to a decision to proceed with a proposed study (Baumrind, 1975; Kimmel, 1991).

The final problem cited by Diener and Crandall is that cost–benefit analyses tend to ignore the substantive rights of individuals in favor of practical, utilitarian considerations. The notion of substantive rights suggests that all persons have certain inalienable rights, such as the rights to free speech and religious freedom. These substantive rights are considered to be inviolable, even if benefits to society could be maximized if such rights were eliminated. The problem here is that cost–benefit analyses take a more pragmatic orientation and may fail to recognize the inviolable nature of human rights.

Collectively, these problems indicate that a cost–benefit approach to ethical decision making alone cannot justify potentially harmful or risky investigations (Diener and Crandall, 1978; Kimmel and Smith, 2001). In fact, a set of ethical principles represents only one important part of the overall machinery needed to effect self-regulation in the research process. APA's original intent in developing the principles was not to mandate a set of constricting, absolute rules that researchers would have to adhere to without regard to the complexities and uniqueness of each research situation. As two members of the task force charged with writing the 2002 revision pointed out (Knapp and VandeCreek, 2003), the development of an ethics code consisting merely of a set of obligatory statements would fail to reflect the complexities of the profession.

Despite the various problems inherent in the cost–benefit approach, the ethical principles provide a workable framework within which psychologists who seek guidance can analyze the issues relevant to the demands of their research. This is a primary function of professional ethical codes. It also is noteworthy that the preamble to psychology's 1973 research principles included the call for consideration of "alternative directions" when planning a research investigation. This reflects the recognition that most research questions in science can be pursued in more than one manner and that the ethical researcher is one who selects the methodological approach that is most likely to satisfy the research goals while minimizing potentially negative consequences. This suggests that the appropriate question for researchers may not be the all-or-none one, between doing and not doing the research, but between doing the research in one way and using the same resources to do a different research project.

Subsequent modifications of the APA principles have included a distinction between "subjects at risk" and "subjects at minimal risk" (which represents one of the ways that professional and governmental guidelines have become more consistent in recent years); a greater emphasis on protecting subjects' right to withdraw from a study, especially when research participants come from "special" populations with limited abilities to understand aspects of the research situation (such as children and the mentally infirm); and a stipulation that investigators should inform their subjects of procedures for contacting them if any stresses or questions emerge after participation (APA, 1981a).

A new code of ethics for psychology – the 2002 APA Ethics Code

The latest revisions of the APA ethics code began in 1986, leading up to a substantially restructured version, which was adopted by the APA's Council of Representatives in 1992 (APA, 1992). Since the first edition of this book, the APA Ethics Code has undergone yet another significant revision. Although the current 2002 APA code (APA, 2002), which went into effect in June 2003, bears broad similarity to its predecessor, there are several noteworthy modifications (see Box 2.4). The 2002 code includes an introduction, a preamble, five general principles (A–E, pertaining, respectively, to beneficence and non-maleficence, fidelity and responsibility, integrity, justice, and respect for people's rights and dignity), and ten areas of specific ethical standards. In distinguishing between the principles and standards, the code clarifies that the former are *aspirational* (and non-enforceable) goals, intended to guide psychologists towards the highest ideals of their profession, whereas the latter are *enforceable* rules for conduct as professional psychologists. One of the problems with earlier versions of the code is that they mixed aspirational and enforceable language (Bales, 1992).

The 15 standards most directly relevant to the conduct of research with human participants appear under the heading "Research and Publication." These standards describe appropriate conduct in reference to the following: (1) institutional approval; (2) informed consent to research; (3) informed consent for recording voices and images in research; (4) research participants; (5) dispensing with informed consent; (6) offering inducements for research participants; (7) deception in research; and (8) debriefing. Other research-related standards classified in this section focus on the care and use of animals in research, the ethical publication and reporting of research results, sharing research data for verification, and plagiarism. The standards pertaining to privacy issues, which in the previous version of the code had been included among these research standards, now comprise a separate section (section 4, "Privacy and Confidentiality").

As in previous revisions, the important ingredients for ethical conduct are informed consent, protection from harm, debriefing, and the safeguarding of privacy and confidentiality rights. However, as in the 1992 revision, some of the vague language evident in earlier versions has been replaced by clearer and more precise rules. For example, separate standards are included to clarify the

Box 2.4   Comparison of the 1992 and 2002 versions of Ethical Principles of Psychologists and Code of Conduct

Despite a great degree of similarity between the latest version of the APA's (2002) ethics code and its 1992 predecessor (APA, 1992) in terms of basic format and structure, the Ethics Committee Task Force (ECTF) significantly improved upon an already formidable document. The APA's website provides a line-by-line comparison of the 1992 and 2002 codes (see www.apa.org/ethics/codecompare.html), although, of course, there is no substitute for reading the codes directly (Knapp and VandeCreek, 2003).

   Among the noteworthy modifications in the current code, only a relative minority stand out with regard to research practices. The first has to do with new conditions under which psychologists may dispense with informed consent (see Box 2.5), consistent with law or regulation. A new standard (8.08c) states that when it becomes apparent that research procedures have harmed a participant, the psychologist is required to take reasonable steps to minimize that harm. The current code also now stipulates that psychologists who request data from other researchers in order to verify a study's substantive claims through reanalysis must use the data only for that purpose, following prior agreement (standard 8.14b). Additionally, a new subsection was added to clarify psychologists' responsibilities when conducting intervention research involving the use of experimental treatments, including the need to obtain the informed consent of intended participants.

   Another significant development reflects an effort by the ECTF to reduce the likelihood that the code could be used to unnecessarily punish psychologists. Concern about the possible punitive uses to which the code could be applied largely stemmed from state psychological associations, licensing boards, malpractice courts, and institutional employers having used previous versions to evaluate the conduct of psychologists. There also was the fear that disgruntled students, research subjects, or colleagues could use the APA code to intimidate or threaten psychologists. A number of changes in wording and deletions thus were made by the ECTF in order to reduce the ways that the code could be used to penalize psychologists unfairly (Knapp and VandeCreek, 2003).

investigator's responsibilities regarding informed consent (standards 8.02, 8.03, and 8.05) and the use of deceptive research techniques (standard 8.07).

   As an illustration of the greater precision in the current code, one need look no farther than the statements regarding the necessity to debrief participants in studies where deception is an integral feature of the research design. Principle 9.e. of the 1981 standards states that the investigator has a responsibility to provide the participants "with sufficient explanation as soon as possible."

Contrast this with the statement in standard 8.07.c of the 2002 code, which maintains that:

> Psychologists explain any deception that is an integral feature of the design and conduct of an experiment to participants as early as is feasible, preferably at the conclusion of their participation, but no later than at the conclusion of the data collection, and permit participants to withdraw their data.

It is also clarified that informed consent is not required in a variety of research situations (referred to in earlier versions of the code as "minimal risk research") (see Box 2.5). Greater attention also is paid in the new code to the confidentiality of research data, especially in terms of the protection of research participants from personal identification. Reflecting recent technological advances, the code also acknowledges the inherent limitations of confidentiality when transmitting information through electronic media. Throughout, the importance of consulting with colleagues and review boards and adhering to federal and state law and regulations is emphasized.

A practical resource for applying the APA code is presently available (Canter et al., 1994). Although intended as a commentary on the 1992 code, it also should prove useful in providing insight into the current code, due to similarities in basic format,

---

Box 2.5   Research situations not requiring informed consent

Current professional and governmental ethical guidelines now enable researchers to submit their research to an expedited review process if the study in question meets certain conditions. Perhaps most significantly, the expedited review may allow researchers to forgo informed consent procedures where those procedures may prove methodologically undesirable or unnecessary. The specific categories of research that may be reviewed according to an expedited process are listed below.

Categories of Expedited Review: APA Ethics Code (2002)

Conditions under which informed consent is not required:

1   The research is not likely to create distress or harm and involves:
   a.   the study of normal educational practices, curricula, or classroom management methods conducted in educational settings;
   b.   only anonymous questionnaires, naturalistic observations, or archival research for which disclosure of responses would not pose any risks to participants and confidentiality is protected;
   c.   organizational effectiveness studies conducted in applied settings where there is no risk to employees and confidentiality is protected.
2   The research is otherwise permitted by law or federal or institutional regulations.

(Continued)

Box 2.5   (Continued)

Categories of Expedited Review: US Federal Regulations (Department of Health and Human Services, 2001a, b)

Behavioral science research activities that present no more than minimal risk to participants are eligible for review by an IRB through an expedited procedure (as described in DHHS policy document Title 45), if the research involves procedures listed in one of the following categories:

1   Research involving data, documents, or records that have been col-
    lected solely for non-research purposes (such as diagnosis);
2   Collection of data from voice, video, digital, or image recordings made
    for research purposes;
3   Research on individual or group characteristics or behavior, including
    research on perception, cognition, motivation, identity, language, com-
    munications, cultural beliefs or practices, and social behavior;
4   Research employing survey, interview, oral history, focus group, pro-
    gram evaluation, human factors evaluation, or quality assurance meth-
    odologies;
5   Continuing review of research previously approved by the IRB (e.g.
    where no new participants are recruited, no additional risks have
    been identified, only data analysis remains).

Assuming that the research is approved for expedited review, the review procedure then would be carried out by the IRB chairperson or by one or more experienced reviewers, as opposed to a formal evaluation conducted by the entire review board.

---

structure, and standards (see Box 2.4). Further clarification regarding the application of the current research standards is available to psychologists from the APA publication *Ethics in Research with Human Participants* (Sales and Folkman, 2000), which is intended to serve as an educational and advisory tool for applying the APA code to ethical issues and dilemmas often faced when conducting research.

The 2002 APA Ethics Code is an impressive document, as evidenced by the apparent care and seriousness that went into its preparation. The code, which is APA's tenth, is the result of a fifty-year history of development and revision, and is presumed to reflect the values of APA members as well as the moral growth of the discipline of psychology (Jones, 2001). While recognizing that "most of the Ethical Standards are written broadly," and that their application "may vary depending on the context," APA (2002, p. 2) took into account earlier criticisms of its research principles and issued a set of statements that are clearer about what psychologists must and must not do in specific circumstances.

Professional codes of ethical conduct also have been developed by a number of psychological associations outside the United States. These are described in detail

in appendix 2. Although all emphasize an overriding respect for research participants and the importance of providing rigorous subject protections, the codes
differ in terms of the degree of specificity with which principles are formulated
and in the basic ethical positions taken, with stronger emphasis placed on either
research benefits or risks to research participants. Such differences are reflective
of cultural variations in value systems, moral judgments, and approaches to
ethical decision making. Consequently, psychologists must be particularly sensitive to foreign ethical guidelines during the conduct of cross-cultural research, as
different standards of acceptable and unacceptable conduct are likely to prevail in
different country contexts.

ETHICS CODES IN OTHER BEHAVIORAL SCIENCE DISCIPLINES

Now that we have reviewed psychology's ethical principles in detail, we can turn
our attention to the ethical activities of professionals in related disciplines. As
illustrations, the focus here is on the ethical principles for the conduct of sociological and anthropological research in the United States.

Sociology

The initial attempts to develop codes of research ethics in the fields of sociology
and anthropology occurred during the 1960s. The American Sociological Association's (ASA) first ethics code was put into effect in 1971, following several years
of study and debate. A standing committee on professional ethics also was
appointed at that time. Unlike the initial guidelines in psychology, which focused
mainly on professional issues, the early ASA ethical standards almost entirely
concerned research, including such issues as objectivity and integrity in research,
respect of the research subject's rights to privacy and dignity, and protection of
subjects from personal harm (ASA, 1971).

Sociology's ethics code was first revised in 1984 following concern that it
emphasized research issues to the exclusion of other professional activities performed by sociologists. Thus, beginning with the 1984 code, sections were included that deal with ethical guidelines relating to research, publication and
review processes, teaching and the rights of students, and relationships among
sociologists. The most recent revision of sociology's ethical principles for research
was approved in June 1997 (ASA, 1999). The revised code was modeled very
closely after recent versions of the APA ethics code; it now includes the identical
distinction between aspirational general principles and enforceable standards and
is similarly structured.

The current ethical principles for sociological research are contained within the
profession's generic *Code of Ethics* (ASA, 1999). The various research standards
(see web link, appendix 1) highlight many of the ethical concerns that we already
identified. Informed consent and confidentiality are incorporated as critical elements of ethical research practice in sociology. However, because sociologists

commonly use non-experimental methodologies as alternatives to controlled laboratory research, the ASA position on informed consent recognizes that the procedure may not be appropriate in many cases. The code (ASA, 1999, p. 14) notes that on rare occasions "sociologists may need to conceal their identity in order to undertake research that could not practicably be carried out were they to be known as researchers." Under such circumstances, the research can proceed if the deception poses no more than minimal risk for participants and if approval has been obtained from an IRB or some other authoritative body. Perhaps as a result of the focus of sociological research on social groups, organizations, communities, and societies, the research principles emphasize the importance of protecting the confidentiality and privacy of the individuals within these contexts who may serve as research participants.

The ASA code does not contain details regarding how the principles are to be interpreted and applied. Thus, researchers must use their own criteria for judging whether the potential risks imposed by a study exceed the risks of everyday situations; they must determine what constitutes culturally appropriate steps for securing informed consent, and so on. In addition to concerns about the lack of specifics regarding interpretation and application of the principles to research situations, the ASA revised code has been criticized on other grounds, including its apparent focus on requirements that are not firmly grounded in moral principle (Mitchell, 1990), a point that similarly applies to most professional ethics codes (Kimmel and Smith, 2001; Smith et al., 2005).

Anthropology

Like their counterparts in psychology and sociology, anthropologists also have taken steps to develop normative guidelines for ethical conduct in research. Most notably, this includes the promulgation of a set of general ethical "position statements" and a more detailed code of ethics. The position statements on ethical problems in research were first made available by the American Anthropological Association (AAA) in 1948, and were more fully articulated in 1967. Based on these early statements, a set of ethical standards detailing the responsibilities of professional anthropologists was adopted by the AAA in May 1971 in a document entitled *Professional Ethics: Statements and Procedures of the American Anthropological Association*. Reissued in 1983 and most recently revised in 1998 as *Code of Ethics of the American Anthropological Association*, these standards presently serve as the primary ethics statement of the AAA and, until recently, the American Association of Physical Anthropologists (AAPA). (The AAPA approved its first *Code of Ethics* in 2003; AAPA, 2003).

The current AAA standards acknowledge that conflicts between the various responsibilities of anthropologists are inevitable and that choices between conflicting values will have to be made. In such cases, it is the anthropologist's responsibility to attempt to resolve such ethical difficulties in ways that are compatible with the established ethical standards. Towards assisting anthropologists in successfully resolving these conflicts, the standards emphasize that priority should be placed on the well-being of research subjects and the integrity of the profession, and that when these conditions cannot be followed, it is best that the research not be carried out (at least as originally proposed). Since 1995, the AAA no longer adjudicates on claims of unethical behavior, preferring to focus on education.

Because anthropological investigations in foreign areas are more likely to give rise to ethical dilemmas than other forms of research in the discipline, the AAA position statements focus on such concerns as freedom of research and support and sponsorship of research. Emphasis is placed on potential threats to governmental and international relations as a function of questionable research practices involving "constraint, deception, and secrecy," which are viewed as having "no place in science" (AAA, 1986). As in related disciplines, the AAA code raises sensitivities to the important ethical issues, but lacks specific recommendations for resolving research dilemmas.

Applied fields

In addition to the codes of ethics detailed above, behavioral scientists also can obtain guidance for research conduct by consulting standards that have been promulgated by other professional groups. For example, survey research codes have been developed by organizations such as the International Chamber of Commerce/European Society for Opinion and Marketing Research (ICC/ESOMAR, 1986), the Council of American Survey Research Organizations (CASRO, 1995), the American Association for Public Opinion Research (AAPOR, 1999), and the Council for Marketing and Opinion and Research (CMOR, 1999). As well as clarifying the rights of respondents, clients, and sponsors and the professional responsibilities of researchers, these codes offer extensive ethical principles in the conduct of public opinion research and in the use of such research for policy and decision making in the public and private sectors. The codes vary in specificity with regard to the range of major ethical issues involving research participants (Smith and Klein, 1999). Bearing in mind that many behavioral scientists are employed in applied settings, it is important to note that corporate codes of conduct have been implemented by a number of companies in North America and Europe (see chapter 7).

GOVERNMENTAL REGULATIONS FOR BEHAVIORAL RESEARCH

Much of the professional activity and concern about ethical issues in research was stimulated by the increasing scope of governmental regulation, policies of the larger scientific community, and new research support requirements. As for the scientific professions, some of the political impetus for regulation of human research resulted from widely publicized accounts of ethical misuse and abuse in biomedical research (e.g. Beecher, 1959).

Details of studies like those described in chapter 1 led to the development of governmental investigatory committees in the United States, and this activity played a role in the eventual formulation of federal regulations for human research. Investigations into controversial studies like the New York cancer cell study typically resulted in the same conclusions – that established policies for reviewing experimental procedures were virtually non-existent in governmental agencies, and that more effective controls were needed to protect the rights of research participants. Federal policy also was stimulated by the following (Frankel, 1975; McCarthy, 1981):

1   widespread acceptance of the Nuremberg Code;
2   publication of the World Medical Association's Declaration of Helsinki in 1964, permitting therapeutic experiments with patients' consent;
3   enactment of the Kefauver–Harris Amendments of the Food, Drug and Cosmetic Act in 1962, which followed hearings into human subject abuses in drug research and resulted in regulations governing the testing of new drugs;
4   recommendations of the National Advisory Health Council (NACH), urging the establishment of governmental standards on human subject research.

Federal safeguards concerning the rights and welfare of human participants in research have been in place as part of US Public Health Service (PHS) policy since 1966, although the initial focus was limited to clinical research in the medical fields (McCarthy, 1981; Seiler and Murtha, 1980). This policy required that a clinical investigation could be PHS funded only after it was first subjected to an institutional ethics review. This review, conducted by a committee consisting of members of the principal investigator's institution, was to include a determination of the rights and welfare of subjects, the adequacy of the procedure for obtaining informed consent, and the risks and potential medical benefits of the proposed study (Frankel, 1975).

Following some confusion as to whether the initial federal policy applied to research in the behavioral and social sciences, Surgeon General Philip Lee issued a statement in May 1969 extending PHS policy to all research involving human participants, including biomedical and behavioral investigations. In addition to assuring greater consistency in interpretation and implementation of the provisions, the revised policy provided greater detail as to what constituted "consent" and acknowledged that certain non-medical benefits could justify a review committee in permitting an informed subject to accept possible risks (Frankel, 1975). The revised policy was amended in 1971 to cover all research activities supported by grant or contract within the Department of Health, Education and Welfare (DHEW, now the Department of Health and Human Services, or DHHS), if the research placed human subjects at risk.

At that time, however, there were several calls for reevaluation of DHHS policy, especially following revelations of research abuses that came to light in hearings before the Senate Health Sub-committee chaired by Senator Edward Kennedy. One of the studies that received particular attention was the Tuskegee syphilis experiment. Another matter to receive scrutiny was the alleged use of psychosurgery and behavioral modification techniques to control violent prisoners. The upshot of these discussions was for Congress to sign into law in July 1974 the National Research Act, creating the National Commission for the Protection of Human Subjects of Biomedical and Behavioral Research.

The primary purpose of the commission was to propose governmental regulations for ensuring the protection of human participants in virtually all behavioral, social, and biomedical research. The commission was composed of eleven members from several fields, including law, medicine, philosophy, the humanities, and theology, who were nominated by their professional organizations and appointed by the Secretary of the DHHS, to whom they were to submit their recommendations. Among the issues considered by the commission were those involving the selection and informed consent of subjects; procedures for investigations involving prisoners or children; and the functioning of ethical review boards (see Seiler and Murtha, 1980, for a critical assessment of the early work of the National Commission).

In addition to creating the National Commission, another major outcome of the National Research Act was to issue regulations requiring the ethical review of human subject research by institutional review boards (IRBs). At first, this requirement for IRB review was applied in an uneven manner. Only DHHS-funded research was to be covered by the regulation, representing a small percentage of the behavioral research carried out in the country. However, if an institution received considerable support from the DHHS for human subject research, even non-funded research carried out at the institution was subject to IRB review (McCarthy, 1981). Non-funded research at institutions receiving only a small amount of DHHS funding was not required to undergo IRB review. This approach was further muddied in 1978 when the National Commission finalized its report on IRBs, which ultimately led to the extension of the requirement for IRB review to all research involving human subjects carried out at an institution receiving DHHS funds. This requirement provoked substantial criticism from those who argued that it was inappropriate for the government to extend its authority to research not directly funded by federal agencies.

These federal developments for regulating research were attacked by behavioral and social scientists on a number of grounds, only one of which involved the confusion over IRB coverage. The arguments reflected fears that the government was exceeding its bounds by implementing increasingly stringent policies to control human subject research. For example, many researchers were wary that investigations would be delayed as project proposals were reviewed by individuals who lacked an awareness of research problems outside their own particular disciplines. Some researchers contended that separate forms of regulation should have been developed for biomedical and behavioral research, and that the application of federal policies for certain categories of research, such as studies involving questionnaires and surveys, threatened the academic freedom of university researchers. Others argued that federal coverage should extend only to human research for which ethical abuses could be documented. The proposed regulations for research involving prisoners, which essentially limited such research to studies offering direct benefits to the participants, also met with disfavor as being overly restrictive. Researchers have viewed the prisoner population as a rich source of willing participants who happen to live under controlled conditions essential for conducting a wide variety of investigations.

The National Commission presented its final recommendations in 1978 along with the two-volume Belmont Report, which included testimony from various experts (National Commission, 1979, appendixes 1 and 2). Hearings then were held on the proposed regulations by the President's Commission for the Study of Ethical Problems in Medicine and Biomedical and Behavioral Research. In drafting its new regulations, the DHHS responded to recommendations of both commissions, public comment, and advice obtained from IRB members and research investigators, breaking sharply with the earlier trend toward greater mandatory IRB coverage of human subject research. The regulations, which first appeared in the January 26, 1981 issue of the *Federal Register*, apply directly only to research projects receiving DHHS funds and no longer apply to unfunded projects. (The Department stressed, however, that institutions seeking DHHS funds should demonstrate their commitment to the protection of human research participants in all non-funded research as well.) Moreover, the regulations substantially reduced the scope of DHHS coverage by exempting broad categories of research that present little or no risk of harm to subjects (so-called minimal risk research), including certain forms of educational research; survey and interview research involving non-sensitive issues; observational studies of public behavior; and research involving the collection or study of existing databases, documents, and records. Additionally, the regulations specify that expedited review (an abbreviated procedure conducted by one IRB member) is appropriate for certain categories of minimal risk research, such as non-manipulative, stress-free studies of individual or group behavior or characteristics.

For the approval of research covered by the federal regulations, an IRB must be established at the institution where the research has been proposed, which is to determine whether the following conditions are met: (1) risks to subjects are minimized by sound research procedures that do not unnecessarily expose subjects to risks; (2) risks to subjects are outweighed sufficiently by anticipated benefits to the subjects and the importance of the knowledge to be gained; (3) the rights and welfare of subjects are adequately protected; (4) the research will be periodically reviewed; and (5) informed consent has been obtained and appropriately documented. (The basic elements of informed consent, as defined in the regulations, are described in chapter 3.) These federal regulations have been in effect since July 27, 1981, and have periodically been revised.

The impact of governmental regulation on human subject research has been substantial. Prior to the establishment of federal regulations, there was very little evidence of any type of committee review of research projects in university departments of medicine (Curran, 1969; Welt, 1961), and probably none at all in social and behavioral science areas (Reynolds, 1979). Today, ethical review boards are commonplace in most research-oriented institutions. While unfunded studies no longer require institutional review according to current federal regulations, it is likely that most universities, hospitals, and other research settings do require some form of review for the approval and monitoring of all human research conducted at those institutions (e.g. Rutecki, Youtsey, and Adelson, 2002).

Ethical review boards are a common feature of human subject research regulation in numerous countries around the world. For example, all members of the European Union adhere to a 2001 European Commission directive (Data Protection Directive 95/46/EC) requiring ethics committees for medical research. The directive is intended to "remove obstacles to the flow of personal data by requiring a high level of protection of fundamental rights (in particular, privacy) in the Member States" (Privireal, 2005). Currently, each participating country implements the directive differently. For example, France has a variety of legal protections for research participants, in addition to implementation of the European directive (via the Huriet-Sérusclat Law of December 20, 1988, which was amended in 2004). French review boards are referred to as Committees for the Protection of Persons (CPPs) and their primary responsibility is to issue an opinion to the investigator regarding protections for proposed studies. There are other types of committees that operate at different levels in the French scientific and health sectors. These include the CNIL (Data Protection Supervisory Authority), which supervises the use of personal data and gives its authorization for the processing of personal data; the National Consultative Ethics Committee, which provides a general reflection on ethical issues, but does not review specific research protocols; and local and institutional ethics committees, which issue decisions on ethical issues, but only rarely review research protocols (Privireal, 2005).

Research Ethics Committees (RECs) have been in existence in the United Kingdom since the mid-1960s, when they were run on a voluntary basis by the UK National Health Service (NHS). There now are two kinds of RECs: (1) Local Research Ethics Committees (LRECs), responsible for reviewing research protocols in their local area; and (2) Multi-Centre Research Ethics Committees (MRECs), responsible for reviewing protocols held in more than four locations. Additional regulations enacted in 2002 gave specific statutory duties to RECs, and in 2004 the United Kingdom Ethics Committee Authority (UKECA) was created by the Medicines for Human Use (Clinical Trials) Regulations to authorize and oversee RECs. The Medicines Regulations also implemented the European directive in 2004. A survey of review procedures in other European member states is available at www.privireal.group.shef.ac.uk. For an overview of research review regulations in Canada, see Seligman and Sorrentino (2002).

The increasing prevalence of ethical review boards, which often are composed of individuals lacking expertise in the areas proposed for investigation, has given rise to serious concerns among investigators. For example, one issue is the apparent lack of consistency of review board decisions, such that a study might or might not receive approval depending upon the particular composition of the committee (Kimmel, 1991; Rosnow et al., 1993). This issue and others related to the ethical review process represent a major focus of chapter 10.

DISTINGUISHING BETWEEN GOVERNMENT REGULATION AND PROFESSIONAL ETHICS

Present federal policy effectively removes much behavioral and social research from IRB scrutiny and shifts the burden of ethical responsibility onto individual investigators and institution officials. Of course, it generally is assumed that investigators will apply their profession's ethical standards in conducting exempted or expedited research or studies not falling under federal coverage. Before concluding this chapter, it might be helpful to distinguish more clearly between professional ethics codes and governmental ethics regulations, clarifying the functions and goals of each.

The development of professional ethical standards and other ethical activities reflect the willingness of a profession to self-regulate the behavior of its members on behalf of the public and the profession. In the context of behavioral research, professional ethics refer to the rules that define the rights and responsibilities of behavioral scientists in their relationships with research subjects, clients, employers, and each other (Chalk et al., 1980). Because researchers work in a variety of scientific disciplines, each having developed its own separate set of standards for guiding and controlling human subject research, no single set of professional rules of conduct presently is available.

By contrast, federal and state laws have emerged as requirements for scientists to take certain precautions or to refrain from engaging in research activities likely to increase the risk of harm to an individual or to society. Government regulations are designed to protect or advance the interests of society and the individuals who make up that society. The mechanism for the enforcement of such regulations is the established system of law in the society.

While sharing the goal of laws and regulations to protect society and its individual members from harm, professional ethics exist primarily to instruct members of the profession in behavior considered appropriate by their peers. In fact, ethical standards can be viewed as a basic means of socializing those entering the profession to normative rules defining acceptable and unacceptable conduct. Nonetheless, under certain research circumstances, professional ethics and legal requirements may not be completely consistent. In such cases, codes of ethics tend to advise the researcher to adhere to the law, after acknowledging their commitment to a professional code of ethics (e.g. APA, 2002).

SUMMARY

In every decision-making situation, a researcher is armed with the ethical maxims of the scientific community, which are intended to provide guidance for dealing with ethical problems. However, unlike governmental regulations, which must be adhered to as directives, an ethical decision may or may not be consistent with the standards of one's profession. Rather, an investigator is free to exercise judgment regarding the appropriate procedures, allowing for exceptions to the ethical standards of the profession if they seem justified by the uniqueness of the situation (Lowman and Soule, 1981).

Professional codes of ethics thus are not guarantees for the full protection of research participants, society, and scientific integrity, but might instead be regarded as workable frameworks providing researchers with guidance in order to analyze the issues relevant to their investigations. In chapter 3 we begin to consider some of these issues in depth by focusing on the ethical dilemmas that arise in the conduct of laboratory research.

3

Ethical Issues in the Conduct of Laboratory Research

"I observed a mature and initially poised businessman enter the laboratory smiling and confident. Within 20 minutes he was reduced to a twitching, stuttering wreck, who was rapidly approaching a point of nervous collapse. He constantly pulled on his earlobe, and twisted his hands. At one point he pushed his fist into his forehead and muttered: "Oh God, let's stop it." And yet he continued to respond to every word of the experimenter, and obeyed to the end."

Stanley Milgram, Behavioral study of obedience

Chapter Topics

☞ Examples of ethically problematic psychology experiments
☞ Arguments for and against using deception in laboratory research
☞ Types of research deceptions
☞ The frequency and magnitude of deception in behavioral research
☞ Debriefing and the removal of negative research effects

I t was not long after publication of Milgram's (1963) "Behavioral study of obedience" in the *Journal of Abnormal and Social Psychology*, in which the above passage appears, that psychologists began to give serious attention to the appropriateness of experimental procedures routinely used in the investigation of human behavior. Psychology experiments rarely elicited the sorts of intense reactions in subjects as those reported by Milgram. Nevertheless, by the mid-1960s, a growing number of critics had begun to question the proliferation of deceptive and potentially harmful manipulations which more and more investigators seemed to be using as a matter of course.

As early as 1954, social psychologist W. Edgar Vinacke took issue with psychology experiments in which research participants were deceived and sometimes exposed to "painful, embarrassing, or worse, experiences." Few, if any, psychologists were ready to deal with Vinacke's concerns at the time, probably because the use of deceptive procedures by psychologists was not particularly widespread (Christensen, 1988). Further, this was the dawn of an increasingly fruitful period for scientific psychology. An experimental research tradition had emerged that many psychologists hoped would rival progress in the more established physical sciences (Rosnow, 1981). A decade later, however, Vinacke's questions about the "proper balance between the interests of science and the thoughtful treatment of the persons who, innocently, supply the data" (p. 155) were raised anew by Diana Baumrind (1964) in response to Milgram's obedience research and a rapidly growing number of other studies involving deception. In her view, Milgram's deceptive procedure, which involved the bogus delivery of electric shocks to a hapless victim, subjected research participants to certain psychological risks. In addition to stress and psychological discomfort, these risks included loss of self-esteem and dignity, and a possible loss of trust in rational authority. Baumrind additionally argued that because of methodological drawbacks, including the questionable representativeness of results obtained from voluntary participants, the research held little potential for serious benefit. She concluded that Milgram should have terminated the experiment as soon as he realized how stressful it was for his subjects. The resulting exchange between the two psychologists over the ethical implications of the obedience research provided a focus for those who had begun to scrutinize the ethical bounds of an experimental approach that had become increasingly prevalent at the time (Rosnow, 1981).

The experimental approach in psychology often involves the observation of human participants in the controlled environment of a psychology laboratory, an artificial setting devised for the sole purpose of studying behavior. In the psychology laboratory, variables of interest to researchers typically can be more carefully manipulated, and behavioral responses more precisely measured, than in non-laboratory (or "natural") settings. However, unlike experimental research in the physical sciences, the investigation of human behavior by psychologists involves complexities inherent in the study of conscious human beings in a social setting defined as a "psychology experiment." A common assumption, described in greater detail below, is that human research subjects often would act differently if they were told the full truth about the experiment (e.g. Silverman, 1977). Since it is often desirable to keep participants naive, behavioral scientists frequently rely on the elaborate use of deceit in order to conceal the true purpose and conditions of their experiments.

This chapter and the next focus on the ethical issues stemming from laboratory experimentation in psychology, giving special emphasis to problems arising from the use of deception. As described in chapter 2, the extant ethics codes do not rule out the use of deception in certain cases, assuming that steps are taken to further protect research participants from harm and that there are no alternative procedures for investigating the research problem under consideration. Below, the various types of deception used in behavioral research are distinguished, along with justifications for their use. Additionally, the nature of informed consent and debriefing is considered. In chapter 4 we turn our attention to the potential threats to research validity imposed by these important ethical procedures and evaluate some suggested alternatives to the use of deception.

THE PROBLEM OF DECEPTION IN
PSYCHOLOGY EXPERIMENTS

In a paper presented at the 1965 American Psychological Association meetings in Chicago, social psychologist Herbert Kelman (1967) helped bring to light just how widespread the use of deception had become in psychology and related fields. Kelman lamented the growing use of deception in psychological research; in addition to discussing Milgram's study, he mentioned several cases of investigations that he felt warranted ethical concern.

Among the studies described by Kelman were experiments by Bramel (1962, 1963) and Bergin (1962), involving undergraduates who were given discrepant information about their sexuality. In the studies by Bramel, heterosexual males were led to believe that they had become sexually aroused by a series of photographs depicting other men. In order to accomplish the manipulation in his studies, Bramel ingeniously used a bogus "psychogalvanic skin response apparatus," which subjects were led to believe was an extremely accurate measure of sexual arousal. Subjects were instructed to record their arousal response level to each photograph projected onto a screen by noting the needle indication on the apparatus, which they were informed would indicate their homosexual arousal to the photograph. Unknown to them, however, was the fact that the experimenter had complete control of the galvanometer readings. Each photograph had been assigned a needle reading in advance, so that photographs portraying "handsome men in states of undress" received higher readings than did those of unattractive and fully clothed men. Despite having taken certain precautions to protect subjects from undue harm, Bramel (1962, p. 123) claimed that the procedure was impressive enough for subjects "that denial of the fact that homosexual arousal was being indicated would be very difficult."

In Bergin's (1962) study, both male and female students were given feedback about their sexuality after completing an extensive series of psychological tests. Perceptions of sexuality were manipulated by falsely informing subjects that their scores on the masculinity factor of a personality test were indicative of the opposite sex. As Bramel had done in his studies, Bergin informed the student participants about the true nature of the research prior to their leaving the laboratory. However, the very fact of having received the false feedback may have caused lasting emotional turmoil in subjects who were particularly sensitive about their sexual identity (Kelman, 1967).

Other, more dramatic illustrations of the potentially harmful effects of deception and the lack of fully informed consent were identified by Kelman. Some of these cases occurred outside the laboratory, such as a series of investigations involving naive army recruits (see Box 5.1). (The implications of using deception in natural settings, where subjects typically are unaware that they are being observed, are described in chapter 5.) In one psychology laboratory study that is often mentioned in discussions of research ethics, Campbell et al. (1964) tested the effects of the classical conditioning of a traumatic fear response in male alcoholic patients who had volunteered to participate in an experiment "connected with a possible therapy for alcoholism." The procedure involved the pairing of a neutral tone with an intense fear response brought on by an injection of the drug Scoline, which produces temporary motor paralysis, causing an inability to move or breathe. Although the effects of the drug were known to have no permanent physical consequences, it was assumed that the temporary interruption of respiration induced by the drug would cause severe stress in unsuspecting patients. Not surprisingly, the inability to breathe (for an average of about two minutes) was reported by the subjects as a terrifying experience, to the extent that all of them believed that they were dying. None of them had been warned in advance about the effect of the drug, and there is no reason to believe that the researchers expected to learn anything about its treatment potential for alcoholism (Diener and Crandall, 1978).

As predicted, by injecting the drug immediately after subjects had heard the neutral tone, Campbell and his colleagues found that the tone by itself had become capable of inducing an extreme stress reaction in the subjects. In fact, the conditioning procedure had been so effective that the researchers later had difficulty eliminating the traumatic reaction to the tone in some patients. Thus, in this study, the researchers recruited volunteers and obtained their consent under false pretenses, withheld important information from them which surely might have influenced their decision to participate, and then subjected them to various risks, including extreme discomfort and possible long-term harm. Evidence suggests that the researchers could have successfully performed the investigation even if the patients had been informed about the effects of the drug, a procedure that would have reduced some of the study's ethical problems. This fact reflects one of the main points in Kelman's early discussion about the use of deception in research. In his view, deception had become a commonplace research procedure that increasingly was being employed even in situations where it was unnecessary.

In psychology, Kelman (1967, p. 2) and others believed, the use of deceptive manipulations had become like a game for many researchers, "often played with great skill and virtuosity." The design of some studies sometimes involves a series of deceptions in which one falsehood is built upon another. "Second-order" deceptions, for example, are procedures in which subjects are observed for the purposes of a study only after they are falsely led to believe that the experiment is over, or that they have been enlisted as the experimenter's accomplice. Both of these sorts of deceptions were utilized in a classic early study on cognitive dissonance theory conducted by Festinger and Carlsmith (1959). The researchers attempted to determine if attitudes towards a boring research task (turning wooden pegs on a board for one hour) would become more favorable if subjects were induced to convey to others that the experiment was interesting and enjoyable. To test this hypothesis, the procedure was designed in such a way that participants were led to believe the study was over after they had completed the boring task. Depending on the experimental condition, subjects then were offered either US$1 or US$20 to misrepresent the task to the next "subject," who really was the experimenter's assistant. The researchers found that subjects who received only $1 (and thus lacked justification for lying about the experiment) later rated it more positively than subjects who received $20 (a sum assumed to have provided sufficient justification for the lie).

Festinger and Carlsmith believed that the results of their study were consistent with the tenets of cognitive dissonance theory. Although this conclusion was contested by other psychologists (e.g. Bem, 1965; Linder et al., 1967), one can readily understand why the investigation also raised ethical concerns. The participants were deceived about the purpose of the study, were falsely informed that the study was over when in fact it was not, and were encouraged to lie to someone they were unaware was in on the experiment in order to receive money. The final insult was that subjects were asked to return the money they had earned for "helping out" the researcher! Such multiple-level deceptions have the potential to undermine the relationship between experimenter and subject, eliminating the possibility of mutual trust and weakening researchers' respect for the very individuals whom they depend on in order to carry out their studies.

Kelman was not alone in criticizing the excessive use of deception in psychological experimentation (e.g. Bok, 1978; Seeman, 1969; Warwick, 1975). Ring (1967, p. 117) similarly attacked the "fun-and-games approach" taken by many psychologists who, in their attempts to create increasingly elaborate deceptions, appeared to be engaged in "a game of 'can you top this?' " Indicative of this tendency is an extreme case cited by Carlson (1971) in which researchers employed 18 deceptions and three additional manipulations in a single experiment (Kiesler et al., 1968). Baumrind (1964, 1975, 1985), another outspoken critic of deception, focused her arguments on the issue of trust. In her view, all cases of deception in human relationships represent violations of human rights that inevitably weaken people's trust in future interactions.

Whatever the specific complaint, the various criticisms leveled against deception often suggest that, because it involves lying and deceit, its use in psychological research is morally reprehensible and may have potentially negative effects on subjects, the profession, and society (Christensen, 1988). Of course, how one feels about research deception ultimately reflects the ethical theory one espouses. Thus, there are those who believe that deception can be ethically justified from a cost–benefit (or "act-utilitarian") perspective, given the methodological requirements of a particular investigation, and provided that certain safeguards are followed, such as debriefing and protection of research participants from harm. This is the position that has been adopted by several professional societies, such as the American Psychological Association (2002). Others, arguing from a deontological (or "rule-utilitarian") ethical position, believe that deception should be eliminated from research settings because its use represents a clear violation of the subject's basic right to informed consent (Baumrind, 1985; Bok, 1978; Goldstein, 1981). Some general examples of ethical and methodological arguments for and against the use of research deception appear in Table 3.1.

Table 3.1 Summary of arguments for and against deception

Arguments for deception

1 Deception enables the researcher to increase the impact of a laboratory setting. The experimental situation can become more realistic, thereby enhancing the internal validity of the study. (example: Berkun et al., 1962)
2 Certain significant areas of human life cannot be experimentally studied in an otherwise ethical manner. Deception can enable the researcher to sidestep this ethical dilemma by creating a reasonable facsimile of the topic of interest. (example: Latané and Darley, 1968)
3 Deception can serve to reduce the effects of subjects' motives and role-playing behavior in the experimental situation. (example: Bramel, 1962)
4 Any potential negative effects resulting from deception (e.g. potentially harmful self-revelations) can be removed through careful post-experimental procedures, such as debriefing. Further, participation in deceptive research can provide an involving learning experience for participants. (example: Milgram, 1964)

Arguments against deception

1 Deception places subjects in a subservient, powerless role in the research context and may lead to a negative attitude regarding participation in the research process.
2 Deception is morally undesirable because it suggests the notion that humans cannot be trusted under otherwise honest and open circumstances.
3 Deception creates poor public relations for the disciplines that utilize it for research purposes.
4 The use of deception may ultimately prove to be self-defeating. That is, as word about its use spreads, subject populations will grow increasingly suspicious of investigators and the research process.

Source: Bassett et al. (1982).

Why deceive?

Strict adherence to the letter of the law regarding ethical standards in the behavioral sciences requires that researchers first obtain voluntary informed consent from their subjects. In the current APA (2002) regulations, for example, the basic elements of informed consent maintain that prospective research participants be informed of (1) the research purpose, duration, and procedures; (2) their freedom to decline participation or withdraw at any time during the investigation; (3) the possible consequences of non-participation; (4) the factors that may influence their decision to participate, such as risks and discomforts; (5) description of any potential research benefits; (6) limits to confidentiality; (7) participation incentives; and (8) information about how and from whom to obtain answers to questions about the study. (For a more complete listing of the components that comprise fully informed consent, see Box 3.1).

The carefully worded criteria that define informed consent in the APA guidelines do not stipulate that researchers must provide subjects with full information about their experimental plans, procedures, and hypotheses. In fact, it is certain of these aspects that researchers often choose to withhold from their subjects or else misinform them about. If they did not, the resulting psychology of human behavior might very well be based on biased research findings. Thus, despite the ethically questionable nature of deception as a research technique, there is

Box 3.1 Informed consent: what is sufficient information?

In a paper prepared for the National Commission for the Protection of Human Subjects of Biomedical and Behavioral Research, Robert Levine (1975) identified 11 types of information that should be communicated to the prospective research participant during the informed consent procedure.

1 Describing the overall purpose of the research.
2 Telling the participant his or her role in the study.
3 Stating why the subject has been chosen (and how).
4 Explaining the procedures, including the time required, the setting, and those with whom the participant will interact.
5 Clearly stating the risks and discomforts.
6 Describing the benefits of the research to the participant, including the inducements.
7 Disclosing alternative procedures, where applicable.
8 Offering to answer any questions.
9 Suggesting that the subject may want to discuss participation with others, especially where substantial research dangers are involved.
10 Stating that the participant may withdraw at any time and that exercising this right will have no negative consequences.
11 Stating that the initial information is incomplete and that further information will be given after the experiment, where applicable.

According to Levine (p. 3.72), "each negotiation for informed consent must be adjusted to meet the requirements of the specific proposed activity and, more particularly, be sufficiently flexible to meet the needs of the individual prospective subject."

widespread agreement that its use in psychological experimentation is often a methodological necessity for many investigations (e.g. Adair et al., 1985; Schuler, 1982; Sharpe et al., 1992; Weber and Cook, 1972).

In order to clarify what is meant by "methodological necessity" and how research results can be biased by fully informed consent, consider the following hypothetical examples suggested by Baron and Byrne (1987). Imagine a study in which subjects are correctly informed at the outset that they are participants in an investigation of the effects of flattery on their liking of strangers. Aware of the purpose of the investigation, it would be difficult to imagine that subjects' feelings towards the strangers from whom they received compliments would be the same as if they were unaware of the study's purpose. Similarly, we might expect many subjects to "bend over backwards" to show how accepting they are of members of other races if aware that they are participants in a study of racial prejudice. The message in both of these cases should be clear: in revealing the exact substance of the research, psychologists would run the risk of distorting the reactions of their subjects and ultimately limiting the applicability of the research findings.

Let us next consider an example that pertains to a series of laboratory investigations that actually were carried out. In order to test certain hypotheses about the conditions affecting whether people will intervene during emergencies, Bibb Latané and John Darley (1970) created research situations in which naive subjects were led to believe that a room next to the laboratory was on fire, that another subject was suffering an epileptic seizure, or that a secretary had fallen from a stepladder in an adjoining room (see Box 3.2). Rather than waiting for such unpredictable events to occur and then observing bystanders' reactions, it was more practical for Latané and Darley to create the events themselves under the more controlled conditions of a psychology laboratory. This, of course,

Box 3.2   Creating emergencies in the laboratory

During the mid-1960s, social psychologists Bibb Latané and John Darley began a series of investigations to determine the conditions leading to prosocial behavior during emergencies. Their interest in this subject matter was sparked by actual incidents involving groups of people who idly stood by, failing to come to the aid of victims in distress. Perhaps the best known example of the perplexing phenomenon of "bystander apathy" was the case involving Catherine "Kitty" Genovese, a 28-year-old bar manager who was brutally murdered near her apartment in Queens, New York, after returning home from work during the early morning hours of March 13, 1964. Thirty-eight bystanders in the neighborhood witnessed the crime but nevertheless failed to take effective action to help her.

Given the number of factors that might underlie such complex behavior, Latané and Darley conducted their initial experiments in the laboratory, where they were able to isolate certain variables of interest. Because of the large number of witnesses present during several of the reported cases of bystander apathy, they reasoned that people may be less apt to intervene when others are present in the situation. But how might an emergency be arranged in a laboratory setting in order to test this hypothesis? One strategy employed by Darley and Latané (1968) was to have college students show up for a study allegedly pertaining to personal problems associated with campus life. Upon arrival in the laboratory, each participant was taken to a small room equipped with an intercom system which would enable communication with other participants (who were actually "figments of the tape recorder"). The subject then was informed that each "participant" in turn would be given two minutes to discuss their school-related adjustment problems, followed by an opportunity to comment on what others had said. The individual comments then would be followed by a free discussion. The experimenter also explained that in order to ensure confidentiality, he would not listen to the discussion and that participants

Box 3.2   (Continued)

would remain anonymous to each other. During the initial round of comments, each prerecorded participant in the discussion, as well as the one naive subject, took their turns and described common adjustment problems. However, the future victim added to his remarks that he was prone to seizures, especially when under stress. When it came time for that individual to speak again, his comments became progressively disoriented and he seemed to be experiencing great distress. Although somewhat incoherent, he then complained that he was having a seizure and needed immediate help. Finally, he choked loudly and then became silent.

In order to manipulate the number of bystanders thought to be present during the emergency, the actual subject was led to believe that the discussion group involved either one other person (the victim), two other persons (the victim and another bystander), or five other persons (the victim and four other bystanders). The results of the study were consistent with expectations that the more people present during an emergency, the less likely they would come to the aid of the victim. Whereas 85 percent of the subjects who believed they alone knew of the "victim's" plight reported the seizure before the victim became silent, only 31 percent of subjects who thought that four other bystanders were present did the same.

Was the use of deception justified in Darley and Latané's study? Critics of deception might argue that the research paradigm exposed subjects to psychological risks, including guilt and a threat to self-esteem for not helping, stress during the emergency itself, and embarrassment at being duped by the researchers. Others might defend the procedure by contending that such risks were far outweighed by the importance of the subject matter and potential gain in knowledge about helping behavior. What do you think?

required the researchers to deceive their participants about the real nature of the situation and the purpose of the investigation. If such facts had been made known to the subjects – that they were participants in a helping experiment or that the situations were not actual emergencies – the researchers clearly would not have been able to learn much about bystander intervention during actual emergencies.

In the examples just described, we can identify some of the more common methodological justifications for the use of deception in behavioral research. Foremost among these is the recognition that if research participants were aware of the true purpose of an investigation, their resulting behavior might be influenced by such knowledge (see Rosnow, 2001; Strohmetz and Rosnow, 2003). Research findings may be systematically biased by altruistic subjects who attempt to confirm the research hypotheses in order to help in the cause of science (the so-called "good subject effect") or by subjects who attempt to put their best foot forward in order to make a good impression on the researcher (a bias known as "evaluation apprehension"). An experimenter's openness may also produce boomerang effects from more suspicious subjects who seek ulterior motives and alternative explanations. These potential threats to validity that stem from the social nature of the experimenter–subject interaction collectively are referred to as "research artifacts."

Confronted by such problems, it is easy to understand why an investigator may feel compelled to mislead subjects about the true nature of the experiment. By doing so, the researcher gains confidence that subjects have responded to the experimental variables under investigation and that the observed behavior has not been influenced by certain motivations associated with participation in the study, such as the good subject effect. In this sense, we would say that deception has the capacity to improve the internal validity of an investigation.

A related methodological advantage of deception is that it can elicit more spontaneous behavior from subjects than otherwise might be the case in a laboratory setting. This possibility can increase the generalizability of the research findings to more natural, everyday situations, thereby improving the external validity of the investigation. Finally, as in the example of the bystander intervention studies, deception can increase the researcher's degree of methodological control over the experimental situation. In their initial investigations, Latané and Darley (1970) were particularly interested in determining whether the number of bystanders present during an emergency would influence the likelihood of intervention by any one bystander. Clearly, they could not have expected an emergency to occur repeatedly in a natural setting under precisely the same circumstances with a different number of bystanders present during each occurrence. It was more feasible for them to systematically manipulate the number of bystanders during a series of carefully contrived "emergencies." By creating "fictional environments" in the laboratory, investigators can manipulate and control the variables of interest with much greater facility than if deception is not used.

In sum, with regard to the use of deception in human subject research, a balance often must be struck between methodological and ethical considerations. Realistically, ethical research procedures such as informed consent are not always the most methodologically sound procedures. In other words, what is the most ethical is not necessarily the most effective. Thus, under certain circumstances, deceiving research participants about the true nature of an investigation may be the only feasible way to collect the necessary data. An absolute rule prohibiting the use of deception in all research would make it impossible for researchers to carry out a wide range of important studies.

Types of research deception

As is apparent in the research examples previously described, various kinds of research deceptions have been utilized by behavioral scientists. Deception may be practiced by researchers within both laboratory and field settings. In laboratory studies, subjects are at least aware that they are participating in a study, whereas participants in field studies may or may not be aware of that fact. In either setting, deception may be of the active or passive sort. "Active deception" is deception by commission, as when the researcher blatantly misleads the subject about some aspect of the investigation (e.g. the purpose of a study or the procedures to be followed). "Passive deception" is deception by omission, as when the researcher purposely withholds relevant information from the subject. With passive deception, a lie is not told; rather, a truth is left unspoken.

   Given this basic distinction between deception by commission and deception by omission, it is possible to classify a variety of deceptive research practices (Arellano-Galdames, 1972). Among the research procedures that represent examples of active deceptions are the following:

1   Misrepresentation of the research purpose.
2   Untrue statements about the researcher's identity.
3   Use of research assistants (called "confederates," "stooges," or "pseudosubjects") who act out predetermined roles.
4   False promises.
5   Violation of the promise of anonymity.
6   Incorrect information about research procedures and instructions.
7   False explanations of scientific equipment and other measurement instruments.
8   False diagnoses and other reports.
9   Use of placebos (i.e. inactive medication) and secret application of medications and drugs.
10 Misleading settings or timing for the investigation (when the study actually begins and ends, its duration, etc.).

Deceptions by omission include the following practices:

1   Concealed observation.
2   Provocation and secret recording of negatively evaluated behavior.
3   Unrecognized participant observation.
4   Use of projective techniques and other personality tests.
5   Unrecognized conditioning of subjects' behavior.

Most of the examples listed in this taxonomy are more likely to be practiced in the laboratory context than in field settings. The list of deceptive procedures is not exhaustive and some deceptive methods might be classified in more than one of the fifteen categories. However, the classification is helpful in pointing out that research deception varies along several dimensions. Gross and Fleming (1982) conducted an analysis of 1,188 studies appearing in leading social psychology journals over a twenty-year period in an effort to determine the frequency with which these types of deceptions were employed by researchers. The provision of a false purpose or cover story represented the most frequently employed deception, followed by incorrect information concerning materials, use of a confederate or actor, and false feedback given to participants. In a more recent study of deceptions reported in published accounts of social psychological research, I found that twenty years after Gross and Fleming's analysis, (a) the provision of a false purpose or cover story and (b) making false statements about the procedure or study materials remained the most prevalent forms of deception utilized by investigators (Kimmel, 2001, 2004a). The employment of confederates or actors is a form of deception that appears to have declined significantly during recent decades.

Additional typologies of deception have been suggested by other researchers (e.g. Lawson, 2001). Sieber (1982a) identified several varieties of deception, including self-deception, third-person deception, offering false information, and offering no information. In addition, she distinguished between three types of "forewarning" (i.e. limited informed consent) by the researcher: (1) consent to the fact that a deception will be employed; (2) consent to be deceived; and (3) obtaining waivers to inform. According to Sieber, whether these forms of deception will result in harm or pose serious risks to participants depends in large part on the nature of the actual experiment. For example, the offering of no information implies that participants are not aware that they are being observed for research purposes. While the appropriateness of this form of deception depends on *what* behavior is being observed, the setting and the purpose of the observation also are critical factors. A research technique in which "lost letters" are dropped in public settings to see how many will be returned poses no risk to participants and the magnitude of the deception is relatively small. In the laboratory, the omission of certain information irrelevant to the subject in a verbal learning experiment likewise would not represent a serious breach of ethical standards.

As the preceding discussion suggests, deceptions vary in terms of their potential consequences. For this reason, the degree of severity of any negative effects must enter into decisions about whether or not to proceed with a study as planned. "Severe deceptions" are those that create false beliefs about central, important issues related to participants' self-concept or personal behavior, as when an experimental manipulation leads participants to believe they lack self-confidence. "Mild deceptions" are those that create false beliefs about relatively unimportant issues peripheral to participants' self-concept, such as misleading them about the research sponsor or study purpose (Toy, Olson, and Wright, 1989). Severe deceptions can be expected to create negative affect both during and after actual participation in the research (e.g. upset or anxiety linked to a reduced self-image), whereas mild deceptions are unlikely to create negative beliefs and affect until the debriefing session at the end of the study (e.g. disappointment that the study was not really supported by an environmental protection group).

The fact that psychologists are more likely to employ severe deceptions that are relevant to the fundamental beliefs and values of research participants than are investigators in related fields, such as marketing and consumer research, to some extent explains why deception has been such a central issue in psychology. Studies involving severe deceptions are harder to justify when ethical principles are applied and are more likely to encounter problems when subjected to committee review. Although mild deceptions are unlikely to cause harm to participants, they can still be morally problematic (Smith, Klein, and Kimmel, 2005). The nature and prevalence of specific effects of deception on research participants are more fully discussed in chapter 4.

When considering potential dilemmas involving the use of deceptive research practices it is important to recognize that the effects of deception may be positive (i.e. beneficial to recipients) or negative (i.e. harmful to recipients), short- or long-term, and immediate or delayed. For example, a research participant may be initially unaffected by the awareness of having been duped into believing that a fictitious organization had sponsored the study, but may experience a short-term loss of self-esteem when later reading a magazine article about how easily people are deceived by researchers. In this case, the deception effects are negative, delayed, and short-term. Although deception is most readily thought of as a practice that is employed during the data collection stage, in fact it may be used at each stage of the research process (see Table 3.2). Further, it is important to recognize that deception can have consequences for each of the parties involved in the research process (see Table 3.3).

Another important distinction pertaining to kinds of deception has to do with the recognition that research deception may be unintentional (Keith-Spiegel and Koocher, 1985). Non-intentional deception, which cannot be entirely avoided, includes absence of full disclosure, failure to inform, and misunderstanding. Intentional deception, on the other hand, includes the withholding of information in order to obtain participation, concealment and staged manipulations in field settings, and deceptive instructions and confederate manipulations in laboratory research. According to Baumrind (1985), absence of full disclosure does not constitute intentional deception, so long as participants agree to the postponement of full disclosure of the research purpose. But when the investigator's purpose is "to take the person unaware by trickery" or to "cause the person to believe the false" for whatever reason (e.g. to induce subjects into agreeing to participate), the study invariably involves the intentional deception of research participants (Baumrind, 1985, p. 165).

Baumrind's notion of non-intentional deception suggests that while full disclosure of all information that may affect an individual's willingness to participate in a study is a worthy ideal, it is not a realistic possibility. Even the investigator with a sincere desire to disclose all relevant aspects of a study's purpose and procedure to subjects nonetheless may fail to reveal certain information. In part, this may be a function of the researcher taking for granted that subjects have a basic level of knowledge about scientific procedures, testing materials, and the research equipment or apparatus used. In other cases, information provided to subjects may not be fully understood. Experimental research procedures can be

Table 3.2 Use of deception at various stages of the research process

Subject recruitment	Research procedure	Post-research/application
Identity of researcher and/or sponsor	Misrepresentation of purpose	Violation of promise of anonymity
Purpose of research	False information about procedures, measures, etc.	Breach of confidentiality
Participation incentives	Withholding information	Misrepresenting implications of research results
Involving people in research without their knowledge	Concealed observation	False feedback during debriefing session

Source: Kimmel (2003).

Table 3.3 Potential costs and benefits of deception studies

Recipient	Benefits	Costs
Participant	Increased understanding of science and the research process Feeling of having contributed to science Self-insight (from personal content revealed by deceptive probes)	Inflicted insight Embarrassment Image of science lowered Mistrust of others
Researcher	Capacity to elicit spontaneous behavior from participants Increased degree of methodological control Enhanced reputation from successful research endeavors	Legal sanctions (e.g. if confidentiality breached) Undermines integrity and commitment to the truth Tarnished image
Profession	Facilitates attempts to determine validity of theories, previous research, and assessment instruments	Exhausts pool of naive participants Jeopardizes community/industry support for the research enterprise
Society	Scientific advancement and progress Increased understanding of behavior Insight into applications towards the betterment of humanity	Undermines trust in expert authorities and science Increased suspiciousness (e.g. self-consciousness in public)

Source: Adapted from Kimmel and Smith (2001)

quite complex and difficult to explain in a language that is understandable to the typical research participant. Further, young children and the mentally impaired have certain cognitive limitations that seriously limit the extent to which fully informed consent can be obtained from these groups (see chapter 8). Finally, due to the imperfect nature of human communication, there is likely to be some degree of misunderstanding between the subject and researcher during the informed consent procedure (Baumrind, 1985).

In sum, deception experiments differ so much in the nature and degree of deception used that even the harshest critic would be hard pressed to state unequivocally that all deception has potentially harmful effects. Indeed, simple generalization about the benefits or harms of deception research is not possible (Sieber, 1982a). Since experimenters can never convey everything about a study to their subjects, it may be that all behavioral research is disguised in one respect or another and that the range of ethical questions related to the use of deception must be thought of as falling on a continuum. The style of the deception is not so much the issue as is its probable effect on the subject.

Frequency and magnitude of deception

Several attempts have been made to gauge the prevalence of intentional deception in human subject research (e.g. Adair et al., 1985; Carlson, 1971; McNamara and Woods, 1977; Menges, 1973; Seeman, 1969; Smith and Richardson, 1983;

Stricker, 1967). Consistent with more casual observation, these early reviews of the published literature revealed that deceptive procedures were regularly used in psychological research and that the frequency of deception had not diminished from its peak in the 1970s (Sharpe et al., 1992). However, there is growing evidence that psychologists have responded to the ethical and methodological concerns linked to the use of deceptive practices and that these practices have begun to decline in recent years.

It is not very surprising to find that a relatively high frequency of deception was evident in psychological research during the 1960s and early 1970s. During this period, psychologists used deceptive procedures as a primary means of coping with research artifacts. One must also bear in mind that separate sets of ethical guidelines for human subject research did not exist until the early 1970s in the behavioral sciences, and there is evidence that ethical regulations in psychology (e.g. as exemplified by the original APA ethics codes) did not initially lead to a reduction in the use of deception (Adair et al., 1985).

Taken together, reviews by Stricker (1967), Seeman (1969), Carlson (1971), and Menges (1973) revealed that nearly one-fifth of the studies appearing in major psychological journals involved incidents of overt deception by experimenters who deliberately told untruths to their subjects. In fact, deceptions involving direct lying to subjects characterized between 19 and 57 percent of the studies published in the areas of social psychology and personality during the period surveyed (1961–71). For example, in an early examination of 457 studies published in the *Journal of Abnormal and Social Psychology*, the *Journal of Personality*, the *Journal of Social Psychology*, and *Sociometry* during 1964, Stricker (1967) reported that subjects were intentionally misled about some aspect of the investigation in 19.3 percent (88) of the investigations. Specifically, subjects were given false information about instruments, stimuli, tasks, and other conditions in 76.1 percent of the deception studies, and about other participants' performance and behavior in 60.2 percent of the studies. The research purpose was misstated in slightly more than half of the investigations.

Stricker also found that the frequency of deception varied greatly according to the specific topical area studied. The use of deception was most pervasive in studies of conformity (81 percent) and cognitive dissonance and balance theory (72 percent). Similarly, Seeman (1969) found that journals emphasizing personality and social psychology had a relatively high incidence of deception in comparison with experimental and clinical psychology publications. Further, Seeman noted a significant rise in the use of deception in the personality and social areas, from 18.5 percent in 1948 to 38.2 percent in 1963. In other surveys, Carlson (1971) and Gross and Fleming (1982) found that participants were rarely given complete and accurate information in studies reported in personality and social psychology journals. It is interesting to note that when psychological journal editors were asked to nominate studies they considered to be empirical landmarks in social psychology, the five most frequently nominated (Asch, 1955; Festinger and Carlsmith, 1959; Milgram, 1963; Schachter and Singer, 1962; Darley and Latané, 1968) involved elaborate laboratory deceptions of the studies' purpose and procedures, and the sixth (Sherif et al., 1961) involved the observation and manipulation in the field of unsuspecting youngsters (Diamond and Morton, 1978; see also Slater, 2004).

The high frequency of deception in personality and social psychology research is understandable, given the nature of the subject matter and the greater potential for threats to validity posed by research artifacts. Many studies involving social and personality topics such as conformity, impression formation, self-esteem, attitude change, helping behavior, and aggression simply could not be carried out without the use of some form of deception. However, deception has not been limited to these areas of psychology. Menges (1973) examined nearly one thousand studies published in 1971 in a variety of psychology journals, including those in abnormal, counseling, and educational psychology, and found that the use of deception was widespread. Subjects received incomplete information in 80 percent of the studies, inaccurate information about the independent variable in 17 percent, and complete information in only 3 percent of the studies.

As previously indicated, the growing attention to ethical issues in psychology during the development of the initial set of APA research principles in the early 1970s did not appear to have a discernible impact on the prevalence of deception during the following decade (McNamara and Woods, 1977; Smith and Richardson, 1983). In order to assess the extent to which psychologists' research practices had been altered by ethical regulations, Adair et al. (1985) evaluated the frequency of the use of deception reported in all empirical studies appearing in the *Journal of Personality and Social Psychology* for 1979. It was found that deception, defined as providing information that actively misled subjects about some aspect of the study, was utilized in 58.5 percent of the examined studies, a percentage which, according to Adair et al. (1985, p. 63), represented a "monotonically increasing function" over previous decades. These results suggested that deception had become a normative practice, especially for research in social psychology.

In addition to the fact that the frequency of deception had not declined following the implementation of more stringent ethical regulations, there is also some evidence that the nature and intensity of the deceptions also remained relatively unchanged. As one indication of the consistency over time in the magnitude of deceptions used, Adair et al. (1985) reported that more than two-thirds of the 1979 studies they assessed employed multiple types of deception. Further, the same authors found that it was relatively easy to identify comparable examples of deception studies in their 1979 sample that matched some of the extreme laboratory experiments cited as problematic by Kelman some fifteen years earlier.

In one study, White (1979) used a typical paradigm for studying the link between aggression and sexual stimuli. Subjects were angered by a confederate who evaluated them in a highly negative and personally insulting way (in order to manipulate frustration levels); they next were assigned to the role of having to give electric shocks to the confederate, after having been given a false cover story as to the purpose of the experiment. Prior to administering the shocks, the angered subjects were asked to rate a series of slides depicting various sexual acts, including some intended to create unpleasant emotional reactions. At this point, the reader should readily recognize some similarities between this approach and Milgram's obedience procedure. However, had Adair et al. selected from studies published in 1977 they would have found an investigation that even more closely matched Milgram's research – a duplication of the obedience procedure carried out by Shanab and Yahya (1977), whose subjects were children as young as six years old.

Recalling certain aspects of Bergin's (1962) sexual identity investigation is a study by Baumeister et al. (1979) in which female subjects were given false feedback informing them that they had scored high on a bogus trait called "surgency." Half of the subjects were led to believe that their score indicated that they were immature, ill adjusted, and possessed a variety of additional negative characteristics. As part of the manipulation, the researchers went on to explain that these traits had resulted from an unusual developmental background which had caused the subjects to be insecure about their femininity. So informed, half of these women then had their surgency score and its presumed meaning publicly disclosed in the presence of a male confederate.

The close match between these experiments and earlier controversial deception studies suggests that the intensity of some deceptive procedures, at least as practiced by social psychologists, had continued even in the years immediately following extensive ethical debate and codification of ethical standards. In fact, extreme cases of deceptive research appeared in the psychological literature as recently as the mid-1980s, as illustrated by the following two examples. In one study, Zimbardo et al. (1981) induced partial deafness in a sample of university students through post-hypnotic suggestion. This procedure was based on the assumption that some elderly individuals become paranoid and fearful because they have hearing problems, not because they are actually suffering from psychological deficits. In the investigation, subjects were misinformed about the purpose of the experiment and the experiences they would undergo. As predicted, it was found that the experience of partial deafness, without awareness of its source, induced changes in the cognitive, emotional, and behavioral functioning of subjects. Specifically, subjects in the deafness-without-awareness treatment condition became more paranoid and were rated by themselves and by others as more irritated, agitated, hostile, and unfriendly than control subjects. Although the experimental sessions were followed by extensive debriefing and attempts to remove any tension or confusion in subjects, lingering effects of the deceptive manipulation cannot be completely ruled out.

Another study involved a variation of Milgram's obedience procedure. Dutch social psychologists Meeus and Raaijmakers (1986) performed an experiment on "administrative obedience" which, rather than commanding subjects to inflict physical harm on another person, required them to engage in behavior intended to cause apparent psychological harm. Subjects were led to believe that they were participating in a study on ability to work under stress and that their task was to administer a series of test questions to a job applicant. Supposedly, the applicant – actually a confederate – would get the job only if he passed the test. However, during the test, subjects were ordered to make an escalating series of fifteen insulting "stress remarks" to the applicant over a microphone from an adjoining room (such as "This job is much too difficult for you. You are more suited for lower functions").

As in Milgram's procedure, the confederate pleaded with the subject to stop, and then angrily refused to tolerate the treatment. The confederate finally pretended to fall into a state of despair, thus apparently losing out on the job for which he was applying. As in Milgram's research, complete obedience was obtained from a majority of subjects (92 percent) in the condition that included an experimenter who ordered them to continue with the procedure. No subject persisted in a control condition lacking a prodding experimenter. In a follow up to this study, Meeus and Raaijmakers (1987) sent another group of subjects a letter prior to their participation forewarning them about the research procedure. Despite the fact that these subjects had ample opportunity to consider the conflict posed by their eventual experimental role, all were completely obedient during the study.

Although Meeus and Raaijmakers eliminated from their studies the use of ominous shock generators and any suggestions that the unsuspecting victim was experiencing intense physical pain, the risks to participants probably were no less than in the original Milgram procedure. Yet despite an increase in sensitivities to ethical issues since Milgram's studies, little attention seems to have been paid to the ethicality of the use of deception in the Dutch replications.

Deception in psychological research: an update

The preceding discussion of deception may paint a somewhat bleak picture of the nature of the research procedures utilized in psychology laboratory research, but the situation appears to be changing. Although rarely implemented during the development period of the discipline, the use of deception increased significantly as subsequent generations of psychologists became more thoroughly committed to the laboratory experiment. In recent years, however, evidence has emerged that the frequency of deception in psychological research has declined. For example, Nicks, Korn, and Mainieri (1997) reviewed articles from journals in personality and social psychology from 1921 to 1994 and found an apparent decrease in the use of active deception (i.e. explicit misstatements of fact) since 1980 as compared to previous decades. Similarly, in his survey of articles appearing in four social psychology journals, Vitelli (1988) reported a decline in the use of deception from 1974 to 1985. Vitelli attributed the decline in deception rates to the formidable array of ethical guidelines and review mechanisms that have evolved in recent decades as well as corresponding changes in theory and research practices in the discipline of psychology.

In light of these findings, I conducted my own assessment of deceptive research practices reported in published psychology studies spanning the past three decades and then compared the results with the research practices described in marketing studies appearing over the same time span (Kimmel, 2001). Despite similar concerns about the use of deception and other ethically sensitive practices in marketing research and other applied fields, criticisms about such research procedures have been rarer and far more muted than those raised in the behavioral sciences and there has been significantly less activity at the professional level to codify principles of research.

I examined all research articles appearing in the *Journal of Personality and Social Psychology* (*JPSP*) for alternative months during the years 1989 and 1996. This analysis was intended to update and extend Adair et al.'s (1985) much-cited descriptive investigation. Additionally, I assessed all studies appearing in the *Journal of Consumer Research* (*JCR*) and the *Journal of Marketing Research* (*JMR*) during three time periods, 1975–76, 1989–90, and 1996–97. Although the findings revealed a rise in deceptive procedures in human participant studies over time in the applied fields, a decline was apparent in the psychology studies. Specifically, evidence of marketing studies employing deception rose from 43 percent in 1975–76 to 56 percent in 1996–97, an increase attributed to the greater use of active deception (i.e. deception by commission), most commonly the misrepresentation of the research purpose and incorrect information about research procedures, equipment, and measuring instruments (see Table 3.4). In a subsequent replication, I observed a continuation of these trends, with fully 66 percent of 108 studies appearing in *JCR* and *JMR* in 2001–02 having employed some form of deception (Kimmel, 2004a). Overall, there was little reporting of ethical practices (e.g. informed consent, freedom to withdraw, protection of confidentiality) in the deception studies and although the reported use of debriefing increased to 21 percent by 1996–97, this rate had fallen to 16 percent in 2001–02. (See chapter 7 for further discussion of research practices and deception rates in consumer research.)

The findings revealed a quite different picture for the psychology studies. Evidence of studies from *JPSP* reporting the use of active deceptions was found to have declined steadily, from 59 percent in 1979 to 33 percent in 1996 (see Table 3.5). A modest increase to 40 percent in studies utilizing active deception was noted during the 2001–02 period (Kimmel, 2004a). The incidence of studies employing passive deceptions was more variable over the periods studied, consistently falling within the 30–35 percent range. These results indicate that although deception still is a rather common practice, at least in social psychological research, it is apparent that psychologists are using deceptive practices less than in earlier periods, and the steady increase in usage noted prior to the development of stricter ethical principles and review processes is no longer evident.

The trends noted in my analyses are consistent with the findings reported by Nicks et al. (1997) and Vitelli (1988) and may be tied to other changes in the

Table 3.4 Percentage of human subject studies employing active and passive deception reported in *JMR* and *JCR*, 1975–2002

	1975–76	1989–90	1996–97	2001–02
N (studies)	83	111	75	108
Deception	43.4	58.5	56.0	66.0
Active deception only	4.8	26.1	16.0	14.0
Passive deception only	32.5	22.5	26.7	27.0
Active and passive deception	6.0	9.9	13.3	25.0
No deception	56.6	41.5	44.0	34.0

Source: Kimmel (2001, 2004a)

72 Chapter 3

Table 3.5 Percentage of human subject studies employing deception reported in *JPSP*, 1979–2002

	1979	1983	1989	1996	2001–02
Active deception studies	58.5	49.7	41.9	32.6	40.0
Passive deception only	–	–	24.7	30.1	26.0
Non-deception studies	41.5	50.3	33.4	37.3	34.0

Source: The percentages for the years 1979 and 1983 were obtained from Adair et al. (1985); the data for 1989, 1996, and 2001–02 were obtained from Kimmel (2001, 2004a).

discipline's research practices. During the 1980s psychological research began to show an increase in the use of non-experimental methods that are less likely to require deception, such as questionnaires and surveys (in contrast to marketing research, which showed the opposite trend). The need for deception is reduced significantly when non-experimental methods are utilized, and field settings tend to be less conducive to the implementation of deceptive manipulations involving staged situations (see chapter 5). Further, coinciding with the increasing pervasiveness of institutional monitoring of research, psychologists may now find it necessary to avoid active deceptions that are likely to be seen as potentially harmful to participants rather than risk the possibility that their research proposals will be rejected by review boards.

ETHICAL SAFEGUARDS IN LABORATORY RESEARCH

In view of the various ethical and methodological problems posed by research practices in the laboratory context, it is essential for the researcher to take special precautions to minimize any negative effects. Before deciding to employ such practices as deception in a study, investigators should give serious consideration to the full range of alternatives that might be employed instead. In the remainder of this chapter we turn our attention to the nature and implications of the important procedure of debriefing as a means of protecting subjects from negative research consequences. Alternatives to the use of deception are considered in chapter 4.

Debriefing

Debriefing is perhaps the most commonly used safeguard when deception studies are carried out in laboratory settings. In its basic form, debriefing (also sometimes referred to as "dehoaxing," "desensitization," or "disabusing") describes the procedure that occurs once data have been collected. The investigator engages the participant in a discussion to clarify various aspects of the study, including its true nature and purpose (see Box 3.3). During the debriefing session the researcher attempts to correct any of the subject's misconceptions about the study, answer the subject's questions honestly, and supply additional information

Box 3.3   Debriefing according to the 2002 APA ethics code

The latest version of the APA ethics code (Principle 8.08) clarifies the following conditions as required for carrying out an effective debriefing of research participants:

a. Psychologists provide a prompt opportunity for participants to obtain appropriate information about the nature, results, and conclusions of the research, and they take reasonable steps to correct any misconceptions that participants may have of which the psychologists are aware.
b. If scientific or humane values justify delaying or withholding this information, psychologists take reasonable measures to reduce the risk of harm.
c. When psychologists become aware that research procedures have harmed a participant, they take reasonable steps to minimize the harm.

Source: APA (2002, p. 1070). Copyright © 2002 by the American Psychological Association. Reprinted with permission.

that may have been purposely withheld. All this information is to be provided sensitively and with the education of the subject in mind.

The debriefing period also provides an opportunity to refer a participant to an appropriately trained provider if something problematic (such as signs of depression) has been revealed during the study. Moreover, in special cases in which confidentiality must be breached (e.g. studies in which it is learned that certain individuals are suicidal or intend to harm others), participants should be reminded about any limitations to confidentiality that were agreed upon during the consent procedure, if feasible (Behnke and Kinscherff, 2002). It also is important to inform individuals how they can contact the researcher if later they have additional concerns or experience negative effects from having participated in the investigation.

Debriefing is considered an important safeguard against the effects of deception because it is during this formal post-experimental interaction that the adverse effects of deception may be detected, including negative reactions (such as embarrassment, upset, and stress), resentment at having been duped, suspiciousness, and the like. From an ethical point of view, the most important function of debriefing is to ensure that no permanent harm will result from subjects' involvement in the study (Schuler, 1982). Along these lines, Kelman (1968, p. 222) stated that "A good rule is that the subject ought not leave the laboratory with greater anxiety or lower self-esteem than he came in with." Others have reiterated this point and added that participants should feel even better about themselves or derive some educational benefit from their laboratory experience. It can be difficult to detect whether these goals have been met and, as described below, in some situations debriefing might do more harm than good. As Tesch (1977,

p. 218) suggested, ethical guidelines that stress the researcher's obligation to detect and remove (or correct) undesirable research consequences are based on the hidden assumption "of magical undoing, of using debriefing as an eraser for emotional and behavioral residues." However, there appear to be at least three necessary steps for maximizing the effectiveness of debriefing in deception studies: (1) a careful debriefing immediately following the subject's participation in the study; (2) a clear explanation of why the deception was necessary; and (3) an expression by the experimenter of regret for having deceived the subject (Kemmelmeier, Davis, and Follette, 2003; Rosenthal and Rosnow, 1991; Tesch, 1977) (see Box 3.4).

Box 3.4   Conducting an effective debriefing

An effective debriefing interview should be treated seriously as an essential element of the research process. The researcher should bear in mind its functions as an educational tool as well as a method for identifying and ameliorating any adverse effects. Although the debriefing procedure typically involves an oral discussion with research participants, it is a good idea for the researcher to plan what to say and what areas will be covered. A thorough debriefing should present, in non-technical language, the purpose of the experiment, various aspects of the procedure that would be helpful to the participants in understanding their role in the experiment (such as the nature of the treatment conditions and the reasons for any deceptions that were included), and the expected results of the investigation. Subjects also should be informed about how they can contact the investigator if needed after leaving the laboratory. By adhering to the following steps, the researcher can increase the likelihood that a debriefing session will satisfy its intended goals:

1   Initially, the researcher should explain the procedures and reasons for them in language that is understandable to participants (this may require pre-testing), including a discussion of the importance of the study and its relevance to understanding behavior.
2   When deception is revealed, the researcher should sensitively explain that the procedure was selected as a last resort, apologize for having used it, and fully explain how the deception was carried out, perhaps by displaying and explaining specific research materials.
3   The researcher should clearly describe any potential delayed effects from participating in the research, their likelihood, and whom to contact should any adverse effects emerge.
4   The participant should be thanked for having taken the time to participate in the study and informed about how the participation was useful and will serve as a valuable contribution to the scientific process. Any promised incentives should be provided at this time (or else it should be explained how they will be delivered later).

Box 3.4   (Continued)

5   During the entire process, one needs to carefully monitor and appro-
    priately respond to the participant's affective reactions and comments,
    while encouraging honest feedback about the study.
6   The researcher should describe the nature of the debriefing process in
    any published accounts of the study. This is to encourage other re-
    searchers to conduct effective debriefings and to eliminate ethical con-
    cerns about the effects of experimental manipulations and deceptions
    on participants (Korn and Bram, 1987).

A useful starting point in developing a more complete debriefing proto-
col is to finish the following paragraph lead ins.
   "The purpose of my experiment is to . . . "
   "The reasons why I misled you or withheld certain information about my
study prior to your participation are . . . "
   "The treatment conditions are . . . "
   "I expect to find . . . "
   "Do you have any questions about the experiment?"
   "For future contacts, I can be reached by . . . "
   "Thank you for participating."

Source: Lead ins adapted from H. O. Kiess (undated) *Experimental psychology learning guide*, unpublished manuscript, Framingham State College,
Framingham, MA. Reprinted by permission.

To be sure, debriefing may serve other functions for the researcher in addition to
the ethical one of identifying and eliminating the harmful effects of deception.
Thus, debriefing is a procedure that also is used in non-deceptive studies.
For example, a subject may have experienced stress or tension as a result of the
experimental manipulations, even if he or she had been informed about them and
agreed to undergo the risk prior to participation. Debriefing in such cases should be
oriented toward assessing any lingering effects from these negative reactions,
helping the subject to better understand and cope with them (see Box 3.5).

In addition to the ethical functions of debriefing, there are two methodological
functions that can be identified (Blanck et al., 1992; Eyde, 2000; Schuler, 1982).
The first has to do with ascertaining whether the experimental manipulations
were successful. As suggested below, one way for the researcher to assess whether
an investigation has high experimental realism is to have subjects reflect on the
study and describe their thoughts about it. In addition to serving as manipulation
checks and providing other insights into the research results, such subject reports
can determine the extent and accuracy of their suspicions, and can verify whether
they construed the research situation as intended and were involved with it
(Aronson and Carlsmith, 1968). Along these lines, Gurman (1994) argued that
in addition to the conventional debriefing of participants, researchers should brief

Box 3.5   To deceive or not to deceive: the case of mood manipulations[1]

Given the various ethical concerns described in this chapter, researchers should proceed with caution in their decision about whether or not to employ a deceptive procedure, bearing in mind that deception always should be used as a last resort. As an illustration of some of the decision-making hurdles that must be overcome to justify deception in a typical laboratory investigation, consider the case of procedures that are often used by researchers to manipulate mood. For example, in one marketing research investigation (Hill and Ward, 1989) participants were instructed to play a computerized game that ostensibly was presented as a promotional game designed for a local automobile dealership. After completing a trial of the game, some subjects were randomly selected to receive positive feedback about their performance (e.g. "Incredible – few people perform that well at this game!"), while others received no feedback. This was done in part to study the effects of the positive mood manipulation on subjects' perceived self-efficacy and subsequent decision making.

Although the deceptions utilized in the marketing study may arouse ethical concerns, few people are likely to have complaints about relatively benign deceptive manipulations that induce subjects to feel better (i.e. that put them in a good mood). However, as many of the examples in this book attest, the mood manipulations utilized by behavioral science investigators often are intended to have the opposite effect – that is, they arouse negative feelings, such as annoyance, anger, sadness, or depressive feelings. Although in each case it may be argued that such mood induction manipulations are justified by the importance of the research and anticipated scientific benefits, the researcher must carefully weigh a variety of considerations before proceeding. In the case of mood manipulation studies, the following questions would be relevant:

1   Is it possible to conduct the experiment in a naturalistic (i.e. non-laboratory) setting in which the desired moods could be expected to be naturally aroused (e.g. a sporting match where a home team win or loss would likely induce positive and negative affect in fans, respectively)?

2   Is there a more acceptable means for inducing the negative mood state? For example, instead of participants being falsely informed that they performed poorly on a task in order to make them feel unhappy, they may be asked to write an essay describing one of the sadder experiences in their lives.

3   Can the hypotheses or research objectives be explored by inducing positive mood states (happiness or tranquility) rather than negative ones (sadness or frustration)?

Box 3.5   (Continued)

4   To what extent will informed consent be obtained from participants at the outset of the investigation? Will they consent to participation in a study involving mood, mood manipulations, and the possibility of deceptive procedures? (For example, when initially enlisting in a subject pool, these possibilities might be presented to participants, who then would have the opportunity to opt out of such studies.)

5   Will participants be compensated and offered an alternative if they decide not to participate?

6   Will participants be screened to check for vulnerabilities to conditions that might be exacerbated by the mood induction (e.g. depression)?

7   Were non-deceptive alternatives considered? If so, why were they rejected?

8   Will participants be thoroughly debriefed and returned to a more positive mood state? Will the deceptions be clearly and fully explained and justified?

9   Will participants be provided with contact information if they suffer lingering effects or have further questions about the study?

10 Is the study likely to be reviewed (and approved) by an institutional review board?

11 Is the researcher fully aware of professional ethical standards, as they apply to the study under question, and is the procedure consistent with the guidelines?

[1]Thanks to N. Craig Smith for suggesting this example. See also Smith et al. (2005).

those persons who did not accept to participate for whatever reason, who are left to ponder the significance and implications of their rejection. Moreover, a briefing of this sort would provide an opportunity to obtain greater understanding of how the study is perceived by prospective participants.

Unfortunately, the extent to which debriefing is capable of detecting procedural problems and subject suspiciousness is questionable in light of evidence suggesting that some subjects are unwilling to confess their prior awareness or to let on that they did not take the procedure seriously (Golding and Lichtenstein, 1970; Newberry, 1973). What may underlie the detection inadequacy of many debriefings is the difficulty for participants to clearly separate the debriefing from the experiment *per se* (Tesch, 1977). That is, subjects may construe the debriefing procedure as merely a continuation of the experiment and continue to play whatever subject role they adopted during the experiment.

A second methodological function of debriefing is that it can operate as a safeguard against the participants' sharing of information about the study with potential subjects. Some researchers have found that pledging subjects to secrecy during the debriefing procedure can limit the extent to which relevant information is passed on to others (see chapter 4). This outcome is especially likely when subjects are given insight as to the problems involved with the loss of naivete

(Horvath, 1986). Of course, some participants are unlikely to keep their knowledge about an experiment confidential, even when they have entered an agreement with the investigator (e.g. Altemeyer, 1972).

There is widespread consensus that debriefing should fulfill an educational function in addition to those functions already described. That is, research subjects should receive some sort of an educational benefit in return for their participation. This might take the form of acquired insight and knowledge of a psychological nature (such as better understanding of the conditions that influence bystander intervention during emergencies), a better appreciation for the scientific process, and self-knowledge. Consider, for example, a study on shyness in which some subjects receive feedback that merely confirms their fears (that they are shy). This sort of self-knowledge could conceivably serve to exacerbate their social anxiety. A more complete and potentially beneficial debriefing would be one in which the researcher provides some insight into the causes of shyness, helps the subject recognize that it is a common but treatable problem, and suggests some steps that might be taken to overcome it.

The extent to which subjects attend to the information provided at the end of a study represents a concern that may limit the educational utility of debriefing. Previous surveys revealed that subjects did not highly value the debriefings they received from researchers (Brody et al., 2000; Gerdes, 1979; Sharpe et al., 1992; Smith and Richardson, 1983). For example, Brody et al. (2000) conducted in-depth interviews with students who had participated in a range of psychological experiments and found that only slightly more than 40 percent viewed their debriefing experiences favorably. The most common complaint, which was shared by 29 percent of the respondents, was that the debriefing was unclear and provided insufficient information. By contrast, positive debriefing experiences were those described as having provided a thorough explanation of the nature of the study, along with information that detailed the broader relevance of the experiment to the field of psychology. Overall, the interviews revealed that debriefings varied greatly in terms of the content, format, and general quality of the experience.

In addition to the possibility that some debriefings are poorly conducted, as suggested, it may also be the case that participants give minimal attention to the debriefing message, assuming that their obligation to the researcher is over. In other words, once subjects have gone through the experimental procedure they are likely to be more interested in obtaining the promised incentive (such as course credit or payment) than in learning about behavioral research (Sharpe et al., 1992). This is especially likely to be the case when debriefings do not appear self-relevant to participants and otherwise do little to pique their interest. Along these lines, Coulter (1986) found that student participants evaluated psychology experiments that posed certain risks more favorably than risk-free studies, presumably because they devoted greater attention to the debriefings in the former case and took the debriefings more seriously.

One interesting approach for overcoming the potential problem of inattentiveness to the debriefing has been recommended by Davis and Fernald (1975). They suggest that successful learning and assimilation of experiments can be maximized by requiring student subjects to compose a laboratory report based on the experiments in which they participate, with the report containing all of the critical information that would appear in a scientific publication. They could also be asked to evaluate the experiments and provide their personal experiences. One limitation to this approach, in addition to the fact that it only applies to participants who are students, is that a common alternative to the research participation requirement in many college courses is for students to write a term paper. Because Davis and Fernald's recommendation would result in a more time-consuming activity for students than participation (or perhaps the term paper) alone, there is the possibility that the university subject pool could be depleted by students who opt for seemingly less demanding alternative options for satisfying course requirements. (Ethical issues pertaining to the research participation requirement are considered in chapter 8.)

There is some concern that the educational functions of debriefing are ignored by researchers, such as when they do not follow through with their promises to subjects that debriefing will occur once all of the data have been collected. In order to limit gossiping about ongoing research investigations among members of the university subject pool, researchers may choose to withhold debriefing until the study is completed. However, as Carroll et al. (1985) have observed, there are certain factors that work against this actually happening. Intact classes of students disperse at the end of the semester and the make-up of the subject pool changes, or the study reveals nothing of significance and subjects do not receive feedback. It is Carroll and colleagues' belief that this is one area in which self-regulation on the part of researchers clearly has failed, and that some form of institutional regulation may be necessary.

Despite the important functions of debriefing, there is not strong evidence that it is practiced by most laboratory researchers. Early analyses revealed that a minority (from 10 percent to 33 percent) of deception experiments mentioned the inclusion of debriefing procedures (Carlson, 1971; Menges, 1973). However, in their survey of studies published in the *Journal of Personality and Social Psychology* in 1979, Adair et al. (1985) found that 66 percent of all of the deception studies and 45 percent of the studies overall (including non-deceptive investigations) reported the use of debriefing, suggesting that the reporting of debriefing had increased over the years. My analyses of studies appearing in the same journal revealed that the prevalence of debriefing was variable over the period from 1975 to 2002, with a mean rate of slightly more than 40 percent of studies reporting that participants were debriefed (Kimmel, 2001, 2004a).

Because most professional ethics codes now require debriefing as a necessary procedure in studies that utilize deceptive manipulations (e.g. APA, 2002), it may be that these figures underestimate the actual amount of debriefing that actually does occur. Adair and Lindsay (1983) found some support for this possibility in a mail survey of the authors of empirical articles in the 1979 volume of the *Journal of Personality and Social Psychology*. Whereas 81 percent of the authors claimed to have included some form of debriefing in their studies, the practice was reported in fewer than half of their published studies. However, descriptions of the nature of the debriefing procedure in published research reports typically are uninformative and often are limited to vague phrases such as "all subjects were fully debriefed" (Adair et al., 1985; Kimmel, 2001, 2004a).

Evaluating debriefing: drawbacks and effectiveness

In chapter 4 we discuss the possibility that debriefing can create certain problems for researchers by influencing the naivete of subjects and thus posing threats to research validity. Other possible drawbacks to the use of debriefing have been identified, which may increase the reluctance of some researchers to include the procedure in their studies. Some concerns have been raised that debriefing may itself cause harm in situations where participants were selected because of some deficit, such as low self-esteem, or if their performance in a deception study revealed embarrassing behavior (Keith-Spiegel and Koocher, 1985). Such "inflicted insight," of course, might not be welcomed by research subjects (Baumrind, 1976). In such cases, it might be a wiser and more ethical course of action for researchers to provide general information about the study instead of a thorough debriefing (Sieber, 1982b). Experimenters might also convey to participants who respond in ways that are socially perceived as negative that their behavior was not atypical and that it is not uncommon for other subjects to respond in kind. (This was Milgram's approach during the debriefing of participants in his obedience studies who believed that they had delivered severe electric shocks.) It is important that researchers take care not to lie to participants when using this approach, as this would undermine the very purpose of debriefing and exacerbate the ethical problems.

There is always the possibility that subjects may not believe that researchers are telling them the truth during the debriefing process. Subjects may simply conjecture that the debriefing is another part of the experiment that involves new deceptions or rather is a therapeutic attempt to relieve any stress, embarrassment, or loss of self-esteem that they have experienced (Carroll et al., 1985; Schuler, 1982). Imagine what might be going on in the mind of a participant who has just left an experiment in which he or she received false feedback about performance on an intelligence test. This participant might think, "I know I was lied to during the experiment, but I'm not sure when: was the poor score I received on the test really a fake, as the researcher confessed at the end of the study, or did the researcher simply make up a story about the test before I left to make me feel better about having received such a horrible score?" The very fact that the subject has these concerns after participation would suggest that the debriefing was not completely effective.

As to the effectiveness of debriefing in eliminating negative consequences, the research is mixed, with some studies revealing that it often does eliminate experimental effects and others suggesting that sometimes it does not (e.g. Holmes, 1976; Ross, Lepper, and Hubbard, 1975; Walster et al., 1967). In one study, Walster et al. (1967) found that a thorough debriefing procedure was not enough to reverse the experimental impairment of self-esteem in subjects prone to low self-evaluations. Ring et al.'s (1970) modified replication of Milgram's obedience experiment demonstrated that certain modes of debriefing apparently are more effective than others. Their comparison revealed that the debriefing that provided subjects with justification for their (obedient) behavior lowered tension more than the debriefing that did not. Overall, careful debriefing of the participants substantially reduced their negative feelings about the use of deception in the study.

The effectiveness of debriefing in successfully correcting a participant's misconceptions resulting from deception is questionable, particularly in cases where the debriefing procedure involves only a cursory attempt by the researcher to inform participants that they were deceived. Effective debriefing may require both "dehoaxing" (i.e. convincing deceived participants that the information they had been given was in fact fraudulent and relieving any anxiety resulting from that information) and "desensitizing" (i e. helping deceived participants deal with new information about themselves acquired as a consequence of their behavior during the study). As previously suggested, it is possible that the realization that one has been deceived could result in a loss of self-esteem and embarrassment, in addition to creating a negative attitude towards the researcher or science (e.g. Baumrind, 1985). In this light, the debriefing process, although designed to resolve ethical problems and provide a methodological check on research methods, paradoxically can have unintended adverse effects on research participants (Toy, Wright, and Olson, 2001). In some cases, for example, it may be appropriate to withhold certain information during the debriefing (e.g. about individual differences) when it is judged that awareness could cause more harm than good to participants.

Unless it is carried out with "care, effort, and vigilance," persons already deceived once may question the validity of the information provided during the debriefing (Holmes, 1976, p. 867). This is one reason why deceptive debriefings are especially ill-advised. The so-called "perseverance process," whereby perceptions and beliefs created during a study continue long after they have been discredited, also may cast doubt on the effectiveness of debriefings to undo the effects of deceptive manipulations. It has been shown that self-relevant and non-self-relevant perceptions (e.g. created by deceptive feedback following experimental tasks) may become cognitively detached from the evidence that created them; as a result, even after the basis for the perceptions is disconfirmed (via a debriefing), individuals may tend to cling to their original beliefs (Ross et al., 1975). It is for these reasons that some researchers have recommended a process approach to debriefing, focusing on the psychological processes that underlie the effects of deception and debriefing and structuring post-experimental procedures accordingly (see Aronson and Carlsmith, 1968; Mills, 1976; and Toy et al. 2001 for specific suggestions for designing thorough process-oriented debriefings). On the whole, it appears that unlike *conventional debriefings*, which involve only a superficial explanation of the deception, *explicit debriefings* (i.e. those that describe the perseverance effect or clearly provide participants with justification for their behavior) can substantially reduce false beliefs or negative feelings linked to the use of deception (e.g. Misra, 1992).

With a consideration of the potential effectiveness of the debriefing process in mind, certain severe deceptions could be seen as preferable to others according to how readily their effects are likely to be reduced or eliminated. Consider, for example, a self-esteem manipulation that has participants write a paragraph about a time when they were proud or not proud of themselves. On the surface, this procedure would seem to be ethically preferable to the more standard one whereby participants are given false feedback about their performance on a test. The paragraph method involves less deception (i.e. although participants are not told that their self-esteem is being manipulated, they are not lied to about their performance abilities) and might appear to have lower potential for harming participants. Nonetheless, in the view of some researchers who have used both procedures, the test manipulation – even though it involves more deception – is preferable to the paragraph approach because it is easier to undo (J. G. Klein, personal communication, October 29, 2002).

For the test manipulation, it is relatively easy to convincingly debrief participants about the bogus nature of the test and the feedback they received (e.g. that the test was impossible to successfully complete, that everyone does very poorly, that the feedback was false). By contrast, there is no straightforward approach for eliminating any residual effects participants might experience from the paragraph manipulation. While researchers may have their participants write a positive paragraph at the end of the study, the effectiveness of this approach for eliminating negative thoughts and feelings induced during the experiment remains uncertain.

Some researchers have maintained that because question marks remain regarding the effectiveness of debriefing in completely removing the negative consequences of experiments, it cannot be used to justify every study. Debriefing should not be over-relied on to eliminate negative effects and it is inappropriate to condone ethically problematic manipulations simply by reference to debriefing (Diener and Crandall, 1978; Schuler, 1982). Whether or not the goals of debriefing are achieved no doubt depends on the seriousness and care taken by the researcher in conducting the procedure. Investigators would be wise to devote as much time to planning their debriefing procedure as they do in designing other aspects of their research, such as elaborate deceptive manipulations.

Removing negative consequences

Researchers are ethically obligated to remove or ameliorate whatever negative consequences arise as a result of research participation, including those that are unforeseen and unintended. At the very least, some attempt should be made to assess whether subjects are experiencing negative effects from having participated in a study and, in cases where potential harm is a major concern, subjects should be followed up at some later point in time. Post-experimental checks and long-term follow-ups are essential for ensuring that negative consequences truly have been removed. Researchers must be particularly sensitive to the possibility that participants from vulnerable populations might experience long-term effects.

Another action that can be taken to assist participants in overcoming the negative effects of deception or other research procedures is to make arrangements for referrals to individuals who are qualified to assist disturbed participants. Monetary compensation mechanisms also have been proposed (President's Commission for the Study of Ethical Problems in Medicine and Biomedical and Behavioral Research, 1982; Silverstein, 1974) and Keith-Spiegel and Koocher (1985) have suggested that "malresearch insurance" may eventually become a reality. Researchers in applied areas also bear an ethical responsibility to untreated control group subjects who have been deprived of a potentially beneficial treatment and who experience this deprivation as a loss. In studies of known positive treatments, these subjects could be offered the treatment once the research is completed, as long as they do not suffer substantially in the meantime as a result of withholding a required treatment. Many researchers no doubt will feel an obligation to aid untreated controls who have assisted them in their research upon completion of a study. (For a more complete discussion of untreated control groups, see chapter 6.)

A related consideration regarding the responsibility of researchers to take steps to assist participants is the possibility that some subjects may be found to have been in a state of preexisting distress prior to their involvement in the research. That is, during the course of an investigation, a researcher might identify potentially depressed or suicidal subjects whose distress had nothing to do with methods used during the study. It is widely acknowledged that researchers have a responsibility to intervene when serious distress is discovered in such cases (e.g. APA, 2002; Burbach et al., 1986; Stanton and New, 1988), by initiating contact with the subject and a significant other or through some other form of intervention. Despite the researcher's duty to promote the welfare of distressed subjects, post-experimental intervention might be viewed by subjects as a violation of their privacy and autonomy rights. One way of allaying this reaction would be to inform subjects before they actually participate in a study of the possibility of follow-up contact by the experimenter. This suggestion, however, may have certain methodological consequences that also must be weighed. For example, Stanton et al. (1991) found that when subjects were presented with the possibility of intrusive follow-up (i.e. experimenter contact with the participant and a significant other) on an informed consent form, they were less likely to report depressive symptoms than subjects expecting a less intrusive follow-up. In light of this finding, Stanton et al. recommend that one way to satisfy both ethical and methodological concerns would be merely to provide all research participants with a list of treatment sources once they have completed their participation in a study.

SUMMARY

When the methodological requirements of a laboratory investigation lead the researcher to conclude that the only way a study can be carried out is by employing deceptive research tactics, the decision to deceive necessarily results in additional ethical responsibilities for the researcher. Deception was once accepted without comment, but it is now accompanied by elaborate justifications and extensive debriefing procedures are required by current ethical codes. Most behavioral scientists, when caught up in situations involving conflicting values, such as whether or not to use deception, are willing to weigh and measure their sins, judging some to be larger than others. Complicating the decision-making process in the context of laboratory research are the various methodological issues related to the use of deception, which we consider next in chapter 4.

4

Methodological Issues in the Use of Deception

"Psychologists always lie!"
Anonymous student cited by M. T. Orne (1962)

Chapter Topics

☞ Assessing the effectiveness of deception
☞ Suspiciousness of research participants
☞ Effects of deceiving subjects
☞ Alternatives to deception and other coping mechanisms

This chapter represents a continuation of our discussion of the issues that emerge in the conduct of laboratory research, with a closer look at the methodological implications of deception. Several methodological issues relating to deception have emerged along with its increased prevalence in research over the years. These issues have become the subject of numerous research studies, many of which have attempted to gain an understanding of how research participants are affected by deceptive practices. Does deception make them more cynical and suspicious of researchers, as the above quotation implies? Do they develop negative feelings about behavioral science research in general? What are the effects of suspiciousness on research results? Are there some alternatives to the use of deception that are both methodologically and ethically sound? These are the questions that are considered in detail below.

EVALUATING DECEPTION FROM A METHODOLOGICAL PERSPECTIVE

The recognition that decisions about particular research questions and associated methodological issues are inextricably bound to ethical considerations is no more apparent than when one considers the inseparable relationship between artifacts and ethics. As described in preceding chapters, ethical developments in psychology were promulgated in large part by the dramatic rise in the use of deceptive methodologies. However, it was not by chance that psychologists turned to deception as a primary research tool. Deception largely emerged as a practical remedy to the experimenter – participant artifact problem – the recognition that participants come to the research setting not as passive automatons who respond mechanistically to the manipulations to which they are subjected, but as conscious, active problem solvers who attempt to guess the investigator's hypotheses in order to do the right (or good) thing. Assistance in this problem-solving activity comes from the multiple sources of demand characteristics available to participants both before (e.g. campus scuttlebutt about ongoing research studies) and during (e.g. research instructions) the actual study (Rosnow, 2002).

The use of deception procedures in behavioral research is predicated upon certain important methodological assumptions, foremost of which are that (1) the level of naivete among research subjects is high, (2) the experimental procedure does not produce cues that are interpretable by participants as indicating that deception is taking place, and (3) subjects' suspiciousness of deception does not alter the experimental effect (Golding and Lichtenstein, 1970). In addition to the ethical implications of using deception for research purposes, concern has focused on these methodological assumptions and the potential shortcomings and limitations of deception as a laboratory research tool. Deception thus has been evaluated in terms of the degree of subject naivete concerning its use, the consequences of suspicion on experimental validity, and the effects of deception on subsequent experimental performance. Some critics have argued that the scientific costs of deception are considerable – that it can lead to such consequences as the depletion of the pool of naive subjects for future research, a reduction in community support for the research enterprise, and an undermining of researchers' commitment to truth (Baumrind, 1985; Ortmann and Hertwig, 2002). We begin our consideration of these potential effects in the following section.

Assessing the effectiveness of deception

The use of deception procedures in laboratory research is largely predicated on the principle that an experimental effect is interpretable only with a naive subject population. Accordingly, most researchers believe that any effects detected that are solely attributable to subject awareness about the study's true nature and purpose should be treated as artifacts of the research setting rather than as sources of meaningful data (Allen, 2004; Rosnow and Rosenthal, 1997). In light of the various methodological problems imposed by research artifacts, current guidelines for the conduct of research necessitate that researchers walk a fine line in responding to scientific and ethical demands. Investigations into widely researched psychological and applied topics such as attitudes, aggression, classical conditioning, prejudice, intimate relationships, group dynamics, impression formation, drug and alcohol use, and social identity represent sensitive areas that typically cannot be studied in traditional ways (e.g. experimental laboratory investigations) with the full awareness of research participants.

It now is rather evident that a completely informed consent obtained during investigations into certain psychological phenomena could cause participants to behave differently in order to present a more socially acceptable (as opposed to a natural or typical) image to the researcher. It has been empirically demonstrated that informing participants of the true purpose and procedures of a study can serve to distort participant responses and severely jeopardize the tenability of inferred causal relationships. This effect has been observed in social psychological research as well as in studies of memory, incidental learning, and cognitive illusions that could not have been carried out without deception (e.g. Broder, 1998; Resnick and Schwartz, 1973). In this light, informed consent essentially operates as an independent variable – studies conducted with or without it may come up with vastly different results. Deception provides a means of distracting the attention of subjects so that their behavior can be more spontaneous and less contrived (Bonetti, 1998a, b). Thus, by opting for deception as a means to reduce demand clarity (e.g. by generating alternative and irrelevant demands), researchers can proceed with greater confidence that participants are responding to the experimental variables under study and not to uncontrolled factors linked to the social nature of the researcher – participant interaction (Rosnow, Strohmetz, and Aditya, 2000; Strohmetz and Rosnow, 2003). In short, if researchers conformed to the letter of the law regarding informed consent and did not deceive participants at all, then many investigations would be impossible to conduct or would result in biased findings.

An obvious criterion for the effectiveness of deception is the extent to which the deception duplicates the essential conditions it is intended to portray (Orne and Holland, 1968). Two important dimensions for evaluating research methods are relevant in this regard: experimental realism and mundane realism. "Experimental realism" refers to the extent to which the experimental situation is realistic to subjects and taken seriously by them. "Mundane realism" refers to the degree of similarity between the events surrounding the research participant in the experimental setting and those that occur in the natural environment. The extent of mundane realism typically varies according to the research setting. An investigation conducted in a field setting in which participants are not aware that their behavior is being investigated has a very high degree of mundane realism (Geller, 1982). At the other extreme are studies conducted in the artificial setting of the laboratory in which subjects are placed in situations that bear little resemblance to their lives outside the research context.

A deception procedure typically will have high experimental realism if it is successfully implemented and the psychological impact of the experimental manipulation on the research subjects is high (Geller, 1982; Rosenthal and Rosnow, 1991). Some critics of Milgram's studies on obedience have argued that the experiments lacked experimental realism because several subjects may have been aware of the deception (e.g. Patten, 1977). Evidence supporting this claim was provided by Orne and Holland (1968) in their description of an unpublished replication of Milgram's research. In post-experimental interviews, participants in the replication claimed that they did not really believe the deception. Further, prior to their participating in the study, two additional groups of subjects were led to believe that things were not what they seemed in the research. In order to raise suspicions, one group was informed that there would be something "fishy" about the experiment but not to "let on" and the other group was prebriefed that the administered level of shock was really only one-tenth the intensity indicated on the shock machine.

Despite these manipulations, the level of obedience for the two groups was not significantly different from Milgram's original study and a "blind" experimenter was unable to ascertain the experimental condition to which subjects belonged. Thus, although Milgram's subjects reported in post-experimental interviews and questionnaires that they believed that victims were receiving painful shocks, they may have been aware of the deception but still behaved as if they were naive. This sort of behavior is consistent with the good subject role described earlier. This role requires that participants pretend to be naive even when they are aware that the researcher is playing tricks on them (Orne and Holland, 1968).

One difficulty in assessing the degree to which an investigation possesses experimental realism has to do with a "pact of ignorance" that sometimes develops between the experimenter and the subject (Orne, 1959). That is, subjects may prefer to conceal the fact that they saw through a deception because it might compromise the value of their participation; in turn, the experimenter may not forcefully attempt to discover evidence that would invalidate subjects' data and delay completion of the investigation. According to Patten (1977), a philosopher with serious reservations about the effectiveness of Milgram's deception, Milgram's disobedient subjects may have been reluctant to say they saw through the hoax because it would have meant giving up the hero status gained by standing up to the malevolent authority and refusing to continue with the experiment.

It is unclear to what extent these methodological points accurately apply to the behavior exhibited by Milgram's subjects. In responding to his critics, Milgram claimed that the obvious signs of tension and stress among a majority of his subjects during the procedure clearly suggest that his method was quite real for the participants. But can researchers better detect whether an experimental manipulation has actually deceived the participants in a study? One proposal is to use quasi-controls, subjects who are asked to step out of their traditional roles and to serve as "co-investigators" in the research process (Orne, 1969).

In essence, *quasi-control subjects* are asked to reflect "clinically" on what is happening during a study and to describe how they think they might be affected by the research context and the experimental events. The intent is to carefully elicit from these subjects their perceptions and beliefs about the research situation, without raising suspicions or prompting their responses. This technique can involve having experimental subjects function as their own quasi-controls. In this case the experimenter would engage the subjects in an exhaustive inquiry following their participation in the experiment or a pilot study. In order to offset the possibility that the interview data are biased by demand characteristics, such subjects would have to be convinced that the formal study is over and that they are now being solicited to serve as aides in the search for knowledge (Rosnow,

2002). The *preinquiry* approach employs quasi-control subjects who are asked to imagine that they are real subjects in the experiment. During the preinquiry, subjects are provided with all of the significant details of the experiment and are asked to predict how they might behave in such a study. A high degree of similarity between their responses and those obtained from real subjects implies that the experimental results could have been caused by subjects' guesses about how they should have responded (Strohmetz and Rosnow, 1995).

There is not much evidence that researchers have made use of quasi-control techniques to assess the adequacy of their deceptive procedures; however, much useful feedback can be obtained from subjects during a judiciously carried out debriefing session. Some of the characteristics of an effective debriefing were described in chapter 3. Without making some attempt to ascertain subjects' reactions to their participation in a study, it is appropriate to ask the question that has been posed by some critics of deception: who is actually being deceived – the subject or the researcher?

Subject suspiciousness

"Psychologists always lie!" This remark, purportedly made to Martin Orne by one of his student subjects, may have been repeated over the years by countless other individuals who have experienced research deceptions firsthand or else learned about such techniques in university courses or from other sources, including friends and the mass media. Orne (1962) lamented that such a comment reflects the concern that subjects' growing sophistication about deceptive practices may cause them to behave unnaturally in behavioral science investigations. As early as the 1960s researchers (e.g. Jourard, 1968; McGuire, 1969; Orne and Holland, 1968) suggested that subjects participating in psychology experiments have considerable awareness of the implicit rules that govern the situation, and have learned to distrust the experimenter because they know that the true purpose of the experiment may be disguised. If the prevalence of deception over the years has decreased naivete among prospective subjects, this would diminish the methodological value of using deception in the first place (Kelman, 1967). It also implies that even honest investigators might not be trusted by subjects who view apparent "openness" with suspicion (Orne, 1962). An anecdote related by MacCoun and Kerr (1987) is enlightening in this regard. During a study in which subjects were asked to serve as members of a mock jury, one of the participants suffered a seizure. Fortunately for this individual, another subject who was trained in emergency procedures offered quick assistance to the victim. What was unsettling, however, was the number of subjects who reported that they initially doubted that the emergency was real. Reflecting a growing suspiciousness among research participants, these subjects misinterpreted the seizure as a staged incident contrived by the experimenter and victim.

There has not been a great deal of research on the extent of subjects' suspiciousness in the research setting and the existing studies present something of a mixed bag. In an early review of deception experiments, Stricker (1967) found that appraisals of the effectiveness of deception were uncommon, and that those that were made tended to be superficial. Only 23.9 percent of the 88 studies utilizing deceptive procedures in 1964 included any attempt to gain some information about suspicion and awareness of deception in the subject samples. The amount of suspicion among subjects in the 21 studies that assessed it was small, ranging from 0 to 23 percent, with an average percentage of only 3.7. However, other investigators have reported high rates of suspiciousness among subjects in conformity studies (as indicated by subjects' comments during post-experimental inquiries), with several estimates reaching as high as 50 to nearly 90 percent (Gallo et al., 1973; Glinski et al., 1970; Stricker et al., 1967; Willis and Willis 1970). Additionally, in an unpublished study of the social conformity literature covering the period 1954–73, Stang found a positive correlation of 0.76 between the amount of reported suspicion in published research and the year, indicating a steady rise in suspicion over the two-decade period (cf. Stang, 1976).

These findings suggest that as the common deception paradigms used to investigate certain topical areas become progressively known among subject populations, research may have to be varied or reinterpreted as dealing with something other than naive behavior. Kenneth Gergen (1973b) theorized that the dissemination of psychological knowledge can alter previous patterns of behavior, which then become difficult to test in an uncontaminated way. Just as powerful drugs to combat virulent diseases can lead to hardier strains of the diseases, which then become immune to the drugs, people may become "immune" to deception as higher rates of suspicion are found among new subject populations (Rosnow, 1978). Thus, researchers might be inclined to increase the number and degree of deceptions in their studies as subject sophistication increases. On the other hand, subject suspiciousness may motivate investigators to orient their attention to new subject populations and to research settings outside the laboratory.

Despite these legitimate concerns, more recent assessments of the extent of subject suspiciousness have revealed that research participants may not be nearly as suspicious as was once feared. For example, in Adair et al.'s (1985) analysis of empirical psychology studies published in 1979, the mean estimate of subjects identified as suspicious ranged from less than 1 percent for studies employing only one type of deception to 6.25 percent for studies employing five types of deception. For all of the deception studies coded, the overall percentage of subjects identified as suspicious was only 1.85 percent. Comparable levels of subject suspiciousness were obtained in my investigation of the research literature (see chapter 3), with an average estimate of suspicious subjects equaling 1.1 percent for marketing research and 2.5 percent for psychological research (Kimmel, 2001). Across 66 investigations reporting suspiciousness checks, only 230 out of 10,028 participants (2.3 percent) were identified as harboring skepticism about the true experimental purpose or manipulations. Because participants cannot always be counted on to be totally forthcoming in revealing their suspicions or knowledge about research procedures and hypotheses, these estimates may well underestimate the overall suspiciousness levels in the subject population. Over the years, there has been little research on the extent of suspiciousness or leakage in the research setting and investigators do not routinely probe levels of participant suspiciousness.

Similarly, the quality of suspiciousness checks by researchers may be called into question, particularly if such efforts represent only half-hearted attempts to demonstrate the soundness of experimental manipulations. In some early investigations, researchers found that when they assessed suspiciousness by asking their participants up to three post-experimental questions, only about 5 percent of the participants were classified as suspicious; this percentage increased to about 40 percent when more extended questioning was utilized (Page, 1973; Spielberger, 1962). More research is needed on the levels and sources of participant suspiciousness and extent of leakage, and investigators need to more carefully evaluate the procedures they use to assess perceptions of their studies and levels of participant suspiciousness (Horvath, 1986; Taylor and Shepperd, 1996).

Sources of suspiciousness

Several potential sources of subject suspiciousness have been identified. Some subjects come to the laboratory setting unaware that deception may take place or else have only a vague knowledge that it is a possibility. In such cases, so-called *demand characteristics* of the experimental situation can cause them to become suspicious. Demand characteristics comprise the mixture of various hints and cues that govern a subject's perceptions of his or her role, the experimenter's hypothesis, and other aspects of the study (Orne and Whitehouse, 2000). For example, certain comments in the instructions to subjects or cues in the laboratory setting itself might suggest that something is going on that is inconsistent with the version given by the experimenter. Subjects who are informed that they are participating in an investigation of verbal learning naturally may become suspicious after happening to notice on the top of a paper held by the researcher a heading that reads "Conformity Experiment."

Subjects may come to the research situation already harboring certain suspicions as a result of demand characteristics encountered in other settings. Cues in the original appeals used to recruit participants, information about behavioral science studies conveyed in college courses, and rumors about ongoing studies represent common sources of demand characteristics outside the laboratory context (see Box 4.1). I can recall how, when I was a student in an introductory psychology course at the University of Maryland, I had to select from among a large number of experiments being carried out on campus in order to fulfill a course requirement for research participation. There was much gossiping about the various studies among my fellow classmates, as they attempted to find out which would be the most interesting (and least time consuming) research experiences. This sort of information transmission within student subject pools apparently is commonplace (Rosnow, 1991). One established principle from research on rumors maintains that uncertainty and anxiety provide optimal conditions for the transmission and reception of rumors (Kimmel, 2004b). These two psychological factors are likely to be high among potential research participants, thus motivating them to gather as much information as possible prior to their

Box 4.1 Demand characteristics and subject performance

An early study by Orne (1959) effectively demonstrated how subjects' behavior in an experiment can be affected by earlier knowledge obtained outside the laboratory. Orne's study involved the presentation of false information to college students about a presumably novel characteristic of hypnosis. He first informed a large college class during a lecture on hypnosis that upon entering a "trance," a hypnotized person will manifest "catalepsy of the dominant hand" – that is, the right hand of a right-handed individual will take on a waxen flexibility or rigidity; for left-handed persons, this effect will be experienced in the left hand. This characteristic, which was fully concocted by Orne, was demonstrated to the class using volunteer students. As a control condition, Orne gave the same lecture and demonstration to another class section, but this time did not include any mention or display of catalepsy of the dominant hand.

Some weeks later, students from both lecture sections were invited to participate as subjects in a study of hypnosis. When they were hypnotized during the study, Orne found that catalepsy was present for nearly all of the students who had learned about it in the previous lecture. By contrast, none of the control subjects exhibited the fictitious characteristic. Apparently, subjects acted on the demand characteristics received prior to their participation in such a way as to confirm what they believed to be the experimenter's hypothesis or to provide the "correct" response to hypnosis.

participation in a study. Such information often might be in the form of suspicion-arousing rumors.

There is evidence that research participants who have been debriefed sometimes communicate the true purpose and other details of the studies in which they have participated to future subjects, even when instructed not to do so. This tendency is referred to as *leakage* (Diener et al., 1972; Farrow et al., 1975; Lipton and Garza, 1978). Some investigators have found that large proportions of subjects leak crucial information into the subject pool, to an extent that could substantially affect the experimental outcome (Glinski et al., 1970; Lichtenstein, 1970; Wuebben, 1967). Apparently, however, information is much less likely to be divulged when research participants are cautioned not to talk about an experiment to others or are asked to make an oral or written agreement with the researcher (e.g. Aronson, 1966; Walsh and Stillman, 1974). Aronson (1966) provided nine subjects with an unusually thorough debriefing following their participation in a deception study, including a vivid description of the consequences of testing sophisticated subjects. None of the subjects revealed the true nature of the experiment when approached by a confederate who attempted to obtain information about the study, suggesting that the nature of the debriefing can offset the possibility of leakage. In their surveys of the *Journal of Personality and Social Psychology*, however, Adair et al. (1985) found that the practice of establishing secrecy agreements with debriefed subjects was infrequent, having been reported in only 13 percent of the deception studies.

One additional potential source of subject suspiciousness that bears mentioning is prior experience in deceptive research. That is, when subjects who participate in multiple investigations are deceived in an early study, they may become less trusting in subsequent studies. Prior experience may operate in such a way as to influence subjects' anticipation of what is going to happen in another study and perhaps affects their performance as well (see below). Research on the effects of prior research experience has been somewhat contradictory, although there is some evidence that suspicions aroused in one study may not generalize to another unless the two have something in common (Brock and Becker, 1966; Cook et al., 1970; Fillenbaum, 1966; Stricker et al., 1967).

Effects of subjects' suspicions

The issue of whether or not deception leads to greater levels of suspiciousness bears little import if, in fact, skepticism regarding research procedures or purpose does not have an impact on experimental performance and it turns out that naive and suspicious individuals behave similarly under the same experimental conditions. Apart from the moral considerations engendered by artifact coping strategies, the potential for suspiciousness to influence research performance probably has aroused the greatest concern among researchers. Mistrust of the experimental procedure could alter participants' reactions enough to cause misleading results or invalidation of an investigation altogether. Research on the effects of distrust on experimental performance has focused on various manifestations of the issue, including the general effects of self-reported suspiciousness (e.g. Stang, 1976; Stricker, 1967), the effects of experimentally induced suspicions through the use of some variation of forewarning (or prebriefing) (e.g. Allen, 1983; Finney, 1987), and the influence of prior experience in deception experiments on subsequent research performance (e.g. Cook and Perrin, 1971; Fillenbaum, 1966).

The effects of suspicion on behavior in an experiment are apt to be varied, depending on the subject's perceptions of the situation and motivations for acting on the suspicions (Allen, 2004). For example, subjects who are aware that they are being deceived by a researcher may resent that fact and thus try to respond in a manner that is counter-compliant with what they believe are the experimenter's expectations. Research participants who approach an investigation with an uncooperative attitude have been referred to as "negativistic subjects" (Masling, 1966). By contrast, subjects who are motivated to cooperate with the researcher might actively seek out additional demand characteristics in order to more successfully play the good subject role (cf. Strohmetz and Rosnow, 1995). Other motivations may be operative in suspicious subjects' minds as they approach the research situation. Awareness that the research procedure is not all that it appears to be may increase subjects' fears about being poorly evaluated; in turn, this can lead to a desire to be more alert and observant in the research situation than under conditions of greater trust.

Research results on the effects of subject distrust are somewhat mixed, with some studies showing that the results produced by suspicious or preinformed participants (who are made aware that deception is to be utilized in the investigation) can differ substantially from those of naive participants (Allen, 1966; Golding and Lichtenstein, 1970; Levy, 1967; Newberry, 1973). In one early conformity study, subjects who were aware of the deception conformed less than those who were deceived, but more than participants in a no deception control group (Allen, 1966). Newberry (1973) carried out two experiments in which individuals who had received prior information from a confederate consistently used it, whether intentionally or not, to improve their performance on various problem-solving tasks. Similarly, Stang (1976) reviewed nine conformity studies that systematically compared suspicious and naive participants (identified via post-experimental interviews) and concluded that suspicious individuals tended to show less conformity than did those classified as non-suspicious.

In addition to the possibility that prior experience in deception studies can serve to increase subject suspicions, there also is some evidence that it can affect performance in subsequent experiments. For example, Silverman et al. (1970) reported that subjects who had been previously deceived in a preliminary experiment differed significantly from naive controls on all measures in a later experiment. The direction of the obtained differences seemed to indicate that prior deception increases the tendency for favorable self-presentation and decreases compliance with demand characteristics. In other words, evaluation apprehension (i.e. "looking good") is more likely to emerge as the predominant motivation of previously deceived subjects, as opposed to the desire to cooperate with the researcher in the cause of science (i.e. "doing good"). Silverman et al.'s results are consistent with other studies that have investigated these two subject artifacts (e.g. Rosnow et al., 1973; Sigall et al., 1970).

Although it appears that previous research experience can play a role in later studies, some researchers have been unable to obtain performance effects from subjects with foreknowledge about an investigation (e.g. Allen, 1983; Brock and Becker, 1966; Fillenbaum, 1966; Wiener and Erker, 1986). Such disparities in the findings likely are linked to a variety of methodological considerations, including the specific procedure utilized for making the relevant comparisons between suspicious and non-suspicious participants, the degree of specificity of the suspicions, the types of persons studied, and the nature and degree of deceptions involved in the research. For example, some studies on the effects of suspiciousness have relied on two immediately consecutive experiments to manipulate degree of experimental naivete. That is, subjects are either debriefed or not debriefed in a first experiment and their performance is then measured in a second experiment. The problem with this sort of procedure is that it does not ensure a great difference in naivete between the comparison groups (Cook et al., 1970).

The degree of intensity of deceptions in a study is an important consideration with respect to the methodological implications of participant suspiciousness.

In chapter 3, the distinction was made between "mild deceptions" (i.e. those involving unimportant issues that are peripheral to participants' self-concept or personal behavior) and "severe deceptions" (i.e. those dealing with central issues that *are* related to participants' self-concept or personal behavior). If a prior deception is seen as mild and legitimate, subjects likely will accept it and proceed faithfully, adhering to the instructions in later studies despite their suspicions. An example of a study involving mild deception would be one in which participants are not informed that they will be asked later to rate their degree of liking for different nonsense syllables on a list they have been asked to memorize. It is unlikely that such a deception would arouse much suspicion for a participant and, even if it did, it is difficult to imagine that it would appear meaningful enough to significantly influence performance on the experimental task. In fact, much research in psychology tends to involve these sorts of mundane procedures, which arouse little interest for the typical undergraduate research participant. In such studies the primary motive may simply be to get it over with in order to receive the promised incentive, without any concern for altering one's natural performance on the research task.

Given the distinction between mild and severe deceptions, we might anticipate different kinds of performance effects depending on which type of deception is used. As described in chapter 3, assuming they have any impact at all on participants, mild deceptions are unlikely to affect performance in the investigation during which they are employed, but could influence performance in subsequent experiments. For severe deceptions, performance could be affected in the ongoing study as well as subsequent ones (Toy et al., 1989).

Another important consideration related to performance effects concerns the empirical issue of whether more (or less) statistical conclusion bias will be created by the decision either to use or not use deception (cf. Shadish, Cook, and Campbell, 2001). That is, even when a researcher chooses not to deceive, this decision will not offset the tendency for participants to conjecture about the true purpose of the study, with each person theoretically generating their own hypotheses. These multiple hypotheses could be seen as operating as a form of error variance to the extent that they influence dependent measure values. In this regard, it might be argued that by opting for deception, a reduction in error variance would result as a function of the deception having led to greater homogeneity among participants.

In addition to these considerations, there is the possibility that suspicion can operate differentially across the conditions of a study (Diener and Crandall, 1978). Because different treatments are likely to cause varying levels of suspicion, apparent treatment effects in some studies may have been caused by the differential suspicion rates. This point raises certain problems for the researcher in terms of the most appropriate means for dealing with data obtained from suspicious subjects (assuming such subjects are identified during a post-experimental interview). The researcher may choose to discard subjects who did not see the experiment as it was intended or simply decide to analyze the data obtained from suspicious and unaware subjects separately (Adair et al., 1985). If the rate of suspicion is not distributed randomly across treatment conditions, omitting the data obtained from suspicious subjects can serve to increase the apparent treatment effects. On the other hand, the decision to eliminate suspicious subjects from the study could lead to the loss of truly random assignment of subjects to conditions. This would make it difficult for the researcher to rule out the possibility that treatment effects were caused by selection biases or, for that matter, undetected suspicion that exists differentially across conditions (Diener and Crandall, 1978). Although there are no easy solutions to these problems, at the very least researchers should attempt to assess the effectiveness of each deception used in an investigation and the extent to which subjects idiosyncratically perceived the experiment and its rationale (Adair et al., 1985).

Before we leave the topic of subject suspicions, an intriguing theoretical issue should be mentioned. This has to do with the possibility that disclosure of information to subjects may turn out to be more stressful than non-disclosure in certain instances (Rosenthal and Rosnow, 1991). Resnick and Schwartz (1973) similarly alluded to a possible drawback of informed consent when they posed the question: "Does being ethical trigger paranoid ideation in otherwise nonsuspicious subjects?" It is possible in some cases that informing subjects will cause more stress and raise more suspicions than leaving subjects in the dark about the nature of the study and its purpose.

Effects of deception

In the preceding section we briefly considered the effects of prior deception on research participants' suspicions and performance in further studies. But what about more general effects? Are subjects harmed by research deceptions? Do deceived subjects become resentful about having been fooled by a researcher? Does deception have an impact on subjects' perceptions about psychology or attitudes about science in general?

Much of the anecdotal and empirical evidence on these and related questions has been encouraging – the negative effects of deception appear to be minimal. For example, Milgram (1964) defended his obedience experiments in part by citing thank you letters he received from some of his subjects and data from a follow-up questionnaire revealing that 84 percent of the subjects were glad they had participated; fewer than 1 percent indicated that they regretted having participated; and 15 percent were neutral or ambivalent. Moreover, thorough interviews were conducted one year after the study and there was no evidence of apparent permanent damage. Short-term effects experienced by some of the subjects were readily dispelled and any remaining discomfort was eliminated through the mailing of an explanatory letter and some preliminary findings to subjects (Errera, 1972).

The results of a replication of Milgram's experiment by Ring et al. (1970) produced a similar picture regarding the lack of negative after-effects resulting from deception. In a follow-up interview, most subjects described the experiment as having been a positive experience for them and claimed that they did not resent the deception. Only 4 percent of the subjects mentioned that they had regretted participating in the experiment. However, some did state that they were experiencing difficulty in trusting adult authorities, and others reported persistent disappointment with themselves or expressed self-doubts.

Subjects' reactions following participation in a bystander intervention experiment also have been assessed (Clark and Word, 1974). A majority of the participants in the experiment viewed the research as valuable (95 percent) and considered the deception unavoidable (94 percent). When surveyed several months later, 92 percent of the subjects claimed that they did not believe that their rights had been violated or that they would rather not have participated in the study.

Based on a review of studies that assessed subjects' reactions to deception experiments (e.g. Finney, 1987; Pihl et al. 1981; Smith, 1981; Smith and Richardson, 1983), Christensen (1988) concluded that subjects who have participated in deception experiments versus non-deception experiments in psychology tend to report that they did not mind being deceived, enjoyed the experience more, received more educational benefit from it, and did not perceive that their privacy had been invaded. More recently, Aguinis and Henle (2001) studied subjects' reactions to the research use of a deceptive technique known as the "bogus pipeline," a fake laboratory apparatus that is presented as capable of detecting when participants are not giving honest responses during an experiment. Although the bogus pipeline has often been criticized on ethical grounds (e.g. Aguinis and Handelsman, 1997; Ostrom, 1973), subjects perceived the technique as a useful and ethical research method, even when other non-deceptive methods are available. Despite their agreement that the technique could have some unpleasant emotional consequences for some participants, subjects perceived the benefits as outweighing the inconveniences and suggested that people would not develop a mistrust of the researcher as a result of participating in bogus pipeline studies. These results may argue for a "situation ethics" approach to solving ethical dilemmas, whereby participants are asked whether they are concerned that certain ethically questionable practices exist after being told the reasons for utilizing them.

The data obtained from the deception after-effects studies have not been readily accepted by some critics of deception. For example, Baumrind (1964) argued that the positive reactions from those who have participated in deception studies may reflect attempts to resolve cognitive dissonance resulting from the deception experience. That is, participation in a deceptive experiment like Milgram's, for example, could have generated negative self-perceptions in subjects as well as unpleasant feelings associated with having been used and tricked by the researcher. In order to cope with these negative outcomes, subjects may have reinterpreted the experiment as being valuable, an interesting learning experience, and so on. Baumrind (1985) also discounted the after-effects evidence as being a product of experimental demands and inadequately conducted post-experimental inquiries, which more properly should be carried out by well-trained clinical interviewers. In her view, self-report questionnaires typically are added to a study as an afterthought and the instruments themselves tend to be poorly constructed.

Despite these criticisms, the results of surveys intended to gauge reactions to deception consistently have shown that most individuals in the general population apparently do not have serious objections to its use for research purposes (Collins et al., 1979; Epstein et al., 1973; Rugg, 1975; Sullivan and Deiker, 1973). Rugg (1975) found this to be the case for several groups of individuals, including college professors and lawyers. Epstein et al. (1973) reported that college students – the very persons who comprise the typical research population and who are likely to experience harm from its use – were generally accepting of deception. A majority of those questioned expected to be deceived as participants in psychological studies. Although they viewed this as personally undesirable, they also believed that deception in research is permissible and appropriate. Similarly, Sullivan and Deiker (1973) found that psychologists tend to have more serious reservations about the use of deception than do college students. When presented with hypothetical experiments that differed in the amount of stress, physical pain, or threat to self-esteem inflicted on subjects, it was the psychologists who turned out to be far more negative towards the practices and the propriety of using deception in each instance than were the students. Perhaps this greater leniency on the part of research participants is simply a reflection of the nature of the times in which we live, where news reports abound about indiscretions, lies, and a wide range of unethical behaviors at the highest levels of government and the boardroom. As a result, people may simply conclude that researchers are no different from other professionals in using deceptive methods to achieve their ends, and that, relatively speaking, the consequences are far less severe.

Another question regarding the use of deception has to do with the belief that such practices reflect poorly on the discipline and cast suspicion on the motives of behavioral scientists. For some time, critics of deception have warned that its frequent and continued use would have an adverse effect on subjects' trust of psychologists and would lead them to adopt a negative attitude towards behavioral research in general (Kelman, 1967; MacCoun and Kerr, 1987). The results of a study by Sharpe et al. (1992) provide little support for these fears. Questionnaire responses obtained from students at the beginning of the 1970 academic year were compared with those of students surveyed at a comparable time in 1989. Data were acquired from both subject samples through the use of the Psychological Research Survey (PRS), a scale that measures attitudes towards psychological research. Scores on the PRS for the two subject samples were found to be similar, suggesting that there had not been a predicted increase in negative attitudes towards psychological research in the subject population as a result of the continued use of deception.

Sharpe et al. also administered the PRS to a third sample of students in 1990, shortly after they had participated in a number of experiments during the academic year. Although these subjects were accepting of arguments justifying the use of deception, their attitude towards psychological research was somewhat more negative than that of subjects in the other samples. According to the researchers, the finding that participants in experiments did not possess a more positive attitude towards research suggests that participation does not facilitate appreciation for the discipline, and thus contradicts a common justification for requiring student research participation (Lindsay and Holden, 1987) (see chapter 8). Previous reports of subjects' positive evaluations of deception experiments may have been due to a contrast effect, with the unfolding deception scenario representing a more engaging experience for subjects – a welcome relief from the more typically mundane and less interesting studies conducted in many university settings. In a more recent investigation of attitudes towards psychological research, Snowden et al. (2003) found that psychology students tended to have more favorable attitudes towards psychological research after having completed a course in research methods where, it is presumed, they learned about the use of and justifications for deceptive research techniques.

Summary: deception in perspective

A review of the literature on the effects of deception, such as whether it results in the contamination of subject pools, the influence of participant suspicions on experimental effects, and the like, leaves more questions unanswered than answered (see Table 4.1). However, despite the sometimes contradictory findings, it is clear that for many research situations, deception does not have the negative methodological effects its critics have long contended. The position that all

Table 4.1 Studies of methodological and disciplinary consequences of deception

Issues linked to deception	Degree of effects[a]	Research evidence
A. *Methodological*		
1 Participant suspiciousness (use of deception leads to an increase in suspiciousness among research subject pools)	Medium to high (>25%) levels of *S* suspicions	Gallo et al. (1973) Glinski et al. (1970) Stricker et al. (1967) Willis & Willis (1970)
	Low (0–25%) levels	Adair et al. (1985) Kimmel (2001, 2004a) Stricker (1967)
2 Leakage (participants divulge crucial information into the subject pool)	Extensive	Diener et al. (1972) Glinski et al. (1970) Lichtenstein (1970) Lipton & Garza (1978)
	Low	Aronson (1966) Walsh & Stillman (1974)
3 Effects of subject suspicions (suspicions linked to the use of deception influence current or future research performance)	Significant effects (between naive and aware participants)	Allen (1966) Cook & Perrin (1971) Golding & Lichtenstein (1970) Levy (1967) Newberry (1973) Silverman et al. (1970)
	No effects	Brock & Becker (1966) Cook & Perrin (1971) Fillenbaum (1966)

Table 4.1   (cont.)

Issues linked to deception	Degree of effects[a]	Research evidence
4 Forewarning (participants' preknowledge of deception alters experimental performance)	Little effect on performance	Allen (1983) Gallo et al. (1973) Wiener & Erker (1986)
	Significant effects (between forewarned Ss and uninformed controls)	Finney (1987) Golding & Lichtenstein (1970) Levy (1967) Turner & Simons (1974)
5 Effectiveness of debriefing on the mitigation of negative deception effects (false beliefs, negative affect, inflicted insight)	Effective (conventional debrief)	Holmes (1973) Holmes & Bennett (1974)
	Ineffective (conventional debrief)	Aronson (1966) Ross et al. (1975) Valins (1974) Walster et al. (1967) Wegner et al. (1985)
	Effective (explicit debrief)	Misra (1992) Ring et al. (1970) Toy et al. (1989)
B. *Disciplinary*		
1 Effects of deception on perceptions of the discipline (deception reflects poorly on the discipline and the image of researchers)	Mixed effects	Sharpe et al. (1992)
	Positive effects	Clark & Word (1974) Gerdes (1979)
2 Participant reactions to deception (participants have adverse reactions to having been deceived, e.g., believe their rights have been violated)	Positive reactions only	Christensen (1988) Clark & Word (1974) Finney (1987) Pihl et al. (1981) Smith (1981) Smith & Richardson (1983)
	Negative reactions	Allen (1983) Cook et al. (1970)
3 General population reactions to deception (objections to the use of deception for research purposes among the general public)	No objections	Collins et al. (1979) Epstein et al. (1973) Farr & Seaver (1975) Rugg (1975) Sullivan & Deiker (1973)
	Objections	Singer (1984)

[a] This column represents the extent to which the anticipated adverse consequences of deception noted in the first column were apparent. For the issues linked to debriefing, this column reflects the extent of debriefing in reducing adverse deception effects or leading to favorable evaluations of the debriefing procedure.

Source: Adapted from Kimmel (2006).

deception is bad and to be avoided is more a moral issue than a methodological one. Certain mundane deceptions that do not have any potential for causing harm or arousing suspicions are acceptable under current ethical codes and represent acceptable recourses for counteracting threats stemming from experimenter – participant artifacts.

The factors that have emerged as particularly relevant to questions related to the impact of deception concern the nature and intensity of the deceptions employed and the quality of the debriefing following a deceptive investigation. Whereas some researchers have chosen to define deception solely in terms of sins of commission, the impact of passive deception is as important to consider as that of active deception. Findings suggest that active and passive deceptions may differentially influence research results and participant reactions to having been deceived, adding credence to Hey's (1998, p. 397) comment that "there is a world of difference between not telling subjects things and telling them the wrong things." As more psychologists move to non-laboratory settings where participants often are unaware of their involvement in a scientific study, issues related to passive deception no doubt will grow in importance in both a methodological and an ethical sense (Sieber, Iannuzzo, and Rodriguez, 1995). From an ethical point of view, sins of omission are generally easier to justify than are instances of intentional lying (e.g. Baumrind, 1985; McDaniel and Starmer, 1998).

Debriefing is a required element for all research employing deception that has the potential to adversely affect participants, yet there still is much to be learned about how to best carry out a post-experimental interview, and how debriefing functions to reduce undesirable methodological and ethical outcomes. Because not all debriefings are alike, the nature of the debriefing protocol can be expected to serve as an important mediating factor in explaining some of the varying effects of deception on participant suspiciousness, attitude towards the investigation and science in general, and performance effects in subsequent research studies.

If, as some research has shown, participants not only evaluate deception research more favorably than do researchers, but also find (non-harmful) deception studies to be more interesting and intellectually stimulating than non-deception studies, this would suggest that deception has the potential to increase the value of the research experience from an ethical perspective (assuming that the deception does not also exacerbate the methodological problems associated with having participants try to figure out the deceptions).

ALTERNATIVES TO DECEPTION

Various alternatives to the use of deception techniques have been proposed, foremost of which are simulations and role playing (see Table 4.2). Other recommended techniques, such as quasi-control groups and forewarning, are not "alternatives" in the strict sense of the word; instead, they are used in conjunction with deception in order to minimize its potential for harmful effects. Each of these approaches is described below.

Table 4.2 Research alternatives to deception and other coping procedures

Research alternative	Methodology
1 Quasi-controls (e.g. Rosenthal & Rosnow, 1991)	Participants are asked to reflect on what is happening during a study and to describe how they think they might be affected by the procedure. If no demand characteristics are detected, the researcher would develop a less deceptive manipulation and have the quasi-controls once again reflect on the study. If they remain unaware of the demands of the study, the researcher could then use this lower level of deception to carry out the intended investigation. (*Key strength:* Deception can be minimized without risking a corresponding increase in demand cues. *Key drawbacks:* Quasi-controls are time consuming and often costly to carry out.)
2 Forewarning (e.g. Allen, 1983)	Prospective research participants are informed before a study begins that deception may be used and are then given the opportunity to agree to place themselves in a situation in which they might be misled or else decline further participation. (*Key strength:* Forewarning reduces the ethical problems associated with deception by having subjects agree to the possibility that they may be misled. *Key drawback:* Forewarning may arouse subjects' search for demand characteristics and efforts to discover procedures involving mistruths.)
3 Simulations (e.g. Geller, 1982)	Conditions are created that mimic the natural environment and participants are asked to pretend or act as if the mock situation were real. Variations include field simulations (simulations in highly realistic staged settings), role-playing simulations (see the next item in this table), and game simulations (participants take on roles in staged situations lasting until a desired outcome has been attained or a specified length of time has passed). (*Key strength:* This approach preserves the key elements thought to underlie the dynamics of the real-world phenomenon under study. *Key drawbacks:* Simulations are sometimes characterized by intrinsic deceptions; mundane realism is sometimes suspect.)
4 Role playing (e.g. Greenberg, 1967)	Research participants are enlisted as active collaborators in the investigation. Each participant is told what the study is about and is then asked to play a role as if actually participating in the actual study. (*Key strengths:* In contrast to deception studies, participants are fully informed; the strategy allows for a wide latitude of response, is capable of exploring complex behavior, and is a more humanistic alternative to deception research. *Key drawback:* Role-playing results may not replicate the results that would have been obtained in traditional research, especially counterintuitive ones.)

Source: Adapted from Kimmel (2006).

Quasi-controls

Previously, we considered the usefulness of quasi-controls as a technique for detecting demand characteristics, thereby providing the researcher with some indication of the effectiveness of a deception manipulation. In addition to their potential methodological utility in assessing the effectiveness of deception procedures, quasi-control subjects can also be used in some studies to minimize the level of deception. For example, researchers can provide a scenario of a study's procedure to respondents representative of those who would participate. After reading the scenario, respondents rate how they would feel about participating in such a study and are then probed with questions such as, "If something were to upset you about this study, what would it be?" In this way, researchers could identify possible harmful aspects of a planned investigation and modify procedures accordingly (or drop the study).

Although quasi-control techniques are time consuming and often costly to carry out, they can be useful to the researcher who is concerned about balancing ethics and artifacts; that is, deception can be minimized without risking a corresponding increase in demand cues. For example, before using a deception, a researcher might first employ a quasi-control group to check for demand characteristics. If none were uncovered, rather than immediately proceeding with the actual experiment, the researcher would develop a less deceptive manipulation and have the quasi-control subjects once again reflect on the study. If they remained unaware of the demands of the study the experimenter could then use this lower level of deception to carry out the intended investigation (Fisher and Fyrberg, 1994; Suls and Rosnow, 1981).

Forewarning

In laboratory studies where deception is deemed necessary, the informed consent process can include a forewarning to prospective participants that some information will be withheld or that certain manipulations will be carried out that cannot be divulged until later. In essence, forewarning is a procedure whereby subjects are informed before they participate that deception may be involved in the investigation. So informed, the researcher then can ask the subjects if they are willing to participate in research that involves deception and include in the sample only those who answer affirmatively (Geller, 1982).

As a form of limited informed consent, forewarning is viewed as ethically preferable to not obtaining consent at all because subjects essentially agree to be deceived and the researcher will not have directly misled them. There is some concern, however, that forewarning will sensitize participants to demand characteristics (Geller, 1982). Subjects may be more inclined to engage in problem-solving behavior in order to determine the nature of the deception than if they had not been forewarned. Despite this possibility, evidence seems to suggest that forewarning subjects does not appear to influence the accuracy of data (Holmes and Bennett, 1974; Horowitz and Rothschild, 1970).

Simulations

A simulation is an experimental strategy that is sometimes used as an alternative to deception in laboratory settings. This technique involves the creation of conditions that mimic the natural environment in some definite way, and participants are asked to pretend or act as if the mock situation were real. Simulations require the scaling down of the natural environment to a size that is conducive to analysis in the laboratory but preserves the key elements thought to underlie the dynamics of the real-world phenomenon under study.

Geller (1982) distinguished between three basic types of simulations: game simulations, field simulations, and role playing. *Game simulations* consist of participants who take on roles in staged situations lasting until a desired outcome has been attained or a specified length of time has passed. Such simulations, which often involve participants working in teams, are popular in research in the areas of business, international relations (including conflict resolution and negotiation), community planning, and education. International simulations or war games, for example, can be used to predict future world events from present national characteristics or conditions. Another popular version of a game simulation is the mock jury study. This approach is intended to closely simulate actual jury procedures and sometimes involves actual cases and real jury candidates and judges. The minimal requirements of such studies are that subjects be brought together in groups in order to read, hear, or see the proceedings of a court case and deliberate as a jury (Bermant et al., 1974; Lamberth and Kimmel, 1981). Subjects indicate their opinions concerning the guilt or culpability of the defendant and may be asked to assess punishment or award damages.

Field simulations are distinguished by their setting. Such simulations are characterized by highly realistic staged settings that encourage participants to believe they are participating in natural situations. A well-known example of a field simulation in psychology is the Stanford prison study (Haney et al., 1973), a mock prison simulation which itself was the subject of much ethical criticism (see Box 4.2). That field simulations can be highly realistic and capable of eliciting spontaneous behavior from participants was effectively demonstrated in an investigation known as the Grindstone experiment (Olson and Christiansen, 1966). Sponsored by the Canadian Friends Service Committee, the study involved the defense of an island under simulated attack. The participants who were to defend the island consisted of Quakers who were committed to pacifist ethics. Although the objective was for the participants to repel the simulated attack through non-violent methods, the study had to be terminated after 31 hours due to the breakdown of behavioral norms of non-violence, which resulted in 13 mock "deaths" (Mixon, 1971).

The *role-playing simulation* has become increasingly used in recent years. According to Geller (1982), role playing has the most developed potential as an alternative to deception and it can be adapted to a wide variety of laboratory settings. Because there has been much scientific debate about the merits of role playing, details pertaining to this approach are presented separately in the following section.

As the Stanford prison study illustrates, the simulation alternative to deception is not free of ethical problems. When effectively carried out, such studies can cause intense emotional involvement and distress in participants, risks that some say should not be condoned for research purposes (Baumrind, 1964; Savin, 1973). Additionally, simulations are not always free of intrinsic deceptions (Geller, 1982). This was true of the Stanford prison study in the sense that

Box 4.2   The Stanford prison study

The Stanford prison study represents one of the most effective and controversial field simulations in the behavioral sciences. Conducted by social
psychologist Philip Zimbardo and two of his graduate students (Craig
Haney and W. Curtis Banks) at Stanford University, the simulation was
intended as an intensive investigation of the behavioral and psychological
effects of imprisonment on the guards who maintain and administer the
prison as well as those who experience it as inmates (Haney et al., 1973;
Zimbardo et al., 1973). The researchers hoped to obtain a better understanding of the processes by which prisoners adapt to this novel and
alienating environment and guards derive social power from their status
in controlling and managing the lives of others.

The researchers decided to conduct their investigation in the context of a
mock prison rather than an actual one for several reasons, including the lack
of outsiders' access to the prison system, the impossibility of separating out
to what extent an individual's behavior is a function of pre-existing personality characteristics or attributed to some aspect of the prison situation, and
the obvious ethical implications of placing innocent people inside a real
prison for the purpose of studying them. As a result, a mock prison (the
Stanford County Prison) was constructed in the basement of the psychology
department building on Stanford's campus. The mock prison was equipped
with iron-barred cells, a solitary-confinement closet, and a recreation area.

The participants for the prison study consisted of 21 college-aged males
who were selected from over 75 volunteers who answered area newspaper
ads promising US$15 a day for a two-week study of prison life (see Box 8.1).
After being tested for psychological well-being – all applicants underwent
extensive psychological testing and psychiatric interviews – 11 subjects
were randomly designated to role play being guards and 10 to be
prisoners. At the outset of the study, the prisoners were unexpectedly
"arrested" at their homes and were booked, fingerprinted, and taken to
the simulated prison by local police officers. Once inside the prison, they
were stripped, searched, and given a loose-fitting smock to wear; they also
were required to wear a stocking over their hair, were told to refer to
themselves by identification number only, and wore a light chain and
padlock around one ankle. These steps were taken in order to minimize
each prisoner's uniqueness and prior identity and to heighten the
prisoners' sense of powerlessness and emasculation. Guards were outfitted
with khaki uniforms, including mirror sunglasses and nightsticks, and were
told to do anything necessary to protect the security of the prison. All of
these details were intended to give as much mundane realism to the
situation as possible.

Although scheduled to run for a two-week period, the study had to be
terminated after only six days because of the extreme psychological effects
experienced by the participants. The guards progressively began to exploit

Box 4.2 (Continued)

their power by behaving abusively toward the prisoners. They woke prisoners in the middle of the night and arbitrarily forced them to do pushups or stand at attention for hours, required them to clean toilets with their bare hands, locked them in solitary confinement, refused to grant them permission to use the bathroom, and cruelly imposed pointless rules. After an initial rebellion, the prisoners became progressively passive, submissive, and depressed. Several prisoners had to be prematurely released – the first after only 36 hours – as a result of suffering severe hysterical reactions, such as uncontrollable crying and disordered thought. Zimbardo himself confessed that he had become seriously affected by his role as warden, autocratically controlling visiting procedures and worrying about rumored "prison breaks." By the sixth day, the remaining prisoners were so obviously shaken by the experience that the researchers concluded that the study had to be prematurely terminated. A series of individual and group debriefing sessions and discussions were conducted and apparently none of the participants showed signs of lasting distress.

Not surprisingly, the prison simulation was subject to much ethical criticism, similar in intensity and kind to those directed at Milgram's obedience experiments (see Savin, 1973). Zimbardo (1973a) countered his critics by pointing out some of the steps that were taken to protect the well-being of his participants, including pre-screening subjects, early termination of the simulation, and extensive debriefing sessions.

According to some, the prison study does not tell us much about prisoners and prison life because of the discrepancies between the simulated prison and real prisons (Forsyth, 1987; Haslam and Reicher, 2003). However, the results of the study provide an impressive illustration of the power of the norms of a situation and of pressures to conform in social life (Mamali, 2004). In a span of only a few days, a group of emotionally stable, law-abiding students were dramatically transformed by their simulated institutional roles. From the Stanford prison study one point is particularly clear: under certain circumstances, a role-playing simulation can become a totally involving life experience for its participants.

One interesting footnote to the Stanford study comes from a recent reflection on the research by Romanian social scientist Catalin Mamali (2004, p. 23). Based on Zimbardo's atypical decision to stop his simulation in advance because of ethical concerns related to the well-being of the participants, Mamali coined the term "Zimbardo's limit" to refer to "a critical interval that marks the level and/or the moment when the experimental procedures, which aim toward the scientific truth, might start to generate unacceptable consequences and costs for the total well being of the participants." As Zimbardo himself admitted, when the investigator becomes an active participant in a simulation, the critical limit may not be as readily apparent as it otherwise might be.

although the subjects had volunteered to role play, they were not told which role they would play (prisoner or guard) until the onset of the study. The participants also were unaware that they would be dramatically "arrested" by local police as part of the study they had volunteered for several weeks earlier.

Another concern about simulations is that their mundane realism is sometimes suspect. This was evident in Allport and Postman's (1947) early laboratory simulations of the rumor transmission process (Kimmel, 2004b). Allport and Postman were interested in the ways rumors change as they are transmitted. Their rumor simulation studies involved a serial transmission chain (similar to the popular game of Telephone) in which a description of an innocuous stimulus (typically a story or picture) is passed along from one person to another and distortions and eliminations in the communication are observed. A participant would describe a picture projected on a screen to another subject who could not see the picture. That subject would then relate everything recalled about the picture to a second subject; the second subject would then convey the description to a third, and so on until the description was transmitted six or seven times. When the accounts were analyzed it was found, consistent with processes of memory, that subjects tended to omit certain details of the communication to simplify the structure (so-called "leveling") and to accentuate or point up other details (so-called "sharpening").

Although Allport and Postman's findings were generally accepted over the years, it is now clear that many rumors do not act that way at all in natural settings; in fact, rumors tend to expand with a growing number of invented facts and details as they circulate (Kimmel, 2004b; Rosnow, 1991). Communications may indeed shrink and become distorted as they are serially reproduced in laboratory simulations; however, such demonstrations may be of limited value for studying rumor transmission. When rumors spread outside the controlled setting of a laboratory many more people are involved who are likely to be emotionally involved in the message content and intrinsically motivated to pass it accurately to others. In everyday interactions there are also opportunities for discussion and clarification of the rumor. Allport and Postman (1947, p. 64) did, in fact, recognize the limitations inherent in their simulation studies: "Laboratory control can be achieved, we admit, only at the expense of oversimplification. By forcing serial reproduction into an artificial setting we sacrifice the spontaneity and naturalness of the rumor situation." Thus, Allport and Postman implied that the mundane realism of their simulations was limited (and in turn their external validity), but apparently decided that it was the best available procedure for their early investigations. Contemporary rumor researchers are more likely to utilize other research strategies, typically in natural settings, in their attempts to uncover what happens to rumors as they are transmitted through interpersonal communication networks.

Role playing

Some researchers who object to deception in any form have recommended the use of an experimental alternative known as *role play*. This alternative to deception in the laboratory involves the diametrically opposed method of enlisting the subject as an active collaborator in the investigation. The subject is told what the experiment is about and is then asked to play a role as if he or she were actually participating in the experiment.

As a method, role playing is quite flexible in terms of setting, participants, and procedure. The essence of a role-playing study is for the participant to pretend that a situation is real when in fact it is not (Geller, 1982). In one application of this approach, subjects may be asked to read a description of an experiment provided by the researcher and to predict how they would respond (similar to the preinquiry method described earlier). In other cases, subjects are asked to play a more active role, from the totally improvised to one in which the experimental scenario is acted out with the aid of a script provided by the researcher. For example, in order to obtain greater insight into marketplace behavior, a consumer researcher may ask subjects to play the role of a seller or customer in a simulated store setting. The person playing the role of customer may be asked to pretend that he or she is dissatisfied with a recent purchase and is trying to return it, and the researcher then can observe how the interaction plays out, perhaps by focusing on the factors that lead to a successful or unsuccessful resolution. In contrast to deception studies, which require that subjects must be kept unaware, participants in role-playing studies must be fully informed. According to proponents of role playing, the strategy allows for a wide latitude of response, is capable of exploring complex behavior, and is a more humanistic alternative to many experiments that typically rely on deception (Forward et al., 1976; Geller, 1982; Mixon, 1972, 1974). One early advocate of the method argued that the behavior of role-playing subjects would more closely approximate life situations than that of deceived subjects (Brown, 1962).

In one of the first attempts to design a role-playing study as an alternative to deception, Greenberg (1967) utilized this technique in a replication of Stanley Schachter's (1959) early affiliation studies. In order to test the hypothesis that fear leads to affiliation, Schachter's initial experiments were designed such that some subjects (the "high-anxiety" group) were led to believe that the experimental procedure would involve painful electric shocks. The deception was accomplished by having a confederate describe the supposed procedure in a frightening way and by prominently displaying ominous-looking equipment in the laboratory. For other subjects (the "low-anxiety" group) the experiment was presented in a non-threatening way as involving no physical discomfort. When the subjects were given the opportunity to wait with others or alone until the experiment actually would get under way, a significantly greater number of high-anxiety subjects chose to wait with others in a similar plight, in support of Schachter's expectation that "misery loves (miserable) company." In a later experiment, Schachter obtained evidence that this effect was more likely to hold for anxious firstborns and only children than for later-borns.

In Greenberg's role-playing experiment, subjects were told to imagine that they were performing in an important experiment and were instructed to "act as if the situation were real." They then were exposed to a scenario that was very closely modeled after Schachter's original design; the threatening apparatus was present for some of the role players and subjects similarly were told that they would soon undergo a painful (or non-painful) procedure. The major results of Greenberg's role-play experiment were consistent with Schachter's findings but not statistically significant. For example, the induction of fear had a lesser effect on affiliation than was expected, but the extent to which high-anxiety subjects chose to affiliate with others was in the predicted direction. Similar results were obtained for the birth-order effect. Supporters of the role-playing approach interpreted the qualified success of this experiment as evidence that role play can replicate more traditional deception experiments. However, because Greenberg had regrouped his data according to perceived fear rather than by experimental manipulation, some critics maintain that his results are suspect and open to alternative interpretations.

Several methodological studies on role play have been carried out since Greenberg's early experiment and they have met with some success, particularly in research on conformity (Horowitz and Rothschild, 1970; Wahl, 1972; Willis and Willis, 1970), obedience (Geller, 1978; Mixon, 1971; O'Leary et al., 1970), and organizational behavior (cf. Greenberg and Eskew, 1993). However, despite these successes and the ethical advantages of role playing, there has been much criticism of it as a research tool (e.g. Freedman, 1969; Miller, 1972), which may account for the paucity of studies that have utilized this approach in recent years. Critics have claimed that the expectation that role playing would replicate general relationships has not been adequately demonstrated. In the same vein, it is argued that role players often cannot duplicate the most interesting findings that come from true experiments, such as counterintuitive ones. It also has been suggested that this technique lacks the capacity to induce involvement in role players when motivational or emotional variables are studied (West and Gunn, 1978).

Opinions continue to be sharply divided over the adequacy of role playing as an alternative to more traditional experimental procedures. Those who have defended its use emphasize the apparent successes of role-play studies and have argued that there is some confusion among critics of the approach as to what actually constitutes role playing. For example, Coutu (1951) distinguished between role playing, which is actual role enactment on the part of the subject in a given situation, and role taking, which is imagining what someone else would do in a particular situation. An example of role taking is suggested by Milgram's (1963) finding that a group of psychiatrists could not accurately predict the outcome of his obedience experiments.

One troubling aspect of role-play studies for their critics is that it is not possible to predict in advance whether the results would have corresponded with the results of non-role-play studies; thus, the best one can conclude after conducting a role-play investigation is that the results might have occurred had truly experimental studies been used (cf. Rosenthal and Rosnow, 1991). According to others, however, discrepancies between role-playing and traditional experimental results are problematic only if one assumes that the latter produce the truth. Indeed, there are enough methodological problems with deception experiments – in addition to concerns that laboratory data often cannot be generalized to everyday behavior – that perhaps deception results should not be used as the criterion against which the value of role playing is considered. As we have learned from the research on subject artifacts, much role playing already seems to occur unintentionally in laboratory experiments.

Given the pros and cons of the role-playing alternative, perhaps the best advice that can be offered to investigators who are considering its use is the suggestion offered by Rosenthal and Rosnow (1991, p. 152) that "researchers must go into this methodology with their eyes open." Role playing can be a useful research technique in certain situations and appears to be an efficient aid to theory development and hypothesis generation (Cooper, 1976). Creative combinations of role playing with the classical experimental approach might be worth exploring, as has been suggested elsewhere (Schuler, 1982). For example, subjects can be required to play various roles while other aspects of the study correspond to usual experimental procedures, such as the withholding of information about certain manipulations. In the long run, few would argue that the role-play approach will completely replace the use of deception in experiments. Nearly thirty years ago, Diener and Crandall (1978) concluded that more information was needed to assess the value of experimentation by means of deception and role playing, in addition to obtaining greater understanding about the roles subjects play in all sorts of investigations. Unfortunately, it appears that Diener and Crandall's conclusion still holds true today.

SUMMARY

This concludes our two-chapter coverage of the ethical issues involved in the conduct of laboratory research and the arguments for and against the use of deception in the laboratory setting. In addition to the numerous ethical implications inherent in the practice of deceiving research subjects, we have seen that there also are a number of difficult methodological issues that need to be weighed by the researcher. Although viewed as morally reprehensible by its critics, there is mounting evidence that deception is not considered to be an unacceptable or aversive methodology from the research participant's point of view and does not appear to have many of the negative effects that its critics have claimed. However, it is also clear that deception has been (and no doubt continues to be) used more out of convention than necessity by behavioral scientists and that the days of experimentally naive subjects are long past. Considering the variety and breadth of existing research alternatives, one only hopes that investigators will progressively explore these potentially rich sources of data.

One alternative to laboratory experimentation that we have not yet considered in depth is for researchers simply to leave the laboratory setting and conduct their investigations "in the streets" – that is, in so-called "real-life" or natural settings. While some of the ethical issues pertinent to research in the laboratory setting also apply to research in the field, there are other ethical dilemmas that present themselves in field settings that are not relevant to traditional research settings. In chapter 5, our focus turns to the ethical issues involved in the conduct of field research.

5

Ethical Issues in the Conduct of Field Research

"In one sense, field experiments are more problematic, more troubling, than lab experiments for the reason that in a lab experiment at least the person knows that he or she is coming for an experiment. It's like going to the theater ... you're not going to know exactly what's happening and, by having decided to participate, you have in a sense consented in a very general way to being subjected to certain strange things that you won't know about. But if you're just walking on the street and, like in some of the helping behavior experiments, some things happen in front of you ... you have not been warned and you have not agreed to participate in an experiment. I think that is a more severe violation of the rights of the subject than the laboratory situation."

Herbert Kelman

Chapter Topics

☞ Field research in perspective
☞ Privacy issues
☞ Non-laboratory methodologies and ethical issues
☞ Ethical issues in ethnographic fieldwork
☞ Conducting research on the Internet

Among the helping behavior experiments that Kelman may have had in mind when he referred to the ethical problems of field research during an informal talk at the 1987 Eastern Psychological Association meeting (cf. Kimmel, 1988b) was a series of studies conducted by Jane and Irving Piliavin during the early 1970s. The studies were designed to test a cost – reward model of bystander behavior based on the assumption that the decision to come to the assistance of a victim is the result of a consideration of the anticipated costs and rewards of helping versus choosing not to help. In one of the Piliavins' experiments a confederate pretended to collapse in a moving subway train (Piliavin and Piliavin, 1972). As the confederate fell, he released a trickle of "blood" from an eyedropper in his mouth; in a control condition, no blood was released. The results of the study supported the expectation that fewer bystanders would come to the aid of the bloody victim because of the greater potential costs involved in assisting an apparently severely injured person. In a later variation of this research, the experimenters had another confederate, who pretended to be just another passenger, stand near the "victim." However, this second confederate wore an intern's jacket, priest's attire, or ordinary street clothes in order to determine how bystanders' reaction would be affected by the presence of a doctor or clergyman.

Although such subway victim studies represent ingenious alternatives to the staged laboratory emergencies that were described in chapter 3, they indeed may be more problematic from an ethical perspective, as Kelman speculated. Because such unexpected events are not common in most persons' lives, they pose certain risks to unsuspecting bystanders. The sight of a victim who appears to be suffering from internal bleeding could cause substantial distress in some onlookers; although unlikely, it is entirely possible that a bystander could faint or even have a heart attack. Those persons who rush to the assistance of the "victim" could be injured in the attempt, and there is the additional possibility that they would experience some embarrassment upon learning that they were fooled for the purpose of a research investigation. Those who choose not to help might experience certain negative effects later, such as guilt or a reduction of self-esteem, when they reflect on their apathetic response.

There are societal implications as well from this type of research. When news spreads that bloody victims are merely research stooges, the public is provided with simply one additional reason for not helping, thus adding to the other forces in society that cause people to be cynical and able to rationalize their failure to assist others (Baumrind, 1977; Jung, 1975; Warwick, 1975). Of course, in defense of the research, there are some who would argue that the studies were specifically intended with the opposite outcome in mind – to provide a better understanding of the forces that work against helping during emergencies – and that awareness of this type of research sensitizes people to the apathetic bystander phenomenon.

Twenty years prior to his remarks at the Eastern Psychological Association meeting, from which this chapter's opening quotation was taken, Kelman brought to public attention some examples of even more dramatic and ethically problematic field investigations in his seminal 1967 paper on deception (see chapter 3). One of these examples involved a series of studies conducted under the auspices of the US army to investigate the psychological effects of stress on performance (Berkun et al., 1962). When brought to public attention, the studies aroused considerable furor because of the powerful stresses that were created in young soldiers (see Box 5.1)

It is important to note, as will become evident throughout this chapter, that most behavioral research in natural settings does not involve the staging of emergencies and other horrific events to see how unsuspecting subjects will react. Other field research procedures are much more benign, such as those that involve the observation and description of naturally occurring public behavior or analyses of the by-products of human behavior (e.g. public records and mass

Box 5.1   The army stress experiments

During the early 1960s, a series of experiments was carried out by a group of US army scientists in order to assess the effects of psychological stress in military settings. Specifically, the researchers were interested in determining whether there is a deterioration of performance during combat as a result of battle stress (Berkun et al., 1962). The subjects in these studies were young army recruits who had not given their prior consent to undergo stress and who were completely unaware that they were being deceived for research purposes. In each of the studies, the subjects were exposed to elaborate and convincing experimental hoaxes that made it appear to them that their lives were in danger or that they were responsible for injuring a fellow soldier.

In one harrowing study, 66 recruits in basic training were aboard a military aircraft that they were led to believe was disabled and about to crash-land. This deception was accomplished when, towards the end of the flight, the subjects saw that one of the plane's propellers had stopped turning and they heard about other malfunctions over the intercom. Subjects then were informed directly that there was an emergency, an announcement reinforced by a simulated pilot-to-tower conversation (which could be heard over their earphones) and by the sight of ambulances and fire trucks on the airstrip.

In order to ascertain whether the recruits' performance would be impaired by these terrifying manipulations, the plane steward distributed two questionnaires that were to be immediately completed. One of the questionnaires was an "emergency form" consisting of deliberately complicated instructions asking about disposition of the soldiers' personal possessions in case of death. The second form included a series of multiple-choice questions intended to test the soldiers' retention of airborne emergency procedures, the results of which supposedly would be furnished to the army's insurance company. Subjects were informed that all of the completed forms would be put in a waterproof container and jettisoned before the crash. Of course, the plane ultimately landed safely. Once they had been informed that their intense ordeal was simply part of a research study, blood and urine samples were collected from the participants. Not surprisingly, post-experimental inquiries revealed that many of the recruits suffered severe anxiety about the possibility of injury or death.

Other studies designed for the project involved new recruits not yet in basic training who were transported to an isolated mountain area where they were to participate in military maneuvers. There they were informed that new concepts of atomic-age warfare were to be tested requiring them to perform individually rather than as a group. Each recruit was taken separately to a remote outpost where, after a short period of time, they were exposed to various experimentally implemented emergencies. For example, one emergency condition involved supposedly misdirected

Box 5.1 (Continued)

artillery shells. This deception was accomplished via radio transmissions contrived to confirm the hazard, and the subjects heard a series of progressively closer explosions intended to simulate the incoming shells. In this condition, a radio transmission suggested that the shells were being fired by gunners who were unaware that anyone else was in the area. In another condition, the subject was deceived into believing that he had caused serious injury to another recruit after setting off an explosion. This condition proved to be the most stressful, perhaps in part because the subject was continually reprimanded by a senior officer for having caused the injury.

In each of these emergency conditions, subjects were led to believe that the only chance of an immediate rescue was to use an elaborate two-way radio to call for help and to report their location. However, in each case, as was pre-arranged, the radio failed to work. The measure of impaired performance in these studies was how long it took the subject to repair the broken radio. After 75 minutes had elapsed, the recruit was picked up at the outpost and blood and urine samples were collected.

Although these dramatic studies no doubt contributed to scientific knowledge by shedding some light on the effects of stress in realistic, non-laboratory settings, they raise a number of significant ethical problems. The uninformed participants were exposed to elaborate deceptions that posed undue or unnecessary risks, including the experience of psychological and physiological harms, invasion of privacy, and disrespect for human dignity. Perhaps the unsuspecting recruits also became less trusting of their army officers as a result of being victimized by the elaborate hoaxes.

Because the army experiments were carried out in an environment in which participants naturally expect a loss of individual freedom, there are some who might argue that the studies were less ethically problematic than had they been conducted in civilian settings. One also could contend that the experience of stress during army basic training is a "given" that recruits naturally come to expect (though perhaps not at the same level as the life-threatening stresses described here). When researchers conduct their investigations in field settings, the extent to which the risks posed are similar to those that individuals experience in their everyday lives is a particularly relevant consideration in evaluating the ethical acceptability of the research.

media content). However, the bystander intervention experiments and the army stress studies serve to illustrate some of the pervasive ethical issues that emerge in research conducted outside of the laboratory. These issues serve as the focus of the current chapter.

FIELD RESEARCH IN PERSPECTIVE

A substantial amount of behavioral science research is conducted "in the field": that is, in naturalistic non-laboratory settings. This is especially true in disciplines such as sociology and anthropology. While laboratory research continues to be the preferred choice of a majority of psychologists, greater attention has been focused on the potential value of field studies for testing psychological hypotheses (e.g. Webb et al., 1981; Yin, 1989) and there is some indication that field research has gradually increased in psychology during recent decades (Adair et al., 1985; Kimmel, 2001, 2004a).

A growing interest in field research as an alternative to laboratory experimentation can be attributed to several factors, largely stemming from some of the methodological problems identified in chapters 3 and 4. The most serious problem that confronted laboratory researchers was the recognition that their "test tubes" were dirty, in the sense that laboratory settings are subject to numerous artifacts that can serve to reduce the validity of the research findings. In short, all of the needs, fears, and intentions that result from subjects' awareness that their behavior is being scrutinized in a scientific investigation represent potential biases in the laboratory. Faced with these problems of "observational reactivity" – a term used to suggest that the act of observing affects that which is being observed or measured – it is easy to understand why many behavioral scientists may choose to study naturally occurring behavior in field settings. In the field, individuals can be studied with or without their awareness that they are research participants.

A second problem with laboratory research leading to an increased interest in field studies is linked to the first. As the methodological problems of experimentation were exposed, elaborate deception manipulations became commonplace as a strategy for coping with potential subject biases. This, in turn, led to a serious consideration of the specific effects of deception (e.g. whether subjects accept the researcher's cover story or instead create their own interpretation of the situation that deviates from the intended manipulation) and the ethical implications of using deception (e.g. whether the research technique represents an abuse of subjects' rights). At a more general level, as soon as the experimental situation began to be viewed as a human interaction situation and researchers began to address the methodological issues created thereby, it became apparent that norms that apply in other human relationships ought also to apply to the research relationship.

Field research offers behavioral researchers a ready alternative to some of the ethical concerns that arise in the laboratory context. Many research hypotheses can be studied in everyday reality without necessitating the deception or manipulation of subjects. Schuler (1982) provides the example of a study intended to investigate the effects on behavior of frustrating experiences. In the laboratory, frustration typically would have to be induced by the researcher through the use of some complex and deceptive manipulation, thereby exposing subjects to risk of harm. (In fact, there is a tradition of such research in the empirical literature on the frustration – aggression hypothesis; see, for example,

Berkowitz, 1969.) Schuler suggests there is no need to induce frustration when one can study many individuals who have been frustrated by events in their natural environments, such as university students who were unable to obtain preferred courses during registration, high-school students who scored poorly on college entrance exams, theater goers who found that the last seats had just been purchased for a hit play, or shoppers who missed out on a desired sale item.

Another reason why some researchers have become increasingly disenchanted with laboratory research has to do with questions about the "ecological validity" of laboratory experiments, a term that is generally used to refer to whether an experimental situation reflects the outside world (Rosnow and Rosenthal, 2005). Experiments that are set up in psychology laboratories often bear little resemblance to the real-world settings they are intended to reflect. Field research represents one possible solution to the limited ecological validity of laboratory research (see Box 5.2). Along these lines, Ellsworth (1977) argued that experimentation in the field actually offers better prospects for revealing complex causal relationships than laboratory experimentation, where so many variables are kept constant that the complex network of interactions operating in everyday life cannot possibly be revealed. Nonetheless, experimental control and precision of measurement are often seriously diminished in field settings (Adair et al., 1985; cf. Shadish et al., 2001).

The recognition that various behaviors are not amenable to investigation in laboratory settings also may have led some researchers to turn their attention to field research (Keith-Spiegel and Koocher, 1985). Behavior as varied as reactions in doctors' waiting rooms, race relations in a community following a highly publicized police beating of a minority group member, and coping behaviors in the aftermath of natural disasters are more appropriately studied in the field than in the laboratory (Sommer and Sommer, 1991). Similarly, the rise of interest in socially relevant research seems to have encouraged many researchers to leave the laboratory and to study social problems where they occur (see chapter 6). Some researchers believe that the investigation of complex social problems like violence and crime, drug abuse, and race relations in the laboratory would result in a reduction of their complexity, a sort of reduced reality from which generalizations would be seriously restricted. Finally, field research is both more relevant and more applicable to the "real-world" problems encountered in professional settings such as industry, commerce, health, and education (Robson, 1993).

It is somewhat ironic that while many early proponents of field research believed it to be an ethical alternative to laboratory deceptions, it now is similarly criticized for the frequent use of deceptive techniques. On the one hand, the fact that subjects usually are unaware that they are being observed in the field (as opposed to the laboratory setting) can be seen as a methodological strength. On the other hand, the manipulation and observation of unsuspecting persons can be viewed as ethically problematic in many situations. Thus, like their counterparts in the laboratory, field researchers must cope with the dilemma of scientific validity versus the ethics of the research methodology used to advance knowledge.

Box 5.2   Studying obedience in the field

In addition to the ethical concerns raised over Milgram's obedience research, there also was a difference in interpretation of the significance of the research, especially in terms of its ecological validity (cf. Blass, 2004). Milgram chose to create a miniature social world within the confines of his laboratory to study obedience to authority. But how might one study such behavior in a more natural setting? An experiment by Leonard Bickman (1974) provides a novel illustration.

In his field study of obedience Bickman manipulated the authority of three male experimenters who gave orders to 153 randomly chosen pedestrians on a street in Brooklyn, New York. The authority level of the experimenter was varied by style of dress. The experimenters wore a sports coat and tie, a milk carrier's uniform, or a guard's uniform closely resembling that of a police officer. The procedure involved having an experimenter give one of the following three arbitrary orders to each chosen subject:

1 *Picking up litter:* the experimenter pointed to a bag lying on the ground and commanded, "Pick up this bag for me!"
2 *Dime and meter:* the experimenter nodded in the direction of a confederate standing nearby at a parking meter and stated, "This fellow is overparked at the meter but doesn't have any change. Give him a dime."
3 *Bus stop:* The experimenter approached a subject waiting for a bus and exclaimed. "Don't you know you have to stand on the other side of the pole? This sign says 'No standing.'"

The results of Bickman's experiment revealed that participants were more likely to be obedient when the experimenter was dressed as a guard rather than as a milk carrier or civilian. Whereas Milgram's laboratory experiments sacrificed realism for experimental control, Bickman's field study sacrificed rigorous control for realism. Because field research is embedded in an existing social situation, it is difficult for the researcher to control other variables that might be capable of influencing the results (Forsyth, 1987).

The fact that Bickman's study was conducted in the field does not mean that the results can be generalized to other natural settings or that it is without ethical problems. Different conclusions might have been obtained had he carried out the study in another area, manipulated authority differently, or used female experimenters (Mook, 1983). The use of deception with participants who were unaware that a study was in progress raises certain ethical issues as well, although perhaps in this case it was the experimenters who were subjected to the greatest risk of harm at the hands of disobedient subjects.

FIELD RESEARCH AND ETHICAL ISSUES

The claim that field studies may be more ethically troublesome than laboratory investigations is open to debate and depends very much on the nature of the investigation. In some field investigations participants are as aware of being observed as those who take part in laboratory investigations. While there are many ethical issues that emerge in non-laboratory settings, two major areas of concern are especially likely to be encountered and can serve as focal points for a discussion of the various field research methodologies. The first concern has to do with the privacy rights of subjects. Because the inherent nature of much field research is to elude the awareness of those who are observed, the possibility that participants' privacy will be invaded must be fully considered by field researchers.

The second area of concern involves the informed consent of those who participate in the research. As in many laboratory studies, informed consent can be problematic in the field because much research simply could not be carried out with the awareness of research subjects. Imagine how ludicrous it would have been to carry out the aforementioned bystander intervention experiments or the army stress studies had the researchers decided first to obtain participants' informed consent. Exacerbating the problem of informed consent in the field are the greater practical problems in carrying out effective subject debriefings.

Privacy

The central ethical issues in field research are likely to revolve around potential invasions of privacy. Privacy, which derives from respect for personal autonomy, has been defined by Alan Westin (1968, p. 7) as "the claim of individuals, groups, or institutions to determine for themselves when, how, and to what extent information about them is communicated to others." Similarly, Ruebhausen and Brim (1966, p. 426) defined privacy as "the freedom of the individual to pick and choose for himself the time and circumstances under which, and most importantly, the extent to which, his attitudes, beliefs, behavior and opinions are to be shared with or withheld from others." These definitions regard privacy, when viewed in terms of the individual's relation to social participation, as voluntary and temporary withdrawal from others through physical or psychological means.

There are major international codes of human rights (such as the United Nations' Universal Declaration of Human Rights and the European Convention on Human Rights) that specify the right to privacy, which also is implicit in various European and American ethical codes for research and professional standards. Some common threads running throughout these codes are a fundamental respect for the person, remedies for violations of privacy, the need for protecting anonymity, and the prohibition of breaches of confidentiality. Confidentiality, which is discussed in greater detail in chapter 7, refers to the right to maintain the privacy of personal data divulged during a professional relationship with a researcher (Folkman, 2000). Attempts to apply the formal privacy and confidentiality standards in certain contexts can give rise to difficult choices. Problems of application are especially evident in research and clinical practice where the need for information conflicts with the reluctance to disclose that information.

The circumstances that characterize participation in field research are such that subjects' freedom to determine whether or not to participate frequently is violated. Participants in the field typically are not informed of their role as subjects and are unaware that a study is in progress. A social contract has not been established with the researcher; as a result, informed consent cannot be given, subjects cannot choose to refuse to participate or leave once the study is in progress, and in many cases they cannot be debriefed or informed of the results once the study has been completed. Under such circumstances, if researchers obtain or reveal (wittingly or unwittingly) information about attitudes, motivations, or behavior that a subject would prefer not to have revealed, the latter's basic right to privacy will have been compromised and an ethical problem will have been encountered.

An individual's desire for privacy is never absolute, and one is continually engaged in a personal adjustment process in which the desire for privacy must be balanced against the desire for disclosure and personal communication with others. This adjustment occurs in the context of various situational forces, including pressures from curious others (such as behavioral scientists), as well as the society's norms and processes of surveillance used to enforce them. Additionally, the nature of privacy demands may change over time along with other social and behavioral developments. For example, with the recent widespread diffusion of the portable telephone and other "nomadic" communication technologies, the privacy of personal conversations is rapidly becoming of a thing of the past. Although there are cultural differences in terms of the propriety of having one's phone conversations overheard by strangers (e.g. Crampton, 2005), the norms concerning privacy rights are certainly undergoing dramatic change in many countries. Moreover, security risks linked to the ongoing fight against terrorism have led to a rapid increase in surveillance equipment, reflecting the fact that the current era is one in which privacy can be expected to be violated. Many people view such violations as legitimate when national interests are at stake (see Box 5.3). In short, under some circumstances or conditions, violations of the right to privacy, when weighed against the right to know, may be viewed as falling within the bounds of ethical propriety.

Webb et al. (1981) have suggested that there is a continuum of situations in which behavior might possibly be observed, anchored at one end by situations in which privacy could not be said to be violated and at the other end by situations in which privacy could be said to be violated. Between these extremes is an area in which the acceptability of violations of privacy will depend upon characteristics of the situation and individual judgment.

One end of the invasion of privacy continuum can best be characterized by the public behavior of public figures. Politicians and celebrities are well aware that their every move may be observed and reported for public consumption. The

Box 5.3   American attitudes towards privacy before and after the 2001 terrorist attacks

Exactly one year prior to the September 11, 2001 terrorist attacks in New York and Washington, the Gallup Organization launched an extensive survey to assess American attitudes towards privacy issues. Overall, some of the key results of that survey revealed that Americans held deep concerns about the potential loss of their privacy rights, especially with regard to their online activities. For example, 82 percent expressed concern about privacy online; 67 percent voiced concerns about the government use of spy software; and 60 percent said that they were worried about the existence of databases allowing access to public records.

Two weeks after the attacks, however, a follow-up Gallup poll suggested that attitudes had been strongly influenced by events: 30 percent of the respondents favored making it easier for legal authorities to access the private communications of citizens, including e-mail and telephone conversations, and 71 percent approved the use of national identification cards. A subsequent Roper Centre analysis of polling data collected by various organizations revealed that although American concerns about personal privacy had steadily risen from 1978 up to the 2001 attacks, they showed a significant decline following the attacks. In the post-September 11 period, the American public was characterized by a greater willingness to forgo privacy guarantees for the sake of security and safety.

Source: Zureik (2004).

nature of what is observed may range from linguistic analyses of political speeches to off-the-cuff remarks made at a dinner party. By nature of their profession, public figures typically recognize that anything they do in public is fair game and reluctantly choose to forgo their right to privacy. When Warren Beatty, the film actor and director, addressed the American Society of Newspaper Editors in 1983, he stated: "Privacy is a simple matter in my case. I don't have any and I don't really expect any" (Friendly, 1983).

Privacy problems are more likely to emerge for non-public figures who presumably are unaware of the possibility that they are being observed, even in public situations. For example, a couple necking on a park bench one sunny day in May, in an open and busy area of the park, surely understand that their behavior can be seen by others. However, they might be offended to learn that strangers were carefully observing them and taking notes of their behavior. This same couple might not mind very much having observers note the amount of time they spend in various aisles of the supermarket while shopping for groceries. Thus, although many observations of public behavior are harmless enough and do not raise ethical problems, researchers need to consider specific behaviors and situations carefully (Webb et al., 1981).

The other extreme of the continuum is characterized by spying on private behavior in situations where people clearly expect their privacy will not be violated, as when they are in their own homes, personal offices, and physicians' examining rooms. The privacy within these settings may fluctuate from time to time (e.g. one's office is not private when workers are present to make repairs), but there is general agreement that these are settings in which invasions of privacy would be deemed inappropriate. While surreptitious observations in private settings might be required in certain criminal situations, they would not be considered legitimate for scientific purposes (Webb et al., 1981). Such observations by behavioral scientists are rare, but have been made. For example, the Wichita Jury Study (see chapter 1) created a national uproar in large part because the researchers had "bugged" the jury room, a private setting that is protected from outside intrusion by laws and tradition.

Falling in the middle of the privacy continuum are public places in which individuals expect some degree of privacy. That is, in some circumstances, public settings are regarded as socially or psychologically private by the persons who temporarily occupy them. For example, returning to our lovers in the park, if they moved from their highly visible bench to a secluded and unoccupied area of the park they no doubt would expect a far greater degree of privacy than they had earlier. If a researcher were to observe the couple through binoculars from a hidden vantage point for a study on interpersonal attraction, the observation is likely to be viewed as a violation of the couple's privacy and not to be condoned.

In other situations in which private behaviors occur in public settings, violations of privacy would be considered even more problematic. For example, despite the "public" nature of public restrooms, people enter such settings with the understanding that their behavior will be respectfully ignored by others. Such expectations in part led to the strong criticisms of Humphreys's "tearoom trade" observations (see chapter 1). Although subjects were well aware that their homosexual activity could be noticed by others present, they did not expect to be observed for research purposes or to have their identities eventually revealed to a researcher. The fact that Humphreys obtained the names and addresses of his subjects through devious means and later interviewed them under false pretenses exacerbated the ethical problems created by his private observations in a public place (Webb et al., 1981).

Another highly controversial study involving observations in public restrooms was conducted by Middlemist et al. (1976). In order to study the hypothesis that crowding leads to stress and discomfort, unsuspecting males were observed while urinating in a campus restroom. The researchers arranged to have a confederate stand either near them (at the next urinal) or farther away (at another urinal); other males were observed urinating alone (the control group). The time of delay before urination and the duration of urination were recorded by an observer hidden in a nearby stall through the use of a periscope device. As predicted, subjects took longer to begin to urinate and urinated for a shorter period of time as the interpersonal space between themselves and the confederate decreased. This study was criticized as trivial research that crossed the bounds of propriety, invaded subjects' privacy, and used up valuable space in an important research journal

(Koocher, 1977). In defense of their research, Middlemist et al. claimed that the invasion of privacy was of the sort that the subjects experience frequently in their everyday lives and that pilot subjects did not object to the observation when they were informed about it afterwards. Further, the researchers stressed that all data obtained in the study were kept anonymous; that is, at no time were individual subjects' identities or behavior made known to others.

While it might also be argued that Middlemist et al's stress hypothesis could have been studied under less invasive conditions, it is important to recognize that their investigation was carried out to test an important theory, there was no intent to demean subjects, safeguards were taken to protect subjects from harm, and no apparent evidence has emerged suggesting that any harm came to the subjects. To a great extent, these points also are relevant in evaluating the ethicality of Humphreys's investigation. As Webb et al. (1981) appropriately observed, the ethical controversies surrounding these studies have involved principles rather than consequences. That is, regardless of the fact that there were no identifiable effects on participants, it has been argued that the studies violated basic ethical principles pertaining to invasion of privacy and should not have been conducted.

In their analysis of privacy issues, Webb et al. (1981) further suggested that four dimensions underlie the placement of different research situations on the invasion of privacy continuum and regularly enter into determinations of the privacy interest. First, there is the element of *publicness in the location of the behavior under study*. People can lay less claim to privacy protections for behavior that takes place in public settings (shopping malls, sports arenas, airports, parks, etc.) as opposed to behavior in private settings such as their own homes. In fact, the value of privacy in the home is recognized by statute and common law. In other settings, as our previous examples illustrate, the distinction between private and public is less clear.

A second dimension underlying privacy considerations is the *publicness of the person studied*. As discussed above, public personalities regularly are subject to observations and reporting that would be considered invasions of privacy by less public individuals.

A third important dimension is the *degree of anonymity provided*, in terms of the explicit identification of the person with particular information. *Anonymity* pertains to a person's desire not to reveal who one is, and the expectation that one will not be personally identified or held to the rules of role or behavior that would operate under normal conditions (Westin, 1968). Privacy is clearly maintained when the linkage between the individual and the information obtained for research purposes has been completely severed. This, as mentioned, was something Middlemist et al. (1977) claimed in defense of their urination study. When information can be linked with a single identifiable person, anonymity will not have been preserved and the risk of privacy invasion is high. Degrees of subject identification falling between these extremes, such as the case in which identification is not immediately available but could be obtained (as in Humphreys's tearoom trade study) also can incur ethical problems.

A final factor in consideration of privacy is the *nature of the information disclosed during a study*. Certain information is likely to be more sensitive and pose greater risks to subjects than other information. For example, in American society, sensitive topics such as those involving birth control practices, income level, bankruptcy events, drinking and driving, cheating on income tax, and child and spousal abuse can be expected to raise privacy concerns. Ethical judgments should take into account the possibility that disclosed information, particularly when it can be associated with individual subjects, may be perceived as an invasion of privacy.

These four considerations can be expected to interact in complex ways. Although not solely applicable to research conducted in the field, they are more likely to influence ethical judgments relevant to the appropriateness of field observations involving participants who have not willingly entered into an agreement with the investigator.

Threats to privacy in cross-cultural research

Although our focus in this chapter emphasizes ethical issues in field research, the protection of subject privacy is a requirement in any research setting in which individuals studied have an interest in controlling other people's access to information about themselves (Folkman, 2000; Sieber, 1992). Threats to privacy can have both ethical and methodological implications in the research context.

Problems pertaining to privacy are particularly likely to emerge in the conduct of cross-cultural research, especially when researchers are not sensitive to the specific needs, attitudes, and behaviors of participants from different backgrounds. There are certain topics that people in different cultures or groups feel it is inappropriate to discuss and behaviors that are too private to reveal. For example, in many cultures, a man will consider it inappropriate to discuss his shaving (and other personal hygiene) habits with anyone, especially a female interviewer (e.g. Kimmel and Tissier-Desbordes, 1999). In the Netherlands and Germany, respondents are notoriously reluctant to divulge information about their personal financial habits; in fact, the Dutch often are more willing to discuss sex than money. Additional examples of privacy issues that emerge in other cultures were suggested by Sieber (1992):

- Attempts to assess attitudes about AIDS through interviews with poor Chicano families residing in southern California are likely to be limited by the fact that such individuals tend to consider it immoral to discuss sexual issues, such as homosexuality, AIDS, and abortion. Many of the respondents are likely to pretend that they do not understand the questions.
- An American study intended to establish the ethnic validity of a psychological measure may be carried out on a sample of Mexicans living in the US southwest, some of whom are likely to be illegal aliens. Given that some of the states in this region prohibit the delivery of publicly funded health care to illegal immigrants, it is likely that there will be potential participants who are unwilling to cooperate with the research. Even if their anonymity is assured, these persons may fear that their status will become known to government officials and have adverse consequences for their families.

As these examples illustrate, various methodological problems are likely to emerge when conflicts related to privacy are not satisfactorily resolved in certain research studies. Threats to privacy can result in biased samples; evasive, incomplete, or inaccurate responses; mistrust; and the loss of potential participants. Such problems can be overcome through careful planning and pretesting, and through the assistance of local persons who can assist in obtaining cooperation from participants in foreign locations (Jeannet and Hennessey, 2004).

Informed consent

It is difficult to consider the ethical issues pertaining to privacy fully without taking into account the principle of informed consent. Even the most private settings can be studied without raising ethical concerns if the people within those settings freely consent to observation once informed of the nature of the investigation. For example, college students might willingly open their dormitory rooms to researchers interested in observing how the rooms are decorated for a study on student interests and lifestyles. Those same students doubtless would view their privacy as having been violated if they were to learn after the fact that researchers had gained access to the rooms for whatever research purpose while the students were out attending classes. Some of the problems associated with the recording of individually identifiable data similarly can be overcome by obtaining subjects' prior voluntary agreement.

The problem with informed consent in field settings, of course, is that much field research involves situations in which informed consent is either not feasible or is detrimental to the interests of the research. These are research activities in which subject awareness might defeat the purposes of the research. On the other hand, informed consent will be irrelevant for many research activities that involve observations of ongoing public behavior or public records. According to Diener and Crandall (1978), when research procedures used in field settings do not significantly affect subjects' lives and do not pose any risks for them, informed consent procedures often become bothersome and time consuming for all parties involved. As a result, obtaining informed consent in such situations may be both ethically and methodologically undesirable. In short, application of the principle of informed consent in field research depends greatly on the nature of the specific research methodologies and the circumstances under which they are employed.

RESEARCH METHODS OUTSIDE THE LABORATORY

Behavioral scientists can choose from a wide variety of research tools and techniques to carry out their investigations in field settings. As a viable solution to the awareness problem encountered in laboratory experiments, field researchers are perhaps most apt to select a research approach that utilizes some form of nonreactive observation or measurement. *Nonreactive research* consists of methods that do not affect what is being studied. In nonreactive (or "unobtrusive") research, participants are unaware that they are being observed or measured for research purposes and thus do not "react" to the research; that is, they remain unaffected by it. Nonreactive methods are particularly useful in situations where the researcher is interested in obtaining an accurate measure of behavior as it naturally occurs. Examples of nonreactive field procedures include descriptive studies involving the simple observation of naturally occurring behaviors, surreptitious field experiments involving unknowing participants, and participant-observation studies in which subjects are unaware of the presence of a researcher. Field researchers also utilize nonreactive measures that do not involve the direct observation of subjects at all, but instead use physical evidence or by-products of behavior (such as archival records).

By contrast, *reactive research* involves obtrusive procedures that affect what is being observed or measured. Among the most common reactive procedures utilized in field settings are surveys, structured observations, and participant observations in which subjects are aware of the presence of the researcher. These techniques avoid some of the ethical issues raised by studying individuals without their knowledge, but are likely to encounter other ethical problems as well as methodological problems associated with observational reactivity.

In the remainder of this chapter we will consider some of these commonly used field research methods, giving particular emphasis to ethical issues involved in the study of individuals without their awareness.

Simple observation

If there is one activity that most people have in common with behavioral scientists it is "people watching." In scientific jargon, this activity is more apt to be referred to as *simple observation*, a research approach that generally has as its goal the careful mapping out (i.e. the description) of what happens behaviorally. Like people watching, simple observation can be fun; it also can be a provocative source of research ideas. As a means of describing behavioral occurrences, simple observation may be casual or systematic in nature. In casual observation, the researcher conducts the observations without prearranged categories or a formal coding or scoring system. For example, the researcher may simply choose to observe people in a particular setting and to note anything that occurs of interest. This is the research approach that most closely approximates everyday, informal people watching.

Systematic observations consist of a more formalized approach to observation and measurement, necessitating that the researcher develop and employ a scoring system with a set of prearranged categories. By "systematic" it is meant that the conditions under which the observations are made are specified in advance and that the observations are carried out in a consistent and orderly way. Typically, this approach requires some sort of a checklist in which information is recorded or tabulated under appropriate headings. Checklist categories, often developed from casual observation, should include examples of observable behavior that one might expect to occur naturally in the situation.

Simple observations of public behavior typically are innocuous and do not raise ethical problems. For example, Sommer and Sommer (1989) carried out systematic observation research in coffee-houses in order to study a basic principle of behavior known as the "social facilitation effect." Social facilitation involves the enhancement of an individual's performance of simple tasks when that person works in the presence of others. This effect was first noted by Norman Triplett in one of the earliest recorded social psychology experiments. Triplett (1897) found that young children wound fishing reels faster in the laboratory when they were joined by other children performing the same task as opposed to when they performed the task alone. This effect has since been replicated in numerous laboratory studies using both humans and non-human species.

In order to test whether social facilitation effects occur among people in their everyday activities, Sommer and Sommer recruited and trained student observers who were assigned to three different coffee-houses – one that was frequented by office workers and business persons, a second that was in a shopping center, and a third located in the college student union. The observers sat in their respective coffee-houses unobtrusively, pretending to be reading a textbook and taking notes. For each session, the observer recorded the duration of stay and amount of beverage consumption for three lone individuals and three people in groups. Across the three settings it was found that facilitation effects were more apparent in length of stay than in beverage consumption, with most patrons drinking only one cup of coffee.

Though carried out with a specific purpose in mind, the coffee-house observations were not much different than the sort of informal people watching that regularly occurs in public places where people eat, drink, and meet with friends. The observations presented no risks to the subjects, did not infringe upon their rights, and the data were recorded anonymously and in aggregate form. In such settings, people come to expect that they may at times be subject to the roving eyes of others, so the research observations can be said to fall within the range of experiences of everyday life. Under such conditions, informed consent is unnecessary and probably would create more problems for the researcher than it would resolve. By obtaining the informed consent of patrons in the coffee-houses, the advantage of observing spontaneous and natural behavior would be lost. At a more practical level, subjects might resent being bothered by a researcher attempting to explain a study that has little consequence for them, and the informed consent procedure would be time consuming and logistically difficult to carry out.

For similar reasons, debriefing subjects once the observations have been made would not be recommended in this type of situation. There is not much a researcher can do if a subject indicates displeasure at being secretly observed, given that the observation already has been carried out. Additionally, the debriefing could serve to raise subjects' level of discomfort or paranoia in other public settings and, without a full understanding of the potential scientific value of the study, could serve to lower their general opinion of scientists who "don't have anything better to do than to watch me drink a cup of coffee!"

In other situations, simple observations may be viewed as more invasive and, as a result, more problematic from an ethical point of view. Thus, this approach does not *a priori* represent an ethical alternative to deceptive laboratory research (Kemmelmeier et al., 2003). It is one thing to observe common non-verbal behavior (e.g. gestures, postures, seating arrangements) in public settings, but another to listen in to the conversations of strangers. Most of us, of course, frequently engage in "people listening" in addition to simply watching people; in fact, with the proliferation of portable phones, we often do not have a choice whether to listen. However, unlike researchers, casual listeners are not apt to take notes or keep careful records of that which they overhear. Indeed, one can find a number of non-reactive studies of conversations in the behavioral science literature, dating back to H. T. Moore's (1922) early investigation of sex differences in conversation.

Moore was convinced that there was a clear mental differentiation between men and women, and so he sought to obtain evidence of this by analyzing the content of their "easy conversations." For several weeks Moore walked along a 22-block area in midtown Manhattan during the early evening hours and jotted down every bit of audible conversation he could overhear. He eventually recorded 174 conversation fragments, which were coded in terms of the sex of the speaker and whether the participants in the conversation were of the same or mixed sex. Moore reported some interesting gender differences, such as the finding that female conversations included many more references to the opposite sex than did male conversations, and his study triggered a number of other hidden-observer language studies.

Moore's observations were restricted to a small area of New York City and thus the conversation fragments he obtained can be questioned in terms of the representativeness of the subjects and their conversations. Other researchers have attempted to overcome such sampling rigidity by obtaining samples of conversation from a wider variety of places and situations. For example, Landis and Burtt (1924) unobtrusively sampled conversations in a broad range of settings, including railroad stations, campuses, parties, department stores, restaurants, theater and hotel lobbies, and streets in both residential and commercial areas. Cameron (1969) had his students listen in on the conversations of more than 3,000 persons in different settings in order to investigate their usage of profanity. Among those most likely to use profane words were factory and construction workers and college students; secretaries tended to swear less often than people in other professions.

Several conversation-sampling studies have been restricted to university campuses, with trained students serving as unobtrusive observers. For example, in their analysis of sex differences in gossip, Levin and Arluke (1985) had students eavesdrop on the conversations of other students in the campus student union. For each instance of overheard gossip (defined as small talk about other persons), the student observers recorded the gender of the gossipers, and the tone (positive or negative) and focus (i.e. who and what the gossip was about) of the gossip fragments. The analysis revealed that the two genders were equally positive and negative in tone, with females devoting only a slighter higher proportion of their conversations to gossip about a third party. The most interesting finding, however, was in content differences: female students were most likely to gossip about close friends, relatives, and their coursework (teachers and classmates), whereas male gossips were most likely to discuss celebrities and distant acquaintances. As is typically the case in nonreactive observations of public behavior, Levin and Arluke's gossip study was carried out as a systematic observation. The student-observers were armed with a coding sheet that required them to check appropriate categories for the overheard gossip fragments. The observers did not record verbatim content of what was said and the identities of the gossipers never were revealed.

In evaluating the propriety of nonreactive conversation research, one must bear in mind that each of the preceding examples took place in public settings where the subjects were aware that what they were saying could have been overheard by strangers in relatively close proximity. We might assume that when people have something very private and personal to discuss they either choose a more isolated setting for their conversation or else lower their voices so that they cannot be overheard. Thus, most nonreactive observation studies of this type can be justified on ethical grounds by the public (and anonymous) nature of the observations, and by the corresponding fact that the risks posed (in this case, having information of a private nature revealed to others) are no greater than those one encounters in daily experience.

By contrast, consider the early case involving surreptitious observations carried out by Henle and Hubble (1938). According to the researchers, "special precautions" were taken to keep the student subjects unaware that their conversations were being recorded verbatim for a research study. As a result, the investigators hid under beds in dormitory rooms, eavesdropped on conversations in washrooms and lounges, and listened to telephone conversations. The researchers also pointed out, without further explanation, that the "unwitting subjects were pursued in the streets, in department stores, and in the home" (p. 230). Without additional details about how Henle and Hubble protected the rights of their participants, it would be difficult to regard the research as ethically acceptable on any of the grounds discussed above. Although the results of the study were presented in statistical summaries without reference to specific individuals, the subjects' privacy (in terms of the observation settings and the potential nature of the information disclosed) was clearly intruded upon.

In many circumstances, the simple observation approach can serve as a more ethically acceptable alternative to surreptitious observations carried out in private settings. The challenge is in finding the appropriate public setting for testing the hypothesis. As an example, consider the researcher who is interested in investigating the relationship between physical attractiveness and the amount of time people spend grooming themselves. The researcher might predict that one's own physical attractiveness is self-reinforcing; that is, people may respond positively to their own physical attractiveness as well as to that of others. There are a number of ways to go about testing this hypothesis, including simply asking people who vary in degrees of attractiveness how much time they spend in front of the mirror on an average morning. Of course, this reactive approach may lead to biased responses in addition to potentially embarrassing the subjects. As an alternative, the researcher might choose to set up a hidden video camera and one-way glass mirror in campus restrooms, thus enabling the observation of unsuspecting subjects. Observers then could record the approximate attractiveness level of each subject (say, on a ten-point scale) and the amount of time each spends gazing in the restroom mirror. While this approach would eliminate the problem of observational reactivity, the researcher would be faced with the ethical problem of having to justify the invasion of subjects' privacy.

As a solution to the problems raised by these approaches, McDonald and Eilenfield (1980) ingeniously exploited an ideal public setting in order to test the attractiveness and mirror-gazing hypothesis. They observed university students as they walked past a mirrored wall on the outside of one of the campus buildings. Hidden observers rated each randomly selected passerby as being low, medium, or high in physical attractiveness and timed how long each subject spent gazing towards his or her reflection. The predicted positive correlation between attractiveness judgments and gazing time was obtained for both male and female subjects. Informed consent and debriefing procedures were not employed by the researchers, a decision that appears to be justified on the basis of the innocuous and public nature of the observations.

Although it may not be possible to overcome the ethical issues raised in the context of most simple observations of private behavior, such studies may be carried out if the researcher judges that certain conditions have been met. Obtaining informed consent from potential participants is the most obvious and effective safeguard when observed behavior is private in nature, although, as described, it is not possible to obtain informed consent and preserve the non-reactive nature of the observation. The researcher should also consider whether there is an alternative research approach that can be implemented in order to obtain the desired data. As McDonald and Eilenfield's (1980) mirror-gazing study illustrates, there may be a more acceptable setting in which to carry out potentially sensitive observations than is first apparent. If an alternative approach is unavailable, researchers should take special care to protect the anonymity of the private information obtained from participants. It also is necessary to consider whether there are legal restrictions barring observation in the intended research setting. Investigators should attempt to establish how private the setting actually is and the degree of sensitivity of the information desired, perhaps by asking individuals from the subject population to consider whether they would view the observations as an invasion of their privacy. When in doubt, it would be wise for the researcher to consult the opinions of colleagues or else to postpone the study until some of the ethical issues can be more effectively resolved.

Nonreactive measures

As an alternative to the direct observation of naturally occurring behavior, researchers may choose to collect data through the use of a variety of nonreactive (or unobtrusive) measures. These measures, along with some of the issues inherent in their use, are fully described in Webb et al.'s (1981) classic compendium, *Nonreactive Measures in the Social Sciences*. Although rarely adequate as a sole means of testing hypotheses – especially causal ones – nonreactive measures are especially suited for the indirect study of behavior in naturalistic settings. Although some ethical problems may be encountered in their application, most nonreactive measures have little or no impact on the research participants and thus are permissible in a majority of situations.

Among the potential sources of nonreactive measures of behavior are physical traces and archival records. Physical trace measures involve the examination of physical evidence or traces of past behavior that have accumulated or built up in the environment (so-called "accretion" measures) or that have selectively deteriorated or worn away (so-called "erosion" measures). Some examples of accretion measures that are revelatory about behavior or a society's lifestyles and values include the accumulation of dust on library books to estimate the extent of their use; the prevalence of politically oriented bumper stickers on automobiles as an indication of interest in an approaching election; analysis of graffiti to investigate social concerns and lifestyle differences in communities differing along socioeconomic lines; and length of discarded cigarette butts to gauge concerns about the health risks of smoking among current smokers. Examples of erosion measures include the selective wearing away of floor tiles to determine the paths most frequently taken by shoppers in supermarkets or other settings; the wear on library books (especially at the corners where pages are turned) to assess their popularity; and estimating the skills and habits of drivers by noting the prevalence of dents, broken glass, and missing ornaments on their automobiles.

As may be evident from some of these examples, subject anonymity typically can be maintained because it is not known who produced the physical traces (such as graffiti and cigarette butts) in the first place. It is the remnants of behavior that are observed rather than the behavior that created the physical traces. However, for some nonreactive measures anonymity cannot be guaranteed. For example, when researchers rummage through the garbage bins in a neighborhood to assess consumption habits, it usually is clear which household has produced what garbage. Even when garbage is collected at a local dumping site, certain contents may contain identifying information (e.g. magazines with address labels still attached, discarded envelopes and letters, and bank statements). Because the contents of garbage may contain sensitive information that the previous owner may not want (or expect to have) revealed to others, privacy concerns need to be considered prior to the carrying out of this form of nonreactive measurement (see Box 5.4).

Archival analysis represents another potentially rich source of data. This type of nonreactive research makes use of data obtained from existing records that were produced for purposes other than behavioral research. Archives may consist of the ongoing, continuous records of a society routinely collected and maintained by government agencies, such as actuarial records (e.g. birth, marriage, death records), political and judicial records (including the voting records and speeches of legislators), other government records (e.g. crime reports, automobile ownership records), and the mass media (e.g. news reports, advertising, editorials).

Box 5.4   Ethics and garbage research

Researchers have found that an analysis of the contents of garbage can be useful for shedding light on certain aspects of a society, including its citizens' habits, interests, and values. An article on "urban archeology" in a 1980 issue of *The Christian Science Monitor* reported that there were about 12 federally funded garbage projects in the United States at the time. One of the longest-running of these investigations is the Garbage Project, directed by William Rathje, a University of Arizona archeologist who believes that the study of garbage represents the study of contemporary material culture (Rathje and Murphy, 2001). When Rathje's team of researchers compare interview data with the actual contents of garbage bags they often find that the verbal reports do not match the garbage. For example, when interviewed, respondents claimed to have healthier eating habits than their garbage revealed.

Despite the informative nature of such research, the garbage studies raise certain ethical problems, particularly in terms of the risk of invading the privacy of the previous owners, the possibility of discovering incriminating material, and problems in maintaining the confidentiality of data. However, these ethical problems may not be as severe as they first appear (Webb et al., 1981). Legally, it seems that once people put things in their garbage cans, the contents are considered abandoned and the previous owners no longer can claim any legal interest in them. Prior to collecting garbage for analysis, the Garbage Project researchers took careful steps to explain the research and obtain community approval. For example, residents in the neighborhoods involved were asked to sign consent forms stating that at some future time their garbage might possibly be collected for study. Later, households are selected at random and the trash is bagged by collectors and taken to an inspection site.

Rathje's student workers also must sign consent forms agreeing in part not to engage in unnecessary inspection or identifying of material. When the studies require that residents be interviewed, garbage collection data are linked with interview responses through the use of codes, which are destroyed once the connection has been made. The Garbage Project received wide publicity in the geographical region in which the studies were conducted and so most residents recognized the risk of discarding any incriminating material.

Other archival records are more episodic and private than running, public records. Some examples include sales records (e.g. casualty insurance sales, sale prices of autographs, sales levels of consumer goods), industrial and institutional records (e.g. job absenteeism and tardiness, accident reports, consumer complaint letters), and various other written documents (such as suicide notes, rumors reported by crisis control centers, journals and diaries).

Research conducted by Phillips (1977) provides a fascinating example of how archival records can be exploited for behavioral research purposes. Phillips reasoned that many driving fatalities may be the result of motorists using their cars to commit suicide, and hypothesized that motor vehicle fatalities, like suicides in general, would increase after a well-publicized suicide story. In order to test this hypothesis, he used running records of automobile accident fatalities kept by the California Highway Patrol and a measure of suicide publicity obtained from California newspapers. The publicity measure was based on the daily circulation of each newspaper and the number of days the suicide story was carried. It was found that the publicity measure indeed correlated significantly with changes in motor vehicle fatalities after each story, with the fatalities increasing significantly during the few days after a well-publicized suicide story. This pattern of fluctuations was not obtained for control periods that were free from suicide stories.

With regard to the ethicality of archival research, at the outset it is clear that the more public the records, the fewer problems will be encountered. For example, in order to determine if there are predictable biases in trial outcomes and prison sentences based on the ethnic status of the accused, a sociologist may decide to consult courtroom records for the necessary data. Such a study would be permissible without having to obtain the informed consent of the individuals involved because the researcher is relying on information recorded in public documents (Diener and Crandall, 1978). In fact, the research use of most archival records, unless they involve private documents, raises very little concern from an ethical point of view.

The potential problems with archives have to do with issues of confidentiality when the researcher gains access to private records or when various data sets can be linked. Webb et al. (1981) described several examples of the misuse of data files. For instance, certain records that may be accessible to particularly enterprising researchers, such as copies of driver's licenses and automobile ownership information, may include a wide range of additional personal data, including height, weight, marital status, whether the person is physically handicapped or is vision or hearing impaired, whether the person had been confined to a mental institution or convicted of felonies, and so on. Hospital records are extremely difficult to gain access to, but typically contain much confidential information about the patient. When data sets are very small, confidentiality becomes difficult, if not impossible, to preserve.

A variety of potential methods for protecting the confidentiality of archival data are available to researchers. An example, which illustrates the kinds of approaches that can be used, pertains to a case involving an investigator who is interested in determining the extent of criminal records among persons with venereal disease (Webb et al., 1981). In order to determine whether there is a link between the variables, the researcher would have to consult two confidential files. One alternative would be to provide police with five lists, each consisting of the names of ten persons treated for venereal disease. Five more lists, each consisting of the names of ten untreated persons, would be provided as a comparison group. The police then could provide the average number of arrests, along with a variability measure, for persons on each list, which could be recoded

Table 5.1   Preserving the confidentiality of qualitative archival data

---

1   Closure (i.e. unavailability) of the material for a specified period.
2   Restricted access, where the material is only available to certain types of researchers, or requests for access are evaluated by persons responsible for maintaining the archive.
3   Protection of anonymity by removal of all personal identifiers on material that will be accessible to users.
4   Users' consent not to breach confidentiality by publishing identifiable information.
5   Recontacting the informants to obtain consent for deposit in a public archive.
6   For current research, secure permission from informants for material to be archived at the time of interview.

Source: Adapted from Corti, Foster, and Thompson (1995).

in such a way that only the designation of treated versus untreated groups is retained. For more complete descriptions of this and other types of confidentiality-preserving techniques, as well as a consideration of their limitations, consult the excellent reviews by Boruch and Cecil (1982), Campbell et al. (1977), and Corti (2003); also see Table 5.1.

In sum, by its very nature, nonreactive measurement tends to raise fewer ethical difficulties than the direct observation of unaware subjects. Nevertheless, each case needs to be considered in terms of whether consent must be obtained and confidentiality of data protected. A study involving the prevalence of empty whiskey bottles or unpaid bills in household garbage containers is more problematic than a study of the erosion of floor tiles (Robson, 1993). Under most circumstances, the confidentiality of data obtained from the use of nonreactive measures can be sufficiently preserved. Perhaps the most compelling question that can be asked about nonreactive measures in general is why they have not been more frequently exploited by researchers as alternatives to deceptive research methodologies.

Contrived observation

Unlike the field research approaches thus far described, contrived observation involves the investigator's intervention in the research setting. By systematically varying aspects of the observational setting it is possible to gain greater control over the variables involved than would be possible in simple observational studies. Contrived observations thus provide the researcher with greater facility for precipitating behavior that otherwise might occur infrequently or unpredictably. There are a number of ways to tamper with nature or intervene in situations for research purposes. Among the contrived methods available to researchers are structured observations, field experiments, and participant-observation studies.

Structured observation

Observations of this kind typically involve a minimal amount of intervention or control over the situation in which the observations are to be carried out. Researchers set up a situation by arranging conditions or controlling antecedent events in such a way that consequent behavior can be readily observed. As an example, in a study of self-awareness in chimpanzees, Gallup (1979) equipped the animals' cages with mirrors and slightly altered their appearance (e.g. by putting a dab of red coloring on their forehead). He then considered the chimpanzees' touching of the altered spot as an indication of their having recognized a change in their appearance. In another study, Zimbardo (1969) left automobiles along the roadside in different settings and made it appear as if the cars were abandoned (the license plates were removed and the hoods were raised). Hidden observers then watched from a distance and recorded any instances of contact with the cars, including acts of vandalism and theft.

As with simple observations, so long as the behavior observed is of a public nature and the risks involved are no greater than those encountered in everyday experience, most structured observations raise few, if any, ethical concerns. For example, although it might be said that the abandoned car study may have encouraged unsuspecting individuals to engage in illicit behavior, the investigation was carried out partly as an attempt to understand behaviors that already were occurring with high frequency in similar settings. To the extent that the structured setting reduces participants' usual range of response or exposes them to certain risks, the research will be more ethically problematic. An early laboratory investigation by Landis and Hunt (1939) may have seemed innocuous at the time, but today may be viewed as more troublesome, especially if replicated as a structured field observation.

Landis and Hunt studied movement responses in subjects by exposing them to various stimuli and filming their gestural response patterns. In one case, when a gun was fired the subjects reacted by drawing the shoulders forward, contracting the abdomen, bending the knees, closing the eyes, and widening the mouth. Imagine the potential problems if an investigator chose to expose subjects in natural settings to the unexpected sound of a gunshot in order to study their behavior free from laboratory contaminations (cf. Webb et al., 1981). Given the high fear of crime and the prevalence of random shootings in contemporary societies, the manipulation might be expected to cause an extreme fear or stress response in some subjects.

Field experiments

As another form of contrived observation, field experiments involve the researcher's attempt to evoke behavior by manipulating an experimental variable or by otherwise modifying some aspect of a naturalistic setting. Despite the potential loss of control over extraneous variables when experiments are conducted in the field, researchers typically gain the ability to observe behavior under conditions presumably free of observational reactivity. This is because for most field experiments the research participants are unaware of the experimental manipulations and recording of their reactions. Thus, from the researcher's perspective, the main advantage of this approach is the high confidence that the observed behavior reflects natural behavior on the part of the participants.

Numerous field experiments have been carried out by behavioral scientists, on such topics as altruism and helping behavior (e.g. the Piliavins' bystander intervention research), social influence, personal space (e.g. Middlemist et al.'s urination study), and community norms. In general, these studies have posed few risks and have placed few demands on the potential participants. For example, Bryan and Test (1967) observed the effects of having either black or white Santas ringing bells next to a charitable organization's donation buckets. All of the passersby (busy shoppers) represented potential subjects, who either donated or did not donate money. Obviously, the researchers could not have expected to obtain the informed consent of each and every person who passed, or tried to debrief them about the study. With the possible exception of momentary guilt for not contributing to charity, there were no risks in this experiment any greater than in everyday life, and all of the donations actually went to the charity.

In a somewhat related study, Crusco and Wetzel (1984) investigated the effect of touching on restaurant diners. It was expected that the size of the gratuity left by the diners would be influenced by the non-verbal behavior of the waitress. Subjects in two restaurants were assigned to one of three conditions: fleeting touch (the waitress twice touched the diner's palm for one-half second while returning change), shoulder touch (the waitress placed her hand briefly on the diner's shoulder while giving back change), and no touch (no physical contact was made with customers). The researchers speculated that touching customers on the hand would produce a positive affect toward the waitress and hence a larger gratuity than the shoulder touch, which might have been viewed as a sign of dominance, especially among male customers. Contrary to prediction, there was no difference between the two touching conditions; both male and female diners gave a significantly larger tip after being touched than when they were not touched. Although the restaurant patrons were not debriefed, we can imagine that some would have voiced resentment towards the researchers for attempting to manipulate the size of the gratuity. Of course, one can argue that the research situation was not fundamentally different from that which normally occurs in restaurants when employees attempt to maximize their tips (Willis-Aronowitz, 2005).

In chapter 3 we considered Latané and Darley's laboratory experiments for investigating bystander intervention during emergencies (see Box 3.2). In order to determine whether similar findings could be obtained in natural settings, the two researchers employed confederates to pose as thieves in a liquor store (Latané and Darley, 1970). As the proprietor (who assisted the experiment) went to the back of the store to search for a requested beverage, one of the confederates picked up a case of beer on the counter and stated "They won't miss this." The two confederates then left the shop. This "theft" was carried out in full view of one or more real customers. As had been found in the laboratory studies, a bystander was more likely to intervene (by informing the proprietor of the theft) when it was believed he or she was the only witness to the crime than when another bystander also was present.

Staged thefts have been utilized by other researchers in order to study bystander reactions (e.g. Bickman and Rosenbaum, 1977; Moriarty, 1975). In Moriarty's (1975) study, a male confederate approached unsuspecting sunbathers at a New York beach and, depending on the experimental condition, either asked them to watch his things on a nearby blanket for a few minutes or asked for a cigarette light before leaving. A few minutes later, a female confederate approached the man's blanket, grabbed his blaring radio, and ran away. It was hypothesized that subjects who agreed to watch the man's things would feel that intervention was their responsibility and would be more inclined to help than bystanders who were asked for a light. This indeed is what happened: 95 percent of the bystanders in the responsibility condition intervened by stopping the thief or by grabbing back the radio, compared with only 20 percent of the bystanders in the no responsibility condition. In contrast to some of the other examples described here, field experiments involving apparent crimes add a degree of physical risk to the situation, to the confederates as well as the subjects.

In addition to staging emergencies and crimes in natural settings, behavioral scientists have designed other procedures for studying helping behavior that are relatively harmless in nature. One of these approaches is the "wrong number technique," in which a researcher telephones individuals selected at random, pretends that a wrong number has been reached, and then explains that he was trying to reach a garage because his car had become disabled on a highway. Claiming that he has no more change for another call, the researcher asks the participant to call a garage for assistance and gives a phone number. The measure of helping behavior consists of whether the participant makes the call; if so, a confederate answers and promises to take a message for the "garage." The researchers who developed this technique attempted to determine what effect the race of the subject and the "victim" would have on helping rates (Gaertner and Bickman, 1971). One finding was that fewer white subjects (evident from vocal characteristics and neighborhood of residence) attempted to help black victims (as manipulated through actual race and vocal characteristics of the caller) than when the victim was white and the subject black.

Another interesting experimental procedure known as the "lost letter technique" has been extensively utilized by field researchers (e.g. Bridges et al., 2002; Jacoby and Aranoff, 1971; Kunz and Fernquist, 1989; Merritt and Fowler, 1948; Milgram et al., 1965; Montanye et al., 1971). This technique involves leaving stamped, addressed letters, containing innocuous messages, in conspicuous locations (e.g. sidewalks, parking lots, under automobile windshield wipers) so that it appears that the letters had been dropped or otherwise lost by the intended sender (Milgram, 1969). The helping measure in studies employing this technique is the number of letters returned to a post-office box (where they can be retrieved by the researcher) under varying conditions. Researchers have assessed a wide variety of attitudes with the lost letter technique, including attitudes towards handicapped children, abortion, gays and lesbians, creationism and Darwinism, the death penalty, busing, and race. In one study, Milgram et al. (1965) planted letters addressed to one of the following: "Friends of the Communist Party," "Friends of the Nazi Party," "Medical Research Associates," and "Mr. Walter Carnap." As expected, fewer of the letters were returned for the first two conditions. Merritt and Fowler (1948) obtained lower return rates for dropped letters that apparently contained a coin (actually a lead slug) than for those that seemed to contain no money. Although a number of variations of the lost-letter technique have been used by researchers, the deceptions typically are minor and pose no risk to participants.

The range of methodologies used in experimental studies of altruism and helping behavior in natural settings provides a useful basis for our evaluation of field experiments in general. When one considers the research examples described here, it is apparent that in most cases only modest demands are placed on the participants, involving relatively trivial, low-cost behavior. Potential participants are asked to mail a lost letter, make a phone call to a mechanic, help a subway passenger to his feet, leave a gratuity, make a donation to charity, report a minor theft, and so on – behavior that rarely exceeds the range of normal public activities. The likelihood of subjects experiencing a high level of physical or psychological stress, embarrassment, or long-term effects is low. Further, the research procedures typically are carried out in a way that ensures anonymity and the confidentiality of response; as a result, the experiments are unlikely to involve intrusions of privacy. Given these considerations, it is not surprising that a majority of adults surveyed in public places about the acceptability of eight nonreactive field studies did not react negatively to the studies (Wilson and Donnerstein, 1976). Among the studies viewed as ethical and non-invasive of privacy were four involving procedures that have been described here – the bloody victim manipulation, the abandoned automobile procedure, and the wrong number and lost-letter techniques.

Because it typically is impractical to obtain the informed consent of participants for field experiments, some researchers have made a special effort to ensure that the persons selected for study do not experience any harmful effects. For instance, in their wrong number experiment, Gaertner and Bickman (1971) attempted to reduce participant guilt for a non-helping response by having the caller, prior to hanging up, say "Here come the police, maybe they can help me." In the Piliavins' bystander intervention studies, the "victim" was always assisted by a confederate if none of the bystanders came to his aid before the next subway stop, suggesting that the "victim" was not seriously injured (Piliavin et al., 1969; Piliavin and Piliavin, 1972). This step may have reduced any lingering after-effects, such as guilt or upset on the part of subjects. Actually, Piliavin and Piliavin's (1972) "bleeding victim" study was quickly terminated because of problems with subway security and the fact that some of the reactions were dramatic and potentially dangerous for passengers.

Despite the low risk of harm in field experiments, it is apparent that the direct potential benefits for participants also appear to be minimal, with the exception of the temporary satisfaction that comes from interacting with others or, as in the case of the helping experiments, engaging in altruistic behavior. Instead, the benefits can more generally be described in terms of scientific interest and the potential practical significance of knowledge gained.

One additional concern regarding field experiments that was alluded to in our consideration of the Piliavins' research pertains to the possibility that surreptitious procedures in natural settings can raise the suspiciousness of ordinary citizens when the events occur naturally. As a result, the tendency to provide help or assistance to others, to obey the orders of legitimate authorities, and the like might be reduced. However, the likelihood of such outcomes probably is small. The number of surreptitious field experiments that have been carried out has not been unduly large, nor have they been particularly well publicized, at least to the extent that they would be expected to have a major effect on ordinary citizens' social reality. Nevertheless, the author knows of a case involving a psychology professor who one day noticed a US$20 bill lying on the floor in the lobby of the psychology building. According to the psychologist, he hesitated for some time prior to pocketing the money, not knowing whether this was his lucky day or whether he instead had unwittingly become a subject in a psychology experi ment. Such reactions may not be atypical among behavioral scientists and per- haps a growing number of non-scientists.

Entrapment studies

In contrast to the relatively innocuous field studies previously described, entrap- ment research is apt to raise serious ethical concerns. Entrapment experiments typically are conducted to investigate moral character by providing opportunities for subjects to engage in dishonest behavior or perform otherwise reprehensible acts. A few examples should suffice to clarify the basic nature of this type of research approach. In one application, Freeman and Ataov (1960) contrived a situation in which students were given a chance to cheat on a classroom test by grading their own examination scoring sheets (which previously had been col- lected and then returned under some pretense). The researchers were interested in determining whether more changed answers would be apparent for different kinds of question formats. In another study, an experimenter pretending to be a foreigner with very limited English and a poor knowledge of the taxi system tested the honesty of New York City cab drivers by requesting a ride to a nearby location and then overpaying the fare (Brill, 1976). As it turned out, the cab drivers were not as apt to cheat their passenger as one may have expected.

In one intriguing entrapment experiment stimulated by the well-known 1972 Watergate break-in, West et al. (1975) attempted to induce participants to agree to take part in a burglary that paralleled the real break-in. The study was intended to test a theory pertaining to the determinants of causal attribution. Consistent with the so-called "actor/observer effect," the researchers noted that participants in the actual Watergate burglary explained their behavior in terms of environ- mental influences external to themselves, whereas observers in the mass media attributed responsibility for the crime to the personal character of those involved.

In order to test the actor/observer hypothesis under more controlled circum- stances, the researchers set up a situation in which criminology students were offered inducements to help take part in the theft of records from a local business firm. The experiment was carried out by having a private detective present the students with an elaborate plan for the burglary. For their part, subjects were offered inducements which included a US$2,000 payment or the chance to perform a patriotic service for the federal government. Other subjects acted as observers in the study; that is, they were given descriptions of the crime and asked to explain why the burglars took part in it. From our perspective, the interesting finding was that a substantial number of the students agreed to take part in the crime (which of course was never carried out).

One of the more serious risks posed by entrapment studies is the possibility that they may change the morals of participants who have been enticed into engaging in disreputable behavior. By the encouragement of dishonest behavior and the creation of opportunities for its convenient occurrence, subjects are placed in situations that differ from their everyday life experiences. Thus, students who find it relatively easy to cheat on an examination during an experiment may be tempted to try again on future occasions, especially if they are not informed about the experiment. Another possibility is that a subject who has either agreed to (or actually performed) a dishonest act such as cheating or a Watergate-like burglary as a result of entrapment might experience subsequent guilt or a loss of self-esteem. Anxiety about the behavior being found out by the experimenter or others (police, college administrators, etc.) is another potential outcome.

Although for a majority of entrapment studies the infractions are so minor or common that serious negative effects are unlikely, the closer the contrived situations are to real life, the more difficult the issues become. Providing students with easy opportunities to commit infractions of the rules in a computer simulation exercise or video game produces fewer risks than enticing them to cheat on an actual course exam. Freeman and Ataov (1960) carried out their cheating study in such a way as to ensure that students' grades were not influenced by their cheating. However, in such studies there is always the possibility that the results can have lingering effects. A professor who learns that students cheated during an experiment or agreed to commit a burglary may become unduly suspicious of their honest academic efforts, and so on. Thus, it is essential that researchers who use this experimental procedure do everything possible to protect the confidentiality of data and take steps to eliminate the likelihood that individual subjects can be identified.

Webb et al. (1981) suggested that entrapment studies may be less troublesome when the honesty of people in positions of public trust, such as taxi drivers, physicians, and automobile mechanics, is studied. Because these individuals occupy roles that have some bearing on public welfare, the potential benefits to society may outweigh the risks involved. Even so, after considering the various issues involved, Webb et al. (1981, p. 270) correctly advised that researchers should be "cautious and sparing in their use of procedures which involve entrapment" because of the potential ethical jeopardy in which participants are placed.

Participant-observation studies

For many aspects of group behavior that do not lend themselves to ready observation, such as delinquency in street gangs, homosexual practices, and the customs of primitive cultures, researchers may elect to gain access by becoming a party to the ongoing activity. *Participant observation* involves a method of observation in which a group or community is studied from within by a researcher who makes systematic notes about what is observed (Rosenthal and Rosnow, 1991). In so doing, it is often possible to grasp the point of view of the participants and to become privy to certain insights about the group (such as its goals or attitudes) that otherwise may not have been available.

Participant observations vary in terms of the researcher's level of involvement in the ongoing activities of the group. The observer may be present without interacting with group members (so-called "passive observation") or may actually engage in the same activities and interact with others as an ordinary participant (so-called "active observation"). Additionally, the extent to which those being studied are aware of the observer can be seen as falling along a disguised–undisguised continuum (Diener and Crandall, 1978). Studies falling at the undisguised end of the continuum are those in which the researcher openly participates in the daily lives of those being studied; the observer's role is something that group members are aware of. An important advantage of the undisguised approach is that after a brief period of adjustment, participants tend to grow used to the presence of the researcher and behave in a natural manner, unaffected by their awareness of the observation. At the disguised end of the continuum are studies in which the individuals who are being observed are unaware of the observer's role or that their behavior is being investigated. Humphreys' (1970) "tearoom trade" investigation is an example of the disguised approach (see chapter 1).

Social psychologist David Rosenhan (1973) utilized the disguised participant-observation approach to investigate the basis of psychiatric diagnosis and the stigmatizing effects of labeling people as "mentally ill." Eight volunteers (including psychologists, a housewife, a pediatrician, and Rosenhan himself) contacted different mental hospitals, misrepresented their identities, and sought admission by claiming to be hearing voices. Once admitted as patients, the researchers stopped complaining of any symptoms and attempted to act normal. Of interest to the observers were patient–staff interactions and the length of time it took before their release from the hospitals. During their stay, the researchers took detailed notes of their interactions with the hospital staff and other patients. Interestingly, the researchers never were recognized as sane by the hospital staff, but eventually were discharged (after a period ranging from 7 to 52 days) as "schizophrenics" whose illness was said to be "in remission." Rosenhan concluded from the results that diagnostic labels tend to stick, regardless of one's subsequent behavior.

As these examples suggest, disguised participant observation is an effective approach for gaining access to phenomena otherwise unavailable to researchers, and has the advantage of minimizing the potentially disruptive effects of the observations on the individuals being studied. The fact that the observations are disguised, however, raises certain issues that are less relevant when the observer is known to the participants. There is the possibility that embarrassment, anger, or other negative reactions may result if participants learn of the deception during the course of the study or if confidential information is made public. Because of the covert nature of the observations, possible invasions of privacy also must be considered, as well as the possibility that individuals will behave in ways that they would rather not have made known to a researcher.

If the criterion of publicness of behavior is applied to considerations of privacy infringement, it is clear that although most disguised observations take place in public settings, there may be a degree of privateness involved (e.g. when observing psychiatric patients). An important related issue has to do with the extent to which subjects' anonymity is protected. It appears that most participant observers are inclined to protect the identity of their participants. Humphreys, for example, kept all identifying names of his participants in locked storage and destroyed them after the completion of the interviews so that identities could not be traced. In fact, although some have argued that disguised participant observations are unethical because of the misrepresentation involved (Erikson, 1967; Jorgenson, 1971), there is substantial evidence that behavioral scientists are aware of the ethical problems and typically take steps to minimize any negative effects (Reynolds, 1979). The potential benefits for the groups involved (e.g. greater sensitivity to the problems experienced by homosexuals or hospitalized mental patients) can be considerable.

ETHNOGRAPHIC RESEARCH

Sociologists, cultural anthropologists, and a growing number of applied researchers are apt to use undisguised participant observations when seeking to describe cultures or groups in their natural context, an approach more commonly referred to as *ethnographic research*. With this approach to naturalistic research, a key ethical requirement is for the researcher to accept the existing social context by acting as an objective observer, rather than attempting to impose one's own norms and values (Oliver, 2003). Because the language of the culture being observed typically is not the native language of the researcher, bilingual assistants may be required in order to frame interview questions in the indigenous language of the culture.

An example of undisguised participant observation is apparent in the work of John Haviland (1977), an anthropologist who lived for ten years in Zinacantan, a small Mexican village. Haviland kept meticulous ethnographic records, including tape recordings of conversations, which he analyzed in order to determine the functions of gossip in the Zinacantan community. Although the participants were aware of his anthropological role, they were not informed that one of Haviland's main interests was their gossip. By living and working within the community as an active participant, Haviland eventually was treated as just another villager and so he was able to record relatively natural conversations.

Despite the apparently benign nature of Haviland's research, the fact that he lived for an extended period of time among the Zinacantan people suggests that their behavior was under continuous, long-term scrutiny. As a result, it is clear that issues of privacy are relevant even when an ethnographic participant observation of this kind is undisguised. The observed individuals can become so comfortable with the researcher that they unintentionally reveal opinions or information that they would have preferred not to have recorded. This is particularly likely to happen in informal contexts, where the researcher may be viewed as having stepped outside of the role of scientist. It also is possible, because of the reactive nature of this approach, that the researcher's presence will affect the behavior of individual group members, thereby influencing their interactions not only with the researcher but with each other as well. Social relationships could be affected and group cohesion weakened.

In order to overcome such shortcomings, researchers may prefer to disguise their observations. Of course, disguised ethnographic research also invites a number of potential ethical problems. This was evident following a study conducted by Carolyn Ellis, a sociologist who periodically resided during a nine-year period among a group of Guinea watermen living in the tidewater region of the American state of Virginia (Allen, 1997). Ellis's interest was to study the kinship network of the Guineamen, which she conjectured to lack external social mechanisms necessary for the subculture to prosper (such as a strong sense of community beyond the extended family, economic cooperation, and commitment to the church). Ellis (1986) ultimately published the prizewinning book *Fisher Folk*, in which she described her ethnographic experience. Although she concealed her subjects' identities by using pseudonyms, the descriptions of the fishing families were not at all flattering – they were described as illiterate, obese, poorly dressed, lacking in basic hygiene, and bearing a characteristic fishy smell. Once the book was brought to the attention of the Guineamen, they were incensed to learn that Ellis, whom they had fed and housed on many occasions, was simply using them for sociological research. In her view, the fact that she never let on that she was a sociologist who was conducting research was indispensable to the success of the research project (Allen, 1997, p. 32):

> I know I did them an injustice. But I couldn't have done the study any other way. My study was predicated on my getting close to them, and if you're constantly reminding people that you're not one of them, you can't do that . . . I didn't want to make people suspicious of me.

The use of qualitative, ethnographic methodologies in such fields as consumer behavior, sociology, urban development, and communication research has brought a growing number of researchers closer to their participants, in terms of physical proximity and intimacy, thereby increasing the salience of various ethical considerations (Sojka and Spangenberg, 1994). In participant observation studies like those conducted by Haviland (undisguised) and Ellis (disguised), the increased involvement in terms of time spent and interactions with research participants lies at the heart of ethical dilemmas encountered by the ethnographer, a point that is emphasized in the following comments by counseling psychologist Beth E. Haverkamp (2005):

> The greater level of engagement offered the researcher is paralleled by a greater level of engagement for participants and is reflected in the characterization of research data as cocreated through the lens of each one's experience. Participants may be involved at intense levels of emotion and disclosure. In some participant observation ethnographies or participatory action studies, they may maintain their involvement over several years and may be collaborators in selecting research questions or analyzing data. As a result, researchers may be faced with difficult decisions about dual relationships, conflicts of interest, and obtaining informed consent.

Several of the difficult decisions to which Haverkamp alluded were identified in interviews with some noted contemporary ethnographers, each of whom is currently using the qualitative, participatory approach in the investigation of consumer behavior (see Box 5.5). One of the problems that was described during the interviews was that of role conflicts that emerge from the researcher's obligations to multiple stakeholders, an issue discussed in greater detail in chapter 6. For example, one ethnographic researcher had been hired by the American aid organization CARE to carry out research in Chad focusing on helping people make the transition from receiving aid to being self-sustaining. The work of CARE was extremely important because it was the only social institution working in Chad at the time. On one occasion, a town merchant showed records to the ethnographer indicating that Chad employees working on the project were diverting aid. Because of the researcher's independence, he was asked if he could do something about this. The researcher was placed in a quandary because the workers were generally very efficient, were delivering a lot of aid, and were just skimming a minimal amount. He eventually went to the CARE staff, told them he had information about aid diversion, and, when asked, provided more information. Nonetheless, the researcher felt that this was an issue of breaching confidentiality.

INTERNET RESEARCH

As an increasing number of behavioral scientists begin to exploit the potential of the Internet and other emerging technologies for research purposes, it is likely that new ethical dilemmas will be encountered and some familiar ones will be recast in a different light (Birnbaum, 2003). In their analysis of issues pertaining to Internet-based research, Nosek, Banaji, and Greenwald (2002) identified three key differences between Internet research and standard laboratory research: (1) the physical absence of a researcher, (2) the questionable adequacy of informed consent and debriefing procedures, and (3) the potential loss of participant anonymity or confidentiality.

The absence of an investigator to a certain extent reduces the potential for coercion and thus represents an ethical benefit of Internet-based research. However, this also means that the researcher likely will be unable to respond to participant concerns or adverse reactions once the study is under way. Moreover, should the participant choose to withdraw early from a study, this will undermine the possibility that an adequate debriefing can be conducted. Thus, special care must be taken to assure that the informed consent process is thorough and includes clear instructions that will enable debriefing for those persons who leave the study early. In order to protect against the possibilities that data may be intercepted by a third party or accessed once stored in files on an Internet-connected server, researchers should take all steps necessary to secure data in order to protect respondent anonymity (Sharf, 1999).

Nosek et al. (2002) recommended several options for debriefing Internet participants, even in situations where they drop out before the completion of a study:

Box 5.5   Ethical conflicts in ethnographic research

A range of ethical conflicts are likely to emerge when researchers become active participants in the cultural or social contexts of persons they investigate. One of the key issues emerges when the researcher must decide whether to use passive deception in terms of informing people that they are part of an ongoing research investigation. This is in large part attributed to the fact that in the natural context, the distinction between everyday life and research often blurs. This is just one of the key points that emerged during the course of informal interviews with five noted ethnographic researchers, and that should be considered prior to the onset of the observational study. Some of their more revealing comments appear below.

- Key issue that is difficult to judge: Where does a conversation end and research begin? Everything that a field researcher sees is potential research. If you have a conversation with someone and later decide to use it as research, do you need to go back to that person and get consent? If filming – it is okay in a public place without getting consent. But what is a public place? How about the campus of a private university?
- Informed consent doesn't always apply. If observing for a year, how often do you get consent? What if you are working with people in developing countries – do they understand consent?
- In videography/photography, IRB would say that data should be destroyed after research is complete. But what if you want to keep a permanent record, or show the material at a conference? At some universities, the Film department or the Journalism school, could collect the same information (films, interviews) as a social scientist, and not have to go through the IRB, because their work is not considered research but art/news. So there is a double standard.
- As a researcher you are supposed to play an objective role. For example, I worked on a project in Thailand on prostitution. A gay male was seeking reassurance that his behavior was safe. You need to be objective for the research, but there is a moral obligation to intervene.
- IRB guidelines don't work well in fieldwork because if you are observing 2000 people, you can't give each of them a consent form. [This ethnographer, who conducts research at specific events, such as conventions, claimed that he does obtain permission from the event holders. When filming an interview he asks permission and uses consent forms.]
- In general, ethnographic research on consumption doesn't use deception. The approach includes letting informants know that we are studying them so they have the maximal possibility of telling us about whatever we are interested in. Since we watch them in their everyday lives over a prolonged period of time, there is little concern that they will go to such efforts to try to deceive us, necessitating our preemptive strategy of deceiving them first.

Source: Based on interviews conducted by consumer behavior researcher Jill Klein, in preparation for an article on deception in consumer research (Smith et al., 2005).

1   Debriefing statements could be forwarded later to an e-mail address provided
    by participants at the outset of the study (assuming the research does not
    require full anonymity).
2   The researcher could include a "leave the study" button on each page, which
    would direct subjects to a debriefing page prior to their dropping out.
3   The computer program could automatically present a debriefing page if the
    participant prematurely closes the browser window.

In addition to these strategies, Nosek et al. suggested that additional debriefing
components could be added that vary across persons, including the provision of a
list of frequently asked questions (FAQs) that address concerns, clarify that such
concerns are common, and emphasize the importance of the research; an e-mail
address for contacting the researcher at a later time; and arranging to have the
researcher available in an online chat room in order to respond interactively to
participants' subsequent questions and concerns.

In recent years, Internet chat groups, bulletin boards, user groups, and listservs
have been studied through the emerging methodology of *netnography*, a research
approach derived from ethnography (i.e. "ethnography on the Internet"), with the
potential to provide researchers with a rich source of qualitative information about
online communities (Kozinets, 1998). Netnography uses information that is publicly available in Internet forums to identify and understand the needs and decision
influences of relevant online groups. Online content has been exploited for research
purposes by researchers in such fields as sociology, cultural studies, and consumer
research and is likely to serve as a focus of research for many years to come. For
example, netnography has been used by marketing researchers to obtain information on the symbolism, meanings, and consumption patterns of consumer groups.

One type of online consumer group that has been the focus of growing interest
is the *brand community*, a non-geographically bound collective of brand admirers
characterized by a structured set of social relations (Muñiz and O'Guinn, 2005).
In recent years, brand communities have evolved for motor vehicles (e.g. Saab,
Jeep, Harley Davidson), TV programs and films (e.g. Star Trek, Star Wars),
beverages (e.g. Pepsi-Cola, Starbucks), and toys (e.g. Barbie). The Internet has
been integral in the development of brand communities, largely because it facili-
tates the means by which community members – who typically have never met –
can communicate and develop strong connections to one another. Thus, the
Internet has proven to be an ideal milieu for researchers to study the brand
community phenomenon.

One of the most salient ethical concerns relevant to the investigation of online
content has to do with the determination of what is public and what is private.
Many people consider the typical chat room to be public behavior, because it is
typically open to anyone who chooses to participate. This is likely to remain the
accepted view, at least until a more complete set of guidelines for Internet-
mediated research is developed. A related concern pertains to how researchers
present themselves online. Although it would be relatively easy to pass oneself off
as just another participant, the general consensus among netnographers appears
to be that researchers should disclose their identities honestly. In research on

brand communities, for example, it has been found that such online groups are quite exclusive and will not admit participants who do not appear to be genuinely committed to the focal brand (Muñiz and O'Guinn, 2005). This would argue against the researcher pretending to be a brand admirer, which in this case would represent a clear case of active deception likely to be perceived as unacceptable by the participants. Brand community members, on the other hand, are apt to respond favorably to receiving attention from a researcher, given that the scientific interest could bring added prestige to the brand.

There currently exist few professional and legislative guidelines for the conduct of online research or netnography (see chapter 7 for a discussion of the Internet standards developed by the American Marketing Association). However, Mathy, Kerr, and Haydin (2003) offered some useful recommendations for Internet-mediated research. In their view, at a minimum, the Internet researcher must carefully adhere to the basic ethical principles of respect for autonomy and non-maleficence (i.e. protection from harm). This can be accomplished in large part through the development of appropriate protocols for obtaining the informed consent of participants, such as the following:

1   Individuals who are willing to participate in a survey investigation could be required to first submit an e-mail request for a copy of the instrument, along with a statement that the study's purpose, risks and benefits, intensity, and duration are clearly understood. This e-mail could then be accepted as an indication of informed consent.

2   It now is possible to have research instruments hosted on a web page, thereby enabling researchers to download responses directly to a database. With cybersurveys of this sort, informed consent is provided on the first web page, which can be designed so that authorized participants must enter a unique password acknowledging that they have read and understand the informed consent protocol. Authorized participants can obtain the password from designated professionals affiliated with the study.

3   The web page address containing the research instrument could be restricted to persons who have specifically been selected to participate in the study. The web page can be designed to include a box that must be checked, indicating that participants have given their informed consent. Only then would it be possible to access the measurement items. However, this approach is possible only when the location of the web page is specifically protected and the host page is not accessible by an Internet search engine.

According to Mathy et al., one of the keys to protecting participants from harm is the guarantee that they are using a computer and Internet access with proper physical safeguards and password protection locks. These are necessary in order to prevent unauthorized disclosure of confidential information that can be disseminated via the Internet.

Taken together, these various recommendations for protecting the rights of participants in online research represent novel strategies for overcoming some of the barriers to informed consent, debriefing, and protection of privacy and confidentiality of data that are imposed by Internet technology. It is essential that researchers continue to search for advanced solutions to these ethical challenges as the technology evolves in years to come.

SUMMARY

It is difficult to arrive at a general conclusion regarding the ethics of field research because of the wide variety of procedures employed by researchers. Some of these procedures involve the simple observation of ongoing behavior in natural settings, while other approaches rely on some form of contrived, covert observation. As a result, the ethicality of each study should be evaluated on an individual basis in light of methodological requirements and participant rights. Because of the tendency for field research techniques to be conducted without the awareness of participants, these approaches have the advantage of causing a minimum of disruption to the behaviors under scrutiny and thereby provide an excellent means for investigating ongoing events and activities. However, because of the covert nature of some of these methods, their potential for infringements of participants' rights to privacy and informed consent must be fully considered prior to undertaking a study.

In a sense, participants in disguised studies, such as simple observations and participant observations, can be seen as indirectly providing their consent to observation when they freely choose to engage in an activity in the presence of another person, especially when the setting is a public one. This point is less applicable to other approaches, such as entrapment studies, in which the contrived situation may vary significantly from the course of participants' everyday life experiences. Regardless of the specific approach, the potential risks posed by field research can be minimized through the use of strategies designed to protect subject anonymity and confidentiality of data.

One problem with many of the research techniques considered to this point is that although they pose few direct negative effects to participants, they may not have much to offer them in the way of direct positive effects either. In chapter 6, we turn our attention to a consideration of issues in research specifically intended to have an impact on society.

6

Applied Research I: Therapeutic and Organizational Research

"The true and lawful goal of the sciences is none other than this: that human life be enriched with new discoveries and powers."

Francis Bacon, *Novum Organum*

"There's nothing as practical as a good theory."

Kurt Lewin, *Problems of Research in Social Psychology*

Chapter Topics

☞ Introduction to applied research
☞ The applied versus basic research distinction
☞ Ethical issues in prevention research
☞ Ethical issues in the helping professions
☞ Organizational research ethics

The application of scientific knowledge to practical issues has long been an important goal of behavioral scientists. The seventeenth-century English philosopher and essayist Francis Bacon was one of the first great thinkers to recognize the value of empirical research as a tool for improving humankind. Similarly, one of the founders of social psychology, Kurt Lewin, firmly believed that theories developed through systematic research are often useful in a practical sense. In the much quoted statement that appears above, Lewin implied that once we have obtained scientific understanding of some aspect of behavior, it should be possible to put that knowledge to practical use. In recent decades, the trend towards application in the behavioral sciences has steadily grown, bringing to the fore a set of special ethical problems inherent in what might be called "real-world" research.

Chapters 6 and 7 focus entirely on the broad range of ethical issues that emerge in the conduct of applied behavioral research, reflecting the steadily increasing involvement of investigators in research activities that are likely to have some sort of impact on society. In this chapter we begin with a brief discussion of the nature and goals of applied research in the behavioral sciences, followed by a description of two illustrative cases of applied studies that have raised ethical issues. The focus then turns to behavioral science applications in some representative applied fields – beginning with social intervention research – in order to illustrate some of the difficult ethical dilemmas that can emerge in applied contexts, along with some suggestions for coping with them.

APPLIED RESEARCH IN PERSPECTIVE

Much of the research that is carried out by behavioral scientists is oriented towards the single goal of understanding a phenomenon, without concern for the relevance or direct usage of the knowledge gained. This is the essence of basic (or "pure") research, which typically is performed in order to obtain knowledge merely for knowledge's sake through the testing of theoretically important hypotheses. For example, researchers might be interested in studying purely scientific questions pertaining to the processes underlying the formation of impressions, the development of group norms, the capacity of short-term memory, and the like.

Applied research, in contrast, is oriented towards the attainment of information that will prove relevant to some practical problem (see Box 6.1). That is, the goal of applied research is to gain knowledge in order to modify or improve the present situation (Shaughnessy and Zechmeister, 1990). Although applied researchers also are interested in discovering the reasons for a phenomenon, their primary goal is to practically apply their findings to "real-life" problems or situations. For example, researchers may carry out studies in order to develop an effective program to reduce racial tensions in a community, to design an advertising campaign for the use of condoms in an attempt to control the spread of AIDS, and so on. In essence, while basic researchers are more interested in comparing what is with what should be in order to determine if a particular theory is adequate, applied researchers attempt to understand the nature of a problem in order to do something to resolve it (Bickman, 1981; Forsyth and Strong, 1986).

The basic and applied facets of scientific inquiry add to the research diversity within each behavioral science discipline. Behavioral scientists examine general questions relevant to their areas of interest, and also seek the solutions to practical problems. For instance, Milgram hoped to obtain the answers to basic questions about the nature of obedience by conducting a series of laboratory investigations to find out who obeys, what social factors influence the level of obedience, and what are the accompanying emotional processes that maintain obedience. His initial interest in examining these questions was stimulated by the atrocities committed during World War II by the Nazis at the direction of malevolent authority.

In addition to shedding light on the psychological variables related to obedience, Milgram's research also yielded insight into socially relevant concerns, suggesting ways that excessive obedience might be prevented. By implying that

Box 6.1   Kurt Lewin and applied research

As an early proponent of the application of behavioral science research to practical problems, Kurt Lewin advanced the idea that theoretical progress and the understanding of social problems are interdependent. Consistent with this notion, Lewin proposed an approach known as "action research" that centers on studying things by changing them and observing the effects of the change. In his view, such an approach could be applied to the analysis of existing social problems and could assist in solving them.

An example of an applied research program carried out by Lewin (1947) during World War II is illustrative of this approach. In a series of experiments, he set out to determine the most effective persuasive techniques for convincing women to contribute to the war effort by changing their families' dietary habits. The goal was to influence the women to change their meat consumption patterns to less desirable, but cheaper and still nutritious, meats; to buy more milk in order to protect the health of family members; and to safeguard the well-being of their newborn babies by feeding them cod liver oil and orange juice.

Lewin compared the effectiveness of two kinds of persuasive appeals by randomly assigning housewives to an experimental condition involving either a lecture or group discussion on the recommended changes. In both cases, the same information about the benefits of the changes was provided. The results of Lewin's research revealed that actively discussing ways to achieve good nutrition resulted in greater changes towards healthier eating habits than passively listening to lectures. For example, 32 percent of those women who participated in a group discussion later reported using the recommended, unfamiliar meats, compared with only 3 percent of the women who had heard a lecture.

Lewin explained the findings by suggesting that group processes had come into play to reinforce the desired normative behavior for those individuals who had participated in the discussions. To some extent, contemporary support groups, such as Alcoholics Anonymous and Weight Watchers, can be seen as part of the legacy of Lewin's wartime research (Brehm and Kassin, 1993).

people who obey malevolent authorities are not necessarily evil and sadistic individuals, his research was useful in revealing the importance of increasing feelings of personal responsibility and recognizing the power of social pressure in combating mindless obedience (Forsyth, 1987). Similarly, some industrial-organizational psychologists are engaged primarily in theoretically based research programs to better understand the factors that are associated with work motivation, job performance, and satisfaction in the workplace – the results of which ultimately might be used to solve practical problems within business and organizational settings.

Behavioral scientists may be employed part- or full-time as applied researchers in industrial settings, market research firms, advertising agencies, hospitals and psychiatric treatment facilities, and government agencies to evaluate the effectiveness of current policies and programs, or to design new ones. For investigators who conduct research in these settings, attention typically is focused on the following kinds of practical questions: What factors help workers resist the adverse effects of job-related stress? How can work be redesigned to maximize efficiency and productivity, without exploiting employees? What variables influence workers' satisfaction with their jobs? Do non-job-relevant personal characteristics such as an applicant's appearance, color, or religion influence the outcomes of job interviews? Which persuasive techniques are likely to influence consumers' interest in a new product? Do special education programs, such as Head Start (a compensatory pre-school program for poor children in the United States), lead to an increase in students' skills (Baron and Byrne, 1994; Forsyth, 1987)?

Another approach to applied research in which investigations are carried out in naturalistic settings is called *social experimentation* (Riecken, 1975). This involves the application of experimental methods to the analysis of social problems and to the development and assessment of interventions to reduce the problems. For example, during the 1970s, the US government experimented with a program designed to assist individuals following their release from prison, in part to help ex-prisoners overcome adjustment problems linked to limited resources and difficulties in finding steady employment (cf. Berk et al., 1987). About two thousand newly released prisoners in Texas and Georgia were randomly assigned to a condition in which they either received or did not receive financial assistance. As is sometimes the case with social experiments, the outcomes of the prison release program were not entirely beneficial. The program resulted in some identifiable positive results, but also was responsible for an increase in crime among some of the financially assisted ex-prisoners, a consequence apparently due to the freedom they were given from having to work.

Social experimentation frequently involves quasi-experimental research designs in which treatments are assigned to subjects on a non-random basis. In essence, *quasi-experiments* resemble true experiments in the sense that they both involve some type of intervention or treatment and outcome measures. Quasi-experimental designs, however, lack the degree of control found in true experiments because there is no random assignment to create comparisons from which treatment-based changes are inferred (Cook and Campbell, 1979). If a researcher wanted to evaluate the effects of low-cost public housing, for instance, it would be difficult or impossible, for administrative and ethical reasons, to randomly assign families to different housing conditions (Rosenthal and Rosnow, 1991). The researcher might instead use a non-equivalent-groups design by comparing families already residing in low-cost housing with families residing in other types of housing.

In one example of an informative quasi-experimental study, researchers investigated the effectiveness of the British breathalyzer crackdown of October 1967, a program initiated as an attempt to reduce drunken driving and, consequently, serious traffic accidents (Ross et al., 1970). A comparison of driving casualties (fatalities plus serious injuries) before and after the breathalyzer crackdown revealed a temporary drop in the accident rate following the onset of the program. In order to rule out alternative interpretations of the data, such as the introduction of safer cars or a police crackdown on speeding, the researchers considered accident rates during the hours British pubs were open (particularly during weekend nights) and during commuting hours when pubs were closed. This analysis revealed a marked drop in the accident rates during weekends and a less notable decline during non-drinking weekday hours.

A follow-up analysis by Ross (1973) served to rule out other possible explanations for the apparent breathalyzer effects and helped to explain why the effects were short lived: the British courts increasingly failed to punish drinkers who had been detected by the breathalyzer. Overall, the breathalyzer crackdown research led to the highly useful conclusion that such a program will help reduce serious traffic accidents when used to discourage drunken driving, but only so long as the courts enforce the drinking and driving laws (Cook and Campbell, 1979; Ross, 1973). Despite some potential technical problems, social experiments have been used effectively in a number of countries for the development and evaluation of a wide range of social programs and policies.

Ethics and the basic versus applied research distinction

That behavioral scientists may choose to direct their scientific activity from a purely theoretical or applied orientation has certain implications in terms of ethical responsibilities and the role of values in the research process. While they share certain fundamental principles of research, the main distinction between these two approaches is that basic science remains unchallenged by practical problems, while applied research is essentially atheoretical in nature (Pepitone, 1981). Basic researchers traditionally have viewed their role as an active one in the discovery of truth but a passive one in determining the societal use of their findings. Underlying this position of scientific non-responsibility is the assumption that although research findings can be used for good or bad ends, knowledge in and of itself is ethically neutral. In this light, basic researchers generally contend that their work is value free and morally neutral – as implied by the labels "basic" and "pure" – because their goal is the impersonal pursuit of scientific knowledge for its own sake.

These views have been criticized on various grounds by those who disagree that basic research is value free and morally neutral. For example, some critics consider it immoral *not* to use the knowledge derived from basic research to attempt to reduce real-life behavioral and social problems (e.g. Baumrin, 1970). Others argue that basic research often entails the use of unethical procedures for obtaining knowledge (as when human subjects are mistreated during the course of a theoretical study) and point out the potential destructiveness of some knowledge for personal and social life, such as the undermining of character and social customs (e.g. Smith, 1978). Indeed, it is possible to find examples of past abuses in applications of "pure knowledge," such as research leading to development of the atomic bomb.

Turning to the applied side of the behavioral sciences, it may be argued that research ethics become increasingly important as the results of investigations acquire public policy and other societal implications outside the research profes- sions. For reasons expressed above, this does not mean that responsibility for knowledge produced can be avoided by restricting one's scientific activity to a basic science approach. Conversely, the view that only applied research is ethical because of its assumed potential for social benefits is also inadequate when we consider that some of the greatest breakthroughs in science have come about through basic theoretical research. In fact, moral distinctions tend to blur when the dichotomy between basic and applied science is more closely evaluated, perhaps because the two types of research are not as different as they first may appear. Applied research often leads to theoretical understanding, and theoretical advances permit practical applications. That is, theory does not arise in a social vacuum apart from the concrete events that gave impetus to it, yet theories of behavior must withstand tests of practical application in order to become established within the scientific community (Georgoudi and Rosnow, 1985; Sarason, 1981).

A shift away from a purely theoretical approach has occurred at various stages in the development of certain behavioral science disciplines, such as psychology and political science. However, each attempt at relevance has brought with it a corresponding set of subtle and complex ethical issues (see Isambert, 1987). It has been suggested that some of these issues may have arisen as a result of researchers having failed to consider the ethical implications of using many of their estab- lished laboratory and field procedures in applied settings. Because so much experimental research in psychology, for example, has been based on the ma- nipulation and control of variables, psychologists who attempt to solve practical problems may similarly try to manipulate and control variables in the natural world, perhaps inappropriately (Argyris, 1975). If so, it is easy to understand why many of the ethical dilemmas encountered in theoretical research (such as those involving informed consent, debriefing, and confidentiality) also have appeared in applied settings.

Illustrative examples of ethics and applied research

In contrast to many theoretical investigations in controlled settings, applied studies often deal with significant aspects of social, psychological, political, and economic functioning, and require considerable resources and staff to be conducted adequately. As with other types of research, informed consent, the protection of subjects' privacy rights, and confidentiality constitute the primary responsibilities of applied researchers in maintaining respect for their research participants. In the event that the participants in applied studies are inadvertently harmed as a result of the research, compensatory measures, including health and medical care, and economic, social, and other types of reparation must be available.

One of the most serious issues to be considered in applied contexts has to do with the possibility that an investigation will have unintended adverse effects. Some applied studies in fact have resulted in unanticipated consequences for research participants or society in general, such as the previously described program to assist ex-prisoners and the Cambridge–Somerville Youth Study (discussed below). These studies serve as stark reminders of the potentially damaging effects of applied research in general. Among the additional ethical issues inherent in applied research are those involving the methodological requirements of random selection and the assignment of participants to experimental conditions. In this regard, the use of volunteer subject groups and the appropriateness of including untreated control groups in social intervention studies have posed ethical problems for researchers. For researchers employed in applied settings, other issues are likely to emerge when the multiple roles and responsibilities inherent in their work give rise to ambiguous and conflicting expectations. A behavioral scientist employed in an organizational setting, for example, might disapprove of the goals and strategies of the organization or question the fairness and justification of certain management decisions (Walton, 1978).

Before we consider these issues in greater detail as they apply to specific applied areas, two brief cases of applied research are presented: (1) the New Jersey negative income tax study and (2) the quality-of-work-life experiment at the Rushton Mining Company. These examples are illustrative of some of the ethical problems that can arise as a result of the applied research process.

The New Jersey negative income tax experiment

This social experiment was designed to assess the impact of guaranteeing poverty-stricken American families a certain minimum income (Allen, 2002; Kershaw and Fair, 1976; Pechman and Timpane, 1975). Despite its positive goals, the study ultimately led to considerable public and governmental concern about privacy issues. The project involved the support of low-income families with monetary sums (i.e. "negative taxes") representing various percentages of the poverty level, ranging from US$1,000 to US$2,000 per year. In order to avoid the disincentive to work, the amount provided was reduced by a graduated percentage of the base level if the family's income rose above the level of the payments.

Because the study could not be distributed randomly on a nationwide basis, the decision was made to restrict it to an area including the state of New Jersey and nearby Pennsylvania cities; however, similar studies also were carried out in other states (see Haveman and Watts, 1976) and Canada (Hum and Simpson, 1991). In the New Jersey study about 1,300 families were randomly divided into seven experimental groups, which differed in terms of income guarantee levels and tax rates assessed on earned income. A no-payment control group also was included, consisting of families who were free to use the regular welfare services available to poor families. (The control families did receive US$10 per month to compensate for time spent completing monthly questionnaires.)

Participants in the study were interviewed before, after, and every three months during the experiment, and were asked to complete detailed questionnaires. One of the most important findings was that the subsidy did not appear to have demoralizing effects on the participants; that is, the families did not stop working when they received a guaranteed minimum income. Nonetheless, the experiment was not without its pitfalls. Although the families had been promised confidentiality, local law enforcement agents viewed the project as an opportunity to check on welfare cheating and attempted to obtain the confidential information in order to expose tax fraud. Individual records containing participant identification and limited information eventually were demanded by a grand jury and a congressional investigating committee. Having promised in good faith to protect respondents' data, the researchers were placed in a difficult position by these actions, and were uncertain as to whether that promise could be kept if a court issued a subpoena. Eventually, the officials were convinced to discontinue their demands for relevant data, but not before the release of 14 records at one site and the identification of 18 families participating in the experiment at a second site.

Despite the lack of serious consequences, the negative income tax experiment illustrates the problems that can arise when external demands are made for the disclosure of information elicited under a promise of confidentiality. Similar conflicts between research requirements and legal standards are prevalent in applied research on other sensitive topics, such as drug use and criminal behavior. One additional consideration regarding the negative tax experiment has to do with the dilemma that occurs when a beneficial experimental program is terminated. For example, the abrupt reduction of family income may have resulted in adverse effects for some of the individuals involved.

The Rushton coal mine experiment

Whereas the negative income tax study mainly involved privacy and confidentiality issues, the Rushton field experiment raised issues concerning perceptions of unfairness relative to the establishment and treatment of experimental groups. Developed on the basis of earlier research carried out in the UK (Trist et al., 1963), the 1973 Rushton project was designed to improve the quality of work life at the Pennsylvania mining company (Blumberg, 1980; Goodman, 1979). Specifically, the researchers hoped to improve employee skills, safety, and level of job satisfaction while at the same time maximizing the company's productivity and earnings (Blumberg and Pringle, 1983).

Following an extended period of preparation, an experimental group of volunteers was organized which was to have full responsibility for the production in one section of the mining operations. The volunteers were encouraged to step out of their traditional roles and were extensively trained in effective mining and safety practices before they were left to coordinate their own work activities. Relative to the other workers in the rest of the mine, the volunteer group had the distinct advantages of being paid at the top rate as the highest-skilled job classification in the section and had greater control over the nature of their work.

At this point, the reader perhaps can imagine what happened next at Rushton. The other workers (i.e. the untreated control group), angered by the "haughty" attitude of the volunteers and suspicious of their receiving additional benefits from the company, developed a strong resentment towards the company and the volunteers. Control subjects complained that the volunteers did not deserve a higher salary than more senior employees in the company. Additionally, rumors began to circulate throughout the mine that the volunteers were "riding the gravy train," that the company was "spoon-feeding" them, and that the researchers were "pinko" college people who intended to "bust the union" (Blumberg and Pringle, 1983). With these signs of impending conflict in the air, a decision was made to abruptly terminate the experiment.

Unlike the other cases that we thus far have considered, the Rushton experiment is unique in the sense that the ethical problems did not emerge as a result of the use of deception, invasion of privacy, or related procedures, but because some participants perceived that they were at a disadvantage relative to others in the experiment. That is, a sizable number of non-volunteers believed that it was unfair not to receive the same benefits enjoyed by the experimental work group. This issue is reflected in related situations, such as in biomedical research that includes placebo-control groups (i.e. comparison conditions consisting of subjects who are administered substances without pharmacological effects as "drugs"). In such studies there are potential ethical costs in not providing treatment to some subjects, particularly if the experimental treatment is shown to be effective. As a result, it may be more ethically appropriate to provide a "common" or "usual" treatment to control subjects.

The negative tax experiment and the Rushton mining project suggest that action research can frequently have its own problems, quite apart from those encountered in more theoretically oriented studies. Some of these problems are described in greater detail below as we turn our attention to other areas of applied research activities.

ETHICAL ISSUES IN PREVENTION RESEARCH

As a form of social intervention, *prevention research* involves the experimental or quasi-experimental investigation of natural behavior in community settings. The overriding goal of such research is the prevention of psychological and related problems, not their treatment once they have become manifest. Unlike most theoretical research programs, the participants in preventive research projects, who often come from low-income and minority populations, stand to benefit directly from their involvement in the research. In essence, prevention research is intended to discover ways to offset human suffering by intervening prior to the appearance of a maladjustment problem.

Prevention studies tend to involve interventions that are educational in nature, oriented towards teaching people different ways to think, behave, and interact in order to protect them from depression (e.g. Cardemil, Reivich, and Seligman, 2002; Le, Muñoz, Ippen, and Stoddard, 2003; Muñoz et al., 1982), difficulties in interpersonal relationships (e.g. Conger, Cui, Bryant, and Elder, 2000; Spivak et al., 1976; Spivak and Shure, 1974), behavior putting them at risk for AIDS (Arp, 2004; Rotheram-Borus, 1991), drug abuse (e.g. Polich et al., 1984), and other potential adjustment problems (e.g. Greenberg, Domitrovich, and Bumbarger, 2001; Lochman, 2000; Nelson, Westhues, and MacLeod, 2003). For example, pre-schoolers from disadvantaged homes, recently divorced people, individuals functioning under high-stress conditions, adolescent runaways, and parents fitting patterns indicating that they may become abusive towards their children might be seen as "at risk" populations. Once such groups are identified, they can be recruited for appropriate intervention programs, including educational, psychotherapeutic, and coping-skills training.

Values play an important role in preventive intervention studies because the ultimate goal is to prevent mental health patterns the researcher believes are potentially damaging to others (Mulvey and Phelps, 1988). As a result, ideologies often enter into decisions as to what should be prevented (Keith-Spiegel and Koocher, 1985). Despite the humanistic intentions of prevention research programs, several complex ethical issues can arise from this research activity (see Table 6.1).

In measuring the success of prevention efforts, it often is necessary to collect data concerning subjects' economic and social status, home and family relationships, and mental and physical well-being longitudinally over extended periods of observation (sometimes lasting for several months or years). Data often must be stored for long periods of time and may become accessible to a variety of persons and interest groups. Thus, ethical problems relevant to invasion of subjects' privacy and the extent to which confidentiality can be guaranteed for future use of data may become particularly salient in ongoing prevention studies (Blanck et al., 1992; Sieber and Sorensen, 1991). To illustrate, one planned investigation involved a private consulting group's attempts to develop a drug prevention program in a local high school (cf. Boruch and Cecil, 1979). The researchers intended to use a personality inventory in order to predict which of the students were likely to become drug abusers. Once identified, the potential drug abusers then were to be referred to supportive services. However, as a result of a civil suit, *Merriken* v. *Cressman*, the court ordered the project to be halted, partly on the grounds that records on the students' propensity to use drugs would not be kept confidential. Despite the researchers' good intentions to the contrary, it was concluded that record dissemination was virtually uncontrollable.

Table 6.1 Ethical issues in prevention research

1 Privacy and confidentiality, especially in longitudinal prevention studies
2 Informed consent and coercion of participants in studies that may significantly affect their life experiences
3 Unanticipated adverse effects resulting from interventions
4 Effects of labeling research participants as "at risk"
5 Creation of dependencies on research-related resources
6 The use of untreated control groups
7 Selection of individuals for participation in preventive programs

Like privacy and confidentiality, informed consent becomes especially important in preventive intervention programs, primarily because individuals may be strongly influenced by the research, much more so than is typical in purely theoretical investigations. When subjects may be permanently changed by an experiment, the importance of voluntary participation is magnified. Special care must be taken to inform potential subjects about their rights and obligations, the procedures they will undergo, potential risks and anticipated benefits, and their freedom to withdraw at any time. When minority group members, children, and non-English-speaking subjects are being studied, informed consent may be especially problematic. For these persons, there are likely to be limited possibilities of articulation and understanding to adequately judge the purpose, risks, and other aspects of the investigation. These limitations further threaten the adequacy of the informed consent process and increase the danger of coercing relatively powerless individuals into prevention programs. (Issues relevant to the use of special populations for research purposes are discussed further in chapter 8.)

Unanticipated consequences of prevention research

There are a number of unforeseen ways in which new research innovations can have harmful effects on individuals, and investigators need to be aware of potential unintended consequences prior to carrying out a prevention study. That preventive research can be damaging to the individuals they are designed to benefit is a danger that can be easily overlooked or minimized (Lorion, 1983). This was apparent in the aforementioned program that led to an increase in crime among financially assisted ex-prisoners. Another illustration was provided by Joan McCord (1978) in her 30-year follow up of the Cambridge–Somerville Youth Study (Powers and Witmer, 1951), a prevention program aimed at delinquent youths. The origins of the Cambridge–Somerville project can be traced to 1939 when Richard Clark Cabot, a social philosopher and physician, began an experimental program intended to prevent delinquency among adolescent males in Boston. Cabot's research involved 506 boys (aged 5 to 13), half of whom had been judged as "difficult" or delinquency prone, with the others considered as "average." An equal number of boys from each group were randomly assigned to a prevention-oriented counseling program, where they received tutoring, medical assistance, and friendly advice for approximately five years. The remainder of the subjects were assigned to a no-treatment control group.

More than 30 years later, McCord and her research team conducted an evaluation of the Cambridge–Somerville project in order to assess its long-term effects. Through the use of official records and personal contacts, the researchers were able to obtain information on 95 percent of the original participants. Although it was found that the subjective evaluations of the program were generally favorable among those who experienced it, the objective criteria revealed a quite different, disturbing picture. None of the matched comparisons between the treatment and control groups showed that Cabot's prevention program had improved the lives of treated subjects; instead, the only significant differences favored those who had *not* experienced the intervention. Subjects who had participated in the delinquency prevention program were more likely than non-treated subjects to have become alcoholics, suffered from more stress-related and mental illnesses, died at a younger age, tended to be employed in lower-prestige occupations, and were more likely to commit second crimes.

In short, McCord's findings revealed not only that the Cambridge–Somerville project failed to achieve one of its basic goals in preventing treated subjects from committing crimes, but also apparently produced negative side effects. Unfortunately, such findings in prevention research are hardly unique. In another community-based intervention program, delinquents and adolescents identified as potential delinquents were matched with adult "buddies" from their neighborhoods (Fo and O'Donnell, 1975). The program apparently helped those with criminal records, but those participants without records of criminal offenses from the year preceding the program committed *more* major offenses in the following year than untreated controls. Other examples of prevention programs that have resulted in unintended negative consequences have been described by Gersten et al. (1979) and Lorion (1984).

Preventive interventions can result in unanticipated consequences in a number of subtle ways. For example, treated subjects in the Cambridge–Somerville project may have become overly dependent on agency assistance, thereby causing them to experience resentment when the outside assistance no longer was forthcoming (McCord, 1978). Further, the treatment program may have increased the likelihood that participants perceived themselves as being in need of help in order to justify receiving the program's services. Fo and O'Donnell (1975) reasoned that treated youngsters in their study with no criminal records may have formed relationships with offenders as a result of their participation in the buddy program, which consequently raised the probability of their committing crimes as well. Thus, exposure to certain uncontrollable features of preventive treatments can produce self-defeating psychological and behavioral effects in research participants.

Some additional explanations for the occurrence of unintended effects in prevention research have been suggested by Muñoz (1983). According to Muñoz, intervention strategies that are targeted to alleviate the incidence of conditions known to place people at high risk for psychological problems might instead serve to increase their occurrence. For instance, a program found to be successful in preventing the negative consequences of divorce, such as a reduced ability to function or traumatic effects on children, could make it easier for people to consider divorce. A similar process could operate to cause a corresponding increase in drug and alcohol abuse or premarital sexual relations as individuals become aware of programs capable of preventing the adverse consequences of those behaviors, such as addiction and sexually communicable diseases, respectively.

Some critics might suggest that prevention programs should not be carried out because of their potential for damaging side-effects; however, it is possible to identify some more appropriate ethical responses to these issues. McCord (1978), for instance, concluded her Cambridge–Somerville follow-up by urging readers not to use the findings as grounds for discontinuing social action programs, but rather as a reminder of the need to conduct pilot studies to assess the potentially damaging effects of preventive treatments before introducing them on a wide-scale basis. Another recommendation for dealing with the problem of unanticipated consequences without reducing research on new treatments is to change the focus of the intervention. For example, rather than directing one's research efforts to the prevention of negative outcomes suffered by divorcees, programs could be devised to assist high-risk couples to achieve more fulfilling marriages or to avoid marriage altogether when there are strong indications that it will fail (Muñoz, 1983). Others have suggested that unintended effects can be avoided if investigators are careful in considering the timing of their interventions. Although certain types of behavior targeted for prevention may be apparent in both risk and non-risk populations, they typically will disappear from non-dysfunctional persons. If a researcher attempts remediation efforts too early, the intervention could cause an interruption of this process and the premature labeling of certain individuals as "at risk" (Gersten et al., 1979; Lorion, 1983).

Labeling effects in prevention research

A common strategy in prevention research is to achieve early identification of persons at risk and to modify their environments in order to reduce that risk. This necessitates that significant persons in the environment typically must be alerted of their at-risk status, such as teachers, parents, employers, and perhaps peers. This early identification and labeling of individuals with apparent mental health or behavioral difficulties represents another sensitive issue for prevention researchers. The "at risk" label can result in a stigma that serves to raise the probability that the initial diagnosis will be confirmed (cf. Mulvey and Phelps, 1988; Rosenthal, 1994a).

Research on the effects of labeling children in the classroom has demonstrated that teachers' expectations can operate as self fulfilling prophesies of their students' intellectual growth (cf. Cooper and Hedges, 1994; Rosenthal, 1991; Rosenthal and Jacobson, 1968). Similarly, treatment by parents, teachers, and peers can produce powerful effects on children who are labeled as high-risk delinquents, drug abusers, and the like. The children could become victims of self-fulfilling prophesies in rating and grading, stereotyping, scapegoating, destructive teasing, name calling, and so on. These potential negative effects were taken into account by the courts in the *Merriken* v. *Cressman* case mentioned previously. The agency responsible for developing the prevention program had not anticipated the possible scapegoating and labeling effects of the process used to predict potential drug abusers.

Designing interventions that minimize or avoid the labeling and stigmatizing process represents one way that the potentially negative unintended effects of preventive research can be counteracted. Towards that end, Jason and Bogat (1983) recommend that an entire classroom of youngsters could be exposed to a treatment, with none identified as the specific target of the project. At the conclusion of the intervention the researchers could ascertain whether those youngsters who initially were lagging in basic skills had progressed in performance. Thus, the success of the intervention would be determined without resulting in potentially damaging labeling effects. Other recommended solutions to the labeling problem, such as regional "broadcast" designs and regression-discontinuity designs, are beyond the scope of this book. Discussions of these strategies can be found in Boruch and Cecil (1979), Shadish et al. (2001), and Trochim (1982).

Untreated control groups

When preventive intervention studies are experimental in nature, ethical issues are likely to emerge regarding the use of untreated control groups and other comparison groups. These issues tend to revolve around questions of fairness in terms of who from among a population of individuals is to receive an experimental treatment when all would stand to benefit from it. Is it ethical to designate some needy persons to an untreated control condition for the purpose of comparing the effectiveness of the treatment under investigation? To a great extent, decisions on such questions must be made on the basis of the relative value of the treatment and current alternatives, as well as the immediate needs of participants.

Applied researchers tend to be in agreement that the random assignment of persons to untreated control groups is an ethical practice, so long as the benefits of the treatment are discovered *after* the results are analyzed (Campbell and Cecil, 1982; Schuler, 1982). However, when some direct loss to untreated control subjects can be foreseen prior to carrying out the study, this approach is more difficult to defend, especially when failing to receive a benefit is experienced as a loss by those persons affected. A methodological problem also may arise as a consequence of the random assignment if untreated control subjects become disappointed about their relative deprivation. Such subjects may drop out of the experiment at a greater rate than treated subjects, thereby making it more difficult to assess the true effect of the treatment.

Decisions about the use of untreated control groups can be based largely on a determination of whether there is good reason to believe (based on evidence obtained from previous research) that the effects of a preventive technique will be highly effective, weak, or unknown. It would be difficult to justify the use of no-treatment groups if, in the consensus of experts, a preponderance of prior evidence suggested that the effects of a prevention technique would be strong. In this case, the experimental treatment should be compared not with a no-treatment control group, but with the best treatment available at the time. This approach is potentially more valuable from a methodological standpoint as well. Rather than making a comparison with the untreated control group and perhaps learning that the intervention is better than nothing, one can determine whether the intervention is better than the current treatment of choice.

The use of untreated controls is likely to be viewed as ethically appropriate, even though the preventive intervention is expected to be strong, in research situations where the beneficial treatment could not reasonably be offered to everyone in need because of limited resources. This point has been used to justify the inclusion of untreated, randomly assigned control subjects in Head Start programs for deprived pre-schoolers (Diener and Crandall, 1978). Although placed at a disadvantage, the control subjects would not be unlike thousands of other disadvantaged children around the nation whom the investigators could not possibly have been expected to help. In fact, one can argue that the perception that one has been deprived of a potentially beneficial intervention is but a "focal deprivation," made salient by the existence of the experimental group (Kimmel, 1988a). Except perceptually, control group participants would not be less deprived if the experiment were canceled and no one received the treatment.

Another case in which untreated control groups would be acceptable is that in which participants can experience a successful treatment once the research is completed, or as soon as the effectiveness of the treatment becomes evident, as long as they do not suffer substantially in the meantime. Researchers should recognize their ethical obligation to assist untreated control subjects to whatever extent possible upon completion of an investigation. When a researcher lacks evidence to substantiate the effects of an untested intervention, having subjects serve in an untreated control group would be justified because it is not known whether they would be in a comparatively deficient condition. For situations in which the effects of a preventive intervention are unknown or doubtful, the key issue is whether treated subjects will be harmed or placed at an unfair disadvantage to persons receiving the current accepted treatments.

Summary

The ethical issues involved in areas of applied science in which research participants may benefit directly are numerous and complex. The issues considered above are representative, but they do not comprise all of the potential problems involved in intervention research. For example, there are additional ethical considerations relating to the use of voluntary participants in prevention programs (see chapter 8). Moreover, issues pertaining to unintended adverse consequences, labeling effects, and untreated control groups are not restricted to intervention studies, but also emerge in other kinds of applied studies. Next, we turn our attention to the helping professions (counseling and psychotherapy) and organizational research in order to briefly survey some of the ethical problems that emerge when behavioral scientists carry out research in such contexts.

ETHICAL ISSUES IN COUNSELING AND PSYCHOTHERAPEUTIC RESEARCH

In helping and human service professions like counseling, social work, and psychotherapy, researchers are apt to encounter many of the ethical issues already discussed in this book. What adds to the significance of these issues, however, is that the consequences of ethical decision making are likely to have a direct impact on participants, who may have certain emotional and psychological vulnerabilities.

Much research in the helping professions is oriented to the development and assessment of diagnostic procedures, interviewing and testing skills, and treatments for adjustment or psychological problems. Counselors and therapists are beholden to research that sheds light on why certain professional practices are more effective than others, what guidelines should be followed in structuring an interview with a client, how to best assess whether a patient is showing improvement, and so on. Because the research methods used in providing this information tend to follow the same rigorous scientific approach one utilizes in the conduct of basic research, similar ethical considerations are relevant. Central to these considerations are those pertaining to deception, confidentiality and the right to privacy, cost–benefit assessments, and protection from harm.

Ethical guidelines for the helping professions

Not surprisingly, APA's *Ethical Principles* (2002) has had a dominant influence in providing guidance for both practitioners and researchers in a range of helping fields. These principles, discussed in detail in chapter 2, are worded broadly enough to pertain to research involving clients and patients in applied settings as well as students and volunteers in basic research settings. Thus, applied researchers are obliged to:

- obtain the informed consent of participants (including a description of the research purpose; right to decline participation; and factors likely to influence the decision to participate, such as potential risks and discomforts);
- protect prospective participants from adverse consequences of declining or withdrawing from the study;
- clarify the nature of any professional services used as an inducement for research participation, as well as their risks, limitations, and obligations;
- avoid the use of deception that is reasonably expected to cause emotional or physical distress;
- fully debrief participants with appropriate information about the research, including any deceptions used and their rationale, and take steps to correct any misconceptions or harms that the procedures may have caused.

In addition to the APA code, each helping field tends to have in place its own more specific set of professional standards that must be followed by practitioners as a basic requirement of their professional affiliation. For example, in the United States, members of the American Counseling Association (ACA) must abide by the ACA *Code of Ethics* (ACA, 2002), which sets out professional standards for counselors who work in a variety of educational and social-service settings (e.g. schools, community agencies, rehabilitation centers, mental health agencies, private practice). The ACA ethics code classifies its 25 research standards under four main headings: (1) research responsibilities, (2) informed consent, (3) reporting results, and (4) publication (see Box 6.2). The ACA recommends that when an ethical issue arises that cannot be sufficiently addressed by its code, counselors should follow a seven-step decision-making model (Forester-Miller

Box 6.2   A selection of research standards from the American Counseling Association's Code of Ethics and Standards of Practice

G.1.   Research Responsibilities

a.   Use of Human Subjects. Counselors plan, design, conduct, and report research in a manner consistent with pertinent ethical principles, federal and state laws, host institutional regulations, and scientific standards governing research with human subjects. Counselors design and conduct research that reflects cultural sensitivity appropriateness.

c.   Precautions to Avoid Injury. Counselors who conduct research with human subjects are responsible for the subjects' welfare throughout the experiment and take reasonable precautions to avoid causing injurious psychological, physical, or social effects to their subjects.

e.   Minimal Interference. Counselors take reasonable precautions to avoid causing disruptions in subjects' lives due to participation in research.

G.2.   Informed Consent

b.   Deception. Counselors do not conduct research involving deception unless alternative procedures are not feasible and the prospective value of the research justifies the deception. When the methodological requirements of a study necessitate concealment or deception, the investigator is required to explain clearly the reasons for this action as soon as possible.

c.   Voluntary Participation. Participation in research is typically voluntary and without any penalty for refusal to participate. Involuntary participation is appropriate only when it can be demonstrated that participation will have no harmful effects on subjects and is essential to the investigation.

d.   Confidentiality of Information. Information obtained about research participants during the course of an investigation is confidential. When the possibility exists that others may obtain access to such information, ethical research practice requires that the possibility, together with the plans for protecting confidentiality, be explained to participants as a part of the procedure for obtaining informed consent.

g.   Explanations After Data Collection. After data are collected, counselors provide participants with full clarification of the nature of the study to remove any misconceptions. Where scientific or human values justify delaying or withholding information, counselors take reasonable measures to avoid causing harm.

(Continued)

Box 6.2   (Continued)

G.3.   Reporting Results

a.   Information Affecting Outcome. When reporting research results, counselors explicitly mention all variables and conditions known to the investigator that may have affected the outcome of a study or the interpretation of data.

c.   Obligation to Report Unfavorable Results. Counselors communicate to other counselors the results of any research judged to be of professional value. Results that reflect unfavorably on institutions, programs, services, prevailing opinions, or vested interests are not withheld.

d.   Identity of Subjects. Counselors who supply data, aid in the research of another person, report research results, or make original data available take due care to disguise the identity of respective subjects in the absence of specific authorization from the subjects to do otherwise.

G.4.   Publication

e.   Professional Review. Counselors who review material submitted for publication, research, or other scholarly purposes respect the confidentiality and proprietary rights of those who submitted it.

Source: Reprinted from American Counseling Association (2002), *ACA Code of Ethics and Standards of Practice*. ACA. Reprinted with permission. No further reproduction authorized without permission from the ACA.

and Davis, 1996): (1) identify the problem; (2) apply the ACA ethics code; (3) determine the nature of the dilemma; (4) generate potential courses of action; (5) consider potential consequences of each action and select a course of action; (6) evaluate the selected course of action; and (7) implement the course of action.

Other professional organizations, such as the American Association for Marriage and Family Therapy, the National Association of Social Workers, and the National Organization for Human Services Education, similarly have adopted standards for professional conduct. Additionally, the National Board for Certified Counselors (NBCC) provides expert online advice on ethical issues encountered by its practicing members (www.expertclick.com).

International organizations also have established guidelines for professionals conducting research outside the United States. For example, the International Association of Family and Marriage Counselors (IAMFC, 2006) developed a code of ethics intended to supplement that of the ACA. The IAMFC research standards represent one section of an ethics framework that also includes separate standards on confidentiality and privacy, competence and professional responsibilities, collaboration and professional relationships, assessment and evaluation, and research and publication (see Box 6.3).

> ## Box 6.3 A selection of research standards from the ethics code of the International Association of Marriage and Family Counselors (Section G Research and Publication, IAMFC, 2006)
>
> 1 Members shall be fully responsible for their choice of research topics and the methods used for investigation, analysis, and reporting. They must be particularly careful that findings do not appear misleading, that the research is planned to allow for the inclusion of alternative hypotheses, and that provision is made for discussion of the limitations of the study.
> 2 Members safeguard the privacy of their research participants. Data about an individual participant are not released unless the individual is informed about the exact nature of the information to be released and gives written permission for disclosure.
> 3 Marriage and family counselors protect the safety of their research participants. Researchers follow guidelines of a peer review committee or institutional research board. Prospective participants are informed, in writing, about any potential risk associated with a study and are notified that they can withdraw at any time.
> 4 Members make their original data available to other researchers. They contribute to the advancement of the field by encouraging the research and publication efforts of colleagues.

Like their basic research counterparts, researchers in the helping professions also are required to adhere to governmental regulations and legal strictures, and typically must have their research protocols first approved by an institutional review board. Again, special care must be taken to protect those persons who participate in research conducted within the counseling and therapy arenas, especially given the likelihood that these persons may have been selected because of their status as patients or clients bearing specific vulnerabilities (see Box 6.4).

One criticism that has been voiced with regard to the ethics codes established by helping organizations is that their standards inadequately address the pragmatic needs of culturally disadvantaged groups, such as racial and ethnic minorities (Corey, Corey, and Callanan, 2003). For example, Casas and Thompson (1991) claimed that the codes generally tend to reflect the individually oriented values of the majority culture and fail to take into account the diversity of values and lifestyles of other cultures, to the detriment of their members. Accordingly, Casas and Thompson proposed a set of recommendations for research in the helping professions. For example, they argued that (a) researchers need to expand their traditional counseling studies so that they are more action-oriented in terms of addressing psychosocial problems; (b) fieldwork studies should be carried out in communities so that they can more readily have an impact on real-life problems; (c) research project priorities should be identified and assigned with the assistance of leaders of minority communities; (d) research assistants should be recruited from among racial and ethnic

> # Box 6.4   Components of ethical behavior for researchers in the helping professions
>
> 1 Understanding and implementing ethical codes.
> 2 Doing what is best for the client.
> 3 Practicing the four core virtues (Meara, Schmidt, and Day, 1996) of:
>   • prudence
>   • integrity
>   • respectfulness
>   • benevolence
> 4 Using moral principles to guide ethical decision making.
> 5 Realizing the importance of intuition, integrity, and honest self-evaluation in ethical decisions.
> 6 Placing client welfare as paramount.
>
> *Source:* Bradley and Hendricks (2004).

minorities; and (e) research findings should provide tangible benefits to the targeted minority community. Similar points have been raised by other counseling experts (e.g. Lee, 1991) and consequently there have been encouraging developments in recent years towards recognizing the importance of adopting a multicultural perspective in the design and conduct of counseling research. Codes of ethics in the helping professions also now acknowledge the need for researchers to remain sensitive to the special needs of diverse cultures.

Ethical issues and dilemmas in the helping professions

The specific ethical issues that emerge in the context of research in the helping professions are strongly tied to one's therapeutic philosophy, the nature of client/therapist relationships, the role of the therapist in the helping context, and the prevailing philosophy about the goals of treatment (Corey et al., 2002). Nonetheless, there are certain ethical considerations that are likely to be relevant to much applied research in helping contexts. These are briefly summarized below.

1. *The obligation to evaluate the effectiveness of psychotherapeutic approaches and techniques.* Ethical decision making should focus not solely on a consideration of the costs and benefits of the decision to carry out a study, but also on the potential impact of the decision *not* to do the research. This issue is perhaps no more salient than in the case of research on untested (or partially tested) psychotherapeutic treatments. According to Corey et al. (2002, p. 214), the question as to whether a given psychotherapeutic approach or technique works is an ethical question, in that the failure to attempt to base a helping practice on empirical research findings "is tantamount to asking consumers to simply trust that practitioners know what they are doing." In short, if practitioners use techniques that have not been empirically validated, the services they render may turn out to be ineffective, they may have adverse effects, and they may be considered deceptive on the part of recipients.

2. *Untreated control groups and labeling effects*. Among the ethical issues and potential dilemmas that may be encountered in the conduct of research in the helping professions, some of those that were discussed in the context of prevention research (see above) are especially relevant. Unlike prevention research, therapeutic studies are more likely to focus on treatments intended to assist individuals who are currently experiencing emotional, psychological, or adjustment problems. However, the problems inherent in the use of untreated control groups and potential labeling effects also are likely to emerge and this possibility must be considered prior to designing an investigation. The labeling of participants as patients or clients also raises problems related to confidentiality and the right to privacy. A case example involving the withholding of treatment from distressed individuals for research purposes appears in Box 6.5.

Box 6.5   Untreated control groups in therapeutic research: a case example

Counseling experts Gerald Corey, Marianne Schneider Corey, and Patrick Callanan (2002) described an interesting hypothetical case involving some of the ethical problems that emerge when treatment is withheld from a particular at-risk group during the course of a research investigation. Their example involves a therapist who works with psychotic depressive patients in a state mental hospital, combining both therapy and research activities. The therapist is interested in assessing the effectiveness of a cognitive-behavioral approach, which she is already using to treat the patients in her hospital ward, because she feels ethically obligated to empirically evaluate the effectiveness of the treatment strategies she is administering. That is, despite her devotion to the treatment approach, she is uncomfortable using it without having clear evidence that it in fact is the cause of her patients' apparent improvement.

The therapist decides that the only way to obtain evidence regarding the efficacy of the therapy is to compare treated patients with a comparable group of patients not receiving the treatment. However, this decision has raised some red flags among members of her hospital's ethics review board who are concerned that it is inappropriate for the therapist to withhold an apparently potent treatment from some of the patients on the ward. Assuming you are a member of the hospital's review board, how would you feel about the use of an untreated control group in this case and what would be your final decision regarding the proposed study? Is it necessary to conduct a formal study at all or is anecdotal evidence regarding the effectiveness of the treatment sufficient? What other ethical protections would you recommend for this study? For further guidance in responding to these questions, the reader is advised to review the discussion on prevention research, which appears earlier in this chapter.

3. *Informed consent.* As previously discussed, informed consent is a fundamental requirement of research with human participants, whether in the basic or applied research context. Informed consent protects the autonomy of participants and provides potential subjects with the information they would need to know in order to make a reasoned judgment about whether or not to participate in the research. One issue that often emerges in the therapeutic research context is that the thinking processes of potential participants may be impaired to the point at which a "reasoned" judgment about participation is not possible. For example, it has been shown that up to half of acutely hospitalized schizophrenic patients may have substantially impaired decision-making abilities, including difficulties in reasoning and understanding (Grisso and Appelbaum, 1995). Moreover, schizo-phrenics commonly tend to lack insight into the presence of their illness and need for treatment (Amador et al. 1994). As a result, they may find it especially difficult to anticipate the consequences of their decisions regarding research participation in a general sense, but also as they relate to the risk of future relapse.

In cases where it is likely that potential research participants suffer from limited or impaired decision making, it is the responsibility of the researcher to develop informed consent procedures that are understandable to such individuals, or else they must seek the informed consent of a legal guardian. Additional protections may be necessary in such cases. Ethical dilemmas related to the informed consent requirement are apt to arise in therapeutic research when the researcher believes that the full provision of information about the study may bias the outcome or make it impossible to conduct the research as planned. Thus, the researcher must judge whether it would be ethically acceptable to withhold key details about the study from participants. As Corey et al. (2002) concluded, because clients are investing themselves emotionally and financially in therapy, they have the right to be informed about their status as research participants and about the specific procedures likely to affect them.

4. *Deception.* In addition to the possibility that researchers may choose to withhold certain key information from the informed consent process – in essence, constituting a passive deception – there are situations in therapeutic research in which participants may be actively misled. For example, in order to evaluate the effectiveness of a pharmaceutical treatment intended to reduce depression, an investigator might choose to compare treated participants with a placebo control group, the latter of which consists of participants who are led to believe that they are receiving the active medication when in fact they are not (e.g. they are given a pill that has no active pharmaceutical ingredients). Placebo controls are often utilized in such research in order to eliminate the possibility that effects obtained within the treated group are not solely a function of participant expectations, but rather the active effects of the drug.

Although the methodological justification for the use of deception in such studies is rather evident, its ethical justification is more problematic because of the preexisting distress of the participants. In addition to the decision that the ends justify the means in this case, the researcher (and, likely, a review board) would need to ensure that special care will be taken to protect the participants from harm and that efforts will be taken once the study is concluded to remove any misconceptions or adverse effects linked to the use of deception. Additionally, a decision must be made as to whether debriefing control subjects about the use of deception could cause more harm than good.

5. *Ethical responsibilities to infirmed research participants.* In chapter 8 we consider the various ethical issues concerning the use of subjects from vulnerable populations. At this juncture, however, it is important to point out that these issues are especially likely to emerge in clinical research settings because research participants are more likely to be suffering from an existing psychological or emotional problem.

In one investigation of investigators' ethical responsibilities to participants in preexisting distress, Stanton and New (1988) reported diverse ethical practices and attitudes among researchers, linked in part to the personal attributes of the investigators and the methodological characteristics of their studies. Overall, 67 percent of the researchers claimed to debrief their subjects and 59 percent stated that they provide information regarding treatment resources to select participants. However, the ethical safeguards utilized by the depression researchers surveyed ranged from doing nothing to initiating contact with both the distressed subject and a significant other. In a follow-up investigation, Stanton, Burker, and Kershaw (1991) found that subjects who could expect to receive the most intrusive intervention (i.e. researcher contact with the subject and a significant other) were less likely to report depressive symptoms than comparison subjects who were led to expect a less intrusive intervention. This finding demonstrates how ethical safeguards utilized in studies involving distressed individuals can have methodological consequences (e.g. by jeopardizing the validity of self-report psychological measures).

Ethical issues in the helping professions: summary

This overview of some of the key ethical concerns in the context of research in the helping professions is intended to provide insight into some of the complex dilemmas that can emerge in applied research settings. Before we conclude this section, it should be added that although there are many risks when research is conducted with the involvement of participants undergoing some form of therapy or counseling, there also is the potential for such participants to obtain certain benefits from their decision to assist in the research process. For example, such individuals may experience an enhanced sense of worth from the awareness that they have assisted in a study that ultimately could reveal better ways of treating psychological problems. This outcome, of course, would be a good thing for persons currently experiencing psychological adjustment problems.

Evidence of the beneficial effects of research participation for psychiatric patients was obtained in a study conducted by Kaminsky, Roberts, and Brody (2003), who interviewed 63 schizophrenics – nearly half of whom had previously participated in research – about their attitudes, beliefs, and experiences with regard to psychiatric research. The interviewees held some distinct views about the research process and their involvement in that process. The key factors that emerged included those associated with openness toward research involvement ("motivators") or else served as "deterrents" to lessen interest in participation. For example, motivator factors included a sense of need and available resources, positive perceptions and greater knowledge of research, relationships established with medical and research professionals, ease of participation, and personal values regarding social responsibility. Deterrent factors included absence of trust in science and in researchers, limited knowledge of research, burdens associated with participation, absence of compensation or opportunities, and dangers associated with research participation. Interestingly, the schizophrenics who had prior experience with biomedical studies were likely to give greater importance to motivating factors than to deterrents. The comments of patients who had previous experience in research protocols suggested that they accrued a variety of benefits from their involvement, including an increase in feelings of hope, increased self-awareness, the opportunity to interact with others, validating oneself and one's experience with schizophrenia, and helping others with schizophrenia. In short, when carried out with special sensitivity to the possible risks involved, the research experience can prove to be a rewarding experience for persons receiving care from health care professionals.

ETHICAL ISSUES IN ORGANIZATIONAL RESEARCH

In the remainder of this chapter, our attention turns to ethical issues in the context of research conducted in the workplace, with a particular focus on areas pertaining to human resources and organizational behavior. These areas generally fall under the general heading of industrial-organizational (I-O) psychology which, like consulting and psychotherapy, represents a flourishing applied field within the behavioral sciences. A primary aim of I-O psychology is to increase understanding of how people relate to work settings, with the aim of bringing about improvements (Dipboye, Smith, and Howell, 1994).

Although not technically considered a helping profession *per se*, in fact the ultimate goal of the field of I-O psychology is to address the problems of human organizations and the utilization of human resources within organizations (Miner, 1992). This is done through the development of approaches that serve to enhance the fit between organizations and workers, maximize job performance, and enhance employee work motivation and job satisfaction. Not surprisingly, applied research within organizations tends to focus on these specific areas of concern. For example, applied behavioral scientists often are employed by organizations to carry out investigations that have as their goal the design and evaluation of programs to improve employee satisfaction and motivation, or to enhance employee performance and relations. Another focus of organizational research is directed toward personnel-related issues, including the validation of selection instruments and the testing of employees for personnel decisions. In essence, these kinds of applied investigations are intended to improve an organization's capacities so that it might realize greater profits, improve its employees' quality of work life, or better manage its impact on other institutions or communities in the larger society (Walton, 1978).

Ethical obligations of organizational researchers

When researchers enter into organizational settings in order to conduct an investigation, they are expected to abide by the ethical standards of conduct set forth by their professional organizations (e.g. the American Psychological Association and its division, the Society for Industrial and Organizational Psychology, or SIOP; the American Society for Personnel Administrators; the UK Institute of Management Consultancy; the Academy of Management) and governmental statutes. Additionally, the APA has developed specific resources for practitioners engaged in applied fieldwork in organizations, including *Specialty Guidelines for the Delivery of Services by Industrial/Organizational Psychologists* (APA, 1981b), a casebook on ethics and standards for the practice of psychology in organizations (Lowman, 1998), *Principles for the Validation and Use of Personnel Selection Procedures* (SIOP, 2004), and *Guidelines on Multicultural Education, Training, Research, Practice, and Organizational Change for Psychologists* (2003). These documents represent useful guides for ethical decision making, but tend to emphasize dilemmas that arise in organizational practice as opposed to research (Aguinis, 2001). In fact, as recently as the late 1990s, Wright and Wright (1999) concluded that the ethical responsibilities of organizational researchers remained a neglected topic.

Like other ethical standards discussed in this book, those pertaining to organizational research highlight the researcher's obligation to protect the rights of the users of psychological services (including job applicants, employees, and the organization employing the researcher) from physical and psychological harm, and to maintain a sensitivity to issues involving informed consent, privacy, deception, and debriefing. Additionally, researchers are obliged to establish a system to protect the confidentiality of records and to anticipate and resolve conflicts of interest that may arise in their professional relationships. However, adherence to professional standards, coupled with the best of moral intentions, is unlikely to prevent many ethical dilemmas from emerging in organizational research. In one's attempt to conduct high quality research, the pressures to comply with both professional and company standards, along with the realities of organizational life, place considerable constraints on the organizational researcher (London and Bray, 1980).

During the conduct of research in organizations, investigators may become entangled in a set of multiple roles that are apt to give rise to ethical concerns. For example, consider the case of a psychologist who has been hired by an organization to conduct a series of studies about how best to maximize performance among the workforce. Once greater insight into the organization's operations is obtained, the psychologist may come to question the fairness of, or justification for, certain managerial actions or perhaps disapprove of the goals and strategies of the management team. Instead, it may be the case that the researcher is asked to implement an intervention having consequences that conflict with his or her values. Perhaps complicating matters, it may be that the psychologist never expected to be asked to implement an intervention when originally hired by the organization. Such inconsistencies are likely to present difficult ethical dilemmas for the organizational researcher (see Box 6.6).

Box 6.6   Ethical dilemmas in organizational research: two examples

Dilemma 1:   Confidentiality and employee theft

In his textbook *Psychology Applied to Work*, I-O psychologist Paul Muchinsky (1983) related an ethical dilemma that he encountered after having been commissioned by a company to survey employee opinions and morale. The employees included in the study had been promised confidentiality, but a problem arose when one survey response revealed the existence of employee theft. Muchinsky thus was faced with the dilemma of having to tell management that some theft had occurred but that the employees involved could not be identified – in fact, identification could have been made with relatively little effort – or, alternatively, to ignore it and fail to tell management about a serious company problem.

Ethical dilemmas such as the one described tend not to have obvious solutions, in large part because of the complexity of the applied contexts in which they arise. Although Muchinsky did not reveal the resolution to this case, it is possible to consider ways in which such a dilemma might have been circumvented. For example, during initial meetings with the management team that hired him to carry out the survey, he might have explained his obligation to adhere to his profession's ethical guidelines regarding confidentiality. Once the nature of confidentiality was clarified, an agreement could have been reached about the proper course of action in the event something turned up during the study that could threaten participant confidentiality. Of course, this would require a careful consideration of the various kinds of information that ultimately could pose problems if revealed. Similarly, Muchinsky could have explained to his participants during the informed consent procedure that under certain circumstances, confidentiality might have to be breached.

Dilemma 2:   Anonymity and a Safety Risk

Imagine how the nature of the dilemma described above may have been different if what was revealed during the employee opinion survey was not about the existence of employee theft, but about an unresolved safety issue in the organization that was potentially life threatening. In this example, described in the APA's casebook on ethical issues in organizations

Box 6.6   (Continued)

(Lowman, 1998), an I-O psychologist guaranteed anonymity to all respondents during an employee opinion survey conducted for a large manufacturing corporation. One of the written comments obtained from a participant, which was included in the survey summary presented to management, described the aforementioned safety issue, but provided few specific details. Because of the urgency of the situation, the company asked the psychologist to obtain more information from the respondent so that an action plan could be developed.

In this case, the psychologist was faced with a dilemma involving whether to ignore the safety issue, thereby protecting the anonymity of the participants, or violating the promise of anonymity by identifying and further questioning the respondent who pointed out the safety problem. Although all names and identifiers were deleted from the comments obtained during the survey, the psychologist could have identified the respondent in question on the basis of available data, such as gender, department, and job position.

The psychologist ultimately decided that the safety issue had to be addressed. Unlike the case of employee theft described in the previous example, the safety concern posed risk of physical harm to the employees, in addition to the financial losses that the company would have incurred from a costly accident. However, the psychologist responded in a way that made it possible to bring the safety concern to the awareness of management without compromising, or appearing to have compromised, respondent anonymity. He used demographic data to identify a subset of employees likely to include the respondent of interest, and sent a memo to each person in this group describing the problem. The company's commitment to preserving anonymity was emphasized in the memo, the safety threat was described, and the respondents were asked to anonymously provide any additional information about the threat to the company's safety director.

Ethical issues in personnel selection research

Organizational psychologists often are called on to assist in the development and validation of selection and assessment instruments for human resource decision making. Such instruments, which typically take the form of paper-and-pencil tests, are used for a variety of employment decisions, including hiring, firing, promotion, job assignments, and salary determinations. Because of the potential impact of testing on the lives of job applicants and current members of the workforce, the ethical implications of personnel research can be profound. In addition to the guidebooks on testing already cited (e.g. SIOP, 2004), there are several ethical standards within the current APA code (APA, 2002) that are pertinent to personnel research activities:

Ethical principle A: Beneficence and Nonmaleficence
Psychologists strive to benefit those with whom they work and take care to do no harm.... Because psychologists' scientific and professional judgments and actions may affect the lives of others, they are alert to and guard against personal, financial, social, organizational, or political factors that might lead to misuse of their influence.

Ethical standard 2.01 Competence
(a) Psychologists... conduct research with populations and in areas only within the boundaries of their competence, based on their education, training, supervised experience, consultation, study, or professional experience.

Ethical standard 3.11 Psychological Services Delivered to or through Organizations
(a) Psychologists delivering services to or through organizations provide information beforehand to clients and when appropriate those directly affected by the services about (1) the nature and objectives of the services, (2) the intended recipients, (3) which of the individuals are clients, (4) the relationship the psychologist will have with each person and the organization, (5) the probable uses of services provided and information obtained, (6) who will have access to the information, and (7) limits of confidentiality. As soon as feasible, they provide information about the results and conclusions of such services to appropriate persons.

Ethical standard 9.05 Test Construction
Psychologists who develop tests and other assessment techniques use appropriate psychometric procedures and current scientific or professional knowledge for test design, standardization, validation, reduction or elimination of bias, and recommendations for use.

Ethical standard 9.06 Interpreting Assessment Results
When interpreting assessment results, including automated interpretations, psychologists take into account the purpose of the assessment as well as the various test factors, test-taking abilities, and other characteristics of the person being assessed, such as situational, personal, linguistic, and cultural differences, that might affect psychologists' judgments or reduce the accuracy of their interpretations. They indicate any significant limitations of their interpretations.

In order to illustrate how these guidelines might apply to an applied research example, Lowman (1998) described a case example involving an I/O psychologist hired to develop a selection system for supervisors working in a plant at a large corporation. The company hired about 15 new MBAs and promoted about 15 in-house employees annually to become supervisors, and at the time of the study its complement of supervisors totaled 450. From the outset, company officials made clear to the researcher that there was considerable pressure to demonstrate the effectiveness of a selection system that could save the corporation a significant amount of money.

The psychologist developed the selection approach by proceeding in the following manner. He first identified a typical applicant group by asking company representatives to identify 15 of the best performing and 15 of the worst performing MBAs. Next, he administered an extensive test battery (including cognitive ability, judgment, and biographical items), projective tests, and a structured interview to this group. Additionally, archival data consisting of educational background information (such as college grades and standardized exam scores) were obtained from each employee's personnel file. The psychologist then chose the eight most discriminating scores from the results, which were selected to represent the items for the final selection instrument. A multiple correlation coefficient based on these items was found to be very high. Finally, the psychologist gave an enthusiastic presentation to the company's management and convincingly argued that the battery would have a 95 percent prediction accuracy in the selection of supervisors. Although optimistic about these results, the client voiced some concern that the system would result in the selection of too many intellectuals. In response to that concern, the psychologist added an additional item to the final battery to measure "organizational fit." The new testing program was implemented by the corporation two months later.

At the core of this case, as Lowman (1998, p. 15) pointed out, is that the psychologist was caught in a conflict between "acting in accordance with sound scientific principles and handling pressures that . . . arise from clients to present impressive research results." The result was that the psychologist's conduct was problematic in various respects, including the sampling approach utilized, his communications with the client, the type of research data used to develop the selection system, and the interpretation of the data. For example, had the psychologist adhered to extant test validation standards, he would have recognized the need to first conduct a job analysis in order to determine the requirements of the job for which the selection system would be used. Additionally, a sampling problem was encountered when the psychologist selected the eight most discriminating scores. Because there were 85 separate scores and only 30 participants representing the extremes, this approach capitalized on statistical chance. Contrary to recommended selection testing methods, the psychologist also used instruments in his analysis that were developed and validated for other purposes, and later changed a selection procedure with demonstrated validity by adding an item based on personal judgment. In short, the psychologist failed in this selection project to employ scientifically appropriate validation methods.

One way to overcome such conflicts is for applied researchers to take care not to oversell the potential outcomes of their research to clients. Instead, it is necessary to communicate before initiating validation and other studies that there is the possibility that the research findings will not support prior expectations or may reveal a selection instrument to be less efficient than desired. Moreover, the applied researcher has a professional obligation to be straightforward when informing the client of the actual results, not the results that the client necessarily wants or expects to hear (see Box 6.7).

Creating ethical relationships in organizational research

The various examples described in the preceding sections further illustrate the ways in which ethical dilemmas arise from applied researchers' multiple and conflicting roles within organization settings. According to Mirvis and Seashore (1979, 1982), the very nature of an organization's social system necessitates that researchers approach their participants and attempt to resolve ethical dilemmas differently than they do in non-applied contexts. This is because organizations

Box 6.7 Avoiding ethical pitfalls in applied research

Even when applied researchers are well-informed about potential ethical problems and are knowledgeable about professional ethical standards and laws, the possibility remains that ethical dilemmas will be encountered in practice. According to Anne Hess, a past member of APA's Ethics Committee, this is because many ethical problems are "stealth dilemmas" – that is, "situations that develop gradually, moving step by small step beyond once firm professional boundaries" (Smith, 2003, p. 50). Although each step may have seemed harmless at the time, practitioners may eventually come to realize that they have landed in deep trouble. Deborah Smith, a writer for APA's monthly newsletter *Monitor on Psychology*, developed a list of recommendations for avoiding ethical pitfalls, based on interviews with leading ethics experts. Some of the key recommendations are summarized below.

1 *Understand what constitutes a multiple relationship*. A multiple relationship would be evident in a situation in which the researcher enters into another personal, financial, professional, or other relationship with clients, supervisors, or others for whom the researcher is already professionally involved. For example, an I-O psychologist may be invited to purchase at a discount products that are produced by the company where he or she is contracted to conduct a research project

The APA 2002 ethics code specifies that psychologists should avoid relationships that could reasonably impair their professional performance or that could potentially exploit or harm another party. In order to evaluate the pros and cons of such situations, three factors can be considered: (1) power (a consideration of the power differential between the researcher and the other party); (2) duration (whether the contact will be brief or continuous or episodic over a long period); and (3) termination (whether the professional relationship is understood by both parties to be permanently concluded).

2 *Protect confidentiality*. Researchers must take care to balance their ethical obligations to protect the confidentiality of information they obtain from participants with requests to provide that information to managers and other clients. According to the APA 2002 ethics code, the researcher is only required to disclose minimum information necessary to provide needed services or to protect the client or others from harm. Four safeguards are recommended to help prevent problems related to confidentiality: (a) discuss the limits of confidentiality; (b) ensure the safe storage of confidential records; (c) know the relevant laws; and (d) obey mandatory reporting laws.

3 *Identify your client and role*. When working with organizations, researchers should understand from the outset exactly who they were hired to assist and what their client expected of them. Moreover, it is

Box 6.7   (Continued)

important that researchers remain transparent about their roles and mindful about their professional boundaries. This typically requires having frank discussions with all parties involved about the relationship they will have with each other.

4 *Record and document.* Documentation is an essential protection should the researcher be charged with an ethical indiscretion by a client. The sorts of information that would be relevant to document in organizational settings include dates of service and fees; informed consent procedures; safeguards for protecting confidentiality and anonymity; and phone calls, e-mails, and out of office contacts.

5 *Practice only where you have expertise.* This is an obvious obligation, but difficulties nonetheless sometimes arise, especially when the researcher agrees to take on a project in emerging areas that lack clear standards. The argument also can be made that research professionals may simply be unaware of what they do not know. As one ethics expert described, "If you find yourself falling back on instruments because you feel confident with them and you don't know which others to use, that means you haven't kept up with the advances in that particular area and need to re-examine what needs to be done to be proficient."

(and other applied settings) consist of individuals who not only have hierarchical positions in relation to one another, but collectively in their identity as an organization have relationships with supporters, consumers, government, unions, and other public institutions.

Research participants in organizations cannot be approached as independent individuals, nor can separate ethical guidelines be applied in dealing with employees, managers, sponsors, or clients, because all of these individuals behave within an interdependent framework of rights and responsibilities. It is likely that these individuals will have overlapping interests that sometimes are in conflict. For example, sponsors of an investigation might hold one set of expectations for the researcher, while the organization that employs the researcher holds another. It thus becomes the researcher's responsibility to clarify his or her own role in the situation. Mirvis and Seashore (1982) suggest that by openly communicating their choice of roles to participants, organizational researchers become better able to define their ethical responsibilities in an applied setting, anticipate the risks and benefits of an investigation, and distinguish the corresponding responsibilities of others.

To illustrate how these notions can be applied to an actual research situation, Mirvis and Seashore (1982) described a field experiment conducted in a branch of a large metropolitan bank. The research team worked with a task force of bank employees to implement a new information system and later evaluated its effects on employees' performance and participation. The information system gathered financial, behavioral, and attitudinal data from the bank's records and directly from employees, and the information was fed back periodically to work groups for problem solving and decision making. Despite the rather straightforward nature of the research, a number of ethical questions nonetheless arose. Certain bank managers who felt that the program usurped some of their managerial powers resented the information system, while others who chose not to actively participate felt they had no choice but to adopt the program. Although steps were taken to protect the confidentiality of data, there were concerns that top management would ask to see the branch reports. Further questions were raised about how voluntary consent, privacy, and confidentiality were to be defined in this context and the means by which benefits were to be weighed against risks of providing treatments or interpretations of data that could negatively affect the status of some employees' jobs.

Most of the problems encountered by the researchers in this example can be traced to conflicting role expectations. From the researchers' role system came a set of expectations defining their professional responsibilities to obtain the voluntary informed consent of participants, protect the confidentiality of data, and involve employees and management participatively in the joint design of the project. But from the outset, managers and employees attempted to fit the researchers into preconceived role models already familiar to the firm. For example, upper management viewed them as inexpensive consultants whose job was to improve branch performance and morale. Accordingly, they felt it appropriate to review confidential reports in order to stimulate further improvements. Employees tended to view the researchers as partisans who offered a direct channel of communication to management and, in one instance, an opportunity to resist a branch manager's decision. This latter situation was viewed by some managers as a threat to their effectiveness and control, and they reacted by using the data to remove uncooperative employees. Thus, throughout the study, the research team was faced with powerful pressures to conform to the competing role expectations of the various parties involved.

The difficulties that arose in the bank project might have been avoided had the researchers first initiated a process of role definition, clarification, and conflict resolution. In Mirvis and Seashore's (1982, p. 91) analysis, it is the investigator's responsibility as an ethical decision maker "to create roles that are mutually clarified and compatible and, in creating them, to affirm general ethical norms governing human research." Should researchers and consultants determine that the values of a client organization are unacceptable and cannot be changed, it may be best to forgo the project entirely. In such cases, subsequent conflicts among role expectations might turn out to be unresolvable.

SUMMARY

As our illustrations within helping professions and organizational settings suggest, applied researchers – like their more theoretically oriented counterparts – must face difficult dilemmas regarding informed consent, deception, confidentiality, privacy issues, and the like, although the ways in which they resolve these dilemmas may have more immediate consequences than are apparent in basic research contexts. Applied studies also differ from purely theoretical ones in that they are more likely to place researchers in positions in which they find themselves caught between conflicting obligations. Although many ethical dilemmas in applied settings will not be readily resolvable – if at all – researchers must be capable of weighing their obligations and choosing a course of action that minimizes the harm to the various parties involved. As Lowman (1998) advised, losing a client may at times be preferable to behaving in ways that compromise the ethical principles of one's profession. In the next chapter, we continue our consideration of applied research by focusing on ethical issues in marketing and survey research.

7

Applied Research II: Marketing and Survey Research

"This [food poisoning] could be the kiss of death for a restaurant. It could be on the front page of the papers with the headline: Some famous guy from Columbia University. Columbia, it's a world-famous institution. It's almost like the White House. This was a very traumatizing experience."

Jean-Claude Baker, owner Chez Josephine restaurant

Chapter Topics

☞ Marketing research objectives
☞ Responsibilities and role relationships in marketing research
☞ Classifications of marketing research issues
☞ Ethical issues and the marketing mix
☞ Deception in consumer research
☞ Conducting ethical marketing surveys

The remarks above were quoted from an unwilling participant in a marketing study to determine how vendors respond to customer complaints. It may be difficult to imagine that such a straightforward and apparently innocuous research goal could give rise to a study that had such dramatic ethical consequences, but that is exactly what happened in this case.

The investigation in question was initiated by a Columbia Business School professor who sent letters on university letterhead stationery to 240 New York City restaurants falsely claiming he had suffered food poisoning after dining at the restaurant in celebration of his wedding anniversary (Kifner, 2001). This was done to provide a context for determining how the restaurant owners would react to a customer complaint. The content of the letter was quite descriptive, with its author explaining how his anniversary celebration turned into a nightmare when he became severely sickened following a visit to the restaurant:

Extended nausea, vomiting, diarrhea and abdominal cramps all pointed to one thing: food poisoning. Our special romantic evening became reduced to my wife watching me curl up in a fetal position on the tiled floor of our bathroom between rounds of throwing up.

The overall emotional impact on the restaurant owners who received the letter was dramatic. Reflecting the adverse consequences induced by the study, an editorial in *The New York Times* ("Spoiling the Broth," 2001) claimed that the resulting review of hygiene procedures "caused a reign of terror in the city's top restaurants." Owners, managers, and chefs of the restaurants who received the letter frantically searched their computers for the professor's reservation and credit card records, reviewed menus and produce deliveries for potentially spoiled foods, questioned kitchen workers for possible lapses, and so on. According to Chez Josephine's chef, "My ego was hurt. I thought we had let Jean-Claude down. I ripped my cooks apart." Reactions to the study resulted in a formal apology from the school's dean and the researcher and prompted the introduction of stricter procedures governing research at Columbia. A letter sent to the restaurants by the researcher explained the true purpose of the fabricated letter and assured that the collected data would not be used for publication. The researcher also promised that he would not conduct similar studies in the future. The business school dean wrote that the entire episode had been "an egregious error in judgment by a junior faculty member [that was] part of an ill-conceived research project." He added that "while the professor initiated this research project on his own, he failed to think through the toll this study would take on its recipients" (Kifner, 2001, p. 1).

The restaurant study represents a stark example of a deceptive marketing study gone awry. At the outset, the design of the study may have seemed an ingenious way of obtaining insight into a growing area of interest in marketing known as customer relationship management (CRM). However, as we have seen in many other cases described in this book, researchers are often blind to the potentially harmful effects of their procedures, especially when they give greater consideration to the anticipated benefits of the research. The critical question regarding the restaurant study is whether equally effective non-deceptive alternatives were available, such as interviewing restaurateurs and dissatisfied customers (who are adequately informed about the nature of the investigation). If, for example, the researcher suspected that respondents would not be forthcoming enough to shed light on the research objectives during face-to-face interviews, even when informed about the importance of the research, another viable alternative approach could be considered, perhaps involving a milder deception than that originally determined. The next step would be for the researcher to assess the relative risks of harm imposed by the alternative deceptive methodologies.

In this chapter, we continue our discussion of applied research by turning our attention more directly to the business side of organizations. Whereas the preceding chapter included a focus on ethical issues in organizational studies specifically pertaining to the workforce, the current chapter emphasizes research considerations more linked to buying, selling, and the assessment of customer opinions. These are considerations that tend to fall within the general realm of marketing and survey research.

ETHICAL ISSUES IN MARKETING RESEARCH

Marketing research is a field of inquiry that covers a wide range of phenomena related to the identification and solution of problems pertaining to consumers and the marketplace. The results of research in marketing are often utilized by marketing managers to facilitate decision making in any of their areas of responsibility. In this regard, marketing research is one of the principal tools for answering such questions as "Will a package change improve brand image?" "How can I monitor my sales and retail trade activities?" "To whom should I target this advertisement?" "Why do shoppers select my brands or those of competitors?" Consumer goods manufacturers often rely on marketing research in order to develop new products or new advertising campaigns for products already available in the marketplace.

In order to satisfy these objectives, marketing researchers rely heavily on the involvement of human participants in the research enterprise, including adult consumers, business professionals, college students and, more recently, children. Accordingly, research in marketing often gives rise to some ethical issues like those encountered in related behavioral science disciplines. Because of the applied nature of much marketing research, ethical conflicts are especially likely to arise because of the number of different parties with some vested interest in the research activity. Marketing researchers may find themselves in an ethical conflict stemming from the divergent interests of clients, suppliers, consumers, and society at large.

The basic marketing concept presumes that the various aspirations and objectives of marketing practitioners are oriented to beneficial outcomes for all parties involved in a marketing exchange. Primarily, marketing is held to play a useful role in helping consumers satisfy their needs, and thereby enables the smooth operation of the exchange relationship between consumers and organizations. This is done through the development of needed products and services that are priced so as to give good value to buyers, while providing profit to the product producer, service provider, and other intermediaries. Consistent with these goals, the essential purpose of marketing research is to improve marketing-related decisions by providing information that can be used to identify and define marketing opportunities and problems.

Marketing research may also be carried out in order to generate and evaluate marketing actions and to monitor current marketing performance (Aaker and Day, 1990). Consumer goods manufacturers often rely on researchers in order to develop new products or new advertising campaigns for products already available in the marketplace. Even radio stations have relied on marketing research in order to determine how to best improve their standing in a highly competitive business area. For example, researchers may interview buyers of CDs and mp3 players or ask them to complete questionnaires detailing their music listening habits. More controlled, laboratory experiments also have been carried out in order to test the effectiveness of various radio advertising appeals. As a more surreptitious approach, some radio stations have even sent researchers out on the road as hitchhikers to obtain more unguarded comments about listener likes and dislikes.

Ethical standards for marketing researchers

Marketing researchers, like their counterparts in related disciplines, have been sensitive to ethics for some time. As early as 1962, the American Marketing Association (AMA), an international society of marketing professionals, adopted a *Marketing Research Code of Ethics*, which was revised in 1972 (see Box 7.1). (A set of standards pertinent to marketing research and practice on the Internet was added in 1997.) The decision to draft a code of ethics came about largely as a result of an apparent rise in research abuses among large and respected business organizations, such as the use of marketing research approaches in order to disguise sales purposes (Twedt, 1963). It was feared that without a code of ethics, such abuses ultimately

---

Box 7.1   Marketing research code of ethics

The American Marketing Association, in furtherance of its central objective of the advancement of science in marketing and in recognition of its obligation to the public, has established these principles of ethical practice of marketing research for the guidance of its members.

Adherence to this code will assure the users of marketing research that the research was done in accordance with acceptable ethical practices. Those engaged in research will find in this code an affirmation of sound and honest basic principles that have developed over the years as the profession has grown.

For Research Users, Practitioners, and Interviewers

1 No individual or organization will undertake any activity which is directly or indirectly represented to be marketing research, but which has as its real purpose the attempted sale of merchandise or services to some or all of the respondents interviewed in the course of the research.
2 If a respondent has been led to believe, directly or indirectly, that he is participating in a marketing research survey and that his anonymity will be protected, his name shall not be made known to anyone outside the research organization or research department, or used for other than research purposes.

For Research Practitioners

1 There will be no intentional or deliberate misrepresentation of research methods or results. An adequate description of methods employed will

(Continued)

Box 7.1   (Continued)

be made available upon request to the sponsor of the research. Evidence that field work has been completed according to specifications will, upon request, be made available to buyers of research.

2 The identity of the survey sponsor and/or the ultimate client for whom a survey is being done will be held in confidence at all times, unless this identity is to be revealed as part of the research design. Research information shall be held in confidence by the research organization or department and not used for personal gain or made available to any outside party unless the client specifically authorizes such release.

3 A research organization shall not undertake marketing studies for competitive clients when such studies would jeopardize the confidential nature of client–agency relationships.

For Users of Marketing Research

1 A user of research shall not knowingly disseminate conclusions from a given research project or service that are inconsistent with or not warranted by the data.

2 To the extent that there is involved in a research project a unique design involving techniques, approaches, or concepts not commonly available to research practitioners, the prospective user of research shall not solicit such a design from one practitioner and deliver it to another for execution without the approval of the design originator.

For Field Interviewers

1 Research assignments and materials received, as well as information obtained from respondents, shall be held in confidence by the interviewer and revealed to no one except the research organization conducting the marketing study.

2 No information gained through a marketing research activity shall be used, directly or indirectly, for the personal gain or advantage of the interviewer.

3 Interviews shall be conducted in strict accordance with specifications and instructions received.

4 An interviewer shall not carry out two or more interviewing assignments simultaneously unless authorized by all contractors or employees concerned.

(This code was adopted by the American Marketing Association in 1962 and includes 1972 revisions.)

would lead to a loss of consumer cooperation with researchers and to substantial deterioration of marketing research in general. This fear has persisted over the years, and to a large extent has been fostered by the activities of unscrupulous persons posing as honest marketing professionals (Langenderfer and Shimp, 2001). However, criticisms have also been directed to legitimate marketing practitioners and researchers because of the inherent nature of the marketing enterprise, which some assert leads to the development of products in the consumer marketplace that essentially exist to provide value to the manufacturer and retailer, without regard to the satisfaction of essential customer needs (Kimmel, in press).

The AMA research code, which supplements a more general code of ethics for association members, is somewhat limited in that it focuses mostly on the researcher and user (or client) relationship and emphasizes problems inherent in survey research, which was the dominant marketing research paradigm at the time the code was drafted. Codes of ethics have been adopted by other professional organizations, such as the Canadian Marketing Association (CMA), the Professional Marketing Forum of Central and Eastern Europe (PM Forum CEE), the Promotional Marketing Council of the European Association of Communications Agencies (EACA), the British Franchise Association (BFA), the International Chamber of Commerce/European Society for Opinion and Marketing Research (ICC/ESOMAR), and the Council for Marketing and Opinion Research (CMOR).

In addition to these, corporate codes of conduct have been implemented by a number of companies in North America and Europe. A *corporate code of conduct* consists of a company's policy statements that define ethical standards for acceptable conduct and typically reflect the underlying core values of the ethical marketer and marketing researcher: responsibility, integrity, honesty, respect, and trust. Despite a great degree of variance in the ways these statements are drafted, adherence to the standards is completely voluntary, although companies may choose to take disciplinary actions against employees who violate them (International Labour Organization, 2005). One recent estimate is that over 90 of the FTSE 100 companies (the top 100 companies listed on the London Stock Exchange) have a code of business ethics, and that 57 percent of the next 250 companies have codes (Institute of Business Ethics, 2005). Such ethics codes typically are designed to serve as instruments for self-regulation, although they may be used by courts as reference documents within the framework of appropriate legally binding regulations.

Marketing ethics codes reflect the commitment of marketing professionals to ethical conduct in all their dealings with persons with whom they interact in the marketing exchange process, including consumers, clients, employees, suppliers, distributors, and the general public. In fact, it has been demonstrated that ethical conduct can pay off for a company in financial terms. A 2003 British study found that companies having a clear commitment to ethical conduct (as indicated by a published code of business ethics) outperformed those that did not over a five-year period on four indicators: economic value added (EVA), market value added (MVA), price/earnings ratio volatility (P/E ratio), and return on capital employed (ROCE) (Institute of Business Ethics, 2005).

Responsibilities and role relationships

When researchers restrict their scientific activities to the investigation of basic research questions, the pertinent ethical issues tend to center on the experimenter–subject relationship. To be sure, when engaging in basic research the experimenter also bears additional ethical responsibilities to his or her discipline and to science in general in terms of the unbiased pursuit of knowledge, and must anticipate attempts by others to apply the research results at a later point in time (Lamberth and Kimmel, 1981). Nevertheless, in the basic research context, the primary ethical responsibilities pertain to the protection of the well-being of the research subjects.

However, as discussed in chapter 6, in applied research fields the ethical issues are compounded by the added relationships into which the researcher enters and the additional role responsibilities these relationships entail. For example, along with the obligation to treat research participants fairly, one must attempt to fulfill the expectations of the client or research user. The researcher also has a responsibility to protect the well-being of the public when the results are put into action. These additional role relationships are emphasized in the AMA code of ethics. Ethical conflicts are more likely to occur in the applied research context as the researcher recognizes that certain duties and responsibilities towards one group are inconsistent with those towards some other group or with his or her own values (see Box 7.2). Ethical dilemmas that involve conflicting role expectations should be anticipated prior to the carrying out of an investigation, especially when entering a relationship with a client whose company priorities may subsequently change, thereby altering the nature of the agreement.

Box 7.2   Applied marketing research and ethics: a case example

A few years ago, the author was hired by Electricité de France (EDF), the French national power company, to carry out an applied research project on rumors about electricity. The project involved a series of open-ended interviews with typical French consumers living in various regions of the country, interviews with some of the company's intermediaries (such as salespersons), an extensive Internet search, and the assessment of archival data. The primary goals of the project were to identify existing misconceptions and false information held by the company's clientele, the extent of belief in rumors related to electricity and the company, and the conditions under which people were transmitting rumors.

One of the company's overriding interests in electricity-related rumors was to identify the kinds of beliefs and fears prevalent among the French consuming public relative to electromagnetic fields (EMFs) emanating from outdoor power plants. When company representatives explained to

Box 7.2   (Continued)

me prior to data collection that their goal was to better inform their consumers and reduce anxieties linked to distorted beliefs about EMFs, I recognized that the company's expectations were consistent with my own. The project enabled me to gain further insight into the social-psychological dynamics underlying the emergence and spread of rumors in the context of an ongoing problem situation, while the company searched for more effective means of communicating with their customers. We shared mutual interests in ultimately being able to reduce public misconceptions and the spread of fear-inducing rumors.

By contrast, imagine how opposing interests or role conflicts could have led to ethical dilemmas in this case. If I had reason to suspect that the company intended to use the results of the research in order to scare homeowners away from areas where the company planned to erect new power stations or to foment the spread of rumors so as to increase the purchase of electrical safety devices, I would not have been able to continue my involvement with the research project. The company's goals would have conflicted with my own moral values and with the ethical standards of my profession, which state that research findings should not be applied to the detriment of individuals or groups.

Another concern, more linked to the research methodology, had to do with the appropriateness of deceiving the company's customers who had agreed to participate in the research. When I obtained the consent of consumers for the interviews, I chose to inform participants that the study pertained to their usage behavior and concerns related to electricity (which, in part, it did), but not that we specifically were interested in rumors. This was to see if participants would spontaneously mention rumors on their own prior to our asking direct rumor-related questions. In our judgment, the use of a passive deception during the recruitment stage was justified because it did not pose any identifiable risks and we presumed that the decision to participate would not have been different had participants known that the study focused on rumors. It would have been more difficult to justify withholding information about the study sponsor, as many of our French participants may have become upset upon having learned after the fact that the research was sponsored by the national utility company.

Source: American Marketing Association (1972) *Code of Ethics*, Chicago: AMA.

Consider the hypothetical case in which a marketing researcher employed by a pharmaceutical company is asked to carry out a study to determine physicians' perceptions of the quality of the pharmaceutical company's products (cf. Aaker and Day, 1990). Suppose that the company insists that the researcher should contact the physicians under the name of a fictitious company and provide a false purpose for the research in order to obtain more objective responses. Let us assume that this situation represents an ethical dilemma for the researcher because it involves conflicting sets of values (the desire to fulfill the company's research needs and the responsibility to protect the respondent's rights to choose and to be sufficiently informed).

Various solutions to this ethical conflict might be selected, depending largely on the strength of the researcher's obligations to the different groups involved. The researcher who feels that it is unethical to blatantly deceive subjects could choose to protect the physicians' right to informed consent. In so doing, there is the possibility that unreliable data will be collected and that the interests of the client will have been sacrificed. Conversely, the researcher could decide to carry out the study as suggested, while taking special care to debrief the physicians about the study's true purpose upon its completion, thereby fulfilling (at least to some extent) the obligation of fairness to the research participants. However, both of these solutions are likely to be viewed as unacceptable compromises. In the first case, the researcher would likely lose a client for failing to comply with the company's desire to remain anonymous to the physicians. The second course of action might be deemed even more unacceptable, given the likelihood that the physicians would react very unfavorably to having been deceived about the study's intent, perhaps to the point of taking legal action against the researcher. The researcher could choose to forewarn the physicians about the possibility that the study might involve some deceptions, but this might lead to the loss of willing participants and, consequently, a non-representative sample.

Perhaps the wisest course in this example would be for the researcher to consider whether a more ethical procedure for obtaining the desired information is available, using an alternative research methodology. The ethical dilemma might have been avoided altogether had the researcher and client clarified their roles and expectations when they first established a professional relationship. That is, the researcher could have clarified his or her professional and scientific obligations to obtain the voluntary informed consent of participants, to protect the confidentiality of data, and to maintain the participants' anonymity, especially if these were conditions by which the agreement to participate was to be obtained. Similar clarifications could have been established with research participants. For example, if the researcher had some suspicions that the study's sponsors might request access to certain confidential information for a follow-up study, potential subjects should have been informed of that possibility during the consent procedure. For additional recommendations for avoiding role conflicts, see Box 7.3.

Classifying ethical issues in marketing research

Several suggestions for classifying the ethical issues in marketing research have been offered by marketing professionals. Perhaps the most basic scheme was presented by Kinnear and Taylor (1995), who distinguished between two general kinds of judgments that are involved in considerations of ethics as related to marketing research: (1) judgments that certain types of research activities are inappropriate (e.g. the use of marketing research as a trick to sell products), and (2) judgments that certain types of activities are required (e.g. the necessity to

Box 7.3 Conflicts of interest and the pharmaceutical industry

In recent decades, the pharmaceutical industry has grown into a multi-billion dollar enterprise and today represents one of the world's most successful business sectors. The industry's contributions in terms of successful healing (e.g. antibiotics), life-enhancing (e.g. pain medications), and life-extending (e.g. insulin for diabetes) medical innovations cannot be debated. However, as the industry's marketing power and financial resources have spiraled upwards, so too have concerns that its influence will increasingly extend to regulatory agencies, professional organizations, research scientists, research journals, medical education, politicians and other influential decision makers, and the media – all to negative effect (Antonuccio, Danton, and McClanahan, 2003). A variety of conflicts of interest are likely to result.

According to Antonuccio and his colleagues, the influence of the pharmaceutical industry is already apparent in a number of ways in the behavioral sciences, especially as a result of the prescription privileges bestowed upon the psychology profession. For example, the authors point out that the American Psychiatric Association annually receives over US$13 million in advertising revenue from the pharmaceutical industry, a sum that is significantly greater than the amount generated by the association's dues-paying members. With such profits at stake, it becomes increasingly difficult for professional journals to publish articles critical of their advertisers' products (Abassi and Smith, 2003). It also has been documented that some new drug advertisements appearing in publications such as the *American Journal of Psychiatry* are often misleading in terms of safety and efficacy (e.g. Wilkes, Doblin, and Shapiro, 1992).

The pharmaceutical industry's influence extends to behavioral and biomedical research in several ways. For example, publication biases that favor pharmaceutical products have been widely acknowledged (e.g. Gilbody and Song, 2000; Lexchin et al., 2003), resulting in an erosion of credibility in the psychiatric and medical literature. Further, data may be withheld or delayed if they reflect negatively on sponsor's products. In one illuminating comparison, estimates of the effectiveness of antidepressants over inert placebos in the published literature were significantly higher than estimates obtained from the US Food and Drug Administration's (FDA) antidepressant database for all drugs in the approval stage (from every study conducted, whether ultimately published or not) (Antonuccio et al. 2003).

Because of the blurring boundaries between psychological science and industry marketing, Antonuccio et al. (2003) proposed that an aspirational "firewall" should be built between the two interests, as a means of preserving the integrity of the science of psychology. Towards that goal they developed a "psychology manifesto," consisting of a set of recommended

(Continued)

Box 7.3   (Continued)

guidelines for professional psychology organizations and psychology training programs. The guidelines (p. 1036) that are most relevant to our focus
on applied research are summarized below:

1   Drug industry advertising should not be permitted in scientific journals.
2   Researchers should conduct and report double-blind tests.
3   Researchers should document concurrent treatments.
4   Internet-accessible databases should be developed.
5   Independent data access should be guaranteed for all participating
    researchers.
6   A writing contribution should be required for the authorship of pub-
    lished or otherwise reported studies.

---

inform the client or research sponsor about certain details of the study's methodology, such as how the subject sample was selected). Although it is a rudimentary
framework, Kinnear and Taylor's distinction reflects the typical thrust of ethics
codes in attempting to delineate acceptable and unacceptable conduct on the part
of researchers towards their subjects and the users of research results.

A second typology of ethical issues in marketing research focuses solely on
issues involving the basic rights of research participants. Drawing on codes of
ethics from other disciplines (such as psychology and sociology), Tybout and
Zaltman (1974) grouped subjects' rights into three general categories: (1) the
right to choose (whether or not to participate in a study), which includes the
right to be aware that one has a choice, to be given sufficient information in order
to be able to decide, and to be given an explicit opportunity to choose; (2) the
right to safety, which includes protection of subjects' anonymity, freedom from
stress, and freedom from deception as to the nature and objectives of the study;
and (3) the right to be informed (after research participation), which includes the
debriefing of subjects and dissemination of data to respondents if desired. As is
apparent, Tybout and Zaltman's classification of issues is limited to a focus on the
relationship between researchers and the participants in their studies, and serves
as an important reminder that researchers in applied settings must be sensitive to
many of the same human subject issues that pertain to basic research.

Shelby Hunt and his colleagues (1984) used an empirical approach to determine the most prevalent ethical problems confronting marketing research practitioners. The researchers asked 460 randomly selected marketing professionals to
identify job situations that posed the most difficult ethical or moral problems for
them. The most frequent responses were classified into the following five areas:

1   Research integrity (33 percent), including such issues as deliberately with-
    holding information, falsifying or ignoring pertinent data, and altering
    research results or misusing statistics in order to support a predetermined
    point of view. The fact that this category emerged as the most frequently

cited source of ethical problems suggests that marketing researchers perceive significant problems in maintaining the integrity of their research.

2   Treating outside clients fairly (11 percent), including issues involving clients outside one's own company, such as the use of hidden charges passed on to the customer.

3   Research confidentiality (9 percent), including issues involved in the protection of data obtained for research purposes (such as the use of data from one project in a related project for a competitor).

4   Marketing mix social issues (8 percent), including issues pertaining to the decision to conduct research within the context of product or advertising decisions that are contrary to the best interests of society, such as advertising to children and the production of products that are hazardous to health.

5   Treating respondents fairly (6 percent), including issues involving the protection of anonymity and the use of deception in order to conceal the purpose or sponsor of the research.

Other sets of problematic practices cited less frequently included interviewer dishonesty, misuse of funds, and the unfair treatment of others in one's company. Hunt et al.'s results are informative in that they help us to recognize the range of actual ethical dilemmas that are likely to confront researchers in applied settings. The findings also suggest that there are two faces to the ethical issues – one dealing with issues that emerge in the conducting of research and the other dealing with considerations relevant to the implied use and application of the research results. Some of the ethical issues that have received particular attention by marketing professionals are listed in Table 7.1. Although this is not an exhaustive listing, these research activities are representative of those most likely to pose ethical dilemmas for the marketing researcher.

As an example of the unanticipated ethical dilemmas that can arise in marketing research, consider the following two hypothetical cases suggested by Charles

Table 7.1 Ethical issues in marketing research

Involvement of individuals in the research process without their knowledge or informed consent
Coercion of individuals to participate in research
Abuse of research participants' rights during the data collection process
Invasion of the privacy of research participants
Threats to research participants' anonymity and confidentiality of data
Failure to debrief research participants
Use of inadequate sampling procedures to increase the likelihood of obtaining desired results
Misrepresentation of non-random subject samples (such as volunteers) as representative
Misrepresentation of research results or dissemination of conclusions that are inconsistent with or not warranted by the data
Use of survey techniques for selling purposes
Use of research strategies to obtain the names and addresses of prospects for direct marketing
Pressure to design research to support a particular marketing decision or to enhance a legal position

Source: Adapted from Day (1975).

Weinberg, Professor of Marketing at the University of British Columbia (Aaker and Day, 1990). In the first case, a study director for a research company develops a questionnaire to be used by a regular client. However, after the questionnaire is sent to the client for final approval, it is returned with numerous modifications, including the addition of leading questions and biased scales. Although the study director does not believe that valid information can be obtained with the revised instrument, the client emphasizes that the questionnaire must be sent out without further changes. In a second example, a marketing research professor assigns a class project in which students have to conduct personal interviews with executives of high technology companies concerning their future plans. The professor assures students that all information relevant to the project is confidential and will only be used in the research course. However, during the project, a student overhears the professor mentioning to a colleague that the findings will be sold to a major technology firm.

There are no uniquely correct resolutions to situations like those described in the preceding paragraph. For such cases, researchers must identify the ethical dilemma involved and be able to justify their decision for resolving the dilemma. For example, the case of the course project illustrates problems involving the unequal distribution of power in research relationships. The professor has a power advantage over the student researchers, who must satisfy course requirements in order to obtain a good grade. Although it might be threatening to individual students to approach the professor (or department chairperson) with their concerns about the use of the project, there often is "safety in numbers." The professor might be more willing to reconsider selling the research when confronted by a group of rebellious students. Another option would be for the students to indicate the potential risk to the executives – the inability to protect the confidentiality of responses – prior to carrying out the interviews. In any case, a promise that the results will be anonymous should not be made if it is unlikely that anonymity can be protected.

Several of the areas of ethical concern appearing in Table 7.1 already have been considered in our discussion of basic research activities (such as deception and informed consent, invasion of privacy and confidentiality of data, and debriefing), while others are described in remaining chapters (such as coercing individuals to participate in research). In order to shed light on some of the ethical issues that are particularly troublesome in marketing research, we next turn our attention to research activities relevant to each of the major content areas of marketing.

Ethical issues and the marketing mix

In what might be considered another approach to classifying ethical issues in marketing research, it is informative to consider the various elements of the marketing enterprise – the so-called *marketing mix* – and the sorts of issues that are relevant to each. By focusing on content areas, essentially we are elaborating on the area of ethical problems identified in Hunt et al.'s (1984) survey as "marketing mix social issues." First, however, it is necessary to clarify what is meant by the marketing mix concept.

The marketing mix has been defined as "the set of marketing tools the firm uses to pursue its marketing objectives in the target market" (Kotler, 2003, p. 15). The concept dates back to a 1964 article written by Neil H. Borden in which he described the marketing manager as a "mixer of ingredients," involved in activities related to product planning, pricing, distribution channels, advertising, packaging, brand management, and the like (Borden, 1964). Borden's early listing of marketing elements has been simplified over the years into four basic categories, known today as the 4 Ps of marketing: product, price, place, and promotion (see Table 7.2).

Apart from issues concerning the ethical treatment of research participants and the protection of participant rights, such as those comprising Tybout and Zaltman's (1974) classification scheme (see above), ethical concerns linked to the 4 Ps of marketing have more to do with the potential uses to which research findings ultimately might be put. Marketing activity is frequently criticized for having adverse consequences for consumers, other businesses, and society as a whole (Kotler, 2003), and it is through applied research that decisions regarding marketing activities typically take shape. One of the most important requirements of

Table 7.2   The 4 P's of marketing: sample research questions

Product
What attributes or benefits are important?
What brand name should be used?
How should the product be styled?
How should the product be packaged and shelved?
Should there be product variations?
Does the product have any safety issues?

Price
What pricing policies are appropriate?
What is the best suggested retail price?
How should price variations be established?
How do consumers perceive prices?
How effective are volume discounts and wholesale prices?
What seasonal pricing strategies should be used?

Place (distribution)
How should the product or service be made available to consumers?
What distribution channels and distribution centers should be established?
How should inventory be managed?
Where should company plants, factories, and warehouses be located?
Should the product or service be available internationally?
What transportation systems should be utilized?

Promotion
What type of advertising should be developed?
Which media should be used for advertising and other promotions?
What influence tactics should be used for face-to-face selling?
How can good public relations for the company best be achieved?
What is the relative effectiveness of different promotional methods (e.g. advertising, coupons and discounts, personal selling, direct marketing)?
How should the marketing communication budget best be managed?

the marketing researcher is the ability to recognize and anticipate these ethical issues prior to the development of marketing strategy. Some examples of issues that arise in the context of each element of the marketing mix are presented below.

Product

According to a 1998 marketing research industry survey jointly conducted by the American Marketing Association (AMA) and the Advertising Research Foundation (ARF), 89 percent of the marketing research directors surveyed indicated that they regularly conduct product and service tests, 88 percent conduct new product tests, and 66 percent conduct research on product name and packaging at their firms (ARF/AMA, 1998). Given that product-related research is a common marketing research activity, it may be said that researchers have an ethical obligation to consider the impact that products have on consumers and society as a whole.

Several ethical issues emerge in the context of the development and management of consumer products. Foremost among these pertain to the argument that many products in the consumer marketplace have been developed primarily to provide value to the manufacturer and retailer, without regard to the satisfaction of essential customer needs. In fact, in most industrialized nations one can observe a proliferation of products that offer little real value to consumers, such as mascara for babies, salted bandages, and a growing range of pet products and services, the latter ranging from Halloween costumes and limousine services for cats and dogs to pet spas, fitness centers, vacation resorts, and retirement homes (Tanikawa, 2004). Although such ostensibly useless products may provide a certain degree of novelty to the purchaser, one may argue that they merely serve to encourage consumers to "buy and have" regardless of the need-satisfying properties of the acquisitions. Further, it is maintained that many products merely add to the creation of false wants and the encouragement of materialistic values and aspirations, thereby influencing consumers to value material objects more than personal development and socially oriented causes.

In determining the proper course of action relative to products, the ethical marketing researcher is well-advised to consider three critical tests that traditionally have been applied to decisions about new product launches: (1) the *concept test* to determine if the intended user really needs the proposed item; (2) the *product use test* to assess whether the item actually developed meets that need; and (3) the *market test* to see if the company has an effective marketing plan. Ethical issues are more likely to be encountered when one or more of these tests cannot be successfully addressed.

Promotion

More than 80 percent of the marketing directors surveyed in the aforementioned ARF/AMA (1998) study claimed to engage in advertising research, with 88 percent carrying out advertising tracking studies (i.e. to assess the effectiveness of an advertising campaign or awareness for specific ads) and 84 percent engaging in advertising copy research (i.e. to assess the effectiveness of varying advertising messages, with "copy" referring to the written or spoken text of an advertisement). In addition to advertising, other promotional tools served as the focus of a significant amount of research activity, including research on sales techniques (44 percent). Promotional research is apt to give rise to several ethical issues, including those pertaining to the creation of deceptive messages and influence techniques. For example, research comparisons of different advertising copy may reveal that one message is better remembered and preferred than the alternatives. However, it may be the case that the more effective message relies on subtle means of misleading message recipients and thus is more problematic from an ethical point of view.

A widely used form of deception in advertising involves the practice of overstating a product's features or performance aspects. In many cases, this practice is rather blatant (e.g. "reverses aging"), whereas in other contexts the deception can be quite implicit. A rather subtle form of deception in advertising was apparent in ads sponsored by producers of drugs used for the treatment of HIV, the virus that causes AIDS. Specifically, in 2001, eight makers of HIV drugs were criticized by regulatory agencies for their ads depicting men with HIV as healthy-looking, robust individuals engaged in strenuous physical activity, such as mountain climbing. Critics argued that such images were not representative of patients with HIV and, among other possible consequences, could affect gay men's decisions about practicing safe sex and their beliefs about the presumed gravity of HIV(Adams and Grimes, 2001).

Another promotional tool, product packaging, serves as a last means of communicating with and persuading shoppers before they make a product or brand choice while in the store. Marketing research can lead to the creation of ethically questionable packaging practices, inducing consumers to select products that will ultimately prove disappointing, unsatisfactory, or harmful. For example, package contents might be exaggerated through subtle design or misleading artwork, product size may be described in misleading terms, and misleading labeling (e.g., "new and improved") might be used. Some products that are specifically intended for adults, such as alcoholic goods, may be packaged in such a way as to appeal to children. This was the case for the product known as Zippers, a fruit-flavored gelatin product with 12 percent alcoholic content. Zippers' packaging consisted of brightly colored plastic containers that closely resembled those of popular gelatin snacks that children often pack in their school lunches. The makers of the product became the target of concerned parents and school administrators who complained that Zippers was being marketed in ways that appealed to underage consumers and made it too easy for children to sneak alcohol into school (GDCADA, 2005).

Price

Pricing represents another important focus of marketing research, with 64 percent of marketing research directors claiming to conduct studies in this area, according to the previously cited ARF/AMA (1998) study. Although the setting of prices is determined by a number of economic and competitive forces, pricing research can be used by companies to influence consumers in ethically questionable ways. This is most evident with regard to the ways that certain pricing tactics may influence consumers into perceiving a price as more attractive than it actually is. For example, the common retail practices of "odd-pricing" and "price partitioning" serve as subtle means of influencing consumers' perceptions of prices. *Odd-pricing* involves the setting of prices for products and services with amounts ending in odd numbers (such as 29.99 euros) rather than rounded figures (such as 30 euros). An odd price tends to be perceived by shoppers as lower than it actually is, apparently because people are more apt to round such prices down, rather than up, and because the larger digit positions in a series of numbers are easier to remember. Thus, a price of 29.99 euros is recalled as closer to 20 euros than to 30 euros and connotes the image of savings.

Partitioned prices are prices that break up the inclusive price into a base price and surcharge. For example, an item of clothing purchased from an e-commerce site is likely to be listed according to its base price (such as 32 euros). The purchaser is unlikely to learn of the total price of the item (such as 39.95 euros, including shipping and handling charges) until proceeding to the site's checkout page. As one might expect, partitioning prices in this way is apt to lead the customer into believing that the overall price is lower because the surcharge (and thus the overall price) tends to be underestimated. Although odd-pricing and partitioned prices may seem like innocuous practices from the marketer's perspective, they highlight the necessity to consider their consequences from the point of view of consumer targets.

Place

An important focus of research related to the fourth element of the marketing mix, place or distribution, has to do with the design of retail settings so that consumers can shop more efficiently and derive greater satisfaction from the shopping experience (e.g. Jones, 1999). However, research also can reveal retailer practices within the physical setting of the store that can effectively influence shoppers in ways that arouse ethical concerns. Subtle tactics often are used to unconsciously influence consumers, including the use of lighting of greater intensity to enhance the perceived quality of supermarket products (such as fresh vegetables and fruits), the shelving at lower heights of products intended to capture the attention of children, the use of loud background music to give the impression that the store is busy and filled with bargains, and organizing the store in such a way that it encourages consumers to pass through more departments or store aisles and thus notice more products. *Olfactory marketing* – the development and use of scents to create shopping environments more conducive to impulsive buying – has grown in popularity in recent years. The ethical concern is whether the use of odors specifically designed to seduce consumers as they shop represents an underhanded means of keeping people in stores longer than they had planned and buying more than they can afford. As the technologies for this and other forms of "subliminal seduction" of shoppers continue to develop, so too will the ethical issues surrounding their development and use.

Some of the ethical issues pertaining to place or distribution cannot be attributed to marketing strategies derived from research. For example, the growing complexity of the distribution process entails certain costs that are passed on to consumers, and the growing intensity of retail competition has diminished the profits that retailers can expect to earn. As large, multinational chains and discounters multiply and gain success in many communities, they threaten the livelihoods of family businesses that have been in operation for decades. In response to these growing problems, marketing researchers should recognize a moral obligation to investigate means by which the distribution system can operate more efficiently and inexpensively, so that costs for the consumer and the threats to small businesses can be reduced.

Deception in consumer research

Before leaving our discussion of ethical issues in marketing research, we return once again to a consideration of deception, this time by focusing on deceptive procedures employed in consumer research. Consumer behavior has been at the center of an enormous amount of research attention, dating back to the mid-1970s when the first empirical journal dedicated to research on the topic – the *Journal of Consumer Research* (*JCR*) – was created. Consumer researchers investigate topics relating to customer loyalty, shopping behavior, brand image, trust, purchase satisfaction, product usage habits, and so on (see Table 7.3). Like other human subject investigators, consumer researchers often deem it necessary to disguise their investigations on these topics in order to minimize demand characteristics and hypothesis guessing (Allen, 2004; Shimp, Hyatt, and Snyder, 1993). As a result, they can find themselves in the position of having to decide whether or not to actively mislead their participants, or to omit pertinent information, as a necessary condition of fulfilling their research objectives.

Recent surveys have revealed that the use of deception is on the rise in consumer studies, as marketing researchers have made increasing use of more traditional behavioral science methodologies, such as laboratory experiments. The reader may recall from chapter 3 the results from the author's content analyses, which revealed an increase in the use of deceptive procedures in marketing studies across four time periods (Kimmel, 2001, 2004a). Specifically, deception rose from 43 percent in 1975–76 to 66 percent in 2001–02, an increase based largely on the employment of active deceptions (see Table 3.4). Across the time periods studied, there was evidence that marketing researchers had turned to experimental laboratory investigations with increasing regularity.

Table 7.3 Common measures of consumer behavior

Product or brand awareness (aided recognition; unaided recall)
Purchase preferences
Degree of brand loyalty
Frequency of purchase
Amount of purchase (expenditure; items bought)
Frequency of shopping trips
Attitudes towards brands, advertisements, shops, etc.
Degree of interest in sales promotions
Advertising awareness and recall
Amount of product wastage

Further evidence of the frequency and nature of deception in consumer research was obtained in a survey conducted by N. Craig Smith, Jill Klein, and myself (Smith et al., 2005). We questioned 112 consumer researchers in attendance at the 2002 Association for Consumer Research (ACR) annual conference in order to determine the extent to which they utilized deceptive methodologies and their attitudes and perceptions regarding the use of deception in the discipline. Deception was reportedly employed by 86 percent of the respondents; 59 percent admitted that they always use deception or use it frequently (in more than half of their studies), and only 42 percent claimed to always debrief deceived participants. On average, our respondents estimated that 52 percent of consumer research investigations involve some form of deception. Nearly one-half of the respondents viewed training in the use of deception as less than adequate in the discipline. Moreover, there was low familiarity with the APA ethics code, which at the time was recommended for ethical guidance by the ACR, and only 14 percent of those not familiar with the APA code said they were familiar with at least one other research code. In sum, these various results suggest that the use of deception is extensive in consumer research, that remedial measures often are not used, and that many researchers appear to be ill-trained to deal with ethical dilemmas pertaining to the use of deception.

Deceptions in consumer research, as in other fields, vary from the mild to the relatively severe (see Box 7.4). For example, mild deceptions are commonly used in studies measuring reaction time and memory, such as when participants are not forewarned that they will be faced with a recall test after exposure to a set of product labels, brand names, or advertisements (e.g. Burke and Srull, 1988). The restaurant study described at the beginning of this chapter represents an example of a more severe deception, especially in light of its impact on persons who were unaware that they were serving as participants. Moreover, the study could have resulted in additional unanticipated consequences: it might have caused embarrassment among the restaurant establishment or resulted in legislation that reduces the profits of vendors. Whereas a researcher might claim that certain research outcomes (such as legislation that is given impetus by publicity surrounding the study) could not reasonably have been anticipated, from the perspective of the aggrieved parties the study might not be viewed as justifiable because it caused them harm.

In another investigation, people were invited by a fictitious online film processing and digitizing company to submit personal photos for a photo album website as part of a supposed "prelaunch beta test" for the company. Shortly after submitting their photos, however, the volunteers were informed that their photos had been lost. This procedure was followed in order to enable the researchers to manipulate key factors related to brand personality and to observe responses to a company's apparent violation of trust. Overall, the participants spent two months interacting with the fictitious firm and, although they were informed three days after the deception that their photos had been found, at least some of the participants may have found the experience to be quite unsettling. The likelihood of consumer studies employing active deceptions of this nature is lower relative to related fields (such as social psychology), but may be expected to

Box 7.4   Deception in the store: the case of mystery shopping

Imagine the following scenario: A shopper enters the new media department of a major electronics retail store and begins to browse the area where there are several new computer speaker systems on display. The shopper clearly appears to be interested in purchasing a speaker system and after several minutes of shifting from one system to another, is finally approached by a salesperson. The seller is cheerful enough, but does not appear to be very motivated to assist the customer – his eyes keep darting in various directions, he responds to an intrusive call on his mobile phone, and he fails to give any advice about the speakers. As the customer asks questions about the speakers, the seller appears evasive, and suddenly disclaims, "Hey, listen, I'd love to help you out here, but I'm really not up on these systems. They just arrived in the store and you really should speak to my colleague, Jerome, who knows a lot more than me about these things. Unfortunately, he's still at lunch." The customer coolly thanks the salesperson and quickly exits the store.

Although this scenario may seem common in the retail sector, there is more to this case than meets the eye. The "customer" actually had no intention of purchasing anything in the store but instead was serving as a "mystery shopper" who was conducting a research study for the store's management in order to assess the quality of service. In this case, the findings were not very encouraging. The seller appeared to be poorly trained, lacking in motivation, and uninformed about the goods he was hired to sell. *Mystery shopping* represents a form of concealed participant observation in which researchers deceive customer-service personnel into believing that they are serving real or potential customers (Ainscough and Motley, 2000; Wilson, 2001). This form of deceptive research, which is rapidly growing worldwide, is used extensively by organizations in retailing, financial services, hotels and catering, public utilities, car dealerships, and government.

The primary aim of the mystery shopping technique is to monitor the consistency and efficiency of customer-service performance in service organizations. Unlike the more open-ended, exploratory nature of ethnographic participant observations in public settings, mystery shopping is based on a structured and systematic format in which checklists and coding forms are used to obtain and measure specific information about service performance (Grove and Fisk, 1992). Based on in-depth interviews with senior managers in various sectors and market research directors who are responsible for commissioning or providing mystery research, Wilson (2001) identified three primary uses of the approach: (1) to serve as a diagnostic tool in order to identify weaknesses and failings in an organization's

(Continued)

Box 7.4   (Continued)

service delivery; (2) to motivate and develop service personnel by linking training, appraisal, and incentives to performance measures; and (3) to assess the competitiveness of an organization's service delivery within the overall industry. Wilson's analysis revealed that mystery shopping activity leads to improvements in service standards, especially when service personnel accept the approach and recognize its ultimate consequences and benefits.

Mystery shopping research has certain clear advantages when compared with the more straightforward customer-satisfaction survey approach. It measures the process rather than the outcomes of a service encounter, focuses on activities and procedures that do or do not occur rather than gathering opinions about the service experience, and tends to provide fuller details about the service encounter as opposed to a global impression. However, as a deceptive research technique, mystery shopping raises obvious ethical concerns, similar to those that emerge in the context of any disguised field observations carried out in public settings. Foremost among the concerns are the risks that participant rights to privacy and freedom from exploitation will be violated. Because services typically are performed in public settings where they can be observed by members of the public other than those persons actually served, the research observations are held by some to require no greater ethical obligations to the service provider than would be expected in normal, everyday circumstances (e.g. Jorgensen, 1989). Nonetheless, there are additional concerns with mystery shopping because service providers' livelihoods may be dramatically affected by the research outcomes and they may regard the technique as distracting and anxiety provoking. Mystery shopping thus must be carried out with sensitivity to these issues.

Based on the findings of his interview study, Wilson (2001) concluded that it is critical that service providers are made aware that their employer will be observing them on occasion in a concealed manner and that they are educated about the benefits and safeguards of the approach before the observations are conducted. Specific guidelines have begun to appear for ethical conduct by mystery shoppers. For example, the Mystery Shopping Providers Association (MSPA), a professional trade organization that offers its services to companies worldwide, obliges its mystery shoppers to adhere to an ethics agreement consisting of 21 specific standards (MSPA, 2005).

increase as a growing number of consumer researchers come to adopt experimental laboratory methodologies.

As for research in other behavioral science fields, when considering the acceptability of carrying out consumer studies that involve more than minimal risk, researchers are advised to first test prospective participants' perceptions of the risk of harm. The quasi-control approach, described in chapter 4, suggests one way that this can be accomplished. Individuals representative of persons likely to participate would be asked to reflect on the proposed study's procedure in order to identify aspects that they would find upsetting or otherwise troublesome. This would suggest potentially harmful aspects of the procedure that would then have to be modified before the actual study is carried out.

Applying this approach to the restaurant study, participants could be required to imagine themselves in the role of a restaurant owner who has received a bogus letter describing a severe case of food poisoning. A variety of possible harms might be foreseen, such as the resulting anxiety experienced by the owner, the loss of time devoted to an investigation of the claim, a rupture in vendor–supplier relationships, a loss of self-esteem at having been duped, and so on. Because they do not have a vested interest in the investigation, the participants might be in a better position to perceive additional harms that the researcher neglected to consider, such as a loss of trust in the research process that could result from unfavorable publicity about the study in the press. By contrast, the role-playing restaurateurs (perhaps consisting of persons who at one time were employed as restaurant workers) might point out that food poisoning claims are not uncommon, that they could not be expected to cause undue duress, and that restaurants would likely have a formal procedure for processing the claims.

Finally, researchers must bear in mind their obligation to use remedial measures to mitigate any harms stemming from the decision to include deception as part of the research procedure. In fact, the current APA ethics code (APA, 2002) requires that all deceptions involving more than minimal risk must be accompanied by appropriate remedial procedures, such as forewarning and debriefing. Although forewarning would not have been possible in the study of restaurant vendors (for obvious reasons), it would be essential that all participants be informed of the deception as soon as possible after reception of the bogus letter. Should the researcher decide that this would negate the possibility of a sufficient window of opportunity for data collection, then the decision would have to be made to forgo the study as planned. In fact, the limited possibility of remedial measures, the likelihood of harm, and the failure to adhere to any extent to the criterion of voluntary participation all argue strongly against carrying out the restaurant study.

Economics research and deception: a radical solution

It is informative to look at how other applied research fields have dealt with similar challenges regarding the acceptability of research deception. In contrast to following psychology's lead in responding to ethical considerations related to research practices, researchers in economics have taken a more aggressive tack. For nearly 20 years, experimental economists have essentially adopted a *de facto* prohibition against the use of deception in research, largely based on concerns that deception contaminates subject pools and may not guarantee that participants will really believe what they have been told about the research environment (Bonetti, 1998a, b; McDaniel and Starmer, 1998). That a similar approach could eventually emerge for all behavioral and social science research is a possibility that has been dreaded by researchers who view increasingly restrictive professional and governmental regulatory mechanisms as significant threats to the research process.

Despite considerable debate about the decision to forbid deception in experimental economics research, it is argued by supporters of the policy that most economics research can be conducted without the use of deception, through the development of alternative procedures (e.g. Bardsley, 2000), guarantees of participant anonymity, and substantial monetary rewards based on outcomes (the latter of which ensures that participants are strongly motivated). Whether forbidding deception would meet with similar success in consumer research is another question entirely, where the range of research questions is broader and more likely to arouse self-relevant concerns and participant role playing.

ETHICAL ISSUES IN THE USE OF MARKETING SURVEYS

Regardless of the discipline, survey studies need to be carried out in ways designed to minimize the risks to research participants to the greatest extent possible. This requires that survey researchers maintain a sensitivity to general ethical considerations that appear in other research contexts, including respondents' right to be informed and the protection of research participants through the proper treatment and use of information obtained from them during the investigation. When marketing and other applied researchers conduct survey studies, additional care must be taken to avoid potential ethical abuses involving the use of survey findings for decision-making purposes.

Informing marketing research participants

Because respondents to marketing surveys generally are voluntary participants, it is important that researchers adequately inform them about the true nature of what they have volunteered for (Fowler, 2001). Thus, the ethical survey researcher typically is expected to provide potential respondents with such information as the name of the organization carrying out the research (and the interviewer's name, if applicable), the research sponsor who is paying for or supporting the research, a brief description of the purposes of the research and issues or topics the research is designed to cover, an accurate description of the extent to which responses will be protected with respect to confidentiality, and the possible threats to or limits on confidentiality. Respondents also should be assured that their cooperation is voluntary, that no negative consequences will result from their participation, and that they are free to decline to respond to any questions that they choose not to answer (Fowler, 2001). Given these obligations, it is clear that it would have been ethically unacceptable for the marketing researcher in the example mentioned previously to adhere to the pharmaceutical company's demands to misrepresent the survey sponsor and purpose (see p. 187).

Although the informed consent process can be relatively straightforward with respect to marketing research surveys, researchers might be tempted to use deception in order to conceal the purpose or sponsor of the research. This typically is done in order to reduce the transparency of the survey or to increase response rates (Levin, 1981). A serious ethical problem emerged in the marketing industry as a result of the use of survey techniques for selling purposes, whereby respondents are led to believe that they are participating in a marketing research survey, only to find out after answering a series of questions that the actual purpose of the interview was to sell or promote a product or service (Day, 1975; Rothenberg, 1990). This practice is known in the marketing industry as "sugging," which means "selling under the guise of market research."

The rationale underlying the use of sugging by marketers is readily apparent, given the fact that the mere mention of certain products and services (such as insurance, magazines, and home improvements) during the early stages of an interview tends to sharply increase the rate of refusal, especially when respondents are contacted by telephone (Day, 1975). It also has been found that prior experience with a false survey increases the tendency of respondents to refuse to participate in subsequent legitimate surveys (Sheets et al., 1974). There is general agreement that this deceptive tactic represents a serious abuse of respondents' rights, and it is prohibited by the AMA's ethics code (though largely unenforceable). The Council for Marketing and Opinion Research (CMOR) also has taken steps to protect legitimate marketing and opinion research and the public opinion from such deceptive tactics, and there is governmental legislation outlawing telemarketing calls selling under the guise of research (see Box 7.5). For example, local US authorities have begun to require licenses and have imposed restrictions on the days and hours when interviewing can be conducted.

Despite these protections, there is some evidence that this practice has been increasing in frequency (see Rothenberg, 1990). For example, a Canadian survey conducted by the Marketing Research and Intelligence Association (MRIA, 2004) revealed that more than half of the respondents (53 percent) claimed to have been contacted for an alleged study that turned out to be an attempt to sell a product or service, and roughly one-in-four (27 percent) had been contacted for a study that turned out to be an attempt to solicit money for a charity or some other cause.

In addition to the ethical problems involved in the use of "surveys" to deceive potential consumers, selling under the guise of research also illustrates a link between methodological and ethical issues in marketing research. This is evident in the widespread fear that the practice increases suspiciousness among potential respondents and ultimately will lead to a reduction in response rates and response quality (see "Methodological issues" below).

Protecting survey respondents

Of all the ethical issues in marketing research listed in Table 7.1, those that are most central to the well-being of survey respondents have to do with privacy concerns and the manner in which the information obtained from respondents

---

Box 7.5   Fighting back against sugging

In December 2004, the Council for Marketing and Opinion Research (CMOR) took aggressive action against a company that had been engaging in the deceptive tactic of selling under the guise of market research (i.e. "sugging"). This involved the filing of a formal complaint against the company with the two main American regulatory bodies, the Federal Communications Commission (FCC) and the Federal Trade Commission (FTC).

The company in question (Emarket Research Group) had been flooding the Internet with offers for free laptops or US$500 gift certificates for participating in an extensive online survey. An investigation by the Marketing Research Association, however, revealed that the actual objective of the company was to sell multiple products and services, rather than to conduct genuine marketing research. The company's website was held to be in violation of the CAN-SPAM Act of 2003, in that it failed to provide substantive information about the firm, where it is located, what it does, or what services it offers. The company also was found to be registered under a fictitious name in at least two US states.

The CAN-SPAM Act is an American law that establishes requirements for those who send commercial e-mail, describes penalties for spammers and companies whose products are advertised in spam if they violate the law, and gives consumers the right to ask e-mailers to stop spamming them (FTC, 2004). Among the law's main provisions are the following: (1) it prohibits false or misleading header information (e.g. the "From" and "To" headings, as well as the originating e-mail address, must be accurate and should identify the person who initiated the e-mail); (2) it prohibits deceptive subject lines describing the content or subject matter of the message; (3) it requires that message recipients are given an opt-out method (i.e. a means is provided for the recipient to choose not to receive further messages); and (4) it requires that commercial e-mail must be clearly identified as an advertisement and include the sender's valid physical address. Violations of these provisions can result in the imposition of heavy fines against the at-fault company. In the case of the Emarket Research Group, the regulatory agencies informed the firm that it must immediately discontinue its deceptive practices and explained the damages done when companies misuse the survey process.

---

is treated. Specifically, researchers must respect the privacy of respondents, especially when the survey involves highly sensitive topics and when personal information is gathered. For example, some marketing researchers utilize in-depth probing techniques during interviews in order to uncover respondents' personal concerns, desires, fears, and anxieties. In other cases, potentially incriminating information might be sought, such as whether consumers have utilized illegal decoding devices in order to obtain free cable television service or have illegally downloaded content from the Internet. Previous research conducted in both the United States and Sweden revealed that concerns about breaches of confidentiality are particularly evident with regard to questions about income and the trustworthiness of institutions (National Academy of Sciences, 1979; National Central Bureau of Statistics, 1977).

For a majority of marketing surveys, respondents' privacy rights can be protected and research cooperation can be obtained under conditions of anonymity and through maintaining the confidentiality of responses (see Table 7.4). Some researchers, for example, attempt to ensure respondent anonymity by utilizing a self-administered questionnaire rather than an approach that requires the presence of an interviewer. The self-administered approach has both methodological and ethical advantages, particularly when it can be assumed that respondents are not suspicious about identifying marks on the questionnaire forms. Other researchers have provided written or verbal assurances of confidentiality in the hope that such a procedure will promote more honest disclosures from participants. Research on the relationship between such assurances and the subsequent quality of data is somewhat equivocal (Blanck et al., 1992).

Table 7.4 Procedures for protecting survey respondents

According to social psychologist Floyd Fowler, Jr. (1993), the key to protecting the privacy of survey respondents lies in the careful treatment of the information they provide. Fowler has suggested several guidelines for minimizing the chances that confidentiality may be breached. These guidelines are summarized below.

1 Commitment to confidentiality should be obtained in writing from all individuals who have access to survey data or who participate in the data collection process.
2 The linkages between survey responses and subject identifiers should be minimized. Respondent names often need not be obtained during any phase of the research process. When specific identifiers, such as names or addresses, are necessary, they can be physically separated from the forms on which the actual survey responses are recorded. (For specific procedures, see Boruch and Cecil, 1979, 1982.)
3 Only those persons who are involved in the survey project should have access to completed surveys.
4 Identifiers should be removed from completed questionnaires as soon as possible.
5 Actual questionnaire responses should not be available to individuals who could identify respondents from their profile of responses.
6 Actual data files usually will include an identification number for each respondent. The linkage between these numbers and other respondent identifiers (such as names and addresses) should not be available to data file users.
7 Special care should be taken when presenting data for very small categories of respondents who might be identifiable.
8 Researchers are responsible for the destruction of completed survey research instruments, or their continuing secure storage, when a project has been completed.

Another means of assuring potential respondents about the legitimacy of a survey is to have a central clearinghouse for registering surveys, assuming they meet certain guidelines, and potential respondents can then be given a toll-free telephone number or e-mail address to check for the legitimacy of a survey they have been asked to complete. A survey registration system of this kind exists in Canada (MRIA, 2004). The aforementioned MRIA Canadian study reported that over half of the respondents (52 percent) agreed that they would be more willing to participate in a survey where study legitimacy could be verified; however, only one in ten respondents were aware of Canada's survey registration system.

Threats to survey respondents' anonymity and confidentiality of data can arise from a number of activities, ranging from pre-coding mail questionnaires with ultraviolet ink to determine the identity of participants to providing subjects' names and addresses to a client after obtaining data under conditions of anonymity. Certain mildly deceptive procedures also represent threats to privacy, including the construction of survey questionnaire items so as to disguise their true intent from respondents or to encourage them to reveal information that they otherwise would not admit (e.g. by requesting year of birth rather than age).

The use of ultraviolet ink on pre-coded mail questionnaires in order to determine the identity of respondents represents a dramatic example of the invasion of privacy in the context of survey research. In a case reported by Boruch and Cecil (1979), a survey contractor engaged in marketing research for the *National Observer* newspaper covertly identified mail questionnaires using invisible ink, despite having included information implying that responses were anonymous. The purpose of the marketing study was innocuous enough – to obtain a statistical description of the newspaper subscribers' demographic characteristics. On the questionnaire sent to subscribers, the researcher promised that responses would be kept confidential and provided additional assurances which likely led most readers to conclude that their anonymity would be protected. For example, no identifying information was requested nor was the questionnaire apparently coded in any way. Eventually, a skeptical recipient exposed the form to ultraviolet light and discovered that an identification number did indeed appear on the questionnaire, resulting in embarrassing publicity about the deception for the survey research firm. The firm admitted the use of the invisible print but claimed that the technique was essential for following up on non-respondents.

The use of secretly pre-coded surveys has been defended by those who have argued that the practice reduces survey costs and response bias, and that the identity of respondents is never disclosed to anyone outside the research organization (Dickson et al., 1977). Regardless of these points, it is difficult to justify the secret coding of questionnaires from either an ethical or methodological perspective. The deceptive practice represents a clear violation of the respondents' right to privacy, and the use of such techniques can serve to raise the level of public mistrust and skepticism regarding all forms of research.

One non-deceptive technique that enables researchers to follow up on non-respondents in a way that also reassures respondents that their questionnaire responses will remain anonymous is to attach a separate postcard with a respond-ent identifier to a questionnaire with no identifier on it. On the postcard a statement addressed to the researcher indicates that the completed questionnaire was mailed at the same time and that the researcher need not send a further reminder urging the respondent to participate in the study. According to Fowler (2001), this procedure apparently does not result in respondents simply returning the postcard alone in order to avoid further reminders; in fact, the number of postcards and questionnaires received tends to be about the same in most studies employing this procedure.

In large-scale survey research, the confidentiality of individual responses can be preserved by application of randomized response methods (Boruch and Cecil, 1982; Fidler and Kleinknecht, 1977; Fox and Tracy, 1980, 1984; Warner, 1965). In a simple variation of this approach, a randomizing device (such as flipping a coin) is used in such a way that interviewers are unable to ascertain which question a respondent is actually answering. As an illustration, this technique can be used to estimate the prevalence of a behavior that is likely to generate a legal risk or embarrassment to a disclosing respondent, such as spousal abuse or cocaine usage. In order to select how to respond to a stigmatizing question (e.g. "Did you beat your wife last month?" "Have you ever used cocaine?") the subject is instructed to flip a coin out of the researcher's sight, and to respond "yes" if it lands heads and to respond truthfully ("yes" or "no") if it lands tails. On a probability basis, it is possible to obtain an estimate of the behavior of interest without compromising the respondent's right to privacy. Knowing that 50 percent of the respondents are expected to get heads to respond "yes," it is then possible to estimate the proportion that actually indicated they had engaged in the sensitive behavior.

In marketing research, the randomized response method might be employed in lifestyle studies involving sensitive and perhaps illegal activities, such as shoplift-ing, gambling, downloading copyrighted material from the Internet, and the procurement of prostitutes within various consumer populations. It should be noted, however, that evidence suggests that if sufficient care is taken to guarantee anonymity, the randomized response technique may not prove more effective than straightforward questioning of respondents in yielding revelations in response to sensitive questions (Linden and Weiss, 1994).

As described in chapter 5, some of these concerns regarding threats to ano-nymity and confidentiality have been raised with increasing frequency with respect to surveys that are conducted electronically. As a result, in recent years there has been a corresponding rise in activity oriented to protecting privacy when new media are used for conducting survey research. For example, the American Marketing Association recently added a set of Internet guidelines to its generic ethics code under the heading *Code of Ethics for Marketing on the Internet*. On the legislative front, the European Union has adopted a directive that requires all EU member states to restrict the export of data to nations lacking adequate privacy protections, prompting the US Congress to enact similar privacy protec-tions (Reid and Priest, 1999).

Methodological issues in marketing research

The linkage between methodological and ethical issues is apparent in marketing research in several ways. As previously discussed, perhaps the most obvious ethical concern stems from the recognition that applied researchers sometimes are pressured by organizations to design research in order to support a particular decision or to enhance a legal position (see Box 7.3). In marketing, revelations pertaining to research sponsored by major American tobacco companies clearly illustrate the difficulties that may be faced by researchers working in applied settings. For example, one tobacco company halted the research of two of the company's scientists who had found preliminary evidence in the early 1980s that a substance in cigarettes increased the addictive power of nicotine (Hilts, 1994a). The company also apparently took steps to block efforts to publish that and other work. One company executive who met with the researchers shortly after they were told to stop their studies and to kill their laboratory rats reportedly asked: "Why should we risk a billion-dollar business for some rats' studies?"

In point of fact, it is relatively easy for marketing researchers to use their methodological skills in order to obtain desired outcomes. Studies can be designed to support a particular decision through the adroit choice of subject samples, biased question wording and placement, and the selective coding and analysis of responses (see Box 7.6).

Box 7.6   Biased questioning in survey research

Sources of bias can enter into the questionnaire data collection process in several ways. An awareness of the effects of question biases can be exploited by unscrupulous researchers in order to increase the likelihood of obtaining desired results. As an example, consider the results of a publicized finding from a survey conducted on behalf of the Burger King hamburger chain. It was reported that consumer respondents preferred Burger King's flame-broiled hamburger to McDonald's fried hamburger by a margin of 3 to 1 (Kinnear and Taylor, 1995). The actual question used by Burger King that led to this result was "Do you prefer your hamburgers flame-broiled or fried?"

When an independent researcher rephrased the question by asking consumers "Do you prefer a hamburger that is grilled on a hot stainless steel grill or cooked by passing the raw meat through an open gas flame?," the results, not surprisingly, were reversed (53 percent of those questioned preferred McDonald's cooking process). This suggests that the initial Burger King survey pitted the most appealing word it could find to describe its cooking process against the most unappealing word for its competitor's cooking process. In short, it was the question semantics that determined the apparent preference for cooking methods, not the actual product.

Box 7.6   (Continued)

Another way that bias can enter into the survey research process is through the use of so-called leading questions. Leading (or "loaded") questions are those that provide respondents with cues as to what the answer should be. For example, the question "Do you own a Sony television set?" would be a leading question if it resulted in a higher reported Sony ownership than when the question simply asked "What brand of television set do you own?" When a brand or company name is included in the question, respondents may assume that company has sponsored the study, thereby resulting in a desire to express positive feelings towards the survey sponsor (Kinnear and Taylor, 1995).

Other examples of biased questions are those including words or phrases that are emotionally charged, provide the respondent with a reason for selecting one of the alternatives, or associate a position with a prestigious (or non-prestigious) person or organization. The following questionnaire items reflect these kinds of hidden (or not-so-hidden) biases (Aaker and Day, 1990; Fowler, 1993):

"Do you agree or disagree that the government should stop wasting money on road construction?" (The researcher's bias is obvious here, and who would ever favor wasting money?)

"Should we increase taxes in order to get more housing and better schools, or should we keep them about the same?" (Despite most individuals' aversion to raising taxes, this question is biased towards an affirmative answer because only the benefits of raising taxes are specified.)

"Do you agree or disagree that the free trade agreement has destroyed the economy?"

"Do you agree that the Mayor has an annoying, confrontational style?" (The use of emotionally charged or negative words, such as "destroyed" or "annoying," can have strong overtones that may overshadow the specific content of the question.)

"Do you agree or disagree with the American Dental Association's position that advertising pre-sweetened cereal to children is harmful?" (In this case the prestigious organization is associated with a particular position.)

Another methodological concern in marketing research has to do with the impact of informed consent procedures on the outcomes of marketing surveys. Research on the effects of informed consent in survey research primarily has focused on the survey response rate and the quality of subjects' responses. In contrast to the situation in the laboratory setting, the power differential between the survey researcher and the potential respondent is somewhat reversed, with the respondent typically in a powerful position to refuse to participate (Sieber, 1982c).

Overall, studies suggest that the negative impact of informed consent on survey research is negligible. With the exception of the request for a signature to document consent (a procedure that is not always necessary), the elements of informed consent do not appear to have much of an effect on response rates or quality of responses to surveys. In one study, Singer (1978) reported that when more detailed, informative, and truthful information about the content of a survey was provided beforehand to potential respondents (such as a description of the content of sensitive questions), neither the overall response rate nor responses to specific survey questions seemed to be affected. In a follow-up study, Singer and Frankel (1982) varied information about the content and purpose of a telephone interview. The results revealed that the manipulated variables did not significantly affect the overall response rate, response to individual survey items, or quality of response. In fact, the highest response rate and fewest refusals were obtained when respondents were provided with the greatest detail about the interview. Similarly, Loo (1982) reported a high level of cooperation among respondents given an opportunity to vent their concerns to respectful and apparently sympathetic investigators.

Despite the apparent lack of significant adverse effects in survey research, researchers should remain cautious of the influence of certain mediating variables that are operative in different consent situations. For example, there is some evidence that respondents may not fully attend to what they are told during the consent procedure (see Singer, 1978), and other research has shown that informed consent can reduce participation and response to specific items in surveys (Lueptow et al., 1977). Additionally, the content and purpose of a survey can interact with sensitive response variables. Informed consent might alert respondents in advance about threatening questions, thereby allowing respondents ample time to think up alternative responses or to decide not to respond at all. Such might be the case when welfare clients are forewarned about income questions or when employees in large corporations are asked about their drinking habits (Singer, 1978).

One of the more pressing methodological concerns in marketing research has to do with the increasing difficulty of obtaining random samples for surveys due to declining rates of participation. Many believe this decline in research participation is due in large part to an increase in suspiciousness among respondents after negative encounters with marketing researchers or with salespersons posing as marketing researchers. As response rates and response quality continue to decline, the long-term statistical reliability of marketing research may be jeopardized. Further, as it becomes more difficult for researchers to obtain random subject samples, there is the additional possibility that they will be tempted to utilize unethical strategies for inducing people into their samples.

Another factor that adversely affects public willingness to cooperate is the increasingly intrusive nature of the research process. In marketing, excessive interviewing in certain districts, such as those that are especially popular for test markets, may be perceived by consumers as violations of their basic right to privacy (Aaker and Day, 1990). This can lead to resentment and a decrease in willingness to fully cooperate, especially if it is believed that participation in one study will result in further research requests.

As with deception, if one were to be absolutist about the principle of privacy in applied research it would be nearly impossible to conduct many meaningful studies because, in a sense, the basic nature of such research – like most behavioral research – is to be intrusive. Ringing a respondent's doorbell or telephone represents an intrusion. After all, much of the information that is sought in studies of human behavior involves human processes that people are trying to protect, defend, or cover up. While respect for the rights of subjects should be held in the highest regard by applied researchers, those rights have to be balanced by the potential benefits and goals within the applied research context.

SUMMARY

This concludes our two-chapter survey of ethical issues in applied research. Clearly, marketing research is fraught with many of the same ethical problems that emerge in more traditional behavioral science research fields, albeit with added complications due to the objectives and goals of the marketing enterprise. Many of these complications can be circumvented when the researcher enters into a professional relationship with a company knowledgeable and up-to-date about the kinds of dilemmas that can emerge in applied contexts, and establishes an agreement with the firm that clearly spells out each party's responsibilities. It is unlikely that the various values, obligations, and goals of company representatives and the research team will be completely compatible, and thus it is essential that potential conflicts be discussed in advance.

Whatever the research situation, it is important for applied researchers to bear in mind that their first obligation is to those persons who cooperate with and participate in the research process. Many of the ethical problems that arise when researchers impose their frames of reference on behavior can be avoided when subjects are treated as partners in the research process. In chapter 8, ethical issues pertinent to the recruitment and selection of research subjects are considered.

8

Recruitment and Selection of Research Subjects

"All students are expected to complete at least three *(3) hours of participation in research studies conducted within the university's Psychology Department in addition to the other course requirements. Sign-up forms describing ongoing studies are located on the bulletin board outside the department secretary's office. Students who do not wish to serve as research subjects may instead complete three written reports (each at least five pages in length) on topics relevant to psychology. All topics must be approved by the instructor."*
Research Participation Requirement on Introductory Psychology Course Syllabus

Chapter Topics

☞ The university subject pool: overview and issues
☞ The ethical use of the subject pool
☞ Ethical and methodological issues associated with volunteer samples
☞ Research incentives
☞ Participants from vulnerable populations

To the best of the author's recollection, the passage that appears above approximates a course requirement that appeared on the syllabus for his first college course as a student of psychology. Many readers may recall a similar passage from the outlines of courses they had taken in psychology, or perhaps have themselves written such a statement on a syllabus for a course they have taught.

It is quite common to find research participation requirements or opportunities for extra credit on introductory course outlines because the university "subject pool" represents a primary source of behavioral science research participants (Higbee and Wells, 1972; Jung, 1969; Landrum and Chastain, 1999; Schultz, 1969; Sieber, 1999; Sieber and Saks, 1989). Surveys show that more than 70 percent of the studies conducted in the areas of personality and social psychology and about 90 percent of cognition and perception studies utilized college students as participants (Korn and Bram, 1987; Sears, 1986). One survey of 366 psychology departments in the United States revealed that

74 percent had student subject pools, with 93.4 percent recruiting subjects from introductory psychology courses and 35.4 percent recruiting from other lower division courses (Sieber and Saks, 1989). Similar results were obtained from a survey of 50 Canadian educational institutions offering programs in psychology (Lindsay and Holden, 1987). These figures represent a continuation of a long-standing tradition in the behavioral sciences, as evidenced by Quinn McNemar's (1946, p. 333) remark, over half a century ago, that "The existing science of human behavior is largely the science of the behavior of sophomores." The fact that college students comprise an overwhelming majority of behavioral science research participants has prompted some writers to refer to them as psychology's human "fruit flies" (Keith-Spiegel and Koocher, 1985; Rubenstein, 1982).

The over-reliance on students for research purposes is not limited to traditional basic research areas in psychology. In other disciplines, including the applied areas of marketing and advertising research, students may be required to serve as experimental subjects as a course requirement, solicited as volunteers, or asked to participate in studies during class time (e.g. by completing questionnaires and the like). Traditionally, marketing researchers have obtained their data by going directly to consumers in non-laboratory settings; however, as early as the mid-1970s, there was growing concern that they were beginning to rely on students as research surrogates. In an analysis of *JMR* articles appearing over a ten-year span (1964–74), Permut, Michel, and Joseph (1976) found that more than one-fifth (21.9 percent) of the subject samples were composed of students, while nearly one-fourth consisted of housewives (12.8 percent) and heads of households (10.4 percent). More recently, McQuarrie (1998) estimated that up to 90 percent of published studies in *JCR* relied on student samples. Based on his own analysis, McQuarrie reported that 67 percent of the laboratory experiments appearing in the *Journal of Advertising Research* (JAR) relied on student samples.

The results of my own research revealed a steady rise in the use of student subject samples over time in studies published in *JCR* and *JMR*, from 25.3 percent (1975–76) to 68 percent (2001–02). Corresponding to the increased use of students in marketing studies, the analysis showed a significant drop in adult consumers (from 54.2 to 32 percent) and business professionals (from 16.9 to 9.5 percent) across the four time periods studied (Kimmel, 2001, 2004). In short, it appears that marketing research samples have progressively come to resemble traditional behavioral science samples in recent years.

Although there are certain educational (and other) benefits that may be gained from research participation, there are ethical and methodological questions that need to be considered with regard to the extensive use of college students as participants in research investigations. For example, are such individuals, who by the nature of their educational status represent a relatively low-power group, unfairly coerced to serve as subjects or is research participation truly voluntary? Do they have freedom of choice to refuse to satisfy a research participation course requirement and are alternative means of completing the coursework offered? Are student participants educationally debriefed, and do the educational and other benefits of participation outweigh the risks for this group? What are the methodological limitations of studying individuals whose behavior in research may not be representative of the general population? Similar kinds of questions are relevant to the use of subjects sampled from other low power or vulnerable groups in society, such as children, the elderly, prisoners, and the institutional-ized, or when research participation is required as part of employment or some other professional relationship with the investigator.

Increasing sensitivity to issues having to do with subject pool policies and procedures has been apparent in recent years, and the importance of voluntary research participation has been emphasized in professional codes of ethics and governmental guidelines. As a guiding principle for framing this chapter's con-sideration of issues pertaining to the recruitment and selection of research parti-cipants, the current APA guideline (standard 8.04) for ensuring freedom from coercion to participate, which the reader may recall from chapter 2, is particularly relevant (APA, 2002, p. 1069):

(a) When psychologists conduct research with clients/patients, students, or subor-dinates as participants, psychologists take steps to protect the prospective par-ticipants from adverse consequences of declining or withdrawing from participation.
(b) When research participation is a course requirement or an opportunity for extra credit, the prospective participant is given the choice of equitable alternative activities.

The investigator's obligation to respect the individual's freedom to decline to participate in or to withdraw from any stage of the research process has been incorporated into the APA code since its earliest versions. However, the applica-tion of this principle is not always straightforward and researchers are apt to encounter ethical dilemmas, particularly when they hold power over prospective subjects or otherwise control desired resources.

THE UNIVERSITY SUBJECT POOL

As mentioned, the preponderance of data obtained in behavioral research with human participants has been provided by college students, a majority of whom were recruited through organized subject pools. University subject pools typically are comprised of all those available students in introductory and other lower-level behavioral science courses who are encouraged (and sometimes required) to participate in campus research in order to obtain some sort of incentive. While the incentive may be monetary in nature, it is more likely to take the form of course credit (e.g. Kimmel, 2001; Lindsay and Holden, 1987). Research partici-pation also may be required merely as a prerequisite to obtaining a course grade; in such cases, an alternative means of satisfying the research requirement typic-ally is made available to students.

Justification for student research participation

Several arguments have been offered to justify the extensive use of students for research participation. One practical consideration has to do with the basic necessity of having a readily available pool of prospective participants for the many research studies that are carried out in university settings during a typical academic year. For academic researchers, a student subject pool represents a convenient, inexpensive study population, thereby eliminating the difficult and costly task of having to recruit participants from outside the university setting. In this regard, undergraduate students stand to benefit society by permitting the carrying out of important research that otherwise might not have been conducted.

Beyond the pragmatic concern for easy attainment of subject samples in research-oriented institutions, an argument can be made that students have an obligation to make a contribution to the discipline that they are studying (Schuler, 1982). By advancing knowledge through participation, students themselves also stand to benefit as that knowledge eventually is conveyed to them during the study of the relevant subject matter in their classes (Bowman and Waite, 2003; Diener and Crandall, 1978; King, 1970). More directly, it is commonly agreed that participation in research can provide clear educational benefits to students by demonstrating firsthand what the research process is like. This common educational justification for requiring student participation is based on the assumption that students can gain a better appreciation of the scientific process by experiencing it directly rather than by having the process described solely through class lectures or readings (Britton, 1987; Coulter, 1986; Rosell et al., 2005). Universities typically require that subject pool participants be educationally debriefed by the researcher or otherwise obtain an explanation of the research purpose and methods.

Despite concerns about coercion and the possibility that students may not receive worthwhile feedback or attend to the feedback that they do receive, surveys generally have shown that students believe that their participation in research was a positive and useful learning experience (Bowman and Waite, 2003; Britton, 1979; Christensen, 1988; Davis and Fernald, 1975; King, 1970; Leak, 1981). Of course, it could be argued that such after-the-fact evaluations on the part of subjects may simply be a means for them to cognitively justify having devoted their time to the research enterprise. Whether or not this is the case, subjects inevitably learn something about the research process through research participation, even if they do not retain specifics about the research design or variables investigated in complex studies (Nummer and Handelsman, 1992).

Further, there is evidence that students' reactions to research participation are especially favorable when an organized effort is made to integrate the research experience into the educational program and when participation is specifically used to introduce and illustrate the nature of the scientific process (Davis and Fernald, 1975; Rosell et al., 2005). For example, Rosell and her colleagues (2005) studied the educational value of participation in psychology experiments by assessing students' perceptions about the science and methodology of psychology at various times during the school term. The researchers attributed the observed improvement of students' understanding of psychology and research procedures over the course of the semester to the combined influence of research participation and course content. As Diener and Crandall (1978) noted, the research experience is not unlike the laboratory section of traditional science courses, with the additional advantage that students are contributing to science and not merely engaging in a learning exercise.

The fact that subject pool participants often are required to participate in multiple studies can have certain methodological disadvantages, especially when subjects become suspicious of the experimenter's intent in later studies following early exposure to deceptive manipulations (see chapter 4). However, Schuler (1982) has suggested that the routine nature of participation for students can actually be seen as having an ethical advantage as well. In his view, by subjects becoming accustomed to the research situation, the overall experience becomes less stressful for them, thereby reducing the researcher's responsibility to some extent. Rather than leading to a cynical attitude on the part of subjects, routine participation can encourage them to adopt the role of research partner in the scientific process.

Ethical concerns about student subject pools

It is clear that subject pools satisfy their primary purpose in providing "grist for the research mill"; nevertheless, ethical concerns have been voiced about the use of college recruits, particularly with regard to the problem of coercion and related forms of exploitation (McCord, 1991; Tickle and Heatherton, 2005). Specifically, there are fears that alternative means of satisfying course requirements may not be offered or else are excessively time consuming or noxious; that students may receive little if any educational debriefing; and that readily accessible complaint procedures are not available to student research participants (Britton, 1979; Keith-Spiegel and Koocher, 1985; Sieber and Saks, 1989). According to one critic of the extensive use of student participants in research, "only a moderate degree of cynicism is required to characterize psychology as a science based on the contributions of a captive population with little power" (Korn, 1988, p. 74).

To date, research on the ethical implementation of university subject pools, the educational outcomes that students derive from participation in research, and students' perceptions of the research requirement is mixed. The results of a comprehensive survey of 366 psychology departments in the United States identified as having both graduate programs and human subject pools seem to justify some of the concerns described above. Sieber and Saks (1989) reported that a number of the surveyed departments were not in full compliance with professional and federal ethical guidelines in terms of protecting students from coercion to participate in research, offering clear educational benefits to research participants, and providing reasonable alternatives to participation.

More recently, Landrum and Chastain (1999) replicated Sieber and Sak's graduate school investigation by conducting a broad survey of 485 undergraduate psychology programs. Perhaps not surprisingly, given the greater emphasis on teaching at the undergraduate level, Landrum and Chastain's study revealed that subject pools were far less common when compared with the earlier graduate school survey (32.7 versus 74.0 percent, respectively). Subject pools were found to be more common at public (40.5 percent) than at private (29.7 percent) undergraduate institutions. With regard to the functioning of the undergraduate subject pools, it was found that 34.7 percent utilized totally volunteer pools, whereas 24.8 percent recruited subjects by offering extra credit. A majority (62.9 percent) of the responding departments revealed that they did not assess the educational value of the students' research experience.

Given the general consensus that subject pools should serve an educational purpose for the numerous students who contribute their time to participate in university research, it is reasonable to expect that formal evaluations to assess the educational value of student research participation should be conducted as a matter of course. Towards that end, Landrum and Chastain (1995) developed the following six-item experimental spot-check assessment instrument, which can be distributed to student-participants at various times during an academic year (responses are given using a five-point scale, ranging from 1 = strongly disagree to 5 = strongly agree):

1   I was treated fairly and with respect during my research session.
2   I learned about psychology by participating in a research project.
3   The research experience is a good way to add variety to introductory psychology.
4   I think that this research experience was a waste of time.
5   I think that participating in this project helped me understand research better.
6   The purpose of this experiment was adequately explained to me.

In one application, Landrum and Chastain administered the spot-check form to 200 psychology subjects at an American university during the 1993–94 academic year and found that students tended to report having favorable reactions to the research requirement. Participants scored above the scale midpoint, on average, for items indicating that participating in research improved their learning about psychology and research, they were treated fairly and with respect, the purpose of the study was adequately explained, and the research experience added variety to their courses.

Returning to the issue of coercion, when students are provided with undesirable and time-consuming alternatives to a research participation requirement, like having to write short term papers or take a quiz, they essentially are left with little choice at all but to participate in the research. Many students are unlikely to select extensive written alternatives to research participation, no matter how unpleasant they may view the research requirement. In addition to the fact that having to write additional papers is an especially noxious choice for many students, who may be overburdened with their regular coursework, they also may fear that their course grade will somehow be adversely affected if they do not choose the instructor's obviously preferred requirement. Such forces are likely to reduce the voluntary nature of participation, and are apt to have a more serious impact in required courses. Voluntary participation also will be seriously threatened when bonus points can be obtained for volunteering for research in situations where there is strong competition for grades.

Despite concerns about coercing students into research participation, it appears that students derive greater satisfaction and educational benefits from the decision to serve as research subjects when given a choice between that option and the term paper alternative. For example, in a comparison of college students' participation in varying research activities, Bowman and Waite (2003) compared students' reactions to volunteering in a research study or writing a short term paper about research. The results revealed that those who volunteered for research participation were more satisfied with their experience and developed more favorable perceptions of psychology and research than those who wrote term papers.

The fact that subject recruitment announcements are characteristically vague exacerbates the problems of undue coercion and exploitation of naive research participants. The solicitation of subject pool participants typically involves the use of sign-up forms posted in the appropriate academic department on campus or distributed during class meetings. Students select a convenient appointment time from those listed on the sheet; their signature essentially serves to establish an agreement with the researcher to participate in the study at the designated time. Often, however, the brief summary of the research on the sign-up form is uninformative and at times misleading, so that students may be left unaware of what they are agreeing to. The decision to participate in one study versus another thus may be based more on the availability of a convenient appointment time than the specific details of what the study apparently will involve.

Subject recruitment announcements may appear rather innocuous, but often belie the true nature of the investigation. For example, the newspaper advertisement used by Philip Zimbardo to solicit participants for his simulated prison experiment (Box 8.1) reflects the passive deception employed throughout the consent phase of that investigation. The announcement for Stanley Milgram's obedience study includes an active deception (the investigation is described as "a scientific study of memory and learning"). It is noteworthy that in these two examples, neither researcher relied on available subject pools for selecting participants; in fact, for the obedience study, Milgram recruited non-students from the

---

Box 8.1   Subject recruitment announcement for the Stanford prison experiment

Male college students needed for psychological study of prison life. $15 per day for 1–2 weeks beginning Aug. 14. For further information and applications, come to Room 248, Jordan Hall, Stanford U.

general population. Milgram's recruitment announcement, which appeared in a local newspaper, offered to pay adult volunteers $4.00 for one hour of their time. The ad specified that the researchers were seeking factory workers, city employees, laborers, businessmen, and others.

When subjects agree to participate in studies that are only vaguely described on recruitment forms, they may find themselves in difficult positions when they appear for their appointment and learn that the research is not quite what they expected. Faced with the decision to withdraw or to go ahead with participation, most students likely opt for participation, viewing their initial agreement to serve as subjects as an obligation that cannot be avoided. Once the initial agreement has been made, demand characteristics of the experimental situation are apt to enhance the perceived power of the investigator and importance of the task at hand, thereby increasing the likelihood of the participant's continued compliance (Kelman, 1972; Orne, 1962; Rosnow, 2002). These forces underline the ethical responsibility of investigators to maintain a sensitivity to their subjects' needs and to cues suggesting that withdrawal is being contemplated. The likelihood of overly vague study descriptions may be diminishing, however, as university administrators and review boards become more sensitive to ethical issues. An examination of subject pool guidelines posted on the Internet suggests that university policies are becoming more rigorous.

In addition to threats to the voluntary nature of research participation, it has been argued that students typically receive dubious educational benefits from their participation in research (Korn, 1988). In fact, for many behavioral science investigations conducted on university campuses, subject pools tend only to provide direct benefits to the researchers who use them. As discussed in our consideration of debriefing techniques in chapter 3, investigators may do little to help make research participation a learning experience for subjects. Many researchers may simply provide subjects with a cursory description of their study on a sheet of paper that is distributed at the end of the experimental session or in the form of an abstract of findings that is mailed to them a few months later (Brody et al., 2000; Coulter, 1986). Moreover, some studies are of such minor significance that they hold little educational potential for participants. By contrast, certain complex, theoretical investigations may be virtually impossible to explain adequately to introductory level students in the short period of time typically allotted to the debriefing session. We earlier considered the possibility that subjects may give minimal attention to the debriefing information they receive after participating in a study. As a result of these factors, some subjects are apt to view their research experience as a trivial and boring waste of their time, perhaps compounding any initial feelings of resentment at having to participate in the first place.

For those students who choose for whatever reason not to satisfy the participation requirement, opting instead to complete an alternative assignment, the educational merits may be even more dubious. In recent years, course instructors have turned to fairer alternatives to research participation that can provide students with relatively equivalent learning experiences. As Landrum and Chastain (1999) reported, instead of extensive term papers, students may be asked to summarize empirical studies appearing in scientific journals, observe an experiment, watch a videotape, attend a conference or colloquium, or complete some other research-related exercise.

Although such activities can offer much to students in the way of educational benefits, they can easily become empty exercises unless they are taken seriously by students and faculty. For example, students might be provided with only minimal feedback from their instructor relative to alternative writing assignments, such as an acknowledgment that they were acceptable (or unacceptable). Instructors rarely have an incentive to grade such reports, which may consist of nothing more than a poor paraphrasing of a journal article or a lecture's key points, and, as a result, instructors may find it easier to simply award bonus points on exams to encourage greater participation in research (Ferrari and McGowan, 2002). In short, although alternative assignments can reduce the likelihood that students are forced into research participation against their will, a poorly implemented program of research alternatives merely adds to concerns about the unfair treatment of student participants.

The ethical use of student subject pools

Several guidelines have been proposed for the ethical use of student subject pools, dating back to the set developed by the American Psychological Association (APA, 1982), summarized in Box 8.2. In addition, a growing number of universities with subject pools have developed specific policies for faculty and student researchers who use them. It should be noted that these guidelines also apply to the general treatment of semi-volunteer research participants solicited in other ways, such as when students are asked to provide questionnaire data during class time.

Outside of North America, however, such policies remain rare. In the United Kingdom, which has led the way in terms of the establishment of ethics committees to oversee research, the National Health Service has implemented a general set of departmental ethics committee standards requiring the ethical and methodological review of all NHS-affiliated research that poses risks to participants (see www.keele.ac.uk). At the time of this writing, the British Psychological Society's Research Board was engaged in work to develop guidelines for the establishment and operation of departmental ethics committees. The Research Board's working group concluded in its initial report that university psychology departments in the UK vary considerably in terms of how they approve and monitor research, and some departments have no procedures at all (Foot and Sanford, 2004). The European Union has lagged in establishing standards for university research; the current Charter of Fundamental Rights of the European Union includes no mention of subject pools or student research participants (see http://europa.eu.int). The rejection of the European constitution by France and the Netherlands in 2005 is likely to serve as a further setback to future ethical developments.

The APA guidelines provide a useful starting point for a consideration of the proper administration of subject pools. These guidelines are intended to apply only to the use of a research participation requirement for studies that offer the

Box 8.2   Suggested guidelines for ethical use of the subject pool (American Psychological Association, 1982)

1   Students should be informed about the research requirement prior to their enrolling in a course.
2   Investigators who intend to use the university subject pool should obtain the prior approval of their research proposals (e.g. by a departmental committee or an Institutional Review Board).
3   Alternative options that are commensurate in time and effort to research participation should be provided so that students may choose the type of research experience, as well as the time and place of participation.
4   A description of the procedures to be employed and the right to withdraw at any time without penalty should be provided and consent sought before the student begins participation.
5   Steps should be taken so that students are treated with respect and courtesy.
6   Students should obtain some sort of reward in return for their participation, at least minimally consisting of as full an explanation of the research purposes as possible.
7   A mechanism should exist by which students may report any mistreatment or questionable conduct related to the research participation requirement.
8   The recruiting procedure should be under constant review, taking into consideration students' evaluations of the research participation requirement.

participant potential educational benefits. An addendum to the APA guidelines suggests that other means of recruiting subjects should be used when the potential for educational gain is missing. For instance, in studies involving long-term participation, the potential for educational gain to subjects typically is exhausted at an early stage in the investigation. In such cases, it is common practice to offer other incentives, such as monetary ones, and to recruit participants from outside the university subject pool. This, in fact, was the approach used by Zimbardo and his colleagues to recruit subjects for what was originally intended as a two-week prison simulation. Because the educational value of research participation may be expected to drop considerably after participation in three or four short-term experiments, the number of total hours for a research requirement should not be too high (Diener and Crandall, 1978).

Turning to the specific APA guidelines, it is suggested that students should be informed of a research participation requirement prior to their enrollment in the course. In essence, this point reflects the necessity for "truth in advertising" for students as they go about making their course selections (Hogan and Kimmel,

1992). Thus, the participation requirement might be stated in the course description in the university catalog. At a minimum, the requirement should appear on the course syllabus distributed at the beginning of the semester when students still have time to decide whether to continue with the class or find an alternative one.

The information that may be provided to students in a description of the subject pool requirement includes the following: the amount of participation required; the available alternatives to participation in research; the general nature of the kinds of studies from which students are expected to choose; the right of students to withdraw from a study without penalty at any time; the penalties for failing to satisfy the requirement or for not fulfilling one's obligations to the researcher; the researcher's obligation to treat subjects ethically and to provide an explanation of the research; procedures to follow if subjects are mistreated; and an explanation of the scientific purposes of research conducted in the departmental laboratories (APA, 1982).

With regard to alternative opportunities for research participation, it is recommended in the discussion accompanying the APA guidelines that students might observe and write about ongoing research or submit a short paper describing published research reports. Other useful suggestions for optional assignments which provide students with educationally beneficial experiences have been offered by researchers. Among the ideas considered at one American university, in addition to allowing students to sign up as observers rather than as participants in selected studies (subject to the investigator's approval), were: (1) scheduling a series of evening research presentations by graduate students and faculty for undergraduates to attend; (2) allowing the customary journal article summary, but with specific articles selected beforehand by faculty based on a determination that they report high-quality, recent studies; and (3) allowing students to assist in an ongoing research project for a specified period of time, by doing data entry and the like (McCord, 1991). These alternatives were selected on the basis of their being essentially equivalent to the research requirement in terms of time, effort, odiousness, and course credit available.

Another possible alternative to research participation would be to have students participate in community volunteer work, perhaps arranged through departmental student organizations, such as Psi Chi (the honors society for psychology students). Raupp and Cohen (1992), for example, have developed a model for incorporating community service volunteering as a course component. Their application involved a course option in which upper-level students were given the opportunity to assist in elementary school tutoring as an alternative to more traditional course requirements. This basic approach surely could be extended to a variety of community volunteer activities in order to provide students in introductory-level courses with an involving and educationally beneficial alternative to research participation. (See Table 8.1 for a summary listing of possible alternatives to the student research requirement.)

Sieber and Saks (1989) have argued that the educational value of subject pools can be maximized when an appropriate *quid pro quo* is established between researcher and student. That is, because the student provides data that yield

Table 8.1   Alternatives to the student research requirement

1	The reading and summarizing of journal articles describing recent, high-quality research
2	Observations of selected, ongoing studies
3	Informal field observations of behavior
4	The viewing of videotapes of laboratory experiments or filmed presentations of how an investigation is carried out, followed by a discussion led by a research assistant
5	Attendance at a research presentation, colloquium, or lecture organized by graduate students and faculty
6	Assisting in an ongoing research project for a specified period of time
7	Attendance at student presentation sessions of research from upper-level courses
8	Conducting a case study using oneself as a participant in some sort of simulation
9	Engaging in volunteer community service activities
10	Readings (e.g. paperback books) about the research process

These recommendations were compiled from the following sources: APA (1982), Diener and Crandall (1978), Landrum and Chastain (1999), McCord (1991), Raupp and Cohen (1992), Sieber and Saks (1989).

knowledge, the researcher should repay the student in kind, not with money or grades, but with interesting and worthwhile knowledge. Additionally, having an opportunity to observe a data collection session or to watch a videotaped presentation of how an investigation is carried out would represent far more inviting and educational alternatives to writing assignments and other course work for students who may choose not to participate in research. Subjects could benefit, following their participation in a study, from instructional feedback devoted to a description of the research design, the hypotheses, and the relevancy of the data collected for testing the hypotheses. Further, participants could be asked to complete evaluation forms by rating the researcher on such qualities as respectful treatment of subjects, clarity and adequacy of informed consent and debriefing, and overall interest and value of the research experience.

As a means for protecting students from unfair coercion, some departments offer research participation not as a course requirement, but rather as one of several things that can be done to earn extra credit points. Although Ferrari and McGowan (2002) studied the influence of exam bonus points where research participation was part of a course requirement, they found that students offered the points began work at an earlier date and completed the research requirement more frequently than students not offered the incentive. Providing students with the opportunity to obtain extra credit through alternative means (such as by writing one-page reviews of articles on library reserve) would avoid the problem of imposing a penalty on non-volunteers. As another protection against coercion, researchers should remain sensitive to the possibility that they are inducing research participation by implying that cooperation will be rewarded by more favorable perceptions of the participant by others.

Collectively, these recommendations for the ethical use of subject pools suggest that (1) attention and effort should be devoted to ensuring that students gain educational value from research participation, and (2) research participation should be available to students as a means for enhancing their course grades rather than jeopardizing grades in any way (Keith-Spiegel and Koocher, 1985).

Thus, students should be informed of the department's subject pool policy prior to enrolling in the course and then again as soon as the course begins. When research participation is made a requirement for successful completion of a course, the alternative means for meeting the requirement should be well-publicized to students, in case they object to participation for whatever reason (Hogan and Kimmel, 1992).

Students also need to be aware of their freedom to withdraw from participation in a study at any time, despite their agreement to serve as subjects. Prospective subjects may show up for a scheduled appointment only to learn that the research involves certain aversive procedures (such as the administration of low-intensity electric shocks) that were not apparent in the original description on the subject sign-up sheet. Some subject pool participants may inaccurately assume that they have no choice but to go through with participation or else lose the promised incentives (such as course credit) as a penalty for withdrawing. The freedom to withdraw from, or refuse to participate in, particular investigations should be explained when the research participation policy is first presented to students and they should be reminded of this right when they arrive for a study. Investigators also are obligated to protect students from adverse consequences attributed to their having declined or withdrawn from research participation (APA, 1992).

Finally, the APA guidelines for the ethical use of subject pools emphasize the importance of having mechanisms in place for reviewing the research participation requirement and for enabling subjects to initiate complaint procedures when they feel that they have been mistreated. Most universities now require that investigators planning on using the subject pool first must have their research proposals approved by a campus subject pool committee or institutional review board. The subject pool application process can serve as a valuable reminder to researchers of their ethical responsibilities to research participants.

Research recruitment procedures can be reviewed and modified based on the regular monitoring of participants' attitudes towards the requirement and investigators' evaluations of the adequacy of the subject pool policy (APA, 1982; Landrum and Chastain, 1999). In some research settings, users of the subject pool are evaluated by subjects in terms of the extent to which ethical guidelines were followed and whether clear and informative feedback was provided. In their survey of undergraduate subject pools, Landrum and Chastain (1999) observed that some psychology departments mandate that student-participants provide feedback about the research experience for additional incentives. In order for participant evaluations to be fair and informative, it undoubtedly is necessary for students to receive some degree of preparation for subject pool participation, in terms of their own and the researcher's ethical obligations. Of course, it is important that this preparation does not merely serve to create false expectations among students about researcher misconduct, leading to self-fulfilling prophecies. However, formal channels should be in place so that subjects are able to address their complaints (should they feel that their rights have been violated by a researcher) and participation-related problems (such as an inability to attend a study for which they have volunteered). Some academic departments have subject pool committees for this purpose, or else designate a research assistant, subject pool administrator, course instructor, or departmental chairperson to handle student concerns (Sieber and Saks, 1989). Repeated complaints about a particular investigator could result in a loss of subject pool usage or other penalties.

The ultimate goal of the subject pool policies described here is to maximize two desirable ends which need not be in conflict: the creation of psychological knowledge and the ethical treatment of student research participants. It is hoped that the ethical use of subject pools will serve to increase the likelihood that future generations of student research participants will view the research option as a valuable and attractive opportunity for learning, rather than as just another course requirement to be avoided.

Ethical responsibilities of research participants

To this point, our emphasis has been placed on the rights of research participants and their appropriate treatment by investigators. As we have seen, participants have the right to be informed of the general purpose of the study and what they will be expected to do; the right to withdraw from a study at any time; the right to receive promised benefits; the right to expect researchers to protect their anonymity and maintain the confidentiality of their responses when these are promised; and the right to know when they have been deceived in a study and why the deception was necessary. Additionally, it is clear that researchers also have certain rights and that research participation carries with it certain obligations. Korn (1988) identified five responsibilities that pertain specifically to the participant's relationship with the researcher (see Table 8.2). These responsibilities are consistent with the contractual nature of the researcher–subject relationship, recognizing that both parties have certain rights and obligations (Carlson, 1971).

Although the responsibilities listed in Table 8.2 are relatively straightforward, a few comments can be made regarding their rationale. For example, unless the participant carefully attends to the researcher and understands what the research involves, a truly informed consent cannot be given. If the researcher is questioned where understanding is lacking both before and after the study is completed, the research experience can be a more rewarding experience for the subject. Researchers also stand to benefit from questions when it becomes clear that participants are misinterpreting certain points.

Table 8.2 Responsibilities of research participants

---

1 Participants have the responsibility to listen carefully to the experimenter and ask questions in order to understand the research
2 Participants should be on time for the research appointment
3 Participants should take the research seriously and cooperate with the experimenter
4 When the study has been completed, participants share the responsibility for understanding what happened
5 Participants have the responsibility for honoring the researcher's request that they not discuss the study with anyone else who might be a participant

---

Source: Korn (1988, p. 77).

Subjects also should be aware of the inconveniences they can cause when they fail to show up for a research appointment at the agreed time. Such behavior is likely to disrupt the schedules of the researcher and other participants. Because the data collection stage of a study can be extremely time consuming for researchers, subjects should make an effort to inform the researcher in advance when an appointment must be canceled so that another participant can be recruited for the time slot. Once an individual has completed participation in an investigation, the importance of maintaining confidentiality about details of the study must be respected. In chapter 4 we described the threats to validity that emerge when suspicious (or pre-informed) subjects participate in research. By reneging on the promise not to discuss a study with others, subjects may in the process invalidate their own and future subjects' performance, thereby resulting in a wasted endeavor for all involved.

Some writers have suggested that research participation can serve as a means for individuals to satisfy their broader social responsibilities. Kimble (1987), for example, suggested that research participation provides one with the opportunity to help solve practical problems and to contribute to knowledge. This view suggests the importance of providing meaningful opportunities for persons who may be interested in volunteering for research participation.

ISSUES INVOLVED IN THE USE OF VOLUNTEERS

On the surface, the use of all-volunteer samples would seem to eliminate the ethical problems that arise when subjects (such as students) are coerced into participating in research. After all, the assumption of voluntary participation lies at the heart of such fundamental ethical regulations as informed consent, freedom to withdraw, and the like. If only it were that easy. As explained below, if all participation were strictly voluntary, researchers would have to cope with methodological problems concerning the representativeness of their samples. They also would be restrained from utilizing certain research approaches, such as nonreactive observation. Thus, the voluntary nature of participation represents yet another issue in which conflicts between methodological and ethical demands are likely to arise. Additionally, there is a gray line between applying undue pressure when recruiting volunteer participants and being an ethical and competent researcher (Blanck et al., 1992). In other words, there is the possibility that researchers may use coercive, sometimes subtle, inducements when recruiting volunteers for research participation, especially when participants are selected from vulnerable populations. In short, the use of volunteers carries with it the potential for several ethical dilemmas.

Volunteers and the representativeness problem

One limitation to using only volunteers for research participation pertains to the fact that persons who volunteer for experiments are likely to differ in significant ways from persons who are forced to participate. As a result of an extensive comparison of studies involving both volunteer and non-volunteer samples, Rosenthal and Rosnow (1975, 1991) found it possible to distinguish volunteers from other research participants on the basis of several personal characteristics. As compared with captive participants or non-volunteers, volunteers tend to be better educated, higher in social class status, more intelligent, more sociable, and have a higher need for social approval. Although the evidence is less strong, it appears that volunteers may also have a greater need for new and exciting experiences, have less conventional attitudes, be less authoritarian, and be more non-conforming, altruistic, and self disclosing than non-volunteers. Situational dimensions, such as the perceived importance of the task, interest in the topic studied, (fewer) hours of employment, (larger) classroom size, and expectations of higher course grades, also have been identified as being positively related to volunteering for research participation (Bowman and Waite, 2003; Rosenthal and Rosnow, 1991; Waite and Bowman, 1999).

Given these differences between volunteers and non-volunteers, it is understandable that researchers may be reluctant to recruit subjects solely on the basis of voluntary participation. To do so would be to raise the possibility that the research conclusions are misleading as a result of volunteer bias. That is, the knowledge that research volunteers are likely to be brighter, less authoritarian, higher in approval need, and so on than non-volunteers can lead one to expect conclusions that are either too liberal or too conservative as a result of the use of volunteer samples.

As an example, imagine a case in which a marketing researcher conducts a study to determine the persuasive impact of a new advertisement prior to recommending its use in a heavily funded television campaign (Rosnow and Rosenthal, 2005). Suppose the researcher finds it most convenient and practical to pilot test the advertisement by recruiting volunteer subjects at various shopping malls and randomly assigning them to an experimental group that is exposed to the new advertisement or a non-treatment control group. The problem with such a study is that its outcome may be contaminated by volunteer bias. Specifically, because volunteers are relatively high in need for approval, and people high in approval need are likely to be more easily influenced that those who are low in approval need (Buckhout, 1965), the combination of these tendencies may lead subjects in the experimental condition to over-react to the treatment. As a result, the possibility would exist that the anticipated effect of the new advertisement in the general population would be exaggerated.

As the previous example illustrates, the generalizability of data obtained from using voluntary subjects exclusively will be threatened to the extent that individual differences between volunteers and non-volunteers are related to the variables under investigation. Thus, because volunteers tend to be more intelligent than non-volunteers, a study involving the establishment of norms for a standardized intelligence test could result in artificially inflated values if only volunteer subjects were studied. Similarly, in prevention research, volunteer subjects might be better able to learn techniques for preventing interpersonal difficulties, depression, and the like than people with similar symptoms who choose not to volunteer. The consequence would be an overestimation of the effectiveness of the prevention program that served as the focus of the study.

Another illustration of the volunteer effect in an applied study was provided by Strohmetz et al. (1990), who examined differences in measures of problem severity among alcoholics who did or did not volunteer to participate in a treatment study. A positive relationship was revealed between patient volunteer status and severity of alcoholism problems reported during the pre-treatment period, such that those individuals who were more willing to participate in the treatment intervention tended to have more severe alcohol-related problems. According to Strohmetz et al., one plausible implication of this result is that patients who agree to participate in an intervention study may somehow be different from the population of interest. A similar concern regarding voluntary self-selection into intervention programs was noted in research involving the adjustment of Vietnam War veterans (King and King, 1991). Awareness of this problem has led some researchers, where possible, to stratify the population of interest into respondents and non-respondents in order to assess the direction of the selection bias (see Blanck et al., 1992; Saks and Blanck, 1992).

In the context of research on prevention programs, the decision to limit participation solely to volunteers raises the possibility that individuals from certain societal groups might not have an opportunity to participate. For example, well-intentioned attempts on the part of researchers not to coerce people into prevention research programs could serve to withhold valuable resources from those most in need. This could occur as a result of recruitment techniques that fail to reach certain segments of the population, or are reaching them through different media (Muñoz, 1983).

Another way that differences between volunteers and non-volunteers can pose a threat to the validity of research conclusions has to do with the higher need for social approval in volunteers. Several studies have demonstrated that because of their higher approval need, volunteer subjects are particularly inclined to comply with an experiment's task-oriented cues (or demand characteristics) in order to play the role of good subject (Horowitz, 1969; Rosnow and Suls, 1970). This problem was apparent in a study carried out by Horowitz (1969) on fear-arousing communications in persuasion. Horowitz reasoned that conflicting findings obtained by attitude change researchers may have been due to whether or not their samples were comprised of volunteer subjects. In his view, volunteers might be more influenced in the expected direction by fear-arousing messages because of a greater sensitivity to demand cues and willingness to comply with them, whereas non-volunteers might behave in an opposite manner in response to forced participation. As predicted, Horowitz obtained a positive relationship between fear arousal and attitude change for volunteers but an inverse relationship for "captive subjects." Apparently, subjects' motivations to comply with the demands of the experiment were influenced by whether or not they had willingly agreed to participate.

The news is not all bad regarding the use of volunteer samples in research. In addition to providing a means of circumventing the coercion problem, the use of volunteer samples also can have positive consequences for research participants.

For example, Bowman and Waite (2003) reported that students who volunteered to participate in out-of-class research studies in order to satisfy a course requirement gained better understanding of psychology and research procedures and developed a greater interest in psychology than students who did not participate. The research participation option was rated as more satisfying and rewarding than alternative options for satisfying the course requirement (i.e. participating in a "mass testing" session or writing a paper). Consistent with previous research (e.g. Holmes, 1967), the number of studies in which students participated was positively associated with the research participation option. Bowman and Waite conjectured that the greater first-hand involvement with research provided students with more opportunities to discuss specifics of the studies with investigators and may have convinced students that they were making a positive contribution to the process.

The problem of inducements to participate

As we have seen, the use of volunteers can serve to upset the delicate balance between the methodological requirements and ethical imperatives of a research study by producing artifacts in the research data (Blanck et al., 1992; Kimmel, 1979; Rosnow, 1997; Suls and Rosnow, 1981; Trice and Bailey, 1986). For this reason alone, recommendations to organize elite subject pools consisting of informed and well-paid volunteers would not be an advisable solution to the ethical problem of coercing people to participate in research (see Box 8.3). Moreover, the use of volunteer-only samples also has statistical implications. Meta-analyses of samples of published studies revealed that the average rate of "no-shows" was approximately one-third of those who volunteered (Aditya, 1996; Rosenthal and Rosnow, 1975). This means that researchers must increase the number of persons recruited by about one-half if they are counting on a specific number of volunteers necessary to satisfy a particular criterion of statistical power (Rosnow, 1997). In light of these considerations, researchers have attempted to cope with threats to external validity due to limited participant samples (e.g. only volunteer subjects) by developing methods for enhancing the diversity of their subjects.

While individuals' freedom to decline to participate is respected, several empirically derived recruitment strategies for inducing more non-volunteers to enter the sampling pool have been proposed. These involve communicating the message to prospective subjects that participation in the research will be interesting, making the appeal for subjects as non-threatening as possible, emphasizing the theoretical and practical importance of the research, offering small courtesy gifts simply for considering participation, and avoiding experimental tasks that could be perceived as psychologically or biologically stressful (Rosenthal and Rosnow, 1975). Such suggestions are based in large part on research findings showing that volunteer rates tend to increase the greater the incentives offered for participation and the less aversive, more interesting, and more important the task. Such methods for stimulating research participation may have certain potential

Box 8.3   "Volunteers for hire"

During the mid-1970s there were indications that graduate students in more than one American university had considered forming organizations along the lines of employment agencies like Manpower, Inc., which would offer volunteer subjects for hire (Rosenthal and Rosnow, 1975). Although the author is not aware of any such groups actually having been formed, it is intriguing to consider the consequences of organized groups of professional volunteers who offer their services for research participation, albeit for a price. Although organizations of this kind might put to rest many ethical anxieties, the generalizability of data obtained from using voluntary subjects exclusively would be threatened to the extent that groups of volunteers differ from the population at large.

Additional problems can arise when professional volunteers consent to participate in experimental studies involving potentially risky tests of medical procedures in order to receive attractive monetary incentives. The practice of offering money for participation in medical studies dates back to the late 1800s, when the renowned army bacteriologist, Walter Reed, offered people US$100 in gold to participate in yellow-fever experiments, and an additional US$100 to their estates if they died. Today, the average stipend for participation in clinical trials in the United States is about US$1000 (Hutt, 2003). An obvious problem inherent in offering large sums of money to willing participants in potentially dangerous medical studies is that there may be no limit to the kinds of risky procedures that some people will agree to undergo if the price is right. Further, because partial completion of a drug study typically results in only partial payment, there apparently are some volunteers who choose not to divulge any adverse side-effects of a drug for fear of being dropped from the study. This tendency to hide the ill effects of an experimental drug could create a false confidence in its safety, ultimately resulting in the approval of a potentially harmful new medicine.

Behavioral scientists generally do not have the resources to offer the kinds of monetary incentives that are used to attract research volunteers by major pharmaceutical companies or the medical research industry. Nevertheless, even when incentives are relatively small, the behavior of voluntary participants may be affected by the prospects of being dropped from a project or missing out on an opportunity to participate in a follow-up study at some later date.

scientific benefits beyond that of drawing a more representative sample and thereby lessening the likelihood of subject selection bias. In addition, these recruitment strategies should make researchers more thoughtful and careful in their appeals for subjects and in the planning of their research, with more emphasis placed on doing important rather than trivial research (Blanck et al., 1992; Rosenthal and Rosnow, 1991).

Some researchers are not totally convinced that improvements in the techniques for recruiting subjects will eliminate the dilemmas inherent in using volunteer samples (e.g. Schuler, 1982). For example, Gross and Fleming (1982) conjectured that research participants who are offered rewards for participation (such as money, entry into a lottery, or course credits) are more likely to be deceived than when they are unpaid and unrewarded volunteers. This potential consequence of inducements to volunteering implies that researchers may assume that offering rewards somehow relieves them of the necessity to be fully straightforward with their participants, because the payment effectively compensates for any embarrassment, discomfort, or loss of self-esteem caused by the deceptive procedure. This same logic would apply to researchers who view the delivery of monetary incentives as justification for not having to provide educational feedback. And, as we have seen, attracting "volunteers for hire" through offers of relatively large monetary inducements can raise certain questions about the validity of the research results (see Box 8.3).

Perhaps the most serious ethical concern involves the point at which the researcher's offers of inducements to participate become coercive, thereby threatening the individual's right and freedom not to participate. To illustrate the kinds of ethical problems that might be encountered in recruiting research subjects, consider the following questions posed by Blanck et al. (1992, pp. 963–4):

1   Is it ethical to employ young, attractive, verbal, and intelligent assistants of ethnic backgrounds similar to the target population in order to recruit participants?
2   Is it ethical to have research assistants spend time in the recruitment site, building a positive reputation, so that the potential participants are familiar with the researchers?
3   May a researcher ethically reward children with a classroom party for returning parental consent forms for a research project, the reward contingent on return of the consent form whether or not the parent granted approval?

Despite the likelihood that each of these strategies would serve to increase participation rates, it is unclear to what extent they present situations involving undue pressure. There are no clear ethical standards for obtaining guidance in such cases beyond the necessity for researchers to maintain a sensitivity to the possibility that they are exerting excessive pressure on targeted participants to enhance recruitment. According to one definition, *undue pressure* "occurs through an offer of an excessive, unwarranted, inappropriate or improper reward or other overture in order to obtain compliance," adding that specific determinations of whether a reward is excessive should be reviewed on a case-by-case basis (National Commission 1979, p. 14).

One subtle coercion that raises ethical issues was alluded to in chapter 6 in our consideration of preventive intervention research – the possibility that the promises made by researchers in their recruitment efforts cannot be carried out. For example, for some intervention programs, individuals from among the most powerless groups in society are invited to participate in voluntary programs that researchers consider to be beneficial to them. To ethically test the effectiveness of the intervention, researchers must be sensitive to the possibility that they are overselling their approach. False hopes about the efficacy of the intervention techniques may be unintentionally created among volunteers, thereby unjustifiably raising their expectations about the potential benefits of participation.

As a means to circumvent the problem of raising false hopes, researchers could communicate to potential subjects the belief that an intervention program has a reasonable chance of positive effects, and little chance of damaging effects, while taking care not to oversell the potential benefits of the approach. For example, in his research on the effectiveness of interventions designed to prevent depression, Muñoz (1983) informed potential participants that the methods have been found helpful in controlling depression that interferes with daily functioning. However, he also warned that the techniques first must be learned by participants and will not necessarily work for all people in all situations. Potential volunteers thus are aware that research involvement may be beneficial to them, but that there is no guarantee that they can be successfully applied to prevent depression.

Other important issues relating to recruitment strategies involve the nature and size of the incentives offered to subjects. People may voluntarily choose to participate in research for several possible reasons, including intellectual curiosity, monetary payment, bonus points in a college class, and the advancement of science (see Box 8.4). Although most researchers would agree that incentives for research should not be excessive, the difficulty becomes one of determining at what point an incentive may be considered "too strong" and thus coercive. One suggestion for assessing whether the strength of an incentive is unacceptable is to offer it to potential subjects in the context of investigations varying in risk. If nearly all agree to participate even when the research poses certain risks, one might conclude that the incentive is excessive (Diener and Crandall, 1978).

Another approach for determining whether incentives may be too strong is to empirically compare their effects on willingness to participate (Reiss, 1976). In a series of three such experiments, Korn and Hogan (1992) investigated the influence of various incentives on college students' willingness to participate in experiments involving aversive procedures. Their results revealed that the incentive offered had an effect on willingness to volunteer for a research study, although it was not as powerful or consistent as the potential aversiveness of the experimental treatment. Students were more willing to participate in a study (whether or not it involved an aversive treatment) for US$10 or 5 percent course credit than for 1 percent course credit or for strictly voluntary purposes. Although incentives increased willingness to participate in two of the three experiments, there were no significant differences related to kind of incentive (course credit or money). On the other hand, students were consistently less willing to participate in research as the aversiveness of the treatment increased.

Korn and Hogan limited their investigation to a range of incentives realistic enough to be considered plausible, rather than including extremely large incentives (such as 50 percent course credit or US$1,000). Their results may have been somewhat limited by the hypothetical nature of the experiments considered. However, the important issue may be not the incentives themselves, but the

Box 8.4   Incentives for research participation

As discussed in this chapter, a variety of incentives have been used by researchers to induce people to serve as participants in scientific investigations. Reflecting the over-representation of student-participants, some of the more common incentives utilized by behavioral researchers are particular to the student population (such as extra credit). Among the different incentive options are the following:

Course credit	research participation as a requirement for receiving a course grade
Extra credit	points are added to the overall course grade
Bonus points	points are added to exam scores
Lottery	all participants are entered into a lottery or drawing, which is carried out once the research is completed; one or more participants are selected to receive a significant gift, usually monetary
Gift	all participants receive a free gift, such as a snack or a free product
Summary of results	participants receive a written summary of the research findings at some point after the study is completed

The use of monetary incentives, which has been recommended as an effective practice for maximizing response rates (American Association for Public Opinion Research 1999; Bearden, Madden, and Uscategui 1998), has increased in psychology over the past decade. Overall, however, a significant proportion of published studies in psychology do not report information about research incentives (Kimmel, 2001, 2004).

investigator's obligations to act responsibly. For example, a college professor who indiscriminately offers 50 percent course credit for research participation would likely undermine his or her obligations as a responsible instructor. A fairer way to implement the incentive would be to first devise the class grade distribution without considering the extra credit option so that non-volunteers will not be at a disadvantage, and then to establish that bonus points will be given only when research participation will provide a learning experience for the students. Finally, a reasonable level of course credit should be established for research participation. As Korn and Hogan demonstrated, incentives need not be very large in order to influence willingness to participate.

Ethical issues concerning the establishment of legitimate levels of incentives for research participation become somewhat more complex when subjects are recruited from special populations, as is the case with prisoner volunteers. In the remainder of this chapter, problems involved in the recruitment of subjects from special populations are considered.

VULNERABLE PARTICIPANTS

Although much of the focus of this chapter has been placed on the recruitment and selection of college students for research participation, it is important to recognize some of the issues underlying the use of other subject populations from which behavioral scientists often draw their samples. For example, many investigators have used prisoners as research subjects for some of the same reasons that students are so prevalent in research – the prison population represents a readily available, captive group of potential participants. Additionally, because of the nature of their investigative interests, behavioral scientists from such disciplines as clinical psychology, developmental psychology, and sociology are apt to select their subjects from certain well-defined, often vulnerable groups, such as children, the elderly, the mentally disabled and handicapped, and under-privileged persons. Individuals within these groups often have certain limited capacities to choose freely whether or not to participate in research, thereby raising some serious ethical issues.

Differing ethical positions on the involvement of research participants from special groups can be traced in large part to a consideration as to whether the research is therapeutic or non-therapeutic in nature (Ramsey, 1976). Therapeutic or clinical research focuses on the treatment of specific problems, and persons typically can anticipate some direct or indirect benefits from research participation. That is, if the methods studied prove to be effective, the participant can expect some improvement. By contrast, participants in non-therapeutic research do not expect to receive any direct benefits relating to their current state, beyond the incentives offered for entering the study (such as monetary payment).

Perhaps with the exception of experimentation with children, the problems inherent in research with vulnerable participants have received considerably greater attention in the context of biomedical research than in behavioral science disciplines (Schuler, 1982). As a result of extensive discussion and debate, special biomedical regulations were developed to protect individuals from special groups whose ability to give informed consent is assumed to be limited. Some of the recruitment and selection issues in using participants from special populations for behavioral science research are described below.

Prisoners

Most of the early research involving prisoner participants consisted of medical experiments on infection, the testing of medical drugs and cosmetics, and related studies, all of which offered minimal direct benefits to the subjects themselves (Jonsen et al., 1977; Reynolds, 1979). For example, one research approach that was commonly used in prison settings is the so-called "patch study" as a means of testing skin sensitivity (Hatfield, 1977). In a typical patch study, one-inch square bandages impregnated with a commercial product (such as perfume, deodorant, or soap) are taped to as many as ten sites on the back or forearm, along with one control site where no substance is used (in order to determine whether the subject is simply reacting to the bandage). A participant typically would wear the patches for up to three or four weeks to determine if the product caused any adverse skin reactions. In other large-scale studies, bath soaps and dandruff shampoos would be provided to volunteer prisoners and used for a period of about three months before the products would be released to retail outlets.

In recent years, such biomedical experiments in prison settings have been severely restricted (e.g. Herbert, 1978). This is largely a result of US recommendations made in 1976 by the National Commission (see chapter 2). There are now severe limits on all research with prisoners that does not contribute to their personal well-being or pertain to the circumstances and conditions of their previous lives. This emphasis on therapeutic research is apt to raise certain role conflicts for behavioral scientists working within institutional settings where the objectives of institutionalization are unclear (Carroll et al., 1985). For example, the roles of prison have included punishment, rehabilitation, deterrence, and protection through detention (Gaylin and Blatte, 1975). In addition to carrying out research in prisons, behavioral scientists often function as therapists, evaluators, administrators, and consultants on matters of control within prisons, and often act as expert witnesses on such matters as parole, competence, sentencing, and dangerousness.

Since World War II, there have been several scandals associated with research conducted in prisons, in some cases involving news of prisoner illness and death, which have prompted formal investigations by various government appointed committees (Hutt, 2003). For example, in 1969 a pharmaceutical industry drug-testing program in Alabama came under scrutiny following newspaper accounts of prison epidemics and sub-standard care of subjects enrolled in the programs. As in previous scandals, a central concern raised by the Alabama case involved large monetary payments to prisoner-subjects that caused some participants to give false information about their medical histories and reactions to the tested drugs. The excessive profits paid to the investigators raised additional concerns.

The American Psychological Association's Task Force on the Role of Psychology in the Criminal Justice System identified confidentiality as a central issue for psychologists working within the prison system (APA, 1978; Clingempeel et al., 1980). Although the focus of the task force was placed on therapeutic practice, it is not difficult to recognize how dilemmas involving confidentiality may arise in research with prisoners. For example, during the course of a study with prisoners an investigator might learn that a subject was smuggling drugs into the prison (Steininger et al., 1984). As discussed in chapter 6, this kind of situation is common in applied studies, where a researcher is often faced with conflicting obligations. In this case, informing prison officials about the drug smuggling would constitute a breach of confidentiality to the prisoner. Although the prison officials are paying for the researcher's services and would desire the information, the prisoner may have volunteered for the research under conditions of anonymity and confidentiality. According to the APA Task Force, most psychologists surveyed tended to prefer not to break promises of confidentiality, citing concern for the potential harm to the prisoners (Clingempeel et al., 1980).

In other cases, such as those involving potential harm to others, researchers' loyalties to their subjects are more seriously challenged. If, during the course of participation in a research study, a prisoner reveals plans to kill or seriously harm another person, most researchers probably would view the need to protect society at large as a more important obligation than any promises of confidentiality made to the prisoner. Such a decision to breach confidentiality when there is clear danger to others is consistent with recommendations by various ethical codes and legal decisions (e.g. the California Supreme Court ruling, *Tarasoff* v. *Regents of the University of California*).

One additional issue to be considered in therapeutic research with prisoners pertains to the view that prisoners (as well as hospitalized patients) should be required to cooperate with research on programs oriented towards their own rehabilitation. The APA (1982, p. 45) advised against this practice on the grounds that the "position is too readily available as a rationalization for exploitation" and because of the possibility that the institutions involved may function more to incarcerate or punish than to rehabilitate inmates.

At the heart of typical objections to non-therapeutic research on prison participants is the concern that consent to participate may rarely be truly voluntary. Prisoners are extremely dependent on material rewards (Hatfield, 1977) and many have hopes that participation in research will lead to an easier or shorter imprisonment. One early critic of the reduction of punishment for criminals who consent to participate in dangerous research was the philosopher Immanuel Kant (1797/1965). Kant believed that the practice would amount to no less than the destruction of legal justice, claiming that "if legal justice perishes, then it is no longer worthwhile for men to remain alive on this earth" (p. 100). While Kant's prediction may have been overly dire, there is wide agreement that early parole should not be given for involvement in a research study. Nonetheless, there is the risk that some prisoners will volunteer for dangerous experiments anyway, believing that in doing so their chances for release will somehow be improved. Undue pressure to participate also can stem from fears that refusing to volunteer for research will somehow lessen the possibility of parole. One recommendation for avoiding these threats to voluntary research involvement is to reward prisoner participants monetarily and to inform them that their participation will not be entered into parole records (Diener and Crandall, 1978).

Researchers must be especially sensitive to the possibility that incentives offered to prisoners are not so strong as to eliminate the freedom of choice in the decision to participate. However, it also should be noted that the opportunity to participate in research provides prisoners with an important means of contributing to society and improving their self-esteem (Hatfield, 1977; Novak et al., 1977). The monetary incentive also allows them to obtain certain amenities through legitimate means and provides a source of contact with the outside world. These positive outcomes are evident in the following comments from an ex-prisoner who participated in several biomedical experiments during the early 1970s (Hatfield, 1977, p. 12):

> In the highly structured environment of prison, where I had no other opportunities to do anything that would give me a substantial monetary and emotional return, medical research gave me a sense of purpose.... Men in prison have few material resources and are denied many aspects of human dignity. Those few opportunities they do have should not be taken away, against their wishes, unless society is prepared to offer a meaningful alternative.

Children

Children represent one of the most widely used special groups for research participation in the behavioral sciences. A primary ethical (and legal) concern, as with other vulnerable groups with potentially limited understanding of information provided by the investigator, pertains to the adequacy of informed consent (Curran and Beecher, 1969) (see Box 8.5). That is, do children understand what they are told about the nature and purpose of a study, and at what age can they be allowed to consent on their own, without the agreement of a legal guardian? A related question is whether children are able to weigh the risks that a study may entail for them. Additionally, children may be particularly prone to pressures to participate in research and have a lower tolerance for potentially risky or deceptive experimental manipulations.

Researchers clearly need to take special care to protect the rights and well-being of less powerful research participants, taking into account subjects' concerns and viewpoints when designing their studies. According to Thompson (1990), it is helpful for researchers to adopt a developmental perspective when planning research with children, by recognizing that although many risks to children decrease with increasing age, others are apt to increase, change in a curvilinear fashion, or remain relatively stable as the child matures. As with other vulnerable groups, the common approach to dealing with the issue of consent is to use parental or proxy consent as a substitute for, or in addition to, obtaining the child's consent. That is, if it is clear that the child cannot give personal consent but stands to benefit directly from the investigation, parents could be asked to provide consent for the child. As a straightforward example, it is not possible to inform a retarded adolescent as one could inform a normal adolescent. In such a case, it is up to the parents or other primary caregivers to decide whether the adolescent should enter an experimental treatment program, based on what is in his or her best interests (Steininger et al., 1984).

The involvement of children in research generally entails fewer ethical problems when the research is therapeutic in nature. Most persons would agree that children should not be prevented from participating in studies that have a chance to improve their health or functioning, assuming that the investigations are well planned and focused. Examples of behavioral science investigations that offer potential therapeutic effects to children include preventive intervention

Box 8.5   Ethical principles for research with participants from special groups: some pertinent examples

American Psychological Association

Principle E. Psychologists respect the dignity and worth of all people, and the rights of individuals to privacy, confidentiality, and self-determination. Psychologists are aware that special safeguards may be necessary to protect the rights and welfare of persons or communities whose vulnerabilities impair autonomous decision making.

3.10(b) For persons who are legally incapable of giving informed consent, psychologists nevertheless provide (1) appropriate explanation, (2) seek the individual's assent, (3) consider such persons' preferences and best interests, and (4) obtain appropriate permission from a legally authorized person, if such substitute consent is permitted or required by law. When consent by a legally authorized person is not permitted or required by law, psychologists take reasonable steps to protect the individual's rights and welfare.

Source: American Psychologist (2002), 57. Copyright © 2002 by the American Psychological Association. Reprinted with permission.

British Psychological Society

3.2   Research with children or with participants who have impairments that will limit understanding and/or communication such that they are unable to give their real consent requires special safe-guarding procedures.

3.3   Where possible, the real consent of children and of adults with impairments in understanding or communication should be obtained. In addition, where research involves any persons under sixteen years of age, consent should be obtained from parents or from those *in loco parentis*. If the nature of the research precludes consent being obtained from parents or permission being obtained from teachers, before proceeding with the research, the investigator must obtain approval from an Ethics Committee.

3.4   Where real consent cannot be obtained from adults with impairments in understanding or communication, wherever possible the investigator should consult a person well-placed to appreciate the participant's reaction, such as a member of the person's family, and must obtain the disinterested approval of the research from independent advisors.

3.5   When research is being conducted with detained persons, particular care should be taken over informed consent, paying attention to the special circumstances which may affect the person's ability to give free informed consent.

Source: British Psychological Society (2005). *Ethical Principles for Conducting Research with Human Participants*. Leicester: BPS.

Box 8.5   (Continued)

Canadian Psychological Association (CPA, 2000)

In adhering to the principle of respect for the dignity of persons, psychologists would:

I.31   Seek an independent and adequate ethical review of human rights issues and protections for any research involving members of vulnerable groups, including persons of diminished capacity to give informed consent, before making a decision to proceed.

I.32   Not use persons of diminished capacity to give informed consent in research studies, if the research involved may be carried out equally well with persons who have a fuller capacity to give informed consent.

I.33   Seek to use methods that maximize the understanding and ability to consent of persons of diminished capacity to give informed consent, and that reduce the need for a substitute decision maker.

I.34   Carry out informed consent processes with those persons who are legally responsible or appointed to give informed consent on behalf of persons not competent to consent on their own behalf, seeking to ensure respect for any previously expressed preferences of persons not competent to consent.

American Sociological Association (ASA, 1999)

12.04 Informed Consent with Children

(a)   In undertaking research with children, sociologists obtain the consent of children to participate, to the extent that they are capable of providing such consent, except under circumstances where consent may not be required as set forth in 12.01(b).

(b)   In undertaking research with children, sociologists obtain the consent of a parent or a legally authorized guardian. Sociologists may seek waivers of parental or guardian consent when (1) the research involves no more than minimal risk for the research participants, and (2) the research could not practicably be carried out were consent to be required, or (3) the consent of a parent or guardian is not a reasonable requirement to protect the child (e.g. neglected or abused children).

(c)   Sociologists recognize that waivers of consent from a child and a parent or guardian require approval from institutional review boards or, in the absence of such boards, from another authoritative body with expertise on the ethics of research. Under such circumstances, the confidentiality of any personally identifiable information must be maintained unless otherwise set forth in 11.02(b).

studies oriented towards improving learning or interpersonal skills, research on techniques to rehabilitate juvenile offenders or drug abusers, and studies to prevent suicide or self-destructive behavior in at-risk youths.

One potential ethical concern in conducting research with children suffering from severe problems is the possibility that the promise of help or an irrational hope for a beneficial outcome will introduce coercive elements into the decision to have the child take part in the research (Carroll et al., 1985). Thus, in addition to clearly describing the anticipated benefits (and potential risks), investigators need to accurately present the likelihood of the experimental outcomes, based on current knowledge, to the adults responsible for the decision to have the child participate in the study. As we saw in the case of the Cambridge–Somerville study (see chapter 6), even the most well-intentioned study can have unantici-pated negative results, a point that the researcher might also convey when obtaining consent. Additionally, when research participation is agreed upon in order to obtain promised therapeutic effects, it is essential that the study actually has the potential to help the individual participant rather than just advancing knowledge about the behavioral problem. Care also must be taken to provide effective procedures to children serving in untreated control groups as quickly as possible so that they do not experience unnecessary delay in receiving treatment.

More stringent safeguards need to be established for therapeutic research with children than for similar research with adults. Although exposure to certain risks may be tolerated in adult studies, it is generally believed that risks should be minimal or non-existent in studies with children. For example, an investigation involving a potentially painful procedure might be judged permissible among freely volunteering, informed adults (APA, 1982). The same procedure would be viewed as unacceptable for children because they are less likely to be familiar with such experiences and, as a result, more fearful of them. Alternative, risk-free procedures need to be explored prior to exposing children to untested research techniques that are intended for therapeutic purposes.

The views regarding children's participation in non-therapeutic research have been quite diverse, not only from an ethical standpoint, but from practical and legal perspectives as well. While some critics have argued against the involvement of children in any type of non-therapeutic research due to their questionable capacity to give consent (e.g. Ramsey, 1976), others have taken the opposite position by suggesting that children would consent if they had full capacities to do so and that research participation provides children with a rare opportunity to benefit others (e.g. Economic and Social Data Service, 2004; McCormick, 1976). The debate is tempered, however, when the research in question clearly eliminates the possibility of harm as a possible consequence of participation. Most researchers would agree that a study of physiological reactions to aversive stimuli, such as physical pain versus negative criticism, would be unacceptable because of children's questionable ability to consent to such an investigation and the poten-tial risks involved (Carroll et al., 1985). By contrast, a perception study involving young children's preferences for colorful and novel stimuli would no doubt be a stimulating and enjoyable experience for them, assuming that the research is conducted in a comfortable, non-fearful environment and parental consent has been freely obtained.

With regard to the issue of consent, parents (or legal guardians) are generally allowed to provide consent for a child in therapeutic studies, but the child's consent also must be obtained when the research is non-therapeutic (BPS, 2005a; Reynolds, 1979). For non-risk, basic research like the perception study just described, researchers often use a consent procedure involving "proxy and parallel consent." This involves obtaining first the fully informed consent of the parents and then the voluntary consent of the child, regardless of the child's age. In other words, the parents or persons legally responsible for the prospective participant are provided with full information about the nature and goals of the investigation. Following their agreement, the child is informed that participation is voluntary, participation can be stopped at any time, and involvement in any phase of the research is not required. The United Kingdom's Market Research Society (MRS) *Guidelines for Research Among Children and Young People* (2000) recommend this method. Specifically, the guidelines state that children under the age of 16 must be approached with their parents' consent, and that information about the investigation must be prepared so that it is suitable for the child and the parent to understand. That is, consent is first obtained from the parent or responsible adult for the child to be approached by researchers, and then the child's consent is sought. The MRS further acknowledges that the consent of other gatekeepers also might have to be obtained before making initial contact with parents, such as persons who control access to children in schools and nurseries. When research is carried out on National Health Service premises in the United Kingdom, the approval of the Local Research Ethics Committee (LREC) must be sought.

In order for procedures like the proxy and parallel consent approach to be ethically sound, the child must be able to understand the researcher's description of the study and should not feel undue pressure to consent simply because parental consent has been obtained. Researchers have wrestled for some time with the question of when a child becomes capable of providing informed consent. Several recommended solutions have focused on the criterion of age, with ages ranging from 6 to 14 years offered as minimal limits for obtaining a child's consent (Curran and Beecher, 1969; Reynolds, 1979). In one review of empirical findings on children's capacity to consent, Abramovitch et al. (1991) reported that most children who were asked to participate in psychological research understood what they would be required to do. However, few children under the age of 12 years believed that their performance would be kept confidential and many felt there would be negative consequences if they ended their participation prematurely.

Prior to carrying out non-therapeutic (as well as therapeutic) investigations with children, researchers should be aware of legal requirements regarding the issue of consent (Annas et al., 1977; ESDS, 2004). As Reynolds (1979) has pointed out, it may be that in some research contexts the investigator will be held responsible for determining whether the child has the intelligence and maturity to understand the research protocol and potential consequences. Some investigators have recommended novel procedures for providing information about a study to children. For example, Levy and Brackbill (1979) have suggested showing to children during the consent procedure a narrated video depicting an investigator and child model going through the various steps in the study. Such a video could serve to clarify the procedure and at the same time reduce any fears the child might be experiencing about the unfamiliar experience.

As an extension of Levy and Brackbill's recommendation, some researchers have begun to address the possibility that children themselves could be trained as researchers, who could then conduct studies with child participants (e.g. Alderson, 2000). In fact, young people have already been used to moderate children's focus groups in marketing research studies. Although the use of children as researchers is likely to raise various methodological and ethical issues, it also would bring certain advantages to the different parties in the research process (ESDS, 2004). For example, it would provide children with opportunities to influence research design, as well as a participatory role in decisions about how research findings are to be disseminated and used. The researcher would have greater access to children, and the views expressed by participants can be more direct and interpreted with greater precision.

To conclude this section on ethical research with children, it is informative to consider the recommendations released in April 2004 by the US Institute of Medicine (http://books.nap.edu/catalog/10958.html). The Institute's report was authorized by the Best Pharmaceuticals for Children Act, which was passed by Congress in January 2002. In addition to its emphasis on the importance of conducting federally and privately funded clinical studies with children, the report offered four specific suggestions for the ethical conduct of such research (Dingfelder, 2004):

1 *Make consent an ongoing process.* Instead of simply obtaining a parent's signature at the outset of the research, fully informed consent would require the investigator to keep parents informed at every step in the study, enabling the parent to voice any concerns throughout the process.
2 *Consider alternative forms of payment.* Monetary incentives may not serve as the best form of compensation for parents or guardians who, because of their work schedule, might prefer instead that investigators use flexible scheduling or provide free transportation so that the child could be driven to the research site.
3 *Communicate with the child.* The research procedure, general purpose, and potential risks should be explained to the child, taking into consideration the child's age and level of understanding.
4 *Request the participant's assent.* The child should be asked whether he or she would like to participate in the study once all of the details have been provided, bearing in mind that the child may be reluctant to decline the request of an authority figure.

Institutionalized individuals

The issues related to research with institutionalized persons, such as mental patients and the mentally handicapped, are similar to those described above in relation to children (Carroll et al., 1985). Some of these issues also were discussed in chapter 6 in our consideration of ethical issues in therapeutic research.

Of foremost concern are potential problems relating to coercion and restrictions on the voluntary decision to participate, protections against research risks, and questions related to competence to give fully informed consent. As in the case of children, it is easier to justify the carrying out of therapeutic research with institutionalized persons than research offering them no direct benefits. According to one critic, non-therapeutic research conducted with mentally infirm participants often is meaningless, with many such studies simply intended to demonstrate that there are differences between people who are institutionalized and people who are not (Haywood, 1976). Certainly, much meaningful basic research can be conducted with institutionalized subjects; however, researchers must carefully evaluate the potential merit of their investigations in order to ensure that they are not taking advantage of captive and distressed participants for the sake of trivial research.

SUMMARY

It is helpful to bear in mind when considering the ethical treatment of research participants that researchers have a fiduciary responsibility to protect the students, patients, volunteers, and other persons who donate their time to contribute to the research process. A *fiduciary relationship* is one in which two unequal individuals interact and the more powerful person is entrusted to protect the best interests of the other (Lemmens and Singer, 1998). The ethical researcher is one who recognizes that the power differential *vis à vis* potential (and actual) research participants can result in unfair coercion and the unacceptable exploitation of persons from vulnerable or dependent groups, and who takes steps to avoid these outcomes. Every person who participates in research is deserving of humane treatment and clearly specified benefits, whether or not the goals of the investigation are therapeutic in nature. Although all potential subjects need to be pre-tested and screened for a study posing certain risk of harm to them, this is particularly true for persons with obvious vulnerabilities. For example, despite the ethical criticisms that were raised about the Stanford prison experiment (see Box 4.2), it must be said that the researchers took special steps to select only those volunteers who fell within the normal range on all measures in an extensive battery of psychological tests. By doing so, the researchers hoped to reduce the possibility of destructive effects (Zimbardo, 1973a, 1973b).

In view of the numerous ethical dilemmas that can arise in the recruitment and selection of research subjects, perhaps the best approach for researchers to take is one that regards the researcher–participant relationship as a collaborative one.

Several researchers have argued for such a model, though it has been rarely implemented in practice (Adair, 1973; Carlson, 1971; Jourard, 1967; Smith et al., 2005). A collaborative relationship would be one in which both the researcher and subjects work together as equals on mutually interesting behavioral research questions. Despite the fact that the collaborative model may represent an unattainable ideal in light of certain practical constraints (see Korn, 1988), the approach argues for a more balanced relationship between investigator and research participants than is currently found in the behavioral sciences. In the view of Rosenthal and Rosnow (1991), by treating subjects as though they were another granting agency, granting researchers their time instead of money, the research relationship can become more reciprocal, research procedures more humane, and the investigations more meaningful for all parties involved.

9

Ethical Issues in Research with Animals

"My first exposure with animal rights was someone who came to the lab and said that the chickens I was working with were suffering anguish. I just dismissed them as silly. I said, "That's emotional nonsense. This is science. This is important," and I just dismissed it."

Animal rights activist, as quoted in H. A. Herzog, Jr., "The movement is my life"

Chapter Topics

☞ Animal research in psychology: current trends
☞ The animal rights and animal welfare movements
☞ Arguments for and against animal research
☞ Approaches for reducing the pain and suffering of research animals
☞ Regulations and guidelines
☞ Alternatives to animal research

In this chapter we turn our attention away from human subject research in order to focus on ethical issues involving research with animals. The use of animals for research purposes has long been considered a legitimate scientific activity, and has played a central role in psychology throughout the twentieth century (Plous, 1996). Millions of animals are studied in research laboratories each year in order to test the effects of experimental treatments that ethical issues prevent from first being tested on humans, and because the behavior of animals is interesting in and of itself. In addition to the widespread use of rodents, such as rats and mice, researchers have carried out investigations on monkeys, dogs, cats, birds, shrews, and fish, because these animals can serve as effective models of many human responses (Rissman, 1995; Shaughnessy and Zechmeister, 1990). Chimpanzees, for example, currently represent the only species of non-human primates in which progress of the HIV virus that causes AIDS can be appropriately studied. Rodents and birds now comprise roughly 90 percent of all non-human research subjects (Bowd and Shapiro, 1993). However, a recent survey of the database of primate research in Asia suggests that few members of the ape species (chimpanzees, gorillas, and bonobos) are currently being used in research, consistent with North American and European findings (Houde, 2004).

A wide range of important questions have been investigated through animal research, including the effects of new drugs intended for human use and of substances meant for release into the environment. Tests of new surgical techniques often are first carried out on animals, and some animal subjects are exposed to diseases so that researchers can observe resulting symptoms and investigate potential cures. In addition to research on the treatment of patients recovering from brain and spinal cord injuries, drug dependencies, and nervous disorders, behavioral scientists have carried out a number of animal studies that have advanced our basic understanding of the relationship between the brain and behavior. Investigators utilizing animal models have studied the neural bases of schizophrenia, amnesia, depression, and other psychological phenomena. There is general agreement that these investigations have yielded valuable contributions not only to human welfare but to the welfare of animals as well (e.g. Azar, 1994b; Baldwin, 1993; Bishop and Nolen, 2001; Miller, 1985; see Box 9.1).

Box 9.1 Animal research and medical progress

Animals make good subjects for research on human disease and health conditions because they share certain biological and genetic similarities with humans. It has been estimated that approximately 35 million animals are used in research each year (Bishop and Nolen, 2001). The United States is the most active country when it comes to animal research, with more than 12 million animals used annually. This extensive research has played a vital role in virtually every major medical advance that has occurred during the past century, for the betterment of both human and animal welfare (Lemon and Dunnett, 2005).

The discovery of insulin as a treatment for diabetes represents a good illustration of the contribution of animal research to medical progress (Bliss, 1984). Insulin was discovered during the early 1920s by the Canadian doctors Frederick Banting and Charles Best. In their research, Banting and Best were able to make an extract of pancreatic cells, which appeared to have anti-diabetic characteristics. The extract contained the hormone insulin, and when the two researchers injected it into diabetic dogs, the dogs' diabetic symptoms were successfully relieved. Only after Banting and Best's research team at the University of Toronto went to work on the production and purification of insulin were the first tests of the insulin injections made on human subjects. Although insulin is not a cure for the dreaded disease, the lives of millions of diabetics have been saved worldwide as a result of its discovery.

As Shaughnessy and Zechmeister (1990) have pointed out, the use of animals as subjects in controlled laboratory studies has often been taken for granted. Although it is possible to invoke the biblical reference to human "dominion" over lower species of animals (e.g. Rollin, 1985) as a justification for animal research, perhaps the strongest argument from a scientific perspective pertains to the need to gain knowledge about phenomena that affect the human condition while at the same time protecting subjects from serious risk of harm. It is difficult to imagine much progress in the fight against such diseases as cancer, AIDS, or muscular dystrophy without first being able to investigate the course of the disease and potential cures in animal subjects.

Despite the numerous scientific advances that have emerged from research on animals, controversy over animal rights and research ethics has given rise to a number of important questions about the appropriateness of using animals for research purposes. Critics have charged researchers with mistreating animal subjects and causing unnecessary suffering, and also have questioned the value of research involving laboratory animals altogether. Behavioral scientists have been especially targeted by these critics, in large part because the benefits of behavioral research involving animals may not be as obvious as in other fields. The public debate over animal research is an emotional one, and logic and reason have often been overshadowed by rhetoric. Examples of the passionate reactions from both supporters and detractors of the use of animals in science are typified by the following comments:

> I can still remember the picture of that little monkey. They had severed his nerves, and he couldn't use his arm. They taped the other arm and made him use the handicapped arm. The monkeys were terrified of the experimenters. (Animal rights advocate, as quoted in Herzog, 1993)

> Animal liberationists do not separate out the human animal. A rat is a pig is a dog is a boy. (Ingrid Newkirk, Director, People for the Ethical Treatment of Animals)

The quotation that appears at the start of this chapter (attributed to a researcher turned animal activist) suggests that even staunch animal researchers ultimately may become conflicted about these issues. As a result of the passions that have been aroused on both sides of the issue, one thing is certain: no longer can research on animals be taken for granted.

In this chapter, the ethical questions pertaining to whether animals should be used for scientific investigations are assessed through a consideration of the philosophical arguments used to support the various positions on the issue, the potential benefits that have been accrued from animal research, and the ethical guidelines and regulations that have been established for protecting the welfare of animal subjects. In addition, the alternatives to animal research that have been proposed are described and evaluated. As we have strived to do throughout this text, an attempt is made to find a reasonable balance for assuring that sound research can be carried out in the most ethical way possible.

BACKGROUND: PSYCHOLOGY AND THE ANIMAL RESEARCH CONTROVERSY

Among the behavioral scientists who conduct research with animal subjects, it is psychologists who are most likely to study animals outside of the species' natural habitats. In fact, certain lower species (such as mice and pigeons) are especially bred by some researchers for the sole purpose of having them serve as laboratory subjects in psychological studies.

While it is difficult to obtain accurate assessments of the percentage of researchers who conduct animal research, it appears that at least within psychology, a minority of researchers are actively engaged in such work. According to one estimate, animals are used in about 8 percent of psychological research (cf. Shapiro, 1991). Similarly, Neal Miller (1985), a strong defender of behavioral research on animals, revealed that only 7 percent of the pages in American Psychological Association research journals reported research primarily on animals, in comparison with 93 percent reporting primarily on human subject research. Elsewhere, Brink and her colleagues conducted a content analysis of the *Canadian Journal of Psychology* and found that 14 percent of the 466 studies published from 1974 to 1992 in the journal included animal subjects, with no discernible trend in use over the period studied (Brink et al., 1995). That is, despite growing concerns about the treatment of research animals and the emergence of animal rights groups during the period, no apparent decrease in the use of animal subjects was apparent. In terms of absolute numbers, Bowd and Shapiro (1993) estimated that roughly one to two million animals may be used in psychological research each year (see Box 9.2).

In recent years, a growing body of evidence has emerged suggesting that the number of animals used in research worldwide has declined, with estimates ranging from 30 to 50 percent (Rowan and Loew, 1995). This decline in animal use includes a 46 percent reduction in the Netherlands (from 1978 to 1991), a 30 percent reduction in Great Britain (from 1980 to 1990), a 55 percent reduction in Italy (from 1978 to 1989), and a 50 percent decline in the United States (since the mid-1970s; not including rats, mice, and birds in the US estimate) (Plous, 1996). C. Gauthier (2004) reported evidence that total animal research use in Canada, the US, and the UK decreased at about the same pace during the 1990s. Most recently, Carlsson, Hagelin, and Hau (2004) reviewed 2800 studies published between 1970 and 2000 in 14 major biomedical journals. Their analysis revealed that despite the total number of articles published in those journals having doubled over the period, the proportion of animal studies had decreased by 30 percent. The average number of animals, in the studies that used them, declined by nearly one-half (see Figure 9.1).

The downward trend in animal research also has become apparent in psychology since the late 1970s, with surveys revealing that between 15 and 25 percent of psychology departments in the United States (e.g. Benedict and Stoloff, 1991; Gallup and Eddy, 1990) and approximately 25 percent in Great Britain (e.g. Thomas and Blackman, 1992) have closed their animal research facilities or

Box 9.2   Animal research and the cosmetics industry

Despite an apparent decline in the use of animals in research during the past 25 years, millions of animals continue to be studied in applied investigations involving safety tests of a variety of products, including industrial chemicals and cosmetics, and other non-psychological research (Eckholm, 1985). For example, approximately 38,000 laboratory animals are killed or maimed in the European Union (EU) nations alone each year in safety tests carried out by cosmetic firms on shampoos, sun creams, and other beauty products.

Since 1998, the testing of cosmetics and their ingredients on animals is banned in the United Kingdom, although a plan to extend this action to the entire EU was postponed because companies lacked alternative testing methods (Brand, 2001). Following 13 years of negotiation, the European Parliament voted in 2003 to phase in a near total ban on the sales of all animal-tested products throughout the EU from 2009 and halt all animal testing. At the time of this writing, only Britain, Austria, and the Netherlands ban cosmetic animal testing, while most of the research continues to be carried out in France and Italy. These moves towards legislation are being fought by the cosmetics industry, with companies claiming that they still lack alternative testing methods. Under pressure from the cosmetics industry, France unsuccessfully attempted to overturn the 2009 European ban on testing, but has continued efforts to appeal the ruling (Carnell, 2005).

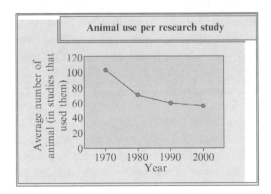

Figure 9.1   The declining use of animals in biomedical research.
Source: Carlsson et al. (2004).

seriously discussed doing so. Declines in the percentage of psychology faculty conducting animal research and in the number of animals used in psychology research also have been noted. A number of factors can be linked to the steady decline in animal research, including the costs of maintaining animal research facilities, increased regulation, the growing concern for animal rights, and the emergence of alternative research approaches not requiring the use of animals (Gallup and Suarez, 1980; Holden, 1982; Plous, 1996).

Psychologists as vulnerable targets

In recent decades, the animal rights movement has done much to raise public consciousness about the rights of animals, and this has contributed to the emergence of stringent controls for animal research. Research proposals are now scrutinized by animal-care committees and peer review for an examination of the scientific merits of the proposed investigation as well as animal care and protection. Most animal research now adheres to the "three R's" concept, which was first proposed in a 1959 book by Russell and Burch, *The Principles of Humane Experimental Technique*. The elements of the "three R's," which inspired the movement towards seeking alternatives to the use of animals for research purposes, are (1) *replacement* of conscious living animals with non-sentient animals or materials, (2) *reduction* of the number of animals utilized in a research study or procedure, and (3) *refinement* of the research techniques and procedures so as to decrease the incidence and amount of animal pain and distress (Carlsson et al., 2004). Although the "three R's" concept has been widely adopted by researchers and animal advocacy organizations, and has been incorporated into the laws of several countries, this has not stopped some proponents of the animal rights movement from threatening and initiating unjustified attacks against behavioral researchers.

Animal research in psychology has been criticized for its invasive procedures, methodological deficiencies, and apparently trivial or repetitive results (Bowd and Shapiro, 1993; Gluck, 2001; Pound et al., 2004; Pratt, 1976; Ryder, 1975; Shapiro, 1998; Singer, 1975). Psychologists who conduct laboratory research on animals are frequently confronted with mistrust and hostility from the public, the media, students, and even fellow researchers (Devenport and Devenport, 1990). Rollin (1981), for example, criticized experimental psychology as "the field most consistently guilty of mindless activity that results in great suffering" (p. 124). At times, the hostility towards psychologists has taken a violent turn as research laboratories have been vandalized and researchers' lives threatened by extreme animal rights activists.

Dr. Marilyn E. Carroll is one researcher who was targeted by animal rights activists in recent years. Carroll was conducting painless, non-surgical research on monkeys to investigate behavioral and pharmacological treatments for drug abuse when she began to receive anonymous death threats (Clay, 1997). This scare tactic quickly escalated to include threats to burn her house, telling her young children that their mother tortured animals, and blocking her garage to prevent her from going to her job at the University of Minnesota. Dr. Ronald W. Wood, another researcher who studies drug dependence in laboratory animals, similarly was targeted by animal rights groups, which circulated false claims that he was a convicted animal abuser who was guilty of scientific misconduct. According to some who follow such cases, it perhaps is not surprising that in recent years many protesters have shifted their attacks from cosmetics researchers to scientists engaged in drug abuse investigations. Animal rights activists tend not to consider drug abusers as a sympathetic group of victims, unlike people suffering from cancer or other potentially deadly diseases. In their view, drug abuse is the result of a moral flaw and is not worthy of research; thus, they advocate using drug addicts rather than monkeys in the experiments.

In contrast to the allegations of some activists, psychologists do not routinely subject their research animals to extreme pain, deprivation, or other inhumane treatment. Yet psychological research has been an early and easy target of animal rights activists. This may be due in large part to the fact that for most people, behavioral research has few easily explained links to specific human health benefits (Baldwin, 1993). Compared with some of the dramatic advances in biomedical animal research, the scientific findings and applications of behavioral research may not be perceived by the lay public as valuable. For example, psychological research that is focused on the development of new therapies for stress disorders likely will not appear to be as effective or as important as medical studies devoted to the discovery of new treatments for a life-threatening disease, such as cancer (Larson, 1982).

Other reasons have been suggested for the distinct vulnerability of psychologists to animal research critics. Because psychological research involves the whole living organism, rather than single cells or specific anatomical structures, researchers often are required to maintain animal subjects for long periods of time and to observe them under a variety of conditions. Some of these conditions can in fact be stressful to the animals involved, and so the duration and circumstances of the studies may contribute to the appearance that they are abusive in nature (Larson, 1982).

Various constraints to the research process itself add to the difficulties of psychologists who conduct animal studies. There often are a number of hypotheses that must first be tested in behavioral research before scientific advances become evident. Studies are done to eliminate the less fruitful hypotheses as well as to discover the more promising ones. As a result, progress in psychology and other behavioral science disciplines tends to be slow and perhaps not readily apparent. Behavioral researchers typically are unable to predict with certainty what the outcomes of their studies will be or what benefits can be expected. For these reasons, researchers choose to maintain a low profile, a tendency that can contribute to the public's misunderstandings and suspicions about the nature of the research that is being carried out (Larson, 1982; Morrison, 2001). Even so, there is evidence that a majority of people generally recognize the need to use animals in experimental research (see Box 9.3).

Emergence of the animal rights movement

Although the modern animal rights movement began to have a clear impact on psychology shortly after publication of Australian philosopher Peter Singer's influential book *Animal Liberation* in 1975, concern about the use of animals in

Box 9.3   Should animal research be allowed?

According to various public opinion polls conducted in the United States, most Americans accept the need for using animals in experimental and medical research. In the mid-1980s, a Media General-Associated Press survey found that eight out of ten people questioned believed it was necessary to use animals in medical research on serious diseases and seven of ten people agreed that animal research was needed for basic scientific research ("Poll finds," 1985). Nearly half of the 1,412 respondents believed that laboratory animals were treated humanely, although another 30 percent did not. Nearly nine in ten respondents had no objection to using rats in research. Similar findings were obtained in a national poll conducted by the National Science Foundation (National Science Board, 1991). In that survey, half of the respondents answered affirmatively to the following question: "Should scientists be allowed to do research that causes pain and injury to animals like dogs and chimpanzees if it produces new information about human health problems?" This finding is particularly interesting in light of the explicit mention of "pain and injury" to two species of popular animals (cf. Kallgren and Kenrick, 1990).

A national survey of 2,000 British adults commissioned by the magazine *New Scientist*, and carried out in May 1999 by Market and Opinion Research International (MORI, 1999), revealed that knowledgeable respondents tend to be more approving about animal research. One of the survey's questions asked respondents, "On balance, do you agree or disagree that scientists should be allowed to conduct any experiments on live animals?" Without additional information, only 24 percent of the "cold start" group agreed with animal research. Other participants were asked the same question, only this time it was preceded by the following: "Some scientists are developing and testing new drugs, or developing new treatments for life-threatening diseases such as leukemia and AIDS. By conducting experiments on animals, scientists believe they can make more rapid progress than would otherwise have been possible." For this "warm start" group of participants, nearly twice as many (45 percent) agreed with animal research. The difference between the two groups suggests that although people may initially be skeptical about the value of animal experimentation, opinions are far from fixed, and most people are willing to be persuaded. Another MORI survey, this time commissioned by the Medical Research Council (MRC), questioned more than 1,000 British on their attitudes about using animals in medicine and science. One finding that stood out was that 84 percent of the respondents favored animal research as long as one or more conditions were met, including that the research be intended for medical or life-saving purposes, that suffering should be minimized, and that there was no alternative.

Another study of public attitudes towards animal research compared reactions in 15 different countries, obtaining some interesting results

Box 9.3   (Continued)

(Pifer, Shimizu, and Pifer, 1994). Respondents from some countries, such as Japan and the United States, expressed low levels of opposition to using animals in scientific research, whereas opposition was much stronger in other countries, such as France, Belgium, and Great Britain. In some Western European nations, opposition to animal research was found to be related to concern about the environment. In all of the 15 nations, more women than men were opposed to animal research.

In addition to these attempts to assess public attitudes towards the use of animals in research, Plous (1996) surveyed the attitudes of nearly 4,000 randomly selected members of the American Psychological Association. Among the findings, it was revealed that a majority of respondents supported animal studies involving observation or confinement, but disapproved of studies involving pain or death. Additionally, there was majority support for the federal protection of animals and mandatory pain assessments.

Taken together, these survey results suggest that most people do not share the goals of animal rights activists who believe that all research involving animals should be eliminated (Baldwin, 1993).

scientific experimentation can be traced back to the Victorian anti-vivisection movement in Britain (Sperling, 1988). This nineteenth-century movement appears to have emerged as a reaction to the rapid scientific and technological changes of the period, which had begun to challenge the prevailing notions of humans' relationship to nature (Baldwin, 1993). The most significant event in the British movement came in 1876 with the passage of the Cruelty to Animals Act, which required licenses for conducting animal research and introduced a "pain rule" to protect domestic animals from cruel and improper treatment. Still in effect today, the law states that there is a limit to the amount of pain that an animal should be allowed to endure for the sake of science (Larson, 1982). There were several challenges to animal research in the ensuing years, but scientists were able to successfully protect their interests and continue using animal subjects.

In the United States, early colonists had introduced a law in 1641 to protect animals from cruelty; however, it was not until 1966 that the first federal legislation intended to safeguard the well-being of research animals was passed in the form of the Animal Welfare Act (see "Regulation and review" below). This legislation, along with subsequent revisions, focused primarily on requirements for housing and breeding research animals rather than on experimental procedures that could cause pain and suffering in the animals.

Public concern over the ethical treatment of animals has increased dramatically since the mid-1970s, apparently sparked by the publication of Singer's (1975) *Animal Liberation* (Baldwin, 1993; Bowd and Shapiro, 1993; Herzog, 1993). A second influential book, Ryder's *Victims of Science*, also appeared in 1975. Both books similarly targeted behavioral researchers for conducting painful and unnecessary experiments on animals. In his book, Singer presented a utilitarian position against animal research and laid the philosophical groundwork for later arguments that animals have rights, including the right not to be used as research subjects. One indication of the impact of these publications on the animal rights movement can be seen in the rapid growth of the leading animal rights organization in the United States, People for the Ethical Treatment of Animals (PETA). The membership of PETA increased from 18 members in 1981 to more than 250,000 members in 1990 (McCabe, 1990). According to the PETA website (www.peta.org), the group currently is the largest animal rights organization in the world, with 850,000 members.

PETA was founded in 1980 by Alexander Pacheco, an animal rights advocate who in 1981 surreptitiously infiltrated Edward Taub's laboratory in order to obtain interviews and photographs relevant to Taub's studies involving deafferented monkeys (see chapter 1). The ensuing controversy over Taub's research also did much to bring animal research issues to the forefront of public awareness and debate (Boffey, 1981; Keith-Spiegel and Koocher, 1985; Larson, 1982). Earlier, considerable media attention had focused on a long-term investigation carried out by an experimental psychologist at the American Museum of Natural History involving the sexual behavior of domestic cats (cf. Shaughnessy and Zechmeister, 1990; Wade, 1976). In order to determine behavioral changes in the cats following the loss of various sensations or brain function, the researchers removed parts of the brains or the testicles of some of their animal subjects. Public awareness of this procedure in 1976 brought a fierce reaction from animal rights groups who believed the experimental manipulations to be cruel and unethical. As a result, activists demonstrated against the museum, pressure was placed on museum contributors to withhold their support, and death threats were received by the researchers.

In addition to PETA, other organized animal protection groups have emerged in recent years. Among these is a more radical group, the Animal Liberation Front (ALF), whose members have harassed and disrupted the work of animal researchers whom they believe to be engaged in cruel and unethical experiments. During a period lasting from early 1984 to May 1985, ALF members carried out raids on more than 20 research centers, freeing experimental animals and destroying laboratory equipment (Eckholm, 1985). It should be noted, however, that only a small minority of animal rights proponents belong to groups like ALF, which advocate and sometimes carry out illegal activities on behalf of research animals (Herzog, 1993). In recent years, the tactics of animal rights activists have become more sophisticated, with activists resorting to the courts and legislative lobbying to stop animal research, and challenging the scientific merit of university animal studies (Azar, 1994c). The existence of animal rights groups is not restricted to the United States. In France, for example, the French National Society for the Defense of Animals (Société Nationale de Défense des Animaux) has actively fought against the suffering inflicted on animals since it was founded in 1972. In addition to the Société, there are approximately 23 other generalist associations that exist to defend animals in France. Recent studies of participants in animal rights groups suggest that there are strong parallels between involvement in the animal rights movement and involvement in religious movements (see Box 9.4).

Box 9.4   Animal rights activists: who are they?

Activists within the animal rights movement seem to come from a diverse range of backgrounds, including scientists who had themselves conducted research on animals at one time and many other individuals who never had expected to become involved in the cause. Only recently have attempts been made to characterize the members of animal welfare groups (Galvin and Herzog, 1992; Jamison and Lunch, 1992; Jasper and Nelkin, 1992; Plous, 1991), and there is scant information available about the social and psychological consequences of involvement in the movement.

The results of a recent participant-observation study conducted within the animal rights movement provide an informative look at the individuals who become active in the movement and the consequences of their activism. Psychologist Harold Herzog (1993) completed extensive interviews with 23 activists in the southern United States, none of whom claimed to belong to radical organizations such as ALF, and accumulated more than 400 pages of transcribed interview data. Sixteen of those interviewed were females, a disparity that reflects the greater representation of women in the movement (Jamison and Lunch, 1992; Jasper and Nelkin, 1992; Plous, 1991). Researchers have found that females tend to be less willing than males to see non-human species used in painful research (Kallgren and Kenrick, 1990). For the three-year period during which Herzog conducted the interviews, he also attended meetings and protest demonstrations in an attempt to learn more about the activists and how their lives were affected by their beliefs.

All of the participants in Herzog's study were committed individuals who had made major lifestyle changes as a result of their beliefs that there is a fundamental equality between humans and other species and that people do not have the right to use animals for their own purposes. Despite this shared world view, however, Herzog found that there was a surprising diversity of attitude and behavior among the activists. Some had come to the movement as a result of the careful evaluation of philosophical arguments, while others were motivated by more emotional reasons; some approved of civil disobedience, while others did not; and a similar diversity characterized the extent to which the activists felt morally superior to non-activists.

One of the most striking findings that resulted from Herzog's investigation was the extent to which the animal rights movement had become the central focus of the lives of nearly all those he interviewed. Most of the activists strove to maintain consistency between their ideals and their actions by refraining from eating meat, boycotting consumer products that had been tested on animals or made from leather, and attempting to spread their message to others. Some participants claimed that the changes in lifestyle brought on by their activism presented serious problems in their family relationships. Interestingly, Herzog noted that some of

(Continued)

Box 9.4   (Continued)

these findings, such as the change in fundamental beliefs evident in most
activists, the dramatic alterations in their lifestyle, and the strong desire to
spread their message, suggest parallels between involvement in the animal
rights movement and religious conversion. The portrait that emerges from
this research nonetheless helps to break down the stereotype of animal
rights activists as overemotional and irrational individuals.

The response from psychologists

It is somewhat ironic that at the same time that the animal rights campaign
against behavioral scientists began to accelerate, psychologists themselves
were beginning to express concern over the welfare of their experimental animals, and the use of animals in research and toxicity tests had begun to decline
(Boffey, 1981; Larson, 1982). During the 1970s, several discussions concerning
the use of animals in research were sponsored by the APA and local psychological
associations, current policy statements were reviewed, and an ethics principle
devoted exclusively to animal experimentation was developed and included in the
1981 *Ethical Principles*. This principle has since undergone minor revisions and
now appears as standard 8.09 in the 2002 APA code (see Box 9.5). Psychologists
in other countries, such as Canada, Great Britain, and Australia, have engaged
in similar activities. A survey conducted by the Institute of Laboratory
Animal Resources of the National Academy of Sciences revealed a 40 percent
decrease in the number of animals used in research during the period, from
33 million birds and mammals in 1968 to 20 million in 1978 (Gallup and
Suarez, 1980).

Despite the fact that psychologists have responded to concerns about their
animal experiments, some critics have argued that discussions within the professional literature have been one-sided and that psychologists in general have
reacted in markedly defensive ways (Bowd and Shapiro, 1993; Phillips and
Sechzer, 1989). According to Baldwin (1993), however, when activists initially
targeted individual psychologists or areas of research that were particularly vulnerable to attack, little or no institutional support was forthcoming; thus,
researchers had little choice but to assume a defensive posture or else ignore
the activists in hopes that they would make their point and then go away. In
short, the research community failed initially to communicate its position effectively and, as a result, public attitudes were shaped by the dramatic images, catchy
slogans, and one-sided arguments provided by the animal rights activists.
Some animal rights supporters nonetheless have argued that the defensive posture taken by psychologists was in part intended as a strategic attempt to trivialize
the issue of animal protection.

Psychologists also were faced with the difficult task of having to explain to an
uninformed public the nature of the scientific method and the fact that one could

Box 9.5 APA's Standards for the Humane Care and Use of Animals in Research

(a) Psychologists acquire, care for, use, and dispose of animals in compliance with current federal, state, and local laws and regulations, and with professional standards.

(b) Psychologists trained in research methods and experienced in the care of laboratory animals supervise all procedures involving animals and are responsible for ensuring appropriate consideration of their comfort, health, and humane treatment.

(c) Psychologists ensure that all individuals under their supervision who are using animals have received instruction in research methods and in the care, maintenance, and handling of the species being used, to the extent appropriate to their role. (See also Standard 2.05, Delegation of Work to Others.)

(d) Psychologists make reasonable efforts to minimize the discomfort, infection, illness, and pain of animal subjects.

(e) Psychologists use a procedure subjecting animals to pain, stress, or privation only when an alternative procedure is unavailable and the goal is justified by its prospective scientific, educational, or applied value.

(f) Psychologists perform surgical procedures under appropriate anesthesia and follow techniques to avoid infection and minimize pain during and after surgery.

(g) When it is appropriate that an animal's life be terminated, psychologists proceed rapidly, with an effort to minimize pain and in accordance with accepted procedures.

These standards form the basis of APA's Committee on Animal Research and Ethics (CARE) stand-alone document *Guidelines for Ethical Conduct in the Care and Use of Animals*, available online at http://www.apa.org/science/anguide.html.

Source: American Psychologist (2002), *57*, p. 1070. Copyright © 2002 by the American Psychological Association. Reprinted with permission.

not expect every animal experiment to produce beneficial results (Baldwin, 1993; Orem, 1990). The inability to respond effectively to growing criticism also failed to allay public fears that psychologists were incapable of self-regulating the care and use of research animals. In recent years, psychologists and other scientists have recognized the need to respond more forcefully and publicly to charges leveled by animal rights activists and have been able to persuasively refute misleading allegations (such as the false claim that animal subjects are routinely subjected to painful electric shocks) (Coile and Miller, 1984; Johnson, 1990; Morrison, 2001). According to Gluck and Bell (2003), for researchers to be able to actively participate in discussions about animal research, they first need to become more knowledgeable about the details of the ethical issues, animal model validation, and the nature of the animals that they study.

It is interesting to note that whereas researchers previously have expressed far more concern about the protection of human subjects in psychological research, it is the public that has been most vocal about animal experimentation (Keith-Spiegel and Koocher, 1985). However, if the rapidly growing psychological literature on ethical issues in animal research is any indication, this claim is less true today than it once was.

ARGUMENTS FOR AND AGAINST ANIMAL RESEARCH

In order to more fully examine the arguments for and against conducting research with animals it first is important to clarify the difference between the goals of animal welfare groups and those of animal rights groups (Baldwin, 1993; Jasper and Nelkin, 1992; Johnson, 1990). Those individuals whose concerns pertain to animal welfare are primarily interested in improving laboratory conditions and reducing the number of animals needed to conduct research studies. These mainstream concerns for the humane treatment of animals are shared by most researchers (Baldwin, 1993). By contrast, the animal rights movement is not mainstream, holding that animals have rights equal to humans and thus should not be used at all as laboratory subjects. The primary goal of animal rights groups is to abolish all laboratory research on animals (Plous, 1991), a goal that researchers and, if responses to national polls are any indication, the general public do not agree with (see Box 9.3).

The philosophical roots of the animal welfare movement can be traced to the Judeo-Christian belief that humans are the stewards of the planet and, as such, are privileged to use its plants and animals as they deem fit (Johnson, 1990). However, this privilege bears a corresponding responsibility to serve as caretakers for that which has been entrusted to them. An important element of Judeo-Christian thought is the belief that humans are qualitatively different from other animal species. In this view, a hierarchy of value exists among the planet's life forms, with human life and welfare having the highest value. By virtue of their unique capacity for moral choice, it is argued that humans can and should be held responsible for their actions towards animals (Robb, 1988). Stemming from these notions are the efforts of animal welfarists to prevent the cruel treatment of animals and to improve their health and well-being. This perspective has a long history in Judeo-Christian thought, in contrast to the relatively recent positions held by animal rights activists.

Although "welfarists" often belong to local humane societies and tend to express sympathy for the plight of animals, they are unlikely to undergo the sorts of lifestyle changes that can be seen in the more committed rights advocates (Herzog, 1993). The latter have been labeled "fundamentalists" to reflect the belief that humans do not have the right to use animals for their own purposes, regardless of the benefits (Jasper and Nelkin, 1992). A similar categorization has been offered by Herzog (1990), who suggests that animal protectionist groups can be distinguished as "reformers," who admit the necessity to utilize animals for research purposes, and the more radical "animal liberators," who believe that animal research is immoral and should be abolished.

The case against animal research

Underlying the various arguments promulgated by animal rights advocates is the recognition that the ethical issues and problems involved in conducting research with animals are different from those involved in human subject research. One essential difference has to do with the fact that animals cannot be informed of the risks posed by a research study or give their consent to participate, and thus they are at the mercy of investigators (Carroll et al., 1985). Because of the near absolute power that researchers hold over their animal subjects, consent requirements and privacy issues essentially are rendered irrelevant in the context of animal research (Keith-Spiegel and Koocher, 1985). In addition to the design and procedure of the investigation, researchers determine and control the conditions under which animals live, including what and how much they are provided to eat. Also, unlike research with humans, the risks of research participation may be far greater for animals and, in some cases, may necessitate the termination of their lives.

Numerous arguments have been put forth by those individuals who believe that animal research should be abolished, although many activists often are unable to articulate the philosophical perspectives that form the basis of their positions (Sperling, 1988). Two of the most influential philosophical positions used to present the case against using animals in research are the utilitarian and the rights arguments. The major points related to these two positions are summarized below.

The utilitarian argument

Described earlier as the basic perspective underlying the development of research principles for human subject research (see chapter 2), the utilitarian position has also been applied to animal research. The basic focus of the utilitarian position is on the consequences of one's actions. According to this perspective, ethical conduct is that which results in the greatest pleasure and happiness, relative to pain and suffering, for the most people. In utilitarian considerations, no one person's happiness is to be held as more important than another's.

In his book *Animal Liberation*, Peter Singer (1975) extended this argument by maintaining that considerations of the greatest good should include animals. At the heart of this view is the "principle of equality" (or "equal consideration of interests"), which holds that all living creatures with the capacity to sense have an equal interest in avoiding pain and suffering. Consistent with this principle is the conclusion that there is no basis for elevating the interests of one species, such as humans, above any other sentient species. In Singer's view, the only relevant moral criterion for distinguishing between species is the capacity to suffer.

Because all sentient animals have that capacity, they are subject to equal moral consideration. Thus, humans and all other sentient animals have an equal interest not to be used in experiments that could cause them harm and suffering.

The critical aspect of the utilitarian argument against the use of animals in research is the claim that it is inappropriate to elevate humans above all other species on the basis of any criterion other than suffering. To do so would be to commit a form of *speciesism*, which is the animal rights supporters' equivalent of racism. In Singer's (1985) terms, speciesism is a prejudicial attitude biased towards the interests of members of one's own species and against the members of other species. Research on animals would be permitted in some circumstances, according to the utilitarian view, but only when the potential value of the study is high and it could also be carried out using human subjects (cf. Herzog, 1990). One problem with this utilitarian position has to do with the difficulty of having to determine where one draws the line between species that suffer and those that do not. On this matter, for example, Singer draws the line at the phylogenetic level of oysters. A second problem with the position is that it does not consider qualitative differences in pain and pleasure across species (cf. Baldwin, 1993).

As is discussed below, another variation of the utilitarian perspective is often used as an argument to *support* the use of animals in research. Researchers have pointed to the numerous examples of animal research applications that have improved human welfare and they have maintained that the benefits to humanity accrued from such research clearly outweigh the costs imposed on the research animals (Miller, 1985). In this view, animals are not given the same degree of consideration as people because of significant differences that exist between humans and other species (e.g. higher intelligence and the capacity for language). Some critics believe that such a cost–benefit approach for justifying animal research is unsatisfactory because any analysis of costs to animals presumes that they are willing participants in the research enterprise (Bowd and Shapiro, 1993). Further, it is argued that whereas the benefits from laboratory research with animals often are uncertain, the costs to animals are obvious and real.

The rights argument

The fundamental assumption of the rights argument against animal research, as articulated by Regan (1983), is that animals possess certain rights based on their "inherent value." That is, it is believed that humans and other sentient animal species have inherent value in equal measure entitling them to certain fundamental rights. Included among these rights are the right to moral consideration, the right to be treated with respect, and the right not to be harmed. Consistent with this argument, it is held that animals have a right not to be used for research by humans, even if the research promises certain direct human benefits. Proponents of this position suggest that animal research should be abolished because scientists tend to treat research animals as renewable resources rather than as creatures with inherent value and rights.

Some proponents of the rights philosophy rely on certain criteria – such as language, higher intelligence, and self-consciousness – for determining who is entitled to fundamental rights. Because non-human species generally do not meet such criteria, it is believed that the rights should be restricted to humans. This philosophical position, however, runs into difficulties when confronted with considerations of the moral status of humans who do not meet the criteria (such as infants and the mentally infirm) and animals that do appear to meet some of the criteria (such as members of primate and cetacean species that have demonstrated some language skills, etc.) (Herzog, 1990). By broadening the criteria to include members of sentient animal species as being morally entitled to fundamental rights, animal rights advocates avoid these concerns. Nonetheless, questions relevant to how the rights in question are defined and who is entitled to them remain at issue for critics of this approach (Baldwin, 1993).

Despite the differences between the utilitarian and rights-based positions against animal research, it is possible to identify some commonalities. At the outset, it is apparent that aside from their somewhat divergent philosophical underpinnings, both positions lead to the same conclusion: that research with animals as it is now conducted should be eliminated. Both views acknowledge the ethical significance of certain similarities between humans and other species (e.g. the capacity for suffering), but downplay the importance of apparent differences (e.g. intelligence level). In so doing, the two positions represent anti-speciesism perspectives on animal research. For many people, however, the utilitarian and rights arguments that human life *per se* is not more important than that of other species are difficult to accept.

Other issues

In addition to the two general philosophical positions described above, other points have been made to bolster the argument that animal research is immoral and should not be allowed. Consistent with the philosophical view that sentient species have the right to be protected from pain and suffering is the accusation that many research animals do in fact experience much pain and suffering during the course of laboratory studies. The controversial test cases involved in charges of animal mistreatment, such as the research on monkeys conducted by Taub, are often cited as evidence supporting accusations of animal abuse inflicted during the course of research.

Despite arguments to the contrary (see "The case for animal research" below), critics have maintained that many animal studies are highly invasive in nature, involving pain, stress, punishment, social and environmental deprivation, as well as experimentally induced emotional and intellectual deficits. Typically cited among the specific research examples are studies of visual deprivation in kittens, infant maternal deprivation and drug addiction in macaque monkeys, brain studies of eating behavior in rats, and the like. Although it is impossible for humans to know with any degree of certainty what members of non-human species experience or feel, animal research critics have argued that considerations of the mistreatment of laboratory animals should include their pre- and post-experimental care (i.e. "husbandry"), in addition to solely focusing on the invasive experimental procedures (Bowd and Shapiro, 1993). For instance, although much of the public outcry over Taub's research focused on the experimental procedure itself (i.e. the deafferentation of limbs), the actual charges against Taub centered on abusive husbandry practices, such as the inadequate care, feeding, and housing of his monkeys (Shapiro, 1989). The customary husbandry practice of housing animals in individual cages is one issue that has aroused concern (Bayne, 1991). Animal critics believe that housing animals of the same species apart deprives them of essential social interaction (Bowd and Shapiro, 1993).

Issues related to the invasive treatment of research animals are exacerbated by additional concerns, such as a lack of apparent value in purely theoretical studies, non-generalizability of animal findings to humans and other species, and the diversion of funds from treatment programs. For example, Bowd (1980) has claimed that many of the findings derived from animal research performed by psychologists are not published, implying that the studies have been deemed insignificant by the investigators' peers. Moreover, one rather consistent theme running through the critiques of animal research has to do with the apparent redundancy in the research that *is* published. According to Bowd (1980, p. 207), "a significant proportion of published research is repetitive or deals with problems to which the answers are self-evident."

Finally, the case against animal research also consists of some arguments that pertain to issues underlying the politics of the debate. While many supporters of animal research would agree that animal rights advocates have successfully mounted a "calculatedly deceptive and seductive campaign to win sympathy and financial support from those who have affection for animals" (Johnson, 1990, p. 213) through the use of shocking posters and the like, the research profession has been similarly criticized for presenting a sanitized and misleading picture of the animal research enterprise (Bowd and Shapiro, 1993). For example, it is argued that the basic media through which students obtain their exposure to animal research (i.e. popular psychology textbooks and audiovisual materials) tend to minimize descriptions of the suffering involved in invasive animal studies, showing instead pictures of cute animals with accompanying text that focuses on the human benefits derived from the research (Field, 1989, 1990). An analysis of leading introductory psychology textbooks, however, revealed that authors rarely make explicit the contributions stemming from research with animals and frequently present major findings from animal research as if they had been obtained from humans (Domjan and Purdy, 1995).

There also have been complaints about the scientific jargon used to refer to invasive procedures in animal research. Bowd (1980), for example, has criticized research psychologists for using language that belies the true nature of the procedures, such as referring to starvation as "deprivation," to the animal participant as an "organism," and describing research animals as being "sacrificed" rather than killed. In Bowd's view, this use of jargon enables many researchers to maintain insensitivity to their treatment of animals.

The case for animal research

As previously described, in recent years researchers and other supporters of animal research have become more forceful in their rebuttals of the arguments summarized in the preceding section. While each of the points raised in favor of eliminating animal research has been countered by researchers (see Table 9.1), the arguments most typically emphasized in defense of that activity are the following: (1) that many benefits to humans and animals have accrued from animal research; (2) that researchers are sensitive to the pain and suffering

Table 9.1 Arguments for and against experiments using animals

Pros	Cons
The potential to reduce human suffering justifies using animals in research and submitting them to discomfort or risky research procedures. That is, animal experimentation can be seen as a means to greater ends, although experiments should be considered on a case-by-case basis.	Animals have rights, including the right not to be used in research experiments. They also have the right to be treated as having value in themselves, and not to be used as a means to human ends. Animals should not be subjected to pain, discomfort, and perhaps death, regardless of the anticipated benefits.
Researchers continue to seek alternatives to using animals in their investigations and the statistics show that animal research is declining. Nonetheless, it is still necessary and justified for pursuing certain research questions.	Animals continue to be used at high rates for research worldwide; however, many animal studies are not published and thus do not show up in analyses of research frequency, or else are redundant and unnecessary.
It is possible to keep animal suffering at an absolute minimum. The reduction of animal suffering has become a central concern for researchers, which is reflected in the use of anesthetics, when necessary, and improvements in keeping animals in clean, comfortable, and healthy conditions.	Regardless of researchers' claims, in practice their experiments on animals are highly invasive, involving pain and suffering. Numerous animals are not anesthetized, are abused by handlers, are kept in isolation or uncomfortable and dirty cages, and an untold number die each year in research experiments.
There is great similarity in the genetic makeup of humans and higher primates (such as chimpanzees), and so animal reactions are a good guide to possible reactions in humans. Even lower species share basic similarities in physiology with humans. Thus, it is morally defensible to conduct certain studies (e.g. on medicines or drug prevention) on animals in order to avoid risking the lives of human subjects.	A large proportion of animal studies in fact utilize lower animals that are vastly different from humans, such as rodents and birds. This is contrary to the argument that anything useful can be determined about human functioning from these studies. Further, the more similar the animal is to a human (such as a chimpanzee), the more immoral it is to submit that animal to harm.
There are a growing number of laws, research guidelines, and review mechanisms (such as institutional review committees) that offer protections for research animals.	Animal protection laws should be replaced by an act that would acknowledge the fundamental rights of animals and prohibit the use of any animals to their detriment.
Animal experimentation can be in the interest of animals as well as humans, because experiments done to test medicines and surgical procedures can often be applied to the betterment of various species of animals.	Unlike human subjects, animals cannot give their consent to medical or other tests. It thus is unacceptable to submit healthy animals to invasive procedures, even if the findings might be used to treat other animals.

Source: Dixon (2000), Slife and Rubenstein (1992).

experienced by animals and use procedures ensuring that animals are humanely treated; and (3) that researchers have developed alternative procedures which have led to a reduction in the use of animals for research purposes. Additionally, researchers have pointed to the practical advantages of using animals rather than human participants in various research contexts. In short, the arguments in favor of animal research tend to reflect the "three R's" (replacement, reduction, and refinement) concept described above.

The philosophical approach underlying most attempts to justify animal research stems from historically early views of humans as being distinct from other species. These views are rooted in Judeo-Christian belief, as well as Cartesian notions found in the philosophy of the seventeenth-century French thinker René Descartes, which differentiated humans from non-humans on the basis of human possession of a "soul" and the capacity for moral choice. Because of their capacity for moral choice, it is maintained that humans can enter into contractual situations with binding rights and responsibilities for both parties (Baldwin, 1993; Robb, 1988). In light of neurological studies demonstrating that there are in fact continuities between human and animal brain structures and functions, it is now acknowledged even within the scientific community that animals experience a broad range of emotions and feelings, and possess psychological features previously ascribed solely to humans (cf. Blumberg and Wasserman, 1995). Nevertheless, one vestige of the early philosophical views of animals that conceptualized them as merely mechanical systems is the utilitarian argument that the use of animals in research is justified by the potential benefits to human welfare. Indicative of this utilitarian perspective is the comment from Herzog (1990, p. 91) that "If it were possible to transplant an organ from a healthy sheep into a dying infant, most of us would readily approve of the operation." In short, this view is consistent with the belief that scientists have a right to attempt to improve human lives through research.

Turning next to the specific arguments that have been raised in support of research on animals, some researchers have emphasized the practical advantages of using animal subjects. In contrast to research with human participants, it is easier in the sense of methodological control to maintain similar manipulated experiences or genetic make up in animal comparison groups. It also is possible to study long-term changes with greater facility in animals due to easier access, more rapid developmental changes, and shorter life spans in various species. It is generally agreed, however, that these practical considerations do not alone serve to justify the use of animal research participants (Shapiro, 1984).

Perhaps the most persuasive argument cited within the research community in defense of animal research is that the research has led to numerous benefits, not only to humans but to other animals as well. Most supporters of animal experimentation contend that these benefits have gone largely unrecognized by animal rights activists. Among the contributions to animals that have accrued from behavioral research are improvements in the environments of captive animals, including modifications in the conditions under which research animals are studied, thereby leading to a reduction of suffering and discomfort during the research experience (Novak and Petto, 1991). Other benefits include biomedical developments in veterinary procedures, vaccines for deadly diseases (e.g. rabies, Lyme disease, feline leukemia), and captive breeding programs that have resulted in saving some animals from the brink of extinction (Baldwin, 1993; King and Yarbrough, 1985). Miller (1983, 1985) has provided several examples of how traditionally lethal methods of controlling animals that damage crops or flocks (e.g. by shooting or poisoning the destructive animals) have begun to be replaced by the application of more humane techniques derived through experimental studies of animal behavior (see Box 9.6).

Research benefits for humans

Although animal rights activists often argue that animal experiments are not really applicable to humans and thus are without any value, the numerous benefits to humans that have come about as a result of research on animals have been clearly documented by others (Bakhle, 2004; Baldwin, 1993; Cole,

---

Box 9.6   Animal research benefits for animals

Psychologist Neal Miller has for more than two decades emphatically presented the case for animal research by documenting the many benefits to animals and humans that have been derived from the research. Among the examples of research benefiting animals described by Miller (1983, 1985) is the application of the so-called "taste-aversion effect," an example of aversive conditioning that causes animals to avoid a nausea-inducing flavor, even if it was tasted several hours before the onset of the nausea. One application of this learned effect involves the administration of a moderately bad-tasting chemical to birds that is reinforced by non-harmful nausea if the birds continue to eat. The administration of the chemical, methiocarb, has proven to be a humane approach to protecting fruit crops and lawns from Canadian geese, and researchers have begun to focus on other possible applications (e.g. to train coyotes to avoid the taste of sheep meat; to better understand the food aversions in children receiving chemotherapy for cancer).

Other behavioral research studies on such topics as imprinting, animal sexual behavior, genetic and experiential factors that control the timing and course of migration, and animal requirements for habitat and for territory have proven essential in efforts to save endangered species from extinction. In one example derived from imprinting research, artificially incubated condor chicks are exposed to and fed by a puppet surrogate of an adult female condor rather than by an undisguised human caretaker. This procedure has been successful in facilitating the young chicks' safe association with wild condors when they are released into their natural habitat.

1992; Comroe, 1983; King and Yarbrough, 1985; Lemon and Dunnett, 2005; Miller, 1983, 1985; Randall, 1983). The fact that animals have played a pivotal role in improving the human condition represents a primary reason why most people claim to support the continued use of animals for research purposes (e.g. Knight et al., 2003; MORI, 1999; National Science Board, 1991; Pifer et al., 1994). It is not our intent here to enumerate all of the benefits that have been cited beyond simply to acknowledge some examples of important contributions that have emerged through animal experimentation. Within biomedical areas alone, the list of contributions attributed to animal research is impressive, including the development of vaccines for a number of diseases (such as typhoid, diphtheria, and polio), antibiotics, antidepressants, local anesthetics, insulin, cancer therapies, and most surgical procedures (Cole, 1992).

The human benefits of behavioral research with animals also are many, although, as described earlier in this chapter, they may not be as apparent to the lay public as the contributions attributed to research in medical fields. Many of the contributions of animal research conducted by behavioral scientists are indeed significant advances, including the rehabilitation of persons suffering from spinal cord injury, stroke, head injuries, and other neuromuscular disorders; the discovery and greater understanding of Alzheimer's disease and eating disorders; improvements in communication with the severely retarded; the discovery of drugs for treating anxiety, psychoses, and Parkinson's disease; the control of chronic anxiety through non-drug therapies; advances in the treatment of premature infants, eye disorders in children, and the problem of enuresis; and improved knowledge about and treatment of alcoholism and other types of substance abuse, obesity, hypertension, memory deficits in the aged, and insomnia (Baldwin, 1993; Miller, 1985). Non-human primate research also has enabled researchers to investigate a variety of complex behaviors, such as aggression, social organization and communication, learning and memory, and growth and development (King and Yarbrough, 1985). Research conducted by Roger Sperry during the 1960s on the "split brain" involved initial animal studies that ultimately led to a better understanding of epilepsy. Today, many epileptic patients who otherwise would have to be confined to hospitals are able to lead relatively normal lives because of Sperry's research (Gazzaniga and LeDoux, 1978; Sperry, 1968).

Given the nature of such benefits, animal research supporters understandably react with great consternation when barriers to animal research arise or when research laboratories are trashed by radical animal rights activists. Thus, the destruction of one psychologist's sudden infant death syndrome (SIDS) laboratory was seen not as a victory for animals, but rather as "a postponement of the day when we will know how to stop babies from dying of SIDS." The loss of an addiction research grant as a result of pressure from animal rights groups was viewed not as a victory for the cats that were to be used in the research, but as a delay in our learning "how to save human beings from lives of drug dependence" (Johnson, 1990, p. 214). Many researchers no doubt would agree with Johnson's overall assessment that "The victories of the animal rights movement can be properly counted only in terms of the human pain and death they have guaranteed."

Reducing the pain and suffering of research animals

In countering the charge by animal research critics that scientists fail to recognize the pain experienced by their laboratory animals, Gallistel (1981) has argued that if that were the case, researchers would not take the care that they do to limit it during experimental procedures. Among the recent steps taken to reduce the possibility that research animals will undergo unnecessary pain or suffering is the establishment of policies at some large research facilities prohibiting the use of muscle paralyzing agents during experimental surgery. So-called "paralytics" (such as curare) have been used to immobilize experimental animals without rendering them unconscious during surgical procedures. Scientists also have become progressively aware that, unless the focus of the research is to study the effects of trauma *per se*, causing animal suffering does not represent good science because the research ultimately will yield invalid, non-generalizable results (Zola et al., 1984).

Further evidence that researchers have grown increasingly sensitive to the concerns of animal rights activists is apparent in the statistics (reviewed above) indicating that the number of animals used in research has sharply declined in recent years. While this reduction also can be attributed somewhat to the increased costs of conducting animal research, it is clear that researchers have been successful in developing methodological alternatives to animal research, such as computer simulations, mechanical models, and the use of tissue and cell cultures (see "Alternatives to animal research" below). There also is increasing evidence that when animals are used in research, the treatment is more likely to be non-invasive (i.e. the study involves minimal pain) as opposed to invasive (i.e. the study includes more or less painful research on conscious animals) (see Table 9.2). For example, in her survey of the database of primate research in Asia for the year 2001, Houde (2004) found that more than half of the investigations (56 percent) consisted of non-invasive procedures involving little or no pain. Similarly, C. Gauthier (2004, p. 275) noted a "sustained downward trend in the number of experiments causing severe pain in unanaesthetized animals" in research conducted in Canada and the US between 1996 and 1999, to a level that is "very low." This included a decrease in the US from 12 to 9 percent in use of the most invasive techniques. Gauthier attributed the observed decline in invasive procedures to newly emergent guidelines designed to ensure better monitoring and care of animals.

Research animals now have greater protections as a result of the appearance in recent years of ethical standards and guidelines, such as those developed by professional associations. The establishment of ethical review committees at research facilities serves as an additional mechanism for overseeing the procedures used for housing animals and for controlling pain, training personnel, and determining the adequacy of the experimental design in terms of costs, benefits, and alternative approaches not requiring the use of animals. Despite these advances, there are some who contend that animal rights activists are not concerned so much with the humane treatment of animals in research as they are with eliminating their use in research entirely (e.g. Johnson, 1990).

Table 9.2   Categories of invasiveness: a pain scale for animal research

Pursuant to the *refinement* element of the "three R's" concept, some organizations (such as the USDA, the Canadian Council on Animal Care or CCAC, and some European bodies) have found it useful to develop pain scales, which categorize the various degrees of invasiveness of different types of animal research experiments. Such scales can be of value to researchers who may be required to assess the degree of pain animals likely would experience in a proposed study, and such scales also can be used in comparative assessments of animal use (Orlans, 1993; Plous, 1996). Animal researchers in Canada are required to assess their research according to the following scale, which is typical of categorizations of this kind:

Category	Degree of invasiveness
B	Little or no discomfort or pain (e.g. studies of invertebrates with complex nervous systems; food or water deprivation studies of a duration similar to that experienced in nature)
C	Minor stress or pain (e.g. minor surgical procedures under anesthesia; use of noxious stimuli from which escape is possible)
D	Moderate to severe stress (e.g. major surgery under anesthesia with recovery, such as brain lesioning or electrode implantation); major stressors such as maternal separation
E	Severe pain (often prohibited) (e.g. use of muscle relaxants for surgical restraint without anesthesia; attempts to induce psychotic-like behavior)

Although Category A is not used in the Canadian system, in other classifications this level is used to refer to experiments involving either no living materials or unobtrusive observations. The USDA scale, which is used for practical purposes but was never formally adopted as a review mechanism, consists of five categories (A – E). Similar to the CCAC scale, the primary consideration differentiating the categories is whether or not anesthetics and analgesics are delivered (C. Gauthier, 2004).

REGULATION AND REVIEW OF ANIMAL RESEARCH

In a relatively short period of time, much has been done to regulate the care and use of animals in behavioral and biomedical research. In the United States, for example, an elaborate system exists for safeguarding the well-being of research animals, consisting of federal regulations, state laws, and professional guidelines and review mechanisms. These safeguards are briefly summarized below.

Governmental regulations

In recent years, the American Congress has played an increasingly involved role in the animal research debate, as is evidenced by the considerable legislation that has been passed. Federal regulations under the Animal Welfare Act and Public Health Service (PHS) policy are now in place, as are state laws governing the availability of pound animals for research. To a great extent, the campaign against animal research launched by animal rights groups during the 1980s was responsible for the emergence of these federal and state requirements, although the

Animal Welfare Act dates back to 1966, when it was first signed into law. The Act has since been amended four times (1970, 1976, 1985, and 1990).

At the center of federal policy regulating the use of animals in research is the Department of Agriculture's (USDA, 1991) Animal Welfare Act (available online at www.nal.usda.gov/awic/legislat/awicregs.htm). Enforced by the USDA's Animal and Plant Health Inspection Service (APHIS), the law consists of guidelines for the care and use of research animals and specifies that unannounced inspections of animal research facilities be carried out periodically by APHIS inspectors. The inspections, which are intended to ensure compliance with the regulations, include assessments of feeding schedules, adequacy of housing, exercise requirements for certain animal species, promotion of the psychological well-being of non-human primates, and so on. The original purpose of the Act was to regulate the care and use of laboratory animals, but it ultimately evolved into the sole US federal law regulating the treatment of animals in research and other activities (such as exhibition and transport). Although there are other laws and policies in the United States pertaining to animal care and use of specifically named animal species, they all refer to the Animal Welfare Act as the minimal standard (USDA, 2000).

The PHS regulations were first published in 1973 and amended in 1979 and 1986. The regulations originally were voluntary and pertained only to standards for animal husbandry. Under the Health Research Extension Act of 1985 (Public Law 99-158) the guidelines became law and now set out requirements for all animal experimentation conducted by federal agencies. The PHS policy is administered by the Office for Laboratory Animal Welfare of the National Institutes of Health (NIH). In addition to the USDA's APHIS inspections, two PHS agencies (the NIH and the Centers for Disease Control) require institutions receiving federal funds to establish a standing Animal Care and Use Committee (ACUC) to review all proposed and ongoing animal research conducted at the institution. These review committees are to comprise at least five members, including a veterinarian, an experienced animal researcher, a non-scientist (e.g. a lawyer or ethicist), and a person who is not affiliated in any way with the institution (Office for Protection from Research Risks, 1986).

Each ACUC review of a research grant proposal is to include a consideration of the justification for the species to be used and the number of animals required to carry out the research; the adequacy of the procedures for controlling pain, housing animals, carrying out euthanasia, and training personnel; any available alternatives to the research; and evidence that the study will not represent an unnecessary replication of previous research. ACUCs also are expected to carry out local inspections of research facilities in order to assess ongoing compliance with state research requirements, and are empowered to investigate complaints about the misuse or mistreatment of animals.

There are some obvious similarities between ACUCs and the NIH regulations requiring the establishment of institutional review boards (IRBs) to review federally funded research with human subjects. Thus, it was not surprising that when legislation was proposed to create ACUC review at PHS grantee institutions, animal researchers reacted with some of the same concerns as those expressed by human subject researchers when IRBs were first created during the 1970s. In fact, although researchers have feared that federal regulations would inhibit research, this appears not to be the case in either the human or animal research context. Rather, institutionalized review seems to have had the effect of improving research design by reducing risk and discomfort for subjects (Mishkin, 1985).

During the early 1990s, several animal rights organizations sued the USDA, arguing that the government's regulations were not strict enough and that more detailed regulations should be issued ("Ruling on animals," 1994). The focus of the lawsuit was on so-called "performance-based" regulations that had been adopted by the USDA in 1991, which placed responsibility for determining the appropriate environment and exercise program for laboratory animals onto each research facility. A judge ruled in favor of the activists in 1993 and ordered the USDA to rewrite the regulations. However, this ruling, which would have required more rigid standards for animal research, was overturned one year later by a unanimous appeals panel decision. It was determined that the animal rights groups did not have legal standing to challenge USDA rules because it could not be shown that they had been directly harmed as a result of USDA actions. The determination also applied to a challenge of USDA's decision not to include rodents and birds in research under the Animal Welfare Act. This court decision was viewed as an important victory for the research community, which had generally supported the reinstated 1991 guidelines ("Ruling on animals," 1994).

Before we leave our consideration of US government regulation of animal research, it is important to note a specific limitation to its coverage of some applied research investigations. It currently is the case that animal research carried out by pharmaceutical companies or genetic engineering firms often falls outside the realm of federal regulation and is not governed by legal requirements. This is so because the research is not supported by federal funds nor does it involve named species. In order to overcome this loophole, the USDA endeavored to have rats, mice, and birds included as species covered by the Animal Welfare Act. This coverage was achieved when a lawsuit filed against the USDA in 1998 (*ARDF* v. *Glickman*) was settled out of court in 2000. Before the USDA drafted the regulations, a Congressional amendment was passed that permanently excluded rats, mice, and birds from Animal Welfare Act coverage (American Association of Anatomists, 2002). This development has been viewed as a significant victory for the biomedical research community, although it is likely that animal rights activists will continue to pursue alternative avenues for further regulation.

Professional developments

Various steps also have been taken within the professions to provide guidelines for the use and care of research animals. Earlier, we alluded to the development of an ethical principle specific to animal research, which was first added to the APA code of ethics in 1981. Similar principles have been adopted by the British and Australian psychological associations. The BPS (2005b) *Guidelines for Psychologists Working with Animals* are based on standards originally published in 1981 by the

Association for the Study of Animal Behaviour and the Animal Behaviour Society. The guidelines, recently revised for the first time since 1995, supplement an earlier BPS statement published as a Report of the Working Party on Animal Experimentation (*Bulletin of The British Psychological Society*, 1979, *32*, 44–52). The intent of the current document (see www.bps.org.uk) is to provide a checklist of points for investigators to carefully consider prior to conducting their experiments with animals.

Regardless of the nature of the research, an overriding BPS principle is that animal researchers have a "general obligation to avoid or at least minimise discomfort to living animals." Additionally, investigators are required to "justify the costs to the animal in terms of the likely benefits of the research" prior to using procedures that are outlined in the guidelines. The guidelines, which adhere to the "three R's concept," are meant to apply to members of the BPS as well as the Experimental Psychological Society (EPS). Moreover, the British Society of Animal Science has enacted its own set of ethical guidelines and has included stipulations pertaining to the protection of research animals as a key element of its publication policy (Jarvis, Day, and Reed, 2003, p. 1):

> The British Society of Animal Science (BSAS) does not publish work that it views as having resulted in unnecessary pain, distress or other forms of suffering to experimental animals. Any experimental work published by BSAS must have been conducted in accordance with relevant national legislation and recommendations relating to the use of animals for experimental purposes.

Regarding professional activity in American psychology, despite the fact that a separate principle devoted to animal research was not added to the *Ethical Principles* until fairly recently, the APA has long been involved in promoting the well-being of animals in psychological research. For example, the original 1981 principle was heavily adapted from an earlier APA policy statement (APA, 1968), which was to be posted in all animal psychology laboratories where animal research was conducted. Guidelines for the use of animals in schools also were detailed in another early APA policy (Committee for the Use of Animals in School Science Behavior Projects, 1972).

The APA Committee on Animal Research and Ethics (CARE) publishes another useful document, *Guidelines for Ethical Conduct in the Care and Use of Animals* (APA, 1993a), which is used widely by researchers in psychology and other scientific fields. Established in 1925, CARE is responsible for reviewing the ethical issues involved in animal research and revising guidelines for the care and use of laboratory animals. Recently, CARE, along with the APA Board of Scientific Affairs, began to release short videos intended to educate high school students about the contributions of laboratory animal research (Dingfelder, 2004). The second video in the series is a 15-minute presentation entitled "The Importance of Laboratory Animal Research in Psychology: Psychopharmacology," which focuses on drug abuse research. The videos are sent to all APA members who teach in secondary schools and are accompanied by a study guide consisting of discussion questions and additional details about the research depicted in the video.

The APA also promotes the well-being of animals in research through membership in an organization known as the American Association for the Accreditation of Laboratory Animal Care (AAALAC), the only such accrediting body recognized by the PHS (Baldwin, 1993). For an institution to receive AAA-LAC accreditation, its animal research facilities must exceed the requirements established by federal policy. To date, more than 670 research institutions in 24 countries have earned AAALAC accreditation (www.aaalac.org). Finally, Psychologists for the Ethical Treatment of Animals (PsyETA), an independent organization of American psychologists who share the concerns of animal welfare groups, was created during the 1980s. Among the goals of this organization – whose members include professionals, students, and activists – are the improvement of the care standards and conditions for animals used in psychological research, the development of educational approaches that contribute to the well-being of research animals, and the maintaining of liaisons between scientific and animal welfare groups (Keith-Spiegel and Koocher, 1985).

Although these professional developments have done much to raise ethical sensitivities within the disciplines, they have not eliminated concerns held by many critics that the scientific community is unable to self-regulate animal research. Reactions to APA's animal research principles are a case in point. These principles, which appear in Box 9.5, have met with some of the same criticisms that were voiced in reaction to the APA's principles for human subject research. For example, Carroll et al. (1985) cautioned that because researchers are always likely to see some value in their own research, they may be prone to rationalize painful procedures as necessary and make little effort to find alternative, painless procedures.

In a more general sense, others have pointed out that the APA's animal research principles deal almost exclusively with the care and treatment of research animals, rather than providing restrictions on their use (Bowd and Shapiro, 1993; Shaughnessy and Zechmeister, 1990). Further, Bowd and Shapiro (1993) noted that only one animal welfare case was considered by the APA Ethics Committee from 1982 to 1990, despite charges by the animal rights movement that several research laboratories had committed specific animal welfare violations during that period. The case that *was* heard by the Ethics Committee involved Taub's research on deafferentation in macaque monkeys.

It is clear that behavioral scientists now take a much more active role in safeguarding their research interests. Groups representing behavioral and biomedical research have begun to form alliances with civil liberties groups and federal agencies to advocate for legislation and other protections for animal researchers. These efforts paid off in the form of passage into law of the Animal Enterprise Protection Act of 1992, more commonly referred to as the "break-in" law ("Animal research," 1992). Among other things, this law makes it a federal offense in the United States to commit acts of vandalism and thefts at animal research facilities on an interstate or international basis that result in more than US$10,000 in damages. This legislation is intended to protect animal researchers from costly and destructive attacks on their laboratories and to reduce fears among researchers whose lives have been threatened by animal rights extremists.

ALTERNATIVES TO ANIMAL RESEARCH

In response to the ethical concerns raised by the use of animals in laboratory research, researchers have been encouraged to develop alternative approaches for carrying out their investigations. While many behavioral scientists continue to believe that a strong defense of current practices is the best policy for responding to their critics, others have questioned whether the use of animals in laboratory research is even the most appropriate approach for studying many behavioral research questions (Devenport and Devenport, 1990). In recent years, a diverse set of alternatives to laboratory animals have emerged and, as a result, the number of animals used for behavioral research purposes in general has continued to decline. Within the behavioral sciences, researchers have employed mathematical simulations, mechanical models, anthropomorphic "dummies," and simulated tissue and body fluids in research situations where at one time animals would have been used as a matter of course.

A growing number of researchers have begun to consider whether research on commonly used animal species could be conducted instead with the use of human subjects or, at the other extreme, lower organisms. Because a major proportion of animal studies are carried out in order to serve as more acceptable alternatives to research situations in which issues of practicality and ethics preclude the use of humans, lower organisms have been increasingly studied (Holden, 1982). For instance, questions relating to behavioral genetics have been investigated through the use of *Drosophila* fruit flies (e.g. Pruzan, 1976; Pruzan et al., 1977), which provide researchers with certain methodological advantages (e.g. accelerated lifespan and generational breeding; ease with which the genetic material can be observed) in addition to alleviating ethical concerns about pain and suffering. Researchers also have begun to identify other alternative species whose nature more closely mirrors human functioning. As an example, Rissman (1995) made the case for the study of the musk shrew (*Suncus murinus*) as an ideal model for investigating the neural and hormonal bases of female sexual behavior.

Other ideas for research alternatives when animals represent the only appropriate subject population have been suggested. Lea (1979) recommended that whenever possible researchers could replace animal stimulation (e.g. of nervous system processes) with mere recording; similarly, stimulation could provide a substitute for lesioning techniques. Such alternative approaches would serve to reduce the amount of discomfort experienced by the animal and limit possible damage to the animal's nervous system. Lea also provided several suggestions for reducing unnecessary degrees of deprivation and other punishments routinely used in learning studies: a food deprivation period of only six hours seems to be as effective for studying learning in rats as a 23-hour deprivation period; rewards can be used instead of punishments in avoidance studies; aversive (but less painful and traumatizing) stimuli, such as loud noises or bright lights, can reduce the need to administer electric shocks. Although such recommendations might not be applicable in physiological studies, Lea observed that the more painful procedures common in physiological research may be justified by the greater likelihood of medical applications derived from the findings.

The reduction in numbers of animal subjects used and the study of animals in their natural habitats represent two of the most basic steps available to researchers for reducing some of the ethical concerns that surround their work. For example, the use of animal subjects in classroom demonstrations can be replaced with films and videotapes, or by having students carry out naturalistic, non-invasive behavioral animal studies (Azar, 1994a). As an alternative to requiring students to conduct repetitive experiments that do not stand to advance science, videotapes could be made for teaching purposes at a relatively low cost and reused for several years (Bowd, 1980). Alternatives to animal research requirements should be provided as a matter of course in teaching contexts, in light of indications that a growing number of students are sensitive to animal rights issues and object to working with animals (Azar, 1994a).

The investigation of animal behavior in its natural habitat has been recommended by those who have questioned the validity of scientific findings derived from laboratory studies (Bowd and Shapiro, 1993; Devenport and Devenport, 1990; Drewett and Kani, 1981). This approach is consistent with the long-standing ethological tradition of observing animal species in their natural environments in order to determine how environmental cues affect behavior. Ethological studies, for example, have provided numerous examples of how physical characteristics and behavior patterns that are adaptive to survival have evolved in species through the process of natural selection (Bernstein et al., 1994).

A classic example of natural habitat observation is evident in the work of Dian Fossey (1981, 1983), a researcher whose life and tragic murder were depicted in the film *Gorillas in the Mist*. Fossey journeyed to Africa in 1967 in order to document a vanishing breed of mountain gorillas for *National Geographic* magazine. Through a procedure known as desensitization, she was able to adapt her animal subjects to the presence of an observer and put them at ease. Over a period of time she gradually moved closer to the gorillas, imitating their movements (such as munching on foliage and scratching herself), until it was possible to sit among them and freely conduct her observations. This enabled Fossey to obtain some fascinating insights into the behavior of her animal subjects.

Ethologists also have used structured observations to investigate the effects of systematic manipulations of various aspects of an animal's natural habitat (Shaughnessy and Zechmeister, 1990). The Nobel Prize winning ethologist Konrad Lorenz employed this method in his well-known research on imprinting, the attachment shown by some animal species to objects they encounter during critical or sensitive periods early in their lives (see Eibl-Eibesfeldt, 1975). Lorenz studied the imprinting response in young graylag goslings, who have a tendency to imprint on their mothers (or almost any moving object in their environment) immediately after hatching. In order to investigate the role of parental signals thought to be naturally attractive to the baby geese, Lorenz created models of male and female parents and tested the young animals' response to the models' movement and honking sounds. In one humorous example of this work, Lorenz squatted and imitated goose noises in front of newborn goslings whose mother was not present; as a result, he himself became an irresistible figure to a gaggle of geese who diligently followed him wherever he went.

Despite some practical limitations inherent in the study of animals in natural settings, the work of Fossey and Lorenz demonstrates how this approach can provide a more accurate picture of the true capacities and normal, instinctual lives of many animal species than that obtained from laboratory-based invasive research. Another interesting application of this methodology, which has been suggested by Devenport and Devenport (1990), involves the use of domestic pets as subjects, with experiments carried out at owners' homes. One important benefit of pet research is the apparent effect it has on improving attitudes about animal experimentation. Based on responses to post-experimental question-naires, Devenport and Devenport found that having a pet participate in research appears to increase interest in science among the owners and provides a better understanding of the research process.

There currently exist several useful resources for the researcher who is interested in pursuing these and other alternatives to animal experimentation. Many of these resources are summarized on the USDA web page entitled "Information Resources for Institutional Animal Care and Use Committees 1985-1999" (www.nal.usda.gov/awic/pubs/IACUC/primary.htm#alt). The British peer-review journal *Alternatives to Laboratory Animals*, with issues dating back to 1983, covers all aspects of the development, introduction, and use of alternatives in animal research and testing. Although the journal includes some highly technical articles, many are understandable to the non-scientist. The Fund for the Replacement of Animals in Medical Experiments (FRAME) also maintains an informative web site relative to the investigation of alternatives to animal research (www.frame.org.uk/index.htm).

SUMMARY

Within the behavioral and biomedical sciences, there is general agreement that until additional alternatives to animal research can be found, research on live animal subjects will continue. Indeed, there are many researchers who believe that the complete elimination of animal research will never be possible (Feeney, 1987; Gallup and Suarez, 1985; Miller, 1985). As a result, researchers must continue to balance the need to carry out potentially valuable investigations against the need for adequate protections in the way animals are treated. As documented in this chapter, much has been done to add safeguards to the treatment and care of laboratory animals, and there is evidence of a steady reduction of animals used for research purposes. Nonetheless, for extreme animal rights groups, these developments have done little to allay their call for a complete halt to animal research and, as others have predicted, researchers will never be rid of the animal rights movement (Morrison, 2001). This being the case, animal researchers and the radical proponents of animal rights must continue to seek common ground, no matter how apparently difficult this objective may be. Additionally, researchers must become more active in public education so as to advance science in an increasingly regulated world.

A useful set of guidelines for reconciling differences between researchers and their animal rights critics was developed in the form of a "peace plan" by animal rights advocate Merritt Clifton (1996). Among Clifton's ten-point proposal are the following recommendations:

- if researchers stop trying to portray animal rights activists as terrorists, then activists will condemn all forms of violent protest;
- if researchers open all animal care and research committee meetings to the public, then activists will promise not to disrupt the meetings or harass participants;
- if researchers show a willingness to police themselves and discipline researchers who abuse animals, then activists will discuss suspected abuses with the institution in question before going to the media;
- if researchers report the number of rats, mice, and birds used in research, then activists will stop using old, inflated estimates of how many animals are used in research;
- if researchers acknowledge criticism respectfully, recognizing that researchers and their critics share common ground, then activists will express criticism respectfully, recognizing that they share common ground with researchers.

As Herzog (1990, p. 93) has noted, "the issue of animal rights is philosophically and psychologically complex ... mired in a milieu of rationality, emotion, convention, ethical intuition, and self-interest." Thus, consistent with Clifton's "peace plan," it is in the best interest of those on both sides of the issue to refrain from perpetuating stereotypes, disseminating propaganda, and engaging in other destructive activities likely to do little to resolve the debate. Further research into the variables influencing moral judgments about animals could provide a better understanding of the different reactions to animal research that have been observed. For example, it has been found that judgments about animals are influenced by individual differences in moral philosophy (Galvin and Herzog, 1992), as well as such factors as animals' phylogenetic distance from humans, their physiognomic similarity to humans, their "cuteness" and perceived intelligence, the affective valence (i.e. perceived goodness or badness) of a species, and the labels we assign to animals (Burghardt and Herzog, 1980; Herzog, 1988; Kallgren and Kenrick, 1990).

Most researchers reject the notion that animals have rights that preclude their use in research, but recognize that scientists have certain responsibilities to the research animals that are studied. Among these responsibilities are the need to ask whether each investigation necessitates the use of animals in the first place and, if so, to use as few animals as possible in the research. Animal researchers must be sensitive to the ethical issues surrounding their work as well as to the professional and governmental requirements that currently are in place. They must proceed in ways that lead to the humane treatment and care of research animals, and to the avoidance of invasive and painful procedures whenever possible. These are common goals of both scientists and animal welfare advocates alike.

10

Ethical Review and the Communication of Results

"The only ethical principle which has made science possible is that the truth shall be told all the time. If we do not penalise false statements made in error, we open up the way, don't you see, for false statements by intention. And of course a false statement of fact, made deliberately, is the most serious crime a scientist can commit."

C. P. Snow, *The Search*

"[An] irony is that researchers are held to a higher standard of ethical accountability than that expected of many designated and self-appointed guardians of human rights."

R. L. Rosnow (1997, p. 345)

Chapter Topics

☞ Ethical review boards: composition and components
☞ The changing nature of IRB review
☞ Assessing the adequacy of the ethical review process
☞ The review of student research
☞ Scientific frauds and honesty in research
☞ Safeguards against scientific misconduct
☞ Accuracy in the reporting of research

When aspiring researchers contemplate what is involved in carrying out an investigation in the behavioral sciences, what no doubt first come to mind are such activities as recruiting subjects and collecting data through implementation of whatever methodological procedures seem most appropriate to the research questions at hand. As a result, the most salient ethical issues may appear to be those directly pertaining to the treatment of the participants during the research process. Is it ethical to deceive subjects? How will subjects be debriefed? Will the privacy of the research participants be protected? Will the experimental procedure inflict unnecessary discomfort on human (or animal) subjects? In preceding chapters, we have attempted to elucidate the scope of these questions and to offer possible solutions to the ethical dilemmas they present.

When we consider the researcher's responsibilities both before and after conducting an investigation, other ethical issues become apparent that need to be addressed with the same level of seriousness as those that arise in the treatment of research participants. In this final chapter we turn our attention to those additional issues pertaining to research activities that take place both before and after data are collected. In particular, problems involved in the ethical review process and in the communication of research findings are considered. Although these research-related activities may at first appear to have little in common, certain similarities can be noted. Most importantly, both activities contribute to the system of "checks and balances" that is built into the scientific research enterprise. That is, the processes of ethical peer review and the public communication of research findings provide, in addition to the sharing of knowledge, means by which research can be evaluated on both methodological and ethical dimensions and a way in which the honesty and integrity of the investigator can be checked.

The first part of this chapter provides a consideration of the review process by focusing on the importance of ethical review, the nature of ethical boards, and threats to objective peer review in light of research on ethical decision making. Next, our focus turns to ethical concerns involving the conduct of student research. We then conclude the book by considering issues relating to integrity in the analysis of data and in the reporting of research results. Although these latter issues do not directly deal with the protection of human rights, they are compelling nonetheless because of their potential impact on science as a body of knowledge (Reese and Fremouw, 1984). Among the specific ethical responsibilities to be discussed are those that arise once an investigation has been completed, such as the accurate reporting of results, assignment of appropriate credit for those who contributed to the research, and ethical conduct in attempts to publish and to protect against the misuse of research.

THE ETHICAL REVIEW PROCESS

Prior to the recruitment and testing of subjects, a thorough search of the relevant literature must be conducted, the investigation must be planned and designed, and the research proposal that emerges from these activities typically must be subjected to review. As discussed in previous chapters, the ethical review of research proposals now is required at most research institutions before the researcher is given the go ahead to carry out a study; review also may occur at various intervals once the data collection process has begun. Some researchers, however, have voiced their concerns about the adequacy of external review in light of subjective biases and vested interests in the decision-making process. Additionally, institutional review boards (IRBs) have been criticized as being overly stringent and conservative in carrying out their gate-keeping function, by unnecessarily restricting scientists in their attempts to investigate sound research questions (see Baumeister and Tice, 1999; Begley, 2002; Ceci et al., 1985; Christakis, 1988; Hansen, 2001; Penner, 2002; Rosnow et al., 1993).

IRB Composition and components of review

In satisfying their responsibilities to ensure the protection and welfare of subjects, ethical review boards typically attempt to ascertain that proposed research conforms to ethical standards (such as informed consent) and that the anticipated benefits are greater than any risks posed to the research participants (and to society at large) (Hansen, 2001; Landrum, 1999). At one time, such systematic evaluations of research studies were not conducted and researchers did not have to concern themselves with ethical standards or IRB review. The IRB concept was first realized during the mid-1960s following recommendations by the National Commission of the United States Department of Health and Human Services (see chapter 2). Prior to that time, there was very little evidence of any type of committee review of research projects in the biomedical or behavioral science fields. The widespread existence of committees to review research with human participants was clearly apparent a few years later, even before enactment of the National Research Act of 1974. The results of a study conducted for the National Commission by the Survey Research Center at the University of Michigan revealed that by 1975 IRBs had been established in 113 medical schools and 424 other research settings (see Gray et al., 1978).

Whereas formal review and external monitoring originally were limited mostly to large, funded research projects, nowadays most studies are subjected to some kind of external review process. (Table 10.1 presents the sorts of questions commonly asked of investigators during a research review.) Universities and other institutions where research with human or animal subjects is conducted now tend to require some form of ethical review for the approval and monitoring of research. For example, a psychology student who intends to conduct an experiment using human subjects might first have to satisfy the requirements of a departmental review committee (Murphy, 1999). Depending on the nature of the study and the degree of risk it entails, the study then might be referred to a university-wide IRB. However, should the study qualify as involving only minimal risk to subjects, it could be approved by the student's course instructor, who has the responsibility to expedite the review process for research falling into certain predefined categories.

Because serious consequences can arise when university, federal, and local review procedures conflict (see Forsyth, 2004; Tedeschi and Rosenfeld, 1981), many officials believe it is a wise policy to have such formal review procedures in place at their institutions. Thus, despite the fact that professional standards tend to place the responsibility for ethical conduct on the individual researcher, the trend in recent years has been for research institutions to adopt the approach typically taken by governments, which is to rely on external enforcement for the approval and monitoring of studies.

Table 10.1 Sample questions for ethical review

Investigator
1 Who is the primary investigator, and who is supervising the study?
2 Will anyone be assisting you in this investigation?
3 Have you or others whose names are listed above had any experience with this kind of research?

Nature of the study
4 What is the purpose of this research? What is it about?
5 What will the research participants be asked to do, or what will be done to them?
6 Will deception be used? If the answer is yes, why is it necessary?
7 What is the nature of the deception, and when will the debriefing (or dehoaxing) take place?
8 Will the participants risk any harm (physical, psychological, legal, or social) by taking part in this research?
9 If there are any risks, how do you justify them? How will you minimize the risks?

Research participants
10 How will you recruit the research participants?
11 How do you plan to explain the research to your potential participants and obtain their informed consent?
12 What should be the general characteristics of your research participants (e.g., age range, sex, and institutional affiliation) and the projected number of participants?
13 What, if any, are the special characteristics you need in your research participants (e.g. children, pregnant women, racial or ethnic minorities, mentally retarded people, prisoners, or alcoholics)?
14 Are other institutions or individuals cooperating in or cosponsoring the study?
15 Do the participants have to be in a particular mental or physical state to participate usefully?

Material
16 If electrical or mechanical equipment will be used, how has it been checked for safety?
17 What standardized tests, if any, will be used? What information will be provided to the participants about their scores on these tests?

Confidentiality
18 What procedure will you use to ensure the confidentiality of the data?

Debriefing
19 How do you plan to debrief the participants?

Source: Rosnow, Ralph L. and Rosenthal, Robert, *Beginning Behavioral Research: A Conceptual Primer.* 5th Edition, © 2005, p. 66. Adapted by permission of Pearson Education, Inc., Upper Saddle River, NJ.

Over the years, membership requirements and review criteria for IRBs have undergone several changes in order to increase their effectiveness and comprehensiveness (Gray and Cooke, 1980; Hansen, 2001; Rosnow et al., 1993). The initial federal regulations requiring IRB review for human subject research in the United States specified that the composition of a review committee was to consist of at least five members with varying backgrounds and fields of expertise (e.g. an IRB could not consist solely of behavioral scientists) (*Federal Register*, March 13, 1975). The committee was also to include at least one member who was not affiliated with the institution, and it could not be comprised of either all men or all women (*Federal Register*, January 26, 1981). Such review committee membership requirements are typical in many university settings, whether external review is required to conform to federal policy or is established on a voluntary basis. It is now common to find responsible individuals from the community, including members of the clergy, lawyers, and nurses, serving on such boards.

In 2001, a United States Presidential advisory board, the National Bioethics Advisory Commission (NBAC) issued several recommendations for improvements in the institutional review process (NBAC, 2001). Although many of the recommendations simply augment IRB procedures that already comprise part of the federal review process, one recommendation was to require IRB review of all human subject research, including research conducted by private individuals, corporations, or other researchers or organizations not receiving federal funds (such as physicians, biotechnology companies, and other business entities). The NBAC recommendations also offered greater precision in terms of the composition of review committees and components of IRB review. For example, IRB members should have relevant experience and expertise commensurate with the types of research reviewed, and at least one-fourth of the IRB membership should consist of persons who represent the perspective of participants, are unaffiliated with the research institution, and are non-scientists. The NBAC also issued recommendations relating to the two essential components of IRB review: risk–benefit assessments and informed consent procedures. An analysis of the risks and benefits was to be applied to all types of covered research, with the standard for "minimal risk" defined as research posing no greater risks than those encountered in daily life. The NBAC report was transmitted to the National Science and Technology Council, a federal body that advises the US President in coordinating national research policy and goals, and has likely had a significant impact on policy discussions relating to the human subject protections (Hansen, 2001).

As a personal example of the committee review process, the author served as an original member of the human studies committee at a college where he previously was employed as a psychology professor and, as it turned out, was the only representative from the social or behavioral sciences serving on the committee. The committee was formed after a faculty member at the college received federal funding to carry out a research project involving human subjects. Other members of the original committee consisted of two physical education professors, two nursing faculty, a college administrator, and a person from the community. Prior to the establishment of the college-wide review committee, an ethical review committee had been formed by the school's behavioral sciences department to review research proposals within the department and to recommend and support campus ethics programs (see Hogan and Kimmel, 1992). For committee review, the investigator first completed an application form for approval of research involving human subjects. If clarifications were needed, the investigator would be invited to meet with the committee, unless it was agreed that the study represented an example of minimal risk research. As is usually the case with such review boards (cf. Gray and Cooke, 1980), studies rarely were disapproved outright; rather, further details regarding the procedure (such as how the subjects were to be debriefed) were often requested or else additional safeguards were suggested (such as the inclusion of a more complete informed consent process).

It probably is not surprising that some behavioral scientists have criticized the usual composition of IRBs, given that committee members are likely to consist of persons who are not researchers themselves and who may not be familiar with the research process (see Box 10.1). That is, it is difficult for some researchers to accept having their proposals reviewed by members of the clergy, lawyers, professors of English, history, physical education, and so on, who may appear to have little appreciation of the potential merits of scientific research and who are likely to be unaware of the methodological difficulties in conducting well-controlled human research while maintaining a strict adherence to ethical regulations. Indeed, some behavioral scientists have argued that a risk–benefit analysis requires certain skills in research methodology (Hansen, 2001; Rosenthal, 1994b). However, a review board entirely staffed by people who are within the same field may be less inclined to ask certain basic questions and may be prejudiced in favor of approving the research of their peers. In this light, it is best that IRBs be composed of a mix of people (Furedy, 2002).

The changing nature of IRB review

The expanded influence of external review has brought with it a growing concern that review boards either do not effectively protect participants from harm or else overstep their intended role in an effort to force behavioral and social research into a biomedical mold, thereby making it increasingly difficult for many researchers to proceed with their studies as intended. Mueller and Furedy (2001) have pointed out some of the problems inherent in attempts to assess review board performance, including the misconception that "a problem found" with a research proposal equates with "an incident avoided." The growing difficulties for behavioral scientists in their efforts to obtain approval from IRBs are reflected by the following comments:

> Let's face it. Getting IRB approval for research projects falls somewhere on a continuum from "downright painful" to "just get it over with." (Hansen, 2001, p. 13)

> I said IRBs were a good idea; I did not say that they were necessarily a good thing in practice.... At some institutions the researcher who submits an IRB application is entering the "Gates of Hell." (Penner, 2002, p. 28)

> Alexander Pope, who opined that "the proper study of man is man," did not have to convince an [IRB] of the wisdom of his words. Just this week I was told that I could not use the question "What city does your romantic partner live in?" to check if the subject was in a long-distance relationship (made the partner too identifiable). (Forsyth, 2004, p. 14)

> IRB ax falls, heads roll. (Baumeister and Tice, 1999, p. 8)

In order to ensure the protection and welfare of participants, review boards typically attempt to ascertain that the anticipated benefits of an investigation are greater than any risks posed and that informed consent procedures are adequate. Where once this formal review process emphasized the protection of participants from "extraordinary risks," the identification of even everyday risk now is obligatory for proposals. Along these lines, Mueller (2003) argued that the

Box 10.1   Reactions to ethical committee review

The following comments were written by an American psychologist in response to a questionnaire intended to assess systematic biases in ethical decision making (Kimmel, 1991). These excerpts reflect a high degree of personal frustration with the external review process; growing evidence suggests that this researcher's experiences may not be uncommon among behavioral scientists.

> I am not very happy with university ethics committees. I had a three-year running feud with the committee at [name of university]. I considered the research I proposed to be risk-free, which they refused to accept. The objections ranged from the ignorant to the absurd. The research involved simple psycho-physical tasks. I noted in my proposal that subjects would take frequent rest intervals to reduce the effects of boredom and fatigue on performance. One committee member felt that boredom was a risk.
>
> The committee in general wanted me to inform my subjects that listening to tones no louder than ordinary speech entailed a slight risk to their welfare. I was not and am not now willing to so stipulate. I have since . . . switched to animal research where the composition of animal welfare committees is a bit more reasonable. I fully recognize and support the need for review of all research involving living subjects. However, when there is no appeal of committee decisions, the review process quickly loses its protective value and the committee instead begins to attempt to *direct* research from their meetings. My chief antagonist on [the university's] committee was a professor in the family resources department who clearly had no idea whatsoever of what laboratory research entailed.

Another candid view of the external review process is taken from an informal talk delivered by Herbert Kelman at the 1987 meeting of the Eastern Psychological Association (see Kimmel, 1988b, p. 157). Unlike the preceding comments, however, Kelman's remarks represent the perspective of an IRB member and reflect the kinds of unintended biases that might enter into evaluations of research in one's own discipline.

> I remember my own experience on an IRB once when we had a proposal for a study, one of those field experiments that involved somebody falling down in the middle of the street and clutching his heart and all of that. I was much more conflicted about saying no to that study than some other people for the simple reason that I saw the study within a tradition. I mean, that's what we've been doing in social psychology and I can understand why this person would want to do this . . . this is part of the traditional way in which work is being done in the field . . . and I had some appreciation for the value of this work. But there were some other people whose immediate reaction was, "This is ridiculous research. Why should one even consider the risks or the ethical violations or the legal problems that might arise out of this for the sake of this worthless kind of enterprise?" Well, I think it's useful to have that corrective there but, on the other hand, I wouldn't want it to be entirely those people. I think you need a kind of dialectic.

regulatory approach commonly followed by many IRBs is to eliminate all risk (including everyday risks such as simple embarrassment), rather than to exercise the best judgment in evaluating research proposals. Similarly, Penner (2002, p. 28) claimed that "the IRB (or its Chair) has little first hand experience with research and is concerned almost exclusively with protecting the institution from possible government censure (or worse) and/or from possible lawsuits by 'aggrieved' research participants." As a consequence of this sort of over-regulation, in the view of some observers, over time participation in research has become much safer than many of the everyday activities in which people engage (Diener, 2001). Rosnow (1997) expressed this sentiment somewhat differently when he noted that contemporary researchers are subjected to a higher level of professional ethical accountability than is the case for other professionals who supposedly represent society's guardians of human rights, such as lawyers, politicians, and journalists, who routinely engage in various forms of deception.

Over the years, the responsibilities of review boards have expanded and the criteria for ethical review have continued to evolve, although for many re-searchers, they remain rather unclear or are poorly understood (see Box 10.2).

Box 10.2   Five myths about institutional review boards (US)

Myth 1.   All IRB Decisions are Based on Federal or Local Statutes or Written Laws

The fact is that many of the formal governmental guidelines pertaining to IRBs are written in complex language that can be interpreted in a number of different ways. The regulations also allow for a substantial degree of discretion in terms of how they are applied, as long as the interpretation is well documented. As a result, many IRB decisions are based on idiosyncratic interpretations of the IRB administrator. If a researcher has difficulty under-standing an IRB decision, it is possible to ask to see the written policies upon which the decision was based.

Myth 2.   The Federal Principles were Originally Developed for Medical Research, and Behavioral Research was Included Later

The fact is that the National Commission's original principles, as presented in the *Belmont Report*, were intended to cover social and behavioral research from the outset. (Several government agencies subsequently gave the force of the law to the National Commission's principles when they adopted the so-called "Common rule" for research with human

Box 10.2   (Continued)

subjects.) When research is reviewed by a medical board, assessments of risks and benefits for non-medical research can be fraught with problems. It therefore is in the interest of the researcher to lobby for separate medical and non-medical IRBs at his or her institution.

Myth 3.   All Research Proposals Must Go Before a Full IRB Board

The fact is that only research that poses more than minimal risk or involves vulnerable groups must be evaluated by the IRB, although an IRB chair has discretion in terms of what kinds of proposals must be reviewed. Research institutions vary greatly in terms of the percentage of proposals that are sent to the full board. Attempts to influence the membership of the IRB could ultimately result in a greater frequency of expedited reviews.

Myth 4.   Deception Research is Not Permitted Under Federal Guidelines

As discussed in previous chapters, the fact is that it is not required that researchers disclose the true purpose of an investigation, as long as participants are aware of what they are required to do and the risks imposed by the procedure, and are debriefed at the conclusion of the research. Clearly, a proposal describing an investigation that includes the use of deceptive procedures is more likely to face certain hurdles prior to approval by an IRB.

Myth 5.   Some Proposals (e.g. Anonymous Surveys) Do Not Need to be Reviewed

Although certain categories of minimal risk research, such as anonymous surveys, are usually exempt from IRB review, this does not mean that they do not need to be reviewed. The fact is that a specific determination will have to be made that the research indeed falls into the exempt category. Thus, a researcher cannot simply conclude that a study is harmless and does not need anyone's formal approval.

Source: Penner (2002).

These developments have been traced in part to a rise in pressures applied by certain advocacy groups, such as groups lobbying for the quicker release of drugs for dying patients, drug companies attempting to gain support for changes enabling research participants to have access to experimental treatments, and researchers pressing for the education of people whose understanding of informed consent is deficient (Mitchell and Steingrub, 1988). According to Rosnow et al.

(1993), such pressures can lead to changes in the criteria ultimately used by IRBs to evaluate research.

Within the research community there are many who believe that IRBs have begun to consider more than is necessary to adequately assess the physical and mental risks to prospective research participants. Indeed, there is mounting evidence that the role of IRBs has changed in recent years to include issues not specifically related to the rights and welfare of research participants in evaluations of research proposals. For instance, the discussion of research design and other methodological considerations is no longer uncommon among IRB members (Rosnow et al., 1993). This development is not necessarily a bad one. Because a poorly designed study can have serious negative ramifications, one might argue that the technical aspects of a proposed investigation in fact should be included as an aspect of external review (Hansen, 2001; Rosenthal, 1994b). To illustrate, Meier (1992) suggested that the design of a large-scale study to examine the efficacy of an experimental drug intended to halt the progression of a fatal illness must provide for clear conclusions to be drawn. This would require that the investigation meet certain standards of control and sample size, considerations that might be incorporated into an IRB decision. In essence, a failure to meet these technical standards likely would result in a significant waste of institutional, public, and other resources.

There remains widespread disagreement over whether technical aspects of investigations ought to be taken into account by IRBs and whether the composition of IRBs should be expanded to include persons with scientific expertise. Some people believe that scientific issues ought to be resolved before a research proposal is submitted to an ethical review committee, or else left to journal referees once the research is submitted for publication (Furedy, 2002; Seligman and Sorrentino, 2002). Additionally, there are potential negative consequences in allowing a consideration of scientific issues into the review process. For example, it has been noted that some IRBs may be prone to apply overly rigorous design standards, such as those that are required for drug trials, to studies in behavioral and social research areas (Rosnow et al., 1993). Further, adding another dimension to the evaluation of research proposals is seen by some researchers as an additional barrier in the pursuit of complex research questions or intention to use less conventional research approaches. Such fears eventually could serve to restrict the kinds of studies that are carried out in certain areas (West and Gunn, 1978).

Another recent development in ethical review is that of the random *research audit*. At any time, a researcher may be asked by an external entity (e.g. the US Food and Drug Administration, the Office for Human Research Protections, or a for-profit research sponsor) or an internal entity (e.g. the local IRB) to provide access to a study's records for the purpose of ascertaining the extent to which the welfare of subjects and the integrity of research data have been protected. The audit may be conducted in order to investigate an allegation (i.e. "for cause") or for random quality control purposes. The audit could focus on the adequacy of informed consent (e.g. through an examination of signed consent forms), adverse event reports, number of participants (including dropouts and premature terminations), the procedures followed by the institutional IRB, and so on. For example, in one university study involving a new HIV medical therapy, an external audit concluded that a significant percentage of subjects were not being visited by members of the research team in adherence with the timelines specified in the approved research protocol, and that subjects were receiving less financial compensation for their participation than had been promised. The audit also found that the informed consent documents were deficient in terms of providing adequate descriptions of the procedures that subjects could expect to undergo.

The consequences of a research audit can be dramatic. A negative evaluation can result in suspension or termination of IRB approval for a study, termination of human subject research privileges, or the specification of corrective actions that must be implemented (with follow-up audit). In the HIV therapy study mentioned above, the decision following the audit required several corrective actions by the principal investigator and the research institution, including an overhaul of the research review process at the university (i.e. requiring mandatory training of local IRB members) and significant revision of the informed consent document (i.e. that it be written in layperson terms that are understandable to participants). In rare cases, an external audit could result in the complete suspension of research at a university (Baumeister and Tice, 1999; Forsyth, 2004).

The possibility of having one's research audited underlines the fact that documentation is an integral and essential component of conducting research with human or animal subjects. According to one university's recommendations for preparing a research audit file, "From the first draft of a protocol application to the completion of a study, much that occurs in between is dependent on the consistency, accuracy and accountability of the study's accumulated documentation" (www.rgs.uci.edu/ora/rp/hrpp.researchauditfile.htm). Documents that should be maintained in a research audit file include any correspondence between the investigator and the IRB, the research sponsor, or funding agency; informed consent forms; case report forms; medical or personal information on subjects; and documents specifying recruitment procedures and compensation of subjects.

Adequacy of the IRB process

Evidence regarding the effectiveness of ethical review committees in protecting the autonomy of research participants and the impact of such committees on research is somewhat mixed. Some informative early results regarding the performance and impact of IRBs were revealed by the aforementioned survey conducted by the Survey Research Center (Gray et al., 1978). More than 2,000 researchers and 800 review board members at 61 research institutions were interviewed about various positive and negative aspects of the functioning of IRBs during a one-year period ending in 1975. One major finding of the survey was that although the IRBs commonly required modifications in the proposed research (usually regarding some aspect of the procedure to obtain consent), the outright rejection of research was rare. Most of the researchers interviewed considered the IRBs' judgments regarding their research proposals as sound; however, approximately half of the researchers reported that they had experienced some delays in undertaking their study or that their research had been impeded in a way that was not balanced by the benefits of the review process. Only 8 percent of the researchers believed that the overall difficulties imposed by IRB review outweighed the benefits of the review process in protecting research participants.

Taken together, the results of the Survey Research Center study do not lend support to the fears often expressed by researchers that the external review process will lead to overly stringent judgments and the frequent rejection of research proposals. Nonetheless, since that study, a growing body of evidence has begun to emerge suggesting that there may be important deficiencies in the performance of some IRBs (Ceci et al., 1985; Goldman and Katz, 1982; Prentice and Antonson, 1987). Specifically, substantial inconsistency has been found in the application of decision standards and in the subsequent recommendations put forth by ethical review committees.

Inconsistencies in ethical decision making

Variability in the evaluation of research proposals among IRBs can stem from several sources, including the composition of the review boards, subjective biases in the assessment of risks and benefits, the nature of interaction among committee members, the types of studies evaluated, committee members' review experience, systematic differences in approval guidelines and community standards, and a failure of institutions to obtain uniformity throughout the external review system. Given these considerations, it is not surprising that inconsistencies in IRB decision making have been reported by researchers who have systematically studied the review process (e.g. Goldman and Katz, 1982).

For example, Eaton (1983) found that experienced reviewers were in agreement about the ethicality of 111 psychological research proposals (in terms of the way subjects were to be treated) only 8 percent of the time. The reviewers who were studied were members of the university psychology department in which the proposals were prepared. More recently, Forsyth (2004) anecdotally described the inconsistency over time in IRB review at his own university, where the rules seem to change according to the season. In Forsyth's view, such shifts in research evaluation are "natural and unavoidable" in that they reflect local events (e.g. the ethics office receives a complaint) and evolving changes in federal requirements.

In an investigation of biases in ethical decision making, the author asked a sample of 259 American psychologists to evaluate several hypothetical studies varying in costs and benefits (Kimmel, 1991). Consistent with previous research on ethical decision making (e.g. Forsyth, 1980; Hamsher and Reznikoff, 1967; Schlenker and Forsyth, 1977), the results were such that it was possible to distinguish between conservative decision makers (i.e. those who emphasized research costs) and liberal decision makers (i.e. those who emphasized research benefits) on the basis of certain individual background characteristics. Respondents who tended to reflect greater conservatism in their ethical evaluations (emphasizing research costs) were primarily female; had recently received the doctoral degree in an applied psychology area, such as counseling, school, or community psychology; and were employed in service-oriented contexts. By contrast, those respondents who tended to be more liberal in their ethical assessments (emphasizing research benefits) were more likely to be male; had held their doctoral degrees in a basic psychology area (such as social, experimental, or developmental psychology) for a longer period of time; and were employed in research-oriented settings. To the extent that these results are generalizable to members of IRBs, there may be predictable biases in the way certain review committees appraise costs and benefits and ultimately decide on the fate of particular research proposals.

In a widely cited investigation of review board decision making, Ceci et al. (1985) demonstrated how personal values can play a critical role in decisions involving socially sensitive research. The researchers had 157 university IRBs review hypothetical proposals differing in terms of their degree of social sensitivity and their level of ethical concern. The proposals described an investigation of employment discrimination and were characterized by a procedure involving varying levels of deception. The results of the study revealed that socially sensitive proposals (intended either to examine discrimination against minorities or to reverse discrimination against white males in corporate hiring practices) were twice as likely to be rejected by the review committees as were non-sensitive proposals. These outcomes did not appear to be influenced by the presence or absence of ethical problems, although the use of deception was most frequently cited as the reason for non-approval of the sensitive proposals. According to Ceci et al., this latter finding seems to suggest that, at least for some studies, IRBs may use whatever reasons are most convenient to justify their review decisions. These results clearly have implications for research studies in other socially sensitive areas, such as AIDS research (Thomas and Quinn, 1991).

The studies described above all pertain to the review of human subject research. In one of the first studies of its kind, Plous and Herzog (2001) found evidence that the approval decisions of university animal use committees are similarly unreliable when it comes to the evaluation of experimental procedures involving animals. Their investigation compared judgments of 50 randomly selected Institutional Animal Care and Use Committees (IACUC) in place at various American universities. Consistency of approval decisions was determined by having the three most recent animal research proposals from the selected universities (for a total of 150) independently evaluated by a second animal care and use committee. The evaluations by the two committees (the original committee and a randomly selected second committee) were found to be statistically unrelated; that is, several proposals that were approved by one committee were disapproved by the other. This inconsistency carried over to separate analyses for specific categories of animals (i.e. dogs, cats, and primates) and procedures (i.e. experiments involving drugs, surgery, pain, or death). In other words, even if the research proposal involved terminal or painful procedures, there still was disagreement among the committee judgments. According to the researchers, the findings suggest that the reliability of proposal reviews is at chance levels – essentially a coin toss – and that the animal review system needs to be fixed.

Given the evidence described here, it is apparent that similar research proposals involving identical levels of risks and benefits may be approved at one institution but not at another. To some extent, local laws, community standards, and institutional restrictions that limit the types of information and degree of acceptable risk to research participants provide indirect sources of inconsistency among IRBs (Rosnow et al., 1993). As a result, luck might sometimes be involved in the approval of a research proposal, especially one that is socially sensitive. A favorable decision might simply be a matter of where one happened to be working when the proposal was submitted for review (Ceci et al., 1985). Rigorous review constraints placed on tests of potential drugs in AIDS vaccine trials already have tempted some AIDS researchers to carry out their studies in developing regions where standards are less strict than in industrialized countries (Rosnow et al., 1993; Thomas and Quinn, 1991).

Recommendations for review

Most researchers appear to accept the concept of external review in principle, but recognize that there is much room for improvement in the review process in actual practice. As an essential mechanism for protecting research participants from major risks of violation of their rights and welfare, whatever steps can be taken to ensure that the review process is adequate and evenhanded would be worthwhile. In the words of one ethicist, "researchers should not be burdened by being victims to an overly zealous IRB any more than subjects should be victims of overly lenient ones" (Veatch, 1982, p. 180). In short, a process is needed for maximizing consistency among IRBs and keeping them informed of emergent issues and shifting standards governing research.

One recommendation that has been offered for achieving these goals is to provide IRB members with a casebook of actual research protocols that have received extensive review and analysis by both investigators and subjects. According to Rosnow et al. (1993), such a casebook could serve as an aid to help sensitize IRB members to relevant costs and benefits of doing and not doing research, while providing them with a means for scrutinizing their own ethical biases. For unique research cases that require novel analysis, Rosnow et al. also suggested that an advisory board could be created within a discipline's professional association. The purpose of the advisory board would be to analyze and review an IRB decision when it is requested due to disagreements among committee members, investigators, and institutions. The advisory board's analysis could either serve an educative function or be binding (assuming the parties involved have agreed to accept the determination as such).

Another approach to improving the review process is to take steps to minimize problems of communication between IRB members and investigators. For example, members of review committees could clarify unclear guidelines and keep investigators fully informed of unfamiliar regulations. This, of course, would require that IRB members be sufficiently prepared for the review process through training sessions and regular communication with other IRBs (Tanke and

Tanke, 1982). It is unlikely that ethical training can produce unanimity in particular judgments, but at least it can provide IRB members with some understanding of the sources of the systematic differences in their ethical decision making. The education of IRB members also can be provided through attendance at regional and national conferences and by exposure to sample review cases in journals. Similarly, investigators can aid the review process by familiarizing themselves with current ethical standards and principles of review. They also need to be straightforward in providing complete and adequate information about the risks and benefits of their proposed studies, especially when potentially sensitive responses are sought from subjects.

Several of the suggestions described here for improving the review process are oriented towards assisting review board members in better understanding the unique characteristics of behavioral and social research (see Box 10.3). Although the review process continues to evolve, it is essential that IRB members recognize that non-medical research should not be evaluated through a biomedical lens, causing unnecessary delays and constraints that do little to protect research participants from actual risks (Azar, 2002).

Box 10.3   Ten steps to improve the institutional review board process

Despite the various problems associated with the current review system for behavioral research, some researchers recently have noted improvements in the ways that review boards operate (cf. Azar, 2002; Forsyth, 2004). This, of course, is in large part attributed to clearer and fairer policies that have evolved over time. Some of the steps that appear to go a long way towards improving IRB functioning are listed below:

1   Training sessions for IRB members and investigators.
2   At least one full-time staff member.
3   A casebook for the evaluation of research protocols.
4   A website including a consent form template and protocol guide.
5   A system for distinguishing between studies that require exempted, expedited, and full-board review.
6   Face-to-face IRB meetings where minutes are taken.
7   A means of responding promptly to subject and researcher complaints.
8   Simplification of the review of modified proposals that had previously been evaluated by the board at an earlier date.
9   Development of written forms in language that is understandable to all relevant parties (review board members, investigators, and subjects).
10 An independent advisory board to assist the IRB in special cases.

The review of student research

Despite the fact that the institutional review process now casts a widespread and extensive net on behavioral and social research, in many academic institutions student research with human participants often escapes the review process. This may be true for any variety of student research projects, including undergraduate course projects, pilot studies, student dissertation and thesis research, and independent study projects. There are various possible reasons for the omission of student research from the review process. In some institutions where IRBs are implemented, the review mechanism only covers projects that are federally mandated to require review or studies in which investigators specifically seek approval for their procedures (Murphy, 1999). In fact, much undergraduate research is conducted at small schools where federally funded studies are unlikely (Kallgren and Tauber, 1996).

Another reason why student research often goes unreviewed is based on the false premise that IRB review is not required for research that is primarily educationally motivated. In other words, there is the presumption among many educators that "student research" is not "real research" requiring pre-approval. As Kallgren and Tauber (1996, p. 20) have clarified, federal IRB guidelines do in fact exempt research that is conducted as an everyday part of the educational process. Specifically, this applies to "research for which data can be collected as part of the normal, day-to-day educational process, such as anonymous course evaluations, course performance measures, or attendance records." The current federal policy in the United States (70 FR 36325, June 23, 2005) is not meant to imply that a review of student research, even that which is educationally motivated, is unnecessary.

Some institutions with IRBs in place take special pains to assure that all research is subject to some form of prior review, whatever the purpose of the research may be. Thus, attempts are made to determine whether each investigation meets standards of informed consent, minimizes risks to subjects, and protects participants' privacy and confidentiality rights. For example, the Vanguard University of Southern California is clear about coverage of its research requirements in its *Handbook for Researchers* (www.vanguard.edu):

> These policies and procedures apply . . . to any research activity that involves human subjects, whether such research is undertaken on a large or small scale, whether it is preliminary or fully designed, whether it is student or faculty research, whether it is externally funded or not, and whether it involves minimal risk or more than minimal risk.

The review of student research is important for several reasons, perhaps foremost being that undergraduate and beginning graduate student-researchers lack the experience in carrying out research and are likely to have only a minimal awareness of the prevailing ethical standards and practices in the field. As Murphy (1999) noted, students with little experience in designing and running studies can be insensitive to ethical issues, including the possibility that participants may be upset by a deceptive procedure; they may not recognize the necessity for carefully designed consent and debriefing procedures; and they may not understand the importance of privacy issues and maintaining the confidentiality of sensitive information. These points similarly were suggested by Kallgren and Tauber (1996), who identified four basic arguments for requiring the review of student research: (1) to protect subject welfare (participants are at risk because student researchers are less likely to identify, anticipate, or respond effectively to ethical problems); (2) to ethically and legally protect instructors (responsibilities are more likely to be shared by the university when student investigations undergo institutional review); (3) to enhance the public reputation of behavioral research (student researchers may form a more positive attitude towards the behavioral sciences as they become aware of the seriousness given to research ethics, and this is likely to be passed on to others; additionally, greater sensitivity to ethical issues is likely to have a positive impact on research participants); and (4) to enrich the educational experience of student researchers (institutional research review can serve as a natural vehicle for teaching ethics to students).

In order to assess undergraduate researchers' perceptions about these issues, Kallgren and Tauber (1996) administered a questionnaire to 53 students who had recently carried out research for an advanced psychology course at a small liberal arts college. All of the students underwent an IRB review for their research. Despite an initial negative reaction upon learning of the review requirement, which the students viewed as "intimidating" and "frustrating," their reactions were quite favorable once they had been through the process. Overall, student researchers admitted that they thought they had learned more by having their research reviewed, felt they had produced a better product, viewed the instructor as more of an ally and reacted to instructor feedback more positively, treated their research more seriously, and indicated that there were more sensitive to ethical issues.

One drawback to having an IRB review student research proposals, especially at large research-oriented universities, is that the committee is likely to be swamped with studies to evaluate (Murphy, 1999). As behavioral science departments continue to grow and the number of student research projects increases, the demands imposed on the IRB will be substantial, resulting in greater delays of graduate student and faculty research and more frustrations for all parties concerned. One way of overcoming such practical concerns is to have departmental committees, as opposed to a university-wide IRB, bear the responsibility for evaluating student proposals. Research reviews conducted by a departmental research committee could be more timely and flexible, and could provide greater opportunities for satisfying certain educational goals (see Box 10.4).

ETHICAL ISSUES IN THE COMMUNICATION OF RESEARCH

The research process does not end once the data have been subjected to statistical analysis and the results have been interpreted by the investigator. In fact, ethical responsibilities extend beyond the actual completion of a study (i.e. the collection

Box 10.4   Developing a departmental review committee

In his case study of the Department of Psychology at the University of Illinois, Gregory Murphy (1999) outlined some useful recommendations for the establishment of a departmental human subjects committee. These recommendations are summarized below.

Committee Objectives

The overall goal of the committee should be to review departmental research proposals for the ethical treatment of human subjects in a timely and complete manner. Review standards should be similar to those that a university IRB would apply to federally funded research.

Coverage of Committee Review

A departmental committee can be designed to oversee class projects, undergraduate research proposals, thesis and other graduate research, and limited research activities carried out by faculty (e.g. in-class question-naires for survey studies). Given that departmental committee members may not have the expertise to sufficiently conduct risk–benefit assessments, committee review should be restricted to minimal-risk research.

Administration of the Departmental Review Process

The committee should develop standardized forms and procedures for review. The committee's policy should be communicated on the depart-ment's website, in printed handbooks and course syllabi, and discussed at the outset of department courses. A formal policy provides for essential documentation should a question arise later about a study, and reinforces the seriousness of the review process.

Although the composition of the committee can vary depending on specific circumstances, members should be selected among faculty from different areas of behavioral research who are active researchers. Other members can be recruited, such as an instructor of the department's intro-ductory course that provides subject pool participants, the subject pool coordinator, faculty from other university departments, a university admin-istrator, and one or two student representatives.

The following steps can be taken to implement the review process:

1   The committee should meet at the beginning of the school year to review and modify policies and ensure that all members interpret the review standards similarly. A department secretary should be assigned the responsibility of coordinating the subject pool and maintaining records.

Box 10.4   (Continued)

2 Written reminders should be sent to all departmental members (faculty, graduate students, postdoctoral students, and visiting professors) at the start of each semester indicating that every study needs approval.

3 A standardized form should be used that poses a series of questions about each proposed study. A full-time faculty member who has agreed to oversee the research and accept responsibility for ethical conduct should be named. The nature and number of subjects to be studied and the subject recruitment procedure should be specified. The form can consist of several checklists so that the investigator can indicate the methods of informed consent and debriefing to be used, whether deception will be employed, and procedures for ensuring confidentiality or anonymity of data collection. Investigators can be asked to attach a detailed description of the study's methodology along with an exemplar of the consent and debriefing forms to be used. Sample forms and a description of the typical components of informed consent and debriefing can be provided in order to assist investigators in preparing their own submissions.

4 When a protocol is received by the committee's coordinator, it should be assigned to a committee member who would then rule within a specified period of time on the study's acceptability. The entire committee would become involved in a judgment regarding a single case only when a unique situation emerges or the investigator objects to a decision by the initial reviewer. Once the protocol is reviewed, one of three decisions can be made: approved, disapproved, or tentative approval. A tentative approval is one that would require either clarification from the investigator or the correction of minor errors. If a proposal is disapproved on ethical grounds, it can be revised and resubmitted. Approval of a project can be valid for a specific duration, such as one year, after which the investigator would be asked whether the project is to continue and if there are any changes to the procedure. The approval can then be extended for another year, if deemed appropriate.

5 The subject pool coordinator would be responsible for retaining files of the proposals and committee reviews. Records should be kept on file for approximately three years after completion of the study as a safeguard in case a question about the treatment of subjects emerges at a later date.

and analysis of data) to include issues involved in the reporting of research and the prevention of the misuse of research results. At the final stage of the research process, peer review comes not from ethical review boards, but rather through the careful scrutiny of the completed research by other members of the scientific community. The nature of this review, however, is fundamentally different from that of ethics committees. Whereas the concerns of review boards focus on the ethical treatment of research participants and the protection of their rights, the nature of peer review following completion of a study emphasizes the scientific quality of the study and professional issues related to honesty and accuracy in the reporting of the research findings. These latter concerns are fundamental to the protection of science as a body of knowledge.

In order for an investigation to have any sort of impact on scientific progress within a discipline or utility in terms of application within specified settings, the research findings must be communicated to others. The details of a study may be communicated to other scientists in various forms, including articles published in scientific journals, chapters in edited books, technical reports, presentations at scientific conferences, and so on. Research findings often are transmitted to the general public through radio or television interviews, newspaper articles, magazine features, public lectures, and the like. Whichever medium is used to report a study to others, certain ethical responsibilities are necessarily imposed on the researcher, who may be held accountable for the consequences of what is reported. As a result, in recent years professional associations have begun to formulate ethical standards for clarifying professional conduct in the reporting and publishing of scientific information. Standards such as those developed by the American Psychological Association (see Box 10.5) can serve as a useful guide for our consideration of some of the ethical issues related to the communication of research results, such as accuracy in the reporting of results and professional issues in research publication.

Box 10.5   Ethical standards for the reporting and publishing of scientific information

The following standards, which deal with the communication of scientific information, were extracted from the American Psychological Association's *Ethical Principles of Psychologists and Code of Conduct* (2002), *American Psychologist*, *57*, 1060–73.

8.10   Reporting Research Results
    (a)   Psychologists do not fabricate data.
    (b)   If psychologists discover significant errors in their published data, they take reasonable steps to correct such errors in a correction, retraction, erratum, or other appropriate publication means.
8.11   Plagiarism
    Psychologists do not present portions of another's work or data as their own, even if the other work or data source is cited occasionally.

Box 10.5 (Continued)

8.12 Publication Credit
   (a) Psychologists take responsibility and credit, including author-ship credit, only for work they have actually performed or to which they have substantially contributed.
   (b) Principal authorship and other publication credits accurately reflect the relative scientific or professional contributions of the individuals involved, regardless of their relative status. Mere possession of an institutional position, such as depart-ment chair, does not justify authorship credit. Minor contribu-tions to the research or to the writing for publications are acknowledged appropriately, such as in footnotes or in an introductory statement.
   (c) Except under exceptional circumstances, a student is listed as principal author on any multiple-authored article that is sub-stantially based on the student's doctoral dissertation. Faculty advisors discuss publication credit with students as early as feas-ible and throughout the research and publication process as appropriate.
8.13 Duplicate Publication of Data
   Psychologists do not publish, as original data, data that have been previously published. This does not preclude republishing data when they are accompanied by proper acknowledgment.
8.14 Sharing Research Data for Verification
   (a) After research results are published, psychologists do not with-hold the data on which their conclusions are based from other competent professionals who seek to verify the substantive claims through reanalysis and who intend to use such data only for that purpose, provided that the confidentiality of the participants can be protected and unless legal rights concerning proprietary data preclude their release. This does not preclude psychologists from requiring that such individuals or groups be responsible for costs associated with the provision of such information.
   (b) Psychologists who request data from other psychologists to verify the substantive claims through reanalysis may use shared data only for the declared purpose. Requesting psycho-logists obtain prior written agreement for all other uses of the data.

Honesty and accuracy in reporting research

If there is one ethical guideline for which there is complete consensus it is the one that maintains that scientists must not falsify their research findings. In fact, the basic rule requiring honesty and accuracy in the conduct and reporting of research is such a "given" in science that it almost may seem absurd to have to mention it at all. After all, one of the basic purposes of conducting research is to build on current scientific knowledge through incremental discovery. Within the research context, the pursuit of truth – in the sense of veracity in the conduct of inquiry – represents the dominant value (Weinstein, 1981). In other words, the norms of scientific inquiry demand honesty throughout the truth-seeking process. Despite the fact that researchers are assumed to be honest and unbiased in their pursuit of scientific truth, instances of fraud and other related forms of scientific misconduct have been revealed throughout the history of science. These issues thus present legitimate ethical concerns for investigators within the behavioral sciences.

Categorizing scientific dishonesty

One of the earliest attempts to delineate various forms of scientific dishonesty came in 1830, when Charles Babbage, a British professor of mathematics at Cambridge University, published a book entitled *Reflections on the Decline of Science in England*. Although Babbage is sometimes referred to as a prophet of the electronic computer, he may be best known for distinguishing in his book between three forms of scientific dishonesty: trimming, cooking, and forging. In contemporary terms, "trimming" refers to the smoothing of irregularities in one's data to make them look more accurate and precise. In essence, trimming is the manipulation of data to make them look better (Babbage, 1830/1969): "in clipping off little bits here and there from those observations which differ most in excess from the mean and in sticking them on to those which are too small." A second type of dishonesty involves the "cooking" of data, which consists of retaining only those results that best fit one's hypothesis or theory and discarding those that do not. "Forging" pertains to the act of inventing some or all of the research data that are reported, and may even include the reporting of experiments that never were conducted. Because it involves instances of complete fabrication of results, forging typically is considered one of the most blatant forms of scientific misconduct.

Of these three research abuses, forging is the most vulnerable to exposure; because it is based on completely fictitious data, it is the most likely to look fake to the knowing eye or to be revealed as a result of unsuccessful attempts to replicate the reported results. Trimming and cooking, on the other hand, may long go undetected, especially if the researcher reaches correct conclusions by illegitimate means. In fact, cooking may be the most difficult to notice given that what it yields is genuine, though only a part of the truth.

One of the most notorious cases of data cooking is the experimental work of the physicist Robert A. Millikan (Sigma Xi, 1984). Early in the twentieth century,

Millikan was involved in an intense controversy with the Viennese physicist Felix Ehrenhaft on the nature of the electronic charge. Following several years of inconclusive and conflicting experiments, Millikan published a major paper in 1913 in which he reported the results of a series of experiments on liquid droplets. Millikan explicitly stated in the paper that the results were based on all of the droplets observed over a period of 60 consecutive days. However, an examination of his laboratory notebooks nearly half a century later revealed that the observations presented in his 1913 article were in fact selected from a much larger total: only 58 out of 140 observations were reported (Holton, 1978). Interestingly, reviewers of Millikan's research have pointed out that his selectivity was unnecessary in that the totality of the research ultimately would have had great scientific importance even if the anomalous values had been reported (Franklin, 1981; Holton, 1978). It is not so much that Millikan's selection of data *per se* was at issue; the unacceptable conduct in this case was his assertion that the published data were based on all the observations.

Although Babbage's categories of scientific dishonesty represent an early typology, they still have relevance today. For example, the debate surrounding the work of Sir Cyril Burt, which was described in chapter 1, involves charges that Burt may have been guilty of engaging in each of the forms of unacceptable conduct identified by Babbage (cf. Green, 1992). Burt's critics have contended that some of his statistical results were "too good to be true," and thus had to have been either trimmed or forged. His studies consistently and overwhelmingly supported his strongly held belief in the heritability of intelligence, suggesting the possibility of data cooking. Further, because he reported some identical correlation values (to three decimal places) in different studies varying in sample size (from 21 to 66), it appears that Burt may have fabricated at least some of the values (Broad and Wade, 1982). It may be recalled from our earlier discussion of this case that Burt even may have "invented" at least two of his research assistants.

The Millikan and Burt cases serve to illustrate how many instances of scientific dishonesty often are neither quickly discovered nor damaging to the perpetrator's ongoing career (Sigma Xi, 1984). Millikan went on to become one of the most influential and renowned scientists in the United States, having received the Nobel Prize in 1923, partly as a result of his early work on the electronic charge. Similarly, Burt acquired a reputation as a pre-eminent researcher and leader in his field, was the first psychologist to be knighted in England, and was the first foreigner to receive the prestigious Thorndike Award from the American Psychological Association. Questions about dishonesty in the work of Millikan and Burt did not emerge until some years after their deaths and, as a result, these men did not have a chance to respond to the charges leveled against them. Similar circumstances characterize some of the well-known early cases of cheating that have been perpetrated during the history of science (see "Cases of scientific fraud" below).

In addition to Babbage's categories of scientific dishonesty, other subtle forms of misconduct in the sciences have been identified. These include the suppression of negative evidence or unsuccessful results; the selective citing of the literature or selective reporting of others' data to bolster one's own position; misrepresentation of others' ideas; the incorrect analysis of research data; misleading descriptions of methodologies; and plagiarism in proposing or reporting research (Mahoney, 1976; Swazey et al., 1993). These forms of abuse often are less blatant than some of the more notorious cases of outright cheating and, as a result, may be more prevalent and difficult to detect. A much grayer area consists of a variety of unprofessional behaviors, such as not sharing resources, maintaining sloppy notebooks or research records, nastiness, non-collegiality, not helping younger colleagues, and professional secrecy. While such misbehavior does not represent scientific misconduct *per se*, its effects may be such that they serve to undermine the scientific endeavor in significant ways (Herman, 1993).

In his 1976 book *Scientist as Subject: The Psychological Imperative*, psychologist Michael Mahoney contends that the portrayal of the scientist as a virtuous, objective, and "passionless purveyor of truth" should be replaced by one that acknowledges the subjective and fallible aspects of human nature. Mahoney argues that the scientist is perhaps the most passionate of professionals: dogmatically tenacious in maintaining opinions; behaving in selfish and ambitious ways; frequently motivated by a desire for personal recognition; and occasionally secretive, suppressing data for personal reasons. A compelling illustration of these tendencies is provided by the research leading up to the discovery of the molecular structure of DNA by James Watson and Francis Crick, which was wrought with secrecy, personal rivalries, animosity, and professional jealousies (Watson, 1969).

Some scientists have gone to great lengths to conceal their discoveries for fear of being "scooped" by professional rivals or of having their ideas stolen by others. For example, Leonardo da Vinci apparently had a penchant for coding his personal notes by writing them backwards, in mirror image, and Galileo is said to have used anagrams as a protection against having his priority claims undermined by others. Interviews with contemporary scientists suggest that secrecy is prevalent in the sciences, although more discreet means of protecting one's work have replaced the rather crude methods used by early scientists (Gaston, 1971; Mahoney, 1976; Mitroff, 1974). One reason for such secrecy, in addition to the fear that one may miss out on an important publication, is the fact that many scientists are concerned about the possibility of having their work stolen. An average of 14 percent of the physical and behavioral scientists interviewed by Mahoney and Kimper felt that their colleagues had plagiarized other's ideas (see Mahoney, 1976).

Cases of scientific fraud

The occurrence of fraud in science is hardly a recent phenomenon. Throughout the annals of science, even some of the most influential scientists of their day have been suspected of falsifying data or engaging in other forms of scientific misconduct. In fact, at one time or another, all of the scientific disciplines have been affected by scandals resulting from the unethical behavior of researchers within their ranks. Many of the cases have appeared in the physical sciences where, because of greater replication and precision, the faking of data may be more readily detectable (Mahoney, 1976).

As interest in scientific honesty has increased in recent decades, historians of science have begun to uncover previously undetected examples of misconduct that may have occurred many years earlier. For instance, more than 1,800 years after the appearance of his influential publication on celestial motions, the renowned Greek astronomer Claudius Ptolemy was accused of having carried out one of the most successful frauds in the history of science. According to the physicist Robert Newton (1977), very few of Ptolemy's observations were his own and those were either fictitious or incorrect. Newton has argued that Ptolemy used a technique that is common among intellectual cheats, which was to work backward to prove the results he wanted to obtain. Ptolemy's key astronomical work (now known as *Almagest*, which is Arabic for "The Greatest") consisted of 13 volumes placing the earth at the center of the solar system and detailed his theory about the motions of the planets and stars. Newton maintained that evidence now points to the likelihood that Ptolemy came up with his theory based on incorrect measurements made by Hipparchus almost 200 years earlier. Despite Ptolemy's claim that he worked for several years to confirm the measurements made by Hipparchus, it appears that he merely took the measurements on faith and never made any of his own. Newton uncovered other discrepancies in Ptolemy's work to support his charges against the astronomer.

Galileo, the famous Italian scientist who is largely credited with overturning Ptolemy's theories of the solar system, has himself been the target of charges that he engaged in scientific misconduct, including the likelihood that he faked some data in order to bolster his own theory of gravity (Cohen, 1957). Galileo's great discovery, based on his use of the newly developed telescope, was that the planets revolve around the sun rather than the earth. The noted contemporary historian of science Richard Westfall charged that Galileo stole the proof for this discovery from a student and used it without acknowledgment to obtain the favors of a patron, the Grand Duke of Tuscany (Broad, 1983). With each challenge to Galileo's reputation as a scientific genius, historians have come to his defense and have attempted to duplicate the experiments he claimed to have conducted. Nonetheless, the accumulation of evidence against Galileo's scientific integrity and questions regarding his personal motives seem to suggest that the greatness of the man perhaps can more readily be found in his ability to conduct "thought experiments," imagining his experimental outcomes instead of actually doing the work to obtain them (Broad, 1983).

During the twentieth century, one can find numerous examples of scandals involving the faking of data that have received widespread attention both within the scientific professions and among the general public. One of the most dramatic cases was the Piltdown hoax, which involved the discovery in 1912 of a primitive skull and jawbone near Piltdown Common, England, by an amateur geologist. The fossil remains, referred to as "Piltdown man," were so different from anything previously known to anthropologists that they quickly threw the discipline into disarray, forcing a rethinking of existing theories of human evolution.

Piltdown man effectively dismayed two generations of anthropologists until the conclusion was reached in the 1950s that a hoax had been perpetrated (Weiner, 1955). Modern tests revealed that a human skull and an ape jawbone from different periods had been altered to simulate the bones of primitive man; for instance, the teeth had been filed in order to give the appearance of having been worn down by chewing. To this day, it is unclear who was responsible for this sophisticated hoax, although one intriguing theory points to none other than the creator of Sherlock Holmes, Sir Arthur Conan Doyle, as a prime suspect ("Arthur Conan Doyle," 1983; Winslow and Meyer, 1983). A comprehensive bibliography of the Piltdown man hoax is maintained online at www.talkorigins.org/faqs/piltdown/piltref.html.

Another famous case involving the altering of a scientific specimen was that of the Austrian biologist Paul Kammerer, who was engaged in research to study the Lamarckian hypothesis of inheritance of acquired characteristics (Weinstein, 1979). Kammerer spent many years attempting to demonstrate that the physical skills and developments acquired by one generation of animals are passed on to their offspring through hereditary processes. Support for this view came when Kammerer reported that salamanders he had raised on a yellow or black background acquired more of the color in their own pigmentation and then passed this acquired characteristic on to their offspring. After World War I, however, when a suspicious investigator examined the preserved specimen of a toad having purportedly acquired a black patch in one of Kammerer's experiments, it was revealed that the specimen had been tampered with. Apparently, the specimen's visible coloration had been produced by India ink, not by pigmentation. The forgery was widely publicized by the media and, as a result, Kammerer's reputation was disgraced and he committed suicide. It never has been established with any certainty whether Kammerer or some other person, such as a research assistant or jealous colleague, was responsible for the fabrication (see Koestler, 1972). In a similar, more recent example, a scientist at the renowned Sloan-Kettering Institute for Cancer Research fabricated his research results after several unsuccessful attempts during the 1970s to graft skin from black mice onto white mice. In what has come to be known as the "painted mice affair," William Summerlin painted black patches on two white mice with a felt-tipped pen so that they would appear to be successful transplants from other animals (Culliton, 1974).

The behavioral sciences have not been immune from cases of scientific fraud. One well-known example surrounds some of the long-term research on extrasensory perception and other psychic phenomena carried out at J. B. Rhine's Institute for Parapsychology in North Carolina. Rhine was a respected researcher on psychic phenomena for many years. As he approached retirement, he appointed a bright young physician named Walter Levy to direct the Institute. Levy proceeded to automate the research laboratories with computers and sophisticated devices in order to eliminate human error in the data collection procedures. Ironically, it eventually was discovered that Levy himself had altered the data in some studies of psychokinesis in laboratory rats. Electrodes had been implanted in the "pleasure centers" of the rats' brains in order to study whether the animals could psychically influence a random generator to deliver pleasurable stimulations. The fraud was revealed when Levy's assistants found that he was surreptitiously unplugging the automated data counter at certain times so that it would appear that the rats had psychokinetically influenced the generator (Asher, 1974). As a result of this revelation, Levy's promising research career abruptly came to an end and parapsychological research, which had begun to gain acceptance within a skeptical scientific community, was once again cast under a cloud of suspicion.

In a lesser known, but perhaps more representative, case of scientific fraud in behavioral research, Stephen Breuning, a psychologist participating in research on the effects of psychotropic medication in mentally retarded patients, admitted to having falsified some of his research reports. Breuning had been working on a research grant awarded to Robert Sprague, a clinical psychologist at the University of Illinois. Sprague's suspicions about the integrity of his young colleague were first aroused by a comment from one of Breuning's research assistants (Sprague, 1993). The assistant stated that Breuning was obtaining perfect agreement between nurses in their independent ratings of the abnormal involuntary movements of patients suffering from a neurological disorder (tardive dyskinesia) due to the long-term use of the medication under investigation. However, such perfect agreement among independent raters of complex movements in patients is highly unlikely.

Subsequently, during his own investigation of Breuning's research, Sprague found clearer evidence of dishonesty. This came in the form of an abstract Breuning had submitted for a symposium on tardive dyskinesia in which he claimed to have examined 45 patients over a two-year period at the research facility where he previously had been employed. Yet Breuning no longer had assistants at that facility and had not traveled there himself during that time to conduct the research. Unable to provide documentation of the examinations, Breuning confessed to having falsified the abstract. After a prolonged investigation conducted by the federal agency that had funded the research, Breuning was indicted for scientific misconduct and sentenced by a federal judge in 1988. According to Sprague (1993), had the misconduct not been revealed, Breuning's fraudulent research reports could have had major policy and medical implications for numerous mentally retarded persons receiving the medication about which he wrote.

In another case, Robert Gallo, a leading AIDS researcher, was found to have falsely stated in a 1984 publication that the French version of the virus that causes AIDS had not been successfully grown in a cell culture, but that his laboratory had achieved success in growing another version of the virus. Actually, both viruses had been grown in cultures in his laboratory, and Gallo was held responsible for having "impeded potential AIDS-research progress" by failing to reveal the utility of the French virus (Herman, 1993). The federal panel that investigated Gallo's laboratory reported a pattern of conduct characterized by a "propensity to misrepresent and mislead in favor of his own research findings or hypotheses" (Herman, 1993, p. 7).

What is particularly disconcerting about the cases of scientific misconduct described here is that a leading (or up-and-coming) scientist was at the center of each scandal. It is unclear whether this can be attributed to the greater pressures placed on the scientist to maintain a lofty status within the field, the fact that research by successful investigators is more likely to be subjected to careful scrutiny within the research community, or the possibility that greater media attention is drawn to celebrated cases involving well-known figures (cf. Bechtel and Pearson, 1985).

Extent of scientific dishonesty

Data fraud is a phenomenon that is considered rare by most scientists, yet as we have seen in the preceding section, scandals continue to be revealed. Little is known about the factors that motivate professional dishonesty, although the desire for money, status, and prestige are likely root causes. The question also remains as to the extent to which the cases that have come to light represent a preponderance of all of the incidents that have occurred or are merely the tip of an iceberg. It has been noted that perceptions of misconduct are probably exaggerated, given that when a case emerges it receives much attention; however, once a case does come to light, it has the potential to do the relevant profession a great deal of harm (Murray, 2002). Although there is general agreement that honesty and accuracy are critical elements of the research enterprise, there are disparate opinions about the extent and significance of scientific misconduct in the research disciplines. It is difficult to estimate just how pervasive fraud and other forms of misconduct are, although concerted efforts have been made in recent years to determine the extent of such practices.

In one attempt to ascertain the extent of cheating in science, anonymous questionnaires were made available to scientists subscribing to the British journal *New Scientist* (St James-Roberts, 1976). A significant percentage of the respondents (92 percent) reported that they had knowledge of "intentional bias" in their scientific disciplines. Another survey on scientific conduct within four disciplines (physics, biology, psychology, and sociology) carried out by Mahoney and Kimper found that 42 percent of the participants knew of at least one instance of data fabrication in their field and nearly half reported knowledge of at least one instance of data suppression (see Mahoney, 1976). Because the survey also revealed much lower estimates of the prevalence of such behavior, it may be that these data were influenced by some well-known scandals. It also must be noted that the generalizability of the results obtained from both of the surveys described here is limited by methodological problems inherent in the data collection procedures.

More recently, researchers from the Acadia Institute Project on Professional Values and Ethical Issues in the Graduate Education of Scientists and Engineers surveyed 2,000 doctoral candidates and 2,000 of their faculty in one of the first major studies of misconduct in science (Swazey et al., 1993). Anonymous questionnaires were returned by about 2,600 of the scientists from 99 graduate departments in chemistry, civil engineering, microbiology, and sociology who were asked about their experiences with 15 different types of ethically questionable behaviors. As is typical in surveys of this kind, the results did not measure the actual frequency of misconduct; rather, rates of exposure to perceived misconduct were obtained. The findings revealed that scientific misconduct may be more pervasive than many scientists believe: 43 percent of the students and 50 percent of the faculty members reported direct knowledge of more than one kind of misconduct in their laboratories. The forms of reported misconduct ranged from faking results to withholding research findings from competitors.

Other findings from the Acadia study revealed that from 6 to 9 percent of the respondents said they had direct knowledge of faculty members who had falsified or plagiarized data; one-third of the faculty members reported that they had direct evidence of such misconduct among students. Reports of questionable research practices (such as inappropriate assignment of authorship in research papers and misusing research money and equipment for personal use) were far more common than reports of outright misconduct. Additionally, striking differences were found between scientists' espoused values and their actual practices. For example, in principle, nearly all of the faculty members endorsed some degree of collective responsibility for the behavior of their graduate students and also claimed some responsibility for their faculty colleagues. Yet, in practice, a relatively small percentage of faculty members believed that they actually exercise their responsibilities to their students (27 percent) or their colleagues (13 percent) to any great extent. Taken together, these results suggest that although misconduct is not rampant in the four scientific disciplines studied, it also cannot be said that it is rare.

One additional finding from the Acadia project is noteworthy. A significant percentage of students (53 percent) and faculty (26 percent) revealed that they were unlikely to report scientific misconduct because they were fearful of reprisals. This finding is consistent with the results of a survey of psychology interns and university faculty in which fear of retaliation emerged as the most frequently given reason for failure to report ethical violations (Holaday and Yost, 1993).

Another approach to estimating the prevalence of research fraud is through the identification of research retractions in the published literature. That is, when questions arise about a researcher having fabricated data or other aspects of a research report, the investigator in question may submit a retraction – if not an outright admission of guilt and apology – to the publication in which the research appeared. In one search of the Medline database, fewer than 300 research retractions appeared since 1966, not all involving misconduct (cf. Murray, 2002). Of course, this approach is likely to underestimate the incidence of fraud because it only identifies cases that have aroused suspicion or where cheating has been revealed. By its very nature, cheating is intended to go undetected. Moreover, the appearance of a retraction does not definitively identify misconduct.

In one recent case, research by renowned Harvard psychologist Karen Ruggiero on the psychological effects of sex and race discrimination was called into question when others attempted to replicate her findings and she failed to show her raw research data to one of her assistants. Following the allegations, Ruggiero issued retractions to two journals that had published her federally funded work, and took full responsibility for having falsified her data. As a consequence, Ruggiero entered an agreement with the US Public Health Service and Harvard barring her from applying for any federal research grants for five years. The case also severely besmirched Ruggiero's reputation as an excellent teacher who had been described in the press as "one of the most promising young psychology professors in the country" (Chow, 2002).

Given the dire consequences that being found out may have on one's professional career, it stands to reason that the rewards can be great for the successful cheat in science. The motivations for these abuses are rather obvious, such as professional advancement, the awarding of research grants, and publications in respected scientific journals (Carroll et al., 1985). The rather low probability of being caught and the ease and opportunity with which data manipulation can be carried out also increase the likelihood of scientific misconduct. It should be added that the tendency to fake or invent data may be attributed to more subtle influences, such as self-deceit and rationalization. For example, researchers might unwittingly convince themselves that the data they have collected cannot possibly be accurate if they vary greatly from what was expected (McNemar, 1960); as a result, they may simply change the data to what was expected. In short, scientists may become so committed to their pet hypotheses that they accept the hypotheses rather than contradictory data when, in fact, they should do the opposite. This possibility is reflected in the following comment from a biochemist at the Max Planck Institute in Germany who admitted to having invented data published in various journal articles: "I published my hypotheses rather than experimentally determined results. The reason was that I was so convinced of my ideas that I simply put them down on paper" ("Researcher admits," 1977). A similar explanation has been offered to explain Cyril Burt's motivations for likely altering the results of his research on the heritability of intelligence (Green, 1992; Hearnshaw, 1979).

Whatever the causes of scientific fraud, it is clear that the consequences of misconduct can be great. In addition to the risks imposed on the unethical researcher (such as professional ostracism if caught or the possibility that the conduct will become more frequent if it is not exposed), violations of scientific honesty can harm science as well. Because the data reported in an investigation are assumed to have intellectual integrity and trustworthiness, falsified data can undermine science by adding purported facts to the existing body of knowledge within a discipline (Reese and Fremouw, 1984). Thus, false results are not merely worthless; they can contaminate scientific knowledge and mislead others working in the same field. In this light, it is no wonder that fraud perpetrated by scientists is considered a very serious offense within the scientific community. In the words of one eminent researcher, "any kind of falsification or fiddling with professedly factual results is rightly regarded as an unforgivable professional crime" (Medawar, 1976).

Student dishonesty

Some early research conducted by Azrin and his colleagues suggests that the falsification of data by young scientists and research assistants may be fairly widespread (Azrin et al., 1961). In one study, the researchers assigned a field experiment on verbal conditioning to 16 students who were to either reinforce the opinions stated by others (by agreeing with them) or to extinguish the opinions (by remaining silent). The procedure of the study, however, was intentionally designed by the researchers to be impossible to carry out in the prescribed way. Despite this fact, all but one of the students reported to their professor that they had successfully completed the experiment. After the one honest student described how it was impossible to run the experiment as intended, eight of the other students admitted to having significantly deviated from the prescribed data collection procedure. In a replication of the verbal conditioning study, 12 out of 19 students approached by a student confederate admitted to him that they had faked at least part of their data and five other students revealed that they had changed the required procedure to make it work (Azrin et al., 1961). Both of these studies were based on an earlier published study (Verplanck, 1955) in which students had collected data. Given the results obtained by Azrin et al., it may be that the original study was comprised of falsified data (Diener and Crandall, 1978).

Student researchers are especially susceptible to dishonest activities – such as falsifying data, making up data for subjects without having run them (a procedure commonly referred to as "dry labbing"), and altering the prescribed research procedure – for some of the same reasons that give rise to cheating in the classroom. Determinants of classroom cheating include pressures for good grades, student stress, need for approval, ineffective deterrents, a belief that cheating is a normal part of life, an overall diminishing sense of academic integrity, and broader social changes (Davis et al., 1992; Lee, 2003; Mahl, 1995). Further, there is evidence that cheating rates among students are as high as 75–87 percent (Baird, 1980; Jendreck, 1989), whereas detection rates are as low as 1.30 percent (Haines et al., 1986), suggesting that academic dishonesty is more likely to be reinforced than punished.

A survey of 12,000 American high school students conducted in 2002 by the Josephson Institute of Ethics (2002) revealed that 74 percent admitted cheating on a classroom exam at least once in the past year, representing a 13 percent increase over estimates obtained in a similar study ten years earlier. Further, 43 percent of the students agreed with the statement "A person has to lie or cheat sometimes in order to succeed," compared with 34 percent who agreed to the same statement in a 2000 survey. According to Michael Josephson, president of the Institute, the steady increase in estimates of student cheating can be partly attributed to new economic pressures and greater rewards for those who succeed in contemporary society (Lee, 2003).

Dishonest behavior that is reinforced in one academic context (the classroom) may readily generalize to other academic activities, such as the carrying out and reporting of research projects in laboratory courses. Thus, students who are pressured for time to complete their coursework may find it relatively easy to invent data that are consistent with the hypothesis or are like data collected from some actual subjects. Similarly, prescribed research procedures can easily be simplified to save time; for example, rather than taking the time to carefully administer written questionnaires to randomly selected participants, student researchers might instead obtain responses over the telephone from a few friends and relatives.

Because student research is generally unlikely to be published, the consequences of faking data are potentially less destructive than when such misconduct is perpetrated by a research professional. Nonetheless, success at falsifying data or other forms of misconduct when one is a student may increase the temptation to engage in such behaviors at a later time should one go on to work in a research field. It thus is important for students and research assistants to recognize the potential impact their work can have on scientific progress and the necessity for maintaining honesty in the reporting of research investigations (see Box 10.6). Of course, it also is essential that young researchers be made aware that they could lose the opportunity to pursue a professional career if they are caught cheating. Just as students may be expelled from the university for cheating, professional researchers run the risk of personal disgrace and expulsion from the scientific community when they are caught falsifying their results.

Safeguards against scientific misconduct

In order to rid the behavioral sciences of scientific fraud and other forms of cheating, a climate in which professional misconduct is clearly unacceptable must be established. Towards that objective, experts agree that it is the shared responsibility of researchers, institutions, funding agencies, and journal editors to take the appropriate preventative measures (see Box 10.7). At present, it is somewhat comforting to recognize that scientific research ideally is self-correcting; that is, there are many checks and balances that can lead to the detection of mistakes and falsified results. The potential harm caused by violations of scientific honesty can be undone by ethical researchers who attempt to replicate the reported results and fail.

In effect, the replication of research findings (i.e. the repeating of an earlier study to see if its findings can be duplicated) and peer review (i.e. a critical evaluation of an investigation by qualified persons within a field) represent the standard means for guarding against dishonesty and error in science. In recent years, however, there has been growing skepticism about the ability of this system to safeguard against scientific misconduct (e.g. Altman, 1986; Sigma Xi, 1984; Weinstein, 1981). In short, it has been argued that current protections against scientific misconduct often fail because findings are infrequently checked in other laboratories and the peer review system frequently depends on misplaced trust ("Fraud in medical research," 1989).

Replication
It has long been assumed that replication provides a kind of "self-cleansing" function in the scientific process, quickly removing error and revealing faked results soon after they appear. Presumably, when important findings are published, they are promptly checked in other laboratories. Such was the case following the initial reports of high temperature superconductivity and low temperature nuclear fusion. Researchers in dozens of laboratories immediately checked and confirmed the initial superconductivity evidence, but failed to confirm the fusion results. Although there was no suspicion of fakery in the latter

Box 10.6 Enhancing the accuracy of student research

Several suggestions have been offered for discouraging cheating in academic settings, including simply informing students not to cheat, explaining why they should not cheat, communicating policies on cheating, distributing separate forms of exams or assignments, physically separating students (e.g. by rearranging seating assignments), maintaining a close vigilance over students, avoiding adversarial relationships with students, and designing classroom demonstrations to illustrate the consequences of cheating (Davis et al., 1992; McBurney, 1996; Riniolo, 1997). Through a serendipitous finding, the author may have stumbled upon a method that enhances to some extent the accuracy of undergraduate student research reports. The method consists of carefully explaining to students prior to their carrying out a required research project that their grades will be independent of their results; that is, a research report could receive a high grade even if the hypotheses tested were not supported by the obtained data.

The potential efficacy of this approach became apparent one semester following the assignment of a research project to two separate sections of an undergraduate course in social psychology that I was teaching. The study represented a simple between-subjects design intended to assess the effects of physical appearance on judgments of guilt and severity of recommended punishment for a fictitious student who had been accused of cheating on an exam. Students in the two class sections were provided with the stimulus material for carrying out the study, including two rudimentary drawings of an "attractive" and "unattractive" female student, a single description of the case of suspected cheating, and rating scales for assessing judgments of guilt and recommended punishment. The student researchers were asked to test three hypotheses: (1) the attractive defendant will be judged as less likely to have cheated; (2) subjects will rate the attractive defendant as less likely to commit the transgression again; and (3) a less severe punishment will be recommended for the attractive defendant.

As I graded the completed research projects, I noticed that an interesting pattern was emerging. It appeared that the student researchers from one class were much more likely to have obtained support for the project's hypotheses than were students from the other section. Once I had finished grading all of the reports I examined this apparent difference more closely. In fact, my initial suspicions were confirmed: 75 percent of the students in one section obtained differences in the predicted direction (i.e. consistent with the hypotheses) as opposed to the remaining students who reported no apparent difference or differences in the opposite direction. In stark

(Continued)

Box 10.6   (*Continued*)

contrast, these percentages were reversed for students in the other section: only 25 percent reported differences in the predicted direction. Given the fact that both class sections had carried out the same research project, it was interesting to ponder what could have caused the varied results.

It eventually occurred to me that the two sections in fact had not received identical instructions for carrying out the study. For one class I recall clearly stating how grades for the research report would not at all be affected by the obtained results. I explained that the evaluation would be based on the clarity of the write-up, the adequacy of the literature review and discussion, and the procedure used to carry out the study. I also added a brief discussion of the importance of honor in science and how falsifying research results represents a serious breach of research ethics. Because of time constraints, this explanation was not provided to the other section and I failed to mention it during subsequent class meetings. Not surprisingly, the students who were not privy to the discussion on honesty and the caveat about the grading criteria comprised the section that was more likely to have obtained support for the hypotheses. It may thus be inferred that at least some of the students may have falsified or invented their data in the direction of the hypotheses in anticipation of receiving a better grade for the project. Of course, such an inference is merely tentative because of the *post hoc* nature of the comparison. It may be that the sections differed in important ways prior to assignment of the project, such that students in the class that tended to find support for the hypotheses were less honest to begin with than students in the other section. Another possibility is that the hypothesis confirming section may have taken greater care in carrying out the study and thus obtained the predicted effects despite the relatively weak manipulation. Nonetheless, the serendipitous finding suggests a possible direction for future research on the effects of teaching students the importance of accuracy in research.

In practice, graduate students and professional researchers are well aware that rewards in the scientific community, such as publications and career advancement, are more likely to be forthcoming when research outcomes are statistically interesting. In essence, professional rewards are clearly linked to meaningful research outcomes (Altman, 1986). As a result, the strategy for enhancing scientific honesty described above would not be very useful for research professionals. However, for younger researchers at the undergraduate level, it could serve as a useful socializing mechanism for encouraging ethical scientific conduct.

case, the failure to replicate the nuclear fusion findings suggested that there were mistakes in the work. Given this system of checking major studies, it is believed that researchers will refrain from fakery because they recognize that if their

Box 10.7   Recommendations for eliminating research fraud

Although the responsibility for scientific misconduct lies first and foremost on the shoulders of the researcher, research institutions and agencies can play a significant role in creating a climate that discourages such unethical conduct. Several recommendations have been offered for eliminating research fraud (cf. Murray, 2002), and these are summarized below.

Institutions and Agencies

1   Educate Students About Research Ethics

Both unintentional (i.e. accidental) and intentional research fraud can be reduced through the ethical education of students. In fact, a growing number of graduate seminars and research methods courses have emerged in recent years that specifically deal with ethical issues. In 1990 the US National Institutes of Health (NIH) mandated that all graduate students who conduct federally funded research must receive training in ethical conduct (Zignego, 2003). Such training is also required for participants in professional psychology programs accredited by APA.

2   Conduct Audits

As described elsewhere in this chapter, research audits have emerged as a new reality of the scientific process. Although it is understandable that researchers may perceive the auditing process as a growing threat, in fact audits represent a strong and potentially effective deterrent against fraud. The awareness that data might be checked at any time is a strong inducement for researchers to maintain the integrity of their research.

3   Investigate Fraud

As with research audits, another deterrent against scientific misconduct is the awareness that all cases of suspected fraud will be thoroughly investigated by professional bodies, such as the APA Ethics Office or an institutional watchdog committee.

Individuals: Researchers and Journal Editors

1   Set Clear Rules for Data Collection and Analysis

If principal investigators set out specific guidelines for the type of data that will and will not be included in a study, there may be less temptation for the trimming or cooking of data. That is, decisions should be made at the outset about how to treat cases of extreme (or highly unexpected) data (so-called "outliers") and the theoretical justification for data elimination. Journal editors also can include specifications about the handling of data in their instructions to authors.

(Continued)

Box 10.7   (Continued)

2   Review Data

It is essential that principal investigators check the raw data collected by their co-investigators or research assistants. An increasing number of journal editors now require researchers to maintain their raw data for a specified period of time in the event that questions later emerge about the integrity of a published study.

3   Explain the Data Analysis Process

Journal editors can require investigators to clarify how they categorized and analyzed their data before accepting to publish empirical studies.

published findings are important, they will promptly be caught and exposed when attempts to replicate their work fail.

In theory, replication ought to serve as a deterrent against scientific dishonesty; in actual practice, there appear to be serious flaws in the effectiveness of this safeguarding mechanism. Not only are replication attempts relatively rare in science, but when they are carried out they may not have much of an impact on exposing inaccurate results. On the one hand, faked research findings indeed might be successfully replicated in cases in which the unethical researcher reached the correct answers through inappropriate means. On the other hand, replications of other scientists' work have become increasing less likely because fewer researchers have the competence to replicate (due to greater specialization in the sciences), funding agencies are unwilling to support "merely" replicative research, and one can expect little recognition as a result of devoting a substantial amount of time to replication research (Mahoney, 1976; Weinstein, 1981). Additionally, replications may be especially rare in cases in which a single study has a strong impact but is so large in scale that a replication would be financially prohibitive (Fisher, 1982). Another factor working against replication research is the reluctance of journal editors and reviewers to favorably consider studies for publication that do not demonstrate new effects. The results of one survey of 80 social science journal reviewers revealed just such a bias against replication studies, with several respondents explaining that they viewed replications as a waste of time, resources, and journal space (Neuliep and Crandall, 1993).

Replications are seldom easy to perform and their results may not be straightforward. Few researchers would be willing to accuse their colleagues of incompetence or dishonesty when the evidence of misconduct is not obvious, such as when the failure to replicate can be explained by other factors. After all, skepticism must be tempered by trust in the honesty of fellow researchers in order for scientific progress to proceed in a relatively smooth fashion (Bronowksi, 1956).

Peer review

As in the case of replication, the effectiveness of the peer review system as a mechanism for safeguarding science from fraud and other forms of research misconduct has been subject to increasing criticism. The conclusions of an investigative panel formed by the Institute of Medicine to study misconduct in biomedical research are typical of recent assessments of the quality of peer review at major research institutions. In its 1989 report, the panel identified an "excessively permissive" attitude by institutions allowing the carrying out of careless and sometimes even fraudulent medical research ("Fraud in medical research," 1989). Few institutions were found to have explicit guidelines for evaluating research; as a result, individual investigators often failed to observe generally accepted practices and academic institutions proved limited in their ability to carry out objective evaluations of misconduct.

Peer review plays a central role in ensuring that the articles published by scientific journals are accurate, methodologically sound, and high enough in quality and innovativeness to merit communication to a larger scientific audience. In most cases, when a research manuscript is submitted to a scientific journal for publication consideration, it is evaluated by one's peers. Assuming the journal editor deems the research worthy of review, he or she will send the manuscript to a few experts (or "referees") for their criticisms and opinions on whether the work represents a contribution to the field and should be published. Such reviews typically are carried out under anonymous conditions; that is, the author's name and institution are left off the reviewed manuscript and the identities of the reviewers are kept secret from the author. Based on the experts' recommendations, the editor makes a final decision as to whether the manuscript should be accepted outright, accepted with revisions, or rejected (see Fogg and Fiske, 1993). It is assumed that this system of peer review prevents the publication of research errors and false claims, improves the quality of accepted papers, prevents duplication among scientific journals, and provides a fair means for the editor to select the most worthy submissions (Altman, 1986).

Unfortunately, adequate measures are unavailable for assessing the effectiveness of the peer review system in achieving the aforementioned goals in research publication (Altman, 1989). Thus, it is not possible to obtain accurate indications as to how many fraudulent research articles are exposed through peer review, how many actually survive the review process, and the extent to which good research is prevented from being published. Despite the fact that about three-fourths of the major scientific journals utilize peer review for assessing at least some of the articles they publish, there have been numerous calls within the sciences for improvements to the system (e.g. Epstein, 1995; Fine, 1996; Rabinovich, 1996). Researchers have complained about the unevenness of the review process (e.g. an article rejected by one journal may well be favorably evaluated by another) and the tendency for the typical journal review to be excessively time consuming (e.g. Bowen et al., 1972; Mahoney, 1976; Zuckerman and Merton, 1971).

In addition to the fact that a previously rejected research manuscript may be accepted for publication as an important contribution to the field by another journal, there is evidence suggesting that research articles also may be differentially evaluated by the *same* journal on different occasions. This possibility was uncovered in an intriguing study carried out by Peters and Ceci (1982). In their investigation of the reviewing process within psychology, Peters and Ceci resubmitted previously published articles to each of 12 prestigious psychology journals. The articles included only cosmetic alterations, including author and institutional affiliation changes. Of the 12 articles resubmitted, only three were detected as resubmissions. Further, eight of the remaining nine articles actually were *rejected* by the journals that previously had published them a short time earlier. The researchers found no evidence that the editorial policies or rejection rates had changed for these journals since the original publication of the articles.

Peters and Ceci's findings, along with research reporting low inter-referee agreement for manuscript review, add credence to the often-voiced charge that the peer review system is capricious and inequitable. In his indictment of the publication process, Mahoney (1976) aptly asserted that the comments made by journal reviewers are often so divergent that one wonders whether they actually had read the same research manuscript. In light of recent research, we can now ask whether journal reviewers read the same manuscript the same way twice.

Another concern has to do with the possibility that personal, institutional, and gender biases may enter into the decisions of editors and reviewers. For example, Campion (1993) surveyed psychology and management research reviewers and found evidence suggesting that reviewers employed in predominantly applied settings (such as consulting and management firms) tend to weight the practical importance of research articles somewhat higher and the theoretical importance somewhat lower than their counterparts in academic settings. These results are consistent with a commonly held assumption that academic-oriented scientists have a greater interest in the theoretical implications of research, while practice-oriented scientists tend to focus on the applied implications of research. Epstein (1995) reported anecdotal evidence suggesting that the more innovative a study, the greater the likelihood that the research report will be rejected for publication.

Other drawbacks attributed to the journal review process include the lack of systematic assessment of the adequacy of reviewers' comments; a tendency to publish only studies with findings that support the researcher's hypotheses; and a proclivity to publish research by prestigious authors (Altman, 1986; Cummings and Frost, 1985; Dickersin et al., 1992; Levenson, 1996; Mahoney, 1976). A revealing anecdote relevant to the influence of a prestigious researcher's name on the likelihood of publication was conveyed by the son of the eminent nineteenth-century scientist Lord Rayleigh (Strutt, 1924). Apparently, Rayleigh's name had either been omitted or accidentally detached from an article on electricity he had submitted to the British Association for the Advancement of Science. The paper was rejected by the committee as having been written by an eccentric theorist. When the authorship of the article was discovered, however, its merits suddenly became apparent and the publication decision was reversed.

Perhaps most troubling from an ethical perspective is the concern that the review system is open to abuse by unscrupulous reviewers who may appropriate ideas from rejected articles or make use of a paper's contents prior to its publication. Also, journal referees who are competing with the authors of reviewed papers for research grants may unfairly evaluate their rivals' work or utilize the knowledge gained in the review process to their own advantage (Altman, 1986).

Again, the extent to which reviewers are guilty of such conduct is impossible to gauge; nonetheless, such activities represent clear abuses of the trust bestowed on those who are invited to take part in the peer review system.

Several recommendations have been offered to improve the peer review process. One suggestion is that journals should develop more explicit guidelines for those who take part in the reviewing of manuscripts, including the establishment of criteria for the selection of referees and for the review of manuscripts (Epstein, 1995). A clear procedure for authors to contest criticism of their work also has been called for (Fine, 1996). For some journals, explicit guidelines for review already have been established, along with steps to speed up the review process and better protect the anonymity of authors and reviewers. Another recommendation is to have more reviewers judge each manuscript (rather than the more typical two or three) in order to overcome possible biases attributed to the background characteristics of reviewers (Campion, 1993).

As suggested in Box 10.7, some individuals within the research community have called for examination of the methods and statistical analyses of submitted studies through audits of investigators' original records and data. In fact, certain journals now require authors to agree that their data will be kept available for consultation for a certain period of time, such as five years, after publication (St James-Roberts, 1976). The widespread adoption of such a requirement could prove informative, especially in light of the findings of an early investigation conducted by Wolins (1962). When Wolins requested original data from the authors of 37 published studies, he obtained data from only seven. When these data were reanalyzed, three included statistical errors large enough to influence the original research conclusions. Further, 21 of the researchers who were contacted claimed that their data had been either misplaced or destroyed. Assuming these results are not atypical, a review process that regularly includes experimental audits of submitted research could prove to be an effective deterrent against scientific misconduct.

Other issues in the publication of research

In addition to the problems inherent in the publication process relative to peer review, researchers have certain ethical responsibilities when they attempt to publish their findings in scientific journals. Among the important issues in communicating knowledge to others that we have not yet considered are those dealing with the proper assignment of publication credit, protection of the anonymity of research participants, and the potential misuse of research results. Each of these issues is briefly addressed below.

Publication authorship assignments
Scholarly publications in the scientific disciplines matter, not only because their contents are assumed to add to scientific knowledge but also because the very act of publishing in reputable (e.g. peer-reviewed) journals is typically taken as a sign that a researcher is productive and is carrying out worthwhile work. In the disciplines of psychology, sociology, and political science, about 80 percent of

the papers submitted for journal publication are rejected (in contrast to the physical sciences where acceptance rates are high) (Zuckerman and Merton, 1971). A recent report of APA journal operations revealed manuscript rejection rates for the association's 26 primary journals ranging from 36 percent (*Experimental and Clinical Psychopharmacology*) to 92 percent (*Journal of Applied Psychology*), with an overall average rejection rate of 72 percent ("Summary Report," 2005). In light of such selectivity in the publication process, "getting published" generally is essential to the academic researcher's professional status and may be used as a criterion for continued employment and job tenure. Unfortunately, this often means that the *quantity* of publications may take on more significance than the *quality* of their content for individual researchers.

A professional emphasis on publication quantity can lead to ethically questionable conduct, such as attempts to publish the same research in multiple journals in order to "fatten" one's curriculum vitae (perhaps by making only minor modifications to the report or by changing its title so that it will not be obvious that the same research has been submitted to more than one journal). On this issue, most professional standards and journal publication policies are clear that the duplicate publication of original manuscripts or data, unless acknowledged as such, is unacceptable (e.g. see Box 10.5). The following statement taken from the *Personality and Social Psychology Bulletin* (www.spsp.org) is typical of journal submission guidelines:

> Journal policy prohibits an author from submitting the same manuscript for consideration by another journal and does not allow publication of a manuscript that has been published in whole or part in another journal. Authors must also verify compliance with APA ethical standards in the treatment of participants, human or animal.

Multiple submissions are generally deplored by journal editors because republishing the same material unnecessarily overburdens the scientific literature and makes it more difficult for scientists to keep up, wastes the time of editors and reviewers, and delays the publication of original manuscripts.

More subtle issues also emerge in the publishing of scholarly research papers, with resolutions that are not always obvious. One of the more difficult areas involves the assignment of publication credit. Although at first glance this would appear to be a relatively straightforward procedure, disputes concerning this issue are among the most common complaints to ethics committees initiated by academic researchers (Holaday and Yost, 1993; Keith-Spiegel and Koocher, 1985). Fairness in authorship assignment also represents one of the most common ethical issues that emerges in the supervision of student research (Goodyear, Crego, and Johnston, 1992). A growing interest in the development of guidelines for authorship credit determination reflects an increase in multiple-authored journal articles (Garfield, 1978). A six-page research report appearing in an issue of the journal *Psychological Science*, for example, was attributed to no fewer than 13 authors (McCloskey et al., 1995).

In general, professional standards maintain that credits are to be assigned proportional to professional contribution, such that the main contributor to a work is listed first. Those who played a minor role in the research, such as persons who assisted in the coding of questionnaires or offered helpful ideas, are usually acknowledged in a footnote. In one survey, substantial agreement was obtained regarding authorship and footnote citation among psychologists who were asked to respond to a set of cases dealing with credit assignment (Spiegel and Keith-Spiegel, 1970). Although no consensus was reached, the respondents typically interpreted "principal contribution" in joint effort research consistent with the following rank-ordering: (1) the person who generated the hypothesis and design; (2) the person who wrote the material for publication; (3) the person who established the procedure and collected the data; and (4) the person who analyzed the data.

Publication credit tends to be an important concern among researchers for reasons that are tied to the vested interests of the individuals involved, such as the need to enhance one's career and to gain status and recognition among one's peers through publication output. "Senior" or first-named authors are often presumed to be the originators and principal contributors to the published work. In certain situations, ethical issues can emerge as a result of the power differential that often exists between collaborators on a research project (Fine and Kurdek, 1993). For example, researchers who have power and authority over their junior co-authors may take advantage of their status to claim senior authorship despite having been only indirectly involved or minor contributors to the research. Another possibility is that lower-status researchers who play a significant role in the research may not be listed by their senior collaborators as co-authors at all, but instead acknowledged in a footnote. Charges along these lines are occasionally voiced by graduate students who claim that their doctoral research advisors unfairly insist on being listed as co-authors of publications based on the dissertation. In some students' views, the advice they receive from their advisors constitutes a teaching obligation and thus should not be considered as a principal contribution (Keith-Spiegel and Koocher, 1985). Others have argued that faculty input into research might not be substantial enough to warrant authorship credit (Crespi, 1994).

In contrast to concerns about the possible exploitation of students in the determination of authorship credit, more recent attention has focused on the issue of providing students with undue credit (Fine and Kurdek, 1993; Thompson, 1994). That is, some faculty researchers might be overly generous in assigning publication credit to promising students in hopes of boosting the students' formative careers. The ethical problem in such cases pertains to the potential risks involved, including false representation of the student's scholarly expertise, providing the student with an unfair professional advantage, and overly inflating expectations for the student's subsequent performance (Fine and Kurdek, 1993).

Although recognizing the ethical implications of these issues, some researchers have advised that the assignment of authorship credit can be fair without requiring the formulation of rigid principles that introduce unnecessary precision, such as proposed point systems evaluating the magnitude of research contribution (see Fine and Kurdek, 1993; Oliver, 2003). Thompson (1994) suggested that the authorship order for research involving two authors, both of whom have made substantial contributions, can be determined in several mutually acceptable ways. For instance, first authorship could be randomly designated, a note could be added to indicate that the authors contributed equally, or it could be decided that one of the authors made a greater contribution. In other cases, such as faculty–student collaborations in which both parties contribute significantly to the work, Thompson recommends giving greater credit to the less established and less powerful contributor. In Thompson's view, although credit in scholarship may not always be fair or precise, the determination of authorship credit should be based on "mutually acceptable agreements that have a rational basis" (p. 1095). Disputes often can be avoided altogether when researchers decide on authorship credit at the outset of a collaboration.

Protecting the anonymity of research participants

The importance of maintaining the anonymity of those individuals who participate in research has been emphasized at various points in this book. Although a researcher may take great pains to protect participants' anonymity and guarantee the confidentiality of research results during the data collection stage of an investigation, it must be recognized that confidentiality can be lost in various ways when the research eventually is communicated to others. The American Psychological Association (1982) identified several situations in which this may occur, including disclosure to third parties (such as parents or friends), to organizations of which the participant is a member (including employers, schools, and clinics), and to professional associates of the investigator. Confidentiality also can be lost as a result of a court order (e.g. when the investigator is legally required to provide information about research participants to the police and the courts) and through research publication.

In most of these cases, researchers often can avoid potential ethical dilemmas by obtaining the participant's permission prior to disclosure and by establishing a clear agreement with the participant and relevant third parties prior to the collection of data. Problems are likely to arise when associates of the participant (such as a teacher or therapist) claim a right to certain information obtained during an investigation, based on the grounds that the communication of data obtained under conditions of confidentiality can be used to the benefit of the participant. Although situations involving the loss of confidentiality on the basis of a court order may be more difficult to handle, it is advised that researchers investigating sensitive topics should explain the potential legal ramifications to the participant in advance and take care to store sensitive data in ways that make the identification of individual subjects impossible (American Psychological Association, 1982).

As mentioned, threats to participant anonymity and the confidentiality of data also can stem from the publication of research results. In behavioral science research in which data are likely to be presented in aggregate form (such as group averages), problems involving the identification of individual participants are rare. However, when case materials on well-known persons or aggregate data on narrowly defined populations (such as organizations or small communities) are published, the identity of specific participants may be revealed, along with sensitive information about them. Although the risks of such revelations usually are not very great, these disclosures may be quite embarrassing to the individuals involved. It may be recalled that this was an outcome following publication of Carolyn Ellis's book describing her participant observations of the Guinea watermen of Virginia (see chapter 5). Another example is provided by a famous field study of the political and social life of a small town in upstate New York, identified by the fictitious name "Springdale" (Vidich and Bensman, 1958). Prior to carrying out their observations, the researchers assured the community's residents that no participants would be identified in published reports of the investigation and that their privacy and anonymity would be protected. In fact, a code of ethics was specifically devised for the purpose of safeguarding the integrity and welfare of the participants and for assuring that all data collected would remain confidential (Bell and Bronfenbrenner, 1959).

Despite the assurances given, publication of *Small Town in Mass Society*, Vidich and Bensman's (1958) book describing the Springdale project, was greeted by vehement objections from the townspeople. Although individuals mentioned in the book were given fictitious names, there were charges that many of the descriptions were embarrassing and failed to effectively disguise the identities of various members of the community. Residents claimed that the researchers' promise of anonymity had been betrayed by the published account of the study, that they had not been treated with respect and dignity in the account, and that the tone of the book was overly condescending and patronizing. Questions also were raised about characterizations of the attitudes and motives of various community members (Reynolds, 1979). The citizens of Springdale further reacted to the published report by publicly lampooning the researchers in a parade and by refusing future cooperation with any social scientists whatsoever, thereby destroying the possibility of replication and long-term follow-up.

The Springdale case serves as a classic example of the potential consequences that can result when attempts to safeguard the anonymity of subjects in published reports are insufficient. When participants can recognize themselves in embarrassing or compromising descriptions in print, resulting negative effects may include a reduction in self-esteem and loss of confidence in the scientific process.

Preventing the misuse of research results

The final issue to be considered with regard to the communication of research findings has to do with the responsibilities of behavioral scientists to protect against the misuse of scientific knowledge derived from their studies. There is always the possibility that misunderstanding, incompetence, or vested interests will result in the improper use of research results by other researchers, business enterprises, politicians, the media, or other individuals. Thus, special care must be taken when publicizing one's research to state conditions pertinent to its usefulness in both theoretical and applied contexts. Of course, simply stating the conditions of application and urging extreme caution in terms that even nonscientists can understand will not always guarantee that research results will be properly used.

Some illustrations of how the misuse of research results can arise were provided by psychologist Stuart Cook (see Judd et al., 1991). One example involves misguided attempts to explain interracial group differences based on studies comparing the achievement test scores of blacks and whites. A beneficial outcome of such comparisons has been to stimulate a search for the causes and remedies of the documented inadequacies in the achievement of lower-class black children. However, some social scientists have warned of the inherent dangers of such research by suggesting that whites may inevitably interpret the results as indicative of inherited black inferiority, without considering numerous other explanations. Such an interpretation could then be used to support segregation and other racially discriminatory social policies. The heated debate that has ensued over publications pertaining to the decline of intelligence test scores, such as Herrnstein and Murray's *The Bell Curve* (1994) and Rushton's *Race, Evolution, and Behavior* (1994), has given rise to similar concerns about the consequences of research on group differences.

As another example of the potential misuse of research, Cook pointed to research conducted on participative decision making in industrial and organizational settings. From this research various factors, such as participation in job-related decision making, have been linked to an increase in worker morale and job satisfaction. There are fears, however, that applications of this research in the development of new management approaches and leadership styles might result in the exploitation of workers. Given that improved morale is sometimes accompanied by an increase in worker productivity, employers could use the research in order to maximize company profits and to increase worker resistance to unionization.

As these two examples suggest, research results can be misinterpreted and used for purposes contrary to the investigator's intentions. Although it appears that many behavioral scientists now feel a greater ethical responsibility than in the past for the knowledge they produce, there is disagreement in the scientific community about the extent of that responsibility and the degree to which researchers should actively promote the utilization of their research findings. While some researchers believe the best they can do to prevent possible misuse is to anticipate likely misinterpretations and to counter them in their published reports, others choose to more actively oppose apparent misapplications of their work. Most behavioral scientists likely would agree that investigators should be held responsible for the adverse effects that result when they fail to inform decision makers of known negative consequences that can accompany application (Reynolds, 1979). The decision not to conduct research because of fears that the findings will be misused is likely to be an unsatisfactory one because of the possible loss of important research benefits (Haywood, 1976).

In recent years, researchers have found it necessary to improve their skills for interacting with journalists so that their research can more thoroughly and accurately be presented to the public through the mass media. Because of extensive public interest in topics and issues that often provide the focus of behavioral science investigations, researchers have increasingly been called on to communicate through mass media channels, including newspapers and magazines ranging from national papers to local weeklies, and radio and television shows that vary from science and public affairs programs to audience call-in shows (in the latter of which the intent may be to have the scientist serve as little more than a scapegoat for public dissection). Some excellent advice is available to scientists interested in sharing their research and knowledge with the public via the mass media. For the interested reader, the following publications are highly recommended: Gastel's *Presenting Science to the Public* (1983), Goldstein's *Handbook for Science Communication* (1986), Miller's *The Scientist's Responsibility for Public Information* (1979), and the quarterly journal *Science Communication*.

SUMMARY

Although the major focus of this chapter has been placed on the problems inherent in the scientific peer review system, this should not be interpreted as suggesting that the review process is so seriously flawed that it does not effectively provide protections against unethical conduct in the behavioral (and other) sciences. In fact, the general consensus among those who have carefully assessed the peer review system in science is that it appears to work quite well in most cases (cf. Altman, 1989; Fogg and Fiske, 1993; Gillespie, 1999). However, like most complex systems, peer review – whether it involves ethics committees, journal editors, research referees, or colleagues – is imperfect and, consequently, mistakes are made. Further investigations are necessary to clarify the impact of ethical guidelines and institutional review on research practice and participant behavior, including whether behavioral scientists have begun to eschew the pursuit of certain research questions for fear that their research proposals never would be approved by an institutional review board. Additionally, review board members need to be sufficiently trained and sensitized about the complex methodological issues inherent in the conduct of rigorous research and about the hazards of imposing unreasonable restrictions on researchers (Colombo, 1995).

In recent years, apparent deficiencies in the approaches taken to protect the rights of research participants and the integrity of science have prompted attempts to ameliorate identifiable flaws within the peer review system. Steps have been taken by institutions to promote responsible research and to evaluate investigations of misconduct; academic departments and granting agencies have been encouraged to adopt new decision-making policies that emphasize the quality of a researcher's work, rather than quantity; and scientific journals have begun to institute policies intended to promote responsible authorship practices.

These developments are typical of ongoing ethical progress in the behavioral sciences. Whenever ethical sensitivities have been raised as a result of an increased attention to moral issues within society or because of publicized research abuses, many positive changes within the scientific disciplines have been sure to follow. Yet one cannot expect too much from the further development of mechanisms for promoting and monitoring the ethicality of behavioral scientists, so long as there are researchers who deem it fit to place personal ambitions before scientific truth. Despite the progress that has been made to improve the process of peer review and the regulation of behavioral research, the burden of responsibility for ethical conduct continues to rest squarely on the shoulders of researchers themselves.

Appendix 1

Annotated List of Web Links to Ethics Codes

1 American Psychological Association

Ethical principles of psychologists and code of conduct (2002)

Web link: www.apa.org/ethics/code2002.html *or* www.apa.org/ethics/code2002.pdf
In addition to its overriding preamble and set of five general principles, the specific ethical standards that are most relevant to the conduct of research with human participants appear in Section 1 (Resolving Ethical Issues), Section 4 (Privacy and Confidentiality) and Section 8 (Research and Publication).
   Web link: www.apa.org/ethics

This APA website provides further details about the code and its history of development.
   Web link: www.apa.org/ethics/codecompare.html

This APA website provides links to detailed comparisons of the 1992 and 2002 versions of the association's ethics code.

Guidelines for Ethical Conduct in the Care and Use of Animals (2002)

Web link: www.apa.org/science/anguide.html
   This site, which is maintained by the APA Board of Scientific Affairs, Committee on Animal Research and Ethics (CARE), provides the current APA guidelines for conducting research on animals.

2 British Psychological Society

Ethical Principles for Conducting Research with Human Participants (2004)

Web link: www.bps.org.uk/the-society/ethics-rules-charter-code-of-conduct/code-of-conduct/ethical-principles-for-conducting-research-with-human-participants.cfm

This site provides a revised set of principles for human subject research, a central component of the BPS *Code of Conduct*. (Further discussion of these principles appears in appendix 2.) Also available on this site are links to other BPS web pages detailing ethical codification by the society.

3   American Sociological Association

Ethical Principles for Conducting Research with Human Participants (1999)

Web link: www.asanet.org/galleries/default-file/Code%20of%20Ethics.pdf

This ASA site provides the generic ethics code for American sociologists, which served as the model for development of the British Sociological Association's *Statement of Ethical Practice* (www.socresonline.org.uk/info/ethguide.html). Ethical standards pertinent to research activities are found in Sections 11 (Confidentiality), 12 (Informed Consent), and 13 (Research Planning, Implementation, and Dissemination).

4   American Anthropological Association

Code of Ethics of the American Anthropological Association (1998)

Web link: www.aaanet.org/committees/ethics/ethcode.htm

This AAA site provides the most recent version of the ethics code for American anthropologists. Responsibilities governing the conduct of anthropological research are detailed in Section III (Research).

5   American Counseling Association

ACA Code of Ethics and Standards of Practice (2002)

Web link: www.counseling.org/resources/codeOfEthics/TP/Home/CT2.aspx

Because the ACA is primarily a service-oriented association, its ethics code has limited guidelines for the conduct of research (Section B.5. Research and Training), but extensively details responsibilities for protecting confidentiality (Section B), in terms of right to privacy (Section B.1) and the maintenance of records (Section B.4). Research guidelines related to testing appear in Section E (Evaluation, Assessment, and Interpretation).

6   National Association of Social Workers

Code of Ethics of the National Association of Social Workers (2005)

Web link: www.socialworkers.org/pubs/code/code.asp

Revised in 1999, the NASW ethics code provides a set of 16 specific research guidelines in Section 5.02 (Evaluation and Research). Other general sections of the ethics code, including Competence (Section 1.04), Informed Consent (Section 1.03), and Privacy and Confidentiality (Section 1.07), also are relevant to research activities.

7   International Chamber of Commerce and the European Society for Opinion and Marketing Research

ICC/ESOMAR International Code of Marketing and Social Research Practice (1986)

Web link: www.esomar.org/web/show/id=43240

This code of ethics, jointly developed by two European bodies, represents an international code for the conduct of marketing and opinion research. Extensive principles (in the form of "rules") detailing the rights of respondents appear in Section B and professional responsibilities of researchers comprise Section C of the code. Specific notes on applying the code were added in 2001 and can also be found at this site.

8   American Association for Public Opinion Research

Code of Professional Ethics and Practices of the American Association for Public Opinion Research (2002)

Web link: www.aapor.org/default.asp?page=about_aapor/bylaws_article9

AAPOR's code of ethics provides a set of four general guidelines for survey research and details standards for minimal disclosure (Section III).

9   Council of American Survey Research Organizations

CASRO Code of Standards and Ethics for Survey Research (2004)

Web link: www.casro.org/codeofstandards.cfm

CASRO's ethics code is intended to apply to researchers working in association with survey research organizations. It includes major sections on responsibilities to respondents (including standards on confidentiality, privacy, and Internet research), clients, the public, and ouside contractors and interviewers. CASRO members also have access to an addendum providing standards pertaining to disclosure of respondents and identifiable data to clients.

10   Center for the Study of Ethics in the Professions

Codes of Ethics Online

Web link: www.iit.edu/departments/csep/codes/codes_index.html

This site is maintained by the Center for the Study of Ethics in the Professions at the Illinois Institute of Technology. This specific web page provides links to ethics codes in 24 professional areas (such as communication, engineering, management, and science) and is regularly updated and expanded.

11   Ethics Codes and Practice Guidelines for Assessment, Therapy, Counseling, and Forensic Practice

Web link: http://kspope.com/ethcodes/index.php

This site presents links to online ethics (and practice) codes for therapy, counseling, and forensic activities developed by professional organizations (e.g. of psychologists, psychiatrists, social workers, marriage and family counselors).

12   Office for Human Research Protections (OHRP, United States Department of Health and Human Services)

Web link: www.hhs.gov/ohrp/

This site provides an extensive directory of links relevant to US federal policies on the conduct of research, including sites for IRB registration, the Belmont Report, current federal research regulations, and international ethics codes and regulatory standards.

13   Europa: Science and Society in Europe

Web link: cordis.europa.eu/science-society//ethics.htm

This website is maintained by Europa (http://europa.eu.int/), a portal site providing up-to-date information about developments in the European Union, including the status of proposed and pending legislation. This site includes numerous links to European ethical legislation and conventions and is intended to "guide researchers towards the most important reference texts in the area of ethics in research." Included among the links are those for the Charter of Fundamental Rights of the European Union (see appendix 2, this volume), universal declarations of the United Nations, opinions on the ethics of research activities, and some examples of codes of conduct. Although many of the linked texts focus on biomedical issues, the site is useful for identifying key research issues in the European community.

14   The Markkula Center for Applied Ethics

Web link: www.scu.edu/ethics/

The Markkula Center for Applied Ethics at Santa Clara University is a leading center for coverage and debate regarding a broad range of ethical issues. This site provides links to several informative articles, cases, briefings, and dialogue that are likely to be of use to the applied researcher. Especially recommended is the link to "decision making," which offers a variety of documents that can assist the researcher in applying ethical guidelines and standards, such as a "framework for ethical decision making" and "calculating consequences."

15   The Institute of Business Ethics: Frequently Asked Questions

Web link: www.ibe.org.uk/faq2.htm

This Institute of Business Ethics web page is invaluable for the applied researcher working within the context of a business setting. It provides links in response to such questions as "How might companies go about producing a code?," "How does an ethical code differ from a code of conduct?," and "What might a code look like?" Although not specifically focused on research issues, these links are useful for ethical codification in applied settings and for better understanding issues at the heart of ethical decision making.

Appendix 2

Psychology Codes of Ethics: An International Survey

Discussions of ethical issues in psychological research have largely been limited to conferences and publications in scientific journals within the United States and other English-speaking nations. Only within recent decades has an interest in these issues begun to emerge in other parts of the world. In 1977 German psychologist Heinz Schuler surveyed a number of the professional organizations for psychology around the world and obtained information about the existence of ethical codes in nine nations, including the United States, Canada, the Federal Republic of Germany, Great Britain, the Netherlands, Poland, Austria, Sweden, and France. According to Schuler, with the exception of the American ethical code, most of the others were labeled as preliminary and in preparation for revision. However, three basic principles were identified in all of the ethical codes for psychological research: (1) protection from physical harm; (2) protection from psychological harm; and (3) confidentiality of data (Schuler, 1982).

Twenty years after Schuler's initial survey of psychology ethics codes, Leach and Harbin (1997) evaluated the ethics codes of 24 different countries and compared them with APA's 1992 version of *Ethical Principles*. Leach and Harbin recognized the likelihood that certain values reflected by the codes' principles and standards would be revealed as consistently important to psychologists in various countries, whereas others would be more unique to particular cultures. For example, although the APA code emphasizes autonomy and individualism as core values, consistent with the importance of these values in American culture, many other regions of the world embrace collectivism as a core cultural value.

Using a systematic approach that compared the specific standards within each code, Leach and Harbin found that Canada's code of ethics was most similar to APA's. In fact, the psychology ethics codes of Canada, Israel, and South Africa shared 100 percent of their general principles (e.g. competence, integrity, concern for human welfare, social responsibility) with the American code. China's code was the most dissimilar, largely because it applied primarily to testing and assessment. Fewer than half of the codes included research standards similar to those appearing in the APA code on institutional approval (32 percent), offering inducements for research participants (21 percent), minimizing invasiveness (11 percent), and providing participants with information about the study (42 percent). However, a majority of the codes similarly addressed such central research standards as informed consent (84 percent), deception (53 percent), planning research (68 percent), and care and use of animals in research (63 percent). Leach and Harbin concluded, consistent with their expectations, that these patterns of similarities and differences among psychology ethics codes are indicative of the different values within the countries surveyed.

For the first edition of this volume, the author conducted an informal follow-up survey of international ethics codes by obtaining the current codes of professional conduct from the following countries included in Schuler's 1977 review: Canada (Canadian Psychological Association, 1991), Great Britain (the British Psychological Society, 1995a), Germany (German Association of Professional Psychologists, 1986), France (French Psychological Society, 1976), the Netherlands (Netherlands Institute of Psychologists, 1988), and the United States (American Psychological Association, 1992). Additionally, codes were obtained from the Australian Psychological Society (1986), the General Assembly for the Scandinavian Psychological Associations (1989), the Psychological Association of Slovenia (1982), the Spanish Psicólogo (Colegio Oficial de Psicólogos, 1993), and the Swiss Federation of Psychologists (Fédération Suisse des Psychologues, 1991). In most cases, it was apparent that the surveyed codes were generic in nature and provided the standards of conduct for psychologists engaged in a variety of professional activities in addition to research, such as consulting and therapy.

A summary of the content of the codes, updated for the current edition, is presented below, focusing especially on the research principles contained within them. One obvious development since the first edition is that several of the codes are now available to the public online.

United States

The activities of the APA in promulgating an ethics code for American psychologists are described at length in chapter 2. That chapter provides a description of the current APA research principles (APA, 2002) and the process by which they were developed. Much attention is given to the APA principles in this text because they have served to a great extent as a model upon which other ethical codes are based.

It should be noted that another important American psychological association, the Association for Psychological Science (APS), chose not to draft a separate code of ethics for its members. This decision was largely based on considerations regarding an enforcement mechanism that would need to be developed as part of a code and the possibility of lawsuits stemming from judgments pertaining to ethical conduct (A. G. Kraut, personal communication, December 8, 1994). In lieu of a formal ethics code, the APS Board of Directors approved the following brief, general statement of principle that is consistent with the society's interests in scientific and personal integrity: "The Board of Directors expects APS members to adhere to all relevant codes of ethical behavior and legal and regulatory requirements."

Australia

The current *Code of Ethics* of the Australian Psychological Society (2005) was adopted in October 1997 and represents the most recent revision of an original code dating back to 1968 (previously known as *Code of Professional Conduct*). Several amendments to the 1997 standards were approved in October 1999 and September 2002. The code sets forth three general principles intended to safeguard the integrity of the profession and the welfare of consumers of Australian psychological services. The principles pertain to (1) responsibility (involving the consequences of professional decisions), (2) competence (in the activities that individual psychologists choose to undertake), and (3) propriety (with regard to the treatment of clients, students, and research participants). In essence, the three Australian principles are akin to the 2002 APA *Principles,* in that they represent unenforceable ideals of the profession. The generic principles are followed by sections providing specific applications in the areas of assessment procedures, consulting relationships, teaching of psychology, supervision and training, research, reporting and publication of research results, public statements, and professional relationships.

Section E of the Australian code contains 18 statements for human subject and animal research, representing a significant expansion of the 11 research principles in the previous (APS, 1986) code. The similarity of these statements to previous versions of the APA research guidelines is striking. Responsibility is placed on the investigator for carefully evaluating the ethicality of a planned study; protection of research participants from psychological risks and disclosures of confidential data is emphasized; and the necessity to obtain participants' voluntary informed consent and to debrief them at appropriate stages of the investigation are included as essential elements of ethical conduct. Among the standards appearing for the first time in the code are those intended to protect against undue coercion of participants. Other new standards require researchers to provide participants with information on services to alleviate any adverse distress resulting from research involvement, and participants to be given the opportunity to obtain information about the study following its conclusion. Researchers also are now required to consult with colleagues and ethics committees prior to deciding that an investigation does not require the written informed consent of participants.

It should be noted that the Australian government, under the rubric of the National Health and Medical Research Council (1999), implemented a detailed national policy for the conduct of human subject research. The *National Statement on Ethical Conduct in Research Involving Humans* policy, which is available online (www7.health.gov.au/nhmrc/publications/_files/e35.pdf), has as its stated purpose "to provide a national reference point for ethical consideration relevant to all research involving humans" (p. 13). The current psychology code requires adherence to this governmental policy, and also maintains that researchers are to follow practices consistent with those outlined in a separate governmental *Statement on Animal Experimentation.*

The Australian *Code of Ethics* is available at www.psychology.org.au

Canada

The *Canadian Code of Ethics for Psychologists* was adopted by the Canadian Psychological Association (CPA) in 1986 and was revised for the first time in 1991. A third edition of the code appeared in 2000, maintaining the basic structure of the earlier editions with minor wording changes throughout. A *Companion Manual* consisting of a variety of materials to assist in the interpretation and application of the code first appeared in 1988; its third edition was published in 2001. The development of the code began during the late 1970s in response to a growing interest among various Canadian groups in having an ethics code that reflected the realities of the nation's research culture (Sinclair et al., 1987). Prior to 1977, Canadian psychologists were expected to adhere to the APA standards for American psychologists, which were adopted with minor changes in wording. The Canadian code was intended, in large part, to further establish the identity of Canadian psychology as a profession and to provide a statement of moral principle for assisting the profession in meeting its responsibilities and for guiding the individual in resolving ethical dilemmas.

A novel approach was utilized to develop the Canadian code. The process began with a careful examination of the 1977 version (and later revisions) of the APA code by a standing CPA committee. Thirty-seven hypothetical ethical dilemmas representing the applied, teaching, and research functions of psychologists then were developed. The dilemmas were used not only to explore how a representative group of CPA members would have responded in the hypothetical situations, but also to gauge the reasoning and ethical principles used in their decision making. Although this approach contrasts with that utilized by the APA, in which psychologists were asked to identify ethical dilemmas they actually had encountered in their research activities, the hypothetical dilemmas were intended to reflect all of the APA ethical principles in place at that time. Of the 125 Canadian psychologists sampled, 59 respondents completed questionnaires that included between two to four of the hypothetical cases. The rationales that were provided for selected courses of action were content analyzed and subsequently categorized into groups of statements representing specific superordinate principles. On this basis, a resulting document emerged containing ethical standards organized around four ethical principles used most consistently by the respondents to resolve the hypothetical dilemmas: (I) respect for the dignity of persons; (II) responsible caring; (III) integrity in relationships; and (IV) responsibility to society. To a large extent, the approach taken in developing the CPA code resulted in clearly articulated principles, values, and standards that constitute a "best practice" model, as opposed to one emphasizing rules, regulations, and proscriptions (Stark, 1998).

The principles are ordered according to the weight each should be given when they conflict, with the highest weight generally given to principle I, "Respect for the dignity of persons," because of its emphasis on individual moral rights, and the lowest weight to principle IV, "Responsibility to society." In other words, although it is assumed that psychologists have a responsibility to work for the benefit of society in ways that do not violate individual rights, when individual welfare conflicts with benefits to society the former is to bear greater ethical weight in decision making. The validity of this hierarchical structure itself has been the subject of research scrutiny, with generally favorable results (Malloy et al., 2002).

Each of the code's four principles is followed by a detailed values statement that serves to give definition to the principle. For example, the statement corresponding to principle I ("Respect for the dignity of persons") emphasizes the responsibility of psychologists to "Respect the dignity of all persons with whom they come in contact in their role as psychologists," especially those in vulnerable positions, such as research participants, clients, and students. A list of specific ethical standards follows each values statement. The standards, which were developed on the basis of an extensive review of ethical codes from other countries and the psychological literature pertaining to ethical guidelines, are intended to illustrate how the principles and values can be applied to the activities of psychologists.

Specific ethical guidelines pertinent to research conduct appear throughout the Canadian code as standards associated with each of the four superordinate ethical principles. Listed under the principle of respect for the dignity of persons are informed consent, freedom of consent, protections for vulnerable persons, privacy, and confidentiality. Standards pertaining to risk–benefit analysis, maximizing benefits, minimizing harm, offsetting/correcting harm, and the care of animals are associated with the principle of responsible caring. The principle of integrity in relationships includes standards pertaining to accuracy/honesty, objectivity/lack of bias, avoidance of incomplete disclosure, and avoidance of conflict of interest. The principle of responsibility to society includes standards associated with the development of knowledge. Some examples of these research-related principles appear in Box A2.1.

   The *Companion Manual* is a comprehensive guide that was developed to assist users of the CPA ethics code. The 2001 manual describes how the code was developed, and provides a running interpretive commentary, followed by a discussion of how the principles and standards might be applied to resolve ethical dilemmas. In the latter section it is suggested that ethical decision making can occur on three levels: (1) ethical behavior that is virtually automatic (that is, ethical decisions that may not appear as such to the decision maker, such as the routine preparation of consent forms); (2) choices that can be made relatively easily by reference to the code (in situations in which training and experience have not

---

Box A2.1   *The Canadian Code of Ethics for Psychologists*: examples of research-related standards

PRINCIPLE I: RESPECT FOR THE DIGNITY OF PERSONS

In adhering to the Principle of Respect for the Dignity of Persons, psychologists would:

Informed Consent

I.17   Recognize that informed consent is the result of a process of reaching an agreement to work collaboratively, rather than of simply having a consent form signed.

I.20   Obtain informed consent for all research activities that involve obtrusive measures, invasion of privacy, more than minimal risk of harm, or any attempt to change the behaviour of research participants.

I.23   Provide, in obtaining informed consent, as much information as reasonable or prudent persons would want to know before making a decision or consenting to the activity. The psychologist would relay this information in language that the persons understand (including providing translation into another language, if necessary) and would take whatever reasonable steps are needed to ensure that the information was, in fact, understood.

Privacy

I.39   Record only that private information necessary for the provision of continuous, coordinated service, or for the goals of the particular research study being conducted, or that is required or justified by law.

Source: Canadian Psychological Association (2000). *Canadian Code of Ethics for Psychologists* (3rd ed.). Ottawa, Ontario.

Table A2.1   *The Canadian Code of Ethics for Psychologists*: steps for ethical decision making

Identification of the individuals and groups potentially affected by the decision

Identification of ethically relevant issues and practices, including the interests, rights, and any relevant characteristics of the individuals and groups involved and of the system or circumstances in which the ethical problem arose.

Consideration of how personal biases, stresses, or self-interest might influence the development of or choice between courses of action.

Development of alternative courses of action.

Analysis of likely short-term, ongoing, and long-term risks and benefits of each course of action on the individual(s)/group(s) involved or likely to be affected (e.g. client, client's family or employees, employing institution, students, research participants, colleagues, the discipline, society, self).

Choice of course of action after conscientious application of existing principles, values, and standards.

Action, with a commitment to assume responsibility for the consequences of the action.

Evaluation of the results of the course of action.

Assumption of responsibility for consequences of action, including correction of negative consequences, if any, or re-engaging in the decision-making process if the ethical issue is not resolved.

Appropriate action, as warranted and feasible, to prevent future occurrences of the dilemma (e.g., communication and problem solving with colleagues; changes in procedures and practices).

Source: Canadian Psychological Association (2000). *Canadian Code of Ethics for Psychologists* (3rd ed.). Ottawa, Ontario.

fully prepared the psychologist, as when a researcher needs to know the elements that constitute adequate informed consent); and (3) dilemmas in which ethical principles seem to conflict (the most difficult situations for which there is no specific standard to guide resolution of the dilemma). Suggestions as to how one might go about resolving difficult ethical dilemmas are provided in the context of a discussion of ten steps for ethical decision making, which appear in the code's preamble (see Table A2.1).

The manual also includes an extensive bibliography on ethics, a set of vignettes of ethical dilemmas, and additional guidelines applied to the use of animals in research, instruction in psychology, and other areas of conduct. The CPA *Companion Manual* may well be the most comprehensive guide for ethical conduct in psychology in existence today.

France

A document entitled *Code de Déontologie des Psychologues* was adopted by the French Psychological Society (Société Française de Psychologie, or SFP) in May 1961, which was applicable to all members of the Society as a code of professional conduct. A new version of the code was ratified in June 1996, following extensive revisions by the SFP, in conjunction with two other French psychology groups, the AEPU (Psychology Association of Professors) and the ANOP (National Association of the Organizations of Psychologists). The code is organized by a preamble and three general "titles": (1) general principles, (2) psychological practice, and (3) training of the psychologist. The initial title presents seven general principles of ethical conduct, including respect for individual rights, competence, responsibility, integrity, and the like. The other two titles are organized according to "chapters" and "articles." Overall, there are 35 articles, which may be considered as specific ethical standards.

An examination of the French code reveals little attention devoted to the conduct of research or specific research principles such as informed consent and debriefing. Instead, emphasis is placed on the fundamental rights of individuals with whom psychologists interact in their helping functions. Also recognized are the basic rights of the psychologist to engage in professional activities, while taking care not to exceed the professional boundaries as defined by current knowledge in the field. To a large extent, the current French code appears to exist primarily to clarify the responsibilities, activities, and necessary training for members of the profession. The principles, although reflecting a greater interest among French psychologists in clinical practice rather than human subject research, are general enough to apply broadly to both practical and scientific endeavors and at least serve to sensitize psychologists to the importance of moral conduct as they engage in their professional activities.

The online version of the current French deontological code of ethics (www.sfpsy.org/index.htm) provides a link to guidelines focusing specifically on the conduct of research, developed by the CERPP (Centre d'Etudes et de Recherche en Psychopathologie). The CERPP site provides four informative links for the researcher: (1) preparing a research thesis, (2) a guide for scientific communication, (3) a model consent form for research participants, and (4) legal standards for professional secrecy.

The situation for French psychologists is somewhat complicated by the fact that research is now covered by French law for medical research (e.g. the recently revised *Code de la Santé Publique*). As a result, researchers are more apt to consult current legal standards than the deontological code of their profession. Prior to the appearance of the current psychology code, some French psychologists began to give greater attention to ethical issues in the conduct of psychological experimentation and the need for more specific ethical principles to guide research psychologists (e.g. Beauvois et al., 1990). Although the new code includes more specific ethical principles pertinent to psychological activity and training, it nonetheless lacks specific guidelines for research conduct.

Germany

The previous code of ethics for German psychologists came into force in 1986 following a three-year period of development by an ethics commission headed by Heinz Schuler. (A new edition with minor revisions was published in 1989.) The previous code, *Professional Obligations for Psychologists*, had been in place since 1967. Like its predecessors, the 1986 *Professional Code of Ethics for Psychologists* was modeled after the APA ethical principles. In addition to including a generic set of ethical principles, the German code of ethics also contained interpretations of a number of statutory requirements affecting German psychologists, such as the Pharmaceutical Publicity Law (which prohibits clinical psychologists from advertising), the "duty of silence" (i.e. professional secrecy), and the adoption of professional titles.

The current code for German psychologists, *Ethical Principles*, was jointly developed by the German Psychological Society (DGP) and the Association of German Professional Psychologists (BDP) (available: www.bdp-verband.org/bdp/verband/clips/ethic.pdf). It was adopted in April 1999 and supersedes the 1987 code. The code is organized into five main sections, including a preamble, which describes in general terms the psychologist's obligation to the profession, responsibility to those who place trust in their professional competencies, and the necessity to maintain competence by keeping informed of developments in the field. The principles that most closely pertain to research appear in the section on "psychology in research and training" (Section C) and are grouped into five subsections: (1) freedom of science and responsibilities to society, (2) principles guiding good scientific practice, (3) principles guiding research with human participants, (4) animals in research and training, and (5) publication of research results. (A sixth subsection pertains to teaching, supervision, and professional development.)

Although broadly stated and accompanied by only a few illustrative examples, the principles address most of the important issues that emerge in the conduct of psychological research with human subjects. The research principles underscore the fact that researchers have a basic right (consistent with the German constitution) to free scientific inquiry, although that right bears certain personal responsibilities, such as the assurance that studies are carried out in compliance with rigorous methodological procedures, a willingness to correct one's errors, and openness to the research achievements of those holding contrary views or beliefs.

In terms of specific research procedures, the principles listed reflect familiar concerns: the researcher's responsibility to subjects, including the obligation not to threaten the dignity and integrity of participants; the necessity to take special precautions when subjects are vulnerable, unable to take responsibility for their own actions, or else placed in a research situation that reduces their ability to act responsibly; the need to guarantee the safety and welfare of research participants and to eliminate the risk of harm to the greatest possible extent; and the requirement that participation in research is based on voluntary informed consent. Voluntary participation is described as requiring the use of language that is reasonably understandable during the consent process, especially regarding research objectives and procedural details (e.g. discomforts or risks that might be associated with participation). Interestingly, the standards require participants to be informed about concealed observers. The code recognizes that there may be "exceptional cases" in which the provision of comprehensive information about the study might jeopardize research objectives. In such cases, researchers are obliged to inform participants as to why complete information cannot be provided at the outset, fully debrief them at the study's conclusion, and take special measures to ensure that they are not endangered by participation. Additional guidelines clarify consent procedures in situations where people are unable to provide full consent themselves.

Another major development in the 1999 code is the expansion of guidelines for the use of animals in research. Six principles are included for animal research, which collectively emphasize the importance of limiting animal research to psychologists who have extensive expertise in experimentation with animals, legal knowledge of the issues involved in animal care, a high degree of sensitivity to ethical issues, and special knowledge as to how to reduce the discomfort, pain, and suffering of animal subjects. Researchers also are required to follow the strictures of animal welfare legislation, as issued by the Senate Commission for Animal Research of the German Society for the Promotion of Research (*Deutsche Forschungsgemeinschaft*).

Great Britain

The British Psychological Society's (BPS) 1992 *Code of Conduct*, in contrast to the ethical codes considered thus far, is unique in the sense that it gives primary attention to research (BPS, 1995a). The first section of the code consists of a set of general principles of conduct in professional practice, covering issues related to competence, the obtaining of consent, confidentiality, and personal conduct. Other sections of the code provide guidelines for the use of non-sexist language, the advertising of psychological services, and the use of professional titles.

The remainder of the code is comprised of standards for the ethical conduct of human and animal research. The Society's "Ethical principles for conducting research with human participants" and "Guidelines for the use of animals in research" appear as two separate sections (www.bps.org.uk). The 15 animal research guidelines were jointly proposed by the Scientific Affairs Board of the BPS and the Committee of the Experimental Psychology Society, having been based on guidelines previously developed by two British animal behavior societies. The animal guidelines, in place since 1985 and recently revised, are discussed in chapter 9 of this volume.

The current principles for human research are a result of the first major revision of the 1978 "Ethical principles." The revision was carried out by a BPS Standing Committee on Ethics in Research with Human Participants and was formally adopted in October 1992. Guiding the Committee during its revision was the recognition that psychologists owe a debt to the individuals who participate in research and that in return those participants should expect to be "treated with the highest standards of consideration and respect."

The issues of deception, debriefing, and risk were of primary concern during the revision process. While acknowledging that many persons view the use of research deception as inappropriate conduct, it was recognized that many psychological processes could not be studied if individuals were fully aware of the research hypothesis. In its attempt to resolve this issue, the Committee distinguished between withholding some details of the research hypothesis and deliberately providing false information to research participants. It was concluded that researchers should attempt to provide as much information as possible to participants and that if deception must be used, the true test of its appropriateness should be the reaction of participants once the deception was revealed to them. The importance of debriefing research participants also was emphasized, especially in cases in which information has been withheld or falsely provided.

Concerning risk, it was recognized that participants must be protected from undue risk, but that to prohibit all research involving risk would serve to make much important research impossible. Thus, the Committee chose to define "undue risk" as varying from the risks that individuals are apt to encounter in their normal lives. This decision was intended to reduce the likelihood that individuals would be induced to take part in research involving greater risks than those normally encountered in their everyday lives.

These considerations are reflected in the "Ethical principles" document, where principles are organized into the following sections: (1) introduction; (2) general; (3) consent; (4) deception; (5) debriefing; (6) withdrawal from the investigation; (7) confidentiality; (8) protection of participants; (9) observational research; (10) giving advice; and (11) colleagues. Each section consists of one ("Colleagues") to nine ("Consent") statements clarifying appropriate conduct. For example, statement 4.2 pertains to proper conduct regarding the use of deliberate deception:

> Intentional deception of the participants over the purpose and general nature of the investigation should be avoided whenever possible. Participants should never be deliberately misled without extremely strong scientific or medical justification. Even then there should be strict controls and the disinterested approval of independent advisors.

As is apparent in this principle, investigators are urged to consult with others when they are unclear as to the appropriate course of conduct in their research endeavors.

Although the 1992 principles to date have not been amended by any subsequent review (personal communication, Felicity Hector, August 31, 2005), a more recent document describing best practice for research governance in psychological research was issued by the BPS Research Board Working Party on Ethical Principles in Psychological Research (BPS, 2004). Recognizing that a majority of human subject research in psychology in the UK is conducted in academic settings, the policy is written with the university psychology department in mind, although the guidelines are meant to be applicable to all research contexts. The guidelines were developed in part through the solicitation of advice from UK psychology departments about ethical issues that should be addressed. The Working Party also drew on the 1992 BPS ethical standards, and guidelines established by other sources, such as European legislation and the UK National Health Service.

At the heart of the Working Party guidelines is a set of 12 general principles, which clarify that all university staff and students must receive prior approval for all research, including studies that do not involve face-to-face interactions with participants (such as mail questionnaires and Internet surveys) and student laboratory/practical exercises. The principles emphasize the importance of adhering to procedures that protect participants from harm, preserve their dignity and rights, safeguard their confidentiality and anonymity, and guarantee voluntary informed consent to research as described in the 1992 BPS human participant guidelines. Additional recommendations are provided for obtaining informed consent. The remainder of the Working Party document details the various available routes for ethical approval (e.g. departmental ethics committee, institutional ethics committees, and external review committees), and provides an exemplar of a psychology department ethical approval form as an optional means for implementing the guidelines (see appendix 3, this volume).

The Netherlands

The Dutch *Code of Ethics* (1998) has a long history behind it, dating back to 1957 when work first began on a professional code. An initial code was accepted in 1960 and underwent minor adjustment in 1976. A completely revised third code was enacted in 1988 as the *Professional Code for Psychologists* of the Netherlands Institute for Psychologists (Nederlands Instituut voor Psychologen, NIP). The current 1998 code was radically reorganized and revised in recognition of legal and professional developments and apparent drawbacks to the structure of the previous code (NIP, 1998). The 1998 code is intended to apply to all psychologists in the Netherlands, including one-third of the practicing psychologists who are not members of the NIP. (Professional sanctions are only possible in the case of psychologists who are members of the NIP.)

As in previous versions, the code is primarily oriented to ethical issues relating to professional practice, although the guidelines are intended to apply to all professional relationships involving treatment, research, advice, or counseling. The code is comprised of a preamble, describing the researcher's personal responsibility to weigh ethical considerations in the conduct of professional activity, including codified principles that may at times conflict. The recognition that the principles are not binding is clarified in the following statement, which appears in the code's general section:

> The psychologist who has valid reason to deviate from the stipulations of the professional code, will, prior to proceeding, thoroughly justify his decision and obtain

expert advice from a colleague who is not directly involved in the professional relationship. His justification demonstrates that although his actions may be contrary to the stipulations of the Code of Ethics, they are concordant with the spirit of the code and were the outcome of thorough deliberation. (Principle I.4.2)

Following the preamble, the code is structured into three major sections: (1) a general section consisting of definition of terms, general stipulations, and exceptional circumstances; (2) a statement of four basic principles (integrity, respect, competence, and responsibility); and (3) the basic principles worked out in guidelines. The third section presents a variety of guidelines for achieving the overriding principles of integrity, respect, competence, and responsibility. For example, guideline III.1.2.1 focuses on the avoidance of deception as a means for maintaining professional integrity: "The psychologist refrains from any form of deception in his professional conduct." Although guidelines such as this do not pertain specifically to research, they are stated broadly enough to apply to more than one professional activity. (In fact, the term "client" is used throughout the code to refer to any person who is the subject of research, advice, counseling, or treatment.) For example, guideline III.2.3.2, which deals with informed consent, can apply to a research, clinical, or counseling professional relationship: "The psychologist gives, prior to and during the professional relationship, information to the client in such a way that the client is able to give his well informed consent to engage in or to continue the professional relationship." Only two of the principles pertain specifically to research activities, one dealing with the collection of research data and the other with confidentiality:

III.1.2.8 Meticulousness in collecting and representing research data
The psychologist is meticulous in collecting research data and in statistically manipulating those. He is not selective in the use of relevant data and in representing and explaining of the results.

III.2.6.4 Information for purposes of scientific research and statistics
The psychologist may, upon request, disclose information to third parties for the purposes of scientific research and statistics. The psychologist ensures the anonymity of his clients when disclosing such information, unless this is impossible in view of the aims of the scientific study. In that case the information only may be given with the client's consent.

The complete NIP code is available online at www.psynip.nl.

Scandinavia

An ethics code for members of the psychological associations in the Nordic countries of Denmark, Norway, Finland, Sweden, and Iceland was approved by the General Assembly for the Scandinavian Psychological Associations in 1989. The code, *Ethical Principles for Scandinavian Psychologists*, was intended to regulate the professional activity of all Scandinavian psychologists, but is administered and interpreted separately by the psychological associations within each participating country.

A revised Nordic code was adopted in the respective Scandinavian countries during 1998 and 2000. The *Meta-Code of Ethics*, which was enacted in 1995 by the European Federation of Psychologists' Associations (EFPA; see www.cop.es/efppa/metacode.htm), was used as the basis for revising the Nordic ethical principles. The EFPA meta-code promotes four overriding ethical principles (respect for a person's rights and dignity, competence, responsibility, and integrity), and sets out specific guidelines for each of these general principles. For example, the guidelines pertinent to respect for a person's rights and dignity include the ethical concerns of privacy and confidentiality (e.g. "Adequate storage and handling of information and records, in any form to ensure confidentiality, including taking reasonable safeguards to make data anonymous when appropriate, and restricting access to reports and records to those who have a legitimate need to know") and informed consent and freedom of consent (e.g. "Clarification and continued discussion of the professional actions, procedures and probable consequences of the psychologist's actions to ensure that a client provides informed consent before and during psychological intervention"). Most pertinent to research procedures are the integrity guidelines of "straightforwardness and openness," which pertain specifically to research deception.

i) General obligation to provide information and avoid deception in research and professional practice.
ii) Obligation not to withhold information or to engage in temporary deception if there are alternative procedures available. If deception has occurred, there is an obligation to inform and re-establish trust.

The EFPA meta-code is intended to provide guidance for the content of ethics codes of association members. The composition of the revised Scandinavian code reflects the structure and spirit of the EFPA principles: it includes a preamble, which is followed by the same four general principles in the EFPA meta-code. Consistent with this structure, the code identifies the importance of confidentiality, informed consent, and avoidance of harm. Although expanding on the EFPA specific guidelines under each of the four principles, the code addresses psychological activities generally, without a specific focus on research:

> The professional ethical principles regulate psychologists' professional activity, which is defined as every situation in which the psychologist practices professional activity in relation to individuals, groups or organizations.
> The psychologist seeks to promote integrity in research, teaching and psychological practice.

Despite the fact that a common set of ethical principles has been in place for the Nordic countries since 1989, it still is the case that the way of interpreting and applying them has varied between the countries, as have the numbers of complaints and sanctions (Aanonsen, 2002).

At the time of this writing, an English version of the revised Scandinavian was unavailable online, but can be obtained on request from the Icelandic Psychological Society (www.sal.is). A Norwegian language version is available at www.psykol.no/?aid=9067069.

Slovenia

A *Code of Ethics for Psychologists* was adopted by the Slovenian Psychological Association in 1982; a revised version appeared in October 2002. The original code consisted of a list of 14 principles intended to serve as guidelines for psychologists in their theoretical and practical work. An emphasis on human dignity, democratic principles, the integrity of the human personality, and the fostering of human relations was apparent throughout the code, which was divided into sections detailing ethical principles in the professional practice of psychologists, such as "psychological aid," "competence," "confidentiality," "professional independence," and "relations with the public." Similarly, the current version of the Slovenian code stresses respect for human rights and dignity, consistent with those guaranteed by the country's democratic laws and constitution, and in accordance with the association codes included within the EFPA.

The ethical principles included in the 2002 code are classified into four main sections: respect for human rights and dignity, the competence of a psychologist, the responsibility of a psychologist, and the integrity of the profession. Although the code does not include a separate section for research, the principles most applicable to research conduct are found in the section on human rights and dignity (section 2), with that section's emphasis on the importance of protecting the rights to privacy, self-determination, and autonomy. Section 2.3 includes nine specific principles pertaining to privacy and confidentiality. For example:

> When reporting, informing, explaining or publishing anything that refers to their clients, psychologists do what is necessary to reasonably restrict the information and preserve their anonymity.

> Regardless of the client's consent psychologists may not publish information that could harm the client in any way.

Five principles dealing with informed consent and freedom of consent comprise section 2.4 of the code. Implicit within the informed consent guidelines is a qualified approach to the use of deception:

> If psychologists wish to include participants from whom they cannot ensure informed consent in their research, they are personally responsible for them. They conduct research with such participants only when it serves an important development of mankind, or when it is advantageous for the participants themselves. If possible, the inclusion of such participants should be avoided . . . If it is impossible to avoid discomfort, harm or danger in the research, psychologists refuse to participate.

Other standards in the code stress the importance of recognizing the limits of methods and procedures used; the proper use of psychodiagnostic techniques; and means for avoiding harm to clients, the profession, and the larger community. The revised code represents a significant expansion of the original code, which consisted of generally stated standards, and can be seen as reflecting the evolution of democracy within the Slovenian Republic.

English-language copies of the Slovenian ethics code are available upon request (psy@-guest.arnes.si).

Spain

The *Deontological Code of the Psychologist* (*Código Deontológico del Psicólogo*) was ratified by a governing body of the Colegio Oficial de Psicólogos in 1987 and received final approval in 1993, following further study and public comment. The Spanish code (which is unavailable in English) consists of 65 "articles" appearing within eight general areas and an introductory section. Section 4 ("De la investigacion y docencia") pertains specifically to research and teaching activities and is made up of six articles (numbers 33 to 38). The code is available online at www.colpsinavarra.org/pdf/codigo.pdf.

The first of the research articles states that an investigation should contribute to the scientific progress and be carried out and communicated in scientifically sound ways. The remaining articles in section 4 describe, respectively, the researcher's responsibility to (1) protect research participants from irreversible or permanent harm; (2) take care not to coerce persons into participating in studies involving temporary discomfort, by obtaining their informed consent and allowing them to discontinue participation at any time; (3) debrief individuals who have participated in research involving deception; (4) respect the dignity of subjects and their sense of decency or modesty, especially when the research involves the investigation of sensitive behaviors; and (5) protect research animals from unnecessary suffering, harm, and pain. Standards pertaining to the confidentiality of information obtained from others and issues of professional secrets appear among the 11 articles in section 5 ("De la obtencion y uso de la informacion"). Section 1 ("Principios generales") articles emphasize the need to protect individual rights and to respect the well-being of persons with whom Spanish psychologists interact in the performance of their professional activities. A final section of the code presents the official regulations of the Comisión Deontológica Estatal del Colegio Oficial de Psicólogos for enforcing the ethical principles and investigating charges of professional misconduct.

Switzerland

The *Deontological Code* (French version) of the Swiss Federation of Psychologists (Fédération Suisse des Psychologues, FSP) was enacted in 1991 and validated most recently in June 2002. (The code is available in French, English, and German versions at www.psychologie.ch). The basic objectives of the code, as described in a preamble, are to provide a means for protecting the public against abusive applications of psychology and to serve as a device for orienting Swiss psychologists in their professional conduct. The code's deontological principles are said to reflect the different aspects of responsibilities of professional psychology in research, teaching, and practice. The principles are divided into sections pertaining to the general responsibilities of Swiss psychologists, professional competence, professional secrets and the protection of data, the establishment of professional relationships, and the advertising of psychological services.

Although the ethical principles are stated broadly enough to be applicable to various aspects of research procedure (such as the protection of confidential information obtained from research participants), there are no specific guidelines directly referring to the conduct of research, beyond a statement that one maintains honesty ("la véracité") in research, teaching, and publishing. Following the ethical principles is a separate section composed of a set of detailed rules and regulations relative to the investigation of complaints by the Swiss Commission of the Professional Order.

In order to address the lack of specificity regarding ethical issues in the conduct of research, teaching, and publication, the Swiss Psychological Society (la Société Suisse de Psychologie, SSP), an affiliate association of the FSP, approved in 2003 a complementary set of principles to address these domains (available at www.ssp-sgp.ch). Section D of the code consists of 21 specific research guidelines, organized according to six sections: (1) methodological competence (e.g. "Psychologists do not use methods that exceed their competencies"), (2) informed consent of experimental subjects (e.g. "Participation in psychology experiments is voluntary"), (3) research deception (e.g. "To mislead an experimental subject is tolerated only when the deception is justified by the expected scientific or practical benefits and when the research objective cannot be attained from a non-deceptive alternative"), (4) debriefing (e.g. "Psychology researchers give the participants, as quickly as possible, the possibility of obtaining information on the topic, the results and the conclusions of the research project. They take care to eliminate possible misunderstandings''), (5) animal experimentation (e.g. ''Psychologists who practice experimentation on animals take care to minimize as much as possible the pains, the suffering as well as the wounds caused to the laboratory animals''), and (6) research missions and expertise (e.g. ''Before each research activity . . . psychologists inform the responsible authorities of the general conditions under which they are ready to work and on the range of their activity''). Certain elements of the SSP guidelines were taken directly from the 2002 APA code, including the components that define a fully informed consent.

Summary

This survey of psychology ethics codes from around the world revealed some similarities as well as differences (see Table A2.2). However, as Schuler (1982) cautioned in his earlier comparison, comparative surveys of ethical codes are limited by a number of considerations, including the differing structures of the codes, which make comparisons difficult; differences in the degree of specificity with which principles are formulated; and differences in the basic positions taken in the codes, with stronger emphasis placed on either research benefits or risks to research participants. Moreover, some codes are based on clearly stated principles and values, whereas others are based on rules, regulations, and proscriptions/prescriptions (J. Gauthier, 2004). Thus, care should be taken in drawing conclusions about the merits of a particular code without first referring to it directly.

One apparent commonality among the codes described here is the fact that a number have been revised or updated on a periodic basis since their initial development. In each case, the revisions tended to reflect newly emergent issues in the discipline (e.g. the rights of student participants; animal welfare), legal developments, or inadequacies noted in the earlier version(s) of the code. Separate research principles were included in most of the codes considered (the USA, Australia, Canada, Great Britain, Germany, Slovenia, Spain), but were merely implied by more broadly stated principles in other codes (France, Scandinavia, the Netherlands). Of those codes that presented research principles apart from those dealing with other professional activities, in some cases the principles were specifically stated with clarifications and examples (the USA, Australia, Canada, Great Britain), while in others they were more generally described (Slovenia, Spain). Only the American and Canadian codes included an accompanying handbook with case examples, applications, and interpretations of the research principles. Interestingly, these were the only two codes developed on the basis of an empirical approach involving members of the profession who had been asked to describe their own approaches to resolving ethical dilemmas. Thus, an empirical approach can be recommended as a critical ingredient in the formulation of specific ethical guidelines of practical use to research scientists for choosing appropriate research procedures.

Also clear from the survey is that a single European perspective on professional ethics does not yet exist, although for years it has been intended to find a common set of regulations. One problem in developing mutually acceptable ethical guidelines among nations has to do with the confounding of professional and ethical topics (Heinz Schuler, personal communication, February 3, 1993). Whereas mutual ethical principles can be formulated rather easily, it is difficult to adopt them on the professional level. This is because in the various European countries, different systems exist for scientific study and different regulatory conditions are in place for obtaining a license for professional practice.

Table A2.2 Ethical codes in psychology: a comparative summary

	USA	Australia	Canada	France	UK	Germany	Netherlands	Scandinavia	Slovenia	Spain	Switzerland[d]
First ethics code	1953	1968	1986	1961	1978	1967	1960	1989	1982	1993[c]	1991
Current revision	2002	1997[b]	2000	1996	1992	1999	1998	1998–2000	2002	NA	NA
Companion manual	Yes[a]	No	Yes	No	No	No	No	No	No	No	No
Empirically based	Yes	No	Yes	No	No	No	No	No	No	No	No
Separate research principles	Yes	Yes	Yes	No	Yes	Yes	No	No	No	Yes	No
Steps or guidelines for ethical decision making	Yes	Yes	Yes	No	No	No	No	Yes	No	No	No

[a] Canter et al. (1994), provides commentary on the 1992 code. See also Sales and Folkman (2000).
[b] Amended 1999, 2002.
[c] Originally ratified in 1987; final approval in 1993.
[d] FSP Code Deontologique (separate research principles included in the complementary SSP code, 2003).

However, with the emergence of the European Union, participating nations have begun to establish common guidelines for the professions. As in the case of the European Federation of Psychologists' Associations meta-code of ethics, the guidelines may serve as minimum common standards of ethical conduct, which then can be fleshed out and expanded by participating member states. One first step towards an international code is the *Charter of Professional Ethics for Psychologists*, a one-page document that briefly outlines general principles of conduct for psychologists in all of their professional activities (available at www.cop.es/efppa/charter.htm). The Charter resulted from a series of meetings involving the participation of Italy, France, Greece, Spain, Portugal, and Malta during the early 1990s. As apparent from the Scandinavian case, however, there are likely to be difficulties in having common standards interpreted and applied in the same way in different countries.

One obvious limitation to the comparison presented here is that attention was given to American and European countries, where individualism tends to be emphasized over community and collective good. Countries that emphasize a more collectivist approach are likely to have different perspectives on deception, informed consent, debriefing, the weighing of risks and benefits, privacy, confidentiality, and professional boundaries. These differences are likely to have implications for ethical codification (J. Gauthier, 2004).

As a final point, each ethics code in the current survey revealed an overriding high regard for the well-being and dignity of research participants and users of psychological services, in addition to recognizing the central values of integrity, responsibility to society, and competence. These emphases were reflected in the attention given to such topics as informed consent (and the related issue of deception), protection from harm, and privacy issues (including confidentiality) in all of the codes.

Appendix 3

Sample Research Application and Informed Consent Forms

Sample form 1: initial research submission form – request for approval (British Psychological Society)

<table>
<tr><td colspan="4">PSYCHOLOGY DEPARTMENT ETHICAL APPROVAL FORM</td></tr>
<tr><td colspan="4">Tick one box: ☐ STAFF project   ☐ POSTGRADUATE project   ☐ UNDERGRADUATE project

Title of project _____

Name of researcher(s) _____

Name of supervisor (for student research)   Date</td></tr>
</table>

		YES	NO	N/A
1	Will you describe the main experimental procedures to participants in advance, so that they are informed about what to expect?			
2	Will you tell participants that their participation is voluntary?			
3	Will you obtain written consent for participation?			
4	If the research is observational, will you ask participants for their consent being observed?			
5	Will your tell participants that they may withdraw from the research at any time and for any reason?			
6	With questionnaires, will you give participants the option of omitting questions they do not want to answer?			
7	Will you tell participants that their data will be treated with full confidentiality and that, if published, it will not be identifiable as theirs?			
8	Will you debrief participants at the end of their participation (i.e. give them a brief explanation of the sturdy)?			

If you have ticked No to any Q1-8, but have ticked box A overleaf, please give an explanation on a separate sheet. [Note: N/A = not applicable]

		YES	NO	N/A
9	Will your project involve deliberately misleading participants in any way?			
10	Is there any realistic risk of any participants experiencing either physical or psychological distress or discomfort? If Yes, give details on a separate sheet and state what you will tell them to do if they should experience any problems (e.g. who they can contact for help).			

If you have ticked Yes to 9 to 10 you should normally tick box B overleaf; if not, please give a full explanation on a separate sheet

			YES	NO	N/A
11	Does your project involve work with animals? If yes, please tick box B overleaf.				
12	Do participants fall into any of the following special groups? If they do, please refer to BPS guidelines, and tick box B overleaf. Note that you may also need to obtain satisfactory CRB clearance (or equivalent for overseas students).	School children (under 18 years of age)			
		People with learning or communication difficulties			
		Patients			
		People in custody			
		People engaged in illegal activities (e.g. drug-taking)			

There is an obligation on the lead researcher to bring to the attention of the Departmental Ethics Committee any issues with ethical implications not clearly covered by the above checklist.

Note 1. How to obtain informed consent: In order that consent be 'informed', consent forms may need to be accompanied by an information sheet for participants setting out information about the proposed study (in lay terms) along with details about the investigators and how they can be contacted. If applicable, this sheet may also make reference to any screening procedures, the confidentiality of the data, any risks involved, and any other points which participants might reasonably expect to know in order to make an informed decision about whether they wish to participate, and which are not included on the informed consent form. A checklist of points on the informed consent form that participants are expected to sign might typically include: **(a)** That their participation is

PLEASE TICK EITHER BOX A OR BOX B BELOW AND PROVIDE THE DETAILS REQUIRED IN
SUPPORT OF YOUR APPLICATION. THEN SIGN THE FORM

Please tick

A. I consider that this project has no significant e thical implications to be brought before the Departmental Ethics Committee.	
Give a brief description of participants and procedure (methods, tests used etc) in up to 150 words. *This form (and any attachments) should be submitted to the Departmental Ethics committee where it will be considered by the Chair before it can be approved.*	

B. I consider that this project may have ethical implications that should be brought before the Departmental
Ethics Committee, and/or it will be carried out with children or other vuluerable populations.

Please provide all the further information listed below in a separate attachment.

1. Title of project.

2. Purpose of project and its academic rationale.

3. Brief description of methods and measurements.

4. Participants: recruitment methods, number, age, gender, exclusion/inclusion criteria.

5. Consent and participant information arrangements, debrieling.

Please attach intended information and consent forms.

6. A clear but concise statement of the ethical considerations raised by the project and how you intend to deal
with them.

7. Estimated start date and duration of project.

This form should be submitted to the Departmental Ethics Committee for consideration.
If any of the above information is missing, your application will be returned to you.

I am familiar with the BPS Guidelines for ethical practices in psychological research (and have discussed them with
the other researchers involved in the project).

Signed ....Print Name................................. Date................
(UG or PG Researcher(s), if applicable)

Signed ....Print Name................................. Date................
(Lead Rescarcher or Supervisor)

STATEMENT OF ETHICAL APPROVAL

This project has been considered using agreed Departmental procedures and is now approved.

Signed   Print Name   Date
(Chair, Departmental Ethics Committee)

voluntary, **(b)** That they are aware of what their participation involves, **(c)** That they are aware of any potential risks (if there are any), **(d)** That all their questions concerning the study have been satisfactorily answered. Documented consent may be signed or initialled (if participants wish to maintain anonymity). In situations where information about the research and participant consent is conveyed verbally, it is recommended that the information be recorded on and read from or cued by a written information sheet; verbal consent should also be taped in order to provide a record.

[*Source:* Reprinted with permission from the British Psychological Society, Leicester, UK.]

Sample form 2:   initial research submission form – request for approval

Department of Psychology
IRB Initial Submission
Faculty Approval cover sheet

PI name: _____

Check one box: ○ Exempt   ○ Expedited review   ○ Full review

Do you wish an editorial reading before this is submitted? ○ YES ○ NO

This sheet must be attached to every NEW application to the IRB; it must be initialed and signed by a regular faculty member of the Department of Psychology. Please affirm by initialing each box that:

☐ I have read and approved this proposal. It is clearly explained and complete.

☐ The methods proposed are consistent with research in this area of psychology.

☐ Risks are minimized by the following:
_____
_____

☐ This work is likely to produce results such that the probable benefits outweigh the potential risks.

☐ Principal risks:
_____
_____

For Expedited reviews only:

☐ Risks are minimal.

For studies using the Subject Pool:

☐ This project is eligible for exempt or expedited review.

☐ There is a debriefing that provides educational value to the participants.

☐ The consent form is headed "Agreement to Participate".

If any relevant boxes are not initialed, please attach an explanation of why not.
Affirmed by:

_____   _____
signature of faculty member   *date*

_____
printed name
                              "Initial review cover sheet" August 30, 2004

[*Source:* Reprinted with permission from the Psychology Department, The University of Illinois at Chicago.]

Sample form 3: informed consent form for student research in experimental psychology

In order to ensure that your rights as a human subject are protected according to the established guidelines of the American Psychological Association, please consider the subjects' rights listed below, all of which you are entitled to expect. After you have finished, you may ask me to explain any issues that are unclear to you. When you are satisfied that you have read and fully understand your guaranteed rights, please sign your name below.

Subjects have the right:

1 to participate voluntarily, free from any coercion

2 to be informed of the general nature of the research

3 not to be deceived unnecessarily or in any way that might be harmful

4 to withdraw from the study at any time, without incurring any penalty

5 to be protected from physical and/or psychological discomfort, harm, and danger

6 to be informed (debriefed) at the conclusion of the study, regarding the intent of the research

7 to expect that any information divulged during the study will be considered confidential and private

8 to expect that reports of the experimental results will reflect group performances rather than individual performances, and that no participant will be individually identified

Subject Consent Form

Researcher (Please read and sign):

I, _____ (name of researcher) agree to abide by all of the guidelines and standards for conducting research with human participants as described by the American Psychological Association.

Date: _____

Subject (Please read and sign:)

I, _____ (name of subject) have been informed about the general nature of this study and agree voluntarily to participate. I have read and understand the Human Subjects' Rights described by the American Psychological Association, and I understand that all such rights will be guaranteed to me.

Date: _____

[*Source:* Reprinted with permission from, the Behavioral Sciences Department, Fitchburg State College, Fitchburg, Massachusetts, USA.]

Sample form 4:   informed consent form for student research

This research is being conducted by_____, Framingham State College, in partial
fulfillment of the requirements of course 42.450 Experimental Psychology.

In agreeing to participate in this research I understand the following:

The experiment will involve [A brief general description of the research is given here. You
need not give specific details of the experiment, but you should give subjects a general
overview of the tasks involved.].

The entire experimentwill take about _____ minutes.

There are no known expected discomforts or risks involved in the experiment. [If
discomfort or risk is expected,youmust indicate the nature of the discomfort and/or risk.]

There are no "disguised" or "trick" procedures involved in the experiment.

All data fromthe experiment will remain anonymous. The data from all subjects shall be
compiled, analyzed, and submitted in a laboratory report to the course instructor. No
participant's data shall be identified by name at any stage of the data analysis or in the
laboratory report.

At the conclusion of my participation in the experiment, I will be given information
concerningmy performance and any questions that I may have will be clearly and fully
answered.

I may withdraw from this experiment at any time.

There are no special benefits to me for participating in this experiment, and it will not
affect my status at Framingham State College.

_____   _____

(Experimenter)   (Experimental Participant)

                                                       _____

                                                        (Date)

[*Source:* Reprinted with permission from the Psychology Department, Framingham State
College, Framingham, Massachusetts, USA.]

References

Aaker, D. A. and Day, G. S. (1990). *Marketing Research* (4th ed.). New York: John Wiley and Sons.

Aanonsen, A. M. (2002). *Professional Codes of Ethics Across National Boundaries: EFPA Metacode and Nordic Code*. Paper presented at the 25th International Congress of Applied Psychology, Singapore, July.

AAPOR (1999). *Best Practices for Survey and Public Opinion Research*. American Association for Public Opinion Research. Available at http://www.aapor.org.

Abassi, K. and Smith, R. (2003). No more free lunches. *British Medical Journal, 326*, 1155–6.

Abramovitch, R., Freedman, J. L., Thoden, K., and Nikolich, C. (1991). Children's capacity to consent to participation in psychological research: Empirical findings. *Child Development, 62*, 1100–9.

Adair, J. G. (1973). *The Human Subject: The Social Psychology of the Psychological Experiment*. Boston: Little, Brown.

Adair, J. G., Dushenko, T. W., and Lindsay, R. C. L. (1985). Ethical regulations and their impact on research practice. *American Psychologist, 40*, 59–72.

Adair, J. G. and Lindsay, R. C. L. (1983). *Debriefing Subjects: A Comparison of Published Reports with a Self-report Survey*. Unpublished manuscript, University of Manitoba, Winnipeg, Canada.

Adair, J. G., Lindsay, R. C. L., and Carlopio, J. (1983). Social artifact research and ethical regulations: Their impact on the teaching of experimental methods in psychology. *Teaching of Psychology, 10*, 159–62.

Adams, C. and Grimes, A. (2001, May 4). FDA faults "misleading" drug-ad images. *The Wall Street Journal*, p. B8.

Aditya, R. N. (1996). *The Not-So-Good Subject: Extent and Correlates of Pseudovolunteering in Research*. Unpublished master's thesis, Department of Psychology, Temple University, Philadelphia.

Advisory Committee on Human Radiation Experiments (1996). *The Human Radiation Experiments: Final Report of the Advisory Committee on Human Radiation Experiments*. New York: Oxford University Press.

Aguinis, H. (2001). Conducting ethical research: Much more than just a good idea. *The Academy of Management's Research Methods Division Newsletter, 16*(1), 1–18.

Aguinis, H. and Handelsman, M. M. (1997). Ethical issues in the use of the bogus pipeline. *Journal of Applied Social Psychology, 27,* 557–73.

Aguinis, H. and Henle, C. A. (2001). Empirical assessment of the ethics of the bogus pipeline. *Journal of Applied Social Psychology, 31,* 352–75.

Aguinis, H. and Henle, C. A. (2004). Ethics in research. In S. G. Rogelberg (ed.), *Handbook of Research Methods in Industrial and Organizational Psychology* (pp. 34–56). Malden, MA: Blackwell.

Ainscough, T. L. and Motley, C. M. (2000). Will you help me please? The effects of race, gender and manner of dress on retail service. *Marketing Letters, 11,* 129–136.

Aitkenhead, M. and Dordoy, J. (1983). Research on the ethics of research. *Bulletin of the British Psychological Society, 36,* 315–18.

Alderson, P. (2000). Children as researchers. In P. Christensen and A. James (eds), *Research with Children* (pp. 241–55). Philadelphia: Falmer Press/Routledge.

Allen, C. (1997). Spies like us: When sociologists deceive their subjects. *Lingua Franca,* November, pp. 31–9.

Allen, C. T. (2004). A theory-based approach for improving demand artifact assessment in advertising experiments. *Journal of Advertising, 33,* 63–73.

Allen, D. F. (1983). Follow-up analysis of use of forewarning and deception in psychology experiments. *Psychological Reports, 52,* 899–906.

Allen, J. T. (2002). Negative income tax. In *The Concise Encyclopedia of Economics.* Available at http://www.econlib.org.

Allen, V. (1966). Effect of knowledge of deception on conformity. *Journal of Social Psychology, 69,* 101–6.

Allport, G. W. and Postman, L. (1947). *The Psychology of Rumor.* New York: Holt.

Altemeyer, R. A. (1972). Subject pool pollution and the postexperimental interview. *Journal of Experimental Research in Personality, 5,* 79–84.

Altman, L. K. (1986, February 25). Peer review is challenged. *The New York Times,* p. C3.

Altman, L. K. (1989, June 6). Errors prompt proposals to improve "peer review" at science journals. *The New York Times,* p. C3.

Amador, X. F., Andreasen, N. C., Strauss, D. H., Yale, S. A., Clark, C. C., and Gorman, J. M. (1994). Awareness of illness in schizophrenia and schizoaffective and mood disorders. *Archives of General Psychiatry, 51,* 826–36.

American Anthropological Association (1983). *Professional Ethics: Statements and Procedures of the American Anthropological Association.* Washington, DC: AAA.

American Anthropological Association (1986). *Statements on Ethics.* Available at http://www.aaanet.org.

American Anthropological Association (1998). *Code of Ethics of the American Anthropological Association.* Available at http://www.aaanet.org/committees/ethics/ethcode.htm.

American Association of Anatomists (2002). *USDA Has No More Say Over Mice, Rats, Birds.* Available at http://www.anatomy.org.

American Association of Physical Anthropologists (2003). *Code of Ethics of the American Association of Physical Anthropologists.* Available at http://www.physanth.org.

American Association for Public Opinion Research (1999). *Best Practices for Survey and Public Opinion Research.* Available at http://www.aapor.org.

American Association of University Professors (1981, December). Regulations governing research on human subjects: academic freedom and the institutional review board. *Academe, 67,* 358–70.

American Counseling Association (2002). *ACA Code of Ethics and Standards of Practice.* Available at http://www.counseling.org.

American Marketing Association (1972). *Code of Ethics.* Chicago: AMA.

American Psychological Association (1968). *Principles for the Care and Use of Animals.* Washington, DC: APA.

American Psychological Association (1973). *Ethical Principles in the Conduct of Research with Human Participants.* Washington, DC: APA.

American Psychological Association (1978). Report of the task force on the role of psychology in the criminal justice system. *American Psychologist, 33,* 1099–113.

American Psychological Association (1981a). Ethical principles of psychologists. *American Psychologist, 36,* 633–8.

American Psychological Association (1981b). Specialty guidelines for the delivery of services by industrial/organizational psychologists. *American Psychologist, 36,* 664–9.

American Psychological Association (1982). *Ethical Principles in the Conduct of Research with Human Participants* (rev. ed.). Washington, DC: APA.

American Psychological Association (1990). Ethical principles of psychologists (amended June 2, 1989). *American Psychologist, 45,* 390–5.

American Psychological Association (1992). Ethical principles of psychologists and code of conduct. *American Psychologist, 47,* 1597–611.

American Psychological Association (1993a). *Guidelines for Ethical Conduct in the Care and Use of Animals.* Washington, DC: APA.

American Psychological Association (1993b). Ethical standards for the reporting and publishing of scientific information. *American Psychologist, 48,* 383.

American Psychological Association (1994). *Publication Manual of the American Psychological Association* (4th ed.). Washington, DC: APA.

American Psychological Association (2002). Ethical principles of psychologists and code of conduct. *American Psychologist, 57,* 1060–73.

American Psychological Association (2003). Guidelines on multicultural education, training, research, practice, and organizational change for psychologists. *American Psychologist, 58,* 337–402.

American Sociological Association (1971). *Code of Ethics.* Washington, DC: ASA.

American Sociological Association (1989). *Code of Ethics.* Washington, DC: ASA.

American Sociological Association (1999). *American Sociological Association Code of Ethics.* Available at http://www.asanet.org.

Angell, M. (1990). The Nazi hypothermia experiments and unethical research today. *New England Journal of Medicine, 322,* 1462–4.

Animal research protection bill approved (1992, September). *APS Observer,* p. 4.

Annas, G. J., Glantz, L. H., and Katz, B. F. (1977). *Informed Consent to Human Experimentation: The Subject's Dilemma.* Cambridge, MA: Ballinger.

Annas, G. J. and Grodin, M. A. (eds) (1995). *The Nazi Doctors and the Nuremberg Code: Human Rights in Human Experimentation.* New York: Oxford University Press.

Antonuccio, D. O., Danton, W. G., and McClanahan, T. M. (2003). Psychology in the prescription era: Building a firewall between marketing and science. *American Psychologist, 58,* 1028–43.

Arellano-Galdames, F. J. (1972). *Some Ethical Problems in Research on Human Subjects.* Unpublished doctoral dissertation, University of New Mexico, Albuquerque.

ARF/AMA (1998). *1998 ARF/AMA Marketing Research Industry Survey.* Available at http://www.marketingpower.com.

Argyris, C. (1975). Dangers in applying results from experimental social psychology. *American Psychologist, 30*, 469–85.

Aronson, E. (1966). Avoidance of inter-subject communication. *Psychological Reports, 19*, 238.

Aronson, E. and Carlsmith, J. M. (1968). Experimentation in social psychology. In G. Lindzey and E. Aronson (eds), *The Handbook of Social Psychology* (Vol. 2). Reading, MA: Addison-Wesley.

Arp, W. (2004). HIV/AIDS and nondecision in Louisiana: A case study of prevention strategy in three black communities. *Journal of Black Studies, 34*, 548–61.

Arthur Conan Doyle is Piltdown suspect (1983, August 2). *The New York Times*, pp. C1, C6.

Asch, S. (1955). Opinions and social pressure. *Scientific American, 193*, 31–5.

Asher, J. (1974, November). Can parapsychology weather the Levy affair? *APA Monitor, 5*, 4.

Association of Professional German Psychologists (1999). *Ethical Principles of the German Psychological Society (DGP) and the Association of German Professional Psychologists (BDP)*. Berlin: BDP.

Atwell, J. (1981). Human rights in human subjects research. In A. J. Kimmel (ed.), *Ethics of Human Subject Research*. San Francisco: Jossey-Bass.

Australian Psychological Society (1986). *Code of Professional Conduct*. Parkville, Victoria: APS.

Australian Psychological Society. (2005). *Code of Ethics*. Available at http://www.psychology.org.au.

Azar, B. (1994a, December). Animal research threatened by activism. *APA Monitor, 25*, 18.

Azar, B. (1994b, December). Research improves lives of animals. *APA Monitor, 25*, 19.

Azar, B. (1994c, December). Tactics of animal activists become more sophisticated. *APA Monitor, 25*, 20.

Azar, B. (2002). Ethics at the cost of research? *Monitor on Psychology, 33*, 38–40.

Azrin, N. H., Holz, W., Ulrich, R., and Goldiamond, I. (1961). The control of the content of conversation through reinforcement. *Journal of the Experimental Analysis of Behavior, 4*, 25–30.

Babbage, C. (1969). *Reflections on the Decline of Science in England, and on Some of Its Causes*. London: Gregg International.

Bacon, F. (1960). *Novum Organum*. New York: Bobbs-Merrill.

Baird, J. S., Jr. (1980). Current trends in college cheating. *Psychology in the Schools, 17*, 515–22.

Bakhle, Y. S. (2004). Missing evidence that animal research benefits humans: Evidence is all around us. *British Medical Journal, 328*, 1017.

Baldwin, E. (1993). The case for animal research in psychology. *Journal of Social Issues, 49*, 121–31.

Bales, J. (1992, November). New ethics code "practical and livable." *APA Monitor, 23*, 6–7.

Bardsley, N. (2000). *Control without Deception*. Tinbergen Institute Discussion Paper, University of Amsterdam.

Baron, R. A. and Byrne, D. (1987). *Social Psychology: Understanding Human Interaction* (5th ed.). Boston: Allyn and Bacon.

Baron, R. A. and Byrne, D. (1994). *Social Psychology: Understanding Human Interaction* (7th ed.). Boston: Allyn and Bacon.

Bassett, R. L., Basinger, D., and Livermore, P. (1982). Lying in the laboratory: Deception in human research from psychological, philosophical, and theological perspectives. *Journal of the American Scientific Affiliation, 34*, 201–12.

Baumeister, R. B. and Tice, D. M. (1999). IRB ax falls, heads roll. *Dialogue, 14*, 8.

Baumeister, R. F., Cooper, J., and Skib, B. A. (1979). Inferior performance as a selective response to expectancy: Taking a dive to make a point. *Journal of Personality and Social Psychology, 37*, 424–32.

Baumrin, B. H. (1970). The immortality of irrelevance: The social role of science. In F. F. Korten, S. S. Cook, and J. I. Lacey (eds), *Psychology and the Problems of Society*. Washington, DC: American Psychological Association.

Baumrind, D. (1964). Some thoughts on ethics of research: after reading Milgram's "Behavioral study of obedience." *American Psychologist, 19*, 421–3.

Baumrind, D. (1971). Principles of ethical conduct in the treatment of subjects: Reaction to the draft report of the Committee on Ethical Standards in Psychological Research. *American Psychologist, 26*, 887–96.

Baumrind, D. (1972). Reactions to the May 1972 draft report of the Ad Hoc Committee on Ethical Standards in Psychological Research. *American Psychologist, 27*, 1083–6.

Baumrind, D. (1975). Metaethical and normative considerations governing the treatment of human subjects in the behavioral sciences. In E. C. Kennedy (ed.), *Human Rights and Psychological Research: A Debate on Psychology and Ethics*. New York: Thomas Y. Crowell.

Baumrind, D. (1976). *Nature and Definition of Informed Consent in Research Involving Deception*. Paper prepared for the National Commission for the Protection of Human Subjects of Biomedical and Behavioral Research, US Department of Health, Education, and Welfare, Bethesda, MD.

Baumrind, D. (1977, April). *Snooping and Duping: The Application of the Principle of Informed Consent to Field Research*. Paper presented at the meeting of the Society for Applied Anthropology, San Diego, CA.

Baumrind, D. (1981, August). The costs of deception. *Society for the Advancement of Social Psychology Newsletter, 7*, 1, 3, 6, 8–10.

Baumrind, D. (1985). Research using intentional deception: ethical issues revisited. *American Psychologist, 40*, 165–74.

Bayne, K. (1991). *National Institutes of Health Nonhuman Primate Management Plan*. Bethesda, MD: Office of Animal Care and Use, National Institutes of Health.

Bearden, W. O., Madden, C. S., and Uscategui, K. (1998). The pool is drying up. *Marketing Research, 10*, 26–33.

Beauvois, J.-L., Roulin, J.-L., and Tiberghien, G. (1990). *Manuel d'Etudes Pratiques de Psychologie I: Pratique de la Recherche*. Paris: Presses Universitaires de France.

Bechtel, H. K., Jr. and Pearson, W., Jr. (1985). Deviant scientists and scientific deviance. *Deviant Behavior, 6*, 237–52.

Beecher, H. K. (1959). *Experimentation in Man*. Springfield, IL: Thomas.

Beecher, H. K. (1966). Ethics and clinical research. *New England Journal of Medicine, 274*, 1354–60.

Begley, S. (2002, November 1). Review boards pose threat to tough work by social scientists. *The Wall Street Journal*, p. B1.

Behnke, S. H. and Kinscherff, R. (2002). Must a psychologist report past child abuse? *Monitor on Psychology, 33*, 56–7.

Bell, E. H. and Bronfenbrenner, U. (1959). Freedom and responsibility in research: comments. *Human Organization, 18*, 49–52.

Bem, D. J. (1965). An experimental analysis of self-persuasion. *Journal of Experimental Social Psychology, 1*, 199–218.

Benedict, J. and Stoloff, M. (1991). Animal laboratory facilities at "America's best" undergraduate colleges. *American Psychologist, 46*, 535–6.

Bentham, J. (1789). *An Introduction to the Principles of Morals and Legislation*. Edinburgh: William Tate.

Bergin, A. E. (1962). The effect of dissonant persuasive communications upon changes in a self-referring attitude. *Journal of Personality, 30*, 423–36.

Berk, R. A., Boruch, R. F., Chambers, D. L., Rossi, P. H., and Witte, A. D. (1987). Social policy experimentation: a position paper. In D. S. Cordray and M. W. Lipsey (eds), *Evaluation Studies Review Annual* (Vol. 11). Newbury Park, CA: Sage.

Berkowitz, L. (1969). The frustration-aggression hypothesis revisited. In L. Berkowitz (ed.), *Roots of Aggression*. New York: Atherton.

Berkun, M., Bialek, H. M., Kern, P. R., and Yagi, K. (1962). Experimental studies of psychological stress in man. *Psychological Monographs: General and Applied, 76*, 1–39.

Bermant, G. and others (1974). The logic of simulation in jury research. *Criminal Justice and Behavior, 1*, 224–33.

Bernstein, D. A., Clarke-Stewart, A., Roy, E. J., Srull, T. K., and Wickens, C. D. (1994). *Psychology* (3rd ed.). Boston: Houghton-Mifflin.

Bickman, L. (1974). The social power of a uniform. *Journal of Applied Social Psychology, 4*, 47–61.

Bickman, L. (1981). Some distinctions between basic and applied approaches. In L. Bickman (ed.), *Applied Social Psychology Annual* (Vol. 2). Beverly Hills, CA: Sage.

Bickman, L. and Rosenbaum, D. P. (1977). Crime reporting as a function of bystander encouragement, surveillance, and credibility. *Journal of Personality and Social Psychology, 35*, 577–86.

Bickman, L. and Zarantonello, M. (1978). The effects of deception and level of obedience on subjects' ratings of the Milgram study. *Personality and Social Psychology Bulletin, 4*, 81–5.

Birnbaum, M. H. (2003). Methodological and ethical issues in conducting social psychology research via the Internet. In C. Sansone, C. C. Morf, and A. T. Panter (eds), *The Sage Handbook of Methods in Social Psychology* (pp. 45–70). Thousand Oaks, CA: Sage.

Bishop, L. J. and Nolen, A. L. (2001). Animals in research and education: Ethical issues. *Kennedy Institute of Ethics Journal, 11*, 91–112.

Blanck, P. D., Bellack, A. S., Rosnow, R. L., Rotheram-Borus, M. J., and Schooler, N. R. (1992). Scientific rewards and conflicts of ethical choices in human subjects research. *American Psychologist, 47*, 959–65.

Blass, T. (2004). *The Man Who Shocked the World: The Life and Legacy of Stanley Milgram*. Cambridge, MA: Basic Books.

Bliss, M. (1984). *The Discovery of Insulin*. Chicago: University of Chicago Press.

Blumberg, M. (1980). Job switching in autonomous work groups: An exploratory study in a Pennsylvania coal mine. *Academy of Management Journal, 23*, 287–306.

Blumberg, M. and Pringle, C. D. (1983). How control groups can cause loss of control in action research: The case of Rushton coal mine. *Journal of Applied Behavioral Science, 19*, 409–25.

Blumberg, M. S. and Wasserman, E. A. (1995). Animal mind and the argument from design. *American Psychologist, 50*, 133–44.

Boffey, P. M. (1981, October 27). Animals in the lab: Protests accelerate, but use is dropping. *The New York Times*, pp. C1–C2.

Bok, S. (1978). *Lying: Moral Choice in Public and Private Life*. New York: Pantheon.

Bok, S. (1992). Deceit. In L. C. Becker and C. B. Becker (eds), *Encyclopedia of Ethics* (pp. 242–5). New York: Garland.

Bonetti, S. (1998a). Experimental economics and deception. *Journal of Economic Psychology, 19*, 377–95.

Bonetti, S. (1998b). Reply to Hay and Starmer and McDaniel. *Journal of Economic Psychology*, *19*, 411–14.

Borden, N. H. (1964). The concept of the marketing mix. *Journal of Advertising Research*, *4*, 2–7.

Boruch, R. F. and Cecil, J. S. (1979). *Assuring the Confidentiality of Social Research Data*. Philadelphia: University of Pennsylvania Press.

Boruch, R. F. and Cecil, J. S. (1982). Statistical strategies for preserving privacy in direct inquiry. In J. E. Sieber (ed.), *The Ethics of Social Research: Surveys and Experiments*. New York: Springer-Verlag.

Bowd, A. D. (1980). Ethical reservations about psychological research with animals. *Psychological Record*, *30*, 201–10.

Bowd, A. D. and Shapiro, K. J. (1993). The case against laboratory animal research in psychology. *Journal of Social Issues*, *49*, 133–42.

Bowen, D. D., Perloff, R., and Jacoby, J. (1972). Improving manuscript evaluation procedures. *American Psychologist*, *27*, 221–5.

Bowman, L. L. and Waite, B. M. (2003). Volunteering in research: Student satisfaction and educational benefits. *Teaching of Psychology*, *30*, 102–6.

Bradley, L. J. and Hendricks, C. B. (2004). *Ethical Issues Encountered by Counselors: Some Solutions*. Paper presented at the American Association of State Counseling Boards conference, Savannah, GA.

Brand, C. (2001, April 3). *EU Votes to Ban Animal-tested Cosmetics*. Available at http://www.vivisectioninfo.org.

Bramel, D. (1962). A dissonance theory approach to defensive projection. *Journal of Abnormal and Social Psychology*, *64*, 121–9.

Bramel, D. (1963). Selection of a target for defensive projection. *Journal of Abnormal and Social Psychology*, *66*, 318–24.

Brehm, S. S. and Kassin, S. M. (1993). *Social Psychology* (2nd ed.). Boston: Houghton Mifflin.

Bridges, F. S., Anzalone, D. A., Ryan, S. W., and Anzalone, F. L. (2002). Extensions of the lost letter technique to divisive issues of creationism, darwinism, sex education, and gay and lesbian affiliations. *Psychological Reports*, *90*, 391–400.

Brink, N., Dulal, N., Paulhus, P., Wolf, S., Chong, C., Barry, S., Andreutti, L., and Saini, S. (1995). Canadian Journal of Psychology: A review of subject, language, funding, experimental vs. clinical, and place of origin of research articles published from 1974 to 1992. Available at http://www.sfu.ca.

Brill, S. (1976, July 19). A New York cabby story you won't believe. *New York*, pp. 8, 10.

British Psychological Society (1995a). *Code of Conduct, Ethical Principles and Guidelines*. Leicester, UK: BPS.

British Psychological Society (1995b). *Guidelines for the Use of Animals in Research*. Leicester, UK: BPS.

British Psychological Society. (2004). *Guidelines for Minimum Standards of Ethical Approval in Psychological Research*. Leicester, UK: BPS.

British Psychological Society (2005a). *Ethical Principles for Conducting Research with Human Participants*. Available at http://www.bps.org.uk.

British Psychological Society (2005b). *Guidelines for Psychologists Working with Animals*. Available at http://www.bps.org.uk.

Britton, B. K. (1979). Ethical and educational aspects of participating as a subject in psychology experiments. *Teaching of Psychology*, *6*, 195–8.

Britton, B. K. (1987). "Academic value of research participation by undergraduates": Comment on Coulter and on Daniel. *American Psychologist*, *42*, 268–9.

Broad, W. and Wade, N. (1982). *Betrayers of the Truth*. New York: Simon and Schuster.

Broad, W. J. (1983, December 13). New attack on Galileo asserts major discovery was stolen. *The New York Times*, pp. C1, C8.

Brock, T. C. and Becker, L. A. (1966). Debriefing and susceptibility to subsequent experimental manipulations. *Journal of Experimental Social Psychology*, *2*, 314–23.

Broder, A. (1998). Deception can be acceptable. *American Psychologist*, *53*, 85–6.

Brody, J. L., Gluck, J. P., and Aragon, A. S. (2000). Participants' understanding of the process of psychological research: Debriefing. *Ethics and Behavior*, *10*, 13–25.

Bronowski, J. (1956). *Science and Human Values*. New York: Messner.

Brown, R. (1962). Models of attitude change. In R. Brown, E. Galanter, E. Hess, and G. Mandler (eds), *New Directions in Psychology: I*. New York: Holt, Rinehart and Winston.

Bryan, J. H. and Test, M. A. (1967). Models and helping: Naturalistic studies in aiding behavior. *Journal of Personality and Social Psychology*, *6*, 400–7.

Buckhout, R. (1965). Need for approval and attitude change. *Journal of Psychology*, *60*, 123–8.

Burbach, D. J., Farha, J. G., and Thorpe, J. S. (1986). Assessing depression in community samples of children using self-report inventories: ethical considerations. *Journal of Abnormal Child Psychology*, *14*, 579–89.

Burghardt, G. M. and Herzog, H. A., Jr. (1980). Beyond conspecifics: Is "Brer Rabbit" our brother? *BioScience*, *30*, 763–7.

Burke, R. R. and Srull, T. K. (1988). Competitive interference and consumer memory for advertising. *Journal of Consumer Research*, *15*, 55–68.

Cameron, P. (1969). Frequency and kinds of words in various social settings, or what the hell's going on? *Pacific Sociological Review*, *12*, 101–4.

Campbell, D., Sanderson, R. E., and Laverty, S. G. (1964). Characteristics of a conditioned response in human subjects during extinction trials following a single traumatic conditioning trial. *Journal of Abnormal and Social Psychology*, *68*, 627–39.

Campbell, D. T., Boruch, R. F., Schwartz, R. D., and Steinberg, J. (1977). Confidentiality-preserving modes of access to files and to interfile exchange for useful statistical analysis. *Evaluation Quarterly*, *1*, 269–300.

Campbell, D. T. and Cecil, J. S. (1982). A proposed system of regulation for the protection of participants in low-risk areas of applied social research. In J. E. Sieber (ed.), *The Ethics of Social Research: Fieldwork, Regulation and Publication*. New York: Springer-Verlag.

Campion, M. A. (1993). Are there differences between reviewers on the criteria they use to evaluate research articles? *The Industrial-Organizational Psychologist*, *31*(2), 29–39.

Canadian Psychological Association (1988). *Canadian Code of Ethics for Psychologists: Companion Maunal*. Old Chelsea, Quebec: CPA.

Canadian Psychological Association (1991). *Canadian Code of Ethics for Psychologists* (rev. ed.). Old Chelsea, Quebec: CPA.

Canadian Psychological Association (2000). *Canadian Code of Ethics for Psychologists* (3rd ed.). Ottawa, Ontario: CPA.

Canadian Psychological Association (2001). *Companion Manual to the Canadian Code of Ethics for Psychologists* (3rd ed.). Ottawa, Ontario: CPA.

Canter, M. B., Bennett, B. E., Jones, S. E., and Nagy, T. F. (1994). *Ethics for Psychologists: A Commentary on the APA Ethics Code*. Washington, DC: American Psychological Association.

Cantwell, A. R. (2001, September/October). The human radiation experiments: How scientists secretly used US citizens as guinea pigs during the Cold War. *New Dawn*, *68*. Available at http://www.newdawnmagazine.com.

Cardemil, E. V., Reivich, K. J., and Seligman, M. E. P. (2002). The prevention of depressive symptoms in low-income minority middle school students. *Prevention and Treatment, 4,* Article 8. Available at http://journals.apa.org.

Carlson, R. (1971). Where is the person in personality research? *Psychological Bulletin, 75,* 203–19.

Carlsson, H.-E., Hagelin, J., and Hau, J. (2004). Implementation of the "three R's" in biomedical research. *The Veterinary Record, 154,* 467–70.

Carnell, B. (2005, May 2). *France Fails in Initial Effort to Overturn European Union Ban on Cosmetics Testing.* Available at http://www.animalrights.net.

Carroll, M. A., Schneider, H. G., and Wesley, G. R. (1985). *Ethics in the Practice of Psychology.* Englewood Cliffs, NJ: Prentice-Hall.

Casas, J. M. and Thompson, C. E. (1991). Ethical principles and standards: A racial-ethnic minority research perspective. *Counseling and Development, 68,* 26–30.

CASRO (1995). *Code of Standards for Survey Research.* Port Jefferson, NY: Council of American Survey Research Organizations.

Ceci, S. J., Peters, D., and Plotkin, J. (1985). Human subjects review, personal values, and the regulation of social science research. *American Psychologist, 40,* 994–1002.

Chalk, R., Frankel, M. S., and Chafer, S. B. (1980). *AAAS Professional Ethics Activities in the Scientific and Engineering Societies.* Washington, DC: American Association for the Advancement of Science.

Chow, C. (2002, January). US government sanctions Harvard prof. for falsifying research. *Accuracy in Academia.* Available at http://www.academia.org.

Christakis, N. A. (1988). Should IRBs monitor research more strictly? *IRB: A Review of Human Subjects Research, 10,* 8–10.

Christensen, L. (1988). Deception in psychological research: When is its use justified? *Personality and Social Psychology Bulletin, 14,* 664–75.

Clark, R. D. and Word, L. E. (1974). Where is the apathetic bystander? Situational characteristcs of the emergency. *Journal of Personality and Social Psychology, 29,* 279–87.

Clay, R. A. (1997). Animal rights activists target psychologists for their research. *APA Monitor, 28,* 30.

Clifton, M. (1996, May). Peace talk. *Animal People,* p. 2.

Clingempeel, W. G., Mulvey, E., and Repucci, N. D. (1980). A national study of ethical dilemmas of psychologists in the criminal justice system. In J. Monahan (ed.), *Who Is the Client?* Washington, DC: American Psychological Association.

CMOR (1999). *Respondent Bill of Rights.* Council for Marketing and Opinion Research. Available at http://www.cmor.org.

Cohen, I. B. (1957). Galileo. In I. B. Cohen (ed.), *Lives in Science.* New York: Simon and Schuster.

Coile, D. C. and Miller, N. E. (1984). How radical animal rights activists try to mislead humane people. *American Psychologist, 39,* 700–1.

Cole, J. R. (1992). Animal rights and wrongs. In B. Slife and J. Rubinstein (eds.), *Taking Sides: Clashing Views on Controversial Psychological Issues* (7th ed.). Guilford, CT: Dushkin.

Colegio Oficial de Psicólogos (1993). *Código Deontológico del Psicólogo* [*Deontological Code of the Psychologist*]. Madrid.

Collins, F. L., Jr., Kuhn, I. F., Jr., and King, G. D. (1979). Variables affecting subjects' ethical ratings of proposed experiments. *Psychological Reports, 44,* 155–64.

Colombo, J. (1995). Cost, utility, and judgments of institutional review boards. *Psychological Science, 6,* 318–19.

Comroe, J. H., Jr. (1983). *Exploring the Heart: Discoveries in Heart Disease and High Blood Pressure*. New York: W. W. Norton.

Committee for the Use of Animals in School Science Behavior Projects (1972). Guidelines for the use of animals in school science behavior projects. *American Psychologist, 27,* 337.

Conger, R. D., Cui, M., Bryant, C. M., and Elder, G. H. (2000). Competence in early adult romantic relationships: A developmental perspective on family influences. *Journal of Personality and Social Psychology, 79,* 224–37.

Cook, T. D., Bean, R. B., Calder, B. J., Frey, R., Krovetz, M. L., and Reisman, S. R. (1970). Demand characteristics and three conceptions of the frequently deceived subject. *Journal of Personality and Social Psychology, 14,* 185–94.

Cook, T. D. and Campbell, D. T. (1979). *Quasi-Experimentation: Design and Analysis Issues for Field Settings*. Boston: Houghton Mifflin.

Cook, T. D. and Perrin, B. F. (1971). The effects of suspiciousness of deception and the perceived legitimacy of deception on task performance in an attitude change experiment. *Journal of Personality, 39,* 204–24.

Cooper, H. and Hedges, L. V. (eds.) (1994). *The Handbook of Research Synthesis*. New York: Russell Sage Foundation.

Cooper, J. (1976). Deception and role playing: on telling the good guys from the bad guys. *American Psychologist, 31,* 605–10.

Corey, G., Corey, M. S., and Callanan, P. (2002). *Issues and Ethics in the Helping Professions* (6th ed.). Belmont, CA: Wadsworth–Thompson Learning.

Corti, L. (2003). Qualitative research data, archiving. In R. L. Miller and J. D. Brewer (eds.), *The A–Z of Social Research: A Dictionary of Key Social Science Concepts* (pp. 69–73). London: Sage.

Corti, L., Foster, J., and Thompson, P. (1995). Archiving qualitative research data. *Social Research Update, 10.* Available at http://www.soc.surrey.ac.uk.

Coulter, X. (1986). Academic value of research participation by undergraduates. *American Psychologist, 41,* 317.

Coutu, W. (1951). Role-playing vs. role-taking: An appeal for clarification. *American Sociological Review, 16,* 180–7.

Crampton, T. (2005, June 11–12). A mobile tale of three cities. *International Herald Tribune,* p. 18.

Crespi, T. D. (1994). Student scholarship: In the best interests of the scholar. *American Psychologist, 49,* 1094–5.

Crusco, A. H. and Wetzel, C. G. (1984). The Midas touch: The effects of interpersonal touch on restaurant tipping. *Personality and Social Psychology Bulletin, 10,* 512–17.

Culliton, B. J. (1974). The Sloan–Kettering affair: A story without a hero. *Science, 184,* 644–50.

Cummings, L. L. and Frost, P. J. (eds.) (1985). *Publishing in the Organizational Sciences*. Homewood, IL: Irwin.

Curran, W. J. (1969). Governmental regulation of the use of human subjects in medical research: The approach of two federal agencies. *Daedalus, 98,* 542–94.

Curran, W. J. and Beecher, H. K. (1969). Experimentation in children. *Journal of the American Medical Association, 10,* 77–83.

Darley, J. M. and Latané, B. (1968). Bystander intervention in emergencies: Diffusion of responsibility. *Journal of Personality and Social Psychology, 8,* 377–83.

Davis, J. R. and Fernald, P. S. (1975). Laboratory experience versus subject pool. *American Psychologist, 30,* 523–4.

Davis, S. F., Grover, C. A., Becker, A. H., and McGregor, L. N. (1992). Academic dishonesty: prevalence, determinants, techniques, and punishments. *Teaching of Psychology, 19,* 16–20.

Day, R. L. (1975). A comment on "Ethics in Marketing Research." *Journal of Marketing Research, 12,* 232–3.

Department of Health and Human Services (2001a). *Categories of Research that May Be Reviewed by the Institutional Review Board (IRB) through an Expedited Review.* Available at http://www.hhs.gov/ohrp.

Department of Health and Human Services (2001b). *Code of Federal Regulations, Title 45, Part 46, Protection of Human Subjects.* Available at http://www.hhs.gov/ohrp.

Devenport, L. D. (1989). Sampling behavior and contextual change. *Learning and Motivation, 20,* 91–114.

Devenport, L. D. and Devenport, J. A. (1990). The laboratory animal dilemma: A solution in our backyards. *Psychological Science, 1,* 215–16.

Diamond, S. S. and Morton, D. R. (1978). Empirical landmarks in social psychology. *Personality and Social Psychology Bulletin, 4,* 217–21.

Dickersin, K., Min, Y., and Meinert, C. L. (1992). Factors influencing publication of research results. *Journal of the American Medical Association, 267,* 374–8.

Dickson, J. P., Casey, M., Wyckoff, D., and Wind, W. (1977). Invisible coding of survey questionnaires. *Public Opinion Quarterly, 41,* 100–6.

Diener, E. (2001). Over-concern with research ethics. *Dialogue, 16,* 2.

Diener, E. and Crandall, R. (1978). *Ethics in Social and Behavioral Research.* Chicago: University of Chicago Press.

Diener, E., Matthews, R., and Smith, R. (1972). Leakage of experimental information to potential future subjects by debriefed subjects. *Journal of Experimental Research in Personality, 6,* 264–7.

Dingfelder, S. (2004). Report on ethical research with children released. *Monitor on Psychology, 35,* 19.

Dipboye, R. L., Smith, C. S., and Howell, W. C. (1994). *Understanding Industrial and Organizationl Psychology: An Integrated Approach.* Fort Worth, TX: Harcourt Brace.

Dixon, T. (2000). Animal experimentation. *Debatabase.* Available at http://www.debatabase.org.

Domjan, M. and Purdy, J. E. (1995). Animal research in psychology: More than mets the eye of the general psychology student. *American Psychologist, 50,* 496–503.

Drewett, R. and Kani, W. (1981). Animal experimentation in the behavioral sciences. In D. Sperlinger (ed.), *Animals in Research.* New York: Wiley.

Eaton, W. O. (1983). The reliability of ethical reviews: Some initial empirical findings. *Canadian Psychologist, 24,* 14–18.

Eckholm, E. (1985, May 7). Fight over animal experiments gains intensity on many fronts. *The New York Times,* pp. C1, C3.

Economic and Social Data Service (2004). *Legal and Ethical Issues in Interviewing Children.* Available at http://www.esds.ac.uk.

Edsall, G. A. (1969). A positive approach to the problem of human experimentation. *Daedalus, 98,* 463–78.

Eibl-Eibesfeldt, I. (1975). *Ethology: The Biology of Behavior.* New York: Holt, Rinehart and Winston.

Ellis, C. (1986). *Fisher Folk: Two Communities on the Chesapeake Bay.* Lexington: University Press of Kentucky.

Ellsworth, P. C. (1977). From abstract ideas to concrete instances. *American Psychologist, 32,* 604–15.

Epstein, S. (1995). What can be done to improve the journal review process. *American Psychologist, 50*, 883–5.

Epstein, Y. M., Suedfeld, P., and Silverstein, S. J. (1973). The experimental contract: Subjects' expectations of and reactions to some behaviors of experimenters. *American Psychologist, 28*, 212–21.

Erikson, K. T. (1967). A comment on disguised observation in sociology. *Social Problems, 14*, 366–73.

Errera, P. (1972). Statement based on interviews with forty "worst cases" in the Milgram obedience experiments. In J. Katz (ed.), *Experimentation with Human Beings*. New York: Russell Sage Foundation.

Evans, S. E. (2004). *Forgotten Crimes: The Holocaust and People with Disabilities*. Chicago: Ivan R. Dee.

Eyde, L. D. (2000). Other responsibilities to participants. In B. D. Sales and S. Folkman (eds.), *Ethics in Research with Human Participants* (pp. 61–73). Washington, DC: American Psychological Association.

Eysenck, H. J. (1981). On the fudging of scientific data. *American Psychologist, 36*, 692.

Faden, R. R. and Beauchamp, T. L. (1986). *A History and Theory of Informed Consent*. New York: Oxford University Press.

Farr, J. L. and Seaver, W. B. (1975). Stress and discomfort in psychological research: Subjects' perception of experimental procedures. *American Psychologist, 30*, 770–3.

Farrow, J. M., Lohss, W. E., Farrow, B. J., and Taub, S. I. (1975). Intersubject communication as a contaminating factor in verbal conditioning. *Perceptual and Motor Skills, 40*, 975–82.

Federal Trade Commission (2004). *The CAN-SPAM Act: Requirements for Commercial Emailers*. Available at http://www.ftc.gov.

Fédération Suisse des Psychologues (1991). *Code Déontologique*. Lausanne, Switzerland: FSP.

Fédération Suisse des Psychologues (2002). *Code Déontologique*. Available at http://www.psychologie.ch.

Feeney, D. (1987). Human rights and animal welfare. *American Psychologist, 42*, 593–9.

Ferrari, J. R. and McGowan, S. (2002). Using exam bonus points as incentive for research participation. *Teaching of Psychology, 29*, 29–32.

Festinger, L. and Carlsmith, J. M. (1959). Cognitive consequences of forced compliance. *Journal of Abnormal and Social Psychology, 58*, 203–10.

Fidler, D. S. and Kleinknecht, R. E. (1977). Randomized response versus direct questioning: Two data-collection methods for sensitive information. *Psychological Bulletin, 84*, 1045–9.

Field, P. B. (1989, October). Animal images in college psychology texts. *The Animals' Agenda*, p. 14.

Field, P. B. (1990). The most invasive animal experiments in psychology textbooks. *PsyETA Bulletin, 9*, 6–8.

Fillenbaum, R. S. (1966). Prior deception and subsequent experimental performance: The faithful subject. *Journal of Personality and Social Psychology, 4*, 532–7.

Fine, M. A. (1996). Reflections on enhancing accountability in the peer review process. *American Psychologist, 51*, 1190–1.

Fine, M. A. and Kurdek, L. A. (1993). Reflections on determining authorship credit and authorship order on faculty–student collaborations. *American Psychologist, 48*, 1141–7.

Finney, P. D. (1987). When consent information refers to risk and deception: Implications for social research. *Journal of Social Behavior and Personality, 2*, 37–48.

Fisher, C. B. and Fyrberg, D. (1994). Participant partners: College students weigh the costs and benefits of deceptive research. *American Psychologist, 49*, 417–27.

Fisher, K. (1982, November). The spreading stain of fraud. *APA Monitor, 13*, 7–8.

Fletcher, R. (1991). *Science, Ideology, and the Media: The Cyril Burt Scandal*. New Brunswick, NJ: Transaction.

Fo, W. S. and O'Donnell, C. R. (1975). The buddy system: Effects of community intervention on delinquent offenses. *Behavior Therapy, 6*, 522–4.

Fogg, L. and Fiske, D. W. (1993). Foretelling the judgments of reviewers and editors. *American Psychologist, 48*, 293–4.

Folkman, S. (2000). Privacy and confidentiality. In B. D. Sales and S. Folkman (eds.), *Ethics in Research with Human Participants* (pp. 49–57). Washington, DC: American Psychological Association.

Foot, H. and Alison, S. (2004). The use and abuse of student participants. *The Psychologist, 17*, 256–9.

Foot, H. and Sanford, A. (2004). *Students as Research Participants: Educationally Valuable or Ethically Suspect?* PLAT 2004 (Psychology Learning and Teaching Conference), Glasgow, UK.

Forester-Miller, H. and Davis, T. E. (1996). *A Practitioner's Guide to Ethical Decision Making*. Alexandria, VA: American Counseling Association.

Forsyth, D. R. (1980). A taxonomy of ethical ideologies. *Journal of Personality and Social Psychology, 39*, 175–84.

Forsyth, D. R. (1987). *Social Psychology*. Pacific Grove, CA: Brooks/Cole.

Forsyth, D. R. and Strong, S. R. (1986). The scientific study of counseling and psychotherapy: a unificationist view. *American Psychologist, 41*, 113–19.

Forsyth, D. (2004). IRBism: Prejudice against institutional review boards. *Dialogue, 19*, 14–15, 29.

Forward, J., Canter, R., and Kirsch, N. (1976). Role enactment and deception methodologies: Alternative paradigms. *American Psychologist, 31*, 595–604.

Fossey, D. (1981). Imperiled giants of the forest. *National Geographic, 159*, 501–23.

Fossey, D. (1983). *Gorillas in the Mist*. Boston: Houghton-Mifflin.

Fowler, F. J., Jr. (1993). *Survey Research Methods* (rev. ed.). Newbury Park, CA: Sage.

Fowler, F. J., Jr. (2001). *Survey Research Methods* (3rd ed.). Thousand Oaks, CA: Sage.

Fox, J. A. and Tracy, P. E. (1980). The randomized response approach. *Evaluation Review, 4*, 601–22.

Fox, J. A. and Tracy, P. E. (1984). Measuring associations with randomized response. *Social Science Research, 13*, 188–97.

Frankel, M. S. (1975). The development of policy guidelines governing human experimentation in the United States. *Ethics in Science and Medicine, 2*, 43–59.

Frankena, W. K. (1973). *Ethics* (2nd ed.). Englewood Cliffs, NJ: Prentice-Hall.

Franklin, A. D. (1981). Milikan's published and unpublished data on oil drops. *Historical Studies in the Physical Sciences, 11*, 185–201.

Fraud in medical research tied to lax rules (1989, February 14). *The New York Times*, p. C2.

Freedman, J. (1969). Role-playing: Psychology by consensus. *Journal of Personality and Social Psychology, 13*, 107–14.

Freeman, L. C. and Ataov, T. (1960). Invalidity of indirect and direct measures of attitude toward cheating. *Journal of Personality, 28*, 443–7.

French Psychological Society (1976). *Code de Déontologie*. Paris: FPS.

Friendly, J. (1983, June 12). Does a "public figure" have a right to privacy? *The New York Times*, p. 8E.

Furedy, J. J. (2002, April). IRBs: Ethics, yes – epistemology, no. *SAFS Newsletter, 31,* 12.

Gaertner, S. L. and Bickman, L. (1971). Effects of race on the elicitation of helping behavior: The wrong number technique. *Journal of Personality and Social Psychology, 20,* 218–22.

Gallistel, C. R. (1981). Bell, Magendie, and the proposals to restrict the use of animals in neurobehavioral research. *American Psychologist, 36,* 357–60.

Gallo, P. S., Smith, S., and Mumford, S. (1973). Effects of deceiving subjects upon experimental results. *Journal of Social Psychology, 89,* 99–107.

Gallup, G. G. (1979). Self-awareness in primates. *American Scientist, 67,* 417–21.

Gallup, G. G. and Suarez, S. (1980). On the use of animals in psychological research. *Psychological Record, 30,* 211–18.

Gallup, G. G., Jr. and Eddy, T. J. (1990). Animal facilities survey. *American Psychologist, 45,* 400–1.

Galvin, S. and Herzog, H. A., Jr. (1992). Ethical ideology, animal rights activism and attitudes toward the treatment of animals. *Ethics and Behavior, 2,* 141–9.

Garfield, E. (1978). The ethics of scientific publication. *Current Contents, 40,* 5–12.

Gastel, B. (1983). *Presenting Science to the Public.* Philadelphia: ISI Press.

Gaston, J. (1971). Secretiveness and competition for priority of discovery in physics. *Minerva, 9,* 472–92.

Gauthier, C. (2004). Overview and analysis of animal use in North America. *ATLA, 32* (Supplement 1), 275–85.

Gauthier, J. (2004). *Toward a Universal Declaration of Ethical Principles for Psychologists: A Progress Report.* Paper presented at the 28th International Congress of Psychology, Beijing, August.

Gaylin, W. and Blatte, H. (1975). Behavior modification in prisons. *American Criminal Law Review, 13,* 11–35.

Gazzaniga, M. S. and LeDoux, J. E. (1978). *The Integrated Mind.* New York: Plenum Press.

GDCADA (2005). *Parents Warned about 24-proof Gelatin.* Available at http://www.gdcada.org.

Geen, R. G. (1968). Effects of frustration, attack, and prior training in aggressiveness upon aggressive behavior. *Journal of Personality and Social Psychology, 9,* 316–21.

Geller, D. M. (1978). Involvement in role-playing simulations: A demonstration with studies on obedience. *Journal of Personality and Social Psychology, 36,* 219–35.

Geller, D. M. (1982). Alternatives to deception: why, what, and how? In J. E. Sieber (ed.), *The Ethics of Social Research: Surveys and Experiments.* New York: Springer-Verlag.

General Assembly for the Scandinavian Psychological Associations. (1989, March). Ethical principles for Scandinavian psychologists. *News From EFPPA, 3*(1).

Georgoudi, M. and Rosnow, R. L. (1985). Notes towards a contextualist understanding of social psychology. *Personality and Social Psychology Bulletin, 11,* 5–22.

Gerdes, E. P. (1979). College students' reactions to social psychological experiments involving deception. *Journal of Social Psychology, 107,* 99–110.

Gergen, K. J. (1973a). The codification of research ethics: Views of a doubting Thomas. *American Psychologist, 28,* 907–12.

Gergen, K. J. (1973b). Social psychology as history. *Journal of Personality and Social Psychology, 26,* 309–20.

German Association of Professional Psychologists (1986). *Professional Code of Ethics for Psychologists.* Bonn: GAPP.

Gersten, J. C., Langner, T. S., and Simcha-Fagan, O. (1979). Developmental patterns of types of behavioral disturbance and secondary prevention. *International Journal of Mental Health, 7,* 132–49.

Gilbody, S. M. and Song, F. (2000). Publication bias and the integrity of psychiatry research. *Psychological Medicine, 30,* 253–8.

Gillespie, J. F. (1999). The why, what, how, and when of effective faculty use of institutional review boards. In G. Chastain and R. E. Landrum (eds.), *Protecting Human Subjects: Departmental Subject Pools and Institutional Review Boards* (pp. 157–77). Washington, DC: American Psychological Association.

Glinski, R. J., Glinski, B. C., and Slatin, P. T. (1970). Nonnaivety contamination in conformity experiments: Sources, effects, and implications for control. *Journal of Personality and Social Psychology, 16,* 478–85.

Gluck, J. P. (2001). Animals in research: For and against. *Quarterly Review of Biology, 76,* 473–4.

Gluck, J. P. and Bell, J. (2003). Ethical issues in the use of animals in biomedical and psychopharmacological research. *Psychopharmacology, 171,* 6–12.

Golding, S. L. and Lichtenstein, E. (1970). Confession of awareness and prior knowledge of deceptions as a function of interview set and approval motivation. *Journal of Personality and Social Psychology, 14,* 213–23.

Goldman, J. and Katz, M. D. (1982). Inconsistency and institutional review boards. *Journal of the American Medical Association, 248,* 197–202.

Goldstein, J. H. (ed.) (1986). *Reporting Science: The Case of Aggression.* Hillsdale, NJ: Erlbaum.

Goldstein, R. (1981). On deceptive rejoinders about deceptive research: a reply to Baron. *IRB: A Review of Human Subjects Research, 3,* 5–6.

Goodman, P. S. (1979). *Assessing Organizational Change: The Rushton Quality of Work Experiment.* New York: Wiley.

Goodyear, R. K., Crego, C. A., and Johnston, M. W. (1992). Ethical issues in the supervision of student research: A study of critical incidents. *Professional Psychology: Research and Practice, 23,* 203–10.

Gray, B. H., Cooke, R. A., and Tannenbaum, A. S. (1978). Research involving human subjects. *Science, 201,* 1094–101.

Gray, B. and Cooke, R. A. (1980). The impact of institutional review boards on research. *Hastings Center Report, 10,* 36–41.

Green, B. F. (1992). Exposé or smear? The Burt affair. *Psychological Science, 3,* 328–31.

Greenberg, J. and Eskew, D. E. (1993). The role of role playing in organizational research. *Journal of Management, 19,* 221–41.

Greenberg, M. (1967). Role-playing: An alternative to deception? *Journal of Personality and Social Psychology, 7,* 152–7.

Greenberg, M.T., Domitrovich, C., and Bumbarger, B. (2001). The prevention of mental disorders in school-aged children: Current state of the field. *Prevention and Treatment, 4,* Article 1. Available at http://journals.apa.org.

Griffin, J. H. (1961). *Black Like Me.* Boston: Houghton Mifflin.

Grisso, T. and Appelbaum, P. S. (1995). The MacArthur treatment competence study III: Abilities of patients to consent to psychiatric and medical treatments. *Law and Human Behavior, 19,* 149–74.

Gross, A. E. and Fleming, I. (1982). Twenty years of deception in social psychology. *Personality and Social Psychology Bulletin, 8,* 402–8.

Grove, S. J. and Fisk, R. (1992). Observational data collection methods for services marketing: An overview. *Journal of the Academy of Marketing Science, 20,* 217–24.

Gurman, E. B. (1994). Debriefing for all concerned: Ethical treatment of human subjects. *Psychological Science, 5,* 139.

Haines, V. J., Diekhoff, G. M., LaBeff, E. E., and Clark, R. E. (1986). College cheating: Immaturity, lack of commitment, and the neutralizing attitude. *Research in Higher Education*, 25, 342–54.

Hamsher, J. H. and Reznikoff, M. (1967). Ethical standards in psychological research and graduate training: A study of attitudes within the profession. *Proceedings of the 75th Annual Convention of the American Psychological Association*, 2, 203–4.

Haney, C., Banks, W. C., and Zimbardo, P. G. (1973). Interpersonal dynamics in a simulated prison. *International Journal of Criminology and Penology*, 1, 69–97.

Hansen, C. (2001). Regulatory changes affecting IRBs and researchers. *APS Observer*, 14, 13–14, 25.

Haslam, S. A. and Reicher, S. (2003). Beyond Stanford: Questioning a role-based explanation of tyranny. *Dialogue*, 18, 22–5.

Hatfield, F. (1977). Prison research: The view from inside. *Hastings Center Report*, 7, 11–12.

Haveman, R. H. and Watts, H. W. (1976). Social experimentation as policy research: A review of negative income tax experiments. In G. Glass (ed.), *Evaluation Studies Review Annual* (Vol. 1). Beverly Hills, CA: Sage.

Haverkamp, B. E. (2005). Ethical perspectives on qualitative research in applied psychology. *Journal of Counseling Psychology*, 52, 146–55.

Haviland, J. B. (1977). Gossip as competition in Zinacantan. *Journal of Communication*, 27, 186–91.

Haywood, H. C. (1976). The ethics of doing research . . . and of not doing it. *American Journal of Mental Deficiency*, 81, 311–17.

Hearnshaw, L. (1979). *Cyril Burt, Psychologist*. New York: Vintage Press.

Henle, M. and Hubble, M. B. (1938). "Egocentricity" in adult conversation. *Journal of Social Psychology*, 9, 227–34.

Herbert, W. (1978, February). HEW tightens regulations on prisoner research. *APA Monitor*, 9, 12–15.

Herman, R. (1993, January 14). US weighs in on ethics as self-regulation fails. *International Herald Tribune*, p. 7.

Herrnstein, R. J. and Murray, C. (1994). *The Bell Curve: Intelligence and Class Structure in American Life*. New York: The Free Press.

Herzog, H. A., Jr. (1988). The moral status of mice. *American Psychologist*, 43, 473–4.

Herzog, H. A., Jr. (1990). Discussing animal rights and animal research in the classroom. *Teaching of Psychology*, 17, 90–4.

Herzog, H. A., Jr. (1993). "The movement is my life": the psychology of animal rights activism. *Journal of Social Issues*, 49, 103–19.

Hey, J. D. (1998). Experimental economics and deception. *Journal of Economic Psychology*, 19, 397–401.

Higbee, K. L. and Wells, M. G. (1972). Some research trends in social psychology during the 1960s. *American Psychologist*, 27, 963–6.

Hill, R. P. and Ward, J. C. (1989). Mood manipulation in marketing research: An examination of potential confounding effects. *Journal of Marketing Research*, 26, 97–104.

Hilts, P. J. (1994a, April 30). Tobacco firm halted nicotine study. *International Herald Tribune*, p. 3.

Hilts, P. J. (1994b, October 13). Human radiation testing wider than US revealed. *International Herald Tribune*, pp. 1, 4.

Hite, S. (1987). *Women and Love: A Cultural Revolution in Progress*. New York: Knopf.

Hochschild, A. R. (1987, November 15). Why can't a man be more like a woman? *The New York Times Book Review*, pp. 3, 34.

Hogan, P. M. and Kimmel, A. J. (1992). Ethical teaching of psychology: One department's attempts at self-regulation. *Teaching of Psychology, 19,* 205–10.

Holaday, M and Yost, T. E. (1993). Publication ethics. *Journal of Social Behavior and Personality, 8,* 557–66.

Holden, C. (1982). New focus on replacing animals in the lab. *Science, 215,* 35–8.

Holden, C. (1986, July). NIH transfers disputed monkeys to regional primate center. *Science, 233,* 154.

Holmes, D. S. (1967). Amount of experience in experiments as a determinant of performance in later experiments. *Journal of Personality and Social Psychology, 7,* 403–7.

Holmes, D. S. (1973). Effectiveness of debriefing after a stress producing deception. *Journal of Research in Personality, 7,* 127–38.

Holmes, D. S. (1976). Debriefing after psychological experiments. *American Psychologist, 31,* 858–75.

Holmes, D. S. and Bennett, D. H. (1974). Experiments to answer questions raised by the use of deception in psychological research. *Journal of Personality and Social Psychology, 29,* 358–67.

Holton, G. (1978). Subelectrons, presuppositions, and the Millikan–Ehrenhaft dispute. *Historical Studies in the Physical Sciences, 9,* 161–224.

Horowitz, I. A. (1969). Effects of volunteering, fear arousal, and number of communications on attitude change. *Journal of Personality and Social Psychology, 11,* 34–7.

Horowitz, I. L. (1967). *The Rise and Fall of Project Camelot.* Cambridge, MA: MIT Press.

Horowitz, I. L. and Rothschild, B. H. (1970). Conformity as a function of deception and role playing. *Journal of Personality and Social Psychology, 14,* 224–6.

Horvath, J. (1986). Detection of suspiciousness as a function of pleas for honesty. *Journal of Personality and Social Psychology, 50,* 921–4.

Houde, L. J. (2004). A data base survey of primate research in Asia. *Journal of Postgraduate Medicine, 50,* 256.

Hum, D. and Simpson, W. (1991). *Income Maintenance, Work Effort, and the Canadian Mincome Experiment.* Ottawa: Economic Council of Canada.

Humphreys, L. (1970). *Tearoom Trade.* Chicago: Aldine.

Hunt, S. D., Chonko, L. B., and Wilcox, J. B. (1984). Ethical problems of marketing researchers. *Journal of Marketing Research, 21,* 309–24.

Hutt, L. E. (2003). Paying research subjects: Historical considerations. *Health Law Review, 12,* 16–21.

ICC/ESOMAR (1986). ICC/ESOMAR international code of marketing and social research practice. In R. M. Worcester and J. Downham (eds.), *Consumer Market Research Handbook.* Amsterdam: North-Holland.

Institute of Business Ethics (2005). *Frequently Asked Questions.* Available at http://www.ibe.org.uk.

International Association of Marriage and Family Counselors (2006). Ethical code for the International Association of Marriage and Family Counseling. *The Family Journal, 14,* 92–98.

International Labour Organization (2005). *Corporate Codes of Conduct.* Available at http://www.itcilo.it.

Isambert, F. A. (1987). L'expérimentation sur l'homme comme pratique et comme représentation [Experiments on man as practice and as representation]. *Actes de la Recherche en Sciences Sociales, 60,* 15–30.

Jacoby, J. and Aranoff, D. (1971). Political polling and the lost-letter technique. *Journal of Social Psychology, 83,* 209–12.

Jamison, W. and Lunch, W. (1992). The rights of animals, science policy, and political activism. *Science, Technology, and Human Values*, 17, 438–58.

Jarvis, S., Day, J. E. L., and Reed, B. (2003). *British Society of Animal Science Ethical Guidelines for Research in Animal Science*. Available at http://www.bsas.org.uk

Jason, L. A. and Bogat, G. A. (1983). Preventive behavioral interventions. In R. D. Felner, L. A. Jason, J. N. Moritsugu, and S. S. Farber (eds.), *Preventive Psychology: Theory, Research and Practice*. Elmsford, NY: Pergamon.

Jasper, J. M. and Nelkin, D. (1992). *The Animal Rights Crusade: The Growth of a Moral Protest*. New York: Free Press.

Jeannet, J.-P. and Hennessey, H. D. (2004). *Global Marketing Strategies*, 6th ed. Boston: Houghton Mifflin.

Jendreck, M. P. (1989). Faculty reactions to academic dishonesty. *Journal of College Student Development*, 30, 401–6.

Jensen, A. R. (1974). Kinship correlations reported by Sir Cyril Burt. *Behavior Genetics*, 4, 1–28.

Jensen, A. R. (1978). Sir Cyril Burt in perspective. *American Psychologist*, 33, 499–503.

Johnson, D. (1990). Animal rights and human lives: time for scientists to right the balance. *Psychological Science*, 1, 213–14.

Jones, J. H. (1993). *Bad Blood: The Tuskegee Syphilis Experiment* (rev. ed.). New York: Free Press.

Jones, M. A. (1999). Entertaining shopping experiences: An exploratory investigation. *Journal of Retailing and Consumer Services*, 6, 129–39.

Jones, S. E. (2001). Ethics code draft published for comment. *Monitor on Psychology*, 32, 76.

Jonsen, A. R., Parker, M. L., Carlson, R. J., and Emmott, C. B. (1977). Biomedical experimentation on prisoners. *Ethics in Science and Medicine*, 4, 1–28.

Jorgensen, D. L. (1989). *Participant Observation: A Methodology for Human Studies*. Newbury Park, CA: Sage.

Jorgenson, J. (1971). On ethics and anthropology. *Current Anthropology*, 12, 347–50.

Josephson Institute of Ethics (2002). *Survey Documents Decade of Moral Deterioration: Kids Today Are More Likely to Cheat, Steal and Lie than Kids 10 Years Ago*. Available at http://www.josephsoninstitute.org.

Jourard, S. M. (1967). Experimenter–subject dialogue: A paradigm for a humanistic science of psychology. In J. F. T. Bugental (ed.), *Challenges of Humanistic Psychology*. New York: McGraw-Hill.

Jourard, S. M. (1968). *Disclosing Man to Himself*. Princeton, NJ: Van Nostrand.

Joynson, R. B. (1989). *The Burt Affair*. London: Routledge.

Judd, C. M., Smith, E. R., and Kidder, L. H. (1991). *Research Methods in Social Relations* (6th ed.). Fort Worth, TX: Holt, Rinehart and Winston.

Jung, J. (1969). Current practices and problems in the use of college students for psychological research. *Canadian Psychologist*, 10, 280–90.

Jung, J. (1975). Snoopology. *Human Behavior*, 4, 56–69.

Kallgren, C. A. and Kenrick, D. T. (1990, March). *Ethical Judgments and Nonhuman Research Subjects: The Effects of Phylogenetic Closeness and Affective Valence*. Paper presented at the Eastern Psychological Association meeting, Philadelphia.

Kallgren, C. A. and Tauber, R. T. (1996). Undergraduate research and the institutional review board: A mismatch or happy marriage? *Teaching of Psychology*, 23, 20–5.

Kamin, L. J. (1974). *The Science and Politics of IQ*. New York: Wiley.

Kaminsky, A., Roberts, L. W., and Brody, J. L. (2003). Influences upon willingness to participate in schizophrenia research: An analysis of narrative data from 63 people with schizophrenia. *Ethics and Behavior*, 13, 279–302.

Kant, I. (1965). *The Metaphysical Elements of Justice* (J. Ladd, trans.). Indianapolis: Bobbs-Merrill.

Katz, J. (1970). The education of the physician-investigator. In P. Freund (ed.), *Experimentation with Human Subjects*. London: Allen and Unwin.

Katz, J. (1972). *Experimentation with Human Beings*. New York: Russell Sage Foundation.

Keen, W. W. (1914). *Animal Experimentation and Medical Progress*. Boston: Houghton Mifflin.

Keith-Spiegel, P. and Koocher, G. P. (1985). *Ethics in Psychology: Professional Standards and Cases*. New York: Random House.

Kelman, H. C. (1967). Human use of human subjects: The problem of deception in social psychological experiments. *Psychological Bulletin, 67*, 1–11.

Kelman, H. C. (1968). *A Time to Speak: On Human Values and Social Research*. San Francisco: Jossey-Bass.

Kelman, H. C. (1972). The rights of the subject in social research: An analysis in terms of relative power and legitimacy. *American Psychologist, 27*, 989–1016.

Kemmelmeier, M., Davis, D., and Follette, W. C. (2003). Seven "sins" of misdirection? Ethical controversies surrounding the use of deception in research. In W. O'Donohue and K. E. Ferguson (eds.), *Handbook of Professional Ethics for Psychologists* (pp. 227–56). Thousand Oaks, CA: Sage.

Kershaw, D. N. and Fair, J. (1976). *The New Jersey Income Maintenance Experiment*. New York: Academic Press.

Kiesler, C. A., Pallak, M. S., and Kanouse, D. E. (1968). Interactive effects of commitment and dissonance. *Journal of Personality and Social Psychology, 8*, 331–8.

Kifner, J. (2001, September 8). Scholar sets off gastronomic false alarm. *The New York Times*, p. 1.

Kimble, G. (1976). *The Role of Risk/Benefit Analysis in the Conduct of Psychological Research*. Paper prepared for the National Commission for the Protection of Human Subjects of Biomedical and Behavioral Research. Bethesda, MD: US Department of Health, Education, and Welfare.

Kimble, G. (1987). The scientific value of undergraduate research participation. *American Psychologist, 42*, 267–8.

Kimmel, A. J. (1979). Ethics and human subjects research: A delicate balance. *American Psychologist, 34*, 633–5.

Kimmel, A. J. (1988a). *Ethics and Values in Applied Social Research*. Newbury Park, CA: Sage.

Kimmel, A. J. (1988b). Herbert Kelman and the ethics of social-psychological research. *Contemporary Social Psychology, 12*, 152–8.

Kimmel, A. J. (1991). Predictable biases in the ethical decision making of American psychologists. *American Psychologist, 46*, 786–8.

Kimmel, A. J. (1998). In defense of deception. *American Psychologist, 53*, 803–5.

Kimmel, A. J. (2001). Ethical trends in marketing and psychological research. *Ethics and Behavior, 11*, 131–49.

Kimmel, A. J. (2003). Ethical issues in social psychology research. In C. Sansone, C. C. Morf, and A. T. Panter (eds.), *The Sage Handbook of Methods in Social Psychology* (pp. 45–70). Thousand Oaks, CA: Sage.

Kimmel, A. J. (2004a). *Ethical Trends in Psychology and Marketing Research: An Update*. Paper presented at the 112th annual convention of the American Psychological Association, Honolulu, Hawaii.

Kimmel, A. J. (2004b). *Rumors and Rumor Control: A Manager's Guide to Understanding and Combatting Rumors*. Mahwah, NJ: LEA.

Kimmel, A. J. (2006). From artifacts to ethics: The delicate balance between methodological and moral concerns in behavioral research. In D. Hantula (ed.), *Advances in Theory and Methodology in Social and Organizational Psychology* (pp. 113–40). Mahwah, NJ: LEA.

Kimmel, A. J. (in press). Marketing, ethics, and society. In C. Michon (ed.), *The Marketer*. London: Pearson.

Kimmel, A. J. and Smith, N. C. (2001). Deception in marketing research: Ethical, methodological, and disciplinary implications. *Psychology and Marketing*, *18*, 663–89.

Kimmel, A. J. and Tissier-Desbordes, E. (1999). Males, masculinity, and consumption: An exploratory investigation. In B. Dubois, T. M. Lowrey, L. J. Shrum, and M. Vanhuele (eds.), *European Advances in Consumer Research* (Vol. 4, pp. 243–51). Provo, UT: Association for Consumer Research.

King, D. J. (1970). The subject pool. *American Psychologist*, *25*, 1179–81.

King, D. W. and King, L. A. (1991). Validity issues in research on Vietnam veteran adjustment. *Psychological Bulletin*, *109*, 107–24.

King, F. A. and Yarbrough, C. J. (1985). Medical and behavioral benefits from primate research. *The Physiologist*, *28*, 75–87.

Kinnear, T. C. and Taylor, J. R. (1995). *Marketing Research: An Applied Approach* (5th ed.). New York: McGraw-Hill.

Kirkpatrick, D. D. (2005, April 9). Responding to consumer and Senate pressure, EPA finally drops CHEERS study. *The New York Times*, p. A15.

Knapp, S. and VandeCreek, L. (2003). An overview of the major changes in the 2002 APA ethics code. *Professional Psychology: Research and Practice*, *34*, 301–8.

Knight, S., Nunkoosing, K., Vrij, A., and Cherryman, J. (2003). Using grounded theory to examine people's attitudes toward how animals are used. *Society and Animals*, *11*, 307–27.

Koestler, A. (1972). *The Case of the Midwife Toad*. New York: Random House.

Komp, C. (2004, November 12). Critics say EPA study would have harmed low-income children. *The New Standard*. Available at http://newstandardnews.net.

Kong, D. (1994, February 20). 1800 tested in radiation experiments. *The Boston Globe*, pp. 1, 22.

Koocher, G. P. (1977). Bathroom behavior and human dignity. *Journal of Personality and Social Psychology*, *35*, 120–1.

Korn, J. H. (1984). Coverage of research ethics in introductory and social psychology textbooks. *Teaching of Psychology*, *11*, 146–9.

Korn, J. H. (1988). Students' roles, rights, and responsibilities as research participants. *Teaching of Psychology*, *15*, 74–8.

Korn, J. H. and Bram, D. R. (1987). What is missing in the Method section of APA journal articles? *American Psychologist*, *43*, 1091–2.

Korn, J. H. and Hogan, K. (1992). Effect of incentives and aversiveness of treatment on willingness to participate in research. *Teaching of Psychology*, *19*, 21–4.

Kotler, P. (2003). *Marketing Management: International Edition*, 11th ed. Upper Saddle River, NJ: Pearson Education.

Kozinets, R. V. (1998). On netnography: Initial reflections on consumer research investigations of cyberculture. *Association for Consumer Research*, *25*, 366–71.

Kunz, P. R. and Fernquist, R. M. (1989). Opinions on abortion as measured by the lost-letter technique. *Psychological Reports*, *65*, 1343–6.

Kuschel, R. (1998). The necessity for code of ethics in research. *Psychiatry Today: Journal of the Yugoslav Psychiatric Association*, *30*, 247–74.

Lamberth, J. and Kimmel, A. J. (1981). Ethical issues and responsibilities in applying scientific behavioral knowledge. In A. J. Kimmel (ed.), *Ethics of Human Subject Research*. San Francisco: Jossey-Bass.

Landis, C. and Hunt, W. A. (1939). *The Startle Pattern*. New York: Farrar and Rinehart.

Landis, M. H. and Burtt, H. E. (1924). A study of conversations. *Journal of Comparative Psychology, 4*, 81–9.

Landrum, R. E. (1999). Introduction. In G. Chastain and R. E. Landrum (eds.), *Protecting Human Subjects: Departmental Subject Pools and Institutional Review Boards* (pp. 3–19). Washington, DC: American Psychological Association.

Landrum, R. E. and Chastain, G. (1995). Experiment spot-checks: A method for assessing the educational value of undergraduate participation in research. *IRB: A Review of Human Subjects Research, 17*, 4–6.

Landrum, R. E. and Chastain, G. (1999). Subject pool policies in undergraduate-only departments: Results from a nationwide survey. In G. Chastain and R. Eric Landrum (eds.), *Protecting Human Subjects: Departmental Subject Pools and Institutional Review Boards* (pp. 25–42). Washington, DC: American Psychological Association.

Langenderfer, J. and Shimp, T. A. (2001). Consumer vulnerability to scams, swindles, and fraud: A new theory of visceral influences on persuasion. *Psychology and Marketing, 18*, 763–84.

Larson, C. C. (1982, January). Animal research: striking a balance. *APA Monitor, 13*, 1, 12–13.

Latané, B. and Darley, J. M. (1970). *The Unresponsive Bystander: Why Doesn't He Help?* New York: Appleton-Century-Crofts.

Lawson, E. (2001). Informational and relational meanings of deception: Implications for deception methods in research. *Ethics and Behavior, 11*, 115–30.

Le, H.-N., Muñoz, R. F., Ippen, C. G., and Stoddard, J. L. (2003). Treatment is not enough: We must prevent major depression in women. *Prevention and Treatment, 4*, Article 10. Available at http://journals.apa.org.

Lea, S. E. G. (1979). Alternatives to the use of painful stimuli in physiological psychology and the study of animal behavior. *ATLA Abstracts, 7*, 20–1.

Leach, M. M. and Harbin, J. J. (1997). Psychological ethics codes: A comparison of twenty-four countries. *International Journal of Psychology, 32*, 181–92.

Leak, G. K. (1981). Student perception of coercion and value from participation in psychological research. *Teaching of Psychology, 8*, 147–9.

Lee, C. C. (1991). New approaches to diversity: Implications for multicultural counselor training and research. In C. C. Lee and B. L. Richardson (eds.), *Multicultural Issues in Counseling: New Approaches to Diversity* (pp. 209–14). Alexandria, VA: American Association for Counseling and Development.

Lee, F. R. (2003, October 4). Are more people cheating? Despite ample accounts of dishonesty, a moral decline is hard to calculate. *The New York Times*, p. B7.

Lemmens, T, and Singer, P. A. (1998). Bioethics for clinicians: Conflict of interest in research, education and patient care. *Canadian Medical Association Journal, 159*, 960–5.

Lemon, R. and Dunnett, S. B. (2005). Surveying the literature from animal experiments. *British Medical Journal, 330*, 977–8.

Levenson, R. L., Jr. (1996). Enhance the journals, not the review process. *American Psychologist, 51*, 1191–3.

Levin, J. (1981). Ethical problems in sociological research. In A. J. Kimmel (ed.), *Ethics of Human Subject Research*. San Francisco: Jossey Bass.

Levin, J. and Arluke, A. (1985). An exploratory analysis of sex differences in gossip. *Sex Roles, 12*, 281–6.

Levine, R. J. (1975). *The Nature and Definition of Informed Consent in Various Research Settings*. Paper prepared for the National Commission for the Protection of Human Subjects of

Biomedical and Behavioral Research. Bethesda, MD: US Department of Health, Education, and Welfare.

Levy, C. M. and Brackbill, Y. (1979, March). Informed consent: Getting the message across to kids. *APA Monitor*, *10*, 3.

Levy, L. H. (1967). Awareness, learning, and the beneficient subject as expert witness. *Journal of Personality and Social Psychology*, *6*, 365–70.

Lewin, K. (1947). Group decision and social change. In T. M. Newcomb and E. L. Hartley (eds.), *Readings in Social Psychology*. New York: Holt.

Lewin, K. (1951). Problems of research in social psychology. In D. Cartwright (ed.), *Field Theory in Social Science*. New York: Harper and Row.

Lexchin, J., Bero, L. A., Djulbegovic, B., and Clark, O. (2003). Pharmaceutical industry sponsorship and research outcome and quality: Systematic review. *British Medical Journal*, *326*, 1167–70.

Lichtenstein, E. (1970). Please don't talk to anyone about this experiment: Disclosure of deception by debriefed subjects. *Psychological Reports*, *26*, 485–6.

Lifton, R. J. (2000). *The Nazi Doctors: Medical Killing and the Psychology of Genocide*. New York: Perseus.

Linden, L. E. and Weiss, D. J. (1994). An empirical assessment of the random response method of sensitive data collection. *Journal of Social Behavior and Personality*, *9*, 823–36.

Linder, D. E., Cooper, J., and Jones, E. E. (1967). Decision freedom as a determinant of the role of incentive magnitude in attitude change. *Journal of Personality and Social Psychology*, *6*, 245–54.

Lindsay, R. C. L. and Holden, R. R. (1987). The introductory psychology subject pool in Canada. *Canadian Psychology*, *28*, 45–52.

Lipton, J. P. and Garza, R. T. (1978). Further evidence for subject pool contamination. *European Journal of Social Psychology*, *6*, 363–70.

Lochman, J. E. (2000). Parent and family skills training in targeted prevention programs for at-risk youth. *Journal of Primary Prevention*, *21*, 253–65.

Locke, E. A. (1993). Found in the SIOP archives: Footnotes that somehow got left out of published manuscripts. *The Industrial-Organizational Psychologist*, *31*(2), 53.

London, M. and Bray, D. W. (1980). Ethical issues in testing and evaluation for personnel decisions. *American Psychologist*, *35*, 890–901.

Loo, C. M. (1982). Vulnerable populations: Case study in crowding research. In J. E. Sieber (ed.), *The Ethics of Social Research: Surveys and Experiments*. New York: Springer-Verlag.

Lorion, R. P. (1983). Evaluating preventive interventions: Guidelines for the serious social change agent. In R. D. Felner, L. A. Jason, J. N. Moritsugu, and S. S. Farber (eds.), *Preventive Psychology: Theory, Research and Practice*. Elmsford, NY: Pergamon.

Lorion, R. P. (1984). Research issues in the design and evaluation of preventive interventions. In J. P. Bowker (ed.), *Education for Primary Prevention in Social Work*. New York: Council on Social Work Education.

Lowman, R. L. (1993). An ethics code for I/O psychology: For what purpose and at what cost? *The Industrial-Organizational Psychologist*, *31*(1), 90–2.

Lowman, R. L. (ed.) (1985). *Casebook on Ethics and Standards for the Practice of Psychology in Organizations*. College Park, MD: Society for Industrial and Organizational Psychology.

Lowman, R. L. (ed.). (1998). *The Ethical Practice of Psychology in Organizations*. Washington, DC: American Psychological Association.

Lowman, R. P. and Soule, L. M. (1981). Professional ethics and the use of humans in research. In A. J. Kimmel (ed.), *Ethics of Human Subject Research*. San Francisco: Jossey-Bass.

Lueptow, L., Mueller, S. A., Hammes, R. R., and Master, L. S. (1977). The impact of informed consent regulations on response rate and response bias. *Sociological Methods and Research, 6,* 183–204.

MacCoun, R. J. and Kerr, N. L. (1987). Suspicion in the psychology laboratory: Kelman's prophesy revisited. *American Psychologist, 42,* 199.

Mackintosh, N. J. (ed.) (1995). *Cyril Burt: Fraud or Framed?* Oxford, UK: Oxford University Press.

Mahl, G. F. (1995). A personal encounter with scientific deviance. *American Psychologist, 50,* 882–3.

Mahoney, M. J. (1976). *Scientist as Subject: The Psychological Imperative.* Cambridge, MA: Ballinger.

Malloy, D. C., Hadjistavropoulos, T., Douaud, P., and Smythe, W. E. (2002). The code of ethics of the Canadian Psychological Association and the Canadian Medical Association: Ethical orientation and functional grammar analysis. *Canadian Psychology, 43,* 244–53.

Malloy, D. C. and Pitter, R. (2006). *Ethics and Values in Community Sport: Interdisciplinary Lessons to Be Learned.* Unpublished manuscript, University of Regina, Regina, Saskatchewan, Canada.

Mamali, C. (2004). Lessons from the epistemic, moral and social richness of Stanford prison experiment. *Dialogue, 19,* 22–3, 28.

Market and Opinion Research International (1999, May 19). *Attitudes Towards Experimentation on Live Animals.* Available at http://www.mori.com.

Marketing Research and Intelligence Association (2004). *Canadian Attitudes to Survey Research.* Available at http://www.mria-arim.ca.

Masling, J. (1966). Role-behavior of the subject and psychologist and its effects upon psychological data. *Nebraska Symposium on Motivation, 14,* 67–103.

Mathy, R. M., Kerr, D. L., and Haydin, B. M. (2003). Methodological rigor and ethical considerations in Internet-mediated research. *Psychotherapy: Theory, Research, Practice, Training, 40,* 77–85.

McAskie, M. (1978). Carelessness or fraud in Sir Cyril Burt's kinship data? A critique of Jensen's analysis. *American Psychologist, 33,* 496–8.

McBurney, D. (1996). Cheating: Preventing and dealing with academic dishonesty. *APS Observer, 9,* 32–5.

McCabe, K. (1990, February). Beyond cruelty. *Washingtonian,* pp. 112–18, 153–7.

McCarthy, C. R. (1981). The development of federal guidelines for social research. In A. J. Kimmel (ed.), *Ethics of Human Subject Research.* San Francisco: Jossey-Bass.

McCloskey, M., Rapp, B., Yantis, S., Rubin, G., Bacon, W. F., Dagnelie, G., Gordon, B., Aliminosa, D., Boatman, D. F., Badeker, W., Johnson, D. N., Tusa, R. J., and Palmer, E. (1995). A developmental deficit in localizing objects from vision. *Psychological Science, 6,* 112–17.

McCord, D. M. (1991). Ethics-sensitive management of the university human subject pool. *American Psychologist, 46,* 151.

McCord, J. (1978). A thirty-year follow-up of treatment effects. *American Psychologist, 33,* 284–9.

McCormick, R. H. (1976). Experimentation on children: Sharing in sociality. *Hastings Center Report, 6,* 41–6.

McDaniel, T. and Starmer, C. (1998). Experimental economics and deception: A comment. *Journal of Economic Psychology, 19,* 403–9.

McDonald, P. J. and Eilenfield, V. C. (1980). Physical attractiveness and the approach/avoidance of self-awareness. *Personality and Social Psychology Bulletin, 6,* 391–5.

McGuire, W. J. (1969). Suspiciousness of experimenter's intent. In R. Rosenthal and R. L. Rosnow (eds.), *Artifact in Behavioral Research*. New York: Academic Press.

McNamara, J. R. and Woods, K. M. (1977). Ethical considerations in psychological research: A comparative review. *Behavior Therapy, 8*, 703–8.

McNemar, Q. (1946). Opinion-attitude methodology. *Psychological Bulletin, 43*, 289–374.

McNemar, Q. (1960). At random: Sense and nonsense. *American Psychologist, 15*, 295–300.

McQuarrie, E. F. (1998). Have laboratory experiments become detached from advertiser goals? A meta-analysis. *Journal of Advertising Research, 38*, 15–25.

Meara, N. M., Schmidt, L. D., and Day, J. D. (1996). Principles and virtues: A foundation for ethical decisions, policies, and character. *The Counseling Psychologist, 24*, 4–77.

Medawar, P. B. (1976, May 22). Science and the patchwork mouse. *Science News, 109*, 335.

Meeus, W. H. J. and Raaijmakers, Q. A. W. (1986). Administrative obedience: Carrying out orders to use psychological-administrative violence. *European Journal of Social Psychology, 16*, 311–24.

Meeus, W. H. J and Raaijmakers, Q. A. W. (1987). Administrative obedience as a social phenomenon. In W. Doise and S. Moscovici (eds.), *Current Issues in European Social Psychology* (Vol. 2). Cambridge: Cambridge University Press.

Mehren, E. (1987, November 16). Controversies surrounding self-proclaimed cultural historian Shere Hite. *The Boston Globe*, p. 2.

Meier, P. (1992, May 12). *Ethical and Scientific Issues in Drug Trials with Human Participants*. Presentation to the APA Committee on Standards in Research, New York.

Menges, R. J. (1973). Openness and honesty versus coercion and deception in psychological research. *American Psychologist, 28*, 1030–4.

Merritt, C. B. and Fowler, R. G. (1948). The pecuniary honesty of the public at large. *Journal of Abnormal and Social Psychology, 43*, 90–3.

Middlemist, D., Knowles, E. S., and Matter, C. F. (1976). Personal space invasions in the laboratory: Suggestive evidence for arousal. *Journal of Personality and Social Psychology, 33*, 541–6.

Middlemist, D., Knowles, E. S., and Matter, C. F. (1977). What to do and what to report: A reply to Koocher. *Journal of Personality and Social Psychology, 35*, 122–4.

Milgram, S. (1963). Behavioral study of obedience. *Journal of Abnormal and Social Psychology, 67*, 371–8.

Milgram, S. (1964). Issues in the study of obedience: A reply to Baumrind. *American Psychologist, 19*, 848–52.

Milgram, S. (1969, June). The lost letter technique. *Psychology Today*, pp. 3, 30ff.

Milgram, S. (1974). *Obedience to Authority*. New York: Harper and Row.

Milgram, S., Mann, L., and Harter, S. (1965). The lost letter technique: A tool of social research. *Public Opinion Quarterly, 29*, 437–8.

Mill, J. S. (1957). *Utilitarianism*. New York: Bobbs-Merrill.

Miller, A. G. (1972). Role playing: An alternative to deception; a review of the evidence. *American Psychologist, 27*, 623–36.

Miller, A. G., Collins, B. E., and Brief, D. E. (1995). Perspectives on obedience to authority: The legacy of the Milgram experiments. *Journal of Social Issues, 51*, 1–19.

Miller, N. E. (1979). *The Scientist's Responsibility for Public Information: A Guide to Effective Communication with the Media*. Washington, DC: Society for Neuroscience.

Miller, N. E. (1983). Understanding the use of animals in behavioral research: Some critical issues. In J. A. Sechzer (ed.), *The Role of Animals in Biomedical Research*. New York: New York Academy of Sciences.

Miller, N. E. (1985). The value of behavioral research on animals. *American Psychologist, 40,* 423–40.

Mills, J. (1976). A procedure for explaining experiments involving deception. *Personality and Social Psychology Bulletin, 2,* 3–13.

Miner, J. (1992). *Industrial-Organizational Psychology.* New York: McGraw-Hill.

Mirvis, P. H. and Seashore, S. E. (1979). Being ethical in organizational research. *American Psychologist, 34,* 766–80.

Mirvis, P. H. and Seashore, S. E. (1982). Creating ethical relationships in organizational research. In J. E. Sieber (ed.), *The Ethics of Social Research: Surveys and Experiments.* New York: Springer-Verlag.

Mishkin, B. (1985). On parallel tracks: Protecting human subjects and animals. *Hastings Center Report, 15,* 36–7.

Misra, S. (1992). Is conventional debriefing adequate? An ethical issue in consumer research. *Journal of the Academy of Marketing Science, 20,* 269–73.

Mitchell, R. G., Jr. (1990). An unprincipled ethic? The missing morality of the ASA code. *The American Sociologist, 21,* 271–4.

Mitchell, S. C. and Steingrub, J. (1988). The changing clinical trials scene: the role of the IRB. *IRB: A Review of Human Subjects Research, 10,* 1–5.

Mitroff, I. I. (1974). Norms and counter-norms in a select group of the Apollo moon scientists: A case study of the ambivalence of scientists. *American Sociological Review, 39,* 579–95.

Mitscherlich, A. and Mielke, F. (eds.) (1960). *Medizin ohne Menschlichkeit.* Frankfurt, Germany: Fischer.

Mixon, D. (1971). Behavior analysis treating subjects as actors rather than organisms. *Journal for the Theory of Social Behavior, 1,* 19–31.

Mixon, D. (1972). Instead of deception. *Journal for the Theory of Social Behavior, 2,* 145–77.

Mixon, D. (1974). If you won't deceive, what can you do? In N. Armistead (ed.), *Reconstructing Social Psychology.* Baltimore, MD: Penguin.

Montanye, T., Mulberry, R. F., and Hardy, K. R. (1971). Assessing prejudice toward Negroes at three universities using the lost-letter technique. *Psychological Reports, 29,* 531–7.

Mook, D. G. (1983). In defense of external validity. *American Psychologist, 38,* 379–87.

Moore, H. T. (1922). Further data concerning sex differences. *Journal of Abnormal and Social Psychology, 17,* 210–14.

Moriarty, T. (1975). Crime, commitment, and the unresponsive bystander: two field experiments. *Journal of Personality and Social Psychology, 31,* 370–6.

Morrison, A. R. (2001). A scientist's perspective on the ethics of using animals in behavioral research. In M. E. Carroll (ed.), *Advancing Human Welfare through Behavioral Science* (pp. 341–56). Washington, DC: American Psychological Association.

Morrow, D. J. (1996, September 30). Human guinea pigs line up to get sick. *The International Herald Tribune,* pp. 1, 7.

Mott, F. W. and Sherrington, C. S. (1895). Experiments on the influence of sensory nerves upon movement and nutrition of the limbs. *Proceedings of the Royal Society, 57,* 481–8.

Muchinsky, P. M. (1983). *Psychology Applied to Work.* Homewood, IL: Dorsey.

Mueller, J. (2003). Overkill by IRBs. *APS Observer, 16*(10), 3.

Mueller, J. H. and Furedy, J. J. (2001). Reviewing for risk: What's the evidence that it works? *APS Observer, 14*(7), 1, 26–8.

Mulvey, E. P. and Phelps, P. (1988). Ethical balances in juvenile justice research and practice. *American Psychologist, 43,* 65–9.

Muñiz, A. M., Jr. and O'Guinn, T. C. (2005). Marketing communications in a world of consumption and brand communities. In A. J. Kimmel (ed.), *Marketing Communication: New Approaches, Technologies, and Styles*. Oxford, UK: Oxford University Press.

Muñoz, R. F. (1983, May). *Prevention Intervention Research: A Sample of Ethical Dilemmas.* Paper presented at the NIMH State of the Art Workshop on Ethics and Primary Prevention, California State University, Northridge.

Muñoz, R. F., Glish, M., Soo-Hoo, T., and Robertson, J. (1982). The San Francisco mood survey project: Preliminary work toward the prevention of depression. *American Journal of Community Psychology, 10,* 317–29.

Murphy, G. L. (1999). A case study of a departmental subject pool and review board. In G. Chastain and R. E. Landrum (eds.), *Protecting Human Subjects: Departmental Subject Pools and Institutional Review Boards* (pp. 131–56). Washington, DC: American Psychological Association.

Murray, B. (2002). Research fraud needn't happen at all. *Monitor on Psychology, 33,* 27–8.

Mystery Shopping Providers Association (2005). *MSPA Code of Professional Standards and Ethics Agreement for Mystery Shoppers.* Available at http://www.mysteryshop.org.

National Academy of Sciences (1979). *Report of the Panel on Privacy and Confidentiality as Factors in Survey Response.* Washington, DC: NAS.

National Bioethics Advisory Commission (2001). *Ethical and Policy Issues in Research Involving Human Participants.* Bethesda, MD: NBAC.

National Central Bureau of Statistics (1977). *The National Central Bureau of Statistics and the General Public: Findings of an Interview Survey Taken in Sweden During the Spring of 1976.* Stockholm: SCB.

National Commission for the Protection of Human Subjects of Biomedical and Behavioral Research (1979). *The Belmont Report: Ethical Principles and Guidelines for the Protection of Human Subjects of Research.* Washington, DC: US Government Printing Office.

National Health and Medical Research Council (1999). *National Statement on Ethical Conduct in Research Involving Humans.* Available at http://www7.health.gov.au.

National Science Board (1991). *Science and Engineering Indicators.* Washington, DC: US Government Printing Office.

Nelson, G., Westhues, A., and MacLeod, J. (2003). A meta-analysis of longitudinal research on preschool prevention programs for children. *Prevention and Treatment, 6,* Article 10. Available at http://journals.apa.org.

Netherlands Institute of Psychologists (1988). *Professional Code for Psychologists.* Amsterdam: NIP.

Netherlands Institute of Psychologists (1998). *Code of Ethics.* Available at http://wwwpsynip.nl.

Neuliep, J. W. and Crandall, R. (1993). Reviewer bias against replication research. In J. W. Neuliep (ed.), *Replication Research in the Social Sciences* [Special Issue]. *Journal of Social Behavior and Personality, 8,* 21–9.

Newberry, B. H. (1973). Truth-telling in subjects with information about experiments: Who is being deceived? *Journal of Personality and Social Psychology, 25,* 369–74.

Newton, R. (1977). *The Crime of Claudius Ptolemy.* Baltimore, MD: Johns Hopkins University Press.

Nicks, S. D., Korn, J. H., and Mainieri, T. (1997). The rise and fall of deception in social psychology and personality research, 1921 to 1994. *Ethics and Behavior, 7,* 69–77.

Nosek, B. A., Banaji, M. R., and Greenwald, A. G. (2002). E-research: Ethics, security, design, and control in psychological research on the Internet. *Journal of Social Issues, 58,* 161–76.

Novak, E., Seckman, C. E., and Stewart, R. D. (1977). Motivations for volunteering as research subjects. *Journal of Clinical Pharmacology, 17,* 365–71.

Novak, M. and Petto, A. J. (eds.) (1991). *Through the Looking Glass: Issues of Psychological Well-Being in Captive Nonhuman Primates.* Washington, DC: American Psychological Association.

Nummer, J. G. and Handelsman, M. M. (1992). Effects of subject pool policy on student attitudes toward psychology and psychological research. *Teaching of Psychology, 19,* 141–4.

Office for Protection from Research Risks (1986). *Public Health Service Policy on Humane Care and Use of Laboratory Animals.* Bethesda, MD: National Institutes of Health.

O'Leary, C., Willis, F., and Tomich, E. (1970). Conformity under deceptive and non-deceptive techniques. *Sociological Quarterly, 11,* 87–93.

Oliver, P. (2003). *The Student's Guide to Research Ethics.* Buckingham, UK: Open University Press.

Olson, T. and Christiansen, G. (1966). *The Grindstone Experiment: Thirty-One Hours.* Toronto: Canadian Friends Service Committee.

Orem, J. M. (1990, March 14). Demands that research be useful threaten to undermine basic science in this country. *The Chronicle of Higher Education,* pp. B2–B3.

Organic Consumers Association (2004). *EPA and Chemical Industry to Study Effects of Known Toxic Chemicals on Children.* Available at http://www.organicconsumers.org.

Orlans, F. B. (1993). *In the Name of Science: Issues in Responsible Animal Experimentation.* New York: Oxford University Press.

Orne, M. T. (1959). The nature of hypnosis: Artifact and essence. *Journal of Abnormal and Social Psychology, 58,* 277–99.

Orne, M. T. (1962). On the social psychology of the psychological experiment: With particular reference to demand characteristics and their implications. *American Psychologist, 17,* 776–83.

Orne, M. T. (1969). Demand characteristics and the concept of quasi-controls. In R. Rosenthal and R. L. Rosnow (eds.), *Artifact in Behavioral Research.* New York: Academic Press.

Orne, M. T. and Holland, C. H. (1968). On the ecological validity of laboratory deceptions. *International Journal of Psychiatry, 6,* 282–93.

Orne, M. T. and Whitehouse, W. G. (2000). Demand characteristics. In A. E. Kazdin (ed.), *Encyclopedia of Psychology* (pp. 469–70). New York: Oxford University Press.

Ortmann, A. and Hertwig, R. (2002). The costs of deception: Evidence from psychology. *Experimental Economics, 5,* 111–31.

Ostrom, T. M. (1973). The bogus pipeline: A new ignis fatuus? *Psychological Bulletin, 79,* 252–9.

Page, M. M. (1973). On detecting demand awareness by postexperimental questionnaire. *Journal of Social Psychology, 91,* 305–23.

Patten, S. C. (1977). Milgram's shocking experiments. *Philosophy, 52,* 425–40.

Pechman, J. A. and Timpane, P. M. (eds.) (1975). *Work Incentives and Income Guarantees: The New Jersey Income Tax Experiment.* Washington, DC: The Brookings Institution.

Penner, L. A. (2002). IRB and U: What institutional review boards are supposed to do. *Dialogue, 17,* 28–9.

Pepitone, A. (1981). Lessons from the history of social psychology. *American Psychologist, 36,* 972–85.

Percival, T. (1803). *Medical Ethics.* Manchester, UK: S. Russell.

Permut, S. E., Michel, A. J., and Joseph, M. (1976). The researcher's sample: A review of the choice of respondents in marketing research. *Journal of Marketing Research, 13,* 278–83.

Peters, D. P. and Ceci, S. J. (1982). Peer review practices of psychological journals: The fate of published articles, submitted again. *The Behavioral and Brain Sciences*, 5, 187–95.

Phillips, D. P. (1977). Motor vehicle fatalities increase just after publicized suicide stories. *Science*, 196, 1464–5.

Phillips, M. T. and Sechzer, J. A. (1989). *Animal Research and Ethical Conflict*. New York: Springer-Verlag.

Pifer, L., Shimizu, K., and Pifer, R. (1994). Public attitudes toward animal research: Some international comparisons. *Society and Animals*, 2, 95–113.

Pihl, R. O., Zacchia, C., and Zeichner, A. (1981). Follow-up analysis of the use of deception and aversive contingencies in psychological experiments. *Psychological Reports*, 48, 927–30.

Piliavin, I. M., Rodin, J., and Piliavin, J. A. (1969). Good Samaritanism: An underground phenomenon? *Journal of Personality and Social Psychology*, 13, 289–99.

Piliavin, J. A. and Piliavin, I. M. (1972). Effects of blood on reactions to a victim. *Journal of Personality and Social Psychology*, 23, 353–61.

Pipes, R. B., Holstein, J. E., and Aguirre, M. G. (2005). Examining the personal–professional distinction: Ethics codes and the difficulty of drawing a boundary. *American Psychologist*, 60, 325–34.

Plous, S. (1991). An attitude survey of animal rights activists. *Psychological Science*, 2, 194–6.

Plous, S. (1996). Attitudes toward the use of animals in psychological research and education. *American Psychologist*, 51, 1167–80.

Plous, S. and Herzog, H. A., Jr. (2001). Reliability of protocol reviews for animal research. *Science*, 293, 608–9.

Polich, J. M., Ellickson, P. L., Reuter, P., and Kahn, J. P. (1984). *Strategies for Controlling Adolescent Drug Use*. Santa Monica, CA: Rand.

Poll finds support for animal tests (1985, October 29). *The New York Times*, p. C4.

Pound, P., Ebrahim, S., Sandercock, P., Bracken, M. B., and Roberts, I. (2004). Where is the evidence that animal research benefits humans? *British Medical Journal*, 328, 514–17.

Powers, E. and Witmer, H. (1951). *An Experiment in the Prevention of Delinquency: The Cambridge–Somerville Youth Study*. New York: Columbia University Press.

Pratt, D. (1976). *Painful Experiments on Animals*. New York: Argus Archives.

Prentice, E. D. and Antonson, D. L. (1987). A protocol review guide to reduce IRB inconsistency. *IRB: A Review of Human Subjects Research*, 9, 9–11.

President's Commission for the Study of Ethical Problems in Medicine and Biomedical and Behavioral Research (1982). *Compensating Research Injuries*. Washington, DC: US Government Printing Office.

Privireal (2005). *Privacy in Research Ethics and Law*. Available at http://www.privireal.group.shef.ac.uk

Proctor, R. N. (1999). *The Nazi War on Cancer*. Princeton, NJ: Princeton University Press.

Pruzan, A. (1976). Effects of age, rearing and mating experiences on frequency dependent sexual selection in *Drosophila pseudoobscura*. *Evolution*, 30, 130–45.

Pruzan, A., Applewhite, P. B., and Bucci, M. J. (1977). Protein synthesis inhibition alters *Drosophila* mating behavior. *Pharmacology, Biochemistry and Behavior*, 6, 355–7.

Psychological Association of Slovenia (1982). *Code of Ethics for Psychologists*. Ljubljana, Slovenia: PAS.

Rabinovich, B. A. (1996). A perspective on the journal review process. *American Psychologist*, 51, 1190.

Ramsey, P. (1976). The enforcement of morals: Nontherapeutic research on children. *Hastings Center Report*, 6, 21–9.

Randall, W. C. (1983). Is medical research in jeopardy? *The Physiologist, 26,* 73–7.

Rathje, W. L. and Murphy. C. (2001). *Rubbish! The Archaeology of Garbage.* Tucson: University of Arizona Press.

Raupp, C. D. and Cohen, D. C. (1992). "A thousand points of light" illuminate the psychology curriculum: volunteering as a learning experience. *Teaching of Psychology, 19,* 25–30.

Ravitch, N., Veatch, R. M., Kohut, T. A., and Lifton, R. J. (1987). Symposium. The Nazi doctors: Medical killing and the psychology of genocide. *The Psychohistory Review, 16,* 3–66.

Reese, H. W. and Fremouw, W. J. (1984). Normal and normative ethics in behavioral sciences. *American Psychologist, 39,* 863–76.

Regan, T. (1983). *The Case for Animal Rights.* Berkeley: University of California Press.

Reid, T. and Priest, L. L. P. (1999). Internet law update: Developments in privacy laws 1999. *FindLaw for Legal Professionals.* Available at http://library.findlaw.com.

Reiss, A. J. (1976). *Selected Issues in Informed Consent and Confidentiality with Special Reference to Behavioral/Social Science Research/Inquiry.* Paper prepared for the National Commission for the Protection of Human Subjects of Biomedical and Behavioral Research. Bethesda, MD: US Department of Health, Education, and Welfare.

Researcher admits he faked journal data (1977, March 5). *Science News, 111,* 150–1.

Resnick, J. H. and Schwartz, T. (1973). Ethical standards as an independent variable in psychological research. *American Psychologist, 28,* 134–9.

Reynolds, P. D. (1979). *Ethical Dilemmas and Social Science Research.* San Francisco: Jossey-Bass.

Riecken, H. W. (1975). Social experimentation. *Society, 12,* 34–41.

Riegel, K. F. (1979). *Foundations of Dialectical Psychology.* New York: Academic Press.

Ring, K. (1967). Experimental social psychology: Some sober questions about some frivolous values. *Journal of Experimental and Social Psychology, 3,* 113–23.

Ring, K., Wallston, K., and Corey, M. (1970). Mode of debriefing as a factor affecting subjective reaction to a Milgram-type obedience experiment: an ethical inquiry. *Representative Research in Social Psychology, 1,* 67–88.

Riniolo, T. C. (1997). Publication bias: A computer-assisted demonstration of excluding nonsignificant results from research interpretation. *Teaching of Psychology, 24,* 279–282

Rissman, E. F. (1995). An alternative animal model for the study of female sexual behavior. *Current Directions in Psychological Science, 4,* 6–10.

Robb, J. W. (1988). Can animal use be ethically justified? In H. N. Guttman, J. A. Mench, and R. C. Simmonds (eds.), *Proceedings from a Conference on Science and Animals: Addressing Contemporary Issues.* Bethesda, MD: Scientists' Center for Animal Welfare.

Robson, C. (1993). *Real World Research: A Resource for Social Scientists and Practitioner-Researchers.* Oxford, UK: Blackwell.

Rollin, B. (1981). *Animal Rights and Human Morality.* Buffalo, NY: Prometheus.

Rollin, B. E. (1985). The moral status of research animals in psychology. *American Psychologist, 40,* 920–6.

Rosell, M. C., Beck, D. M., Luther, K. E., Goedert, K. M., Shore, W. J., and Anderson, D. D. (2005). The pedagogical value of experimental participation paired with course content. *Teaching of Psychology, 32,* 95–9.

Rosenhan, D. I. (1973). On being sane in insane places. *Science, 179,* 250–8.

Rosenthal, R. (1991). Teacher expectancy effects: A brief update 25 years after the Pygmalion experiment. *Journal of Research in Education, 1,* 3–12.

Rosenthal, R. (1994a). Interpersonal expectancy effects: A 30-year perspective. *Current Directions in Psychological Science, 3,* 176–9.

Rosenthal, R. (1994b). Science and ethics in conducting, analyzing, and reporting psychological research. *Psychological Science*, 5, 127–34.

Rosenthal, R. and Jacobson, L. (1968). *Pygmalion in the Classroom*. New York: Holt.

Rosenthal, R. and Rosnow, R. L. (1975). *The Volunteer Subject*. New York: Wiley.

Rosenthal, R. and Rosnow, R. L. (1984). Applying Hamlet's question to the ethical conduct of research: a conceptual addendum. *American Psychologist*, 39, 561–3.

Rosenthal, R. and Rosnow, R. L. (1991). *Essentials of Behavioral Research: Methods and Data Analysis* (2nd ed.). New York: McGraw-Hill.

Rosnow, R. L. (1978). The prophetic vision of Giambattista Vico: Implications for the state of social psychological theory. *Journal of Personality and Social Psychology*, 36, 1322–31.

Rosnow, R. L. (1981). *Paradigms in Transition: The Methodology of Social Inquiry*. New York: Oxford University Press.

Rosnow, R. L. (1991). Inside rumor: A personal journey. *American Psychologist*, 46, 484–96.

Rosnow, R. L. (1997). Hedgehogs, foxes, and the evolving social contract in psychological science: Ethical challenges and methodological opportunities. *Psychological Methods*, 2, 345–56.

Rosnow, R. L. (2001). Experimenter and subject artifacts: Methodology. In N. J. Smelser and P. B. Baltes (eds.), *International Encyclopedia of the Social and Behavioral Sciences* (pp. 5120–4). Oxford, UK: Pergamon.

Rosnow, R. L. (2002). The nature and role of demand characteristics in scientific inquiry. *Prevention and Treatment*, 5 (Article pre0050037c). Available at http://journals.apa.org.

Rosnow, R. L., Goodstadt, B. E., Suls, J. M., and Gitter, A. G. (1973). More on the social psychology of the experiment: When compliance turns to self-defense. *Journal of Personality and Social Psychology*, 27, 337–43.

Rosnow, R. L. and Rosenthal, R. (1997). *People Studying People: Artifacts and Ethics in Behavioral Research*. New York: W. H. Freeman.

Rosnow, R. L. and Rosenthal, R. (2005). *Beginning Behavioral Research: A Conceptual Primer*, 5th ed. Upper Saddle River, NJ: Pearson.

Rosnow, R. L., Rotheram-Borus, M. J., Ceci, S. J., Blanck, P. D., and Koocher, G. P. (1993). The institutional review board as a mirror of scientific and ethical standards. *American Psychologist*, 48, 821–6.

Rosnow, R. L., Strohmetz, D. B., and Aditya, R. N. (2000). Artifact in research. In A. E. Kazdin (ed.), *Encyclopedia of Psychology* (Vol. 1, pp. 242–5). New York: Oxford University Press.

Rosnow, R. L. and Suls, J. M. (1970). Reactive effects of pretesting in attitude research. *Journal of Personality and Social Psychology*, 15, 338–43.

Ross, H. L. (1973). Law, science and accidents: The British Road Safety Act of 1967. *Journal of Legal Studies*, 2, 1–75.

Ross, H. L., Campbell, D. T., and Glass, G. V. (1970). Determining the social effects of legal reform: The British "breathalyser" crackdown of 1967. *American Behavioral Scientist*, 13, 493–509.

Ross, L., Lepper, M. R., and Hubbard, M. (1975). Perseverance in self-perception and social perception: Biased attributional processes in the debriefing paradigm. *Journal of Personality and Social Psychology*, 32, 880–92.

Rothenberg, R. (1990, October 5). Surveys proliferate, but answers dwindle. *The New York Times*, pp. A1, D4.

Rotherham-Borus, M. (1991). *HIV Interventions for Adolescents*. Washington, DC: Surgeon General's Panel on HIV.

Rowan, A. N. and Loew, F. M. (1995). *The Animal Research Controversy: Protest, Process and Public Policy*. North Grafton, MA: Tufts University, Center for Animals and Public Policy.

Rubenstein, C. (1982). Psychology's fruit flies. *Psychology Today, 16*, 83–4.

Ruebhausen, O. M. and Brim, O. G., Jr. (1966). Privacy and behavioral research. *American Psychologist, 21*, 423–37.

Rugg, E. A. (1975). *Ethical Judgments of Social Research Involving Experimental Deception*. Doctoral dissertation, George Peabody College for Teachers, Nashville, TN.

Ruling on animals in research is struck down (1994, September). *APS Observer*, p. 12.

Rushton, J. P. (1994). *Race, Evolution, and Behavior: A Life History Perspective*. New Brunswick, NJ: Transaction.

Russell, W. M. S. and Burch, R. L. (1959). *The Principles of Humane Experimental Technique*. London: Methuen.

Rutecki, G. W., Youtsey, M., and Adelson, B. (2002). The institutional review board: A critical revisit to the protection of human subjects. *Ethics and Medicine, 18*, 135–44.

Ryder, R. (1975). *Victims of Science: The Use of Animals in Research*. London: Davis-Poynter.

St James-Roberts, I. (1976). Cheating in science. *New Scientist, 60*, 466–9.

Saks, M. J. and Blanck, P. D. (1992). Justice improved: The unrecognized benefits of aggregation and sampling in the trial of mass torts. *Stanford Law Review, 44*, 815–51.

Sales, B. D. and Folkman, S. (2000). *Ethics in Research with Human Participants*. Washington, DC: American Psychological Association.

Sarason, S. B. (1981). *Psychology Misdirected*. New York: Free Press.

Savin, H. B. (1973). Professors and psychological researchers: Conflicting values in conflicting roles. *Cognition, 2*, 147–9.

Schachter, S. (1959). *The Psychology of Affiliation*. Stanford, CA: Stanford University Press.

Schachter, S. and Singer, J. (1962). Cognitive, social, and physiological determinants of the emotional state. *Psychological Review, 69*, 379–99.

Schlenker, B. R. and Forsyth, D. R. (1977). On the ethics of psychological research. *Journal of Experimental Social Psychology, 13*, 369–96.

Schuler, H. (1982). *Ethical Problems in Psychological Research*. New York: Academic Press.

Schultz, D. P. (1969). The human subject in psychological research. *Psychological Bulletin, 72*, 214–28.

Sears, D. O. (1986). College sophomores in the laboratory: Influences of a narrow data base on psychology's view of human nature. *Journal of Personality and Social Psychology, 51*, 515–30.

Seberhagen, L. W. (1993). An ethics code for statisticians – what next? *The Industrial-Organizational Psychologist, 30*, 71–4.

Seeman, J. (1969). Deception in psychological research. *American Psychologist, 24*, 1025–8.

Seiler, L. H. and Murtha, J. M. (1980). Federal regulation of social research using "human subjects": a critical assessment. *The American Sociologist, 15*, 146–57.

Seligman, C. and Sorrentino, R. M. (2002). The control agenda in Canada's governance of ethical review of human research. *Dialogue, 17*, 22–4.

Shadish, W. R., Cook, T. D., and Campbell, D. T. (2001). *Experimental and Quasi-experimental Designs for Generalized Causal Inference*. Boston: Houghton-Mifflin.

Shanab, M. E. and Yahya, K. A. (1977). A behavioral study of obedience in children. *Journal of Personality and Social Psychology, 35*, 530–6.

Shapiro, K. (1983). Psychology and its animal subjects. *International Journal for the Study of Animal Problems, 4*, 188–91.

Shapiro, K. (1984). Response to APA's "Why animals?" *Psychology in Maine, 1*, 1–2.

Shapiro, K. J. (1989). The Silver Springs monkeys and APA. *PsyETA Bulletin, 8*, 1–6.

Shapiro, K. J. (1991, July). Use morality as basis for animal treatment. *APA Monitor, 22*, 5.

Shapiro, K. J. (1998). *Animal Models of Human Psychology: Critique of Science, Ethics and Policy.* Cambridge, MA: Hogrefe & Huber.

Sharf, B. F. (1999). Beyond netiquette. In S. Jones (ed.), *Doing Internet Research: Critical Issues and Methods for Examining the Net.* Thousand Oaks, CA: Sage.

Sharpe, D., Adair, J. G., and Roese, N. J. (1992). Twenty years of deception research: a decline in subjects' trust? *Personality and Social Psychology Bulletin, 18*, 585–90.

Shaughnessy, J. J. and Zechmeister, E. B. (1990). *Research Methods in Psychology* (2nd ed.). New York: McGraw-Hill.

Sheets, T., Radlinski, A., Kohne, J., and Brunner, G. A. (1974). Deceived respondents: once bitten, twice shy. *Public Opinion Quaterly, 36*, 261–2.

Sherif, M., Harvey, O. J., White, B. J., Hood, W. E., and Sherif, C. W. (1961). *Intergroup Conflict and Cooperation: The Robbers Cave Experiment.* Norman, OK: Institute of Group Relations.

Sherrington, C. S. (1906). *The Integrative Action of the Nervous System.* New Haven, CT: Yale University Press.

Shimp, T. A., Hyatt, E. M., and Snyder, D. J. (1993). A critique of Darley and Lim's "alternative perspective." *Journal of Consumer Research, 20*, 496–501.

Shubin, S. (1981, January). Research behind bars: Prisoners as experimental subjects. *The Sciences, 21*, 10–13, 29.

Sieber, J. E. (1982a). Deception in social research I: Kinds of deception and the wrongs they may involve. *IRB: A Review of Human Subjects Research, 4*, 1–6.

Sieber, J. E. (1982b). Deception in social research III: The nature and limits of debriefing. *IRB: A Review of Human Subjects Research, 6*, 1–4.

Sieber, J. E. (1982c). Ethical dilemmas in social research. In J. E. Sieber (ed.), *The Ethics of Social Research: Surveys and Experiments.* New York: Springer-Verlag.

Sieber, J. E. (1992). *Planning Ethically Responsible Research.* Newbury Park, CA: Sage.

Sieber, J. E. (1999). What makes a subject pool (un)ethical? In G. Chastain and R. Eric Landrum (eds.), *Protecting Human Subjects: Departmental Subject Pools and Institutional Review Boards* (pp. 43–64). Washington, DC: American Psychological Association.

Sieber, J. E., Iannuzzo, R., and Rodriguez, B. (1995). Deception methods in psychology: Have they changed in 23 years? *Ethics and Behavior, 5*, 67–85.

Sieber, J. E. and Saks, M. J. (1989). A census of subject pool characteristics. *American Psychologist, 44*, 1053–61.

Sieber, J. E. and Sorensen, J. L. (1991). Ethical issues in community-based research and intervention. In J. Edwards, R. S. Tindale, L. Heath, and E. J. Posavac (eds.), *Social Psychological Applications to Social Issues.* Vol. 2: *Methodological Issues in Applied Social Psychology.* New York: Plenum Press.

Sigall, H., Aronson, E., and Van Hoose, T. (1970). The cooperative subject: myth or reality? *Journal of Experimental Social Psychology, 6*, 1–10.

Sigma Xi, The Scientific Research Society (1984). *Honor in Science.* New Haven, CT: Sigma Xi.

Silverman, I. (1977). *The Human Subject in the Psychological Experiment.* New York: Pergamon.

Silverman, I., Shulman, A. D., and Wiesenthal, D. L. (1970). Effects of deceiving and debriefing psychological subjects on performance in later experiments. *Journal of Personality and Social Psychology, 14*, 203–12.

Silverstein, A. J. (1974). Compensating those injured through experimentation. *Federal Bar Journal, 33*, 322–30.

Sinclair, C., Poizner, S., Gilmour-Barrett, K., and Randall, D. (1987). The development of a code of ethics for Canadian psychologists. *Canadian Psychology, 28*, 1–8.

Singer, E. (1978). Informed consent: Consequences for response rate and response quality in social surveys. *American Sociological Review, 43*, 144–62.

Singer, E. (1984). Public reactions to some ethical issues of social research: Attitudes and behavior. *Journal of Consumer Research, 11*, 501–9.

Singer, E. and Frankel, M. R. (1982). Informed consent procedures in telephone interviews. *American Sociological Review, 47*, 416–27.

Singer, P. (1975). *Animal Liberation*. New York: Avon.

Singer, P. (ed.) (1985). *In Defence of Animals*. Oxford, UK: Blackwell.

Sjoberg, G. (1967). Project Camelot: Selected reactions and personal reflections. In G. Sjoberg (ed.), *Ethics, Politics, and Social Research*. Cambridge, MA: Schenkman.

Slater, L. (2004). *Opening Skinner's Box: Great Psychological Experiments of the Twentieth Century*. New York: W. W. Norton.

Slife, B. and Rubinstein, J. (1992). *Taking Sides: Clashing Views on Controversial Psychological Issues* (7th ed.). Guilford, CT: Dushkin.

Slovenian Psychological Association (2002). *The Code of Professional Ethics of Slovene Psychologists*. Ljubljana: SPA.

Smith, C. P. (1981). How (un)acceptable is research involving deception? *IRB: A Review of Human Subjects Research, 3*, 1–4.

Smith, D. (2003). Ten ways practitioners can avoid frequent ethical pitfalls. *Monitor on Psychology, 34*, 50–5.

Smith, D. H. (1978). Scientific knowledge and forbidden truths – are there things we should not know? *Hastings Center Report, 8*, 30–5.

Smith, M. B. (1976). Some perspectives on ethical/political issues in social research. *Personality and Social Psychology Bulletin, 2*, 445–53.

Smith, N. C. and Klein, J. G. (1999). *Ethics in Marketing Research and the Use of Remedial Measures to Mitigate the Deception of Respondents*. Unpublished manuscript, McDonough School of Business, Georgetown University.

Smith, N. C., Klein, J. G., and Kimmel, A. J. (2005). *The Ethics of Deception in Consumer Research*. Unpublished manuscript, London Business School, UK.

Smith, N. L. (1985). Some characteristics of moral problems in evaluation practice. *Evaluation and Program Planning, 8*, 5–11.

Smith, S. S. and Richardson, D. (1983). Amelioration of deception and harm in psychological research: The important role of debriefing. *Journal of Personality and Social Psychology, 44*, 1075–82.

Snow, C. P. (1959). *The Search* (rev. ed.). New York: Charles Scribner's Sons.

Snowden, J. L., Debbaut, N., Jachym, L., Gardner, J., and Lecci, L. (2003). *Students' Implicit and Explicit Attitudes towards Psychological Research and Practice*. Poster presented at the 15th annual convention of the American Psychological Society, Atlanta.

Society for Industrial and Organizational Psychology (2004). *Principles for the Validation and Use of Personnel Selection Procedures*, 4th ed. Bowling Green, OH: SIOP.

Sojka, J. and Spangenberg, E. R. (1994). Ethical concerns in marketing research. In C. T. Allen and D. Roedder (eds.), *Advances in Consumer Research* (Vol. 21, pp. 392–6). Provo, UT: Association for Consumer Research.

Sommer, B. and Sommer, R. (1991). *A Practical Guide to Behavioral Research: Tools and Techniques* (3rd ed.). New York: Oxford University Press.

Sommer, R. and Sommer, B. (1989). Social facilitation effects in coffee-houses. *Environment and Behavior, 21*, 651–66.

Sperling, S. (1988). *Animal Liberators: Research and Morality*. Berkeley: University of California Press.

Sperry, R. W. (1968). Hemisphere deconnection and unity in conscious awareness. *American Psychologist, 23*, 723–33.

Spiegel, D. and Keith-Spiegel, P. (1970). Assignment of publication credits: Ethics and practices of psychologists. *American Psychologist, 25*, 738–47.

Spielberger, C. D. (1962). The role of awareness in verbal conditioning. *Journal of Personality, 30*, 73–101.

Spivak, G., Platt, J. J., and Shure, M. B. (1976). *The Problem-solving Approach to Adjustment*. San Francisco: Jossey-Bass.

Spivak, G. and Shure, M. B. (1974). *Social Adjustment of Young Children: A Cognitive Approach to Solving Real-life Problems*. San Francisco: Jossey-Bass.

Spoiling the broth (2001, September 11). *The New York Times*, Op-ed page.

Sprague, R. L. (1993). Whistleblowing: A very unpleasant avocation. *Ethics and Behavior, 3*, 103–33.

Stang, D. J. (1976). Ineffective deception in conformity research: Some causes and consequences. *European Journal of Social Psychology, 6*, 353–67.

Stanley, B. and Sieber, J. (eds.) (1992). *Social Research on Children and Adolescents: Ethical Issues*. Newbury Park, CA: Sage.

Stanton, A. L., Burker, E. J., and Kershaw, D. (1991). Effects of researcher follow-up of distressed subjects: Tradeoff between validity and ethical responsibility? *Ethics and Behavior, 1*, 105–12.

Stanton, A. L. and New, M. J. (1988). Ethical responsibilities to depressed research participants. *Professional Psychology: Research and Practice, 19*, 279–85.

Stark, C. (1998). Ethics in the research context: Misinterpretations and misplaced misgivings. *Canadian Psychology, 39*, 202–11.

Steininger, M., Newell, J. D., and Garcia, L. T. (1984). *Ethical Issues in Psychology*. Homewood, IL: Dorsey.

Stoke, S. M. and West, E. D. (1931). Sex differences in conversational interests. *Journal of Social Psychology, 2*, 120–26.

Stricker, L. J. (1967). The true deceiver. *Psychological Bulletin, 68*, 13–20.

Stricker, L. J., Messick, S., and Jackson, D. N. (1967). Suspicion of deception: implications for conformity research. *Journal of Personality and Social Psychology, 5*, 379–89.

Strohmetz, D. B., Alterman, A. I., and Walter, D. (1990). Subject selection bias in alcoholics volunteering for a treatment study. *Alcoholism: Clinical and Experimental Research, 14*, 736–8.

Strohmetz, D. B. and Rosnow, R. L. (1995). A mediational model of research artifacts. In J. Brzezinski (ed.), *Probability in Theory Building: Experimental and Nonexperimental Models of Scientific Research in Behavioral Sciences*. Amsterdam: Editions Rodopi.

Strohmetz, D. B. and Rosnow, R. L. (2003). Artifacts in research process. In M. S. Lewis-Beck, A. E. Bryman, and T. F. Liao (eds.), *The Sage Encyclopedia of Social Science Research Methods*. Thousand Oaks, CA: Sage.

Strutt, R. J. (1924). *John William Strutt, Third Baron Rayleigh*. London: Arnold.

Sullivan, D. S. and Deiker, T. A. (1973). Subject-experimenter perceptions of ethical issues in human research. *American Psychologist, 28*, 587–91.

Suls, J. M. and Rosnow, R. L. (1981). The delicate balance between ethics and artifacts in behavioral research. In A. J. Kimmel (ed.), *Ethics of Human Subject Research*. San Francisco: Jossey-Bass.

Summary Report of Journal Operations, 2004 (2005). *American Psychologist, 60*, 560–1.

Swazey, J. P., Anderson, M. S., and Lewis, K. S. (1993). Ethical problems in academic research. *American Scientist, 81,* 542–53.

Tanikawa, M. (2004, October 23). The unleashing of the pet industry. *International Herald Tribune,* pp. 16–17.

Tanke, E. D. and Tanke, T. J. (1982). Regulation and education: The role of the institutional review board in social science research. In J. E. Sieber (ed.), *The Ethics of Social Research: Fieldwork, Regulation and Publication.* New York: Springer-Verlag.

Tarde, G. de (1901). *L'Opinion et la Foule.* Paris: Felix Alcan.

Taub, E., Bacon, R., and Berman, A. J. (1965). The acquisition of a trace-conditioned avoidance response after deafferentation of the responding limb. *Journal of Comparative and Physiological Psychology, 58,* 275–9

Taylor, K. M. and Shepperd, J. A. (1996). Probing suspicion among participants in deception research. *American Psychologist, 51,* 886–7.

Tedeschi, J. T. and Rosenfeld, P. (1981). The experimental research controversy at SUNY: A case study. In A. J. Kimmel (ed.), *Ethics of Human Subject Research.* San Francisco: Jossey-Bass.

Tesch, F. (1977). Debriefing research participants: Though this be method there is madness to it. *Journal of Personality and Social Psychology, 35,* 217–24.

Thomas, G. V. and Blackman, D. (1992). The future of animal studies in psychology. *American Psychologist, 47,* 1679.

Thomas, S. B. and Quinn, S. C. (1991). The Tuskegee syphilis study, 1932 to 1972: Implications for HIV education and AIDS risk education programs in the Black community. *American Journal of Public Health, 81,* 1498–1505.

Thompson, B. (1994). The big picture(s) in deciding authorship order. *American Psychologist, 49,* 1095–6.

Thompson, R. A. (1990). Vulnerability in research: A developmental perspective on research risk. *Child Development, 61,* 1–16.

Tickle, J. J. and Heatherton, T. F. (2005). Research on college students. In R. J. Amdur and E. A. Bankert (eds.), *Institutional Review Board: Management and Function* (2nd ed.). Sudbury, MA: Jones & Bartlett.

Toy, D., Olson, J., and Wright, L. (1989). Effects of debriefing in marketing research involving "mild" deceptions. *Psychology and Marketing, 6,* 69–85.

Toy, D., Wright, L., and Olson, J. (2001). A conceptual framework for analyzing deception and debriefing effects in marketing research. *Psychology and Marketing, 18,* 663–89.

Tracy, P. E. and Fox, J. A. (1981). The validity of randomized response for sensitive measurements. *American Sociological Review, 46,* 187–200.

Trice, A. D. and Bailey, B. H. (1986). Informed consent: II. Withdrawal-without-prejudice clauses may increase no-shows. *Journal of General Psychology, 113,* 285–7.

Triplett, N. (1897). The dynamogenic factors in pacemaking and competition. *American Journal of Psychology, 9,* 507–33.

Trist, E. L., Higgin, G. W., Murray, H., and Pollack, A. B. (1963). *Organizational Choice: Capabilities of Groups at the Coal Face Under Changing Technologies.* London: Tavistock.

Trochim, W. (1982). *Research Design for Program Intervention: The Regression-Discontinuity Approach.* Beverly Hills, CA: Sage.

Tucker, W. H. (1997). Re-considering Burt: Beyond a reasonable doubt. *Journal of the History of the Behavioral Sciences, 33,* 145–62.

Turner, C. W. and Simons, L. S. (1974). Effects of subject sophistication and evaluation apprehension on aggressive responses to weapons. *Journal of Personality and Social Psychology, 30,* 341–8.

Twedt, D. T. (1963). Why a marketing research code of ethics? *Journal of Marketing, 27,* 48–50.

Tybout, A. M. and Zaltman, G. (1974). Ethics in marketing research: Their practical relevance. *Journal of Marketing Research, 11,* 357–68.

Tybout, A. M. and Zaltman, G. (1975). A reply to comments on "Ethics in marketing research: Their practical relevance." *Journal of Marketing Research, 12,* 234–7.

US Department of Agriculture (1991, February 15). Animal welfare; standards; final rule. *Federal Register,* pp. 6426–505.

Valins, S. (1974). Persistent effects of information about reactions: Ineffectiveness of debriefing. In H. London and R. Nisbett (eds.), *Thought and Feeling* (pp. 116–24). Chicago: Aldine.

Veatch, R. M. (1982). Problems with institutional review board inconsistency. *Journal of the American Medical Association, 248,* 179–80.

Verplanck, W. S. (1955). The control of the content of conversation: reinforcement of statements of opinion. *Journal of Abnormal and Social Psychology, 55,* 668–76.

Vidich, A. J. and Bensman, J. (1958). *Small Town in Mass Society: Class, Power, and Religion in a Rural Community.* Princeton, NJ: Princeton University Press.

Vinacke, W. E. (1954). Deceiving experimental subjects. *American Psychologist, 9,* 155.

Vitelli, R. (1988). The crisis issue assessed: An empirical analysis. *Basic and Applied Social Psychology, 9,* 301–9.

Wade, N. (1976). Animal rights: NIH cat sex study brings grief to New York museum. *Science, 194,* 162–67.

Wahl, J. M. (1972). *Role Playing vs. Deception: Differences in Experimental Realism as Measured by Subject's Level of Involvement and Level of Suspicion.* Doctoral dissertation, University of Oregon, Eugene, OR.

Waite, B. M. and Bowman, L. L. (1999). Research participation among general psychology students at a metropolitan comprehensive public university. In G. Chastain and R. Eric Landrum (eds.), *Protecting Human Subjects: Departmental Subject Pools and Institutional Review Boards* (pp. 69–85). Washington, DC: American Psychological Association.

Walsh, W. B. and Stillman, S. M. (1974). Disclosure of deception by debriefed subjects. *Journal of Counseling Psychology, 21,* 315–19.

Walster, E., Berscheid, E., Abrahams, D., and Aronson, V. (1967). Effectiveness of debriefing following deception experiments. *Journal of Personality and Social Psychology, 6,* 371–80.

Walton, R. E. (1978). Ethical issues in the practice of organization development. In G. Bermant, H. C. Kelman, and D. P. Warwick (eds.), *The Ethics of Social Intervention.* Washington, DC: Hemisphere.

Warner, S. L. (1965). Randomized response: A survey technique for eliminating evasive answer bias. *Journal of the American Statistical Association, 60,* 63–9.

Warwick, D. P. (1975, February). Social scientists ought to stop lying. *Psychology Today, 8,* 38, 40, 105–6.

Waterman, A. S. (1974). The civil liberties of the participants in psychological research. *American Psychologist, 29,* 470–1.

Watson, J. D. (1969). *The Double Helix.* New York: New American Library.

Webb, E. J., Campbell, D. T., Schwartz, R. D., Sechrest, L., and Grove, J. B. (1981). *Nonreactive Measures in the Social Sciences* (2nd ed.). Boston: Houghton Mifflin.

Weber, S. J. and Cook, T. D. (1972). Subject effects in laboratory research: an examination of subject roles, demand characteristics, and valid inferences. *Psychological Bulletin, 77,* 273–95.

Wegner, D., Coulton, G., and Wenzlaff, R. (1985). The transparency of denial: Briefing in the debriefing paradigm. *Journal of Personality and Social Psychology, 49*, 338–46.

Weiner, J. S. (1955). *The Piltdown Forgery*. London: Oxford University Press.

Weinstein, D. (1979). Fraud in science. *Social Science Quarterly, 59*, 639–52.

Weinstein, D. (1981). *Scientific Fraud and Scientific Ethics* (CSEP Occasional Papers: No. 4). Chicago: Center for the Study of Ethics in the Professions.

Welsome, E. (1993). The plutonium experiment [special reprint]. *The Albuquerque Tribune*, 47 pp.

Welsome E. (1999). *The Plutonium Files: America's Secret Medical Experiments in the Cold War*. New York: The Dial Press.

Welt, L. G. (1961). Reflections on the problems of human experimentation. *Connecticut Medicine, 25*, 75–9.

West, S. G. and Gunn, S. P. (1978). Some issues of ethics and social psychology. *American Psychologist, 33*, 30–8.

West, S. G., Gunn, S. P., and Chernicky, P. (1975). Ubiquitous Watergate: an attributional analysis. *Journal of Personality and Social Psychology, 32*, 55–65.

Westin, A. F. (1968). *Privacy and Freedom*. New York: Atheneum.

White, L. A. (1979). Erotica and aggression: The influence of sexual arousal, positive affect, and negative affect on aggressive behavior. *Journal of Personality and Social Psychology, 37*, 591–601.

Wiener, R. L. and Erker, P. V. (1986). The effects of prebriefing misinformed research participants on their attributions of responsibility. *Journal of Psychology, 120*, 397–410.

Wilkes, M. S., Doblin, B. H., and Shapiro, M. F. (1992). Pharmaceutical advertisements in leading medical journals: Experts' assessments. *Annals of Internal Medicine, 116*, 912–19.

Willis, R. H. and Willis, Y. A. (1970). Role playing versus deception: an experimental comparison. *Journal of Personality and Social Psychology, 16*, 472–7.

Willis-Aronowitz, N. (2005, August 17–23). The tipping point. *Village Voice*, p. 12.

Wilson, A. M. (2001). Mystery shopping: Using deception to measure service performance. *Psychology and Marketing, 18*, 721–34.

Wilson, D. W. and Donnerstein, E. (1976). Legal and ethical aspects of nonreactive social psychological research: An excursion into the public mind. *American Psychologist, 31*, 765–73.

Winslow, J. H. and Meyer, A. (1983, September). The perpetrator at Piltdown. *Science, 83*, 32–43.

Wolins, L. (1962). Responsibility for raw data. *American Psychologist, 17*, 657–8.

Wright, T. A. and Wright, V. P. (1999). Ethical responsibility and the organizational researcher: A committed-to-participant research perspective. *Journal of Organizational Behavior, 20*, 1107–12.

Wuebben, P. L. (1967). Honesty of subjects and birth order. *Journal of Personality and Social Psychology, 5*, 350–2.

Yin, R. K. (1989). *Case Study Research: Design and Methods* (rev. ed.). Newbury Park, CA: Sage.

Young, S. C., Herrenkohl, L. R., Bibace, R., and Lin, A. W. (1995, March). *Shifting from "Experimenter Subject" to "Researcher Participant" Relationships. Conceptual and Methodological Implications*. Paper presented at the Eastern Psychological Association meeting, Boston.

Zak, S. (1989, March). Ethics and animals. *The Atlantic, 273*, 68–74.

Zicklin, E. (1994, March). I. V. league. *Spy*, pp. 18–19.

Zignego, V. (2003, October 29). University research ethics. *The Badger Herald*. Available at http://www.badgerherald.com.

Zimbardo, P. (1969). The human choice: Individuation, reason and order versus deindividuation, impulse and chaos. In W. J. Arnold and D. Levine (eds.), *Nebraska Symposium on Motivation* (Vol. 17). Lincoln: University of Nebraska Press.

Zimbardo, P. (1973a). On the ethics of intervention in human psychological research: With special reference to the Stanford prison experiment. *Cognition*, *2*, 243–56.

Zimbardo, P. (1973b). The psychological power and pathology of imprisonment. In E. Aronson and R. Helmreich (eds.), *Social Psychology*. New York: Van Nostrand.

Zimbardo, P., Anderson, S. M., and Kabat, L. G. (1981). Induced hearing deficit generates experimental paranoia. *Science*, *212*, 1529–31.

Zimbardo, P., Haney, C., Banks, W., and Jaffe, D. (1973, April 8). The mind is a formidable jailer: A Pirandellian prison. *The New York Times Magazine*, pp. 38–60.

Zola, J. C., Sechzer, J. A., Sieber, J. E., and Griffin, A. (1984). Animal experimentation: issues for the 1980s. *Science, Technology, and Human Values*, *9*, 40–50.

Zuckerman, H. and Merton, R. K. (1971). Patterns of evaluation in science: Institutionalisation, structure, and functions of the referee system. *Minerva*, *9*, 66–100.

Zureik, E. (2004). *Appendix A: Overview of Public Opinion Research Regarding Privacy*. Available at http://www.queensu.ca/sociology/Surveillance.

Subject Index

Name Index